Frommer's®

Vietnam

3rd Edition

by Sherisse Pham

Wiley Publishing, Inc.

ABOUT THE AUTHOR

Sherisse Pham was a Beijing-based freelance journalist for over 4 years but recently relocated to New York to study at Columbia University's Graduate School of Journalism. She has contributed to several Frommer's guides and has written for *WWD, The South China Morning Post, People Magazine,* CNN.com, and *Zagat Survey* among others. She graduates in 2010 and hopes to eventually return to Asia to continue reporting on the region.

Published by:

WILEY PUBLISHING, INC.

111 River St.
Hoboken, NJ 07030-5774

ISBN 978-0-470-52660-6

Editor: Michael Kelly, with Alexia Travaglini
Production Editor: Michael Brumitt
Cartographer: Andrew Dolan
Photo Editor: Richard Fox
Production by Wiley Indianapolis Composition Services
Front cover photo: Fisherwomen at sunset © Alex Bramwell / iStock Photo.
Back cover photo: Rice paddy in Sa Pa, Lao Cai Province © Pichai Khaola / iStock Photo.

For information on our other products and services or to obtain technical support, please contact our Customer Care Department within the U.S. at 877/762-2974, outside the U.S. at 317/572-3993 or fax 317/572-4002.

Wiley also publishes its books in a variety of electronic formats. Some content that appears in print may not be available in electronic formats.

Manufactured in the United States of America

5 4 3 2 1

CONTENTS

LIST OF MAPS vi

1 THE BEST OF VIETNAM 1

1 The Best Vietnam Experiences......1
2 The Best Sites (According to UNESCO)..........................2
3 The Best Temples & Archaeological Sites 2
4 The Best Museums.................3
5 The Best Beaches 3
6 The Best of the Outdoors...........3
7 The Best Luxury Accommodations....4
8 The Best Midrange Accommodations..................5
9 The Best Dining....................6

2 VIETNAM IN DEPTH 7

1 Who Are the Vietnamese?..........7
2 Vietnamese Religion 9
3 A Look at the Past: Vietnam the Country, Not the War 9

3 PLANNING YOUR TRIP TO VIETNAM 18

1 When to Go.......................18
Vietnam Calendar of Events 19
Less Is More: Packing & Clothing in the Tropics 20
2 Entry Requirements...............22
3 Getting There & Getting Around ...23
4 Money & Costs....................26
What Things Cost in Vietnam.......27
5 Health 27
AIDS in Vietnam 31
6 Safety............................33
Responsible Tourism 34
7 Specialized Travel Resources 36
8 Sustainable Tourism...............41
General Resources for Green Travel...42
9 Special-Interest & Escorted General-Interest Tours.............43
Tours for Vietnam Veterans 44
10 Staying Connected................48
11 Tips on Accommodations.........49

4 SUGGESTED ITINERARIES IN VIETNAM 52

1 The Regions in Brief 53
2 Doing It All: Vietnam & Cambodia in 28 Days 54
3 Vietnam in 14 Days: North to South 59
4 World Heritage Tour (9 Days) 61
5 Get Your Motor Runnin'—Vietnam by Motorcycle or Jeep 62
6 A Side Trip to Cambodia 63

5 HANOI 65

Flying Dragons & Thieving Turtles: Hanoi's Founding 66
1 Orientation 67
Make Friends with Vietnam Heritage 70
The Neighborhoods in Brief 71
2 Getting Around 72
Rigged Taxi Meters 72
Fast Facts: Hanoi 74
3 Where to Stay 77
4 Where to Dine 88
The Best Authentic Local Fare 90
Have You Tried the Snake? 99
5 Exploring Hanoi 100
Walking Tour: The Old Quarter 103
6 Outdoor Activities & Other Fitness Pursuits 114
7 Shopping 116
8 Hanoi After Dark 123
9 Day Trips from Hanoi 126

6 THE NORTHERN HIGHLANDS 128

1 Lao Cai 128
Hilltribes in Northern Vietnam 130
2 Sapa 132
3 The Dien Bien Phu Loop 141
The Minsk: A Guide to Renting & Enjoying Your Big Honkin' Soviet Motorbike 144
4 The Northeastern Highlands Loop 152

7 NORTHEASTERN COAST 157

1 Haiphong 157
2 Halong City 161
3 Halong Bay 163
4 Cat Ba Island 167

8 NORTH-CENTRAL VIETNAM 173

1 Ninh Binh 173
2 Vinh 179
Who Was "Uncle Ho"? 180

9 CENTRAL VIETNAM 184

1 Hue . . . 184

Fast Facts: Hue . . . 188

2 The Demilitarized Zone (DMZ) . . . 199

3 Bach Ma National Park . . . 203

4 Lang Co Beach . . . 204

5 Danang . . . 205

Fast Facts: Danang . . . 208

Who Are the Cham? . . . 206

6 Hoi An . . . 211

Fast Facts: Hoi An . . . 212

10 THE CENTRAL HIGHLANDS 232

1 Dalat . . . 232

Central Highland Ethnic Minority Hilltribes . . . 234

Fast Facts: Dalat . . . 239

2 Buon Ma Thuot . . . 249

3 Pleiku & Kontum . . . 255

11 SOUTH-CENTRAL VIETNAM 261

1 Quy Nhon . . . 261

Fast Facts: Quy Nhon . . . 264

Revisit the My Lai Massacre . . . 267

2 Nha Trang . . . 268

Fast Facts: Nha Trang . . . 271

3 Outside Nha Trang . . . 283

4 Phan Thiet Town & Mui Ne Beach . . . 285

Fast Facts: Phan Thiet & Mui Ne . . . 285

12 HO CHI MINH CITY (SAIGON) 291

A Veteran's Trip Back . . . 292

1 Orientation . . . 294

Fast Facts: Ho Chi Minh City . . . 298

2 Where to Stay . . . 300

3 Where to Dine . . . 313

Quest for the Perfect Noodle . . . 319

4 Exploring Ho Chi Minh City . . . 320

5 Shopping . . . 329

6 Saigon After Dark . . . 333

7 Side Trips from Ho Chi Minh City . . . 335

13 THE MEKONG DELTA 349

1 Visitor Information . . . 349

2 My Tho . . . 353

3 Can Tho . . . 353

Fast Facts: Can Tho . . . 354

4 Chau Doc . . . 357

Fast Facts: Chau Doc . . . 358

5 Phu Quoc Island . . . 360

A Unique Breed: The Phu Quoc Ridgeback . . . 361

Fast Facts: Phu Quoc . . . 363

14 CAMBODIA 368

1 Getting to Know Cambodia 369
2 Planning Your Trip to Cambodia ... 374
Some Important Safety Tips 377
Fast Facts: Cambodia 381
Telephone Dialing Information at a Glance 383
3 Phnom Penh 383
Fast Facts: Phnom Penh 386
4 Southern Cambodia 399
5 Siem Reap & Angkor Wat 405
Give of "Yourself" in Siem Reap 406
Fast Facts: Siem Reap 410
The Magic Hours at Angkor Wat ... 427
6 Battambang 436

15 FAST FACTS 441

1 Fast Facts: Vietnam 441
2 Airline, Hotel & Car Rental Websites 445

16 THE VIETNAMESE LANGUAGE 447

1 The Basics 447
2 Getting Around 451

17 VIETNAMESE CUISINE 454

1 Typical Ingredients 454
2 Dining & Etiquette 455
Eew, What's That?! 459

INDEX 460

LIST OF MAPS

Suggested Itineraries **55**
Hanoi **78**
Hanoi: Old Quarter **85**
Walking Tour: The Old Quarter ... **105**
The Northern Highlands **129**
Sapa **133**
Northeastern Coast **159**
Haiphong **161**
North-Central Vietnam **175**
Central Vietnam **185**
Hue **187**
Danang **207**
Hoi An **215**
Central Highlands **233**
Dalat **237**
South-Central Coast **263**
Nha Trang **269**
Ho Chi Minh City (Saigon) **302**
Mekong Delta **351**
Cambodia **371**
Phnom Penh **385**
Siem Reap **407**
Angkor Wat **423**

ACKNOWLEDGMENTS

I would like to thank Phan Ho Nam for her excellent support work as a fact-checker and occasional translator.

—Sherisse Pham

HOW TO CONTACT US

In researching this book, we discovered many wonderful places—hotels, restaurants, shops, and more. We're sure you'll find others. Please tell us about them, so we can share the information with your fellow travelers in upcoming editions. If you were disappointed with a recommendation, we'd love to know that, too. Please write to:

Frommer's Vietnam, 3rd Edition
Wiley Publishing, Inc. • 111 River St. • Hoboken, NJ 07030-5774

AN ADDITIONAL NOTE

Please be advised that travel information is subject to change at any time—and this is especially true of prices. We therefore suggest that you write or call ahead for confirmation when making your travel plans. The authors, editors, and publisher cannot be held responsible for the experiences of readers while traveling. Your safety is important to us, however, so we encourage you to stay alert and be aware of your surroundings. Keep a close eye on cameras, purses, and wallets, all favorite targets of thieves and pickpockets.

FROMMER'S STAR RATINGS, ICONS & ABBREVIATIONS

Every hotel, restaurant, and attraction listing in this guide has been ranked for quality, value, service, amenities, and special features using a **star-rating system.** In country, state, and regional guides, we also rate towns and regions to help you narrow down your choices and budget your time accordingly. Hotels and restaurants are rated on a scale of zero (recommended) to three stars (exceptional). Attractions, shopping, nightlife, towns, and regions are rated according to the following scale: zero stars (recommended), one star (highly recommended), two stars (very highly recommended), and three stars (must-see).

In addition to the star-rating system, we also use **eight feature icons** that point you to the great deals, in-the-know advice, and unique experiences that separate travelers from tourists. Throughout the book, look for:

Finds	Special finds—those places only insiders know about
Fun Facts	Fun facts—details that make travelers more informed and their trips more fun
Kids	Best bets for kids, and advice for the whole family
Moments	Special moments—those experiences that memories are made of
Overrated	Places or experiences not worth your time or money
Tips	Insider tips—great ways to save time and money
Value	Great values—where to get the best deals
Warning!	Warning—traveler's advisories are usually in effect

The following **abbreviations** are used for credit cards:

AE	American Express	**MC**	MasterCard
DC	Diners Club	**V**	Visa

TRAVEL RESOURCES AT FROMMERS.COM

Frommer's travel resources don't end with this guide. Frommer's website, **www.frommers.com** has travel information on more than 4,000 destinations. We update features regularly, giving you access to the most current trip-planning information and the best airfare, lodging, and car-rental bargains. You can also listen to podcasts, connect with other Frommers.com members through our active-reader forums, share your travel photos, read blogs from guidebook editors and fellow travelers, and much more.

The Best of Vietnam

1

Vietnam offers adventures and curiosities around every corner. Be ready for a wild ride in a colorful and chaotic land—along the way, you'll discover tranquil places and opportunities to connect with local people. Below is the best Vietnam has to offer, from fine dining to off-the-beaten-track oddities.

1 THE BEST VIETNAM EXPERIENCES

- **Eat on the Street:** "Real" Vietnamese food is best at street side or in small market areas, and though it might be a little grungy or off-putting to some, dining alfresco in old Indochina offers the most authentic and delicious meals. Prepare yourself for some adventurous dining. If you're in Ho Chi Minh City, try Quan An Ngon Restaurant (p. 318) for a safe overview of Vietnamese fare. See the "Where to Dine" sections in following chapters.
- **Get Lost in the Markets:** In Vietnam, the market—spelled *Cho* and pronounced like the beginning of the word *could*—is the epicenter of culture and commerce. The best market for tourists is Ben Thanh Market (p. 321) in Saigon, which caters to foreign visitors with low-cost T-shirts, souvenirs, and local treats. Every town has a market: Dalat's market, with its delicious strawberry preserves; Hoi An's busy riverside fish market and wholesale silk market; Hanoi's sprawling Dong Xuan Market (p. 122); and the hilltribe markets of Sapa and Bac Ha in the far north.
- **Visit Hilltribe Groups:** Vietnam's remote mountain regions, the Central Highlands and the far north, are home to a patchwork of ethnic minorities. Ethnic hilltribe people still practice their own brands of animistic religion and wear colorful traditional clothing. Travelers among them, in places like Sapa and Bac Ha in the far north or near Buon Ma Thuot or Kontum in the Central Highlands, can even experience a homestay in some villages through certain eco-tours and trekking companies. See chapters 6 and 10.
- **See the Water Puppets of Hanoi:** Okay, this is one for the tour buses, but the Thang Long Water Puppet Theater (p. 123) in Hanoi is magical. Intricate puppets emerge from the surface of a small watery stage as if by magic, telling tales of old Vietnam. Don't miss it.
- **Take a Wild Ride:** Whether through Hanoi's narrow alleyways and mazelike neighborhoods or on the broad boulevards of busy Ho Chi Minh City, the traffic in Vietnam is a trip. Darwinian road rules mean that any ride by motorcycle, car, or bus is a test of faith, as drivers swerve and angle through some of the world's craziest traffic. In Vietnam, "getting there" is an adventure in itself. See "Getting There" sections in the following chapters for more information.
- **Celebrate the Tet Holiday:** This Lunar New Year celebration (p. 20) in early February is the most important event on the calendar. Should you be in Vietnam at this time of year, the greatest gift you could get is an invite to a family's

Tet celebration. Bring a little something to eat as a contribution, and enjoy some of the most unique hospitality in the world.

2 THE BEST SITES (ACCORDING TO UNESCO)

- **Halong Bay:** Just a short few hours from Hanoi, the bay at Halong, with its craggy limestone towers dotting the wide-open bay all the way to the horizon, has long inspired Vietnamese poets and philosophers. A ride on the bay these days is a rather busy, crowded affair, but some luxury tours and a few eco-tour operators can take you to the back of beyond, exploring little-known caves by kayak. See chapter 7.
- **Phong Nha—Ke Bang National Park:** These massive caves (more or less an off-the-track site popular with backpackers) are about halfway between Hue and Vinh. You have to arrange your own transport or go with a tour. See p. 183.
- **Hoi An:** Tourism has exploded on the ancient streets of Hoi An. A hub of international craft and commerce since the 14th century, this is where Vietnamese, Chinese, and even Japanese tradesmen made and sold their designer wares. Many shops are still-operational wood, stone, and ceramic workshops, but now among them are fine-dining outlets, funky little hotels (as well as new resorts on the outlying beach area of Cua Dai), and lots of bespoke tailors. Shoppers swoon. See section 6, "Hoi An," in chapter 9.
- **My Son Sanctuary:** The Cham people, an Indonesian group who arrived by ship from the Malay Peninsula, held sway over most of central Vietnam and built arching hilltop towers. My Son is the finest example. See "An Excursion to My Son," in chapter 9.
- **Hue Monuments:** The Nguyen Kings—the last and perhaps the most glorious (or grandiose) of Vietnam's dynastic rulers—built grand monuments to themselves in and around the massive Hue Citadel. Hue's sights, particularly the elaborate kings' tombs, make for a very interesting visit. See section 1, "Hue," in chapter 9.

3 THE BEST TEMPLES & ARCHAEOLOGICAL SITES

- **The Cao Dai Holy See:** The spiritual home base of the Cao Dai religion, a unique contemporary faith, the Holy See is a fantasyland of colored mosaics and elaborate painting. Followers are dressed in white turbans during the picturesque daily procession. See p. 327.
- **Tomb of Khai Dinh:** The egotistical, eccentric emperor Khai Dinh left behind a tomb that is a gaudy mix of Gothic, baroque, and classical Chinese architecture. Quite unique. See p. 197.
- **The Tunnels of Vinh Moc and Cu Chi:** Faced with devastating air raids, both of these sites supported large groups of soldiers and civilians who used the tunnels as supply lines, as escape routes, and as bases for waging a devastating guerilla campaign against U.S. forces. Day trips to either site are memorable. See p. 202 and 328.
- **Hoa Lo Prison (aka Hanoi Hilton):** Home to U.S. pilots—including John McCain—who were shot down during

the Vietnamese war with the U.S., Hoa Lo Prison is now a small museum (most of it was demolished for a high-rise). A good glimpse into Vietnam's grisly past. See p. 111.

- **Reunification Palace:** In 1975 tanks rolled over the gates of the prime minister's palace, signaling an end to the Vietnam War. You can see the actual tanks on-site. See p. 322.

4 THE BEST MUSEUMS

- **War Remnants Museum** (Ho Chi Minh City): Formerly called the Museum of American War Crimes, this ever-evolving collection is the face of Vietnam's war past. Exhibits are insightful and certainly rife with rhetoric, but offer a unique glimpse at propaganda from "the other side," and a yin to the heavy yang of Western reporting and documentation of the war years. A unique perspective and a must-see. See p. 325.
- **The Cham Museum** (Danang): This open-air colonial structure houses the largest collection of Cham sculpture in the world. Many of the 300-plus Hindu-inspired carvings are captivating. See p. 210.
- **Vietnam National Museum of Fine Arts** (Hanoi): This large colonial structure houses a fine collection of new works, historical lacquer and silk paintings, woodblocks, and folk and expressive works in oil. See p. 109.
- **Ho Chi Minh Museum** (Hanoi): Like the War Remnants Museum, the Ho Chi Minh Museum is a battleground of ideology. Located adjacent to his very tomb, the museum tells the tale of the revolutionary from cradle to grave. See p. 108.

5 THE BEST BEACHES

- **Nha Trang:** Vietnam's Ocean City is very crowded in the summertime with domestic tourists, but it's a great escape. The city has a few worthy sights—otherwise a cluttered market town—but there are some great new resorts and the best seafood going. See p. 268.
- **Mui Ne Beach, Phan Thiet:** Just a few hours from Saigon, Phan Thiet is the perfect getaway for Saigon residents. There's a golf course designed by Nick Faldo, the seafood is good, and there are some great day trips to remote sand dunes and smaller fishing villages. See p. 285.
- **Phu Quoc Island:** Phu Quoc boasts vast tracts of interior forestland and far-flung beaches great for exploring by motorbike. There's a small clutch of mid- to low-end resorts and La Veranda, an affordable luxury resort, but the times they are a-changin' and development is on the way. Get here fast. See p. 360.

6 THE BEST OF THE OUTDOORS

- **Kayaking in Halong Bay:** Often in conjunction with luxury cruises, kayaking in Halong Bay means going through low caves at low tide to get to the collapsed center of huge limestone and volcanic rings, where walls of jungle vegetation tower hundreds of feet overhead and crawl with monkeys, snakes, and rare animals. Kayaks are the only way to get up close. See chapter 7.

- **Multisports in the Central Highlands:** Opportunities abound for trekking, climbing, and mountain biking. Just contact one of the many small outfitters in Dalat (all are a copy of Phat Tire, a Vietnam pioneer). See chapter 10.
- **Cycling the Mekong Delta:** The best part about cycling in Vietnam is that, with some exceptions, the routes are quite flat. Adventure-tour outfitters out of both Hanoi and Ho Chi Minh City (see "Visitor Information & Tours," in chapters 5 and 12) can make any arrangements for a tour of any length, even providing a support van, and going by bike gives you a close-up view of it all. See chapter 13.
- **The Central Highlands or the Far North by Motorbike:** The rural roads of Vietnam beg to be explored, and going by motorbike, though dangerous, is a great way to do it. From Dalat in the Central Highlands, arrange a ride with an Easy Rider (p. 238), motorcycle guides who can take you up the Ho Chi Minh Trail (now a highway) and as far as Danang and Hoi An. In the far north, the Russian Minsk motorbike is the workhorse of the hills, and you can rent your own bike or go with a guide out of Hanoi and visit some incredible terrain. See chapter 10.
- **Taking On Fansipan or Trekking the Far North:** The very top of Vietnam, **Mount Fansipan** (p. 134) is a multiday adventure and only for the hearty, but the views afforded and the experience itself are amazing. There are lots of outfitters in the popular tourist town of Sapa, and you can arrange any number of treks to ethnic hilltribe villages, even overnights and homestays. See chapter 6.
- **Sail or Kite-Surf on the South China Sea:** Opportunities for watersports and sailing are many as you travel along Vietnam's coast. Most resorts have boats for rent, and Nha Trang is a good bet, as is the area off Mui Ne Beach near Phan Thiet, which is becoming a very popular wind- and kite-surfing spot. See chapter 11.
- **Cuc Phuong National Park:** A great little overnight from Hanoi for nature lovers, Cuc Phuong hosts a unique primate-research center, has good basic accommodations, and offers lots of hiking trails. Good guides are on hand to assist or hire for the day. See p. 177.
- **Cat Tien National Park:** Bird-watcher heaven, little Cat Tien is halfway between Saigon and Dalat, and an overnight stay includes night spotting, rustic accommodations, and a morning hike. The place is crawling with jungle animals, birds, and lots of naturalists and ornithologists chasing after them with binoculars. See p. 346.

7 THE BEST LUXURY ACCOMMODATIONS

- **InterContinental Hanoi Westlake** (© **04/6270-8888;** www.intercontinental.com): With rounded villas dotted around West Lake and a chic outdoor bar overlooking the water, this new resort is a perfect escape from the city. See p. 80.
- **Sofitel Metropole Hanoi** (© **04/3826-6919;** www.sofitel.com): The best hotel in Vietnam for luxury, service, style, and a connection to the history of Hanoi. See p. 81.
- **The Nam Hai** (Hoi An; © **0510/394-0000;** www.ghmhotels.com): This

resort is the most luxurious, over-the-top destination in Vietnam. A premier spa, three outdoor infinity pools, and private pool villas highlight a list that goes on and on. See p. 213.

- **Ana Mandara Villas Dalat** (✆ **063/355-5888;** www.anamandara-resort.com): This is the most charming hotel in Vietnam, with 17 lovingly restored French colonial villas nestled upon a hill in the Central Highlands. See p. 240.
- **Sofitel Dalat Palace** (✆ **063/382-5444;** www.sofitel.com): There's nothing like it anywhere, really, this converted palace of the last emperor of Vietnam, Bao Dai. Retro-style rooms come with fireplaces, divan beds, claw-foot tubs, and great artwork. Fine dining and a high standard of service round out the package. One of those special finds in the world. See p. 240.
- **Evason Hideaway Ana Mandara** (Nha Trang; ✆ **058/372-8222;** www.sixsenses.com): Think the Ana Mandara done to perfection, but set on a far-flung beach with the country's most high-end pool villas. See p. 272.
- **Princess d'Annam** (Phan Thiet; ✆ **062/368-2222;** www.princessannam.com): This brand-new resort is an absolute dream for southern Vietnam. Luxurious suites and villas are nestled around a tropical garden, with picturesque oceanside dining, an outdoor infinity pool, and a three-story spa rounding out the indulgence. See p. 286.
- **Grand Mercure La Veranda** (Duong Dong Beach; ✆ **077/398-2988;** www.mercure-asia.com): This stately colonial resort with pristine views of the ocean is Vietnam's premier island getaway. See p. 365.
- **Park Hyatt Saigon** (✆ **08/3824-1234;** www.saigon.park.hyatt.com): This new luxury hotel has a prime downtown location overlooking the Saigon Opera House. The interior is sophisticated and modern, and the decor is luxurious without being chintzy. The hotel also has some of the best dining options in Saigon. See p. 304.
- **Sheraton Saigon** (✆ **08/3827-2828;** www.sheraton.com/saigon): Come here for glitzy surroundings and big conferences. It's a popular place for business travelers. See p. 305.

8 THE BEST MIDRANGE ACCOMMODATIONS

- **Maison d'Hanoi** (✆ **04/3938-0999;** www.hanovahotel.com): This is a stylish hotel in the center of Hanoi, just south of Hoan Kiem, with a compact setup and high standard. An affordable boutique downtown hotel. See p. 83.
- **Topas Ecolodge** (✆ **020/387-1331;** www.topasecolodge.com): Topas Ecolodge has the best mountain and rice paddy views in Sapa. Nestled in a misty valley away from the din of Sapa town, the lodge is also an ideal jumping-off point for treks and hikes. See p. 136.
- **Life Resort Hoi An and Quy Nhon** (www.life-resorts.com): Whether at the more isolated beachside resort in Quy Nhon (✆ **056/384-0132**) or at the fine resort in Hoi An (✆ **0510/391-4555**)—the very closest resort to town—Life Resort sets a new standard. See p. 214 and 264.
- **Blue Ocean Resort** (Phan Thiet; ✆ **062/384-7322;** www.blueoceanresort.com): The recent face-lift has done marvels for this resort. Stand-alone bungalows, with balconies overlooking the ocean and private outdoor tubs, are your best bet here. Great spa, too. See p. 288.

- **Palace Hotel** (Ho Chi Minh City; ✆ **08/3824-4231;** www.bongsencorporation.com): A recent renovation has left this place with a cool Art Deco look and modern, comfortable rooms. Fold in the ideal downtown location, and this hotel is a real bargain. See p. 309.
- **Victoria Chau Doc and Can Tho** (www.victoriahotels-asia.com): These two riverside classics are worth the trip. Chau Doc (✆ **076/386-5010**) is a renovated old administration building, and Can Tho (✆ **0710/381-0111**) is a retrofitted grande dame. Take great day trips and enjoy slow, riverside living. See p. 359 and 355.

9 THE BEST DINING

- **Cha Ca La Vong** (Hanoi; ✆ **04/3825-3929**): A Vietnamese institution and a tourist rite of passage, really. A meal here is a memorable, do-it-yourself affair on the beat-up second floor of a restaurant as old as the hills (and it looks like it has never been painted). The food does all the talking: a unique dish of whitefish flash-fried in lots of peanut oil with dill and turmeric. See p. 90.
- **La Badiane** (Hanoi; ✆ **04/3942-4509**): The hottest table in town, La Badiane offers affordable French cuisine in an atmospheric colonial mansion. See p. 89.
- **Mango Rooms** (Hoi An; ✆ **0510/391-0839**): The atmosphere is fast and furious as hip young owner Duc slings a unique brand of Asian-fusion fare, heavy on grilled items and delicious light ingredients. See p. 222.
- **Le Rabelais** (Dalat; ✆ **063/382-5444**): Fine French cuisine served with real panache at one of Vietnam's most luxurious rural hotels. See p. 243.
- **Quan An Ngon Restaurant** (Ho Chi Minh City; ✆ **08/3829-9449**): Its popularity has spawned a number of small offshoots, including a specialty restaurant focused on northern rice dishes and another new outlet for buffet dinners, but the original restaurant near the Reunification Palace is the best. A virtual survey course of authentic Vietnamese cuisine from every region of the country, this restaurant is the town's most atmospheric, friendly, and busy. See p. 318.

2

Vietnam in Depth

Despite its "in-depth" subtitle, this chapter only briefly skims the surface of a rather deep reservoir; literary and nonfiction works about the Vietnam War era alone are legion, and Vietnam's cultural heritage goes back thousands of years. The Vietnamese are careful to distinguish their cultural traditions from those of its neighbor China. With its distinct, very sophisticated traditions of painting (particularly lacquer painting), crafts such as weaving and woodcarving, theater, opera, dance, and water puppetry, Vietnam's own cultural landscape is as varied and colorful as its topography. And despite centuries of occupation by foreigners, Vietnamese cultural traditions have survived. Opportunities abound to explore trade villages, learn about Vietnamese cooking, witness the country's performing arts like water puppetry (in Hanoi), court dance (in Hue), catch a traditional opera, or look over the shoulder of artists at work in studios or at street side. ***Note:*** Please see chapter 16 for information about the Vietnamese language and chapter 17 for an overview on Vietnamese cuisine.

1 WHO ARE THE VIETNAMESE?

Over 90% of Vietnamese people are Viet, or *Kinh,* people, descendants of the indigenous race, but with the many violent and migratory incursions over the centuries, as well as the southward expansion of Vietnamese territory into Cambodia, modern Vietnamese are a combination of many races and cultural influences. Chinese, Khmer (or Cambodian), Cham, and indigenous groups in the north, central mountains and coast, and far south were all one-time enemies turned allies and comprise the melting pot of modern Vietnamese.

So who are the Vietnamese? A people trying to find that out themselves, really. With the opening of their doors in the late 1980s, capitalism came trickling in and now flows like a tidal wave, and the "comrades" of old now elbow their way to becoming "consumers" and participating in the global market. The contradictions are sometimes absurd.

The dominant group, the ethnic Viet or Kinh people, inhabit the prime lowland rice-growing territories and are a very lopsided majority. Kinh people are descendants of inhabitants of the provinces of southern China.

Vietnam's tapestry of ethnic minorities spreads across the vast tracts of the Central Highlands and the far north (for more information about the specific hilltribe groups in each region, see the related boxes in chapters 6 and 10). Known under French governance and during the U.S. war years as Montagnards, ethnic hilltribe people and their myriad subgroups in Vietnam divide the mountainous areas of the country into a colorful patchwork of disparate languages, cultures, and traditions. A visit to the regions in the far north or Central Highlands, best when accompanied by a guide who can make introductions, is a unique glimpse of the diversity and fortitude of these resilient groups who have been immigrating from China and nearby Laos for hundreds of years. Ethnic Khmer, or Cambodian people, live in large communities in the south, mostly along the Cambodian border and on the

Mekong Delta. Ethnic Cham people, the Muslim descendants of the 15th-century Champa Kingdom that once ruled the far south, live mostly in isolated fishing communities in the coastal south.

A few million ethnic Chinese make up a strong merchant class centered in the major cities. Ho Chi Minh City has a teeming and prosperous Chinatown, and Chinese merchants have lived for generations and plied the same trades for hundreds of years in Hanoi's Old Quarter. As one-time conquerors and colonists, and contemporary enemies, ethnic Chinese have been persecuted since the expulsion of American forces and reunification of Vietnam in 1975. Many Chinese in Vietnam fled, joining the deluge of Vietnamese "boat people" escaping persecution.

Today ethnic tensions in Vietnam are limited to the majority government, with its fear of and disputes with ethnic minority people in the Central Highlands and the far north. Only recently, a contingent of refugees fleeing persecution in Laos—Vietnam's cousin in paranoia about hilltribe insurgency—found refuge in the Central Highlands, only to suffer suspicion, searches, and bullying from the Vietnamese. Still smiting from hilltribe group complicity with French and U.S. forces during the Vietnam War, the government is wary of these stubborn, autonomous people, placing them into controlled village units of "enforced primitivism."

Vietnamese family units are tight. Generations live together and practice the same trade, usually rural farming, but merchants and shopkeepers also work together generation after generation. Population density is high because wherever there are no mountains, the land is either developed or cultivated; flat, arable ground is at a premium. Collectivization and cooperation in villages have always been the norm—some argue that some form of socialism was inherent in the Vietnamese makeup. Vietnam nearly collapsed in abject poverty under Communism, but with its return to the market economy, village units have formed again and rural life has improved. Although material wealth eludes most (many Vietnamese still live in abject poverty), the standard of living is on the rise. Though the country is in a mad dash of modernization, the economy has remained largely agrarian, with farmers, fishermen, and forestry workers accounting for three-quarters of the workforce in a mostly rural demographic. The Vietnamese have a strong sense of family and of community, and are accustomed to close human contact and far-reaching relationships around large patriarchal family groups.

The French categorized the country into three distinct regions—Cochin China in the south, Annam in the center, and Tonkin in the north—and it's important to note that Vietnam was unified under one name only after the departure of Japanese and French troops at the end of World War II. It took years of fighting—first with the French, then with the Americans—before the nation was united, and even today Vietnamese from the north and the south are quite distinct.

Traditional village life once centered on the *dinh,* or small shrine honored as the god of the village or the mountains, now a Confucian altar to the generations that came before. Young Vietnamese are increasingly seeking higher-paying jobs in cities, but most return home or support their extended families from afar.

Hospitality is very important to Vietnamese, and travelers often find themselves as guests in local homes and offered the choicest pieces of a humble repast, or sharing rice whiskey and laughter. Vietnamese are very kind and playful. Children are doted upon. Families are close and supportive, and adopt new members all the time (you'll be taken in, too). Accept invites whenever possible.

It's easy to know a lot about Vietnam and Vietnamese culture, but much harder to really *understand,* say many longtime expats. Learning about the concept of "saving face," for example, often takes some painful lessons in "losing face," but a trip to Vietnam is a great way to get perspective on our own cultural programming.

2 VIETNAMESE RELIGION

Religion in Vietnam influences every aspect of daily living but is loosely practiced at a temple. Over 75% of Vietnamese follow a mix of **Confucianism** and its tenets of ancestor worship, as well as **Buddhism** and **Daoism.** Buddhism came to the region via China in the 2nd century A.D., a form of Mahayana Buddhism, or "The Big Vehicle," in which the belief is that all sentient beings will attain enlightenment en masse. There are some pockets of Theravada Buddhists, mostly among ethnic Khmer communities in the south, who are proponents of the "Small Vehicle" belief—inherited from India via Thailand and Cambodia—in enlightenment on a person-by-person basis. Daoism, a Chinese traditional belief in the harmony of nature, also influences belief, and a small sect of Hoa Hao Buddhists believes strongly in ancestor worship.

Only a small percentage of Vietnamese are **Protestant,** but **Catholicism** came ashore with missionaries as early as the 17th century and found a firmament in Vietnam that lasts to this day, particularly in the south (in fact, after the withdrawal of the French and partitioning of the country at the 17th Parallel, the majority of northern Catholics fled south). There are a number of Catholic vestiges in the Central Highlands and far north where missionaries did some of their hardest work, and devotion to this day, now led by a Vietnamese bishop, is still strong. Every city has a Catholic cathedral, and church services are well attended and quite fervent.

Unique is the **Cao Dai** faith, a homegrown religion that embraces all faiths and philosophies, and even ranks scientists like Pasteur as saints. There are more than two million Cao Dai worshipers in Vietnam, predominantly in the south, and their very colorful Holy See near Tay Ninh is a popular day trip from Ho Chi Minh City.

A small percentage of Vietnamese, mostly the Cham people living along the coast in central Vietnam, follow the tenets of **Islam.**

3 A LOOK AT THE PAST: VIETNAM THE COUNTRY, NOT THE WAR

The war in Vietnam is written large on the collective consciousness of the last few generations in the West, but Vietnam's scope of history spans thousands of years and has seen the rise and fall of many empires and conquerors. Not to minimize the devastating effects on both sides during what the Vietnamese call "The American War," but the conflict that ended now more than 30 years ago is far in the past for most Vietnamese, many of whom consider the time as just another in a very long series of incursions by a foreign foe. Search for volumes of Vietnamese history in your local library in the West, and you'll find literally hundreds of tomes about the war with the United States but little about the scope of Vietnam's 1,000 years of struggle with foreign powers. Vietnam's recent struggles are so close, so well documented, that our image of the country is intimately connected to footage of napalm-strafed hillocks, suicide attacks in Saigon, prolonged bombing campaigns, prisoners of war in the most desperate straits, the Vietnamese "boat people" of the 1970s and 1980s, or returning U.S. veterans with PTSD (post-traumatic stress disorder), the likes of Robert De Niro in the *Deer Hunter* or *Rambo.* But talk to Vietnamese about the "American War," and you'll hear little recrimination. In fact, Vietnam's war record and persistence in the face of an economically superior foe is its greatest source of strength in a long history of prevailing against the odds—or an "ongoing revolution," according to Marxism.

Vietnamese history can be broken into six distinct eras: 1) prehistory up until the first of the vaunted Hung Kings (like the British legends of Arthur); 2) the Chinese millennium from 189 B.C. to A.D. 939; 3) 1,000 years of Vietnamese autonomy and wars with the Khmer and the Cham to the south, as well as ongoing border scraps with China until the late 19th century; 4) colonization of Vietnam, again, under the French for 80 years; 5) war with the United States; and 6) years of hard-fought independence that began with Ho Chi Minh's Declaration of Independence but wasn't cemented until the fall of Saigon in 1975 and a unified Vietnam.

EARLY HISTORY

Early history is steeped in legend, and even the most reliable documents are but secondhand musings in the footnotes of ancient Chinese texts. The earliest kingdom, the Van Lang, was formed by the legendary **King Huong Vuong,** the Vietnamese equivalent of Arthur and his Knights of the Round Table. For some 2,000 years until the 3rd century B.C., the mythical Hung dynasty prospered in the Red River Delta concurrently with early Bronze Age cultures, and later the Dong Son Bronze Age culture, which dated from 850 to 300 B.C. (see the box on Dong Son culture, below).

Legend has it that Hung kings had magical powers and their story is shrouded in myth and legend, but, particularly under the later Hung kings, there was relative stability and progress. Communal life centered on wet rice cultivation, a model that has stood through the ages, and early Vietnamese under the Hung also raised cattle; fostered the growth of weaving, pottery, and building skills; and developed intricate bronze-smith technology. The Hung dynasty crumbled under repeated incursions from China in the 3rd century B.C. (culminating in collapse in 258 B.C.).

Under the leadership of **An Duong Vuong,** the King Arthur of Vietnam, a small kingdom of ethnic Viet tribes called **Au Lac** formed in the 3rd century B.C. The tiny kingdom centered on the ancient capital near Co Loa, north of present-day Hanoi. The Au Lac were eventually absorbed into the Chinese Qin dynasty in 221 B.C., but as that dynasty crumpled, a Chinese general by the name of Chao Tuo, or Trieu Da in Vietnamese, conquered the northern regions in 207 B.C. and established Nan Yueh, a Chinese term meaning "Far South" (called *Nam Viet* in Vietnamese), an autonomous principality that would be handled as a "rogue territory" by the Chinese for hundreds of years to come.

THE CHINESE MILLENNIUM

From 111 B.C., Vietnam was under Chinese rule, this time as part of the Han Empire. Vietnam would remain part of greater China for the next thousand years. The Chinese form of writing was adopted (to be replaced by a Roman alphabet in the 17th c.), Confucianism was instated as the leading ideology, and Chinese governors were installed as local rulers. The

Dong Son Culture: Vietnam's Non-Chinese Origins

First discovered in 1924 near the Ma River in the far north near Dong Son (thus the name), Dong Son Drums are large, ornate brass kettles supposedly dating as far back as the 7th century B.C. But early research of these sites was shoddy, and the French Ecole d'Extrème Orient used some rather loose evidence to posit the existence of a unified society throughout the region and named the culture Dong Son after its first discovery. So the truth about these ancient and obviously well-organized civilizations is still in question, and although Vietnamese cling to the Dong Son Drum as evidence of an early, very advanced, and, most important, autonomous (read "not Chinese") civilization, questions remain. Many archaeologists believe that the Dong Son cultures originated from outside incursions of Austronesian groups.

What we do know for sure is that the drums were produced by a very advanced early civilization (from the 7th c. B.C. to the 1st and 2nd c. A.D.) and made from sandstone and terra-cotta molds. Each drum is unique, with some commonalities, like the small sculptures of frogs around the faces of some drums, as well as images of the sun and of the Lac Bird.

Chinese were heavy-handed colonists, seeking to profit on the backs of the conquered Vietnamese, imposing forced labor, and extracting high taxes at sword point.

For centuries, few effectively challenged Chinese rule until the **Ba Trung** sisters, Trung Trac and Trung Nhi, took the place of their executed dissident husbands and, in a wave of popular support and revolutionary spirit that is revered to this day, staged the **Hai Ba Trung Rebellion** (literally, the "Two Sister's Rebellion") in A.D. 39. The sisters, leading an angry horde, expelled the Chinese and ruled the northern kingdom for just 3 years before the Chinese resumed control and the sisters, in their shame, drowned themselves. The Hai Ba Trung Rebellion stands out only because of its brief success and was really just an early incarnation of the many rebellions against Chinese rule that would follow through the long Chinese control—rebellions that, despite their tenacity, all ended under the brutal thumb of tyrannical Chinese rule.

THE VIETNAMESE MILLENNIUM

One of the greatest triumphs of the loosely unified Viet people came in 939 B.C. when **Ngo Quyen** defeated the Chinese at **Bach Dang,** a naval battle of legend in which the Vietnamese surprised their enemy by placing massive pikes in the waters of Halong Bay, where the Chinese boats were run aground and ransacked. Although Ngo Quyen died and Vietnam fell into a prolonged civil war under the Ngo dynasty, Vietnam was finally free of China.

In 968 B.C., **Dinh Bo Linh** pacified, unified, and made extensive treaties to keep Vietnam a fully autonomous Chinese vassal state. So began the ascendancy of Vietnam's mandarins, a high caste of intelligentsia who created special schools for promising Vietnamese to be groomed into the country's elite. All education was conducted in Chinese by Chinese (see "Temple of Literature and National University [Van Mieu–Quoc Tu Giam]" in chapter 5), and Mandarins exerted great influence. These concessions meant that Vietnam was free to run its affairs independent of the Chinese, other than the regular tolls it paid to mother China. Vietnam benefited from this adoption of China's educational system, as well as inherited technologies of math and science, the lunar calendar, and both legal and educational systems. The Chinese imprint is still visible today in Vietnam's Confucian traditions, architecture, and even today's pell-mell thrust toward a market economy.

Vietnam's long period of autonomy was not without peril, however, as incursions from the Cham in what is now central Vietnam and the Khmer in the far south put pressure on the burgeoning united state. The kingdom flourished and strengthened, enough for the Vietnamese to repel the intrusion of Mongol invaders under Kublai Khan from the north, and armies from the kingdom of Champa from Danang and the east, in the mid–13th century. Vietnam gradually absorbed the Cham Empire and made progressive claims on Khmer land as far as the Mekong Delta.

In 1400, China once again occupied Hanoi, reclaiming its foundering vassal as its own, until, in that same year, a peasant uprising changed everything, something like the popular movement of the two Trung sisters. Socialist historians pointed to this as evidence of the true revolutionary spirit among Vietnamese.

Even after the shortest trip in Vietnam, you'll recognize the name **Le Loi** from street signs everywhere. Le Loi was a rich landowner who organized resistance to the occupying Chinese forces from a base high in the mountains. In 1426 he achieved a great military victory at Sontay and at Lam Son in the far north, vanquishing the Chinese and paving the way to his becoming emperor, renaming himself **Le Thai To.** He reigned from 1428 to 1527 and heralded what many call a "golden age" in Vietnam under the Le Kings, a time where the country came into its own, developing a new education system and penal code, especially under the rule of **Emperor Le Thanh Tong.**

Instability at court was rife, however, and the country was eventually split along north-south lines in 1545; the north followed the Le dynasty, and the south followed the Nguyen, with ongoing conflict between the two.

Europeans, particularly the French, seized upon Vietnamese instability and Catholic missions, and European traders began to come ashore. French Jesuit Alexandre de Rhodes arrived in Vietnam in the 17th century and created a Romanized Vietnamese script, an important milestone in Vietnamese literacy and accessibility to the West.

Continued clan tension between the north and south led to numerous failed peasant revolts, until the **Tay Son Rebellion** in central Vietnam near the town of Quy Nhon saw the ascendancy of **Nguyen Hue,** who proclaimed himself the **Emperor Quang Trung** and fought to obliterate the Nguyen in the south and the Trinh in the north, effectively uniting Vietnam under one banner.

When Quang Trung died without an heir in 1792, **Nguyen Anh,** a southerner, declared himself king in 1802 and adopted the name **Gia Long.** For the first time, he called the country **Vietnam.** The **Nguyen Capital** was in **Hue,** and the Citadel and grand tombs of the fallen Nguyen kings still stand.

By the 1850s, the French had already settled in the region, the arms of the Catholic Church reaching far and wide and exacting more and more influence. The French pressed for further control and, in 1847, attacked Danang, which became the French city of Tourane. Three decades later—after first capturing Saigon, then Cambodia, then central Vietnam (or Anam), and later the north—France signed a treaty as the official protectorate of Vietnam in 1883. And so began some

80 years of colonial rule once again in Vietnam.

FRENCH COLONIAL RULE & THE FIRST WAR OF INDOCHINA

Some recent media, the likes of Graham Green's *The Quiet American* (made into a film with Michael Caine in 2001) or *Indochine,* portray colonial Vietnam as an ephemeral time of gentle European eccentrics and explorers in starched white collars (usually sweaty) traipsing around an exotic landscape of cacophonous streets or padding about dark opium dens among erotic temptresses in the traditional *ao dai* dress, a romanticized image of Vietnam as a land of exotic pleasures. Missing are scenes of Vietnamese under the lash of the colonists. Missing are scenes of desperate peasant revolts, poverty, and forced labor. By the 1900s, a general equanimity was reached between the Vietnamese and their occupiers, who painted themselves as benevolent benefactors of culture and education. But it was that education, and the writings of French patriots like Rousseau and Voltaire, that fueled Vietnamese ire over French subjugation. The fighting was soon to follow.

Early-20th-century resistance, like the **Quan Phuc Hoi** movement that sought restoration of an autonomous Vietnam or the **Tonkin Free School Movement** that preached ascendancy of Vietnamese traditions and culture, imminently failed or were brutally crushed by the French, and the numbers in the notorious prisons, like the **Hanoi Hilton,** swelled to breaking points. The proud people of Vietnam bristled under colonial rule, and in 1930 revolution found fertile ground to establish a nationalist movement, especially with the return of **Nguyen Tat Thanh,** otherwise known as **Ho Chi Minh.** Uncle Ho rose from relative obscurity and a long life as an expatriate and exile (read the story of Ho Chi Minh in chapter 8). He overcame the limitations of his rather frail carriage and bearing to become the leader of decades of struggle. World War II and occupation by the Japanese in 1940 helped fuel the movement by creating chaos and nationalist fervor, and in celebration of the retreat of the Japanese, Ho Chi Minh declared Vietnam an independent nation in August 1945.

However, the French, in defiance of international pressure, returned to Vietnam at the end of World War II and took the north as their own once again, infuriating Communists who had, but briefly, seen a window of opportunity for self-governance. The French didn't agree with Ho Chi Minh's cleverly versed plea for autonomy and democracy. On September 2, 1945, he began with the famed quote from the U.S. declaration that "All men are created equal." Despite international pressure for full French withdrawal from their interests in Indochina, the French—under leadership of plucky Gen. Charles de Gaulle in an effort to restore French colonial glory—sent a large expeditionary force. Guerilla fighting in all of the provinces escalated, and in November 1946, in reaction to Vietnamese attacks, the French shelled Haiphong, the major port city in the far north, killing an estimated 6,000 and heralding a new colonial struggle, this time by a highly motivated Viet Minh with popular support and credibility. After 7 years of French/Viet Minh conflict—and despite heavy backing by Eisenhower (the U.S. supplied planes and 80% of the war costs)—the French, dug in at Dien Bien Phu, made the fatal blunder of being cavalier about their enemy's capacities: They chose a wide, shallow valley where they assumed that their superior artillery could handle any attack.

General Giap, Vietnam's top strategist, had acquired heavy artillery from China and, with a huge heroic effort of human will, hauled his new hardware over mountain passes to surround the wide valley at

Dien Bien Phu. The French were completely surprised. In short order, the airstrip was destroyed and the French were cut off. Supplies and new troops arrived via airlift, but the Viet Minh were relentless, engaging a vicious trench ground war—Vietnamese proudly declare that the siege of Dien Bien Phu was won not by bullets and bombs, but with Vietnamese resolve and the shovel. The battle lasted 25 days, with Viet Minh troops winning by inches, but with heavy casualties on both sides. Brave French and South Vietnamese paratroopers dropped into the battle site in the 11th hour when hope was surely lost, but on May 7, 1954, the Viet Minh made their final assault. When the smoke cleared, North Vietnamese rejoiced to what looked like the end of a foreign empire.

Meeting in Geneva, all sides agreed that Vietnam would be partitioned at the 17th parallel (a line that would come to mark the front in the next war), and the country would hold free elections 2 years hence. The north would be ruled in the interim by Ho Chi Minh, the leader of the Viet Minh, and the south by Ngo Dinh Diem, a U.S.-backed expatriate politician.

When election time arrived, Diem, facing likely defeat from the populist candidate Ho Chi Minh, withdrew from the election, breaking his promise at the Geneva Convention, and so began the struggle that pitted a reluctant superpower against a headstrong nationalist movement. The Viet Minh became the Viet Cong, and the war of attrition was on.

THE SECOND WAR OF INDOCHINA: VIETNAM & THE UNITED STATES

In 1961, in the hopes of supporting democracy in South Vietnam, President John F. Kennedy tentatively escalated U.S. involvement in Vietnam based on fears of the domino effect, a phrase set forth by former President Eisenhower and popularized by Robert McNamara, then U.S. secretary of defense. The idea was that, with the support of "Red China," the countries of Southeast Asia, mostly poor, developing nations with large rural populations, were susceptible to Communist ideology, then the world's greatest perceived evil. Vietnam—being closest to China and heavily reliant on Chinese aid—would, the theory went, be the first to fall. The domino effect meant that Vietnam's fall would trigger grass-roots Communist movements in neighboring Laos, Cambodia, Thailand, and Burma, and on to the rest of south Asia. Vietnam, and specifically the 17th Parallel, is where U.S. ideologues chose to draw the line in the mud.

In its earliest stages, U.S. involvement was meant to "win the hearts and minds of the people." Hoping to model the benefits of capitalism and lead the fight with humanitarian efforts, there were many doctors and educators among early advisors, but most met with skepticism and armed resistance from a peasantry well versed in taking bonbons from imperial forces by day and practicing subterfuge by night.

Southern president Diem was an unpopular, heavy-handed ruler. In the early 1960s, southern Buddhists began to protest against Diem's unfairness and persecution of Buddhists and rural people (Diem was a staunch Catholic). In a famous image from the war, an elder monk set himself aflame in Saigon on June 11, 1963. Unrest in the south was growing, but the U.S. still backed Diem right up until the coup d'état in November 1963 and Diem's demise. Three weeks later, President Kennedy was assassinated.

The **Gulf of Tonkin Incident** was a watershed moment in the Vietnam War. Reports vary, and many believe that the U.S. engineered or exaggerated the events of August 1964 in the Gulf of Tonkin, when two U.S. ships, the *Maddox* and the *Turner Joy*, were reportedly attacked while patrolling the Gulf of Tonkin near Hanoi. In response, President Lyndon Johnson bombed Hanoi, the first of many large-scale bombing campaigns; the U.S. Congress also passed the Gulf of Tonkin Resolution, giving the U.S. president broad powers to wage war in Vietnam. Though hardly the sinking of the *Lusitania* or the attack on Pearl Harbor, the incident at Tonkin set off an irreversible chain of events. U.S. bombing campaigns increased in 1965 with the hopes that the North Vietnamese would just surrender or come to the bargaining table—in fact, they never would, and the many civilian deaths caused by **Operation Rolling Thunder** merely steeled northern resolve. War protests in the U.S. began as early as 1965 with the Students for a Democratic Society march on Washington, D.C.

Official war was never declared in Vietnam, but on March 8, 1965, President Johnson dispatched the first full contingent of over 3,000 American combat troops to Danang to prop up the south. The Soviet Union and China weighed in with assistance to the north. The rest is history. You couldn't turn the channel on what would be called the "Living Room War," the first combat to be reported on television nightly, and the first to be so hotly debated in public consciousness. Americans had always believed that they fought, and won, wars that were justified, but Vietnam was a confounding exception. Early images of U.S. troops burning villages raised more questions than support at home, and just as the number of U.S. casualties increased, so did youthful protest and dissent. Vietnam divided the United States for generations, and many see the years of discord between political "hawks and doves" as molding political consciousness and public activism in America.

The statistics tell this story best: Two and a half million U.S. military personnel served during the 15-year conflict—58,000 gave their lives in action, some 300,000 were wounded, and countless numbers suffered post-traumatic stress disorder (PTSD). The war cost the United States over $900 billion. U.S. planes dropped 8 billion pounds of bombs (more than four times the tonnage of all of World War II), and along with Operation Ranch Hand, the systematic spraying of carcinogenic defoliants, Vietnam was left nearly a wasteland.

Three million lives were lost on the Vietnamese side—more than half were civilians. After the war, hundreds of thousands of South Vietnamese were put in reeducation camps, and an untold number of "boat people" fleeing oppression died at sea due to storms or at the hands of the South China Sea's rabid pirates (most of the lucky few who made it languished in a refugee camp for years before being able to find placement abroad). Tens of thousands of deaths were due to land mines and UXO (unexploded ordinances) in Vietnam since 1975, and tens of thousands more still suffer deformities because of exposure to U.S. chemical defoliants.

Troops numbered just 200,000 in 1965, but by the end of 1968, the totals were over 540,000. In November 1965, the United States had a flying success in the first open battle of the war in the Ia Drang Valley in the Central Highlands. With its superior fire power and air support, the United States succeeded in herding Viet Cong troops into the open, and though the United States suffered heavy casualties, the success at Ia Drang bolstered U.S. resolve that the war could be won.

But Vietnam was a guerilla war, an episodic war against an enemy happy to win by inches, to suffer major casualties in order to break American resolve, to attack, retreat, and wait. The Viet Cong troops, with basic support from China, could subsist, they said, on a cup of rice and a cup of bullets each day, and the Ho Chi

Minh supply line, a trail "complex" more than a road, could never be stopped by U.S. might. The North Vietnamese also were able to attack and retreat into neighboring Laos and Cambodia. Clever "tiger traps" and anti-personnel mines and snares set by the North Vietnamese troops were also demoralizing to a mostly drafted (that is, nonvoluntary) U.S. force. The Vietnamese built elaborate tunnel complexes and had many spies in the ranks of the south.

The mountainous jungles of Vietnam meant that the United States could not use tanks or armored personnel carriers in combat. U.S. techniques were to use defoliants, establish defoliated perimeters around fixed positions, and patrol to hunt down an enemy—tactics that played right into the Vietnamese strategy of attack and retreat.

U.S. soldiers fought valiantly, but the strategy of a "limited war" meant that the army had to fight one-handed and was unable to mount a full attack, mostly for fear of reprisals from nearby China or the Soviet Union. The U.S. was losing the "war of attrition" to a highly motivated North Vietnamese force, while the Army of the Republic of Vietnam (ARVN), the troops who fought alongside the U.S. GIs, was notoriously indifferent.

The tide of the war turned with the **Tet Offensive** in late 1968. U.S. Gen. William Westmoreland put all of his eggs in one basket, amassing the bulk of U.S. forces along the demilitarized zone (DMZ) at the 17th Parallel in expectation of a full frontal attack from the north. U.S. forces faced devastating attacks near Khe San in the months leading up to it, but after major diversionary attacks at Hue, just north of the DMZ, North Vietnamese forces instead made an end run through neighboring Laos and Cambodia, connected with troops loyal to the revolution embedded in the south, and penetrated into the heart of Saigon, even taking the U.S. Embassy briefly. Northern General Giap's tactics were a great risk, and losses on the North Vietnamese side were heavy, but the Tet Offensive was the beginning of the end of the war—at home in the United States and on the ground in Vietnam.

After Tet came the devastating My Lai Massacre on March 16, 1968, where a platoon led by Lieut. William Calley went on a rampage that left 500 villagers dead and a world wondering what was happening in Vietnam. "The whole world is watching!" the demonstrators shouted at the 1968 Democratic convention—and it was. U.S. troops returning to the United States were met with jeers. There were "two wars," actually: the military war of bombs and guns in Vietnam, and the political war in the United States, a country undergoing drastic social changes.

The Paris Peace Talks began in the same year that the U.S. election brought Richard Nixon to the stage, and troop reductions began just a year later. Ho Chi Minh died in 1969 of natural causes, but his memory was a rallying cry, while back in the United States, protests became violent in Kent State University, where national guardsmen shot and killed four unarmed protestors. The **Paris Peace Accords** finally became a success, and the United States ceased bombing North Vietnam. A massive exchange of prisoners took place at the DMZ, and "Vietnamization" of the war began—in other words, U.S. combat ended and turned the war over to the South Vietnamese.

After more than a decade of fighting, the Communists took Saigon on April 30, 1975, and in 1976 the north and south were officially reunited.

MODERN VIETNAM

Rather than enjoying the newfound peace after driving out the United States, Vietnam invaded Cambodia after border skirmishes in 1978. China, friend of Cambodia, then invaded Vietnam in 1979.

At home, Communist ideology made for empty stomachs, and international trade embargoes and faltering support from the Soviet Union made life difficult for the Vietnamese. Though postwar Vietnam was autonomous, proud, and full of principles, the rice hampers were empty. By 1988, all Soviet aid was gone. Millions were starving and inflation neared 1,000%. Desperate boat people, many of the unfortunate Vietnamese who had complied with the Americans, took to the seas on leaky boats, and many met horrible fates at the hands of the South China Sea's deadly pirates.

Faced with disaster, the Vietnamese government began implementing the new ideas of ***Doi Moi,*** a free-market policy that decentralized business, allowing private citizens and farmers to own land and the Vietnamese currency to trade on international markets. To ingratiate itself with the international community in the hope of aid and trade, Vietnam withdrew its army from Cambodia in 1989, and as the 1990s began, the country began opening to the world. After peace with Cambodia and Vietnam's move to market economy, the United States lifted its long-standing trade embargo against Vietnam in 1994, and the two countries established diplomatic relations in 1995. Vietnam also joined ASEAN (Association of Southeast Asian Nations), and recent years have seen one milestone after another toward cooperation: a visit by President Bill Clinton in 2000, huge economic aid packages and commitments to cooperation, answers to long-standing questions about U.S. POWs, and U.S. assistance to victims of Agent Orange. Vietnam hosted the Asian Games in 2003, putting its best foot forward in what was a coup for international opinion. American Secretary of Defense Donald Rumsfeld met with Vietnam's defense minister in Washington, D.C., in 2003, and the USS *Vandergrift* pulled into port in Ho Chi Minh City at about the same time, the first U.S. Navy ship to dock in a Vietnamese port since hasty withdrawal in 1975. Telling signs, indeed.

The per-capita income of Vietnam (less than $800) may seem low by Western standards, but the number is steadily rising each year. Unfortunately, the gap between urban and rural incomes remains noticeably large: Recent data indicates the per-capita income of the entire nation is $726, while Ho Chi Minh City's is a whopping $1,800. The country's stated goal—to become a middle-class country by 2010—means raising per-capita income to at least $1,000. Economic analysts believe this goal is attainable. Meanwhile, the country's status as an Asian "Tiger Economy" was solidified with its ascension to the World Trade Organization in early 2007. Shortly afterward, President Nguyen Minh Triet became the first Vietnamese head of state to visit Washington since the war ended. These are exciting times for Vietnam. And while Communist rhetoric still exists as an all-encompassing nationalism, the Vietnamese look toward a bright and very different future in the free market.

3

Planning Your Trip to Vietnam

Obtaining a prearranged visa and following some important medical guidelines is all that's required for a safe and exciting trip to Vietnam. But the information below helps you plan your finances, decide whether to go on your own or by tour, and learn about what to expect in Vietnamese hotels and restaurants. For the lowdown on taking a side trip to Cambodia, see chapter 14.

1 WHEN TO GO

Think Vietnam and you might imagine a steamy jungle and hot sun—and you'd be mostly right. But even though Vietnam is tropical, you'll find a real range, from chilly mountaintops and cool highland areas to sun-drenched coastline and, yes, that steamy jungle, too, laced with the swampy rivers you've seen in movies.

Opposing monsoon seasons in the north and south mean that seasonal changes are different in north, central, and south Vietnam. The good news for travelers is that this means it's always high season *somewhere* in Vietnam, and the tropical south is always warm. Vietnam can be broken into three **distinct geographical and climatic zones** as follows: north, central, and south.

The **north** is cooler than the rest of the country. Winter months, from November until January, can be quite cool, especially in mountainous areas. Northern temperatures range from 60°F to 90°F (16°C–32°C). If you are going far north to **Sapa** or **Dien Bien Phu** along the China/Laos border, be sure to bring one extra layer of warmth (a pullover will do); near Sapa is Fansipan, Vietnam's highest point, and there is even the occasional freeze and snow at this altitude. **Hanoi,** the capital and in the north, as well as nearby coastal regions around **Haiphong** and **Halong Bay,** experience relatively high humidity year-round and a rainy season from May to October. Winter months are cool (as low as 57°F/14°C) and somewhat damp, but the heat starts to pick up in April and makes for a hot, wet summer (many Hanoians get out of town, to the mountain towns or nearby beaches off Haiphong or Vinh). The best time to visit the north, though cold in midwinter, is from November to the end of April.

The **Central Coast** follows an opposing monsoon pattern to the north, with warmer weather during the July-to-October high season on, and wet, colder weather from November to May. **Coastal Vietnam**—Quy Nhon and Nha Trang—experiences steamy temperatures like the far south (70°F–90°F/21°C–32°C), but coastal wind can have a cooling effect. Raging storms and frequently large typhoons strike the coast in summer months, from July to November; often during this season, the surf is too rough for swimming.

The **Central Highlands,** just inland and on the southern end of the **Annamese Cordillera** range, receives nearly double the rainfall of the national average, and this plateau, in towns like **Dalat** and **Pleiku,** is cool throughout the year.

The **south,** the region around **Ho Chi Minh City** and the **Mekong Delta,** is steamy hot year-round with only periods of rainy and dry weather. Temperatures range from 70°F to 90°F (21°C–32°C), with a hot, dry period from March to May seeing temperatures in the 90s (30s Celsius). Summers are hot, humid, and rainy.

Because of the regional variations in weather, a part of the country is seasonable at any time of year. Most travelers in Vietnam trace a north-south or south-north route with flights connecting on either end (or adding continued travel to Cambodia or China). Depending on the duration of your stay, you can plan to "follow" the good weather, hitting Saigon in February or March and tracing warmer weather up the coast.

Note: **Avoid travel during the Tet holiday** in January and February (see calendar of events below). Tet is a Christmas and New Year's celebration rolled into one, and anyone and everyone is going "over the river and through the woods" to their respective grandmother's house. Transport is always fully booked. Unless you're lucky enough to enjoy Tet with a Vietnamese family, be forewarned: During this time, many travelers find themselves stranded, hotels completely full, and roadways crowded with traffic and revelers.

Below are the monthly weather charts for the major cities of the northern, central, and southern regions of Vietnam (Hanoi, Danang, and Saigon, respectively). Rainfall daily averages are accurate to within 1 millimeter.

Average Daily Temperatures (°F/°C) & Monthly Rainfall (mm/in.)

		Jan	Feb	Mar	Apr	May	June	July	Aug	Sept	Oct	Nov	Dec
Hanoi	**Highs**	66/19	67/19	72/22	80/27	87/31	90/32	90/32	89/32	88/32	82/28	76/24	71/22
	Lows	58/14	60/16	65/18	71/22	77/25	80/27	80/27	80/27	78/26	73/23	66/19	60/16
	Rainfall	18/ 0.7	28/ 1.1	38/ 1.5	81/ 3.2	196/ 7.7	239/ 9.4	323/ 12.7	343/ 13.5	254/ 10.0	99/ 3.9	43/ 1.7	20/ 0.8
Danang	**Highs**	77/31	79/32	83/34	87/34	91/33	93/31	93/30	92/30	89/30	85/31	81/30	77/30
	Lows	67/16	69/21	71/24	75/24	78/24	79/24	79/24	78/24	76/23	75/23	72/23	68/19
	Rainfall	102/ 4.0	31/ 1.2	12/ 0.5	18/ 0.7	47/ 1.9	42/ 1.7	99/ 3.9	117/ 4.6	447/ 17.6	530/ 20.1	221/ 8.7	209/ 8.2
Ho Chi Minh City	**Highs**	88/31	90/32	92/33	93/34	92/33	89/32	89/32	88/31	88/31	87/31	87/31	87/31
	Lows	72/22	73/23	76/24	79/26	79/26	77/25	77/25	77/25	76/24	76/24	74/23	72/22
	Rainfall	15.2/ 0.6	2.5/ 0.1	10.2/ 0.4	50.8/ 2.0	213.4/ 8.4	309.9/ 12.2	294.6/ 11.6	271.8/ 10.7	342.9/ 13.5	261.6/ 10.3	119.4/ 4.7	45.7/ 1.8

VIETNAM CALENDAR OF EVENTS

In their daily lives, Vietnamese people follow the standard 12-month calendar, otherwise known as the Gregorian or solar calendar used in the West. However, most of Vietnam's small village fetes and holidays follow the traditional Chinese calendar, which has 355 days and adds a "leap month" every 3 years or so to keep up with the solar calendar. Following the Chinese lunar calendar means that most holidays correspond with the full moon (on the 15th of each lunar month) or no moon (on the 1st); it also means that holidays fall on different calendar dates each year. For example: **Tet,** the Lunar New Year and Vietnam's biggest holiday, will be on February 14, 2010; February 3, 2011; January 23, 2012; and February 10, 2013.

There is a variety of regional celebrations and local festivals among the ethnic majority Vietnamese. Add to that the many disparate holidays and practices of Vietnam's 54 ethnic groups, and you have holidays left and right; any rural trip means a

Less Is More: Packing & Clothing in the Tropics

Keep it light and loose. You are sure to hit hot, sticky weather on any route in Vietnam. The old traveler rule "Less is more" applies here; bulky luggage is an albatross in Vietnam. Fast and light is best. Loose, long-sleeve shirts and long pants, preferably cotton, are recommended. Shorts are good for swimming but not great for the backcountry, where mosquitoes are ferocious. Also note that shorts are generally worn by children, not adults (although long shorts are more accepted, especially for young men), and for women only rarely (with sporting events being the exception). Foreign visitors are somewhat exempt from these conventions, but why not go local where we can? A wide-brimmed hat is essential protection from the sun, and some even carry an umbrella to be used either as a parasol or as cover from sporadic rains. Sandals are acceptable in most arenas. Affordable laundry service is available everywhere, and thin cotton dries quite quickly—great for a bit of sink-washing instead of carrying around heaps of laundry.

good chance of stumbling onto something interesting. Vietnamese are inclusive about their celebrations; **Tet,** for example, is a family holiday, but a few shouts of *Chuc Mung Nam Moi* (Happy New Year!) usually mean getting swept up in the fervor. Surrender to it.

Be sure to ask around about market days in the Northern Highland areas—when a big, traveling goods market comes into town (usually Sun). Also look for the likes of modern city festivals, like the hugely popular **Hue Festival** (see the box in the Hue section of chapter 9). Below are the major national holidays and festivals.

January/February

New Year's Day. Everything but Dick Clark. January 1.

Anniversary of the Founding of the Communist Party. Nationwide. Celebrated everywhere; expect parade grounds in any city to be busy with cultural shows and speechmaking. Waving massive red flags in open-air shows in the evening is always the finale. February 3.

Vietnam Traditional Lunar New Year Festival (Tet Nguyen Dan): Countrywide. This 4-day national holiday, Tet, usually falls between January and February. The festivities begin on New Year's Eve and the first 3 days of a Lunar New Year, but most people celebrate for a week or more. It's a time to be with family members. For detailed information, see the box on Tet, below. The first day of the first lunar month (Feb 14, 2010; Feb 3, 2011; Jan 23, 2012; and Feb 10, 2013).

March/April

Festival at the Perfume Pagoda. Near Hanoi. Buddhists from all over Vietnam make a pilgrimage to the deep cave at the apex of this holy mountain at the half-moon of the second lunar month (Mar 30, 2010; Mar 19, 2011; Mar 7, 2012; and Mar 26, 2013).

Hmong Spring Festival. In the far north. Hmong populations across the north converge for colorful parades and market days. Fifth day of the third lunar month (Apr 18, 2010; Apr 7, 2011; Mar 26, 2012; and Apr 14, 2013).

Gio To Hung Vuong. This new nationwide holiday (added in 2007) commemorates the death of Emperor

Hung. According to legend, Emperor Hung ruled over what is now modern Vietnam some 50 centuries ago. Tenth day of the third lunar month (Apr 23, 2010; Apr 12, 2011; Mar 31, 2012; and Apr 19, 2013).

Saigon Liberation Day. Celebrated nationwide with lots of parades and commemorative TV programming. Apr 30.

May

International Labor Day. The communist marching day around the world. Celebrations and parades in central squares nationwide. May Day, May 1.

Birthday of President Ho Chi Minh. Nationwide. Cultural performances and candlelight vigils are held across the country. The major sights in Vinh, Ho Chi Minh's birthplace, are overrun, and Hanoi's Citadel area, where Ho's body is held in state, is mobbed. May 19.

August/September/October

Tet Trung Nguyen. Nationwide. A time to give thanks to the ancestors. Families gather, remember those who have died, eat, and visit grave sites. Half-moon of the seventh lunar month (Aug 24, 2010; Aug 14, 2011; Aug 31, 2012; and Aug 21, 2013).

National Day. Celebrates the rise of the Socialist Republic of Vietnam. Local parades, pomp, and circumstance. Sept 2.

Do Son Buffalo Fighting Festival. Near Haiphong. A riot for everyone (except the buffalos). The ninth day of the eighth lunar month (Sept 16, 2010; Sept 6, 2011; Sept 24, 2012; and Sept 13, 2013).

Mid-Autumn Festival. Nationwide. This colorful celebration is a popular one for kids, with dance and special sweet cakes. Half-moon of the eighth lunar month (Sept 22, 2010; Sept 12, 2011; Sept 30, 2012; and Sept 19, 2013).

December

Christmas. Nationwide, but most widely celebrated in the south, where Christian populations are largest.

The Tet Holiday: "Over the Rice Field & Through the Jungle . . ."

Imagine an American Thanksgiving, Christmas, New Year's Eve, and Easter all rolled into one—that's Tet. This megaholiday on the Vietnamese calendar is a time for pilgrimage to the family stamping grounds. Everyone, including the many young Vietnamese who have left the rice fields for work in the big cities, goes home (travel is a nightmare and best avoided). Food is the focus, and everyone hustles home to try Grandma's *chung* cakes—a small square cake made of glutinous rice—after a real feast of down-home cooking (regional variations are many). This is a time to honor ancestors; offerings of fruit and flowers, whole feasts even, are placed on family altars. The 23rd day of the 12th lunar month hosts a ceremony of farewell for last year's "Kitchen God." The 29th and 30th days are a time to say farewell to the old year and hello to the new, with all the fanfare and hoopla you can muster; streets are crowded with motorbikes, and the rice wine and *bia hoi* (local draft beer) flows freely. Folks go a-visiting on the first day of the lunar new year, sharing food and fellowship among neighbors. Tet is also a celebration of Vietnamese strength and autonomy. On the fifth day of the Tet holiday, people raise a glass (or two) to freedom fighter **Quang Trung,** who defeated the Chinese at Dong Da near Hanoi, and spurred them on with cries of, "And then we'll go home for some of Grandma's *chung cakes*!" Bonsai!

Although Vietnam's recent plunge into capitalism means more and more American-style Santa-focused decorations and shopping in the major cities, you can still expect some Ho Ho Ho Chi Minh style. Dec 25.

For an exhaustive list of events beyond those listed here, check http://events.frommers.com, where you'll find a searchable, up-to-the-minute roster of what's happening in cities all over the world.

2 ENTRY REQUIREMENTS

PASSPORTS

For information on how to get a passport, see "Passports" in the "Fast Facts: Vietnam" section in chapter 15—the websites listed provide downloadable passport applications, as well as the current fees for processing passport applications. For an up-to-date, country-by-country listing of passport requirements around the world, go to the "Foreign Entry Requirement" Web page of the U.S. State Department at **http://travel.state.gov**.

VISAS

Vietnam recently began granting **5-year visa exemptions** to all overseas Vietnamese in over 90 countries. The exemption applies to individuals who have Vietnamese nationality and foreign nationals of Vietnamese origin. If you are the spouse or child of someone who qualifies, you can have your very own visa-free status, so long as your husband, wife, or parent has obtained the exemption first. Check out http://mienthithucvk.mofa.gov.vn for instructions and regulations. It can be a lengthy process, so apply at your nearest Vietnamese embassy or consulate well ahead of your trip.

Residents of the United States, Canada, Australia, New Zealand, and the United Kingdom need both a passport and a **prearranged visa** to enter Vietnam. A tourist visa lasts for 30 days and costs $65. You'll pay a bit more through an agent but will save yourself some paper shuffling. ***Note:*** If you're planning a side trip to Angkor Wat but your return flight leaves from Vietnam, make sure to get a multiple-entry visa to get back into the country. A multiple-entry 30-day visa costs $110. A visa takes 5 to 7 days to process. Applicants must submit an application, a passport, and two passport photos. U.S. citizens can obtain a visa application from the Vietnam Embassy in Washington, D.C., online at www.vietnamembassy-usa.org, or by calling ✆ **202/861-1297.** Mail the completed application with your passport and your passport photos using an express carrier (Federal Express, US Express, or Priority Mail with delivery confirmation) to the embassy (1233 20th St. NW, Ste. 400, Washington, DC 20036), including a self-addressed stamped envelope from an express carrier (with delivery confirmation). Processing time is usually 5 days, but for a small fee, you can expedite it to as few as 2 days, and even less in last-minute circumstances (call to see what you can arrange). The embassy is open Monday to Friday from 9:30am to 12:30pm. The fax number is 202/861-1297.

Although there's no official policy, once inside Vietnam, most tourists can extend their visa twice, each time for 30 days, but this is done on a case-by-case basis, and it's possible only through a travel agent (government-owned Saigontourist is a good bet; for more information, call ✆ **08/3824-4554** or go to www.saigontourist.net). If someone gives you trouble about extending your visa, stick to your guns and ask around. Multiple-entry business visas that are valid for up to 3 months are available, but you must have a sponsoring agency in Vietnam and it can take much longer to process. For short business trips, it's less complicated simply to enter as a tourist.

You no longer need to specify an entry point; Vietnam visas are good for any legal port of entry—land, sea, or air—but remember that your visa begins on the date that you specify on your application.

In a bid to boost investment and cooperation, Vietnam has lifted visa requirements for Japanese and Koreans—a good sign that visa restrictions for Western visitors might loosen up soon.

For more information on obtaining a visa, please see the "Fast Facts: Vietnam" section in chapter 15.

CUSTOMS

What You Can Bring into Vietnam

The first and most important thing to remember is, **don't lose your entry/exit slip,** the white piece of paper that will be clipped to your passport upon arrival. If you do, you might be fined. If you are entering the country as a tourist, you do not need to declare electronic goods and jewelry if these things are for personal use. Declaration forms are only to make sure you're not importing goods without paying a tariff. You must declare cash in excess of $3,000 or the equivalent. You can also import 200 cigarettes, 2 liters of alcohol, and perfume for personal use.

It is unlikely that you will be hassled in Vietnam for bringing anything in, but be careful if bringing excessive equipment. Adventurers with bicycles or special kites for kite surfing will have to prove that they will be taking their expensive items home with them and not selling them in Vietnam. Commercial photographers or amateurs who work with professional, high-end equipment should be wary of bringing the whole studio with them. The atmosphere is lightening up, but foreign journalists still provoke fear (the Communist Party still hopes to maintain their information vacuum). More than 30 rolls of film is suspect, but just play dumb and there'll be no problem.

What You Can Take Home from Vietnam

For information on what you're allowed to bring home, contact one of the following agencies:

U.S. Citizens: U.S. Customs & Border Protection (CBP), 1300 Pennsylvania Ave., NW, Washington, DC 20229 (✆ **877/287-8667;** www.cbp.gov).

Canadian Citizens: Canada Border Services Agency (✆ **800/461-9999** in Canada, or 204/983-3500; www.cbsa-asfc.gc.ca).

U.K. Citizens: HM Customs & Excise at ✆ **0845/010-9000** (from outside the U.K., 020/8929-0152), or consult their website at **www.hmce.gov.uk**.

Australian Citizens: Australian Customs Service at ✆ **1300/363-263,** or log on to **www.customs.gov.au**.

New Zealand Citizens: New Zealand Customs, The Customhouse, 17–21 Whitmore St., Box 2218, Wellington (✆ **04/473-6099** or 0800/428-786; **www.customs.govt.nz**).

MEDICAL REQUIREMENTS

There are no specific health requirements for entry into Vietnam.

3 GETTING THERE & GETTING AROUND

GETTING TO VIETNAM

By Plane

The three international airports in Vietnam are **Tan Son Nhat International (SGN)** in Ho Chi Minh City, **Noi Bai International (HAN)** in Hanoi, and **Danang International (DAT)** in Danang (central Vietnam). Vietnam Airlines has hubs in both Tan Son Nhat and Noi Boi. Most carriers connect to Vietnam's three international airports via **Singapore, Bangkok** (Thailand), **Hong Kong, Taipei** (Taiwan), or **Seoul** (South Korea).

To find out which airlines travel to Vietnam, please see "Airline, Hotel & Car Rental Websites," p. 445.

Getting into Town from the Airport

In Hanoi, taxis queue up just outside the arrivals door and will zip you into town for 230,000 VND to 250,000 VND. Taxis to and from Danang's airport will set you back 60,000 VND. Down south, a ride into Ho Chi Minh City is around 180,000 VND.

By Car

The overland route from Phnom Penh to Vietnam is reportedly safe and quite accessible. You can arrange transfers with any of the Phnom Penh travel agencies, the best of which is budget **Capitol Tour,** #14 Rd. 182, Phnom Penh (✆ **023/217-627**), which cooperates with the Vietnamese budget-cafe tour operator **Sinh Café** to make for a relatively fluid connection between the Cambodian capital and Ho Chi Minh City. ***Note:*** You must have a prearranged Vietnamese visa when entering Vietnam (visa on arrival is available in the other direction, from Vietnam to Cambodia). Buses leave from the Capitol Tour office in the early morning, arriving in Ho Chi Minh in the midafternoon, depending on the efficiency of the connection. (Note that you'll have to lug your own bags through the long border checkpoint here.)

You can do this same trip by rented car with driver, but you'll have to make separate arrangements on either side of the border, since vehicles cannot cross.

From Laos

I wouldn't really recommend this long overnight road trip from Vientiane or Savannakhet. You're dropped off smack in the center of Vietnam, at Dong Ha Province just north of Hue (makes for a more limited itinerary or backtracking). It's better to fly from Vientiane to Hanoi or Ho Chi Minh City on Vietnam Airlines or Laos Aviation. Note that any connections with the city of Luang Prabang must go through the Laos capital, Vientiane.

By Train

There are regular connections between Vietnam and China at the border areas of Lang Son and Lao Cai, both in the far north. Note that you need prearranged visas for entrance into China and Vietnam, so be sure to plan ahead if traveling in either direction. Trains do not make direct connections to both border points (Lao Cai is far more efficient); you must take short taxi/motorbike taxi rides on either side of the border to get to public transport.

By Boat

You can cross to Vietnam by boat from a port near the Cambodian capital of Phnom Penh to Chau Doc, a small Vietnamese border town in the Mekong Delta. Contact budget **Capitol Tour** in Cambodia for connections.

A unique new option is the weeklong cruise from Angkor Wat all the way to Can Tho or My Tho on one of the luxury, shallow draft **Pandaw Cruise Boats** (www.pandaw.com). Shared rooms on the vessel start at $2,069 for the 1-week duration.

GETTING AROUND VIETNAM

With many transport options, you'll find good local travel agencies in every tourist stop in Vietnam, all ready to book your plane, bus, and boat tickets or to rent cars. Competition among service providers works to your advantage, and you can find affordable deals for getting around with just a bit of shopping.

By Plane

It's a good idea to fly the longer hops along Vietnam's length: from Hanoi to Hue, from Danang to Nha Trang, and from Nha Trang to Ho Chi Minh City (or vice versa). Vietnam Airlines runs the most domestic routes in Vietnam, while budget carrier Jet Star Asia offers healthy competition on the tourist routes (namely to-and-fros btw. Hanoi, Ho Chi Minh City, Danang, and Nha Trang). Domestic departure tax is included in most fares.

By Car

If you've got the budget for it, going by car is the best and safest way to see Vietnam. Self-driving is unwise. There are rules on the road, but to the uninitiated, driving is chaotic. Your international driver's license holds up—in fact, any piece of paper with English writing will do most of the time—and right-lane driving might look familiar and easy to some, but that's where the similarity ends.

Turn it over to a driver, available for hire anywhere and for as little as $10 per day. For car-rental options, see "Visitor Information & Tours" in each destination section. Most hotels will rent wheels for day trips at inflated rates; budget hotels and guesthouses offer the best rates. Budget travelers often pitch in for a rented car between sites (from Hue to Nha Trang, for example), where going by private car means you can set your own schedule and stop at places like Bach Ma National Park, Lang Co Beach, and atop Hai Van Pass.

By Train

The Reunification Express runs the entire length of Vietnam's coast—from Ho Chi Minh to Hanoi, with routes out of Hanoi to the likes of Sapa, Lang Son, and coastal Haiphong. Riding the length of the country takes nearly 40 hours. The most popular hops are from Hanoi up to Sapa, where special luxury trains with dining cars cover the route, or from Hanoi down the coast to the old capital of Hue, and from there to Danang (less popular) or all the way to Nha Trang and Ho Chi Minh. Improved road travel is making the train obsolete in most parts, except for the mountainous far north. There are a number of classes, from third-class hard seat to air-conditioned cushioned seat to sleeper, but in general the more comfortable seats are affordable. Be warned that you need to book trains a few days in advance, especially for weekend travel. Popular trips to Sapa are best organized through a tour company (for a small fee) from home or well in advance when on the ground in Vietnam.

By Bus

Local buses are either a nightmare or a delight, depending on your expectations. If you're prepared to be the main character in a piece of bad, chaotic performance, then your appetite will be pleased; if you want grist for the travel journal, you will find it; if you want to get somewhere efficiently and with all of your sensory nerve endings intact, you will be disappointed.

Local buses depart from stations usually a good distance from the town center (it usually requires a ride on the back of a motorbike taxi to get there), and station touts are all over you, pulling you this way and that (this is the best piece of "bad performance art"). Buses leave only when full—and "full" means that everyone is uncomfortable, two to a seat, produce hanging, bags under your feet and, bird flu be damned, chickens in bags and on people's laps. Just when you think the bus is completely full, when not one more person could possibly squeeze in, the driver pulls to the side of the road and, like a circus clown car, the bus swallows one more body. All buses honk wildly as they navigate the chaotic traffic of Vietnam's bumpy roads, and all transport travels at a lumbering 50kmph (31 mph).

In the bigger cities and on longer routes, you'll find regular schedules and bus stations with ticket booths and marked prices, but when you're out in countryside, you often have to negotiate a price with the driver or bus tout—a frustrating operation when you just want to catch the

@#%# bus. It is a real visceral adventure, and going by local bus is the best way to meet Vietnamese people and learn the local language, but it can be too overwhelming for some.

One good alternative is to buy a ticket with assigned seat on the **small air-conditioned minivans** that ply most major routes in Vietnam (the **Mai Linh Express** is a reliable option). Ask at any hotel front desk, and expect to pay often double the local bus price (still very affordable) and ride in relative style among locals but without the hassles.

The **"open tour" ticket** is a way to plan your overland travel all the way down the coast of Vietnam; it is a one-way, multi-stop ticket, and you can catch buses from each town going from Hanoi south, all the way to Ho Chi Minh City. It sounds like a great idea, and folks in the sales offices will regale you with tales of ease and comfort as you explore the length of the Vietnam coast, but don't be fooled: These are rock-bottom budget tours, and though the buses are usually in pretty good shape and have air-conditioning, it can be a pretty unpleasant cattle-herding situation among lots of complaining backpackers. Buses stop only at big tourist-shopping complexes, and you get little interaction with locals. That said, these tour buses are good for short hops between cities, but I try to mix it up, catching the train where possible (especially on long hauls from Hanoi to Hue or Danang to Nha Trang), and even getting together with fellow travelers and hiring your own car for a day along the coast (not much more costly). Don't be taken in by the easy "open tour" ticket, as, for just a few bucks extra, you can buy individual journeys from each town as you head south.

4 MONEY & COSTS

The Value of Vietnam Dong (VND) vs. Other Popular Currencies

VND	US$	Can$	UK£	Euro (€)	Aus$	NZ$
10,000	$0.56	C$0.62	£0.34	€0.40	A$0.69	NZ$0.89

Frommer's lists exact prices in the local currency wherever possible, though the **U.S. dollar is used widely** in both Vietnam and Cambodia: In fact, the dollar is the de facto currency in Cambodia, and packing some U.S. greenbacks will come in very handy. The currency conversions quoted above were correct at press time. However, rates fluctuate, so before departing, consult a currency exchange website such as **www.oanda.com/convert/classic** to check up-to-the-minute rates.

Tips Small Change

When you change money, ask for some small bills or loose change. Petty cash will come in handy for tipping and public transportation. Consider keeping the change separate from your larger bills so that it's readily accessible and you'll be less of a target for theft. Keep a good supply of $1 bills and/or 20,000 VND bills; these will come in handy when paying for cab and motorcycle rides.

What Things Cost in Vietnam

Cup of coffee	10,000 VND–15,000 VND
Taxi from the airport	180,000 VND–260,000 VND
Three-course dinner without alcohol	250,000 VND–450,000 VND
Moderately priced hotel	1,060,000 VND–1,800,000 VND

Note: Prices vary in smaller towns.

During your trip, the most useful Vietnam Dong bills will be upwards of 10,000 VND. There are smaller bills (which are also physically smaller than the more frequently used bills of 10,000 VND and up) of 1,000 VND, 2,000 VND, and 5,000 VND, which are handy when buying snacks from street vendors or if you want to give exact change to cabdrivers. Every now and again, a bronze 5,000 VND coin will land your way. For the most part, bills are distinguishable by color: The 500,000 VND is light blue, 100,000 VND is green, and 20,000 VND is dark blue. Be mindful of the 10,000 VND, 50,000 VND, and 200,000 VND notes—all are done in pinkish-red hues that are quite similar to each other.

ATM service is good in most cities and the machines accept four-digit PINs. If heading off into the countryside, bring cash. Credit cards are also widely accepted, though many smaller companies, such as tour agencies or boutique hotels, will charge a 2% or 3% commission. For now, the traditional swipe credit cards are still widely accepted. All hotels can do business in U.S. dollars. In some parts, everybody down to the smallest shop vendor quotes prices in U.S. dollars, and particularly the big-ticket items are best handled with greenbacks instead of large stacks of local currency.

While dealing in U.S. dollars can make things less complicated, always keep in mind local currency values so that you know if you're being charged the correct amount or are given the correct change (usually in Vietnamese currency). In this book, I've listed **hotel, restaurant, and attraction rates** in whatever form the establishments quoted them—in local currencies where those were used, and in U.S. dollars (designated by the dollar sign: $) where those were quoted.

5 HEALTH

STAYING HEALTHY

Health concerns should comprise an important piece of your preparation for a trip to Vietnam, and staying healthy on the road takes vigilance. Make it a priority. Tropical heat and mosquitoes are the biggest dangers, other than motor vehicle accidents, and travelers should exercise caution over the extreme change in diet and sanitary standards in Vietnam—especially if eating at local joints. But with just a few pretrip precautions and general prudence, you can enjoy a safe and healthy trip. Consult with a health practitioner or someone specializing in travel health before your trip about inoculations. Stay abreast of international monitors, such as the U.S. **Centers for Disease Control and Prevention** (**© 877/FYI-TRIP** [394-8747]; www.cdc.gov) or the **International Association for Medical Assistance to Travelers** (**IAMAT; © 716/754-4883,** or 416/652-0137 in Canada;

www.iamat.org) for tips on travel and health concerns, as well as the most current information on any outbreaks of infectious diseases in the region.

General Availability of Healthcare

The only high-quality healthcare facilities are located in Hanoi and Ho Chi Minh City (Saigon)—for specific listings, see "Hospitals" in the "Fast Facts: Vietnam" section in chapter 15, or also in chapters 5 and 12. Hanoi and Ho Chi Minh City each have a branch of the International SOS clinic. Hanoi also supports the Hanoi Family Medical Practice, as well as the Hanoi French Hospital. Your options in rural areas are quite limited, and any major medical issue usually means an uncomfortable transfer to one of these centers or an evacuation to Singapore, Bangkok, or Hong Kong.

In rural areas, the local apothecary shop often acts as a catchall triage for what ails you, and over-the-counter medications are available anywhere from small storefront pharmacists who, with little more than a brief chat and description of a problem (with the use of a phrase book or some creative charades), will dole out affordable prescriptions for anything from antibiotics to sleeping pills. However, there are a lot of fake medicines for sale, and storage conditions may be poor. I would recommend calling SOS, Family Practice, or your home country's embassy for recommendations of reliable pharmacies.

When you're far from good healthcare, I recommend bringing a small kit of medicines that includes antidiarrhea medication, rehydration salts for the ubiquitous bout with the trots, antibacterial cream and bandages, and a pain reliever like ibuprofen or acetaminophen.

COMMON AILMENTS

Tropical Illnesses

Most of the real "baddies" in Vietnam and Cambodia are tropical diseases carried by mosquitoes: the likes of **malaria, dengue fever,** and **Japanese encephalitis.** Quite simply, the best way to avoid mosquito-borne diseases is to avoid being bitten. Repellents that contain between 25% and 50% **DEET** are the most effective. The more gentle alternatives, including oil of eucalyptus (see baby-care products in any pharmacy) provide terrific DEET-free mosquito protection but are not as effective. A new product on the market, picaridin, also offers DEET-free protection. It's an excellent repellent, but at 7% concentration, it may last for a shorter period of time. Also be aware that malaria mosquitoes bite most frequently around dawn and dusk, so exercise caution especially at those hours (wearing long sleeves and long trousers and burning mosquito coils is a good idea). Dengue-fever mosquitoes bite during the day. Always sleep under a mosquito net where needed—and if they are needed, they are usually provided—and make sure it has no holes (or at least patch them up with tape). If you are purchasing your own mosquito net, it is most effective if it has been pretreated with permethrin, which is a very safe insecticide.

MALARIA Three hundred million people are infected with malaria yearly, with over one million deaths, particularly in developing countries. The disease has four strains, including deadly cerebral malaria (common in Africa), but all are life threatening. Malaria is caused by a one-cell parasite transmitted by the female Anopheles mosquito. The parasite travels into the liver, lies dormant, and grows; then symptoms occur when the parasite enters the bloodstream. Symptoms include high fever, painful headaches in the front of the head, nausea, vomiting, dizziness, and confusion. If experiencing any degree of these indicators, seek treatment. Keep in mind that malaria symptoms look like a number of diseases (even just a flu).

Malaria is a concern for travelers in Vietnam. But don't stress out over the bogus information you might hear and read—the kind of stuff that would keep you up all night listening for skeeters or vacationing somewhere else. Arm yourself with correct information, and forget the rest.

First, know that visitors to the major cities and standard coastal tour areas in Vietnam have a very low chance of contracting malaria—very low. Travelers venturing off the track and up into the bush in the Central Highlands or the interior in the central, north, or Mekong Delta will want to take a **malaria prophylaxis.** A standard course of mefloquine (brand name Lariam) or atovaquone/proguanil (brand name Malarone) will cover you. In farther "off-the-track" border regions near Myanmar, Laos, and Cambodia—areas where a resistance to standard medications has developed—travelers should take Doxycycline.

Your best insurance is to take care when sleeping: Ensure that windows are closed (when you have air-conditioning) and that you have a good mosquito net when needed (typically provided). Also, cover up in Vietnam—wear a long-sleeve shirt and trousers in the evening; this not only keeps the mosquitoes at bay, but moderate attire is also the social norm in conservative Vietnam (and also much cooler in the hot months). Put bug spray (preferably with DEET) on exposed areas of the skin, and avoid swampy marshes or heavy jungle at dawn and dusk. Don't let fears of malaria ruin your trip, and don't buy into the paranoia going around. Take these precautions—as needed—and all will be well.

However, no antimalarial drug is 100% effective. If you develop fever and chills while traveling or after your return home, seek medical care and tell the provider that you have traveled to a malarious area and need to be checked.

DENGUE FEVER **Dengue fever** is possible to contract just about anywhere in Southeast Asia. Dengue is a viral infection spread by the Aedes-Aegypti mosquito. Symptoms include headache, high fever, and muscle pain. Unlike malaria and Japanese encephalitis, which survive and spread mostly out in rural areas, dengue knows no bounds and urban outbreaks are common. There is no prophylaxis and no treatment—and some cases are fatal—but with dengue, it is just a matter of suffering it out with cold compresses, fever-reducing pain relievers, and lots of hydration. A real drag.

JAPANESE ENCEPHALITIS **Japanese encephalitis** is viral, transmitted by mosquitoes, and is endemic to the region—especially after rainy season (July–Aug). Symptoms include headache, fever, nausea, upset stomach, and confusion—all quite similar to malaria and dengue fever. When outbreaks occur, or if traveling widely in rural parts, vaccination is recommended, but note that vaccination is not 100% effective.

Hepatitis

Another common but preventable ailment in Vietnam is **hepatitis A,** which causes inflammation of the liver. Hepatitis A is contracted from contaminated water or food, and the pathogen of hep A is rather stalwart, staying alive in the air and on the skin for some time. The best preventative is to wash your hands thoroughly before eating and stick to bottled water and food cooked to order (not sitting out). Symptoms include fever, general ill health (nausea and vomiting), lack of appetite, and jaundice.

For anyone over the age of 2 traveling in Vietnam, I'd recommend a hepatitis A vaccination. The inoculation requires just one shot and a booster after 6 months.

Hepatitis B is contracted through contact with blood of an infected person (needle, sexual contact, splashed blood, or even sharing a toothbrush or razor—insist on a new razor if you get a haircut and shave). Nurses, for example, are commonly immunized in any country, and the three shots (over a 6-month period) are recommended for a longer stay in the region.

Rabies

Rabies is a fatal viral infection carried by animals. The disease is transmitted by a bite or contact with the saliva of an infected animal. Rabies is a concern in rural Vietnam, among populations of dogs, as well as monkeys and bats. If exposed in any way—a puncture wound of any kind from a suspected animal who exhibits strange behaviors such as foaming at the mouth or ataxia—seek treatment immediately and follow a series of vaccinations over a 1-month period—commonly the Verorab brand. Adventure travelers or health workers who will spend lots of time in the countryside and the bush might just want to consider a **pre-exposure vaccination,** which makes post-exposure treatment far more simple, as it decreases the number of shots required as well as prevents the need for rabies immune globulin, which may not be available and thus may require a trip elsewhere for care (for example, Bangkok). Another group at high risk is children. They are more likely to touch or play with stray dogs and are less likely to report a bite.

Typhoid

A bacterial illness that is transmitted through contaminated food, typhoid is life threatening, especially to children and the elderly, but early detection and a course of antibiotics is usually enough to avoid any serious complications. There are a few different vaccinations available in both oral and injectable forms. Though they are only between 55% and 70% effective, the vaccine is recommended for travelers in the region.

Tuberculosis

As in so many developing countries, tuberculosis is quite common, especially in rural Vietnam. Caused by poor hygiene and unventilated overcrowding, TB is a bacterial infection of the lungs that can spread to other parts of the body and, if left untreated, kill. The vaccination requires a TB screening 6 months prior to inoculation.

Sexually Transmitted Diseases

Anyone contemplating **sexual activity** in Vietnam should be aware that **HIV,** the virus that causes AIDS, is rampant in many Southeast Asian countries, including Vietnam. Also concerning are other **sexually transmitted diseases (STDs),** such as gonorrhea, syphilis, herpes, and hepatitis B. A latex condom is recommended second to abstinence. For more information on AIDS, see the AIDS sidebar below.

Other Diseases

Other diseases common in the region include schistosomiasis and giardia, both of which are parasitic diseases that can be contracted from swimming in or drinking from stagnant or untreated water in lakes or streams. **Cholera** epidemics sometimes occur in remote areas. Keep an eye on the CDC website or other international health monitors to stay informed of any health hot spots.

DIETARY RED FLAGS

Unless you intend to confine your travels to the big cities and dine only at restaurants that serve Western-style food, you'll likely sample some new cuisine. Initially, this could cause an upset stomach or diarrhea, but it usually lasts just a few days as your body adapts to the change in your diet.

Always drink bottled water (never use tap water for drinking). To be safe, you should even brush your teeth with bottled water. The old adage of "Boil it, cook it, peel it, or forget it" is important to remember in Vietnam. Be sure to peel all fruits and vegetables and avoid raw shellfish and seafood. Also beware of ice unless

AIDS in Vietnam

Statistics on AIDS in Vietnam are unreliable because of limited testing, but with increased border crossings from China and rampant prostitution—including, sadly, a great deal of child prostitution—the prognosis is not good. Estimates report that about 0.5% of the general population in Vietnam is infected with HIV. However, this proportion can be much higher in commercial sex workers (possibly up to 60%–70% in some areas) and intravenous drug users (possibly up to 60%–80% in some areas).

Unprotected sex with an anonymous partner is very risky behavior. Although condoms are widely available in Vietnam, be aware that certain groups still have very high HIV/AIDS infection rates. International monitors with the U.S. Centers for Disease Control and Prevention and other agencies are working with the Hanoi government on HIV/AIDS prevention, care, and treatment. An increasing campaign is promoting the use of condoms—you'll see lots of signs with cartoon character condoms smiling and waving from the roadside, needle users underneath skull and crossbones, or a happy young couple embracing, a condom in the young man's hand. But generally speaking, Vietnam's remaining fears of outside influence and continued tight control on information—combined with a certain shame over even talking about issues of sex—are ripe ground for the disease to spread. Time will tell.

it is made from purified water. Any suspicious water can be purified by boiling for 10 minutes or treating with purifying tablets. If you're a vegetarian, you will find that Vietnam is a great place to travel; vegetarian dishes abound throughout the region (just say *Toi ahn jai,* which means "I eat vegetarian").

In terms of hygiene, restaurants are generally better options than street stalls. But don't forgo good local cuisine just because it's served from a cart or dining is on squat stools at street side—this is where you'll find some of the best food in Vietnam, as well as the highest likelihood of a stomach cootie. It is acceptable—in fact, customary—to wipe down utensils in restaurants, and in some places locals request a glass of hot water for just that purpose. Carrying antiseptic hand-washing liquid is also not a bad idea.

So how can you tell if something will upset your stomach before you eat it? Trust your instincts. Avoid buffet-style places, especially on the street, and be sure that all food is cooked thoroughly and made to order. I've been plenty sick my share of times and have found that each time I get into trouble, I've usually felt a certain sense of dread from the start. If your gut tells you not to eat that gelatinous chicken foot, don't eat it. If your hosts insist but you're still nervous, explain about your "foreign stomach" with a regretful smile and accept a cup of tea instead. Be careful of raw ingredients, common as garnish on Vietnamese dishes. Questions like, "Are these vegetables washed in clean water?" are inappropriate anywhere. Use your best judgment or simply decline.

BUGS, BITES & OTHER WILDLIFE CONCERNS

All kinds of creepy critters live in a tropical climate. Mosquito nets in rural accommodations are often required and, if so, are always provided by hoteliers. Check your shoes in the morning (or wear sandals) just in case some little ugly thing is taking a nap in your Nikes. Keep an eye out for snakes and poisonous spiders when in jungle terrain or when doing any trekking. Having a guide doesn't preclude exercising caution. **Rabies** is a concern in rural areas of Vietnam, and extreme care should be taken when walking rural roads, especially at night, when you might want to carry a walking stick or umbrella as a deterrent to any mangy mutts. Vietnamese street mutts, the ones who escape the stew pot, have all been hit with stones; if you are threatened by a dog, the very act of reaching to the ground for a handful of stones is often enough to send the beast packing. Some travelers, especially those spending a lot of time in the back of beyond, get a **rabies pre-exposure vaccine** (for more information, see the "Common Ailments" section, above). If you are bitten, wash the wound immediately and, even if you suffer just the slightest puncture or scrape, seek medical attention and a series of rabies shots (now quite a simple affair of injections in the arm in a few installments over several weeks). The best advice: Stay away from dogs.

RESPIRATORY ILLNESSES

SARS hit the region hard in the winter and spring of 2003. Singapore reported some cases and essentially closed to tourism, and though most other countries in the region reported no cases of the disease, places like Thailand, Vietnam, and Cambodia suffered the fallout of the region-wide scare. At press time, there are no new cases in the region.

Following right on the heels of the SARS crisis, which was devastating to tourism in Vietnam, the **avian influenza,** also called the "bird flu," caused another public-relations nightmare throughout the region. The danger of humans contracting bird flu is still rather low, and limited to people working in poultry slaughterhouses. Millions of chickens suspected of carrying the illness have been culled, and the countries affected have been unusually forthright about reporting new cases and combating outbreak. Human-to-human transmissions—caused by a mutation of the poultry-borne disease—have not been reported. For more information, check the CDC website for the most up-to-date information about the disease. It is important to note that you cannot contract bird flu from consuming cooked chicken.

Air quality is not good in the larger cities like Ho Chi Minh City, Hanoi, Haiphong, and Danang; with no emissions standards, buses, trucks, and cars belch some toxic stuff. Visitors with respiratory concerns or sensitivity should take caution. **Tuberculosis** is a concern in more remote areas where testing is still uncommon.

SUN/ELEMENTS/ EXTREME WEATHER EXPOSURE

Sun and heatstroke are a major concern in Vietnam. Locals wear those cool conical hats and long-sleeve shirts and trousers for a reason. Limit your exposure to the sun, especially during the first few days of your trip and, thereafter, from 11am to 2pm. Use a sunscreen with a high protection factor and apply it liberally. Asian people are still big fans of parasols, so don't be shy about using an umbrella to shade yourself (all the Buddhist monks do), but note that it is a decidedly feminine choice of accessory. Remember that children need more protection than adults.

Always be sure to drink plenty of bottled water, which is the best defense against heat exhaustion and the more serious, life-threatening heatstroke. Coffee, tea, soft drinks, and alcoholic beverages should not be substituted for water; they are diuretics that dehydrate the body. In extremely hot and humid weather, try to stay out of the midday heat, and confine most of your daytime traveling to early morning and late afternoon. If you ever feel weak, fatigued, dizzy, or disoriented, get out of the sun immediately and go to a shady, cool place. To prevent sunburn, always wear a hat and apply sunscreen to all exposed areas of skin.

Be aware of major weather patterns; many island destinations are prone to typhoons or severe storms.

WHAT TO DO IF YOU GET SICK AWAY FROM HOME

Reliable emergency service is limited to Hanoi and Ho Chi Minh (see the "Hospitals" listing in the "Fast Facts: Vietnam" section in chapter 15). Any foreign consulate can provide a list of area doctors who speak English. If you get sick, consider asking your hotel concierge to recommend a local doctor or nearby pharmacist. Some larger hotels and resorts have on-call nurses and doctors available for "room calls." Do not get involved with local hospitals, many of which have an archaic standard of care, unless in the most dire situation or as a base for an evacuation.

For travel abroad, you may have to pay all medical costs upfront and be reimbursed later. Medicare and Medicaid do not provide coverage for medical costs outside the U.S. Before leaving home, find out what medical services your health insurance covers. To protect yourself, consider buying medical travel insurance. (For information on traveler's insurance, trip cancellation insurance, and medical insurance while traveling, please visit www.frommers.com/planning.)

Very few health insurance plans pay for medical evacuation back to the U.S. (which can cost $10,000 and up). A number of companies offer medical evacuation services anywhere in the world. If you're ever hospitalized more than 150 miles from home, **MedjetAssist** (© **800/527-7478;** www.medjetassistance.com) will pick you up and fly you to the hospital of your choice virtually anywhere in the world in a medically equipped and staffed aircraft 24 hours a day, 7 days a week. Annual memberships are $225 individual, $350 family; you can also purchase short-term memberships.

U.K. nationals will need a **European Health Insurance Card (EHIC)** to receive free or reduced-cost health benefits during a visit to a European Economic Area (EEA) country (European Union countries plus Iceland, Liechtenstein, and Norway) or Switzerland. The European Health Insurance Card replaces the E111 form, which is no longer valid. For advice, ask at your local post office or see www.dh.gov.uk/travellers.

I list **hospitals** and **emergency numbers** in the "Fast Facts: Vietnam" section in chapter 15.

If you suffer from a chronic illness, consult your doctor before your departure. Pack **prescription medications** in your carry-on luggage, and carry them in their original containers, with pharmacy labels—otherwise, they won't make it through airport security. Carry the generic name of prescription medicines, in case a local pharmacist is unfamiliar with the brand name.

6 SAFETY

An old Asia hand I know says this: "Your best insurance policy for any trip in Vietnam is to stay off motorbikes. Don't ride one yourself. Don't ride on the back. And watch out for them on the streets."

He's right, but the sad fact is that motorbikes and motorbike taxis are the best and most common way to get around most Vietnamese towns. In some cases, a ride on a bike is the only choice for covering short

Responsible Tourism

Tourists in Vietnam are a relatively new species, and it's important to respect local culture and try to minimize our impact on the country. In Vietnam, try to keep personal ideologies and political debate quiet. Vietnamese are proud of their triumph over outside threats, autonomy that came at a great cost in lives and suffering, and the doors are just opening after a long period of isolation (because of both external sanctions and internal policies). The common sentiment among Vietnamese, more than half of whom were born after the end of conflict with the United States, is to forget the past and push on into an ever brighter future, economically and socially. There are, however, many monuments to Vietnam's years of struggle. When visiting monuments to war—or one of the many sights that depict or revisit the years of struggle against the Chinese, French, or Americans—it's important to practice restraint. Refrain from jokes, try to go in smaller groups, and engage in debates or personal feelings in discreet tones or at a later time. In places like **Ho Chi Minh's Mausoleum** in Hanoi, the monument to the **My Lai Massacre** in central Vietnam, the tunnels of **Cu Chi** and **Vinh Moch,** the **Hanoi Hilton,** or the **War Remnants Museum,** discretion is not only requested, it's often enforced (visitors have been known to receive actual hand slaps and barked orders at Ho Chi Minh's Mausoleum, for example).

Our strongest impact as visitors is through our money and how we spend it. Giving gifts in Vietnam, particularly to young people or the many who approach foreign visitors with calls of help, is a double-edged sword. Where it might gratify in the short term to help someone and fill a few outstretched hands with sweets or school supplies, it sets up a harmful precedent and props up the image of foreign visitors as walking ATMs—to be bilked, begged, and bamboozled at every turn. You will be followed and harried in Vietnam quite a bit, and in some areas, particularly Hanoi, the young book-and-postcard salesmen and touts are part of organized gangs and very persistent (although the hard sell has lessened with the increased number of tourists). Saying a polite but firm "No" to persistent hawkers goes a long way to alleviating the problem.

city hops or getting to the bus station, for example. The decision is yours, of course, but be careful: Tuck your knees in, wear a helmet, and ask the driver to slow down (say *dii cham* or give a thumbs-down gesture) if he gets going too fast.

The greatest danger to your safety when traveling Vietnam is, in fact, road travel: Getting around by car or bus means throwing your lot into a system where might is right, and the fastest vehicles or the ones that look and sound most like the apocalypse have the right of way. Even major highways are narrow and require a bit of "chicken"—or "forced giving way"—when opposing vehicles meet. An estimated 30 people die every day on roads in Ho Chi Minh alone.

The good news is that anonymous violent crime is almost nonexistent in Vietnam. Petty thievery and pickpocketing is an issue, but you'll have no problems if

Among **Vietnam's ethnic minorities** in the Central Highlands and the far north, be most careful about your impact. These are communities that are on the fringes of Vietnamese culture, distinct enclaves where ancient practices of animistic faiths still hold sway. Photographers should be sure to ask before snapping portraits or images of ceremonial sights; increasingly, asking for permission to photograph is met with pleas for money, but say "No" and move on. It's important not to assault locals with a camera, however uniquely attired and exotic they may be. Gifts of clothes or medicines might seem helpful but only diminish already-eroding ancient cultures and customs of clothing manufacture—where, in fact, one's clothing is an integral part of status in the community—and traditional medicines, erasing ancient traditions passed on from the time of migration from China. Learn about these people and their traditions as much as you can before traveling among them—in fact, your knowledge about any place that you travel makes you less likely to make uncomfortable blunders. Keep an open mind, and be ready to learn, not teach. Below are a few good guidelines for environmental and cultural stewardship.

Don't litter: Sounds simple, but in a country where you will rarely find a public trash receptacle (most things are discarded on the street and swept up *en masse*), it is difficult. As unimportant as it might feel to drop a gum wrapper, more important is your example of *not* dropping a gum wrapper. On rural hiking trails or in national parks, tie a garbage bag to the outside of your pack and pick up wrappers along the way. Don't preach, but if locals ask what you are doing—and they certainly will—explain that you are keeping the park clean and that it is something that anyone can do.

Wherever possible, try to **support the local economy**—eat at local joints, buy essentials like bottled water and soap at small mom-and-pop shops instead of big air-conditioned department stores, even try public transport (if you are a hearty soul). Don't buy any animal products, even the likes of snake wines or lizard-skin bags, and try to find out if souvenirs are produced locally.

Your behavior as a tourist also reflects on the many tourists who will come after you. Set a good precedent, even when if doesn't feel important.

you practice some vigilance with valuables (keep passport and cash in a concealed travel wallet or in a hotel safe). Also, try to stick more to the well-traveled roads, especially at night—walking down dark alleys is never safe in any country. In general, foreign visitors have no problems with crime in Vietnam unless they're doing something wrong themselves.

Vietnam is politically very stable, so don't worry about getting caught up in any insurgency, though tensions and mistrust do continue between Vietnam's ethnic hilltribe communities and the central Vietnam administration. Terrorism is nonexistent because the visa restrictions are so tight, and because anyone doing anything funny under the watchful eye of the Party—and that means you—just gets the boot. There have been a number of cases of journalists and members of evangelical religious denominations being detained and having materials confiscated. Whatever you're doing in Vietnam, just make it look like tourism and you should be okay.

Corruption in government on all levels is rife, and, if you find yourself talking with the local constabulary, know that you won't be "protected and served" in Vietnam, but "harassed and collected from." Road violations are usually handled with an expected small bribe at curbside, for example, and you can typically bribe your way out of—or into—any situation. In general, however, local law agents don't want anything to do with foreigners unless there is a clear road to a quick profit. If in doubt in any circumstance, contact your country's embassy or consulate.

Marijuana may appear legal in Vietnam, considering its widespread availability—especially in beach towns like Nha Trang—but don't be fooled. The same guy who sold it to you collects a few dong for informing a crooked cop, who then collects his dong bounty and a few dollars from you—or, worse, jail time if you can't produce the requisite bribe. Not worth it.

DEALING WITH DISCRIMINATION

Western visitors of all races are treated as a collective oddity in Vietnam; no one gets particular attention, really. In certain rural parts, the arrival of a Westerner draws a crowd. Foreign visitors are greeted everywhere with spastic shouts of "Hello"—often genuine, but for local kids, especially, it's usually something like shouting "punch buggy" when you see a Volkswagen. Say "Hi" back and you've made someone's day, but responding to everyone—especially when it's not too genuine—is a bit much. Vietnamese are motivated by a friendly curiosity with foreigners, and that often translates to pushing boundaries of physical space: tugging at arm hair (not unusual for Vietnamese) or grabbing at your personal items (not to steal, just to see). It's okay to push people away, but know that Vietnamese are motivated by curiosity and operate under different definitions of personal space.

Women alone rarely run into any special problems in Vietnam, but all should take caution when alone at night. If unmarried, or traveling sans spouse, the pity is laid on pretty thick.

Gay travelers should note that there are laws against homosexuality in Vietnam, but the laws are more or less institutionalized prejudice—and the impetus for harassment and police blackmailing scams. Raids on homosexual establishments are not uncommon. Beware of homosexual touts and escorts, many of whom act in cahoots with police on scams. A large gay culture does exist in the big cities, but it's kept well under the table.

7 SPECIALIZED TRAVEL RESOURCES

In addition to the destination-specific resources listed below, please visit Frommers.com for additional specialized travel resources.

GAY & LESBIAN TRAVELERS

Vietnam is a very conservative country, something like the West was before the 1960s. Marriage is a child-bearing operation that happens early in life, with generations of a family living together. Imagine Hillary Clinton's proverbial "village" (as in "It takes a village"), but here, there's little leeway for anything short of providing for the next generation and no tolerance of alternative lifestyles. Attitudes toward homosexuality, despite growing notions that people are "born" so, are archaic and discriminatory.

In fact, there are laws against homosexuality in Vietnam, and any gay activity or nightclub is watched closely for "aberrant behavior" of what is officially considered a great "social evil." Police have been known to raid men's clubs, massage parlors, and saunas, imposing fines and "re-education courses" on Vietnamese offenders. Sadly, police often target foreign gay visitors in the big cities and sometimes work with dangerous gay touts and escorts to set up gay travelers (and sex tourists) for blackmail and scams.

The efforts of local and international NGOs to educate about condom use has met with some success, as there is a low reportage of HIV infections among gay males (though statistics are unreliable). In general, an increase in sex tourism in Vietnam has been reported, including gay sex tourism—the sad truth is that many of these visitors have pointedly forgotten what they know about HIV and AIDS prevention.

You won't find any parades or openly gay-friendly destinations in Vietnam because all gay nightlife is underground, but there is a gay scene in Hanoi and Ho Chi Minh, as well as at some beach destinations. Check the regional Utopia Asia website (www.utopia-asia.com) for information about nightspots and gay-friendly accommodations, or try the international sources below.

The **International Gay and Lesbian Travel Association (IGLTA; ✆ 800/448-8550** or 954/776-2626; www.iglta.org) is the trade association for the gay and lesbian travel industry, and offers an online directory of gay- and lesbian-friendly travel businesses and tour operators.

Many agencies offer tours and travel itineraries specifically for gay and lesbian travelers. San Francisco–based **Now, Voyager** (**✆ 800/255-6951;** www.nowvoyager.com) offers worldwide trips and cruises, and **Olivia** (**✆ 800/631-6277;** www.olivia.com) offers lesbian cruises and resort vacations.

Gay.com Travel (**✆ 800/929-2268** or 415/644-8044; www.gay.com/travel or www.outandabout.com) is an excellent online successor to the popular ***Out & About*** print magazine. It provides regularly updated information about gay-owned, gay-oriented, and gay-friendly lodging, dining, sightseeing, nightlife, and shopping establishments in every important destination worldwide. British travelers should click on the "Travel" link at **www.uk.gay.com** for advice and gay-friendly trip ideas.

The Canadian website **GayTraveler** (**www.gaytraveler.ca**) offers ideas and advice for gay travel all over the world.

The following travel guides are available at many bookstores, or you can order them from any online bookseller: ***Spartacus International Gay Guide, 35th Edition*** (Bruno Gmünder Verlag; www.spartacusworld.com/gayguide); ***Odysseus: The International Gay Travel Planner, 17th Edition*** (Odysseus Enterprises, Ltd.); and the ***Damron*** guides (www.damron.com), with separate annual books for gay men and lesbians.

TRAVELERS WITH DISABILITIES

Most disabilities shouldn't stop anyone from traveling. There are more options and resources out there than ever before. Most major hotels in the large cities of Vietnam—Ho Chi Minh City and Hanoi—can accommodate travelers with wheelchairs, but hotels in rural areas are unlikely to provide such services. Ramps are uncommon.

Organizations that offer a vast range of resources and assistance to travelers with disabilities include **MossRehab** (**✆ 800/CALL-MOSS** [225-5667]; www.mossresourcenet.org), the **American Foundation for the Blind** (**AFB; ✆ 800/232-5463;** www.afb.org), and **SATH** (Society for Accessible Travel & Hospitality; **✆ 212/447-7284;** www.sath.org). **AirAmbulanceCard.com** is now partnered with SATH and allows you to preselect top-notch hospitals in case of an emergency.

Access-Able Travel Source (**© 303/232-2979;** www.access-able.com) offers a comprehensive database on travel agents from around the world with experience in accessible travel; destination-specific access information; and links to such resources as service animals, equipment rentals, and access guides.

Many travel agencies offer customized tours and itineraries for travelers with disabilities. Among them are **Flying Wheels Travel** (**© 507/451-5005;** www.flyingwheelstravel.com) and **Accessible Journeys** (**© 800/846-4537** or 610/521-0339; www.disabilitytravel.com).

Flying with Disability (www.flying-with-disability.org) is a comprehensive information source on airplane travel. **Avis Rent a Car** (**© 888/879-4273**) has an Avis Access program that offers services for customers with special travel needs. These include specially outfitted vehicles with swivel seats, spinner knobs, and hand controls; mobility scooter rentals; and accessible bus service. Be sure to reserve well in advance.

The "Accessible Travel" link at **Mobility-Advisor.com** (www.mobility-advisor.com) offers a variety of travel resources to those with disabilities.

British travelers should contact **Holiday Care** (**© 0845/124-9971** in U.K. only; www.holidaycare.org.uk) to access a wide range of travel information and resources for the elderly and those with disabilities.

FAMILY TRAVEL

If you have enough trouble getting your kids out of the house in the morning, dragging them thousands of miles away might seem like an insurmountable challenge. But family travel can be immensely rewarding, giving you new ways of seeing the world through smaller pairs of eyes.

The rough roads of Vietnam can be a bit much for little ones, and concerns about communicable diseases in rural areas should certainly be weighed (be sure to check with your healthcare provider and be vigilant about updating all vaccinations). However, more accessible destinations and larger cities offer a glimpse into ancient civilization and varied culture that delights the kid in all of us.

Traveling families report no unique hassles to bringing the kids along to Vietnam. Most families choose to fly from place to place within the country, though, and avoid overcrowded local transport (though the trains, especially to Sapa in the far north, are pretty doable and a good adventure). Most hotels can arrange extra beds at little additional cost, and connecting-room capability is common. To locate accommodations, restaurants, and attractions that are particularly kid friendly, refer to the "Kids" icon throughout this guide.

The larger resort destinations—the better hotels in **Nha Trang, Hoi An,** and the **Furama Resort in Danang**—are quite kid friendly. Many families choose a comfortable hotel and make **culturally rich Hanoi** a hub for trips to **Halong Bay** and **Sapa,** but the whole length of Vietnam's coast is open to exploration by the adventurous traveling brood. Kids love eating ice cream in the many open-air joints surrounding Hoan Kiem Lake in Hanoi, and war tourism seems to spark something in boys (of all ages). The **War Museum** in Ho Chi Minh City—with tanks, planes, and artillery in the large courtyard—seems to delight kids and is a highlight, but be forewarned: There are also many grisly images in this museum. Kids love crawling through the tunnels in **Cu Chi** or **Vinh Moc** and the Central Highlands town of **Dalat,** which, with its tattered Disney-like sights and fun day hikes, is a favorite for kids. Kids always enjoy rapping with the **hilltribe people in Sapa**—a fun clash of culture because the young ethnic hilltribe folks speak English well and are eager to chat with foreigners their age—this also means that your kids might come home with a few words of Hmong, Dao, or Vietnamese, and maybe even a pen pal.

The big hotels all have pools, oceanside resorts are great places to play, and every major city has a big water park that, though sometimes a bit grungy, appeals to both parents and kids wanting to escape from the heat and connect with locals. You'll find willing—and affordable—babysitters in even the smallest hotel or guesthouse, and Vietnamese dote on children, meaning your clan will get lots of attention everywhere you go. Some parents are surprised at how easily kids adapt—much better than parents sometimes—adventurously hopping on boats and fearlessly meeting with locals.

A note of warning: People generally love kids in Vietnam, and foreign children are sure to attract lots of attention—sometimes far too much, actually, and it can be a bit overwhelming. With the most friendly of intentions, Vietnamese often like to touch foreign kids, tousle their hair, or brush a cheek and dote like your favorite auntie does back home, which can be disconcerting or confusing for kids (even from auntie). It's a good idea to warn your kids that this might happen, and it's also okay to step in front of people and kindly but firmly say "No" or *Khong tich* (he/she doesn't like that) while brushing away a hand. You might also find yourself in "walking zoo" moments, where groups of Vietnamese tourists want photos of themselves—and this is most common at the big sights—with foreign people. Again, this can be overwhelming, and saying no is fine, but you can also just warn your child about it and roll with the punches. As much as possible, talk with people; this takes away the freaky "sideshow" vibe and puts you on a level of "relating," as all parents do, rather than comparing your differences.

For further details on requirements for children traveling abroad, go to the U.S. State Department website (http://travel.state.gov).

Recommended family-travel Internet sites include **Family Travel Forum** (www.familytravelforum.com), a comprehensive site that offers customized trip planning; **Family Travel Network** (www.familytravelnetwork.com), an award-winning site that offers travel features, deals, and tips; **Traveling Internationally with Your Kids** (www.travelwithyourkids.com), a comprehensive site offering sound advice for long-distance and international travel with children; and **Family Travel Files** (www.thefamilytravelfiles.com), which offers an online magazine and a directory of off-the-beaten-path tours and tour operators for families.

WOMEN TRAVELERS

Women traveling alone in Vietnam face no particular safety issues, and common sense should keep anyone safe. If alone, female travelers in Vietnam (everyone, really) are repeatedly grilled about their marital status and, if single, pitied—a bit exhausting after a while. Some women even revert to wearing wedding bands to end those conversations before they begin. No particular vigilance is required for female travelers, as violent crime is minimal in Vietnam, but the usual precautions about walking alone at night and hitchhiking certainly apply, as anywhere. "Catcalling" happens but is rarely sinister or followed by any action.

For general travel resources for women, go to www.frommers.com/planning.

RETURNING WAR VETERANS

American (and Australian) veterans of the Vietnam War who have put off this trip for years think about the past with regret or remorse and imagine they might find harsh recrimination from Vietnamese people—the same kind of harsh recrimination that many experienced when returning to their home country (which they thought they'd been fighting for). Instead, most veterans who return to Vietnam find healing. Many of the hundreds of thousands of U.S. soldiers who found themselves lost and confused on a steaming tarmac so far from home were no more than kids at the time, and many have carried baggage about the war for a lifetime. A trip to Vietnam, and an experience of Vietnamese hospitality, might just close the chapter.

Vietnamese people who lived through the war will certainly never forget it—but what they endured, and the autonomy that they earned through those years of trial, is a source of pride—and most folks you meet are eager to let go of the past. And though Vietnamese nationalism is at once worn proudly in public displays—like big brass-band ceremonies on National Day and May Day—on the personal level, you'll rarely find Vietnamese talking about the war with strutting bravado. Popular for U.S. veterans are humanitarian-aid tours, where groups bring resources and their own elbow grease back to the very rural people they wanted to help so many years ago. Veterans tours often include a meet-and-greet, through a translator, with North Vietnamese veterans, and these times of connection with the one-time enemy bring solace to many. Visiting old wartime posts or cities where they were billeted, veterans also speak of a connection with the rich Vietnamese language and culture on their second go-around. For more information on tours for veterans, see the sidebar "Tours for Vietnam Veterans," in section 9, "Special-Interest & Escorted General-Interest Tours," below.

To read about the experience of one returning veteran, see the box called "A Veteran's Trip Back" in chapter 12.

SENIOR TRAVEL

Seniors traveling in Vietnam might bask in the glow of filial piety and enjoy the Vietnamese idea—from Confucianism—of respect for elders, but senior travelers are less likely to enjoy the major discounts found in the West. But do mention the fact that you're a senior when you make your travel reservations. Although all of the major U.S. airlines except America West have canceled their senior discount and coupon book programs, many hotels still offer discounts for seniors.

Members of **AARP,** 601 E St. NW, Washington, DC 20049 (© **888/687-2277;** www.aarp.org), get discounts on hotels, airfares, and car rentals. AARP offers members a wide range of benefits, including *AARP The Magazine* and a monthly newsletter. Anyone over 50 can join.

Many reliable agencies and organizations target the 50-plus market. **Elderhostel** (© **800/454-5768;** www.elderhostel.org) arranges worldwide study programs for those aged 55 and over. **ElderTreks** (© **800/741-7956** or 416/558-5000 outside North America; www.eldertreks.com) offers small-group tours to off-the-beaten-path or adventure-travel locations, restricted to travelers 50 and older.

Recommended publications offering travel resources and discounts for seniors include the quarterly magazine ***Travel 50 & Beyond*** (www.travel50andbeyond.com) and the best-selling paperback ***Unbelievably Good Deals and Great Adventures That You Absolutely Can't Get Unless You're Over 50 2009–2010, 18th Edition*** (McGraw-Hill), by Joan Rattner Heilman.

STUDENT TRAVEL

Vietnam is a hot destination for budget-minded (I didn't say *poor*) students. Commonly, young backpackers hit the shores in Southeast Asia and travel for extended periods of time, with Vietnam just one stop on an extended tour. Starting from bases like Hanoi's Old Quarter, Saigon's Pham Ngu Lao area, or over on Khao San Road in Bangkok, budget travelers have roamed the rugged highways and byways of Vietnam and broader Indochina for years, paving the way for high-end tourism. More remote areas are relegated to this hearty horde, and rural roads still beckon with the promise of friendships (often through shared strife) and broadening experiences.

Any discounts to be found in Vietnam and Southeast Asia come from hard bargaining or tolerance for the most basic accommodations, but it's not a bad idea to have an **International Student Identity Card (ISIC),** which offers substantial savings on rail passes, plane tickets, and entrance fees. It also provides you with basic health and life insurance and a 24-hour help line. The card is available for $22 from **STA Travel** (✆ **800/781-4040** in North America; www.statravel.com), the biggest student travel agency in the world. If you're no longer a student but are still under 26, you can get an **International Youth Travel Card (IYTC)** for the same price from the same people, which entitles you to some discounts (but not on museum admissions). (***Note:*** In 2002, STA Travel bought competitors **Council Travel** and **USIT Campus** after they went bankrupt. It's still operating some offices under the Council name, but it's owned by STA.) **Travel CUTS** (✆ **866/246-9762;** www.travelcuts.com) offers similar services for both Canadians and U.S. residents. Irish students may prefer to turn to **USIT** (✆ **01/602-1904;** www.usitnow.ie), an Ireland-based specialist in student, youth, and independent travel.

SINGLE TRAVELERS

By and large, travelers in Vietnam and the other countries of Southeast Asia are seekers of some kind, whether for an exotic location or an unbending of their cultural norm, or to reconnect with their past and come to terms with it. Many prefer to travel in Vietnam alone. For independent travelers, solo journeys are opportunities to make friends and meet locals. Groups of tourists are intimidating, but single travelers—though better targets for touts and shysters—also look like they need help ("sympathy touring," a friend of mine calls it) and will likely be pitied (however unfounded) and offered hospitality by kind Vietnamese families.

A certain camaraderie also develops on long bus rides or in the uncertainty and wonder we share with fellow travelers from the West, and a trip that might start out solo often ends in friendships that last a lifetime.

Travel Buddies Singles Travel Club (✆ **800/998-9099;** www.travelbuddies worldwide.com), based in Canada, runs small, intimate, singles-friendly group trips and will match you with a roommate free of charge. **TravelChums** (✆ **212/787-2621;** www.travelchums.com) is an Internet-only travel-companion matching service with elements of an online personals-type site, hosted by the respected New York–based Shaw Guides travel service.

Many reputable tour companies offer singles-only trips. **Singles Travel International** (✆ **877/765-6874;** www.singles travelintl.com) offers singles-only escorted tours to places like London, Alaska, Fiji, and the Greek Islands. **Backroads** (✆ **800/462-2848;** www.backroads.com) offers "Singles + Solos" active-travel trips to destinations worldwide.

For more information on traveling single, go to www.frommers.com/planning.

8 SUSTAINABLE TOURISM

As a relatively new vacation destination—and a developing country, to boot—Vietnam puts little pressure on the tourism industry to develop sustainable practices. There is virtually no backlash for hotels' and resorts' profligate energy usage. Meanwhile, the enthusiasm of international hotel chains and local developers has led to

General Resources for Green Travel

The following websites provide valuable wide-ranging information on sustainable travel. For a list of even more sustainable resources, as well as tips and explanations on how to travel greener, visit www.frommers.com/planning.

- **Responsible Travel** (www.responsibletravel.com) is a great source of sustainable travel ideas; the site is run by a spokesperson for ethical tourism in the travel industry. **Sustainable Travel International** (www.sustainable travelinternational.org) promotes ethical tourism practices and manages an extensive directory of sustainable properties and tour operators around the world.
- In the U.K., **Tourism Concern** (www.tourismconcern.org.uk) works to reduce social and environmental problems connected to tourism. The **Association of Independent Tour Operators** (**AITO;** www.aito.co.uk) is a group of specialist operators leading the field in making holidays sustainable.
- In Canada, **www.greenlivingonline.com** offers extensive content on how to travel sustainably, including a travel and transport section and profiles of the best green shops and services in Toronto, Vancouver, and Calgary.
- In Australia, the national body which sets guidelines and standards for eco-tourism is **Ecotourism Australia** (www.ecotourism.org.au). **The Green Directory** (www.thegreendirectory.com.au), **Green Pages** (www.thegreen pages.com.au), and **Eco Directory** (www.ecodirectory.com.au) offer sustainable travel tips and directories of green businesses.
- **Carbonfund** (www.carbonfund.org), **TerraPass** (www.terrapass.org), and **Carbon Neutral** (www.carbonneutral.org) provide info on "carbon offsetting," or offsetting the greenhouse gas emitted during flights.
- **Greenhotels** (www.greenhotels.com) recommends green-rated member hotels around the world that fulfill the company's stringent environmental requirements. **Environmentally Friendly Hotels** (www.environmentally friendlyhotels.com) offers more green accommodations ratings. The **Hotel Association of Canada** (www.hacgreenhotels.com) has a Green Key Eco-Rating Program, which audits the environmental performance of Canadian hotels, motels, and resorts.
- **Sustain Lane** (www.sustainlane.com) lists sustainable eating and drinking choices around the U.S.; also visit **www.eatwellguide.org** for tips on eating sustainably in the U.S. and Canada.
- For information on animal-friendly issues throughout the world, visit **Tread Lightly** (www.treadlightly.org). For information about the ethics of swimming with dolphins, visit the **Whale and Dolphin Conservation Society** (www.wdcs.org).
- **Volunteer International** (www.volunteerinternational.org) has a list of questions to help you determine the intentions and nature of a volunteer program. For general info on volunteer travel, visit **www.volunteerabroad.org** and **www.idealist.org**.

massive development of once-public, pristine beaches in Phan Thiet, Mui Ne, and Danang. The end result may well be ghettos of five-star resorts and golf courses guzzling large quantities of energy.

For individual travelers, cranking up the air-conditioning is a knee-jerk reaction when vacationing in Vietnam. Sure, there are some cool respites in the north and central parts of the country, but for the most part, your vacation is going to be a hot one. But bear in mind that it takes massive amounts of energy to keep hotel rooms and indoor areas cool. To make your Vietnam vacation a little bit greener, take the initiative and turn down the air-conditioning when staying at high-end hotels—these places often keep rooms at a chilly 66°F (19°C).

A few notable outfits are also making conscious efforts to reduce their impact on the surrounding environs. The guys at **Vietnam Vespa Adventure** (see chapter 12) use biodiesel made from refined vegetable oil waste to run their multiday tours on vintage Vespa scooters. Over in Phnom Penh, the **Quay** (see chapter 14) bills itself as a "carbon-friendly" boutique hotel, buying carbon credits to offset the hotel's emissions.

Finally, when traveling to far-flung places, be mindful of local customs. Be very cautious about taking photographs among Vietnam's ethnic hilltribe minorities in the far north and Central Highlands. Ask first, respect an answer of "no" (true anywhere), and avoid photographing sacred shrines of hilltribe people.

9 SPECIAL-INTEREST & ESCORTED GENERAL-INTEREST TOURS

SPECIAL-INTEREST TRIPS

Academic Trips & Language Classes

A visit just to **Hanoi** puts vast resources at your fingertips—from museums to vestiges of architecture as far back as the 13th century. Walking tours of the Old Quarter, an area of the city that a curious traveler could literally pick apart block by block, are like a giant textbook. Here you'll learn about early Vietnamese commerce, the colonial administration of the French, early Vietnamese unrest, and eventual insurgency, not to mention the more heavy-handed legacy of a triumphant Vietnam under the leadership of Ho Chi Minh in the vestiges of his mausoleum and museum.

Asia Transpacific Journeys (see the listing under "Escorted General-Interest Tours," below) is quite typical of the many international tour agencies running trips to Vietnam. They offer specialized itineraries focused on Vietnamese culture—such as the ancients, the Cham people, vestiges of the Chinese millennia, and the years under French colonialism.

Hanoi Language and Culture Tours (✆ **09/1352-2605;** www.hanoilanguagetours.com) offers multiday courses that range from quick 2-day affairs to arm you with Vietnamese basics, to language and travel courses that that offer the opportunity to practice your newly learned linguistic skills in a Vietnamese homestay.

Adventure & Wellness Trips

If you like to get out into the countryside, you can find much to do in Vietnam. Consider first the kind of terrain you'd like to explore—ranging from dense jungle to high mountains, coastal estuaries to inland rivers on flooded rice plains. Next, choose your weapon: kayak, mountain bike, motorcycle, jeep, hiking boots, or flip-flops.

The best areas for some good trekking are in the **far north** and **Central Highlands**

Tours for Vietnam Veterans

A good percentage of visitors to Vietnam are American Vietnam War veterans. It's not unusual to run across groups or individuals as you make your way across the country, some simply seeing how the story ended or others on more somber missions, such as staging memorial services.

But why would a veteran want to return to Vietnam, the scene of such tragic events? Most say they seek closure and that only by finally crossing the 17th Parallel can they find that; many also say that a trip to Vietnam gives them a chance to truly experience Vietnamese culture this second time around and visit peaceful villages devoid of barbed wire, mines, and terror.

Tours of Peace (TOP), a nonprofit organization started by Jess DeVaney, a retired U.S. Marine, arranges tours of Vietnam for veterans not only to come to terms with their past, but also to participate in the future. DeVaney's tours bring friends and family to points of historical or personal significance, but what is unique here is their humanitarian focus: The folks at TOP believe that through helping others, we heal ourselves, so humanitarian-aid projects are part of every tour. TOP visits orphanages, homes for the elderly and the homeless, poor rural villages, and schools, providing food, medicines, and supplies that save lives and give hope. Participants have a chance to return again as jolly green giants of yore, only this time able to help and spread kindness. Trip participants say that the tour is a great step in their recovery and toward acceptance of the past.

According to a spokesperson, "TOP participants come home from Vietnam this time feeling whole and understood. Vietnam is no longer a secret and a source of nightmares for them. A Tour of Peace helps participants exorcise the

of Vietnam; both regions have large populations of minority ethnic hilltribes, and the scenery—rice terraces and spiked peaks—is stunning. Highlights include visiting **Halong Bay** and the country's many national parks.

In the north of Vietnam, the folks at **Handspan** (© **04/3926-0581;** www.handspan.com), as well as **Buffalo Tours** (© **04/3828-0702;** www.buffalotours.com), put together exciting kayaking adventures in Halong Bay. In the far north, they offer good hiking trips to Sapa and by jeep up to Dien Bien Phu. In central Vietnam, the old French colonial hill station of Dalat plays host to a great outfitter, **Phat Tire Ventures** (© **063/3829-422;** www.phattireventures.com), where you can rock-climb, mountain-bike, or trek with the most professional guides and experienced technicians.

Off-road adventures on **motorbike** and **by jeep** abound along the length of Vietnam. See chapter 6 for more extensive information on motorbike and jeep touring north of Hanoi along the **Dien Bien Phu Loop** or up to **Cao Bang.** Small outfitters in Hanoi can help with rentals or guide hires.

In the **Central Highlands,** hiring an **Easy Rider** motorcycle guide out of Dalat is all the rage. (See chapter 10 for contact information.) Riding a big (for Vietnam) 125cc Honda Bonus—you sit on the back—the Easy Riders, most of whom demons of war and find peace of mind." TOP offers financial assistance for those who need it (an application is on its website) and organizes tours year-round.

Applications for a Tour of Peace can be printed from TOP's website, **www.topvietnamveterans.org**, or by writing to TOP Vietnam Veterans, 8000 S. Kolb Rd., Ste. 43, Tucson, AZ 85706.

Also consider **Vets with a Mission,** a large nonprofit that has been in business some 17 years and runs annual trips, for veterans only, to Vietnam. Like Tours of Peace, Vets with a Mission—as their name suggests—is a group out to make a difference on their trips, and they bring large medical donations and services. The group helps veterans cut through the outmoded notion of heavy remorse and gives vets a chance to weigh in with their actions. Go to **www.vwam.com** or contact the group by e-mail at vetswithamission@backroads.net or by snail mail at: Vets with a Mission, P.O. Box 202, Newberry, SC 29108.

A few tour operators cater to veterans and can tailor individual tours to follow a division's history or customize travel for a returning veteran's wishes. Most groups visit general operating areas. An itinerary may start out in Saigon with an excursion to the Cu Chi Tunnels, going down to the Mekong Delta, then heading up to Qui Nhon and to the Central Highlands and Pleiku, and then moving on to Danang, China Beach, Hue, and, of course, the demilitarized zone (DMZ).

Contact the **Global Spectrum,** 5683 Columbia Pike, Ste. 101, Falls Church, VA 22041 (✆ **800/419-4446** or 703/671-9619; fax 703/671-5747; www.asianpassages.com).

retired from the South Vietnamese Army and speak English well, will take you across the ridge of the highlands all the way through **Ban Ma Thuot** and on to **Kontum,** where the Ho Chi Minh Trail (now a major highway) leads as far as Danang or Hue. Easy Rider can make arrangements for groups and even rent motorbikes if some members of the group want to ride their own bikes alongside a guide. The same routes can also be done by jeep.

In **Ho Chi Minh City,** seek out **Vietnam Vespa Adventure** for a memorable trip on a lovingly restored vintage Vespa scooter (see chapter 12 for contact information). These guys will take you off the beaten track along the coast of Phan Thiet and Mui Ne, or up north to Nha Trang.

Food & Wine Trips

Sampling Vietnamese cuisine is a highlight of any trip, so why not learn to make it yourself? The **Hanoi Cooking Centre** (✆ **04/3715-0088;** www.hanoicookingcentre.com) is a new and popular choice in the nation's capital. The city's first purpose-built cooking center runs hands-on classes out of a restored colonial building near Truc Bach Lake. In Hoi An, in central Vietnam, Ms. Vy at **Morning Glory Restaurant and Cooking School** (✆ **0510/324-1555;** www.hoianhospitality.com) runs great programs of varying length.

ESCORTED GENERAL-INTEREST TOURS

Escorted tours are structured group tours with a group leader. The price usually includes everything from airfare to hotels, meals, tours, admission costs, and local transportation.

Whether you want to ride an elephant through the jungle, trek among indigenous people, shake hands with a gibbon, swim beneath a waterfall, snorkel in a clear blue lagoon, lounge on a white-sand beach, or wander through exotic markets, there's a Vietnam tour packager for you, offering a wide range of travel options using the finest and most reliable travel services available in the region.

Among the most experienced and knowledgeable tour operators specializing in Vietnam and Southeast Asia are **Absolute Asia** and **Asia Transpacific Journeys.** In-country tour providers **Diethelm** and **Exotissimo** can do anything from arranging deluxe tours to just helping out with any small details or bookings. Most companies allow clients to design their own trips or deviate from exact schedules (often at a small cost). Companies like **Intrepid,** among others, offer unique itineraries for solo travelers. Many in-country tour operators are listed in the book's following chapters, but here are the top outfitters:

ABERCROMBIE & KENT Well-known luxury-tour operator Abercrombie & Kent offers Southeast Asia programs with numerous comprehensive itineraries, including expansive tours to Vietnam and Cambodia. A journey with A & K includes the best dining and luxury transport, as well as high-end stays at the finest hotels in Southeast Asia and Vietnam, such as the Metropole in Hanoi or the finer beach resorts near Nha Trang. In the United States: 1520 Kensington Rd., Ste. 212, Oakbrook, IL 60523-2141; ✆ **800/323-7308;** fax 630/954-3324; www.aandktours.com.

ABSOLUTE ASIA Founded in 1989, Absolute Asia offers an array of innovative itineraries, specializing in individual or small-group tours customized to your interests, with experienced local guides and excellent accommodations. Talk to them about tours that feature art, cuisine, religion, antiques, photography, wildlife study, archaeology, and soft adventure—they can plan a specialized trip to see just about anything you can dream up for any length of time. They can also book you on excellent coach programs in Vietnam or throughout Indochina. In the United States: 180 Varick St., 16 Floor, New York, NY 10014; ✆ **800/736-8187;** fax 212/627-4090; www.absoluteasia.com.

ASIA TRANSPACIFIC JOURNEYS Coordinating tours to every corner of South and Southeast Asia and the Pacific, Asia Transpacific Journeys deals with small groups and custom programs that include luxury hotel accommodations. The flagship package, the 23-day Passage to Indochina tour, takes you through Laos, Vietnam, and Cambodia's major attractions with a well-planned itinerary that also promotes cultural understanding. A highly recommended choice. In the United States: 2995 Center Green Court, Boulder, CO 80301; ✆ **800/642-2742** or 303/443-6789; fax 303/443-7078; www.asiatranspacific.com.

BACKROADS For those who want to explore Vietnam by bike, cycling and hiking specialist Backroads has a 12-day Vietnam tour, among others. Check out their website; they're always coming up with new innovative itineraries in the region. In the United States: 801 Cedar St., Berkeley, CA 94710-1800; ✆ **800/462-2848** or 510/527-1555; fax 510/527-1444; www.backroads.com.

EXOTISSIMO A French outfit and outbound (in-country) agency with offices in every major city in the region, Exotissimo has excellent guides on-site. Agents can arrange all-inclusive tours and help with all travel details, from ticketing to visas. See the office locations in each relevant chapter. In France: 40 bis, Rue du fg Poissonniére, 75010 Paris; ✆ **(33)149/490-360;** fax (33)149/490-369. In Vietnam: Saigon Trade Center, 37 Ton Duc Thang, District 1, Ho Chi Minh City; ✆ **08/825-1723;** fax 08/828-2146; www.exotissimo.com.

IMAGINATIVE TRAVELLER This U.K.-based firm gets rave reviews every time for organizing all sorts of cycling, trekking, and motorcycling adventures throughout the region, particularly in Vietnam and Cambodia. In the U.K.: 1 Betts Ave., Martlesham Heath, Suffolk IP5 3RH; ✆ **0800/316-2717;** www.imaginative-traveller.com.

INTREPID This popular Australian operator is a good choice for getting off the beaten track on a tour of Vietnam. Intrepid caters tours for the culturally discerning, those with humanitarian goals, adventurers, and people on a budget. Their motto is their name, and with some of the best guides in Asia, these folks will take you to the back of beyond safely, in style, and with lots of laughs. A fun, fraternal vibe pervades these tours; it's especially great for the hearty adventurer looking to join a group. In Australia: Fitzroy, DC VIC 3065, 11 Spring St., Fitzroy, Victoria; ✆ **613/9473-2626;** fax 613/9419-4426; www.intrepidtravel.com. In the U.S.: **877/448-1616.**

Pros & Cons of Escorted Tours

Many people like the ease and security of escorted trips. Escorted tours—whether by bus, motorcoach, train, or boat—let travelers sit back and enjoy their trip without having to spend lots of time behind the wheel or worrying about details. You know your costs upfront, and there are few surprises. Escorted tours can take you to the maximum number of sights in the minimum amount of time with the least amount of hassle—you don't have to sweat over the plotting and planning of a vacation schedule. Escorted tours are particularly convenient for people with limited mobility. They can also be a great way to make new friends.

On the downside, an escorted tour often requires a big deposit upfront, and lodging and dining choices are predetermined. You'll get little opportunity for serendipitous interactions with locals. The tours can be jampacked with activities, leaving little room for individual sightseeing, whim, or adventure—plus they also often focus only on the heavily visited sites, so you miss out on the lesser-known gems.

Before you invest in an escorted tour, ask about the **cancellation policy:** Is a deposit required? Can they cancel the trip if they don't get enough people? Do you get a refund if they cancel? If *you* cancel? How late can you cancel if you are unable to go? When do you pay in full?

Note: If you choose an escorted tour, think strongly about purchasing trip-cancellation insurance, especially if the tour operator asks you to pay upfront. (For information on traveler's insurance, trip cancellation insurance, and medical insurance while traveling, please visit www.frommers.com/planning.)

You'll also want to get a complete **schedule** of the trip to find out how much sightseeing is planned each day and whether enough time has been allotted for relaxing or wandering solo.

The **size** of the group is also important to know upfront. Generally, the smaller the group, the more flexible the itinerary, and the less time you'll spend waiting for people to get on and off the bus. Find out the **demographics** of the group as well. What is the age range? What is the gender breakdown? Is this mostly a trip for couples or singles?

Discuss what's included in the **price.** You may have to pay for transportation to and from the airport. A box lunch may be included in an excursion, but drinks might cost extra. Tips may not be included. Find out if you will be charged if you decide to opt out of certain activities or meals.

Before you invest in a package tour, get some answers. Ask about the **accommodations choices** and prices for each. Then look up the hotels' reviews in a Frommer's guide and check their rates online for your specific dates of travel. You'll also want to find out what **type of room** you get. If you need a certain type of room, ask for it; don't take whatever is thrown your way. Request a nonsmoking room, a quiet room, a room with a view, or whatever you fancy.

Finally, if you plan to travel alone, you'll need to know if a **single supplement** will be charged and if the company can match you up with a roommate.

For more information on escorted general-interest tours, including questions to ask before booking your trip, see www.frommers.com/planning.

10 STAYING CONNECTED

CELLPHONES

The three letters that define much of the world's wireless capabilities are **GSM** (Global System for Mobile Communications), a big, seamless network that makes for easy cross-border cellphone use throughout Europe and dozens of other countries worldwide. In the U.S., T-Mobile, AT&T Wireless, and Cingular use this quasi-universal system; in Canada, Microcell and some Rogers customers are GSM, and all Europeans and most Australians use GSM. GSM phones function with a removable plastic SIM card, encoded with your phone number and account information. If your cellphone is on a GSM system and you have a world-capable multiband phone such as many Sony Ericsson, Motorola, or Samsung models, you can make and receive calls across civilized areas around much of the globe. Just call your wireless operator and ask for "international roaming" to be activated on your account. Unfortunately, per-minute charges can be high—usually $1 to $1.50 in western Europe and up to $5 in places like Russia and Indonesia.

The best way to get connected with your own hand-phone in Vietnam is to **buy an affordable GSM phone** and set up a simple prepaid account. Local calls are less than 10¢ per minute, and incoming calls are free.

Most cellphone operators in the West sell "locked" phones that restrict you from using any other removable computer memory phone chip card (called a **SIM card**) other than the ones they supply. Buy an **unlocked phone** that accepts a prepaid SIM card (found at a local retailer for as little as $40) that gives you a new account and phone number and can be exchanged for a new card in your next destination (like nearby Cambodia or Thailand). Buy new and reconditioned mobile phones at local department stores in the major cities or in any of the small storefront vendors popping up everywhere. When signing up for a local calling plan (for as little as $20, including a first batch of anytime minutes) you will get a local phone number and the staff can help you set it up (be sure to ask for help getting the phone set to "English," or *tien Anh,* if searching the LCD monitor yourself). In Vietnam, service providers include **Vinaphone,** with main offices at 1–3 Nguyen Van Binh in Ho Chi Minh (✆ **08/3823-9001**), and cards are sold at retailers around the city. **Mobiphone** is a similar service and is best for good service in urban areas, but not as effective as Vinaphone out in the provinces. Retailers for these popular providers are just about anywhere, and at any post office in the country.

Note: **Phone rental** is unavailable in Vietnam; buying a phone and setting up a prepaid account is the way to go.

INTERNET & E-MAIL

Without Your Own Computer

Internet cafes are just about anywhere in Vietnam—I've even been to an Internet cafe with a thatched roof in a rural hamlet. The quality of connections varies. In big cities like Hanoi or Ho Chi Minh City, you can find fast, affordable ADSL service for as low as 4,000 VND per hour. The Internet is controlled by the government post office in any town, and most post offices now have adjoining cybercafes that are a good bet for fast, affordable service. In rural areas, it can get frustrating; the good ADSL line that starts at the post office gets split and spliced in its path to rural parts, creating patchy service or, if someone's been digging in the wrong place, unavailable service. The other drawback is that these places are often smoky and very crowded with screaming kids playing online shoot-'em-up games. Check the listings in individual chapters, or inquire at any hotel front desk to find an Internet cafe.

To find cybercafes in your destination, check **www.cybercaptive.com** and **www.cybercafe.com**.

Most major airports have **Internet kiosks** that provide basic Web access for a per-minute fee that's usually higher than cybercafe prices.

With Your Own Computer

Wi-Fi (wireless fidelity) is the buzzword in computer access, and many of the larger high-end hotels in Vietnam are signing on as wireless "hotspots" from where you can get high-speed connection without cable wires, networking hardware, or a phone line (see below). You can get Wi-Fi connection one of several ways. Many laptops sold in the last few years have built-in Wi-Fi capability (an 802.11b wireless Ethernet connection). Mac owners have their own networking technology, called Apple AirPort. For those with older computers, an 802.11b/**Wi-Fi card** (around $50) can be plugged into your laptop. Many of Vietnam's wireless hotspots, in cafes or major hotels, are available for free. Prepaid plans are likely to follow.

Most business-class hotels in Vietnam offer dataports for laptop modems and increasingly offer high-speed Internet access using an Ethernet network cable or in-room Wi-Fi. You can bring your own cables, but most hotels will gladly loan them. A number of hotels in Vietnam offer free in-room Internet service.

Wherever you go, bring a **connection kit** of power and phone adapters, a spare phone cord, and a spare Ethernet network cable (some of the better city hotels can provide what you need). The current in Vietnam is 220V. Most laptops can plug directly into Vietnamese outlets, but bring a three-prong-to-two-prong adapter and a surge protector.

11 TIPS ON ACCOMMODATIONS

Affordable luxury is the name of the game in Vietnam. For what you'd pay to get a cracker-box room in U.S. and European big cities, you get to go in style in Indochina. Pay over $100 and you are royalty. Budget travelers and young backpackers flock to the region, and a big part of the charm is spending $5 to $7 per night. If your trip is short, live it up! Go for a luxury room; take advantage of affordable health and beauty or spa treatments (for a fraction of what you'd pay elsewhere). Midrange boutique hotels and rustic eco-friendly rural resorts are also a new trend as developers discover that "refurbished" is cool and that location—whether overlooking the Mekong or set in a tropical rainforest—is everything.

Many of the major chains are in the region. **Sheraton** and the **Mövenpick** have hotels in Ho Chi Minh City and Hanoi. **Hilton** has properties in Hanoi, and there's a **Park Hyatt** in Ho Chi Minh City. The French hoteliers at **Accor** host a number of **Sofitel** and **Mercure** hotels in Vietnam. Many of the big-city properties are aimed at the business market, but in Vietnam, the unique, refurbished **Sofitel Metropole** takes the cake. There are also a number of good individual brands in Vietnam: the likes of **Daewoo** in Hanoi, or the **Rex** and the **Caravelle** in Ho Chi Minh City.

Budget accommodations mean the ubiquitous **minihotel.** Quality varies, but these small Chinese-style hotels usually have air-conditioning, hot water, and cable TV starting at just $15. Some minihotels in Hanoi and Ho Chi Minh are going boutique, a good trend. **Maison d'Hanoi** hotel in Hanoi is a good bet for a boutique hotel in a good location.

Whatever your financial situation, you will be greeted by high standards with good amenities and services at low cost in Vietnam.

SURFING FOR HOTELS

In addition to the online travel booking sites **Travelocity, Expedia, Orbitz, Priceline,** and **Hotwire,** you can book hotels through **Hotels.com, Quikbook** (www.quikbook.com), and **Travelaxe** (www.travelaxe.net).

HotelChatter.com is a daily webzine offering smart coverage and critiques of hotels worldwide. Go to **TripAdvisor.com** or **HotelShark.com** for helpful independent consumer reviews of hotels and resort properties.

It's a good idea to **get a confirmation number** and **make a printout** of any online booking transaction.

Another good way to secure an affordable room is booking through an **on-the-ground tour agent in Vietnam.** Check the "Visitor Information & Tours" sections of specific destination chapters in this book. Travel agents do, of course, tack on a fee for their services, but that's on top of a very low contract rate they have negotiated directly with the hotel. Vietnam-based online hotel booking is a singularly dodgy affair, but many report success with small local consolidators, exemplified by the likes of **www.asia-hotels.com** or **www.vietnamrooms.com**.

SAVING ON YOUR HOTEL ROOM

The **rack rate** is the maximum rate that a hotel charges for a room. Hardly anybody pays this price, however, except in high season or on holidays. To lower the cost of your room:

- **Ask about special rates or other discounts.** You may qualify for corporate, student, military, senior, frequent-flier, trade union, or other discounts.
- **Dial direct.** When booking a room in a chain hotel, you'll often get a better deal by calling the individual hotel's reservation desk rather than the chain's main number.
- **Book online.** Many hotels offer Internet-only discounts, or supply rooms to Priceline, Hotwire, or Expedia at rates much lower you can get through the hotel itself.
- **Remember the law of supply and demand.** You can save big on hotel rooms by traveling in a destination's off season or shoulder seasons, when rates typically drop, even at luxury properties.
- **Look into group or long-stay discounts.** If you come as part of a large group, you should be able to negotiate

a bargain rate. Likewise, if you're planning a long stay (at least 5 days), you might qualify for a discount. As a general rule, expect 1 night free after a 7-night stay.

- **Sidestep excess surcharges and hidden costs.** Many hotels have adopted the unpleasant practice of nickel-and-diming guests with opaque surcharges. When you book a room, ask what is included in the room rate and what is extra. Avoid dialing direct from hotel phones, which can have exorbitant rates. And don't be tempted by the room's minibar offerings: Most hotels charge through the nose for water, soda, and snacks. Finally, ask about local taxes and service charges, which can increase the cost of a room by 15% or more.
- **Carefully consider your hotel's meal plan.** If you enjoy eating out and sampling the local cuisine, it makes sense to choose a **Continental Plan (CP),** which includes breakfast only, or a **European Plan (EP),** which doesn't include any meals and allows you maximum flexibility. If you're more interested in saving money, opt for a **Modified American Plan (MAP),** which includes breakfast and one meal, or the **American Plan (AP),** which includes three meals. If you must choose a MAP, see if you can get a free lunch at your hotel if you decide to do dinner out.
- **Consider enrolling in hotel chains' "frequent-stay" programs,** which are upping the ante lately to win the loyalty of repeat customers. Frequent guests can now accumulate points or credits to earn free hotel nights, airline miles, in-room amenities, merchandise, tickets to concerts and events, discounts on sporting facilities—and even credit toward stock in the participating hotel, in the case of the Jameson Inn hotel group. Perks are awarded not only by many chain hotels and motels (Accor's AClub, Hilton HHonors, and Sheraton's Starwood Preferred Guest, to name a few), but individual inns and B&Bs. Many chain hotels partner with other hotel chains, car-rental firms, airlines, and credit card companies to give consumers additional incentive to do repeat business.

LANDING THE BEST ROOM

Somebody has to get the best room in the house. It might as well be you. You can start by joining the hotel's frequent-guest program, which may make you eligible for upgrades. A hotel-branded credit card usually gives its owner "silver" or "gold" status in frequent-guest programs for free. Always ask about a corner room. They're often larger and quieter, with more windows and light, and they often cost the same as standard rooms. When you make your reservation, ask if the hotel is renovating; if it is, request a room away from the construction. Ask about nonsmoking rooms and rooms with views. Be sure to request your choice of twin, queen-, or king-size beds. If you're a light sleeper, ask for a quiet room away from vending or ice machines, elevators, restaurants, bars, and discos. Ask for a recently renovated or refurbished room.

If you aren't happy with your room when you arrive, ask for another one. Most lodgings will be willing to accommodate you.

4

Suggested Itineraries in Vietnam

The narrow S-curve of coastal Vietnam makes itinerary planning quite simple: You're going either south to north or north to south. Hearty backpackers take at least a month (if not more) going by "open tour bus" and/or other local transport, while jet-hopping tour groups cover the highlights in as little as a week to 10 days.

If you have just 4 or 5 days, base yourself out of either Hanoi or Ho Chi Minh City and choose from the day trips and overnights listed in chapters 5 and 12. With any itinerary, try to give yourself a good amount of flextime for days of rest at a beach, tummy trouble, or chance meetings, side trips, and inspirations along the way.

Some international flights land in Danang, and some travelers cross over land from Laos to Vinh or Hue—which are midway along the coast—or to Ho Chi Minh City from Phnom Penh, Cambodia. But most people arrive in Vietnam by air into Hanoi or Ho Chi Minh City. Most tours of Vietnam start off in one of these two busy cities. First-timers are often overwhelmed by the chaotic traffic, busy markets, pesky touts, and hot weather—hang in there, it just takes a bit of getting used to.

The most important thing to consider is weather. The country's opposing monsoonal systems in the north and south may sound a bit complicated, but here's what you need to know, in a nutshell:

The south, including **Ho Chi Minh City (Saigon)** and the **Mekong Delta,** is always hot, with a rainy season (ranging from afternoon thunderstorms to all-day downpours) from May to October. The **Central Highlands** is best during their "somewhat" dry season from January to May. Along the coast in **central Vietnam,** the monsoon season is inverted, and though the temperature is steady and warm, you can experience rain from October to February (and some tropical storms in between). The **north** is much cooler, with a wet and cold winter from December through February (quite cold in the mountains, and there's even snow), and a very hot summer with rains (best time to visit is in the fall, Sept–Oct). Consult individual destination chapters for more details. You can catch high season in multiple regions if you visit on the cusp of seasons: For example, travel in the north in November before you head south.

Important note: If you're landing directly in Vietnam after a long-haul flight from Europe or the U.S., know that **jet lag** is a formidable foe. You might hit the ground running on your first day and then feel exhausted on day 2 or 3—especially due to the heat and chaos of urban Vietnam. Try to get onto Vietnamese time immediately (go to bed at a reasonable hour even if you're not tired, and wake up in the morning); some people also say that taking melatonin, an herbal supplement, helps with jet lag. All of the itineraries below assume that you're rested and ready to go, so you might want to factor in some downtime at the start of your trip to get rested.

1 THE REGIONS IN BRIEF

THE LAY OF THE LAND

Vietnam is an S-shape peninsula that borders China to the north, Laos to the west, and Cambodia to the southwest. Covering about 331,520 sq. km (129,293 sq. miles), it's roughly the size of Italy, but only a small percentage of the land is arable and habitable because of the Annamese Cordillera and other steep mountain ranges and mountain terrain. Vietnam has a varied and lush topography, with two massive deltas (one in the north and one in the south), tropical forests, craggy mountains and rock formations, and stunning coastline. Vietnam is only about 1,613km (1,000 miles) north to south as the crow flies, but by road and along the stretch of coastal highway, it's about 3,260km (2,021 miles). Vietnam also claims thousands of islands off its coast.

Rice is the staple of Vietnam, and the economy and society relies heavily on its production. The shape of Vietnam is often compared to a common sight in any Vietnamese market: the tenuous balancing of a bamboo pole slung over one woman's shoulder as she hangs pendulous bundles on either side of her body. The thin central coast of the country is the bamboo shaft of the fragile contraption, and the productive rice-growing regions of the Red River Delta in the north and the fertile Mekong Delta in the far south are the overflowing "bread baskets" that hang from the pole. But drawn to scale, it might be a bit lopsided—the Mekong is exponentially more productive.

THE NORTH *Bac Bo* is the Vietnamese term for the north, the cradle of Vietnamese civilization along the country's own version of the Tigris and Euphrates, the **Red River Delta.** Called the *Song Hong* in Vietnamese, the river is the epicenter of prehistoric culture and early empires, where organized wet rice cultivation, done on flooded paddies and requiring extensive community cooperation, began. The Red River Delta gave birth to the first Au Lac dynasty and earliest capital at Co Loa—just north of Vietnam's current capital, **Hanoi,** which lies at the heart of the region. Just east of Hanoi, the busy port of Haiphong leads the way to the 3,000 islands of the stunning **Halong Bay;** most of the islands are unlivable but are a stunning set piece of towering karst, or limestone, formations shrouded in jungle. Where Hanoi's creation myth speaks of the ascending dragon *Thang Long,* the mountains of the bay are said to be the footprints of the descending dragon, or *Ha Long,* as it went to its home in the ocean deep.

The northern highlands, occupying the northwest tip of Vietnam, are known for their beauty, with jagged mountains rising over sweeping green valleys. The inhabitants are mostly ethnic minority hilltribes still somewhat isolated from civilization. Popular tourism destinations are **Sapa, Lao Cai,** and **Dien Bien Phu.** Vietnam's tallest mountain, Fansipan (3,143 m/10,309 ft.), overlooks Sapa, part of the mountain range the French dubbed "The Tonkinese Alps."

CENTRAL Central Vietnam, or *Trung Bo,* flanks the long line of the Trung Son Mountain range, also called the Annamese Cordillera. In this volume, I divide the center into the north center, where you'll find the cities of Vinh, Hue, Danang, and historic Hoi An, and the south center, where you'll find the beach community of Nha Trang, as well as the temperate, hilly Central Highlands region, with small towns like Pleiku and the city of Dalat.

Traveling south from Hanoi, visitors trace the central coastline, location of major cities Hue, Danang, and Hoi An. The small town of **Vinh,** birthplace of Ho Chi Minh, is just halfway between Hanoi and Hue. And **Hue** (pronounced *Hway*), a name familiar from the war years for its strategic location near the 17th Parallel, is Vietnam's former capital and imperial city (1802–1945). Going south from Hue, crossing over the high Hai Van Pass before dropping back to the coast and the small beach area of Lang Co and nearby Bach Ma National Park, is **Danang,** Vietnam's fourth-largest city and a port town whose major attractions include the museum of Cham antiquities and nearby China Beach. Nearby **Hoi An,** a major trading center from the mid–16th century, shows the architectural influences of Chinese and Japanese traders who passed through and settled here, leaving perfectly preserved buildings. It is now once again a center of cultural exchange and commerce, but is tourist-focused with souvenir centers and tailor shops (also lots of new resorts on nearby Cua Dai Beach).

Tracing the coast farther south from Hoi An, pass through the small port city of **Quy Nhon,** uninteresting but for a few nice new resort offerings, and then on to **Nha Trang,** Vietnam's preeminent sea resort, where new upmarket offerings are popping up like mushrooms on a log. Just inland from the south-central coast area, you'll find the Central Highlands area, a temperate, hilly region occupied by many of Vietnam's ethnic minorities. Most popular and developed for tourists is historic **Dalat,** a resort town nestled in the Lang Bien Plateau, established by the French at the turn of the 20th century as a recreation and convalescence center. The scenery looks something like Switzerland in summer, with high hills studded with tall pines and peppered with quaint, French contemporary villas, most in a sad state of decay. North of Dalat, the Annamese Cordillera mountain range hosts the little hill town of Buon Ma Thuot, Pleiku, and Kontum, all names familiar from the war era and home to some of the hottest fighting at that time.

THE SOUTH Southern Vietnam, called *Nam Bo,* is home to Vietnam's largest city, bustling **Ho Chi Minh City,** also known as **Saigon.** Vietnam's largest cosmopolitan area is like a region unto itself, with a population of more than eight million spreading out over a wide area of urban and suburban sprawl. **Tay Ninh** is a town just to the north and west of Saigon that's home to the unique Cao Dai sect and the end of the Ho Chi Minh Trail at the Black Mountain. Some of the heaviest fighting during the war took place here, much of it planned from the tunnels of **Cu Chi.** The south is hotter, in climate as well as cuisine.

South of Ho Chi Minh City is the **Mekong Delta,** where, after a 4,500km (2,790-mile) journey from the mountains of Tibet, the mighty Mekong splits into nine smaller branches and a wide alluvial plain as it deposits its silt on the way to the South China Sea. The well-irrigated delta is the most agriculturally productive region of Vietnam, where most of the country's rice is grown, and where the population has swelled in recent years with increased productivity and industries like fish farming and shrimp cultivation. The climate of the delta is tropical; the lower delta is untamed swampland. The region shows the influences of ancient Funan and Khmer cultures, as well as the scars from recent wars (the Viet Cong used the delta as a secret base) and battles with neighboring Cambodia.

2 DOING IT ALL: VIETNAM & CAMBODIA IN 28 DAYS

The following tour is the most comprehensive one in this chapter, and it still hits only the highlights. You can combine any itineraries listed with the side trips and specialty itineraries at the end of this chapter, and lots of Vietnamese destinations are conducive to further in-depth study or relaxed lingering.

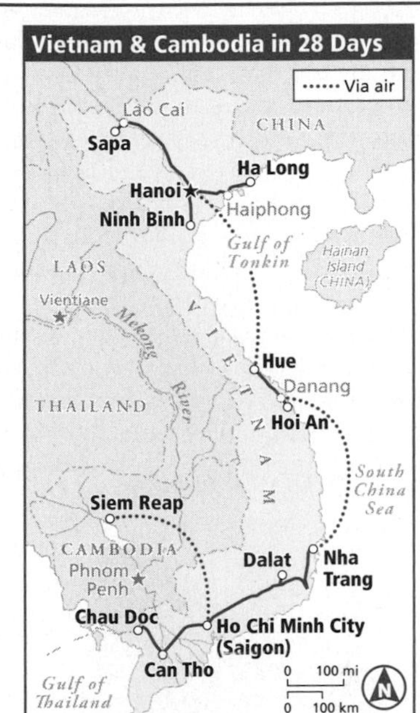
Vietnam & Cambodia in 28 Days
Via air
Lao Cai
CHINA
Sapa
Ha Long
Hanoi
Haiphong
Ninh Binh
Gulf of Tonkin
Hainan Island (CHINA)
LAOS
Vientiane
Mekong River
VIETNAM
Hue
Danang
THAILAND
Hoi An
South China Sea
Siem Reap
CAMBODIA
Dalat
Nha Trang
Phnom Penh
Chau Doc
Ho Chi Minh City (Saigon)
Can Tho
Gulf of Thailand
0 100 mi
0 100 km
N

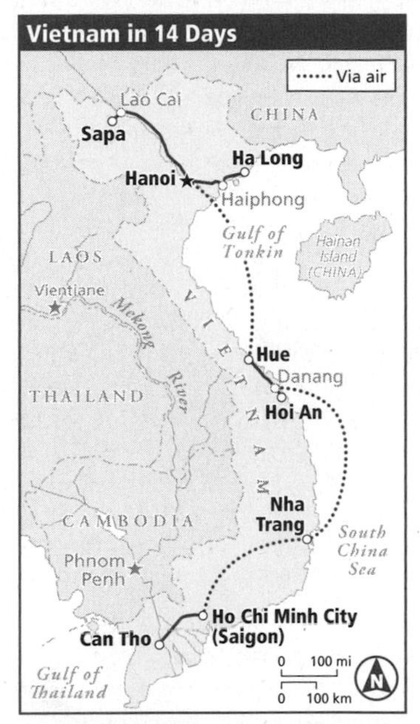
Vietnam in 14 Days
Via air
Lao Cai
CHINA
Sapa
Ha Long
Hanoi
Haiphong
Gulf of Tonkin
Hainan Island (CHINA)
LAOS
Vientiane
Mekong River
VIETNAM
Hue
Danang
THAILAND
Hoi An
Nha Trang
CAMBODIA
South China Sea
Phnom Penh
Ho Chi Minh City (Saigon)
Can Tho
Gulf of Thailand
0 100 mi
0 100 km
N

World Heritage Tour (9 days)
Via air
CHINA
Hanoi
Ha Long
Haiphong
Gulf of Tonkin
Hainan Island (CHINA)
LAOS
Vientiane
Mekong River
Hue
Danang
THAILAND
My Son
Hoi An
VIETNAM
South China Sea
CAMBODIA
Phnom Penh
Ho Chi Minh City (Saigon)
Gulf of Thailand
0 100 mi
0 100 km
N

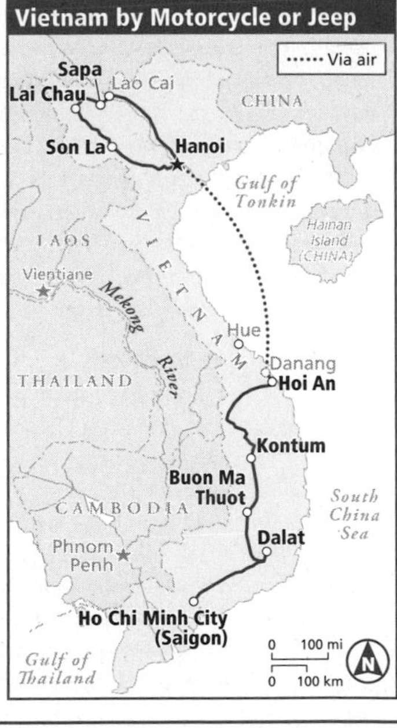
Vietnam by Motorcycle or Jeep
Via air
Sapa
Lao Cai
Lai Chau
CHINA
Son La
Hanoi
Gulf of Tonkin
Hainan Island (CHINA)
LAOS
VIETNAM
Vientiane
Mekong River
Hue
Danang
THAILAND
Hoi An
Kontum
Buon Ma Thuot
CAMBODIA
South China Sea
Dalat
Phnom Penh
Ho Chi Minh City (Saigon)
Gulf of Thailand
0 100 mi
0 100 km
N

Day 1: Arrive in Hanoi

"Honey, were there five people on that motorcycle?" Yes, dear, there were. Welcome to Hanoi. Even your ride from the airport can be tiring; plan to rest a bit when you first arrive. If you can swing it, stay at the **Sofitel Metropole** (p. 81) in the heart of the city. Explore the **Old Quarter** (p. 100) in the evening.

Day 2: Hanoi

Take a Hanoi City Tour starting at the Hanoi Citadel, including the **Ho Chi Minh Mausoleum, House,** and **Museum** (p. 108) as well as the **One-Pillar Pagoda** (p. 109). Then hit **Van Mieu,** the Temple of Literature (p. 110), in the afternoon. Take a tour of the **Old Quarter** (p. 100) on foot (with or without a guide) or by cyclo. In the evening, take in the **Thang Long Water Puppet show** (p. 123). Then collapse.

Day 3: Hanoi to Halong Bay

Leave early in the morning for a 3-hour drive to the pier at Halong City (p. 161) and then board an overnight boat in the bay—best is the luxury ***Emeraude,*** and one notch down is Buffalo Tour's ***Jewel of the Bay*** or Handspan Tour's ***Dragon's Pearl*** (p. 165). You will lunch aboard the ship, cruise for a few hours with stops at various cave sites, and then sleep onboard the boat moored in a quiet bay. Itineraries vary, but most include time for kayaking to caves and island lagoons and swimming.

Day 4: Halong Bay to Hanoi

Awaken to sunlight reflecting off the high limestone formations of stunning Halong Bay. Most trips include a morning kayak adventure and a few stops before returning to the pier and making the 3-hour road connection to Hanoi. Overnight in Hanoi. ***Note:*** Some adventure itineraries include extra days for more far-ranging kayak exploration, or include an extra night on **Cat Ba Island** (p. 167).

Day 5: Hanoi

Enjoy another near full day in Hanoi. Wake up early (dawn) and exercise with locals around **Hoan Kiem Lake** (p. 111), check out the lakeside temples, and explore the Old Quarter. Here you can shop, check out the old prison known as the **Hanoi Hilton** (p. 111), take in one of Hanoi's museums—the **Vietnam National Museum of Fine Arts** (p. 109) is quite good—see the **Opera House** (p. 111), and spend some time near **Nha Tho,** the Catholic cathedral of Hanoi, with its many shops and cafes along Nha Tho Street. In the evening, catch the overnight train from Hanoi to Lao Cai (p. 134).

Day 6: Lao Cai to Sapa

Arrive in Lao Cai at 6am and hop on a bus for transfer to Sapa. Check in to your hotel—I recommend the **Victoria Sapa** (p. 136)—and take an afternoon walk down into the valley lined with rice terraces to the **Cat Cat Village** (p. 140).

Day 7: Sapa

Spend a full day trekking—best arranged through an outfitter in Hanoi or with **Handspan** or **Topas** (p. 135) in Sapa. The **Lao Cai–to–Ta Van Walk** is popular, but there are many options to visit Hmong and Dao villages. Explore the Sapa market in the afternoon and take in a dance performance of local hilltribe people in the evening.

Day 8: Sapa to Hanoi

Should you time it right on a Sunday, you can make a round-trip to the **Bac Ha Market** (p. 139) in the early morning before returning by overnight train to Hanoi. Otherwise, arrange a short day trek, rent a Minsk motorcycle to explore on your own, or take a self-tour through the valley from Sapa before you get on the overnight train from Lao Cai back to Hanoi.

Day 9: Hanoi

When you arrive in Hanoi, you'll likely be tired after trekking and the overnight train. Rest in the capital for the morning and then take a day trip to the **handicraft villages** outside of Hanoi.

Day 10: Ninh Binh (or the Perfume Pagoda)

Take a day trip out of the big city. Connect with a good tour provider for a full-day trip south of the city to the **Ninh Binh** area, with the high grottoes of **Tam Coc** (similar to Halong Bay's, but along a river), and nearby **Bich Dong Temple,** or visit **Ken Ga,** a riverside village. You can also include a visit to **Cuc Phuong National Park,** though it's best as an overnight so that you can go jungle trekking in the morning, when it's cool and the wildlife is active. Another option is to take a full-day tour to the **Perfume Pagoda** just south of Hanoi. Return to Hanoi for your last evening and some more exploration and shopping.

Day 11: Hanoi to Hue

Fly to Hue in the morning. After checking in at your hotel, take a tour by bicycle or cyclo to the central **Hue Citadel** (p. 195) and the ruins of the old **Imperial City** (p. 195). In the afternoon, you can ride a bicycle—a little far—or arrange a car to visit a few sights on the outskirts of town, including a few temples and the **Tomb of Tu Duc** or other imperial tombs if you have time (p. 197). In the evening, enjoy dinner at **Tropical Garden** (p. 193). After your meal, stroll along the **Perfume River** near the **Trang Tien Bridge** (p. 186).

Day 12: Hue to Hoi An

In the morning, take a boat trip to the **Thien Mu Pagoda** (p. 198) and visit a few of Hue's many **imperial tombs**—best are the tombs of **Khai Dinh** and **Minh Mang.** In the afternoon, leave by car or minivan for **Danang** (p. 205). Along the way, stop at **Lang Co Beach** (p. 204) and the overlook at **Hai Van Pass** (p. 202). Visit the **Cham Museum** (p. 210) in Danang and, time permitting, the **Marble Mountains** (p. 211). Overnight in Hoi An. If you arrive before the shops close, place an order for your tailored clothes.

Day 13: Hoi An

Take an all-day tour of the central area of Hoi An (p. 211), stopping at **ancient attractions** including the Chinese pagodas and congregation halls, the Japanese Bridge, and the many museums and old shop houses. In the afternoon and evening, take in the old town or scoot out to **Cua Dai Beach** (p. 228), a short car ride from town, to dip your toes in the South China Sea. Shop 'til you drop in the evening until around 9pm, when shops close.

Day 14: Hoi An

Take a day of leisure and shopping—get that suit fitted properly—or beachcombing at **Cua Dai Beach,** or opt for the all-day jaunt to **My Son** (p. 228), the most famous relics of Cham civilization.

Day 15: Hoi An to Nha Trang

Fly from Danang (via a trip to the **Marble Mountains,** p. 211, in the morning if you've yet to go) and get settled in Nha Trang for a few days of beach time. Rest and relax at the **Ana Mandara** (p. 271) if you can afford it; if not, good budget options abound, too.

Day 16: Nha Trang

Enjoy the beach, take a scuba course, hop on an all-day boat trip to outlying islands, or hit the city's few nearby sights (the **Po Ngar Cham Towers,** p. 280, or the **Alexandre Yersin Museum,** p. 279). Morning trips to the city market or the fish market (p. 280) near the Po Ngar Cham Towers are popular for photographers. But don't feel pressed—Nha Trang is a place to kick back, eat good seafood, and rest.

Day 17: Nha Trang to Dalat (or Stay in Nha Trang)

Note: This trip to Dalat is optional; you might prefer to spend an extra night in

Nha Trang before flying to Ho Chi Minh City. A 3-hour drive on a spanking new highway takes you to mountainous **Dalat** (p. 232). If your budget allows for it, stay at the luxurious **Sofitel Dalat Palace** (p. 240) or the **Ana Mandara Villas Dalat,** tucked away on a hilltop overlooking the city center (p. 240).

Day ⓲: Dalat

Take a fun day tour of the breathtaking (some rather hokey) sights around Dalat. Hire an **Easy Rider** (p. 238) and watch out for the bugs hitting your teeth as you smile, bouncing around hilly Dalat on the back of a motorbike (tour options by van and car are also available; see p. 238). Alternatively, try an all-day adventure of trekking, canyoneering, or mountain biking with **Phat Tire Ventures** (p. 239).

Day ⓳: Dalat to Ho Chi Minh City (Saigon)

Starting in the morning, drive overland from Dalat. (***Note:*** Naturalists, birders, and nature photographers will want to add a day at the **Cat Tien National Park,** about halfway btw. Dalat and Saigon; see p. 346.) Arrive in **Ho Chi Minh City** (p. 291) in the late afternoon, check in somewhere near central **Dong Khoi Street,** and then explore the downtown area near **Lam Son Square,** the central **Opera House,** and busy **Le Loi Street.** Lots of good shopping, dining, and nightlife.

Day ⓴: Ho Chi Minh City Tour

In the morning, get an early start at **Giac Lam Pagoda** (p. 326), Ho Chi Minh City's oldest pagoda, and then tour **Chinatown** (p. 325) and some temples, as well as the large Chinese market, **Binh Te Market** (all in far-off District 5), before returning to the city center and **Ben Thanh Market** (p. 321)—a good place to wander and pick up a few trinkets and stop for lunch at **Pho 2000** (p. 319), just adjacent to the market. In the afternoon, hit the **War Remnants Museum** (p. 325) and, time permitting, the **Reunification Palace** (p. 322). In the evening, enjoy a meal at **Quan An Ngon Restaurant** (p. 318), Vietnam's finest purveyor of authentic Vietnamese cuisine in an authentic local setting (there are lots of gussied-up high-end Vietnamese restaurants in town, but funky Ngon takes the cake).

Day ㉑: Cu Chi Tunnels and the Cao Dai Holy See

Leave early to catch a midmorning service of the unique world religion of **Cao Daism** (p. 327), in their Technicolor temple. Then make your way to the **Cu Chi Tunnels** (p. 328), where North Vietnamese guerrillas waged war on American and South Vietnamese forces from a vast, undetectable complex of tunnels near the terminus of the Ho Chi Minh Trail.

Day ㉒: Ho Chi Minh City to Chau Doc

Note: Take a guided tour to the Mekong Delta. Most tour providers offer different versions of the same trips, with 1-, 2-, or 3-night stays. Go for at least 2 nights. For more information on tour operators, see p. 349.

Early in the morning, head for the delta—the rice bowl of Vietnam. Make your first stop the **Cai Be Floating Market** (p. 352) for a boat ride among the busy river throngs, and then go all the way down to **Chau Doc** (stay at the **Victoria Chau Doc,** p. 359)—a full day's drive with stops and little side trips.

Day ㉓: Chau Doc to Can Tho

In the morning, take a boat trip along the canal to the floating villages of ethnic **Cham** (p. 352)—you'll see fish farms and riverside temples and mosques near Chau Doc. Then, time permitting, trek up little **Sam Mountain** (p. 360), a Buddhist pilgrimage peak with views all the way to Cambodia. Afterward, make your way to Can Tho. Overnight at the **Victoria Can Tho** (p. 355).

Day ㉔: Can Tho to Saigon
Take a morning boat tour along the many canals around Can Tho (p. 353), visiting craft communities, rice-cake and toffee factories, and raw-rice granaries (photographers will be click-click-clicking) before making your way back to Saigon.

Days ㉕ to ㉘: Saigon to Siem Reap (Angkor Wat)
Take a morning flight from Saigon to Siem Reap, the support town for the stunning temples of Angkor Wat. Give yourself a few days to take in all of the sights at Angkor (see "A Side Trip to Cambodia," later in this chapter, and "Siem Reap & Angkor Wat," in chapter 14). Some include further travels in Cambodia; you might consider going to Angkor Wat from Saigon via the Cambodian capital of Phnom Penh (you can go by boat from Chau Doc on the Mekong Delta).

Important note: Once you leave Vietnam, you will have to secure a prearranged tourist visa to reenter. You can enter and exit Cambodia at designated points (overland or by air) and receive a visa upon arrival. You can fly from Siem Reap to Bangkok for onward international connection.

3 VIETNAM IN 14 DAYS: NORTH TO SOUTH

This is a truncated version of the 28-day itinerary. You can see quite a lot in a few weeks and catch the major sights along the coast. See information at the bottom of this section for advice on doing this same itinerary in reverse, from south to north.

Day ❶: Arrive in Hanoi
Get settled somewhere cozy (I recommend the **Sofitel Metropole,** p. 81), and then take a walk (or cyclo ride) around the **Old Quarter** and **Hoan Kiem Lake** (p. 100 and 111).

Day ❷: Hanoi to Lao Cai (Sapa)
Enjoy a morning of touring the main sights in the Hanoi Citadel, including **Ho Chi Minh's Mausoleum** (before 11am), **House,** and **Museum** (p. 108), and the **One-Pillar Pagoda** (p. 109). In the early evening, catch the overnight train for Lao Cai (best on a **Victoria** sleeper car; see p. 134).

Day ❸: Lao Cai to Sapa
Arrive in Lao Cai at 6am and hop on a bus for transfer to Sapa. Check in to your hotel—I recommend the **Topas Ecolodge** (p. 136)—and take an afternoon walk down into the valley lined with rice terraces to the **Cat Cat Village** (p. 140), or hire a guide for an all-day hike (after a short jeep ride) from **Lao Cai to Ta Van.** Alternatively, just take in the little town of Sapa, the rice-terraced valley below, and the central market crowded with Hmong people.

Day ❹: Sapa to Bac Ha and back to Hanoi
If it's a Sunday, take a day trip to the market town outside of Lao Cai called **Bac Ha** (p. 139), the region's most colorful hilltribe market. Otherwise, plan to spend part of the day trekking (contact **Topas** or **Handspan,** p. 135), and then catch an early evening overnight train from Lao Cai back to Hanoi (factor in the few hours from Bac Ha or Sapa to Lao Cai station).

Day ❺: Lao Cai to Hanoi
Arrive at 6am in the capital and take some time to rest in comfy city digs. Explore the **Old Quarter** and **Hoan Kiem,** and maybe do a bit of shopping. Catch a show at the **Thang Long Water Puppet Theater** (p. 123) in the evening, or hit some of the town's fine-dining establishments or nightlife (see chapter 5).

Day 6: Hanoi to Halong Bay

Leave early in the morning for a 3-hour drive to the pier at Halong City, and then board an overnight boat in the bay—best aboard the luxury ***Emeraude*** or ***Halong Ginger;*** one notch down is Buffalo Tour's ***Jewel of the Bay*** or Handspan Tour's ***Dragon's Pearl*** (p. 165). You'll lunch aboard the ship, cruise for a few hours with stops at various cave sites, and then sleep aboard the boat moored in a quiet bay. Itineraries vary, and most include time for kayaking to caves and island lagoons and swimming.

Day 7: Halong Bay to Hanoi and on to Hue

Awake to sunlight reflecting off the high limestone formations of stunning Halong Bay. Most trips include a morning kayak adventure and a few stops before returning to the pier and making the 3-hour road connection to Hanoi. Catch the afternoon (4:30pm) flight from Hanoi to Hue (or overnight in Hanoi and fly in the morning).

Day 8: Hue

Set out on a tour by bicycle or cyclo to the central **Hue Citadel** (p. 195) and the ruins of the old **Imperial City** (p. 195). In the afternoon, you can ride a bike—though it's slightly far—or arrange a car to a few sights on the outskirts of town. You can arrange a boat to see the likes of the **Thien Mu Pagoda** (p. 198) and a few of Hue's many **imperial tombs**—best are the tombs of **Khai Dinh** and **Minh Mang Tomb** or **Tu Duc.** In the evening, enjoy dinner at **Tropical Garden** or **Club Garden** (p. 193 and 193), and then stroll along the **Perfume River** near the **Trang Tien Bridge** (p. 186).

Day 9: Hue to Hoi An

In the afternoon, leave by car or minivan for **Hoi An** (p. 211). Along the way, stop at **Lang Co Beach** (p. 204), the overlook at **Hai Van Pass** (p. 202), the **Cham Museum** in Danang (p. 210), and, time permitting, the **Marble Mountains** (p. 211). Overnight in Hoi An (p. 213). If you arrive before the shops close, place an order for your tailored clothes.

Day 10: Hoi An

Follow **Day 13** in the 28-day itinerary, above, hitting the beach or exploring town.

Day 11: Hoi An to Nha Trang (via Danang)

Fly from Danang (via a trip to the **Marble Mountains,** p. 211, in the morning if you've yet to go) and settle in Nha Trang for a few days of beach time. Rest and relax at the **Evason Ana Mandara Resort** (p. 271) or one of the many good budget options around (see chapter 11).

Day 12: Nha Trang

Enjoy the beach, take a scuba course, hop on an all-day boat trip to outlying islands, or hit the city's few nearby sights (the **Po Ngar Cham Towers,** p. 280, or the **Alexandre Yersin Museum,** p. 279). Morning trips to the city market or the fish market (p. 280) near the **Po Ngar Cham Towers** are popular for photographers. But don't feel pressed—Nha Trang is a place to kick back, eat good seafood, and rest.

Day 13: Nha Trang to Ho Chi Minh City

You might consider adding a few days at this point and scoot up to the temperate hill town of **Dalat** or tour part of the **Central Highlands.** Otherwise, fly to Ho Chi Minh City.

Day 14: Ho Chi Minh City

In the morning, get an early start at **Giac Lam Pagoda** (p. 326), Ho Chi Minh City's oldest, and then tour **Chinatown** (p. 325) and some temples, as well as the large Chinese market, **Binh Te Market** (all in far-off District 5), before returning to the city center and **Ben Thanh Market** (p. 321)—a good place to wander and pick up a few ditties. Stop for lunch at

Pho 2000 (p. 319), just adjacent to the market. Time permitting, hit the **War Remnants Museum** (p. 325) or the **Reunification Palace** (p. 322). Enjoy a meal at **Quan An Ngon Restaurant** (p. 318), Vietnam's finest purveyor of authentic Vietnamese cuisine in an authentic local setting (there are lots of gussied-up high-end Vietnamese restaurants in town, but funky Ngon takes the cake). Depart.

GOING SOUTH TO NORTH

Note: If arriving in the south (most likely in Ho Chi Minh City), you can reverse this 2-week itinerary. Many travelers include a trip to the **Mekong Delta,** staying 1 night in **Can Tho** and exploring the river markets in the area (see **Days 22 and 23** in the 28-day itinerary, above) instead of going to Sapa in the far north.

4 WORLD HERITAGE TOUR (9 DAYS)

This trip takes you to the main **UNESCO World Heritage Sites** of Vietnam, including **Halong Bay, Hue, Hoi An,** and **My Son.**

Day ❶: Hanoi

After you arrive and settle in to your hotel, take a cyclo tour or walk around Hanoi's busy **Old Quarter** (p. 100). See the **Thang Long Water Puppet show** (p. 123) in the evening.

Day ❷: Hanoi to Halong

In the early morning, take a walk around central **Hoan Kiem Lake** (p. 111) and the **Old Quarter** (p. 100), and then visit the Hanoi Citadel—with **Ho Chi Minh's Mausoleum, House,** and **Museum** (p. 108), as well as the **One-Pillar Pagoda** (p. 109). In the late afternoon, head to **Halong City** (p. 161) for an overnight. (***Note:*** My preference is to overnight on one of Halong's better boat trips, but this journey requires a full 2 days.)

Day ❸: Halong to Hanoi

Take an early morning boat cruise on **Halong Bay,** stopping at some of the main cave sights (p. 166). Check out **Thien Cung Grotto (Heavenly Cave)** or **Surprise Cave,** and enjoy lunch aboard the ship before returning to Hanoi in the late afternoon.

Day ❹: Hanoi to Hue

Take a morning flight to **Hue** (p. 184), the old Imperial City in central Vietnam. Visit the **Hue Citadel** (p. 195), the **Thien Mu Pagoda** (p. 198), and the tomb of **Tu Duc** or other tombs outside of town. Enjoy Hue cuisine at one of the popular downtown tour restaurants (see "Where to Dine" in chapter 9, section 1, "Hue").

Day ❺: Hue to Hoi An

Take a morning to catch any sights you might have missed on the previous day, or visit the more far-flung temples like the **Tomb of Minh Mang** (p. 197). In the afternoon, leave by car or minivan for **Hoi An.** Along the way, stop at **Lang Co Beach** and **Hai Van Pass.** Overnight in Hoi An. (If you get here in time, place an order for your tailored clothes.)

Day ❻: Hoi An

Take an all-day tour of the **Ancient Town,** stopping at Chinese pagodas and congregation halls, the Japanese Bridge, and the many museums and old shop houses. In the afternoon and evening, take in the old town or scoot out to **Cua Dai Beach** to dip your toes in the sand. Shop 'til you drop in the evening.

Day 7: Hoi An to My Son

Set out in the morning for an all-day trip to the hilltop temples of stunning **My Son** before returning to Hoi An.

Day 8: Hoi An to Hanoi (via Danang)

Head to Danang in the morning, making stops at the **Marble Mountains, China Beach,** and the **Cham Museum,** where you'll see all the relics that were removed from My Son, before flying from Danang to Hanoi.

Day 9: Hanoi

Spend your last morning before departure in Hanoi (maybe doing some last-minute shopping).

5 GET YOUR MOTOR RUNNIN'—VIETNAM BY MOTORCYCLE OR JEEP

To rent your own motorbike and drive the length of the country, contact tour agencies in Ho Chi Minh City and Hanoi. If you go this route, Vietnam is your oyster—you can go where the road takes you. Below is a trip that includes two good overland tours in the **Central Highlands** and the **Northern Highlands**—both doable by rented jeep as well. So start your engines and prepare for some memorable adventures.

Day 1: Arrive in Ho Chi Minh City (Saigon)

Get acclimated and explore the downtown area of Ho Chi Minh City, along Dong Khoi. If time permits, go to the **Reunification Palace** (p. 322) or **War Remnants Museum** (p. 325).

Day 2: Saigon to Dalat

Fly or drive from Saigon to the mountain town of Dalat, and then head straight for **Peace Cafe** (p. 245), to arrange your trip with an **Easy Rider** (expect to pay about $35 per day to ride on the back with a guide, budget accommodations included). In the evening, check out the **Dalat Market** (p. 246).

Day 3: Dalat to Buon Ma Thuot

Start early, catching the sights outside of Dalat that interest you (check out the **Crazy House,** p. 247, or the temples and monasteries outside of town). Then follow rolling hills of coffee plants and stunning pine-dotted vistas as you ride to **Buon Ma Thuot** (p. 249). Pass through **Lak Lake** (p. 254) in the late afternoon and visit **M'nong Communities** (p. 254). Rugged travelers spend an overnight at Lak Lake or at the nearby **Hotel Biet Dien** (p. 254). For something less rustic, press on to Buon Ma Thuot and the **Damsan Hotel** (p. 251).

Day 4: Buon Ma Thuot to Kontum

Stop at a number of battle sites during the all-day drive, and pass through the city of Pleiku. Overnight at **Family Hotel** (p. 257) in Kontum.

Day 5: Kontum to Hoi An

Visit **Dak To** (p. 259) and **Charlie Hill** (p. 259), two important battle sites, before hopping on Hwy. 14 for a ride all the way to Hoi An. For an overnight stay, try one of the resorts along **Cua Dai Beach** (p. 281), and settle in for a day of well-earned relaxation.

Day 6: Hoi An

Take a tour of the **ancient town** (p. 212) or head to little **Cua Dai Beach** (p. 228).

Day 7: Hoi An to Hanoi

Fly to the capital via Danang. Get oriented with a cyclo or walking tour of the **Old Quarter** (p. 100).

Day 8: Hanoi

Take a tour of Hanoi starting at the Hanoi Citadel, including the **Ho Chi Minh Mausoleum, House,** and **Museum** (p. 108), and the **One-Pillar Pagoda** (p. 109). See **Van Mieu,** the Temple of Literature (p. 110), in the afternoon. In the evening, take in the **Thang Long Water Puppet show** (p. 123). Collapse.

Day 9: Hanoi to Son La

Hit the highway on your rented **Minsk** motorcycle, with or without a guide (check with rental agencies in Hanoi; p. 144). Breeze through little **Mai Chau** (p. 142), take a walk to the ethnic villages outside of town, and then spend the night in Son La at the **Trade Union Hotel** (p. 146). If you have time, visit the **Son La Prison** (p. 147).

Day 10: Son La to Lai Chau

Follow **Route 6** in its most dynamic climb up from Tuan Giao and along a high mountain area to the town of **Lai Chau** (p. 151). Stay at the little **Lan Anh Hotel** (p. 151) and take a late-afternoon (or tomorrow-morning) trek to the many **White Thai villages** (p. 151).

Day 11: Lai Chau to Sapa

The all-day ride from Lai Chau to **Sapa** (p. 132) follows the **Dong Da River** (p. 151) along a very picturesque stretch. Just before Sapa, you'll climb up stunning **Tram Ton Pass** (p. 152), which offers some of the most picturesque landscape in Vietnam. Put your feet up in Sapa (I recommend **Topas Ecolodge,** p. 136) and swap tales of your adventure.

Day 12: Sapa

Enjoy a full day of trekking—best arranged through an outfitter in Hanoi or with **Handspan** or **Topas** (p. 135) in Sapa. The **Lao Cai–to–Ta Van Walk** is popular, but there are many options to visit Hmong and Dao villages. Explore the Sapa market in the afternoon and take in a dance performance of local hilltribe people in the evening.

Day 13: Sapa to Hanoi

If it is a Sunday, check out the **market** (p. 139) in the town of **Bac Ha.** Otherwise, explore the hills around Sapa before the short few hours to **Lao Cai** (p. 128). From here, you can put your motorcycle on the train for Hanoi and ride in comfort on the overnight, best in a luxury sleeper car.

Intrepid riders who didn't get enough of the open road can forgo the train back to Hanoi from Lao Cai and head east, reaching **Ha Giang**—a small town that connects the two routes of Dien Bien Phu Loop and Cao Bang—or even continuing farther to **Cao Bang** (p. 153) in a day.

The waterfall outside of **Cao Bang** is spectacular and the road to **Lang Son** (p. 155) is a great ride (lots of hilltribe markets). From **Lang Son** to Hanoi is a wide highway (for trade with China). Budget 3 extra days of hard riding if you want to include Cao Bang and Lang Son on your way back to Hanoi.

Day 14: Hanoi

Arrive in Hanoi station at 6am. After a day's stay at a hotel to get cleaned up and do some last-minute shopping, depart for your next destination.

6 A SIDE TRIP TO CAMBODIA

The majestic temples of Angkor Wat are just a short flight from Ho Chi Minh City or Hanoi, and many travelers extend their trip to visit this archaeological wonder.

Day ❶: Ho Chi Minh City/Hanoi to Siem Reap

Fly from Hanoi or Ho Chi Minh City to **Siem Reap.** Get comfortable at your hotel: The **Raffles Grand Hotel d'Angkor** (p. 412) is a palace, and **Hôtel de la Paix** in town (p. 411) is a contemporary luxury.

Day ❷: Angkor Wat

Set out for the temples before dawn, taking in the morning glow from atop **Bakeng Hill** (p. 424). Visit the main temples, including the many sights of **Angkor Thom** (p. 425)—including the **Bayon,** the **Baphuon,** the **Terrace of the Leper King,** and the **Elephant Terrace**—and then hit **Preah Khan** (if you have time) before lunch. In the afternoon, take in the jungle temple and everyone's favorite, **Ta Prohm** (p. 429). Make a few more stops, maybe at **Banteay Kdei** (p. 429) and **Sras Srang** (p. 427), before sinking your teeth into the big temple, **Angkor Wat** (p. 424), where you can spend hours going through the relief carvings like the **Churning of the Ocean of Milk.** Take a guided tour to get the most out of this experience. Climb the three tiers of the temple and enjoy the sunset from the top.

Head back to **Siem Reap** (p. 417) to enjoy a fine meal (for local food, try **Khmer Kitchen,** p. 420), beers, and backpacker babbling. If it's a Saturday, take in the show by **Beat Beatocello at the Kantha Bopha Foundation** (p. 435), where Beat (aka Dr. Richner) entertains an audience with his cello while telling of the foundation's aid work and begging for funds (all in good fun).

Day ❸: Angkor Wat

Watch the sunrise from Sras Srang or **Angkor Wat,** and then hit your favorite temple again or any you missed in the main Angkor compound. Many use Day 3 for trips out to the likes of the **Roluos Group** (p. 431) or as far as the crumbling jungle temple of **Beng Melea** (p. 430). See the sunset from Bakeng Hill. Catch a morning or afternoon flight back to Ho Chi Minh City or Hanoi.

Option: Add an extra day and hop on a flight to the crumbly old colonial **Phnom Penh** (p. 383) and visit the city's rather grim sights focused on the genocide in Cambodia: **Tuol Sleng Museum** (p. 396) and the **Killing Fields** (p. 395). Explore the city's large **Central Market** (p. 395) and maze of dusty streets, or enjoy a walk along the riverside Sisowath Quay or a ride across the Japanese Bridge for a night at a local minstrel show.

5

Hanoi

Cleaving the yellow walls of a centuries-old Chinese temple, an old gnarled banyan tree is adorned with flowers and offerings of rice wine and incense. Adjacent to the tree is a designer boutique and gallery; farther on is an Internet cafe; and out front, an endless stream of honking motorbikes whiz by, rustling the tree's leaves.

If the 200-year-old banyan could speak, it might tell stories of the 19th-century tradesmen who worked on the avenue out front, the arrival of the French, or the introduction of the automobile. It could speak of the years when revolutionary murmurs became skirmishes and barricades lined the streets of the Old Quarter, or of a time—years later—when a full-scale war, with an enemy that attacked from the skies, almost completely evacuated the city. It might talk about the quiet years after peace in 1975, years of austerity. And then it might tell of one-time enemies returning as investors, bringing recent years of capitalistic excess.

The most obvious reminders of the past in Hanoi are written in the vestiges of precolonial and colonial buildings—low facades tucked beneath towers of concrete, especially in the city's Old Quarter. But even these centuries-old structures are recent, considering the rich history here that dates back thousands of years. Through it all, stalwart and struggling for its patch of ground, the old banyan looks on, ready for whatever changes come its way and grappling its crooked arms around new hunks of pavement, choking on motorbike fumes.

Hanoi ranks among the world's most attractive and interesting cities. Originally named Thang Long, or "City of the Ascending Dragon," the city was first the capital of Vietnam in A.D. 1010 and has had many names until its current incarnation. The name Hanoi, in fact, means "Bend in the River" and denotes the city's strategic location along the vital waterway. Historians liken the life-giving Red River—its banks crowded with green rice paddies and farms—to the Tigris and Euphrates rivers, a cradle of civilization. Even when the nation's capital moved to Hue under the Nguyen dynasty in 1802, the city of Hanoi continued to flourish, especially after the French took control in 1888 and modeled the city's architecture to their tastes, lending an important aesthetic to the city's rich stylistic heritage, even expanding the city and adding rail connections over the Long Bien Bridge in 1902. In 1954, after the French departed, Hanoi was declared Vietnam's capital once again. The city boasts more than 1,000 years of history, and that of the past few hundred years is marvelously preserved.

Hanoi has a reputation, doubtless accrued from the Vietnam War years, as a dour northern political outpost. The city is certainly smaller, slower, and far less developed than chaotic Saigon, but Hanoi's 3.5 million residents still seem to be in constant motion—an endless stream of motorbike and bicycle traffic. You'll see some vestiges of Soviet-influenced concrete monolith architecture here, along with plenty of beautiful, quiet streets and tranquil neighborhoods to explore. The city's placid air gives it a gracious, almost regal flavor. Hanoi is dotted with dozens of lakes—small and large—around which you can usually find a cafe, a pagoda or two, and absorbing vignettes of street life.

Flying Dragons & Thieving Turtles: Hanoi's Founding

Originally, at its prehistoric founding as Thang Long, Hanoi was called **"The Ascending Dragon."** The dragon that ascended, so the story goes, created civilization as we know it along the Red River Valley and then plunged to his sleep in Halong Bay, thereby creating the grand karst slopes—today a UNESCO World Heritage Site. The dragon is the symbol of the city, and you'll find references to it wherever you go.

Hanoi's other important creation myth is one oddly echoed by the legend of King Arthur and his rise to the throne after receiving the sword Excalibur from the Lady of the Lake. "Strange women lying in ponds distributing swords is no basis for a system of government," says Michael Palin's character in *Monty Python and the Holy Grail,* the spoof of the Arthur legend, and Hanoi's mandate granted by a giant turtle in Hoan Kiem is equally ridiculous, but a great one for putting the kids to bed at night.

Le Loi, the first king of a united Viet people, asked the powers in heaven to help him vanquish the Chinese in the 2nd century A.D. His answer came from a giant turtle that rose from the depths of Hoan Kiem Lake and offered him the sword that he would use to drive the Chinese out. (Vietnamese history is full of valiant tales about driving the Chinese out.) When Le Loi returned to the lake to give thanks, the turtle rose again out of the water and took a firm jaw hold of the sword and dragged it to the watery depths, a sign that the citizens could lay down their arms and the city would prosper in peace. The turtle fooled old Le Loi, because the Vietnamese would suffer under Chinese oppression for centuries to come. The myth is best depicted at the Thang Long Water Puppet Theater (p. 123). And keep an eye out for a unique breed of lake turtles—you'll see them basking on the central island. See the "Hoan Kiem District" section under "Attractions," later in this chapter, for details on the lake's temples and sights, and note that most addresses in this chapter are given in relation to the lake, so you should get to know it during your stay in the Vietnamese capital.

Among Hanoi's sightseeing highlights are the **Ho Chi Minh Mausoleum** and **Museum;** the **National Art Museum;** the grisly **Hoa Lo Prison** (also known as the infamous Hanoi Hilton); central **Hoan Kiem Lake,** where Hanoians enjoy brisk morning walks or tai chi in a tranquil city landmark that symbolizes the city's mythical origins (see the box, "Flying Dragons & Thieving Turtles: Hanoi's Founding," above); and the **Old Quarter,** whose narrow winding streets are named after the individual trades practiced here since the 15th century. Hanoi is Vietnam's cultural center, and the galleries, puppetry, music, and dance performances are worth taking in.

You might also want to use the city as a base for excursions throughout the north to **Halong Bay** and **Cat Ba Island,** to the **Ninh Binh** area south of Hanoi and **Tam Coc,** the "Halong Bay in the rice fields," or for a primate encounter at **Cuc Phuong National Park.** In addition, Hanoi is a jumping-off point for rugged travel in the highlands of the northwest, among hill-tribes and along high passes lined with lush terraced rice farms in a loop that includes historic **Dien Bien Phu** and the old French holiday escape of **Sapa,** the most popular town in the north, easily reached by overnight train from Hanoi (see chapter 6).

1 ORIENTATION

GETTING THERE & AWAY

By Plane

Hanoi, along with Ho Chi Minh City, is a major international gateway. Hanoi's **Noi Bai International Airport** (✆ **04/3886-5047**) is about a 45-minute drive outside the city. If you haven't booked a hotel transfer through your hotel, an airport taxi costs 230,000 VND for a sedan taxi, 250,000 VND for a van. To save a few dollars, you can take the Vietnam Airlines minivan into town. It costs $2 for a drop-off at the Vietnam Airlines office, but sometimes for an extra buck you can get the driver to drop you at your hotel if it's along the way. From town to the airport, shuttles depart from the Vietnam Airlines office and cost 20,000 VND. Call ✆ **04/3825-0872** to get departure times.

To contact international carriers in Hanoi, try the following: **Aeroflot,** 360 Kim Ma (✆ 04/3771-8742); **Air France,** which has a helpful customer service desk on the southwestern edge of Hoan Kiem Lake, 1 Ba Trieu (✆ 04/3825-3484); **All Nippon Airways (ANA),** 9 Dao Duy Anh (✆ 04/3934-7237); **British Airways,** 9 Dao Duy Anh (✆ 04/3934-7239); **Cathay Pacific,** 49 Hai Ba Trung (✆ 04/3826-7298); **China Airlines,** 6B Trang Tien St. (✆ 04/936-6364); **Czech Airlines,** 65 Quan Su (✆ 04/3941-1320); **Emirates Airlines,** 9 Dao Duy Anh (✆ 04/3934-7240); **Japan Airlines (JAL),** 63 Ly Thai To (✆ 04/826-6693); **Lao Airlines,** 68 Tran Quoc (✆ 04/822-9951); **Malaysia Airlines,** 1/F Hanoi Towers, 49 Hai Ba Trung (✆ 04/3934-2304); **Pacific Airlines,** 152 Le Duan (✆ 04/3851-5350); **Qantas Airways,** fourth floor at 9 Dinh Le (✆ 04/3933-3026); or **Singapore Airlines,** 17 Ngo Quyen (✆ 04/3826-8888). Note that if you work with a local ground operator for day tours and trips in Vietnam, most will help with any reconfirmation or flight changes free of charge or for just the cost of necessary local calls.

For domestic connections, your only option (luckily, a good and affordable one) is **Vietnam Airlines.** The main, and most convenient, Vietnam Airlines office in Hanoi is at 1 Quang Trung St., a street that runs directly west from the southern end of Hoan Kiem Lake (✆ **04/3832-0320**). Ticket purchases are made on the second floor (at a good discount from prices quoted at storefront travel agents), and it's an orderly business where you pick a number and wait for the next teller. They accept major credit cards as well as either U.S. dollars or Vietnam dong. The office is open from 7am to 6:30pm Monday to Friday, and in front of the building is a convenient stand of minivans that make regular connections with the airport for just 20,000 VND. A tourist information kiosk is also at the airport, as well as a **lost and found** (✆ **04/3884-0008**).

By Train

Hanoi Railway Station, on the western edge of Hoan Kiem District (120 Le Duan; ✆ **04/3942-3697;** ticket office ✆ 04/3942-3949), is a terminal stop on the Reunification Railroad. A comfortable, air-conditioned soft berth to Hue costs 460,000 VND, and it's 1,003,000 VND to Ho Chi Minh City. Buying tickets at the station is easy (but time-consuming), and any travel agent can handle it for a small fee. Both standard and luxury trains from Hanoi to Lao Cai, the jumping-off point for the popular hill town of Sapa, can be booked at traveler cafes in the Old Quarter and from any travel agent; often you can get a special rate on a deluxe overnight train to Lao Cai and your overnight accommodations in Sapa. Slow trains also connect with Haiphong and even to Cao Bang and Lang Son, but these are the kinds of rides that are for train buffs only.

By Bus

Budget traveler cafes in the Old Quarter, mostly along Hang Bac or Hang Be streets, offer low-luxe seat-in-coach tours. Services and prices are similar: About 690,000 VND earns you an open-tour ticket from Hanoi to Saigon with all stops in between. See the section "Budget Tourist Cafes & Open Tours," below.

Local buses arrive at and depart from the following stations: **Gia Lam Station** (Nguyen Van Cu St., Long Bien District—across the Long Bien Bridge and a few clicks to the east of town) runs minibuses and coaches to Haiphong, Halong Bay, Lang Son, and some destinations in the far northwest; **Ben Xe Nam Hanoi (Southern Bus Station;** 5km/3 miles south of the city) runs regularly to all stops along the southern coast, starting with Ninh Binh and going as far as Ho Chi Minh City, as well as to Dien Bien Phu and the far northwest; **Ha Dong Station** is north of town and runs buses regularly to Lao Cai (near Sapa).

VISITOR INFORMATION & TOURS

There are a number of good, high-end tour operators in Hanoi, all offering similar tours throughout the north—to Halong Bay, Ninh Binh, and the Dien Bien Phu loop. Operators can usually assist with city day tours and arrange internal flights, hotels, and countrywide tours, as well as handle any onward connections in the region or back home. Most visitors contact these providers before arriving in Vietnam, but if you land at their counter on any given day, the folks at the tour companies below can help. With prices only a hitch above the midrange operators, the following five providers are a cut above others in their efficient service, creative and adventurous itineraries, and quality guides.

- **Ann Tours,** 77 Pham Hong Thai St., Truc Bach Ward, Ba Dinh District (✆ **04/3715-0950;** www.anntours.com). Based in Ho Chi Minh City, Ann Tours also has an office in Hanoi and offers private deluxe tours to Halong Bay and elsewhere. Frommer's readers have written to share their good experiences with this operation.
- **Buffalo Tours,** 94 Ma May (✆ **04/3828-0702;** fax 04/3926-3126; www.buffalotours.com). This reputable outfit offers a range of standard tours and some good eco-adventures, including cycling, trekking, and kayaking trips from the Mekong Delta in the south to the hilltribe hills along the China border in the far north. Their boat, the *Jewel of the Bay,* is a great choice for trips in Halong. The friendly and professional staff can handle any eventuality, including onward travel and connections in the region.
- **Exotissimo,** 26 Tran Nhat Duat (✆ **04/3828-2150;** fax 04/3828-2146; www.exotissimo.com). You'll get comprehensive service throughout the region from this company.
- **Handspan,** 80 Ma May St. (✆ **04/3926-0581;** fax 04/3926-2383; www.handspan.com). This is an excellent option for organized trips around Hanoi, in the northern hills, and to Halong Bay, plus some great adventure options. Their Halong Bay boat is one of the most popular, and their eco-friendly adventures throughout Vietnam

usually mean you'll break a sweat and get out to see "real" Vietnam. They have an office at the popular Tamarind Café (p. 97).

- **Topas Outdoor Adventures,** 52 To Ngoc Van St. (✆ **04/3715-1005;** fax 04/3715-1007; www.topas-adventure-vietnam.com). This Danish company is very professional and extremely friendly. They are best known for their outdoor/trekking tours (to Sapa and other parts of Vietnam), but they also offer the standard selection of 1-day city tours. Their guides are well trained and knowledgeable.

Midrange Local Tour Operations

- **I Love Vietnam,** 25 Hang Be St., in the Old Quarter (✆ **04/3926-2451;** www.ilovevietnamtravel.com). Spawned as a hypothetical on the blackboard of a travel and tourism course, I Love Vietnam is a popular new tour agent with good local and regional tours for small groups. A Canadian-Vietnamese joint venture, their offices are on the second floor of **Le Pub,** a popular storefront bar on the eastern end of the Old Quarter. The helpful staff can make any arrangements.
- **TNK Travel,** 85 Hang Bac (✆ **04/3926-2378;** fax 04/3926-2377; www.tnktravel.com). Offering all basic services, including budget transportation options like those offered at Hanoi's tourist cafes (see below), TNK leads good private tours.
- **Asiana Travel Mate,** 7 Dinh Tien Hoang St., Hoan Kiem District (✆ **04/3926-3370;** fax 04/3926-3367; www.asianatravelmate.com). Begun in 2006, this operator offers the standard set of day trips and excursions. Although their motto is "Responsible Travel and Sharing," they do not have any eco-specific tours. They are a government-run travel agency, however, so service is a lower quality than most privately owned operators.
- **A–Z Queen Salute Café Travel,** 50 Hang Be St., in the Old Quarter (✆ **04/3826-7356;** fax 04/3926-2214; www.salutehotels.com). A local budget cafe that's gone upmarket, the Queen Salute Café hosts their usual roster of "Cheap Charlie" tours (see the section "Budget Tourist Cafes & Open Tours," below) and now also provides specialized services and private tours. The company runs a few popular downtown hotels as well, and you can book directly with them on all-inclusive tours, to get significant discounts at their hotels.
- **ET Pumpkin,** 89 Ma May St. (✆ **04/3926-0739;** fax 04/3926-2085; www.et-pumpkin.com). Offering adventure travel and all of the usual northern itineraries (in fact, the company has a branch office in Lao Cai, the access town for travel in Sapa), ET Pumpkin is a dependable organization catering to groups and individuals.
- **Queen Travel,** 65 Hang Bac St. (✆ **04/3826-0860;** fax 04/3826-0300; www.queencafe.com.vn). With upmarket private tours at midmarket prices, Queen Travel is an old standby in the Old Quarter. The company can arrange almost anything and put together specialized itineraries on demand.
- **Kangaroo Cafe,** 18 Pho Bao Khanh, east of Hoan Kiem Lake (✆ **04/3828-9931;** www.kangaroocafe.com). A long-popular tour operator and cafe run by Australian expats, the Kangaroo Cafe is a good, safe choice for midmarket tours anywhere in the north and in southern Vietnam as well. The staff speaks a cool Aussie slang, some mixed with a nasal Vietnamese accent, and they make you feel at home (their breakfasts aren't too bad, either).
- **Hidden Hanoi,** 137 Nghi Tam (✆ **04/3719-1746;** www.hiddenhanoi.com.vn). Hidden indeed, this small tour provider runs unique walking tours around the Old Citadel (which now houses Ho Chi Minh's mausoleum and museum) and the Old

Make Friends with Vietnam Heritage

Friends of Vietnam Heritage (www.fvheritage.org) is a group of Hanoi residents and expatriates who get together to celebrate Vietnamese culture and history in informal gatherings in the hopes of preserving its rich tapestry and introducing it to the uninitiated. They hold events, show films, and host special lectures, in addition to offering many group meetings: a pottery group, a museum group, a cultural history and civilizations group, a traditional-medicine group, and a Buddhist group, among other informal gatherings. The organization has published a few useful guides to local temples and pagodas, and sponsors a small meeting room and free lending library at 63 Ly Thai To St. (on the ground floor of the Development Center; ask for "Friends of Vietnam Heritage"), which is open from 9am to 5pm Monday through Friday. It's a great way to connect with some friendly and very engaged Hanoi residents and expatriates.

Quarter. With a focus on connecting with Vietnamese culture, the company teaches language and cooking at their center north of the city near West Lake. Arrange to meet up with their good walking tours in town at preordained meeting places.

Budget Tourist Cafes & Open Tours

Tourist cafes are small eateries/Internet cafes and travel agents all rolled into one. Tours are often bare-bones and services are basic—and often crowded—but the cafes are a good option for tours and transport or for 1- or 2-day excursions to sights like Halong Bay, the Ninh Binh area, or the far north. For higher-quality information and service, I recommend the companies in the sections above. But tourist cafes get you where you want to go, have consistent daily departures, and cost just peanuts.

Hanoi is the home base of many of Vietnam's large **tourist cafes** that sell budget **"Open-Tour Tickets,"** which are no-frills seat-in-coach tours to just about anywhere along the country's length (for more information, see "Getting There & Getting Around" in chapter 3). Below are the best of the many:

- **Sinh Café,** 52 Luong Ngoc Quyen St. (✆ **04/3926-1568;** fax 04/3926-1621; www.sinhcafevn.com). This is the biggest and most popular cafe tour company in all of Vietnam. Their services are good throughout the country, and their offices are quite helpful elsewhere; sadly, in the north, things get a little confusing with this outfit. Just about anybody with red paint and a paintbrush is putting up the distinct Sinh Café logo above shops in the Old Quarter. Most do, in fact, act as consolidators for the company, but often what you get is not the genuine item or, worse, a really bad local company taking advantage of you. What complicates the matter is that Sinh Café is in cahoots with Hanoi Toserco, a big government travel agency, and the two cooperate in a number of offices, the largest at 48 Hang Bac St. I've heard some bad reports about the Toserco trips, so try to book through the main Sinh office on Luong Ngoc Quyen.
- **An Phu Tours,** 50 Yen Phu, Hanoi (✆ **04/3927-3585;** fax 04/3927-4135; www.anphutour.com). Like the other tourist cafes, the folks at An Phu have reliable

transport services. Their office in Hanoi is just an outpost, really: Their operation is based in the center and south, particularly in Hoi An, where they offer more extensive services and budget day tours.

CITY LAYOUT

Hanoi is divided into four main sectors: Hoan Kiem, Ba Dinh, Hai Ba Trung, and Dong Da (see the section, "The Neighborhoods in Brief," below). Metropolitan Hanoi includes a number of outlying areas that were once provinces, but as the population expands in number and large-scale development seeks new land, the city's perimeter widens.

THE NEIGHBORHOODS IN BRIEF

Hoan Kiem District Most foreign visitors to Vietnam spend their time in the heart of Vietnam's ancient capital, Hoan Kiem District. Between the shops and restaurants around busy central **Hoan Kiem Lake,** the very lungs of the city and the most popular strolling spot in town, and the **Old Quarter,** there is wandering aplenty. Most of the prewar colonial buildings in this area are still intact, even if exteriors are faded and crumbling or being encroached on or crowded out by newer concrete construction. Hanoians are getting hip to the historical cache they have in this district, and you'll find more and more buildings being preserved for the public, whether as restaurants or as tour sights (for details, see "Walking Tour: The Old Quarter," in the "Exploring Hanoi" section, later in this chapter). In and among the Old Quarter's busy streets, you'll find the guildhalls of each individual trade once practiced there, as well as community halls and Chinese temples tucked behind ancient willow trees and down quiet alleys. Hoan Kiem hosts a number of markets, including Dong Xuan, the city's largest. The southern edge of Hoan Kiem District is the French Quarter, where streets were reordered under French rule. Here you'll find the old **Opera House** and a number of museums. On the western edge of Hoan Kiem, you'll see a number of important pagodas, including the city's most prominent, **Quan Su,** as well as the famous prison the **Hanoi Hilton,** now mostly replaced by an office complex. Traffic in this busy district is about as busy as it gets.

Ba Dinh District The farthest northwest sector of Hanoi, Ba Dinh begins at the line demarcated by the train station and train line running north-south through the city. This is where you'll find the **Hanoi Citadel,** now rebuilt and housing the **Ho Chi Minh Mausoleum,** as well as his house and an adjoining museum. The nearby **One-Pillar Pagoda** is one of the city's oldest, dating from the 11th century. The **Army Museum** and **Fine Art Museum** are also in Ba Dinh.

Hai Ba Trung District Once where foreign visitors were more or less sequestered (or limited to), this area to the south of Hanoi is where you'll find **Thong Nhat Park** (formerly Lenin Park).

Dong Da District Where Quang Trung, one of the leaders of the Tay Son Rebellion, defeated the Chinese—the event is celebrated every year during the Tet holiday—Dong Da is also home to the city's **Van Mieu Temple of Literature,** the home base of the Mandarins who once governed Vietnam.

2 GETTING AROUND

Hanoi is divided into districts. Most sights and accommodations are in Hoan Kiem District (downtown), centered around picturesque Hoan Kiem Lake, and Ba Dinh (west of town) or Hai Ba Trung (south) districts. Most addresses include a district name. You'll want to plan your travels accordingly because getting from district to district can be time-consuming and expensive.

BY BUS

Hanoi has a number of local **buses** that ply regular routes through the city, but Hanoi's smoke-belching lorries are extremely crowded, and using them is difficult if you don't speak Vietnamese. With the ready availability of fast, affordable local motorbike taxis and good metered taxis (see below), few tourists bother with local buses.

BY TAXI

Taxis can be hailed on the street, at hotels, and at major attractions. The meter should read between 10,000 VND and 15,000 VND (depending on the company and size of the cab) to start, and 4,000 VND to 6,500 VND for every kilometer (about ½ mile) thereafter. The three most reputable companies are **Hanoi Taxi** (✆ **04/853-5353**), **Hanoi Tourist Taxi** (✆ **04/856-5656**), and **Mai Linh** (✆ **04/822-2555**). You (or the concierge) can call ahead for pickup. Make sure the cabbie turns on the meter. Be sure to get your change; drivers often seek a surreptitious tip by claiming that they don't have the right amount to give back. Smile. Tell the driver that you'll wait until it's obtained, and it will materialize. Tips are greatly appreciated, but don't feel pressed to give any certain percent; just round up the meter or offer 5,000 VND, and you are being quite generous by local standards.

BY CAR

Renting a car is convenient, but driving yourself is not recommended. Book a car with a driver from $40 a day (or $5 per hour, minimum 3 hr.). If an upscale hotel quotes you more, call one of the **tourist cafes** or any of the travel agents listed above. A rented car or shared taxi is a great way to make your own itinerary around the city or to destinations throughout the north. Note that in the city center, however, a big car can get stymied by the heavy traffic, so if your constitution is hearty and you like to throw caution to the wind, go for a cheap and maneuverable motorbike taxi to get you through the city traffic and small alleyways of the city (see below).

Warning! Rigged Taxi Meters

Be sure to go with an accredited taxi company, either one mentioned above or a company connected with your hotel. Smaller companies and individual operators sometimes rig the meter and charge up to double the price. If you protest, these shifty characters just point to the meter as evidence. If you think you're being overcharged, don't pay, but ask the driver to wait while you get someone from the front desk of your hotel to verify the rate.

BY MOTORBIKE

Motorbike taxis are a cheap and easy way to get around the city, but drivers go like madmen. ***Be forewarned:*** This is transportation for the brave. Haggle hard with these guys. No matter the distance, drivers will start off asking for a few dollars, but with relentless haggling (you'll have to walk away a few times) they'll come down as far as 15,000 VND for short trips. Motorbike taxi drivers have a pretty hard lot, though, and most expats and longtime Vietnam travelers usually compromise and pay a little extra, 10,000 VND to 15,000 VND, to avoid a long time spent haggling. Motorbike taxi drivers in Hanoi can also be hired by the hour for 30,000 VND to 40,000 VND, and showing the driver the written address of where you want to go is a better alternative than trying to have your bad Vietnamese understood. I've even given a driver a day's worth of addresses and had him create my itinerary because these drivers know the streets and the traffic best. Give a tip and you've got a friend for life, or at least someone who'll show up at your hotel the next day to see if you need any further assistance.

If you're feeling especially brave, you can **rent your own motorbike.** Navigating Hanoi's busy streets is harrowing, though, and most motorbike riders use their rented two wheels to get out of town instead of around in town (see chapter 6 for more detailed information on motorbike touring in the north). Most tourist cafes and mid- to low-range hotels can arrange rentals, and there are a few good storefront rental agencies. Try **Mr. Cuong's Motorbike Adventure,** at 1 Luong Ngoc Quyen St., on the east side of the Old Quarter near the city's major ring road (✆ **04/3926-1534**)—the best place to rent a big honkin' Russian Minsk motorbike for $7 per day—or **Mr. Hung's Vietnam Adventure Tour,** at his in-town office just north of Hoan Kiem Lake, 5A Dinh Liet St. (✆ **04/3926-0938**), or at his repair shop on the city ring road at 162 Tran Quang Khai St. (Mr. Hung's provides bike rentals as well as comprehensive in-town and rural tour options and guides.) One-day rentals of 100cc motorbikes start at $6. A 1-month rental of a little hair dryer–style model (a Honda Dream or Wave) can cost as little as $50. Wear a helmet (it's now a well-enforced law, and all the locals are doing it), go slow, honk to alert other vehicles when passing, and stay alert. Inexperienced riders might want to think twice about cutting their teeth on a motorbike in crazy Hanoi traffic.

Warning: Riding on a motorbike, whether your own or on the back, presents a Catch-22: It's the fastest and most affordable way to navigate city roads, but it's also your best bet for a trip to the emergency room or worse. Take caution and, wherever possible, try to put as much steel between you and the chaos of the road as possible. In other words, take buses and cars when possible.

BY CYCLO

Cyclos are two-seated carts powered by a man on a foot-pedal bike riding behind you. You can flag them down anywhere, particularly near hotels and tourist attractions, where they're certain to find (or follow) you. Being trundled along among whizzing motorbikes isn't always very comfortable, but it can be a nice choice for touring the Old Quarter's narrow streets. Bargain with the driver before setting out. You can pay as little as 20,000 VND for a short ride, and 30,000 VND for a longer haul. You can also hire by the hour for about $2. If you're inclined, most drivers will even let you take a short ride—around the block or so—just for fun.

BY BICYCLE

Rental costs for a bike are about $1 per day from a hotel or tourist cafe. The traffic is daunting, but the brave quickly learn how to just stay to the right and join the flow. Helmets are generally not available.

Fast Facts Hanoi

ATMs Most major banks in Hanoi and even countrywide now offer ATM service. Look for **Vietcombank** and **Incombank** branch locations throughout the city. New ATMs are popping up all over. Ask any hotel concierge where to find one. Consult with your bank office at home to inquire about international ATM usage fees. Most range from just $1 to $1.50. For more information, see the "Money & Costs" section in chapter 3.

Banks & Currency Exchange The best service (24-hr. ATMs with guards) is at the **Australia New Zealand Bank (ANZ),** 14 Le Thai To St. (✆ **04/825-8190**); **Citibank,** 17 Ngo Quyen St. (✆ **04/3825-1950**); and **Vietcombank,** 198 Tran Quan Khai (✆ **04/3934-3137**). Most banks will exchange foreign currency, either U.S. dollars or euros, during normal banking hours. You'll also find a few money-changing storefronts along Hang Bac Street in the Old Quarter and around the edge of Hoan Kiem Lake. **Hanoi Sacombank,** 88 Ly Thuong Kiet (✆ **04/3942-8095**), is one to try.

Avoid exchanging on the black market. Black-market money-changers will approach you outside of the major banks; in the past, you could get a much improved rate from them, but today the advantage is nominal and travelers often find themselves left with a few counterfeit or out-of-circulation notes in the mix—it's not worth the trouble.

Business Hours Most Hanoi shops and offices are closed for lunch, usually from 11 or 11:30am to 12:30 or 1pm. Hanoians wake up very early to take advantage of cooler weather, and an early lunch is followed by some rest time in the heat of the day. Most offices close at 5pm and are shut on Sunday.

Car Rentals Contact any tour operator or hotel concierge about booking a car with driver for day trips or to sights farther afield. Expect to pay about $30 to $40 per day, and $10 for a guide to accompany you.

Climate Hanoi experiences relatively high humidity all year and a rainy season from May to October. Winter months are cool and damp (rarely below 57°F/14°C), but the heat starts to pick up in April and makes for a hot, wet summer (a popular time to hit cooler climates like Sapa in the far north or enjoy the offshore breezes in Halong).

Doctors & Hospitals **International SOS,** at 31 Hai Ba Trung, just south of Hoan Kiem, is your best bet for emergency services and travel illness. Contact their 24-hour service center at ✆ **04/3934-0555** or their clinic at ✆ **04/3934-0666,** or visit the website at www.internationalsos.com. International SOS is part of a worldwide international service that you can join for a fee and be covered anywhere they offer services. The organization has a capable staff of expatriate and Vietnamese doctors, with specialists ranging from pre- and post-natal care to tropical infectious disease experts, good eye doctors, and dentists. They work in collusion with most major insurance companies and can contact your provider to let you know if you are covered. The cost of an initial visit is $69 with an expatriate doctor or $59 with a Vietnamese doctor.

Hanoi Family Medical Practice, at Van Phuc Diplomatic Compound, 298 Kim Ma (✆ **04/3843-0748**), is another walk-in clinic, like International SOS, that caters to Hanoi's growing expatriate community. They have a good dental center.

Another good choice for comprehensive service is the **Hanoi French Hospital,** south of the town center at 1 Phuong Mai (✆ **04/3574-0740**). As the name suggests, the hospital caters to Francophones, and a knowledge of French is a plus, but doctors and staff can speak English as well. Service is very professional, efficient, and much more accessible and affordable than at the town's two international clinics.

Embassies & Consulates Your country's embassy is your home base in the event of any instability, political situation, or emergency (either medical or legal). It's not a bad idea to register with your embassy when you arrive in Hanoi or Ho Chi Minh City, or through the embassy website before you leave home. Embassies are also a good place to pick up the most current information on regional crises, health issues, political hot spots, and advice on travel. If you are in Vietnam during one of your country's national holidays, check for any special events held at an embassy compound (there's nothing like Thanksgiving among Americans or Victoria Day with fellow Canadians, for example). The following is a list of the major international embassies in Hanoi: **Australia,** 8 Dao Tan (✆ 04/3831-7755); **Canada,** 31 Hung Vuong (✆ 04/3734-5000); **European Union,** 83B Ly Thuong Kiet (✆ 04/3946-1702); **New Zealand,** 63 Ly Thai To (✆ 04/3824-1481); **United Kingdom,** 31 Hai Ba Trung (✆ 04/3936-0500); **United States,** 7 Lang Ha (✆ 04/3772-1510).

Note that most storefront travel agents can handle visa services for a nominal fee, but when arranging visas and gathering information about travel in nearby countries, you can also contact the following embassies: **China,** 46 Hoang Dieu (✆ 04/3845-3736); **India,** 58–60 Tran Hung Dao (✆ 04/3824-4989); **Japan,** 27 Lieu Giai (✆ 04/3846-3000); **Laos,** 22 Tran Binh Trong (✆ 04/3942-4576); **Malaysia,** 45 Dien Bien Phu (✆ 04/3734-3836); **Myanmar,** A3 Van Phuc Compound (✆ 04/3845-3369); **The Philippines,** 27B Tran Hung Dao (✆ 04/3943-7948); **South Korea,** 360 Kim Ma (✆ 04/3831-5111); **Thailand,** 63–65 Hoang Dieu (✆ 04/3823-5092).

Internet Internet service in Hanoi is affordable and found on nearly every street corner, especially in the Old Quarter, where so many budget travelers dwell. Service is usually a speedy ADSL connection and costs about 3,000 VND per hour. The **Tourist Information Center** at the north end of Hoan Kiem Lake (7 Dinh Tien Hoang St.; ✆ **04/3926-3368**) offers some free Internet access. Small Internet storefronts are numerous in the Old Quarter on Hang Bac or Hang Be, and in all traveler cafes: In fact, many include some free connection time if you book a trip at their storefront. **A–Z Queen Salute Travel Café,** at 65 Hang Bac (✆ **04/3826-0860**), is a good bet with affordable service and a pay-as-you-use honor system. On Ma May Street in the Old Quarter, try the corner shop at **66 Ma May** (just north of the Tamarind Café): Always crowded, it has good, fast ADSL service and sells affordable prepaid Internet phone cards. **Amazing Internet,** at 15 Hang Non (✆ **04/3828-6193**), on the east side of the Old Quarter, is rather proud of itself, and for good reason, considering its fast service and very helpful staff.

Maps The **Tourist Information Center** (7 Dinh Tien Hoang St.; ✆ **04/3926-3368**) has excellent free tourist maps. If setting out into the country on motorbike or by hired car, be sure to pick up a detailed map—look for the **Vietnam Tourism Travel Atlas** (costs 85,000 VND), which has good regional maps and detailed city maps of the major towns.

Newspapers & Magazines The ***Vietnam News*** is available free at most upmarket hotels and can be purchased at most bookstores and at magazine shops near Hoan Kiem Lake; written by Vietnamese, its local news is more or less propaganda ("We are successful and our economy is growing"), but the paper does cover the major international wire-service news items of the day and lists current events in the country.

A number of cheap and/or free local magazines are geared toward tourists and business visitors. You can pick up any of the following at airline offices, travel agents, popular restaurants, hotel lobbies, and bookstores: the ***Guide,*** which is a travel and tourism glossy supplement published monthly by the ***Vietnam Economic Times*** that provides useful listings of hotels, restaurants, and happenings (pick it up for free or for 16,000 VND in some locales); ***Vietnam Discovery,*** which sells for 15,000 VND and is a monthly magazine listing hotels, published by the Vietnam National Administration of Tourism, similar to the *Guide;* ***Vietnam Pathfinder,*** which is a small tourism magazine with an expatriate section featuring good insider tips on tours, travel, dining, and shopping; and the ***Guidebook*** (www.theguidebook.com), another one with good local listings for Hanoi and Ho Chi Minh City. ***East&West,*** a new glossy publication, zeroes in on new high-end fashion, shopping, and hotel news in Vietnam and Southeast Asia. You can pick up copies at select boutiques and high-end hotels. Check their website (www.east-westmag.com) for distribution.

Pharmacies Vietnamese pharmacies are the "diagnose yourself" variety. Got a bad cough and think it's an infection? Pound the table and ask for antibiotics. So much for discouraging antibiotic-resistant illnesses. Pharmacies are on every street corner and, even if the folks there don't speak English, they can help if you mime your disease (I once did an interpretive dance I call "nonstop diarrhea"), or for the less theatrical, they usually have an English-to-Vietnamese dictionary with medical terms listed. Ask for foreign-made drugs, best from France, as Vietnamese versions of medicines, though cheap, are often inferior. I recommend heading to the SOS International Clinic, which has a pharmacy on-site (see "Doctors & Hospitals," above).

Police Yes, you may call them if you have something stolen, and they can fill out a report for insurance purposes, but the Hanoi police are best avoided; in fact, the only reason to see them is if you're bribing your way out of something (a traffic violation, for example). In Vietnam's rapidly changing economic and social climate, laws are mutable and, in fact, the rule of law is still uncertain. Traffic police crack down on motorbike drivers without helmets, but in general, foreign visitors have no contact with the grim lads in khaki.

Post Office The **General Post Office** is located at 6 Dinh Le St., Hoan Kiem District (✆ **04/3825-7036**). It's open daily from 6:30am to 10pm. You can also send faxes and make international phone calls there. **FedEx** (✆ **04/3719-8787;** daily 8am–6pm) is located in the same building as the post office but has its own storefront just around the corner. You can also find a **UPS** storefront on the same block at 10 Le Thach St. (✆ **04/3824-6483;** daily 7:30am–6pm) and a branch of **EMS** at 12 Le Thach St. (✆ **04/3824-1271;** daily 7am–9pm). Expect to pay anywhere from $29 to $74 per kilo, depending on expediency of service.

Safety Hanoi, like the rest of Vietnam, is safe. The only concerns for visitors are pickpockets and minor local scams (see "Rigged Taxi Meters," under "Getting Around," earlier in this chapter). Keep an eye on your valuables; store traveler's checks and money in your hotel safe or, if you must bring them with you, keep cash and important documents safe in a travel wallet under clothing and out of sight of the clever hands of thieves. Take care if out clubbing late in Hanoi, and avoid dark streets and walking alone, as you might in any place in the world. But in general, you're free from violence in the Vietnamese capital.

The city is not without hassles, though. You will be harassed by book, magazine, and souvenir sellers. The entreaties of these relentless entrepreneurs can get pretty tiresome. Remember that they're just kids, most of whom work under the pressure of local mafia, and it is their job to sell you; take time to talk with them if you have it, but remember that any conversation is geared toward getting the greenbacks out of your pocket. If you're not interested in their goods, let them know, but these guys rarely leave it at that. A firm "No!" doesn't hurt anyone's feelings. If you stop at intersections and look at maps, know that the motorbike taxi guys will swarm you. I always try to have a look at the map before I get to any intersection so that I know what street I'm looking for and can proceed through intersections like I know where I'm going.

Telephone The city code for Hanoi is 04. Most hotels provide **international direct dialing (IDD),** although none allow you to access an international operator or AT&T (whose Vietnam access code is ✆ **01/201-0288**). To do that, you will have to go to the post office. You'll find public phone booths throughout the city for local calls that accept phone cards purchased from the post office. **Internet "telephony"** is the cheapest option and is available in Internet cafes throughout the city. Connecting through a designated ADSL line, phone service through the Internet from Hanoi is quite good, with the annoying delay effect at a bare minimum. Try the corner shop at **66 Ma May** or one of the other small Internet cafes in the Old Quarter.

3 WHERE TO STAY

From historic charm to slick efficiency to budget hole-in-the-wall accommodations, you'll find what you want in Hanoi. Amenities and cleanliness levels are high across-the-board, and your dollar, yen, or euro goes quite far, so indulge in an upgrade! Most hotels over $15 a night will have a phone, air-conditioning, in-room safes, and hair dryers. Children 11 and under usually stay free. Ask for discounts. Prices shown here are high-season rack rates; discounts of up to 50% are available. Hotels charge a VAT of up to 20% except where noted.

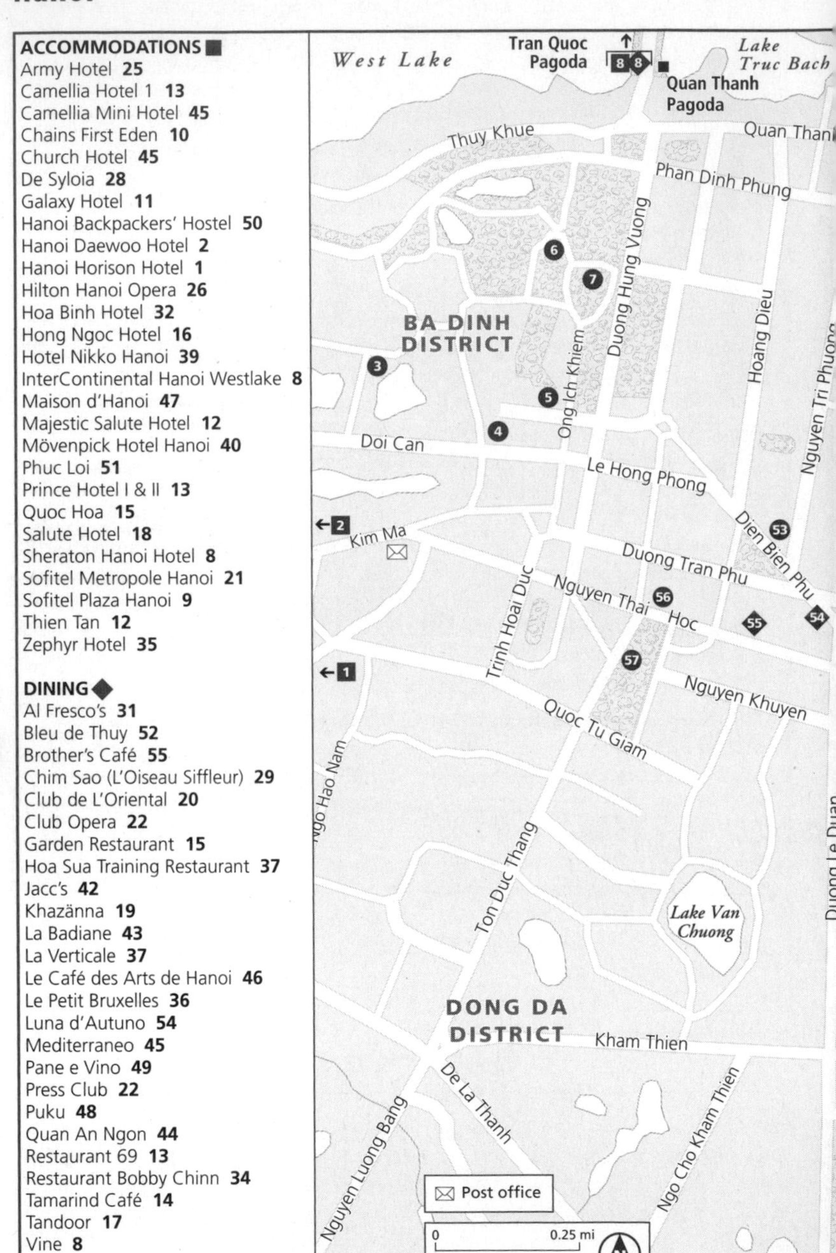
ACCOMMODATIONS ■
Army Hotel 25
Camellia Hotel 1 13
Camellia Mini Hotel 45
Chains First Eden 10
Church Hotel 45
De Syloia 28
Galaxy Hotel 11
Hanoi Backpackers' Hostel 50
Hanoi Daewoo Hotel 2
Hanoi Horison Hotel 1
Hilton Hanoi Opera 26
Hoa Binh Hotel 32
Hong Ngoc Hotel 16
Hotel Nikko Hanoi 39
InterContinental Hanoi Westlake 8
Maison d'Hanoi 47
Majestic Salute Hotel 12
Mövenpick Hotel Hanoi 40
Phuc Loi 51
Prince Hotel I & II 13
Quoc Hoa 15
Salute Hotel 18
Sheraton Hanoi Hotel 8
Sofitel Metropole Hanoi 21
Sofitel Plaza Hanoi 9
Thien Tan 12
Zephyr Hotel 35
DINING ◆
Al Fresco's 31
Bleu de Thuy 52
Brother's Café 55
Chim Sao (L'Oiseau Siffleur) 29
Club de L'Oriental 20
Club Opera 22
Garden Restaurant 15
Hoa Sua Training Restaurant 37
Jacc's 42
Khazänna 19
La Badiane 43
La Verticale 37
Le Café des Arts de Hanoi 46
Le Petit Bruxelles 36
Luna d'Autuno 54
Mediterraneo 45
Pane e Vino 49
Press Club 22
Puku 48
Quan An Ngon 44
Restaurant 69 13
Restaurant Bobby Chinn 34
Tamarind Café 14
Tandoor 17
Vine 8
Wild Lotus 38
Wild Rice (Lá Luá) 30
West Lake
Tran Quoc Pagoda
Lake Truc Bach
Quan Thanh Pagoda
Thuy Khue
Quan Thanh
Phan Dinh Phung
Duong Hung Vuong
Hoang Dieu
Nguyen Tri Phuong
BA DINH DISTRICT
Ong Ich Khiem
Doi Can
Le Hong Phong
Dien Bien Phu
Kim Ma
Duong Tran Phu
Nguyen Thai Hoc
Trinh Hoai Duc
Nguyen Khuyen
Quoc Tu Giam
Ngo Hao Nam
Ton Duc Thang
Lake Van Chuong
Duong Le Duan
DONG DA DISTRICT
Kham Thien
De La Thanh
Nguyen Luong Bang
Ngo Cho Kham Thien
Post office
0 0.25 mi
0 0.25 km
N
Lake Ba Mau

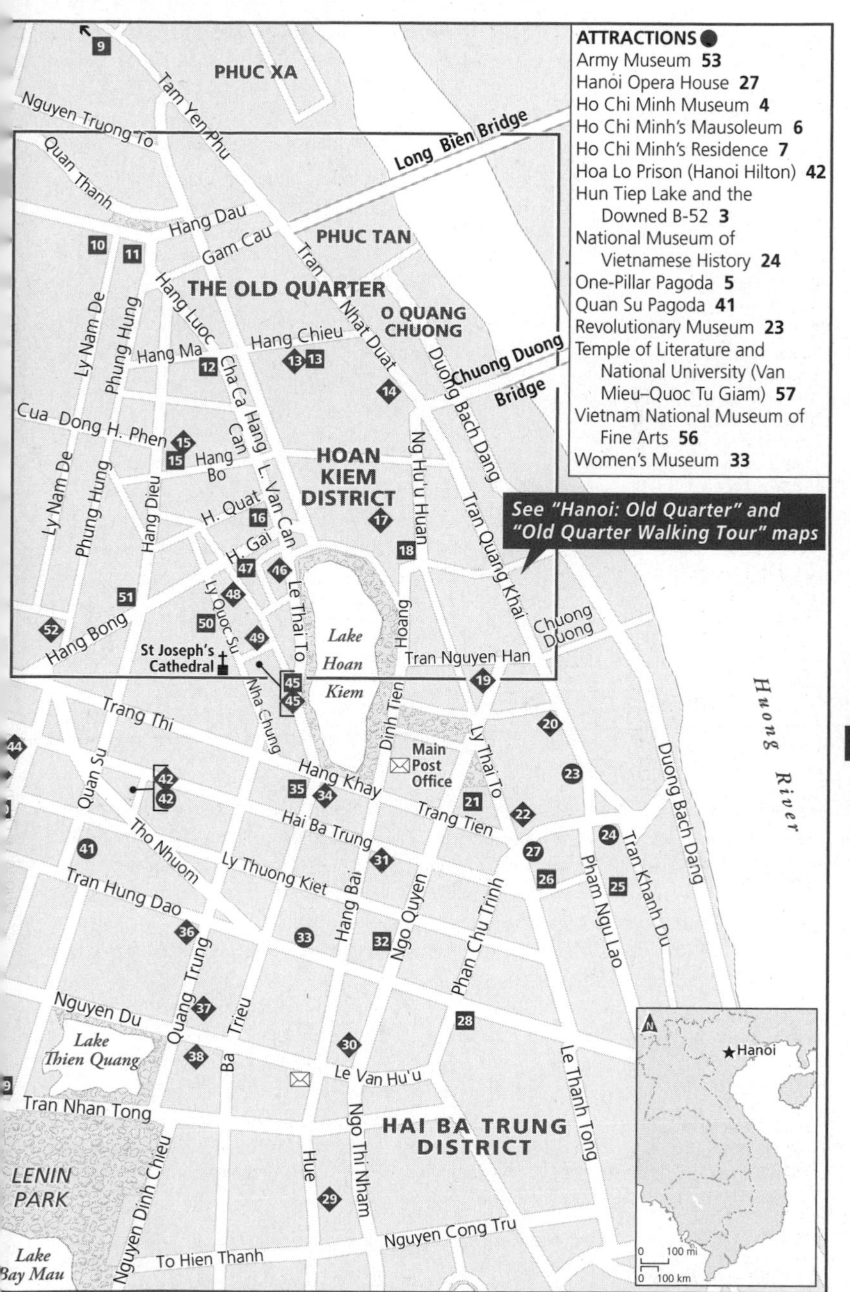
ATTRACTIONS
Army Museum 53
Hanoi Opera House 27
Ho Chi Minh Museum 4
Ho Chi Minh's Mausoleum 6
Ho Chi Minh's Residence 7
Hoa Lo Prison (Hanoi Hilton) 42
Hun Tiep Lake and the Downed B-52 3
National Museum of Vietnamese History 24
One-Pillar Pagoda 5
Quan Su Pagoda 41
Revolutionary Museum 23
Temple of Literature and National University (Van Mieu–Quoc Tu Giam) 57
Vietnam National Museum of Fine Arts 56
Women's Museum 33
See "Hanoi: Old Quarter" and "Old Quarter Walking Tour" maps
PHUC XA
PHUC TAN
THE OLD QUARTER
O QUANG CHUONG
HOAN KIEM DISTRICT
HAI BA TRUNG DISTRICT
LENIN PARK
Long Bien Bridge
Chuong Duong Bridge
Huong River
Lake Hoan Kiem
Lake Thien Quang
Lake Bay Mau
St Joseph's Cathedral
Main Post Office
Nguyen Truong To
Tam Yen Phu
Quan Thanh
Hang Dau
Gam Cau
Tran Nhat Duat
Hang Luoc
Ly Nam De
Phung Hung
Hang Ma
Hang Chieu
Cha Ca
Hang Can
Duong Bach Dang
Cua Dong
H. Phen
Hang Bo
L. Van Can
Ng Hu'u Huan
Hang Dieu
H. Quat
H. Gai
Tran Quang Khai
Ly Quoc Su
Le Thai To
Hang Bong
Chuong Duong
Tran Nguyen Han
Hoang
Dinh Tien
Nha Chung
Trang Thi
Quan Su
Hang Khay
Ly Thai To
Trang Tien
Hai Ba Trung
Tho Nhuom
Ly Thuong Kiet
Tran Khanh Du
Pham Ngu Lao
Tran Hung Dao
Hang Bai
Ngo Quyen
Phan Chu Trinh
Quang Trung
Nguyen Du
Ba Trieu
Le Van Hu'u
Le Thanh Tong
Tran Nhan Tong
Ngo Thi Nham
Hue
Nguyen Dinh Chieu
Nguyen Cong Tru
To Hien Thanh
Hanoi
0 100 mi
0 100 km

VERY EXPENSIVE

Hanoi Daewoo Hotel ★ The Daewoo has a popular guest list (heads of state and dignitaries including Bill Clinton and Jiang Zemin have stayed here) but an unfortunate location. It's far away from the action of the Old Quarter and lacks any sort of social scene. Everything is done large—the lobby, the bars, the rooms with king-size beds, and the 80m (262-ft.) curving pool. All interior space is tessellated in marble, deep-toned wood, or sumptuous fabrics. It's almost a bit *too* much. Bathrooms are surprisingly small in the lower-end rooms but are still quite well appointed.

360 Kim Ma St., Ba Dinh District, Hanoi. ✆ **04/3831-5000.** Fax 04/3831-5010. www.hanoi-daewoohotel.com. 411 units. $199 double; $319 executive-floor double; $329–$1,500 suite. AE, DC, MC, V. **Amenities:** 4 restaurants; 2 bars; babysitting; concierge; family play program; elegant health club; Internet; Jacuzzi; room service; sauna; spa. *In room:* A/C, satellite TV, fridge, hair dryer, minibar.

Hilton Hanoi Opera ★★ Not to be confused with the famed "Hanoi Hilton" that housed American POWs (see "Attractions," later in this chapter), the Hilton is a reproduction colonial that describes an elegant arc around the perimeter of the splendid Hanoi Opera building. The inside matches the fine facade, with a lobby showcasing up-and-coming Vietnamese artists (Nguyan Tuan Ngoc was on display at the time of writing) done on a grand scale. Rooms are carpeted in rich, contrasting colors with unique cushioned wallpaper, subdued lighting, and faux Chinese lacquer cabinets. Rooms on the fifth floor have balconies. The hotel also has plenty of special features for vacation travelers, including in-house tour services through Exotissimo (www.exotissimo.com) and a helpful concierge. You'll find fine Vietnamese dining at Ba Mien, and gourmet sandwiches and baked goods at Café Opera. Hotel breakfasts are tops, and JJ's Sports Bar is a good place to catch up on scores or play a game of pool. The courtyard pool is always a couple degrees cooler than the stuffy Hanoi air and overlooks the nearby Opera House.

1 Le Thanh Tong St., Hoan Kiem, Hanoi. ✆ **800/774-1500** or 04/3933-0500. Fax 04/3933-0530. www.hilton.com. 269 units. $210–$230 double; $250 executive room. AE, MC, V. **Amenities:** 2 restaurants; bar; cafe; 2 club lounges; babysitting; fitness center; outdoor pool; room service; rooms for those w/limited mobility. *In room:* A/C, TV, hair dryer, Wi-Fi.

Hotel Nikko Hanoi ★★ The folks at the Hotel Nikko take care of the most discerning of all international visitors: the high-powered Japanese businessman. As a result, the place has every detail right—an immaculate, modern, streamlined design throughout, rooms so tidy you could eat sushi right off the floor, and comfort at a premium. Dining outlets are superb. It is a business hotel, but I include it here for the discerning travelers who like their accommodations peppered with a little bit of Wabi Sabi: the Japanese way of precision, quiet, and emptiness (with a little bling-bling thrown in). Nikko is located on the north end of sprawling Thong Nhat Park (formerly Lenin Park) overlooking Bay Mau Lake, a good distance south of the busy tourist area of Hanoi, but that might be one of the hotel's greatest assets. They have good live jazz performances regularly in their lobby lounge.

84 Tran Nhan Tong St., Hai Ba Trung District, Hanoi. ✆ **04/3822-3535.** Fax 04/822-3555. www.hotelnikkohanoi.com.vn. 255 units. $180–$300 double; $400–$820 suite. AE, MC, V. **Amenities:** 3 restaurants (Japanese, Chinese, and Continental); 2 bars; babysitting; concierge; health club; outdoor pool (4th floor); room service; spa. *In room:* A/C, satellite TV, fridge, hair dryer, minibar.

InterContinental Hanoi Westlake ★★ The InterContinental offers a sweet resortlike atmosphere in busy little Hanoi. The hotel is Hanoi's newest and best five-star. For a romantic treat, splurge on a suite on one of the island pavilions connected to the main building via Venetian-style bridges. All rooms come with private balconies, and most have fabulous views of West Lake. Rooms on the top floor ("Atelier rooms") have high, sloping ceilings, giving the space a cozy cabin feel. Located about a 20-minute cab ride away from Hanoi's Old Quarter, this hotel is a perfect getaway from the hustle and bustle of city life. The outdoor Sunset Bar is a popular destination for hip locals and expats alike.

1A Nghi Tam, Tay Ho District, Hanoi. ✆ **04/6270-8888.** Fax 04/6270-9999. www.intercontinental.com. 359 units. $185–$305 double; suites from $415. AE, MC, V. **Amenities:** 3 restaurants; outdoor bar; cafe; lounge; babysitting; concierge; executive-level rooms; health club; Jacuzzi; outdoor pool; room service; sauna; smoke-free rooms; spa. *In room:* A/C, satellite TV, fridge, hair dryer, minibar, Wi-Fi.

Mövenpick Hotel Hanoi ★★ The newly renovated Mövenpick is a sleek affair of modern comforts and swish decor. This is a better deal than other hotels in this category, such as the Hilton and the Daewoo, which look and feel quite dated in comparison. Rooms are spacious, with warm, dark wood–finish floors and splashy accent furniture like French-style dressers painted in silver and gray, and black Art Deco rugs with a bit of lime thrown in. It's a careful balance of classic and contemporary, and the overall feel is excellent. Bathrooms are a bit on the small side, with no separate tubs, but there is a good-size shower cubicle outfitted with a rain shower. Watch out for the water temperature—it gets hot very quickly. The service is very friendly, if sometimes a bit eager.

83A Ly Thuong Kiet St., Hanoi. ✆ **04/3822-2800.** Fax 04/3822-2822. 154 units (some with shower only, some with shower and tub). $220–$250 double; $280–$320 suite. AE, MC, V. **Amenities:** Restaurant; bar; concierge; health club; dry sauna; smoke-free floors. *In room:* A/C, satellite TV, fridge, hair dryer, minibar.

Sheraton Hanoi Hotel ★★ Just a 10-minute ride north of town, this smart, upscale hotel sits on a peninsula jutting out into Hanoi's picturesque West Lake in a neighborhood popular with the local expat community (which means good restaurants and services in the area). The hotel makes up for any inconvenience to town by being completely self-contained, with fine-dining options and hotel services that cover all bases, from local touring to business support. Rooms are done in an ultratidy, contemporary style typical of Sheraton hotels—certainly nothing to write home about, but cozy and familiar. All rooms have fine views of the lake. Bathrooms are large, with big bathtubs, separate glass shower, and fine wood and granite detail. In-house dining is tops, and transport to town is available 24 hours. The hotel is just reopening after a delay of some 7 years due to the economic collapse in 1997. Construction, though, is ongoing, with promises of more rooms as the upper floors are completed.

K5 Nghi Tam, 11 Xuan Dieu Rd., Tay Ho District, Hanoi. ✆ **04/3719-9000.** Fax 04/3719-9001. www.sheraton.com. 299 units. $200–$270 double; from $320 suite. AE, MC, V. **Amenities:** 2 restaurants; bar; babysitting; concierge; club-level rooms; health club; Jacuzzi; outdoor pool; room service; sauna; smoke-free rooms; tennis court. *In room:* A/C, satellite TV, fridge, hair dryer, minibar.

Sofitel Metropole Hanoi ★★★ Hanoi's top choice. Built in 1901, the Metropole is a historical treasure. It was here that invading, liberating, or civil armies found billet and raised their flags; the first film was shown in Indochina; Jane Fonda and Joan Baez took cover in a bomb shelter; and heads of state and embassy officials have resided over the years. The Metropole has been through numerous renovations, including the Opera wing (so named because it is nearer to the Hanoi Opera House), which was first added in 1996. Currently, the hotel is developing an executive floor geared to business visitors; the entire wing was closed for the renovation at the time of writing. Rooms in the newer wing are more spacious, but go for the old wing and walk into a bit of history (keep an eye out for ghosts) in these medium-size rooms with wood floors, cane furniture, classic fixtures, and high ceilings. Modern bathrooms are large and have little touches like wood-frame mirrors, fresh flowers, and a fine line of in-house products. The staff couldn't be nicer or more efficient. The pool is small but nice, the in-house health club is top-notch, and the adjoining Bamboo lounge is an oasis of calm in the city center. Le Beaulieu is popular in Hanoi for classic French fare, and the Spices Garden is a great place to sample local delights. The lunch buffet is a safe and tasty place to try Hanoi street fare like *pho* (Vietnamese noodle soup). The Sofitel's Met Pub is a casual spot to have a beer and listen to live music. The downtown location can't be beat, and there's a nice mix of tourists and businesspeople here.

15 Ngo Quyen St., Hanoi. ✆ **800/221-4542** or 04/3826-6919. Fax 04/826-6920. www.sofitel.com. 363 units. $220–$300 double; from $551 suite. AE, DC, MC, V. **Amenities:** 3 restaurants; 3 bars; concierge; health club; courtyard pool. *In room:* TV, DVD, fridge, hair dryer, minibar, Wi-Fi.

Sofitel Plaza Hanoi ★ If you've come to Hanoi for real Sofitel charm, your best bet is the downtown Sofitel Metropole (see above). The big drawback of this hotel is location, which resembles a Florida suburb, but for familiar comfort and a bit of breathing room from downtown chaos, the Sofitel Plaza is a good bet. The hotel towers over the southern end of West Lake, which is about a 10-minute ride on Hanoi's ring road to the north of downtown, but this hulking plaza hosts such a high standard of rooms and services that you won't mind the slight inconvenience. Views from upper floors to the nearby lake and surrounding city (no buildings obstruct the views from here) are great. Rooms are large and decked out in sumptuous fabrics, rich rugs, and fine furnishings. The commute to the Old Quarter is about 40,000 VND in a taxi, and after wandering around there, you might be pleased to be whisked out of the chaos to air-conditioned comfort.

1 Thanh Nien Rd., Ba Dinh District, Hanoi. ✆ **04/3823-8888.** Fax 04/3829-3888. www.accor.com. 317 units. $180–$200 double; $250–$1,000 suite. AE, MC, V. **Amenities:** 2 restaurants; 2 bars; concierge; health club; Jacuzzi; outdoor pool; room service; spa. *In room:* A/C, satellite TV, fridge, hair dryer, high-speed Internet, minibar.

EXPENSIVE

De Syloia ★ The De Syloia is a cozy little treasure just south of the city center. Rooms aren't especially luxurious for the price, but they're large, clean, and comfortable, with tidy carpet and dark-wood furniture. The large bathrooms have tubs (deluxe rooms and suites have Jacuzzis). The lobby is compact and clean but not particularly atmospheric, and the whole setup is a Hanoi minihotel gone upscale. Amenities are limited, but the staff is friendly on a good day, and this is a popular choice away from the downtown traffic. Check the website for discounted rates.

17A Tran Hung Dao St., Hoan Kiem District, Hanoi. ✆ **04/3824-5346.** Fax 04/3824-1083. www.desyloia.com. 33 units. $116–$138 double; $171 deluxe; $182 suite. AE, MC, V. **Amenities:** Restaurant; bar; minigym; Internet. *In room:* A/C, satellite TV, fridge, hair dryer, minibar.

Hanoi Horison Hotel ★ This massive midrange number is far south of the tourist area of Hanoi, but the Hanoi Horison attracts international businesspeople (mostly a high-end regional market from Singapore or nearby China), as well as a burgeoning leisure market, and covers all the bases. This is a good choice for comfort and, for some, a welcome distance from "tourist Hanoi" (but just a short cab ride to the sights). Horison is built around a 14-story tower of glass, with an elevator open to the views of the busy street scene below and two massive wings extending from the glass centerpiece. The lobby is grand and the service is effusive from the moment someone opens the door for you. Deluxe rooms are very large, and a much higher standard than superior, certainly worth the upgrade. Furnishings are a little nicked and scraped from use, but the rooms are decorated in a cozy, contemporary style with funky white floor lamps that shine mellow, indirect light and big, comfy beds. Swimming in the pool gives you a commanding view of the busy intersection below.

40 Cat Linh St., Dong Da District, Hanoi. ✆ **04/3733-0808.** Fax 04/3733-0888. www.swiss-belhotel.com. 247 units. $190 superior; $210 deluxe; $395–$2,300 suite. AE, MC, V. **Amenities:** 2 restaurants; 2 bars; concierge; concierge-/club-level rooms; health club; Jacuzzi; outdoor pool w/vanishing edge and city view; room service; sauna; smoke-free rooms; spa; tennis court. *In room:* A/C, satellite TV, fridge, hair dryer, Internet, minibar.

Maison d'Hanoi ★★ This is the best new hotel in town. Opened in December 2008, the Maison d'Hanoi has all the fun stuff you expect from a boutique property in Hanoi—contemporary decor with a flair of Vietnamese style, comfy wood floors, and great service. Bathrooms are small but comfortable. Double rooms are spacious, and the beds come with mattress pads that leave them incredibly soft and comfortable. Oversize, thick silk headboards are both sleek and functional, doing a good job of muffling sounds of nearby rooms. The breakfast is nothing to write home about, but there's enough available to satisfy morning hunger pangs. Tea and coffee are served throughout the day.

35–37 Hang Trong St., Hoan Kiem District, Hanoi. ✆ **04/3938-0999.** Fax 04/3938-0989. www.hanovahotel.com. 55 units. $140–$160 double; $180–$220 suite. AE, MC, V. **Amenities:** Restaurant; bar. *In room:* A/C, satellite TV, fridge, high-speed Internet, minibar.

Zephyr Hotel ★ This compact gem overlooks the southern end of central Hoan Kiem Lake. Style throughout is neat but getting a bit dated after 4 years of operation. It's still a good choice for those who want to be in the middle of things but can't bear the thought of an Old Quarter minihotel. The Zephyr can also meet the demands of business travelers. Thin office-style carpets in rooms are a drawback, but beds have big fluffy duvets, and the built-in wooden cabinetry is stylish. Deluxe rooms are quite large and luxurious, and two of them have balconies. Upper floors are best—some have great views. The eighth floor is a cool lounge area with windows overlooking the city and cool, regal high-backed lounge chairs. The first-floor restaurant serves good international fare and a very good buffet breakfast.

4–6 Ba Trieu St., Hoan Kiem District, Hanoi. ✆ **04/3934-1256.** Fax 04/3934-1262. www.zephyrhotel.com.vn. 43 units. $123 double; $143 deluxe; $178 Zephyr suite. AE, MC, V. **Amenities:** Restaurant; bar; small fitness area. *In room:* A/C, satellite TV, fridge, hair dryer, high-speed Internet, minibar.

MODERATE

Army Hotel ★★ Value In a sprawling complex owned by the Vietnamese military—thus the name—there's no need to salute here and the friendly staff won't ask you to drop for 20 push-ups. For comfort and value close to downtown (and a nice pool), the Army Hotel is a find. Located on a quiet street just a short walk east of downtown (behind the Opera House), Army is popular with long-term visitors, especially couples who come to adopt children in Vietnam. Rooms vary, so ask to see one before you check in; most are large and clean, with tile floors and nice-size bathrooms with a tub/shower. Each room has a balcony, some with direct pool access. The staff is friendly, the lobby business center is convenient, and the pool is inviting and unique in this price range. Ask about their eclectic suites, some with Japanese-style rooms, and a larger private balcony.

33C Pham Ngu Lao St., Hanoi (just behind the Opera House). ✆ **04/3825-2896.** Fax 04/3825-9276. armyhotel@fpt.vn. 70 units. $50 double; $80 suite. AE, MC, V. **Amenities:** Restaurant; babysitting; exercise room; outdoor pool; sauna; room service. *In room:* A/C, TV, fridge, hair dryer, Internet.

Chains First Eden Just adjacent to the Galaxy Hotel in the far north end of the Old Quarter, Chains First Eden is a longtime popular budget choice in Hanoi (about 10 years old now). The place is a little worn and the rooms aren't spectacular, but the price is right. Everything is "good enough," and the location is perfect for exploring the Old Quarter. Rooms are a worn, familiar standard, like a larger minihotel room with thin office carpeting and Chinese furnishings. All bathrooms have tub/showers and plenty of counter space. The hotel is popular with groups, and the friendly staff speaks English well. Discounts are available for longer stays.

3A Phan Dinh Phung St., Hoan Kiem District, Hanoi. ✆ **04/3828-3896.** Fax 04/3828-4066. 42 units. $40–$60 double. MC, V. **Amenities:** Restaurant; bar; health club; room service. *In room:* A/C, satellite TV, fridge, minibar.

Church Hotel This was the first of the downtown, boutique hotel trend in the nation's capital. And while I would like to stay loyal to original purveyors, it is getting hard to ignore the past few years' slip in quality. Rooms are beginning to show their age, with marked walls, scratched floors, and small water stains in the bathroom. Staff members are helpful, but somewhat begrudgingly so. However, the hotel still sits right in the middle of the action on busy Nha Tho Street, a popular cafe-and-shopping area near Hanoi's large Catholic cathedral. The lobby is spotlessly clean, with modern Vietnamese oil paintings adorning the walls. It remains a good choice for comfort and downtown convenience.

9 Nha Tho St., Hoan Kiem District, Hanoi. ✆ **04/3928-8118.** Fax 04/3828-5793. www.churchhotel.com.vn. 16 units. $50–$55 double; $82 suite. Rates include breakfast. MC, V. **Amenities:** Restaurant. *In room:* A/C, satellite TV, fridge, hair dryer, high-speed Internet.

Galaxy Hotel ★★ Popular with tour groups, the Galaxy is on a busy corner just north of the Old Quarter—a good spot to begin exploring this colorful part of the city. Converted from a 1929 factory, the recently renovated building is colorless but comfortable. The paneled-wood decor is plain overall and getting a bit tattered. Tile bathrooms are small but neat. Corner suites are a great option, with windows facing two directions over the Old Quarter. A good Asian restaurant is on the premises, as well as an inviting lobby bar. Friendly staff members will remember your name and can suggest good places to dine and city tours.

1 Phan Dinh Phung St., Hanoi. ✆ **04/3828-2888.** Fax 04/3828-2466. galaxyhtl@vnn.vn. 60 units. $70 double; $90 suite. Rates include breakfast. AE, DC, MC, V. **Amenities:** Restaurant; bar; babysitting; room service. *In room:* A/C, satellite TV, fridge, hair dryer, minibar.

Hoa Binh Hotel ★ Built in 1926 and recently renovated, the Hoa Binh is a good, atmospheric choice. Comfort and history meet here, and whether you're walking up the big, creaky grand staircase or opening French doors onto a balcony overlooking the busy street, you know that you're in Hanoi. Sizable rooms have original light fixtures, molded ceilings, and gloss-wood furniture. Everything is done a bit "low luxe," but the shiny polyester bedspreads, velveteen drapes, and spongy mattresses detract from the overall effect. Bathrooms are plain and small but spotless. The hotel, popular with tour groups, is in a prime downtown location, and the bar has a view of the city. Ask to see a room before checking in, because they vary in size, shape, and degree of smoke.

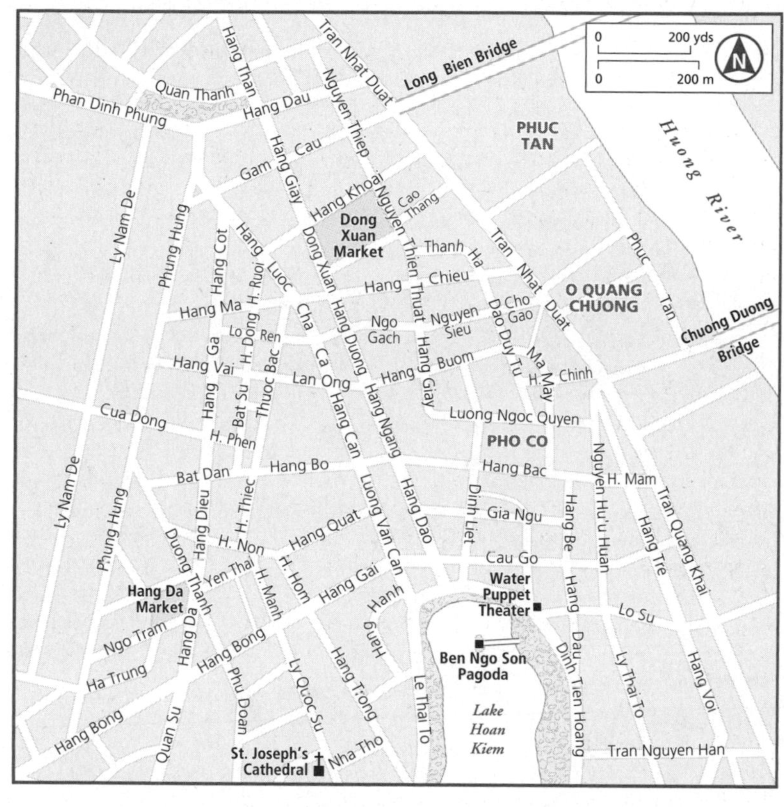

27 Ly Thuong Kiet St., Hoan Kiem District, Hanoi. ✆ **04/3825-3315** or 3825-3692. Fax 04/3826-9818. www.hoabinhhotel.com. 100 units. $80 double; $130–$150 suite. Rates include breakfast. AE, MC, V. **Amenities:** 2 restaurants; 2 bars; concierge; room service; sauna; smoke-free rooms. *In room:* A/C, TV, fridge, hair dryer, Internet, minibar.

Majestic Salute Hotel ★ The Majestic Salute is the flagship of the A–Z Salute Café empire—a little streetside traveler cafe that's grown in increments over the years to own guesthouses, a minihotel, and now this midrange venture. The Majestic's lobby has a funky 1960s retro feel, the kind of place where Austin Powers might feel at ease after a night at the clubs. Rooms are large and cozy, a basic high-end minihotel standard. The thin office-style carpeting in both public and private spaces is unfortunate, but some rooms have neat anterooms and are quite spacious. The hotel is just north of the main action in the Old Quarter, with entrances onto both Hang Duong, a street that becomes a walking district on weekend nights, and Cha Ca Street (near the popular restaurant Cha Ca La Vong, a Hanoi institution). Double-glazed windows throughout the hotel mean that though the hotel is sandwiched between some of the Old Quarter's busiest (honk-honk) streets, rooms are quite quiet.

54–56 Hang Duong/19 Cha Ca St., Hoan Kiem District, Hanoi. ✆ **04/3923-0036.** Fax 04/3923-0037. www.majesticsalutehotel.com. 37 units. $85–$102 double; $120 suite. MC, V. **Amenities:** 2 restaurants; lobby lounge bar; health club; room service. *In room:* A/C, satellite TV, fridge, minibar.

Quoc Hoa ★ The Quoc Hoa is a cozier, more upmarket choice than your average Old Quarter minihotel. The branding is something like the little Church Hotel (see above). Standard rooms are clean and have many amenities, but they're cramped into a smaller space. Superior rooms are worth the extra $20: They're larger and have nicer furnishing and amenities. Deluxe rooms are just slightly larger than standard rooms. The contemporary design isn't flashy, but crisp and inviting. Service is good—in fact, the Quoc Hoa caters to a large contingent of Swiss and Japanese business visitors on a regular basis—some long-staying customers—and the front-desk staff really snaps to and even anticipates guests' needs. A tiny fitness center is on the top floor, and the casual restaurant is inviting. Your minihotel neighbors will be envious.

10 Bat Dan St., Hoan Kiem District, Hanoi. ✆ **04/3828-4528.** Fax 04/3826-7424. www.quochoahotel.com. 37 units. $71–$100 double; $143 suite. MC, V. **Amenities:** Restaurant; bar; fitness center; Jacuzzi; room service. *In room:* A/C, satellite TV, fridge, hair dryer, minibar.

Thien Tan ★ From the same folks who gave the city Church Hotel (see above), this tiny boutique hotel opened in March 2007. The entrance is marked by a narrow spiral staircase, which is quaint, unless you have to drag heavy luggage up to your fourth-floor room. Rooms are actually more spacious, have more natural lighting, and are in overall better condition than at their sister hotel. The service staff is super friendly and genuinely concerned about meeting your needs (a very distraught woman at the front desk worried over the quality of breakfast when I couldn't quite finish the heaps of bacon, eggs, and toast).

12 Cha Ca St., Hoan Kiem District, Hanoi. ✆ **04/3824-4005.** Fax 04/824-4004. thientanhotel@viettel.com.vn. 5 units. $40 double. MC, V. **Amenities:** Restaurant. *In room:* A/C, satellite TV, fridge, hair dryer, high-speed Internet, minibar.

INEXPENSIVE

Camellia Hotel Group Run in conjunction with **ODC Travel,** a Hanoi-based tour company, the folks at the Camellia Group manage a number of good, basic budget stops in the city's Old Quarter. They are not affiliated with the Camellia Mini Hotel below. Here you'll find basic rooms, friendly service, and little else. The best of the six properties is Camellia II on Long Ngoc Quyen. These hotels are always booked, so be sure to contact them in advance. If Hotel II is booked, try their nearby Anh Dao Hotel. All of these properties have good Internet terminals in the lobby and offer a host of tour itineraries. In fact, most big groups staying here—usually French budget tours—have organized their journey through ODC.

Camellia Hotel 1: 12 Pho Hue St. ✆ **04/3822-5140.** 35 units. Camellia Hotel III: 31 Hang Dieu. ✆ **04/3828-5704.** 16 units. Camellia Hotel IV (Phan Thai Hotel): 44 Hang Giay St. ✆ **04/3824-3667.** 20 units. Camellia Hotel V: 81 Thuoc Bac St. ✆ **04/3828-2376.** 18 units. www.camellia-hotels.com. $35–$80 double. MC, V. **Amenities:** Restaurant; bikes; Internet. *In room:* A/C, satellite TV, fridge, Internet.

The Camellia Mini Hotel ★ For simplicity and comfort, this minihotel, just a short walk north of Nha Tho Street and the old Catholic cathedral—now a popular gallery-and-cafe area—is a no-frills choice that fires on all cylinders. Camellia, not to be confused with the growing Camellia hotel empire in the backpacker area of the Old Quarter (see above), is down a quiet side street and offers guests a clean, quiet room with air-conditioning, hot water, and cable television. Doubles with a balcony and windows facing the street are just 750,000 VND. Breakfast is included. Staffers are very helpful, will take care of any extra bags you leave while on overnight trips, and are very prompt about laundry service. A great choice for a simple, affordable home base while traveling the north. Should you speak French—or Chinese—you might even make a few new friends, as the little lobby is always abuzz with expat comings and goings.

12 Chan Cam St. (just north of St. Joseph's Cathedral), Hanoi. ✆ **04/3828-5936.** Fax 04/828-9409. 17 units. 300,000 VND–750,000 VND double. No credit cards. **Amenities:** Restaurant (breakfast only). *In room:* A/C, satellite TV, fridge.

Hanoi Backpackers' Hostel Here's a budget choice and the first real-deal youth hostel in Vietnam. There are three dorm rooms for up to 10 folks, one room for 12, and one set aside for ladies only (one they like to call the "Nunnery"). This is a great place to meet other folks (no other choice, really) in a hearty, wholesome environment. There's self-service cooking in the first-floor kitchen, and folks here—both staff and fellow travelers—are very helpful, passing on information about routes outside of the city. Beds are clean and spacious, with nice thick duvets and air-conditioning for summer months. Yes, it's a hostel, but everything is in tiptop shape and very clean. The rooftop bar, called Charlie Don't Surf, is also a barbecue area, rocks late some nights, and is a mellow place to put your feet up on others.

48 Ngo Huyen St. (down a small lane just north of St. Joseph's, the big Catholic cathedral), Hoan Kiem District, Hanoi. ✆ **04/828-5372.** www.hanoibackpackershostel.com. $7.50 dorm bed; $18–$36 double. No credit cards. **Amenities:** Restaurant (breakfast only) and shared kitchen; Internet; tour services. *In room:* A/C, no phone.

Hong Ngoc Hotel ★★ With four locations right in the heart of the Old Quarter, this is a good no-frills option close to Hoan Kiem Lake. The staff has an amazingly friendly, can-do attitude and can help you with any detail, like renting a car, motorbike, or bicycle. Rooms are compact but all have the quality amenities of a proper hotel. For those traveling with their own computers, the budget locations (Hang Bac St. and Ma May St.) offer in-room wireless connections; the other locations have faster ADSL connections. Larger suites are a good choice, and all rooms are done in dark wooden trim. Bathrooms are small and clean. This is an affordable minihotel with attitude—like a terrier who thinks himself a Great Dane.

14 Luong Van Can St., Hoan Kiem District, Hanoi. ✆ **04/3826-7566.** Fax 04/3824-5362. 34 Hang Manh St., Hoan Kiem. ✆ **04/3828-5053.** Fax 04/3828-5054. 99 Ma May St. Hoan Kiem. ✆ **04/3828-3631.** 39 Hang Bac St., Hoan Kiem. ✆ **04/3926-0322.** 97 Nguyen Truong To. ✆ **04/3829-2025.** hongngochotel@hn.vnn.vn. Total of 110 units. $25–$30 double at the budget locations; $50–$125 double at other locations. MC, V. **Amenities:** Restaurant; Internet; room service. *In room:* A/C, satellite TV, fridge, Internet, minibar.

Phuc Loi ★ This is a standard Old Quarter minihotel, but everything here is supertidy and ornate. Rooms are small but spotless, with faux-wood floors and high ceilings. This place is relatively new and everything is in good shape. The fine-size bathrooms provide tub/showers, granite counters, and patterned wall tiles. Try for one of the three large split-level VIP rooms—they're very comfortable and a steal at $35. Rooms on higher floors have great views of the Old Quarter. The staff is friendly and helpful.

128 Hang Bong St., Old Quarter, Hanoi. ✆ **04/3928-5235.** Fax 04/3828-9897. phucloihotel@fpt.vn. 22 units. $35–$70 double. MC, V. **Amenities:** Bar; bikes; small gym. *In room:* A/C, satellite TV, fridge, hair dryer, minibar.

Prince Hotel I & II This is a classic old minihotel in the Old Quarter. Nothing frilly, rooms at the Prince Hotels (both 1 and 2) are basic decorless spaces with dark-wood furnishings, tile floors, air-conditioning, and hot water. The front-desk staff might at first appear helpful until you realize they're trying to sell you the kitchen sink in terms of tours and rentals, but that's their job. The place is a good budget base for exploring the Old Quarter. Rooms at the back, away from the busy street, are your best bet. They have two addresses, both nearby in the heart of the Old Quarter.

Prince I: 51 Luong Ngoc Quyen St., Old Quarter, Hanoi. ✆ **04/3828-0155.** Fax 04/3828-0156. Prince II: 42B Hang Giay St., Old Quarter, Hanoi. ✆ **04/3926-1203.** Fax 04/3828-0156. www.hanoiprincehotel.com. $15–$25 double. Total of 26 units. MC, V. *In room:* A/C, satellite TV, fridge, minibar.

Salute Hotel Downtown, in the heart of the Old Quarter chaos on Hang Dau Street (just north of Hoan Kiem Lake), is Salute Hotel—the first and most humble offering by the friendly folks at A–Z Salute Café. A huge two-room suite goes for $45. There's an elevator, unique in minihotels, and the lobby is enclosed and air-conditioned. Popular with Australian travelers, the hotel is staffed by a very friendly lot who can help out with any detail.

7 Hang Dau St., Hoan Kiem District, Hanoi. ✆ **04/3825-8003.** Fax 04/3934-3607. 15 units. $30–$80 double. MC, V. **Amenities:** Restaurant; bar. *In room:* A/C, satellite TV, fridge, hair dryer, Internet, minibar.

4 WHERE TO DINE

It's hard to have a bad meal in Hanoi. Almost every ethnic food variation is well represented in the city—from Italian, to Indian, to vegetarian options, to familiar Western fare. Years of brutal colonial rule by the French left many resentments, but no amount of anti-foreign revolutionary zeal could overcome Vietnamese culinary traditions borrowed from their one-time oppressors. The baguette lives on, and the legacy of fine French cuisine can be found in every quarter (and the French chefs are coming back to train this next generation as well). In Hanoi, look out for both classical French and Vietnamese fusion fare, all priced for varying budgets. The city now hosts a number of fine high-end Vietnamese restaurants where you can try local specialties without worrying about getting dysentery. But for authentic Vietnamese fare, try the squat stool places at streetside. Check the special sidebar below for good no-frills local dining options. Hanoi is a great place to eat adventurously and belly-up to good local cuisine.

EXPENSIVE

Bleu de Thuy ★★ (Finds) FUSION This gem of a restaurant is set in a gorgeous converted French colonial house. The main floor is done in warm yellows and blue trim. Upstairs offers terrace seating, and on cooler nights, the side patio sandwiched between the restaurant and an exposed brick wall offers cozy private dining. Their imaginative dishes are crisp and light, and beautifully presented. An order of sea bass is topped with a tiger prawn wrapped in crisp strips of deep-fried lotus and tastes even better than it looks. They also have nothing to hide with their open kitchen—no need to hesitate when ordering their salmon tartar, which is minced to perfection. The menu is updated every month; ask for suggestions or opt for their degustation (or "tasting") menu, which is billed as the ultimate culinary journey.

28 Tong Duy Tan St., Hoan Kiem District. ✆ **04/3928-5900.** Main courses 180,000 VND–252,000 VND. MC, V. Daily 11:30am–2pm and 6-11pm.

Club de L'Oriental ★★★ VIETNAMESE This is upscale Vietnamese food at its best—beautiful colonial decor, properly trained staff, and amazing food. The fresh spring rolls are the best in town, though I can never choose between those and the deep-fried

Imperial-style spring rolls, so I often order both and end up stuffing myself before the entrees arrive. For mains, I highly recommend the grilled chicken in lemon leaves served with a dipping plate of salt and pepper in a sprinkle of lime juice, a light but savory dish. On the richer side, try the sautéed prawns in tamarind sauce. The main floor has a handful of tables set up around an open kitchen, seats around which are perfect for couples or single diners. For an intimate but chilly experience, reserve a table in the wine cellar.

22 Tong Dan, Hoan Kiem District. ✆ **04/3826-8801.** Reservations recommended. Main courses $8.25–$15; set menu $29 lunch, from $35 dinner. AE, MC, V. Daily 11am–2pm and 6–11pm.

La Badiane ★★ FRENCH Local chef Benjamin Rascalou's new restaurant is a tasty addition to Hanoi's fine-dining scene. La Badiane is housed in an old colonial villa divided into a small garden courtyard on the ground floor and a pair of intimate dining rooms upstairs. The three set-price dinner menus include flavorful options like coffee-marinated lamb. Service is also top-notch here, which is quite an accomplishment for such an intimate place. This is Rascalou's first restaurant, but he is well respected in the local foodie community for his stunning work at the Green Tangerine, where he served as head chef for 6 years prior to opening La Badiane.

10 Nam Ngu St. ✆ **04/3942-4509.** Reservations recommended. Main courses $14–$18; set menus $11 lunch, $23–$29 dinner. AE, MC, V. Daily 11:30am–2pm and 6–10pm.

La Verticale ★★ FUSION Chef and owner Didier Corlou has lived in Vietnam for 18 years and has a clear love affair with spices. Not only do magical spice combinations make appearances in La Verticale's tasty food, but they are also infused into the restaurant's decor—tables are sprinkled with star anise, chopsticks rest on curls of cinnamon, and colorful peppercorns lie in shallow bowls. The menu changes by season, but expect to find inventive dishes marked with a strong Vietnamese base. If it's available, I highly recommend the pork served five ways. The succulent fatty cubes braised in red sauce is divine, as is the thin loin strip marinated in soy sauce.

19 Ngo Van So St. ✆ **04/3944-6317.** Reservations recommended. Main courses $17–$36. AE, MC, V. Daily 11:30am–2pm and 6–10pm.

Press Club ★ CONTINENTAL Don't be fooled by the elite address and elegant atmosphere: The Press Club is the kind of place that impresses, but it's far more affordable and accessible than its reputation and stylish dining room might indicate. The old-boys' network still digs it, but the Press Club is also attracting a younger, hipper crowd. The indoor restaurant is sizable yet private, done in dark tones of maroon and forest green with solid wood furniture and detailing. Outdoor seating is available on the terrace facing a large stage that features regular live music acts. The service is impeccable. The menu is full of sumptuous Continental standards: antipasto starters, goat-cheese salad, tuna steak, and various wood-grilled imported steaks and meat dishes. Savory entrees include the filet of barramundi with clam crust Creole sauce and rice croquette, roasted salmon specials, and imported spatchcock served with sweet potatoes in a Dauphinoise and citrus sauce. For dessert, try the white-chocolate sticky rice or rich rice pudding. On the ground floor, there's a casual and cozy coffee corner called the **Deli** (see "Snacks & Cafes," later in this chapter).

59A Ly Thai To St., Hoan Kiem District. ✆ **04/3934-0888.** www.hanoi-pressclub.com. Reservations recommended. Main courses $16–$40. AE, MC, V. Daily 11am–2pm and 6–10:30pm.

Vine ★ FUSION All good things must come to an end. For about 5 years, Vine reigned supreme as *the* place to find a fabulous meal in Hanoi any day of the week. But ownership

The Best Authentic Local Fare

Hanoi's local cuisine is some of the best in Vietnam, and the finest local dishes are served at small one-dish restaurants, usually just open-air joints at street side, where you might wonder why there's a line out the door. To Vietnamese, it's about the food, not the atmosphere. Some of the best meals in the capital—or anywhere in Vietnam, for that matter—are eaten on squat stools with disposable chopsticks. Standards of hygiene might appear poor, but do as locals do and wipe down bowls and chopsticks with a napkin before tucking in. Yes, eating on the street does mean you might have some tummy trouble, but if you stick to the few places recommended below, you should be okay.

The ubiquitous *pho*—noodle soup served with slices of beef *(bo)* or chicken *(ga),* fresh bean sprouts, and condiments—can be found anywhere. And don't miss *cha ca,* Hanoi's famed spicy fish fry-up (see below).

Banh Cuon ★, 14 Hang Ga St. (✆ **04/3828-0108**), consists of minced pork and mushrooms rolled into soft rice crepes topped with crispy fried garlic and coriander. Cut-up pieces are dipped in a tasty fish sauce. The stuffing-to-crepe ratio at this streetside eatery is a bit on the low side, but it is still great value for money, at 20,000 VND a plate.

Bun Bo Nam Bo ★★, 67 Hang Dieu St. (✆ **04/3923-0701**), serves only one main course: *bun bo,* a dish of fresh rice noodles topped with crisp fried garlic, bean sprouts, peanuts, basil, and beef, that costs only 30,000 VND. Sound simple? It is. It is the subtlety of the flavors of this dish and the stock that brings 'em here in droves. Just order by holding up as many fingers as you want bowls of *bun bo,* take a seat at the low tables in the brightly lit interior, and wait. A spartan atmosphere, but a rich and delicious dish worth hunting down. No credit cards. Daily 7am to 10:30pm.

Cha Ca La Vong ★★, 14 Cha Ca St. (✆ **04/3825-3929**), is on a street called Cha Ca, and it serves one dish . . . you guessed it . . . *cha ca* (100,000 VND per person). So what's the story with *cha ca?* Very simple: It's a delicate whitefish, fried at high heat in peanut oil with dill, turmeric, rice noodles, and peanuts—and it's delicious. The place is pretty grungy, and to call the service "indifferent" would be to sing its praises, but that's the beauty here: It's all about the food. You order by saying how many you are and how many bottles of beer or soda you'd like. Then it's do-it-yourself, with some gruff guidance, as you stir in the ingredients on a frying pan over a charcoal hibachi right at the table. It's a rich dish and great with some hot sauce (go easy on it at first), and it makes for a fun and interesting evening. Just say "Cha Ca" and any cabdriver can take you there. Avoid copycats: There are a few copycat "Cha Ca La Vong" restaurants on the same street serving this dish on electric grills, so make sure you've got the right address before you sit down and order. No credit cards. Daily 11am to 2pm and 5 to 9pm.

Gia Thuyen Pho (Noodle Soup) ★★, 49 Bat Dan St. (on the west side of the Old Quarter near the old citadel wall), is a very popular storefront *pho* noodle soup stand in Hanoi's Old Quarter. If you've seen the Japanese film *Tampopo,* about the making of the perfect noodle soup, or saw the *Seinfeld* episode about New York City's "Soup Nazi" who, because of his quality broth, chose his customers instead of vice versa, you'll have an idea what it's like. The line is around the block day and night, as Hanoians of all stripes humbly cue up for a taste of the best. The formula is simple: delicious cured beef, fresh noodles, and spices—done the same way, over and over, for years. Just order "One please" (it is *pho* with beef or nothing) and pay the surly lady, who might even let a few customers go ahead of you if she doesn't like the cut of your jib. Unlike in most *pho* joints, no one serves you, so you have to carry your own bowl to an open slot at a crowded table (if you come with a friend, you might have to separate), and the place is as grotty as any little noodle stand, but when you pull those first noodles off the chopsticks and follow with a spoonful of broth, you'll know why you came. No phone. One bowl of beef *pho* is 25,000 VND. Daily 6 to 11am and 6 to 11pm.

Nguyen Sinh Restaurant Francais, 17–19 Ly Quoc St., directly north on the street that runs in front of the Nha Tho Cathedral (✆ **04/3826-5234**). What is so Vietnamese about this French restaurant? Everything. Founded in 1950, these folks were the ones (among many) who kept alive the art of baking bread and cooking French foods. Vietnamese French has its own bend, say French expats, and in Hanoi it's a cuisine of its own. This little storefront offers good imported cheese and wine; it's sort of like Hanoi's de facto New York deli (it'll do in a pinch, anyway, for that late-night snack). Here you can get a delicious baguette with cheese and pâté for just 35,000 VND, or a savory steak fry-up French style. You'll find locals in berets trying out their newest licks on the saxophone, and French expats getting a little taste of home, chatting with the Francophone clientele. Très chic. Daily 7am to 10pm.

Restaurant Lau Tu Xuyen, 163 Yen Phu, with another location at 199 Duong Nghi Tam (✆ **04/3714-0289**), is a fun adventure. Way out on the eastern shore of West Lake (about 30,000 VND by taxi from the city center), this big warehouse of a restaurant is the best place in town to enjoy the real *lau,* or Vietnamese hot pot. Go with a Vietnamese friend or be open to some creative charades with your waitress; there's no English menu, and foreign visitors are rare. The official directions for cooking hot pot? As my friend says, "You just put." Add whatever you like—fresh seafood, beef, poultry, and vegetables—to a shared pot of boiling broth on a hot plate in the center of the table. They also can bring out a barbecue setup for small kabobs. You order like you would order dim sum, choosing plates of raw ingredients off a tray. The place is packed in the evenings, especially in the winter (this is Vietnam's version of stew) and on weekends. The entry is just adjacent to the Thang Loi Lakeside hotel. The local draft beer flows freely and costs little. Make a night of it and end with a walk in this busy expat neighborhood. Expect to pay about $5 per person in a group. No credit cards. Daily 11am to 10pm.

squabbles and staff departures spell bad times for this West Lake restaurant. For now, signature dishes like the tuna tartare and lobster bisque remain unrivaled in the city. Mains are starting to slip, though; their famed pizza lacked the crispy, savory zip of previous times, and the vegetarian lasagna was full of bitter mushrooms, stingy on spinach, and buried in far too much cheese. Memorable evenings can still be had, especially if you reserve a table in the wine cellar or grab one of the corner getaways on the second floor.

1A Xuan Dieu, Tay Ho District. ✆ **04/3719-8000.** Main courses $11–$85. AE, MC, V. Daily 9am until last order.

Wild Lotus ★★ CONTEMPORARY VIETNAMESE City sounds—and smells—melt away as you climb up a marble staircase, past two small lotus ponds and a waterfall, to get to the main floor of this restaurant, housed inside an old French building. The ambience is upscale Asian chic, with a bouquet of lotuses on every table, wooden furniture, and original art pieces on the wall by established Vietnamese artists like Vo Van Long. From the kitchen comes gorgeous Vietnamese food with added hints of spices from Thailand. I highly recommend the peanut-crusted shrimp with green mango salad, and grilled fish tikka in pandanus leaves with tartar and sweet chili. Both are light dishes that carry just the right amount of spunk, thanks to the tart green mango and sweet chili sauce. ***Tip:*** The restaurant serves portions that are meant to be shared, so if dining alone, ask about half-portions so you can try more than one dish.

55A Nguyen Du St. ✆ **04/3943-9342.** Fax 04/3943-9341. Main courses 120,000 VND–200,000 VND. MC, V. Daily 11am–11pm.

Wild Rice (Lá Luá) ★ ASIAN FUSION Nothing about Lá Luá portends to be authentic Vietnamese; everything from the decor to the dining is, in fact, an amalgam of traditions and customs. The place looks like an upmarket L.A. bistro borrowing Japanese themes, with tall stands of bamboo encased in glass, slate floors, and bright white walls that shine with the mellow glow of indirect lighting. The food is good Vietnamese-influenced fare. My grilled chicken in chili with lemon grass was deliciously spicy and savory. Try the barbecued squid or beef with coconut. Presentation is Zen simple: white linen with black chopsticks, a plate, a bowl, and a candle on the table, and it's as if the staff is playing a game of chess on your table, rearranging things as if they'd rather not disturb the utensil still life. It's all a bit studied, really, but the food is very good.

6 Ngo Thi Nham St., Ba Trung. ✆ **04/3943-8896.** Fax 04/3943-6299. Main courses $16–$60. AE, MC, V. Daily 11am–2pm and 6–10pm.

MODERATE

Al Fresco's (Kids) TEX-MEX Run by Australian expats, Al Fresco's two floors of friendly, casual dining is sort of like a T.G.I. Friday's reincarnated in Vietnam. With checkered tablecloths, good oldies music, and a great view from the second floor to the street below, this is the place to bring the kids (or yourself) when they're in need of a slice of home. The only reason to visit this place is for the ribs, which are a house specialty. Desserts are good standbys like brownies a la mode. The wine list is heavy on Australian and inexpensive South American reds. If you've had enough of fried rice or noodle soup, come here for something to stick to your ribs.

23L Hai Ba Trung St., Hoan Kiem District. ✆ **04/3826-7782.** Main courses 150,000 VND–180,000 VND. MC, V. Daily 9:30am–11pm.

Brother's Café VIETNAMESE Buffet only, Brother's is an inexpensive starting point to explore gourmet Vietnamese cuisine. Lunch includes dishes such as salted chicken, sweet-and-sour bean sprouts, shrimp, noodles, and spring rolls; a full dessert table of sweet tofu, sweet baby rice, dragon fruit, and other exotic offerings; and fresh lemon or melon juice. Dinner features grilled items—shrimp, fish, lamb, and pork—and a glass of wine. There are faux street stalls encircling the garden, with Vietnamese favorites like *pho* (noodle soup) and *bun cha* (cold rice noodles, spring rolls, and lettuce eaten by dipping into a slightly sweet sauce with meat). But be forewarned: The place is virtually overrun by tourist buses during peak lunch- and dinnertimes.

26 Nguyen Thai Hoc. ✆ **04/3733-3866.** www.brothercafe.com. Lunch $11; dinner $17. AE, DC, MC, V. Daily 11:30am–2pm and 6:15–10:30pm.

Club Opera ★ VIETNAMESE Just next to the Press Club and across from the Sofitel Metropole, this exclusive little bistro, like its sister, the Emperor, serves delicious Vietnamese food that's a bit dolled up for the foreign palate—and priced to the foreign wallet. They have all kinds of Vietnamese fare, from Hue specials like crispy fried spring rolls to delicate, smaller versions of *banh khoi* (fried doughy pancakes filled with vegetables, herbs, and shrimp). You'll also find stir-fries and hot-pot specials, as well as grilled chicken in lemon grass and rich fried squid. The atmosphere is a retro French villa, with lots of cozy romantic nooks and candlelight.

59 Ly Thai To St., Hoan Kiem District. ✆ **04/3824-6950.** Main courses $9.50–$16. AE, MC, V. Daily 11am–2pm and 6–10:30pm.

Garden Restaurant ★ VIETNAMESE The Garden Restaurant is a low-luxe, authentic Vietnamese restaurant that attracts a few tourists (and small tour groups) in the know. With cool courtyard seating and cozy inside dining, this is a good place to try real Hanoi cuisine—stir-fries and roast dishes, as well as curries and specialties like whole fried river fish or "drunken shrimp," a dish of live prawns cooked in flaming rice whiskey and put under a cover to simmer (they flip and flop like crazy, and when they stop moving, you know the dish is done). Bring friends and settle in for a long repast. The young waitstaff are eager to practice their English and aim to please.

36 Hang Manh (west of the lake and just north of Hang Gai). ✆ **04/3824-3402.** www.hanoigarden.com. Main courses 120,000 VND–150,000 VND. MC, V. Daily 10am–2pm and 5–10pm.

Hoa Sua Training Restaurant ★ VIETNAMESE/FRENCH Do a good deed, enjoy a great feed. You'll find lots of good French and Vietnamese dishes at this popular cafe in the south end of town. Started in 1995, Hoa Sua is also an NGO and training school for disadvantaged youth, and it now has over 1,700 graduates who have gone on to all kinds of careers. Because working at the restaurant is like a final exam for these students, the young staff is as friendly as they come and every detail is well attended to. The food is great, the atmosphere in the courtyard or on one of the patios in this sprawling faux colonial is very laid-back, and the price is right. Lunch and dinner specials are written on a chalkboard, and everything—from good steak and chips, to sandwiches, to Vietnamese curry specials or fried seafood—is delicious. Best of all, the profits go to good use, providing scholarships for students and upgrading the school's service standard.

28 Ha Hoi St. ✆ **04/3942-4448.** www.hoasuaschool.com. Main courses 45,000 VND–180,000 VND. MC, V. Daily 11am–10:30pm.

Jacc's ★ INTERNATIONAL Originator of many of Hanoi's popular restaurants, Jacc's friendly Australian proprietor has hung his hat at this popular expat restaurant. Set on the fourth floor of Hanoi Towers, a popular executive service building and apartment block, Jacc's is a busy bar—elbow to elbow during post-work happy hours—and the menu features great imported steaks, fry-ups, pizzas, and some good local offerings. The glass-and-steel open area of the restaurant overlooks the nearby pool. In the evening, it's popular for dinner, drinks, and negotiations between international partners, and in the morning, it's the spot for a good fry-up breakfast.

4th floor, Hanoi Tower, 49 Hai Ba Trung. ✆ **04/3934-8325.** Main courses 150,000 VND–450,000 VND. MC, V. Daily 6:30am–midnight.

Khazänna ★★ NORTHERN INDIAN This restaurant changes names and owners every 2 years, but the current incarnation serves a fine menu of good north Indian dishes. You'll find tidy Indian-themed Western decor here with excellent service and presentation: The curries are served in small metal crocks with brass ladles. The affordable lunch menu brings in crowds of businesspeople. In the evening, choose from an extensive menu of curries, grilled dishes, and good nan breads.

1C Tong Dan St., Hoan Kiem District. ✆ **04/3934-5657.** Main courses $5–$10. MC, V. Daily 11am–2pm and 6–10pm.

Le Petit Bruxelles ★ CONTINENTAL "Little Brussels" is just that—a home away from home for Belgian and French expats. The open-air restaurant's two stories are just off of Ba Trieu in the south end of town, and the building is tucked back away from the main street to slightly deaden the many beep-beeps. The menu offers good cold starters like fresh tomato with imported mozzarella and niçoise salad. The steak and chips with fries, chicken with mushrooms in cream sauce, and steak tartare top the long list of choices (and the effusive owner is always happy to spin up something special for you). Dessert is real French *glaces,* crème caramel, or fresh fruit. The downstairs open patio area with a bar is a great spot for a drink or a coffee and chat, and at night, with candlelight, the place is romantic. It's reminiscent of something like, well, a little streetside cafe in the heart of Brussels. The good, hearty Belgian beer flows freely (but not cheaply), and special fondues are available for groups and parties.

58B Tran Quoc Toan. ✆ **04/3942-5958.** www.le-petit-bruxelles.com. Main courses $5–$12. No credit cards. Daily 11am–2pm and 5–11pm.

Luna d' Autuno ★★ ITALIAN It's all about pizza here, and it's good stuff, popular with Hanoi expats and families. In a laid-back little courtyard, connected to a popular wine bar out front, Luna d' Autuno is just the ticket for a casual meal and beers after work, a treat for the kids, or a casual night out. The portions are big, and all ingredients are good and fresh. The wood-fired, thin-crust pizza (you can specify how crunchy) lets the ingredients do the talking. You'll find no pretensions here, and the atmosphere is very casual. The staff is welcoming, and the international language of pizza overrides any language barriers. Don't miss the cool Luna Lounge, a wine bar on the second floor.

11B Dien Bien Phu. ✆ **04/3823-7338.** Main courses $6–$14. MC, V. Daily 11am–11pm.

Pane e Vino ★ ITALIAN The vaulted ceiling and huge front windows filtering in plenty of light make for fabulous ambience in this Italian restaurant. The three-course set lunch menu is an excellent value, at $7, and more than enough to fuel a traveler who's been walking all over Hanoi for the better part of 4 hours. The front table and upstairs balcony overlook the busy Old Quarter street outside, making this a perfect place for air-conditioned people-watching. Or you can reach into their basket of board games and while away some time playing Vietnamese-vocabulary Scrabble.

98 Hang Trong. ✆ **04/3928-6329.** Main courses $4–$18. MC, V. Daily 7:30am–11pm.

Tips Restaurant Tip

Note that many upscale restaurants in Hanoi levy a 5% service charge on top of the 10% government tax.

Restaurant Bobby Chinn ★★ CALIFORNIA/VIETNAMESE/FRENCH It was a sad day when Bobby Chinn had to close up the restaurant on the southwest corner of Hoan Kiem Lake, which had served for years as the place to see and be seen in Hanoi. Thankfully, Bobby took the opportunity to rework the restaurant to reflect budget-conscious times. The new place out in Xuan Dieu is a mini replica of the style and panache that made him famous in the Old Quarter, and the new streamlined menu is significantly cheaper. The main floor, with its cozy gray couches and intimate bar, is perfect for predinner cocktails. At the time of writing, only one small dining room had been set up on the second floor, though a second is on the way. Maroon cloths hang in twisted knots from the ceiling and are draped over walls, providing stark backgrounds to the restaurant's stylish selection of local art. As for food, vegetarian quesadillas served with mango salsa are an excellent starter, and while the menu offers a wonderful selection of fusion dishes, my favorite entree is the decidedly Western rack of lamb and mashed potatoes. Polish the meal off with the trio of crème brûlée and one last cocktail downstairs, and you won't regret schlepping out to the new location. Bobby doesn't drop in at the restaurant like he used to, but when he's around, he's sure to make the rounds, charming and chatting with guests (or offering a zany serenade with his acoustic guitar). He's become a small celebrity with his new cooking show on the Discovery Channel, and guests do occasionally ask for an autograph.

77 Xuan Dieu, Ba Dinh District. ✆ **04/3934-8577.** Reservations recommended. Main courses $8–$20. AE, MC, V. Daily 11am–midnight. Bar until 11:30pm.

INEXPENSIVE

Chim Sao (L'Oiseau Siffleur) ★ Finds VIETNAMESE This charming restaurant serves authentic Vietnamese dishes in a home-style ambience. Rotating art hangs on unfinished walls, and guests have to remove footwear before heading upstairs to sit on floor pillows and dine over squat tables. The English translations of dishes rarely do them justice—the "tofu with egg salted" is actually a delightful dish of cubed, battered tofu that is flash-fried for a crisp exterior. Other must-try dishes are the caramelized pork served in a piping hot clay pot, and the "mountainous flower rice," which is sticky rice served with a sprinkle of crispy fried garlic.

65 Ngo Hue, Hoan Kiem District. ✆ **04/3976-0633.** Main courses 60,000 VND–90,000 VND. No credit cards. Daily 11am–2pm and 5:30–10pm.

Le Café des Arts de Hanoi ★ BISTRO/CONTINENTAL After strolling around Hoan Kiem Lake, stop off at its northwest end for a drink or a bite at this friendly bistro-style eatery, run by French expats and open all day. Spacious, with tiled floors and shuttered windows looking into the narrow Old Quarter street below, the cafe has casual rattan furniture and a long, inviting bar, and it doubles as an art gallery, which explains the interesting paintings hanging throughout. The Vietnamese art crowd also provides some attractive local color. Most inviting, however, is the excellent food. Ask for the special of the day, and stick to bistro standbys like the omelets or a *croque madame*—toasted bread and cheese sautéed in egg—and house specialty *salade bressare* (fresh chicken and vegetables in a light mayonnaise sauce). There are also excellent lunch set specials and good house wine by the glass.

11B Ngo Bao Khanh, Hoan Kiem District (in the Old Quarter). ✆ **04/3828-7207.** Main courses $12–$22. No credit cards. Daily 11am–11pm. Bar open until midnight.

Mediterraneo ★ ITALIAN A tasty but typical range of northern Italian fare is served at this mellow streetside cafe on Nha Tho, Hanoi's stylish cafe area (called Church St.). Prosciutto with melon, and tomato and mozzarella are good starters. Follow with homemade pasta, a grilled dish, or pizza. You'll also find here daily specials and a good wine list. This is an affordable, cozy, and casual spot.

23 Nha Tho St., Hoan Kiem (near the Old Church). ✆ **04/3826-6288.** Main courses $5–$14. MC, V. Daily 9am–11pm.

Puku ★ Finds NEW ZEALAND This hidden gem of a cafe is a growing hit with local expats. The interior is bohemian eclectic; an unfinished coat of peacock-blue paint adorns the walls, and lamps made from what looks like inverted rice bowls are suspended from the ceiling with scarlet-colored velvet ropes. There's outdoor bar-stool seating on their small balcony, or you can curl up on their blue-and-orange couch. The music matches the zany decor. A folk singer's acoustic rendition of Beyoncé's "Crazy in Love" was playing as I waited for my meal. Puku, which means "Belly" in Maori, the language of the indigenous New Zealand people of the same name, serves up hearty open sandwiches, pastas, and pastries. The Kia sandwich, a grilled open-faced sandwich topped with pesto, chicken, and cheese, and served with saffron mayo and a small green salad, is a hearty lunch of champions. To get to the restaurant, head into the small door to the right of the big gallery located at the same address, head down the corridor, and take the first set of stairs to your left.

60 Hang Trong St., Hoan Kiem District. ✆ **04/3928-5244.** Main courses 50,000 VND–70,000 VND. No credit cards. Daily 7:30am–10:30pm.

Quan An Ngon ★★★ VIETNAMESE *Ngon* means "delicious" in Vietnamese, and this lively restaurant and its extensive menu live up to its name. Sit at the elbow-to-elbow tables in the open air or else inside, where it's cooler and quieter. The bustling courtyard, filled with Vietnamese professionals and students, is surrounded by well-stocked, clean food stalls, reminiscent of what you might find, at random, on the street, but without some of the, uh, hygiene concerns. My personal favorites are the pounded shrimp fried on sugar cane, served with greens that you then wrap in the accompanying rice paper, and the sautéed beef with salad greens. The spring rolls are a bit dry here, but still tasty. Prices are incredibly reasonable, and you can go to the cooking stations on the sides to check out tasty options; this is a great place to explore a wide-ranging sample of Vietnamese fare.

18 Phan Boi Chau St., Hoan Kiem District. ✆ **04/3942-8162.** Main courses 26,000 VND–115,000 VND. MC, V. Daily 7am–10pm.

Restaurant 69 ★ VIETNAMESE The number is just the address on busy little Ma May Street, right in the heart of the Old Quarter tourist area. Set in an old converted traditional shop house, Restaurant 69 is worth it if only for the atmosphere. Go for a table on the second-floor balcony, if you can. There's a novella of a menu with lots of local specials, anything from *pho* (Vietnamese noodle soup) and *bun bo Hue* (a dish of rice vermicelli and beef popular in the town of Hue in central Vietnam), to good stir-fries and seafood hot pots. The clay-pot dishes are popular, too. Soups, salads, and sandwiches pretty much cover all the bases, and the friendly staff makes this a welcome place to beat the heat (or get warm) and have a snack while touring the Old Quarter.

69 Ma May St., Hoan Kiem. ✆ **04/3926-1720.** Main courses $4–$6. No credit cards. Daily 9am–11pm.

Tamarind Café ★★ VEGETARIAN Tamarind is a laid-back, friendly spot, and, even if you're not a vegetarian, this welcoming cafe's inventive menu will tickle your fancy. Soups like vegetarian wonton and two-color soup (spinach and sweet potato) take the chill off Hanoi winter nights and go great with the selection of sandwiches. Other inventive options here include "Ratatofu," ratatouille over tofu, and the Tamarind salad—diced onions, cucumber, tomatoes, mango, and avocado over a bed of crisp lettuce served with honey vinaigrette—is a fabulous summer lunch. Fruit shakes and excellent teas round out the meal. It's not only a great place to take a break from the hectic traffic of the Old Quarter and relax, but also a good place to meet other travelers and pick up advice. The cafe is full early in the morning, when large groups of travelers setting out with **Handspan Travel** meet here for breakfast before their trips.

80 Ma May St., Hoan Kiem District. ✆ **04/3926-0580.** Main courses $5–$6. MC, V. Daily 6am–11pm.

Tandoor ★ INDIAN Tandoor is a long-popular Indian-food enclave, popular with both young travelers looking for a bit of a curry fix after weeks on the road with nothing but rice and noodle dishes, as well as expats feeding a family (they have free delivery service and takeout). The same owners run another popular Indian joint across town, called **Dakshin,** at 94 Hang Trong St. (just north of the church, Nha Tho; ✆ **04/3928-6872**), which is focused on vegetarian cuisine. Try the delicious kabobs served from an authentic *tandoor* oven—hence the name—and any of the delicious curries. Daily set menus for lunch and dinner are affordable and offer a good range of dishes, hitting all the right points on your palate, from spicy, to salty, to sweet. Go for the prime balcony table on the second floor overlooking the busy street out front.

24 Hang Be St., Hoan Kiem District. ✆ **04/3824-5359.** Main courses 45,000 VND–250,000 VND. MC, V. Daily 11am–2:30pm and 6–10:30pm.

SNACKS & CAFES

Life moves fast in the busy city, but Hanoians are fond of their coffee and taking time to sit back and watch it go by. Below are just a few of the many cafes in town. Hanoi's cafes open early for breakfast (about 7am) and close around 9pm. Bring cash; only larger restaurants accept credit cards.

Ciao Café An outlet of this popular Saigon chain, Ciao Café is a cool two-story place just south of the lake, with cozy booths and a funky, Art Deco style all its own. It attracts mostly locals, making it a fun hangout and people-watching perch.

2 Hang Bai St. ✆ **04/3934-1494.** Daily 7am–11pm.

Finds A Scoop

Check out the **local ice-cream shops** along Trang Tien Street between the lake and the Dan Chu Hotel. For 3,000 VND, enjoy a cone and be part of the local scene.

The Deli Located on the first floor of the Press Club (p. 89), the Deli—along with its adjacent coffee corner, Le Comptoire—is a good place to grab a local or international paper and enjoy a relaxed lunch of sandwiches and gourmet pizzas, not to mention the Aussie pie with chips or "Mom's Meatloaf." It's a bit pricey, but there's free Wi-Fi, so bring your laptop and get connected.

59A Ly Thai To St., Hoan Kiem District. ✆ **04/3934-0888.** www.hanoi-pressclub.com. Daily 7am–10pm.

Fanny's Ice Cream ★★ One of the main attractions around Hoan Kiem Lake (for me) is Fanny's Ice Cream on the west side of the lake. They serve exquisite gelato-style ice cream.

48 Le Thai To (on the western edge of Hoan Kiem Lake). ✆ **04/3828-5689.** Daily 10am–10pm.

Highland's Coffee ★ Highland's is the local version of Starbucks—a popular place to beat the heat and have a good, strong cup of coffee. The best location is lakeside on the sixth floor of the massive wedge-shaped building that overlooks a busy traffic circle and the north end of the lake. Red couches are set up in intimate arrangements on platforms overlooking the busy anthill below: a good meeting point. Alternatively, head to their hip outdoor courtyard between the Hilton and the Hanoi Opera House (✆ **04/3 933-4947**). This is a great place to enjoy any kind of espresso or cappuccino, Italian sodas, snacks, sandwiches, pizzas, and good breakfasts, all while looking out over the lake or watching the hustle and flow of traffic below.

3/F 1-3-5 Dinh Tien Hoang St. (across the street from northeast corner of Hoan Kiem Lake). ✆ **04/3936-3228.** Daily 7am–9pm.

KOTO (Know One Teach One) ★ Why not put your ice-cream money to work for a good cause? KOTO is an acronym for "Know One Teach One," and like Hoa Sua (p. 93), the cafe is just one arm of a grass-roots humanitarian program to train Hanoi kids in the service industry. Australian expats run the program and teach English, comportment, food preparation, and service skills at their cozy little storefront. Just around the corner from the Temple of Literature in Dong Da District (p. 110), KOTO is the best choice for refreshment after touring the sight. Pop in for good soups and sandwiches, as well as a host of sweet treats and good coffee.

59 Van Mieu St., Dong Da District. ✆ **04/3747-0337.** Fax 04/3747-0339. www.streetvoices.com.au. Daily 7am–10pm.

La Place Tucked in a quiet alleyway just off the square out in front of St. Joseph's Cathedral (Nha Tho), La Place is a lounge cafe with good coffees, mellow music, great breakfasts, and desserts.

4 Au Trieu. ✆ **04/3928-5859.** Daily 7:30am–10:30pm.

Little Hanoi Just north of the lake, this local-style fast-food joint has a basic but tidy bamboo-and-wood decor. Overlooking the busy street, it's a good place for breakfast and to watch the world go by on roaring motorbikes. A limited menu offers local favorites like banana flower salad and noodle soup, and Little Hanoi makes a good central meeting point. They deliver, too.

21 Hang Gai St. ✆ **04/3828-8333.** Daily 7:30am–11pm.

Moca Café ★ For some good coffee and desserts, or to just sit, rest, and watch the world go by along busy Nha Tho Street, stop in at Moca Café, one of the city's popular

Finds Have You Tried the Snake?

Six kilometers (3¾ miles) to the east of Hanoi, across the Red River, is the town of Le Mat, also known as the "Snake Village." Among shanty houses and winding alleyways, you'll find Chinese-style roofs sheltering elegant dining areas, all strangely tucked away. What's the big secret? This town is the hub of the very taboo snake industry, and it's the place to try fresh ***Tit Ran,*** or snake meat. The Vietnamese taboo is not much different than that in the West—something like "Eat snake? Ooooh, yuck!" Snake is also considered a male aphrodisiac, a kind of fried Viagra, so at night it's not uncommon to see groups of businessmen drunk as skunks piling into these places for a bit of medicine.

Here's the drill: Finding it is half the battle (or adventure). Any taxi driver will be happy to take you to his friend's place in anticipation of a commission. Feel free to ask to see another restaurant (some of them are pretty grotty), but expect to pay about $5 to get there. There are lots of restaurants in Le Mat, but one to try is **O Sin** (✆ **04/3827-2984**).

You'll be greeted by a friendly owner who'll usher you back to the cages and put on quite a show of stirring up the snakes before selecting one he thinks will feed your party. He'll then quote you a ridiculous price, but expect to pay somewhere between $5 and $10 per person after bargaining.

Then the show begins. You'll be seated and, before your eyes, the owner will adeptly kill the snake, drain the blood into a jar of rice whiskey, and systematically disembowel the animal, extracting the liver and showing you the still-beating heart before adding it to the whiskey/blood concoction. The guest of honor eats the heart and takes the first sip of whiskey before circulating the bottle. Thus begins a lengthy seven-course meal, starting with fried snake skin, grilled snake filet, snake spring rolls, snake soup with rice cake, minced snake dumpling, copious amounts of rice whiskey, and orange wedges for dessert. It's a decent meal, really, and certainly something to write home about.

Be warned that many of these places are part of the underground market in endangered species, selling bear paws and rare jungle animals thought to have medicinal benefits, but the snakes are common cobras found everywhere in Vietnam, and a trip here makes for an interesting night. Be clear with the driver about where you want to go (for example, not to a brothel afterward), and don't pay until you arrive at the destination.

traveler hangouts. This area is infamous for its bohemian community of artists and expatriate English teachers (many of whom use the cafe to give private lessons).

14–16 Nha Tho. ✆ **04/3825-6334.** Daily 7am–11pm.

Paris Deli ★ Just across from the Moca (see above) on Hanoi's tranquil and chic little "Church Street," you'll find this well-liked air-conditioned storefront that serves good pastry, proper croissants, breads, and deli sandwiches, plus all the coffee and cool fruit drinks you'll need to wash it down. This is a good place to beat the heat and take a rest from shopping or walking the city center.

13 Nha Tho St. ✆ **04/3928-6697.** Daily 7:30am–11pm.

Pepperoni's Pepperoni's serves tasty comfort food in the popular Bao Khanh Street area (across from Le Café des Arts in and among many popular nightlife spots). There's a salad bar, but because the place is open air, stuff flies all over it. Stick to the pizza and good pasta.

29 Ly Quoc Su. ✆ **04/3928-5246.** Daily 8am–11pm.

Pho 24 This popular national chain serves good Vietnamese *pho* (noodle soup) as you like it—make your own creation by ticking boxes off a punch list of ingredient choices. The beauty at Pho 24 is its high standard of cleanliness.

1 Hang Khay St. (at the southern end of Hoan Kiem Lake). ✆ **04/3936-5259.** Daily 7am–10:30pm.

Thuy Ta Cafe On the water at the northwest end of the lake, this cafe has great views and an extensive menu. The best choice is just a good ice cream or coffee while taking in the lake's scenery. Unlike most others listed here, Thuy Ta is more popular with locals than tourists.

1 Le Thai To St., Hoan Kiem District. ✆ **04/3828-8148.** www.thuyta.com. Daily 6am–11pm.

5 EXPLORING HANOI

Hanoi is a good place to get out and tour on your own. Start in the Old Quarter with a morning walking tour—especially in the summer months, when you'll want to take advantage of cooler weather. If you're game, get up really early and join in with morning exercise at lakeside. If sleeping a bit later sounds better, start at Hoan Kiem, hit the major sights in the Old Quarter, including **Bach Ma Temple,** and then take in the Hanoi Citadel area. ***Remember:*** If you want to catch a glimpse of the embalmed Ho Chi Minh in his mausoleum in the very center of the Citadel, you have to get there before 11am. Catch Ho's mausoleum, museum, and his very spartan home, as well as the One-Pillar Pagoda. Then hit the Temple of Literature, a short cab/motorbike ride away. From there, it's a matter of preference: shopping options galore around the central lake, French colonial buildings south of the lake and the Opera Building, a trip to the Catholic cathedral of Nha Tho and the surrounding cafe area, or further exploration of the Old Quarter or the Dong Xuan Market. You can get well acquainted with Hanoi in a day or two, but it takes a lifetime to know.

While sightseeing, remember that state-owned attractions will usually close for lunch from 11:30am to 1:30pm. Be sure not to accept any extraneous pamphlets or unwanted guides at sights; all come with a nominal, but frustrating, fee.

THE OLD QUARTER

Hanoi would not be Hanoi without its **Old Quarter,** a maze of streets dating back to the 13th century, its present-day chaos just a different version of the old chaos, when specialized trade guilds were responsible for each street. The quarter is exhausting ("What's with all the honking?!" my friend asks) and crowded; you'll be jostled by passing motorbikes, cyclos, and hawkers with shoulder-poles hanging pendulous burdens of local produce. The quarter is one of those places in the world that grows on you the more you experience it.

Said to resemble a tree sprouting from the cool waters of Hoan Kiem Lake, the streets are like chaotic branches and tendrils as they fan out in jagged patterns across the area north of Hanoi's famed lake. Limited on one side by the Red River and on the other by the once-great Hanoi Citadel, whose walls are still standing in some areas, the Old Quarter is, as the name denotes, the oldest area of the town and has long been an important economic center. In its earliest inceptions, the Old Quarter was accessed by a series of canals on its northeast edge that lead to regional waterways. The western end of the quarter was developed in the early 19th century when the completion of the Hanoi Citadel left open areas that were settled by outlying villages and tradespeople. The quarter hosts the city's largest market, Dong Xuan, and welcomes the bulk of foreign visitors to the city with its maze of streets, multitude of services, and great hotel and restaurant "finds." Getting lost in the maze is one of the biggest joys of Hanoi.

Most interesting are the **Communal Houses** set up by the guilds in each area. Like small temples to honor a local god, many to the Bach Ma, or "White Horse," who represents the city of Hanoi, these little courtyard areas are usually protected from the street and have often hidden entrances or just humble low roofs out front that give way to elaborate interior courtyards and temple buildings. Aside from communal houses, you find standard **Buddhist and Daoist temples** among the city's crooked streets. Most notable is the **Bach Ma Temple** in the eastern end of the quarter.

Keep an eye out for the classic Old Quarter **tube house,** the best and most accessible example of which is at 87 Ma May St. or at 38 Hang Dao (directly north of the lake). Tube houses are so named because they are just that: a long, narrow tube of space that is subdivided into sections that served the family's every need. Why so narrow? And, in fact, why do Vietnamese still build so narrow and high today? Properties were taxed on the basis of their street frontage, and real estate has always been expensive in this bustling quarter (real estate prices in Hanoi rival any city in the West these days). Tube houses are divided into sections. The front is the business office, where any goods are displayed and where business is conducted. In a succession of courtyards and interior spaces, some two stories, a tube house has areas set aside for gardening and for servants, and, at the back, private family quarters with the kitchen and the loo, which was traditionally nothing more than a large latrine pot that fit into a nook and had to be emptied regularly. You can spot traditional homes by their low tile roofs parallel to the street.

European buildings of the French are more elaborate, usually two-story structures, with architectural flourishes like overhanging bay windows and a high sloping roof, some of the mansard variety. The more time you spend in the Old Quarter, the more adept you get at finding the old among the new. In fact, many shops with the most modern, neon-lit storefronts on the first floor are, in fact, old colonials, so be sure to keep an eye on the roofline to spot some antique gems among the clutter.

The Old Quarter evolved from workshop villages organized by trades, or guilds, and even today, streets are dedicated to a product or trade. Some streets still offer the services of old—for example **Hang Thiec Street,** or Tinsmith Street, is still the place to buy tin receptacles and for sheet-metal work—but others have changed: **Hang Vai,** or Cloth Street, is now home to the bamboo trade, and many old streets support new trades. You won't find anything named "Motorcycle Seat Repair Street" or "Cheap Plastic Toys Imported from China Street," but they do exist. It's a fascinating slice of centuries-old life in Hanoi, including markets that are so crowded that the streets themselves narrow to a few feet.

Hanoi's Old Quarter is also where the seeds of Communist revolution were sown—starting in 1907 with the Tonkin Free School Movement, a program of study at a school in the Old Quarter, just north of Hoan Kiem Lake, which focused on Vietnamese traditions instead of the *de rigueur* French curriculum. The Old Quarter school was closed down by French officials, but the patriotic zeal that founded it would never die and instead produced small workers' strikes throughout the 1920s, many of which brought bloodshed. Old Quarter trade guilds were fertile ground for the worker's revolution, spawning independent presses; over time, Communist cells emerged that would unite during the August Revolution of 1945. The Old Quarter was, in fact, Vietnamese turf during violent skirmishes with the colonial French in their bid to control the upstart colony from 1945 until complete Vietnamese victory at Dien Bien Phu and French withdrawal.

The following is a translation of just some of the streets and the trades that were practiced in the Old Quarter. Some of the streets below still sell or produce the same items; others have evolved to more modern goods, but the clumps-of-industry principle remains. Look for the following:

Street Name Translations of Old Quarter Trades

Street Name	Trade	Street Name	Trade
Hang Bac	silver	Hang Giay	paper
Hang Be	rattan rafts	Hang Hom	coffins
Hang Bo	baskets	Hang Khoai	sweet potatoes
Hang Bong	cotton	Hang Luoc	combs
Hang Buom	sails	Hang Ma	paper replicas/toys
Hang Ca	fish	Hang Mam	fish
Hang Can	scales	Hang Manh	bamboo shades
Hang Cot	bamboo mats	Hang Muoi	salt
Hang Da	leather	Hang Non	conical hats
Hang Dao	silk	Hang Quat	fans
Hang Dau	beans	Hang Than	charcoal
Hang Dieu	bongs and pipes	Hang Thiec	tin
Hang Dong	brass	Hang Thung	barrels
Hang Duong	sugar	Hang Tre	bamboo
Hang Ga	chicken	Hang Trong	drums
Hang Gai	hemp and rope	Hang Vai	cloth

I had the good fortune of meeting an American *Viet Kieu,* or returning Vietnamese, on a trip in Halong Bay and hearing about his life in old Hanoi and his impressions now. Born on Hang Bong (Cotton St.) in the Old Quarter, he grew up in a house near West Lake but had spent a lot of his youth careening about the commercial streets at the town center while his mother worked as a seamstress. Asked what was different between the old Hanoi and the new (this was the his first time back since taking flight after the Geneva Accords divided the country), the kind gentleman talked only of the similarities, saying that his home out near West Lake is just as it was (and the owner abruptly slammed the door on him when he told her why he'd knocked, for fear he'd come back to re-claim his house). He said that the Old Quarter, barring the proliferation of motorbikes, neon, and improved pavement, was exactly as it was when he left Vietnam in the mid-1950s. For those who decry the cacophony and chaos of motorbikes, cars, and trucks in the district, it's important to remember that the Old Quarter is a market area, a place for business, and business in Vietnam is conducted at high decibels. The streets of the Old Quarter have always been busy and noisy, only now it is modern traffic that makes the racket, not shouting hawkers pulling bullock carts.

Note: There is an initiative to make the Old Quarter a pedestrian-only zone, and on weekend nights, the length of pavement along central Hang Ngang and Hang Duong is closed to car and motorbike traffic. A night market has opened up with lots of flea market–style sellers of tourist trinkets.

WALKING TOUR THE OLD QUARTER

START: North end of Hoan Kiem Lake (at the Ngoc Son Pagoda).

FINISH: Return to the north end of Hoan Kiem Lake (to Dong Kinh Nghia Thuc Sq.).

TIME: 1½ hours without stops; up to 3 hours with exploring, coffee, and chatting.

BEST TIMES: From early morning.

WORST TIMES: Middle of the day (too hot).

The best way to really experience Hanoi's Old Quarter is on foot. As you explore the route below, stop for coffee at a local cafe or a storefront geared to tourists in the backpacker area of the quarter. Stop for a chat; folks are busy but friendly if you take the time to connect. Photographers will want to set out early and catch the dynamic colors of the morning sun, which set off the rich yellowed plaster of older buildings and make the colors of produce in the markets more vibrant.

This route is a large clockwise circle through the Old Quarter. Walking times vary depending on your clip and your interest in the details, but generally, allow a few hours. ***Note:*** Try to study the map discreetly and know your next turn before arriving at an intersection. If you ask for directions, motorbike taxi drivers will just implore you to hire them for a ride and even try to confuse you. Learn to look for distinct rooflines. Just a short time in the Old Quarter will have you distinguishing a Chinese temple or community house from a tube house or more French-influenced construction.

❶ Hoan Kiem Lake

Start with a visit to the **Ngoc Son** pagoda on the north end of the lake. Cross the red **Bridge of the Rising Sun** to reach the temple. From this most prominent point in the city, follow the northern edge of the lake heading west and cross over the busy traffic circle. This busy square is known as the **Dong Kinh Nghia Thuc Square** (the **Tonkin Free School Movement Sq.**), named for the early-20th-century nationalist movement that would eventually spawn grass-roots Communism in Vietnam.

West from the square is:

❷ Hang Gai Street (Hemp St.)

This busy avenue marks the southern boundary of the Old Quarter. Hang Gai no longer supports hemp outlets as in days of old (the street would also host print shops and bookstores in the 19th c.), but is lined with boutique shopping, galleries, and silk tailors. Just a few hundred meters west of the traffic circle (on the left), you'll find a large **banyan tree** out in front of what was once a prominent communal house at no. 85 Hang Gai. The tree is one of the finest specimens of an old banyan in the city, a perfect example of nature's adaptability as heavy roots cleave large stones, and masons have built around the old tree for centuries. The sight is like a small temple, with sticks of incense wedged between knobs of the tree and offerings of rice whiskey lining the base of the tree.

Turn right off of Hang Gai and look for a small street sign pointing to:

❸ Tam Thuong Alley

Follow a few crooks in this quiet little alley, and you come to the **Yen Thai Communal House,** a classic low tile roof over a wooden entry that gives way to a quiet courtyard. Just across the street are a few guesthouses popular with French backpackers. Tam Thuong terminates at **Yen Thai Street,** where you'll make a left and, in the morning, walk through a small open-air market with great morning light for photography.

Turn right at the end of Yen Thai Street onto Hang Da Street:

❹ Hang Da Market and Hang Dieu Street

At the intersection of Yen Thai and Hang Da is the former site of **Hang Da Market,** a large, local dry-goods and clothing market. Sadly, the old four-story yellow stone building was recently torn down, and the new Hang Da Market will be a sterile shopping mall. After a quick look, head north on Hang Da—don't miss the large **bird shop** with a wall of bamboo cages on the northern corner of Hang Da and Hang Dieu.

Continuing north, Hang Da becomes Hang Dieu Street. Hang Dieu was traditionally the area for tobacco and pipe sellers; keep an eye out for the filigreed colonial edifices at no. 66 and no. 77 Hang Dieu (you'll have to look up to distinguish these from the concrete clutter).

TAKE A BREAK
Bun Bo Nam Bo, at 67 Hang Dieu St. (**✆ 04/3923-0701**), serves one of Hanoi's most popular one-dish noodle specialties.

Turn right off of Hang Dieu onto:

❻ Bat Dan Street

This street once housed sellers of clay bowls that were brought to the city from riverside workshops along the Red River. No. 33 Bat Dan is a very ornate and colorful communal house.

Turn left (go north) on Thuoc Bac Street, once an area for traditional medicines. Then turn left (west) on:

❼ Hang Phen Street

At the corner of Hang Phen and Bat Su, look for a preserved traditional house, characterized by its low tile roofline, at **no. 52 Bat Su** (also note the cozy little coffee shop on the corner, good for a rest and to watch the busy street life).

Carry on along Hang Phen until it becomes **Cua Dong Street,** which brings you to the eastern edge and wall of the Hanoi Citadel built by the Nguyen dynasty in the 1800s. Cua Dong Street terminates at the wall of the Hanoi Citadel.

Turn right off of Cua Dong onto:

❽ Phung Hung Street

Running along the wall of the city's old citadel, what marks the western edge of the Old Quarter, Phung Hung Street is a notable sight among Vietnamese tourists for the publication offices of an important Communist paper at **no. 105 Phung Hung.** There's a plaque that notes this spot as a historical vestige, but if you spend too much time studying the shuttered colonial edifice, local folks might get edgy, thinking you're a spy of sorts.

Turn right off of Phung Hung onto:

❾ Hang Vai

Translated as "Cloth Street," Hang Vai is the **bamboo district.** The busy exteriors

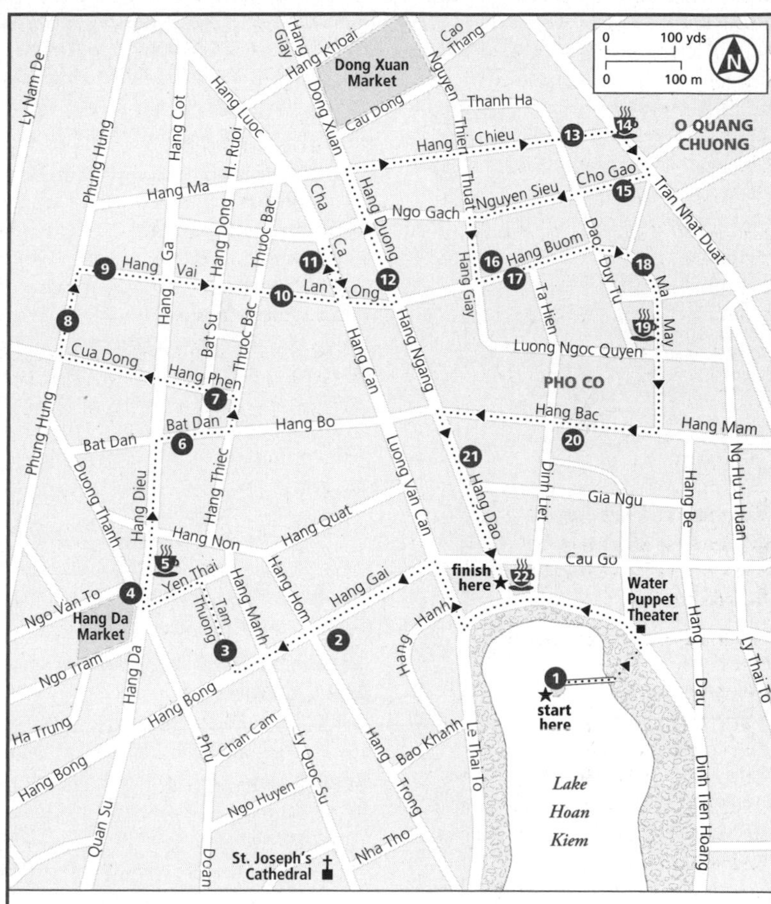

1 Ngoc Son pagoda and the Bridge of the Rising Sun
2 Bayan tree at #85 Hang Gai Street
3 Tam Thuong Alley
4 Hang Da Market and Hang Dieu Street
5 Bun Bo Nam Bo
6 Bat Dan Street
7 Hang Phen Street
8 Phung Hung Street
9 Hang Vai (the bamboo district)
10 Lan Ong Street
11 Cha Ca La Vong
12 Hang Duong Street
13 Quan Chuong Gate
14 *Bia hoi* stand
15 Co Luong Communal House on Nguyen Sieu Street
16 Bach Ma Temple (The White Horse Temple)
17 Hang Buom Street
18 Ma May Street
19 Tamarind Café
20 Chuong Vang Theater
21 #38 Hang Dao Street
22 Highlands Coffee

of small warehouses are lined with stands of cut bamboo poles, some more than two stories in height. This is the raw material for those wonderful Dr. Seuss scaffoldings you see on construction sites. The shops also sell bamboo tobacco pipes of the "bong" variety, some quite elaborate. At the corner of Hang Vai and north-south Hang Ga, keep an eye out for the **communal house** at no. 16D Hang Ga St.: A corner door cut into the white plaster and flanked by Chinese script ushers you into a small courtyard area with banyan trees and a small temple to Bach Ma, the "White Horse," a god associated with Hanoi (see Bach Ma Temple, below). Carrying on east on Hang Vai, look for the entrance to the **communal house** at **no. 7 Hang Vai.**

Heading east, Hang Vai becomes:

⑩ Lan Ong Street

One of the most interesting parts of the Old Quarter, Lan Ong Street is still home to a large enclave of ethnic Chinese who sell the herbs and medicines of old from small storefronts that date back to the origins of the quarter. The best shops are on the right side as you head east. Here you'll find picturesque little interiors with walls lined in massive dark-wood cabinets with tiny drawers and buckets and bins all around, with the most curious assortment of dried goods you'll ever see. This is the kind of place where, sadly, you might be able to buy a bear's gall bladder or a monkey's paw. The buildings all along this short stretch are originals dating back as far as the 17th century. Look for the busy elementary school at **no. 40 Lan Ong,** which was once the **communal house** of the area's Chinese population. Just across from the converted communal house and all along the length of the street, look for low roofs and narrow entries, especially those with tile roofs covered in moss, as these are original Chinese homes.

A quick left (north) turn brings you to:

⑪ Cha Ca Street

Following Lan Ong Street, heading east, cross the famous **Cha Ca Street (Fish St.).** Make a left (north) and look for the **Cha Ca La Vong restaurant** (p. 90), which serves one of Hanoi's most famed dishes.

Returning to eastbound Lan Ong, turn left (north) onto Hang Duong.

⑫ Hang Duong Street

Hang Duong Street (Sugar St.) is lined with traditional constructions, foremost of which is the **communal house** on the left as you go north at **no. 38 Hang Duong St.** It has a stunning banyan tree in the courtyard and a dark, alluring charm to its smoky interior. ***Note:*** Hang Duong is a **pedestrian area** on weekend nights and becomes a busy little market for tourist trinkets and local goods.

A short detour off of Hang Duong is the 13th-century **Thanh Ha Communal House,** just a short walk east on **Ngo Gach Street (Brick St.).**

Continue north on Hang Duong, and then turn right on:

⑬ Hang Chieu

Follow **Hang Chieu** east across the northern end of the Old Quarter to **Quan Chuong Gate,** the only remaining gate of the city's once-formidable fortifications. From here, go right (south) onto **Dao Duy Tu Street** and look for the small entrance to the **Huong Nghia Communal House** on the left side near the corner of Cho Gao Street. The communal house has an entrance open to visitors who bring offerings and light incense.

> **14 TAKE A BREAK**
> Tired? Thirsty? On the corner adjacent to the communal house on Hang Chieu is a popular ***bia hoi* stand** and restaurant where you can get a mug of local brew and get out of the heat for just 3,000 VND.

Turn right onto Nguyen Sieu.

⓯ Nguyen Sieu Street

Nguyen Sieu is a street named for a noted 18th-century scholar and lined with colonial buildings (your architecture-spotting muscles must be strong by now). On the right, keep an eye out for the small alley entrance to the **Co Luong Communal House,** a colorful temple surrounded by modern relief sculptures, some of quite fanciful *Alice in Wonderland* mushrooms and frightening demons.

Turn left (south) on Hang Giay Street. Go straight 1 block. Then turn left on Hang Buom Street. Immediately on your left is the important:

⓰ Bach Ma Temple (The White Horse Temple)

Located at no. 76 Hang Buom St., the Bach Ma Temple is open from 8 to 11am and 2 to 5pm daily (until 9pm on holidays). Built in A.D. 1010, the temple is dedicated to the White Horse of legend, which, it is said, helped the early king of the Viet people, Ly, decide where and how to defend his city. The temple interior is a grand courtyard of massive red pillars and large Buddhist statuary and altars.

Continue east along:

⓱ Hang Buom Street

From the Bach Ma Temple, continue east on Hang Buom (Sail St.). Once adjacent to a small tributary of the To Lich River, which brought goods to the city, Hang Buom was where local merchant vessels came to refit their ships. Look for the many colonial buildings and traditional Vietnamese houses, as well as a communal house at **no. 22 Hang Buom.**

As Hang Buom curves to the right (south), it becomes:

⓲ Ma May Street

Ma May is the beginning of the busiest budget tourist areas of the Old Quarter. In and among Internet cafes and tourist restaurants (often one and the same), you'll find good examples of traditional and colonial buildings. The **Huong Tuong Communal House** is at **no. 64 Ma May,** and one of the most interesting sights in the city can be found at **no. 87 Ma May,** a refurbished and restored traditional house. Here, for a fee of just 5,000 VND, a young docent dressed in a traditional flowing *ao dai* gown will take you on an informative tour of the building and can explain important details about life in the Old Quarter in centuries past. With the careful renovations done by a UNESCO-funded, French- and Canadian-backed organization, this classic home offers a unique opportunity to have a close look at the interior detail of a traditional Old Quarter home. Also see the similarly renovated property at 38 Hang Dao St. (see below).

19 TAKE A BREAK

Ma May is home to the popular **Tamarind Café** (p. 97), a perfect place to kick off your shoes, order a fresh fruit smoothie, and recharge for the last leg of this walking tour.

Heading south on Ma May, turn right at its terminus with:

⓴ Hang Bac Street

Heading west on Hang Bac, you're in the heart of the backpacker area. Here you're sure to be assailed on all sides by touts and hucksters and have your pick of budget tours from the many storefronts that line this busy street. Hang Bac means "Silver Street," and the silver these days is mostly the stuff coming from your pocket and falling into tour operators' hands, though you still can find some silver (and gold) jewelry makers and sellers.

As you approach the intersection of Dinh Liet Street, look right and you'll see the large **Chuong Vang Theater** at **no. 72 Hang Bac,** which was the stronghold of troops who laid siege to the French after the August Revolution in 1945.

You'll find good shopping and lots of goods and services in this area. You can finish the tour here or check out one more sight worth seeing.

Head west on Hang Bac. Turn left (south) on:

21 Hang Dao

Immediately on your right, don't miss another fine example of a **restored traditional Old Quarter house,** much like the one on Ma May (and run by the same folks). **No. 38 Hang Dao** is a two-story home that was once owned by silk merchants. It's quite spacious and elaborate (silk merchants were wealthy); you'll see how an Old Quarter house was set up, including where the worship area was set (now an office), as well as where the family lived, cooked, and worked. Helpful docents guide you through for a fee of 20,000 VND (or for free, if you've got your ticket from Ma May St.).

Hang Dao continues south and ends at Hang Gai and the **Dong Kinh Nghia Thuc Square** (the **Tonkin Free School Movement Sq.**). Look for the large ocean-liner-shaped building that overlooks the square and Hoan Kiem Lake to the south.

22 TAKE A BREAK

On the fourth floor of the most prominent building on Dong Kinh Nghia Thuc Square, find the popular **Highland's Coffee,** a good place to meet up after your walk or to rest your bones after completing the circle.

ATTRACTIONS

Ba Dinh District

Army Museum ★★ This museum presents the Vietnamese side of the country's struggle against colonial powers. There are three buildings of odds and ends from both the French and American wars here, including evocative photos. Most interesting, though, is the actual war equipment on display, including aircraft, tanks, bombs, and big guns, some with signs indicating just how many of which enemy the piece took out. There's a tank belonging to the troops that crashed through the Presidential Palace gates on April 30, 1975, Vietnamese Liberation Day. Outside sits a spectacular, room-size bouquet of downed French and U.S. aircraft wreckage. Also on the grounds is Hanoi's ancient flag tower (Cot Co), constructed from 1805 to 1812. The exhibits have English translations, which makes this an easy and worthwhile visit.

28A Dien Bien Phu St. ✆ **04/3823-4264.** Admission 20,000 VND. Tues–Thurs and Sat–Sun 8–11:30am and 1:30–4:30pm.

Ho Chi Minh Museum ★★ English-language explanations help to piece together the fragments of Ho's life and cause at this museum tribute, and there are personal items, photos, and documents detailing the rise of the nation's Communist revolution. The rhetoric is laid on a bit thick, but all in all it's an interesting and informative display. Completely unique to Vietnam are the conceptual displays symbolizing freedom, reunification, and social progress through flowers, fruit, and mirrors.

3 Ngoc Ha (left of One-Pillar Pagoda, near Ba Dinh Sq.), Ba Dinh District. ✆ **04/3846-3757.** Admission 12,000 VND. Tues–Sun 8–11:30am and 1:30–4pm.

Ho Chi Minh's Mausoleum ★★ In an imposing, somber, granite-and-concrete structure modeled on Lenin's tomb, Ho lies in state, embalmed and dressed in his favored khaki suit. He asked to be cremated, but his wish was not heeded. A respectful demeanor is required, and the dress code mandates no shorts or sleeveless shirts. Note that the mausoleum is usually closed in October and November, when Ho goes to Russia for body maintenance of an undisclosed nature. The museum might be closed during this period as well. Note that the mausoleum is open only in the mornings.

On Ba Dinh Sq., Ba Dinh District. Free admission. Tues–Thurs and Sat 8–11am. Last visitors admitted at 10:15am.

Ho Chi Minh's Residence ★★ Ho's residence, the well-known house on stilts, is behind the Presidential Palace, a gorgeous French colonial building built in 1901 for the resident French governor. Shunning the glorious structure nearby, Ho instead chose to live here from 1958 to 1969. Facing an exquisite landscaped lake, the structure does have its charm, and the spartan room is an interesting glimpse into the life of this enigmatic national hero. The basement was a meeting place for the politburo; upstairs are the bedroom and a study, and little details like his phone and walking cane are kept behind glass. Behind the house is a garden of fruit trees, many of them exotics imported from other lands, including miniature rosebushes and areca trees from the Caribbean.

Behind the Presidential Palace at Ba Dinh Sq. Guided tour 5,000 VND. Tues–Sun 8–11am and 1:30–4:30pm.

Hun Tiep Lake and the Downed B-52 This is not a sight that will knock you off your feet for its size or beauty: In fact, what brings many here is that it's an ordinary neighborhood, a maze of quiet lanes broken only by a small pond and, in the brackish water, the wreckage of an American B-52 shot down during the Christmas air raids of 1972. Many folks, veterans among them, find that a visit here puts a perspective on the war and that the rusting wreckage brings our abstract historical impressions back to the concrete present; others see landing gear, struts, and metal sheathing in a grungy pond. There's a partly submerged memorial plaque, and the area is cordoned off; entrance fees are soon to follow, no doubt. Most taxi drivers know it, or some creative charades will get the point across. Drivers will drop you off at the head of the alley (Lane 55) leading to the sight (a handwritten sign reads B-52 with an arrow).

Located just south of West Lake along Hoang Hoa Tham Rd., and a short walk down Lane 55 heading south. Free admission.

One-Pillar Pagoda ★ To the right of the Ho Chi Minh Museum is the unique One-Pillar Pagoda, a wooden structure built in 1049 that sits on stilts over a lake. A king of the Ly Dynasty, Ly Thai Thong King had it built after having a dream in which Bodhisattva Avalokitesvara, the goddess of mercy, presented him with a lotus flower. The existing pagoda is a miniature reproduction of the original, which was said to represent a lotus emerging from the water. It is certainly interesting, and a prayer here is said to bring fertility and good health. It's best to wear something full-length (skirt or trousers), not shorts.

Right of Ho Chi Minh Museum, near Ba Dinh Sq., Ba Dinh District. Free admission. Daily 6–11:30am and 2–6pm.

Vietnam National Museum of Fine Arts ★★ This very worthwhile arts museum features Vietnamese art of the 20th century, up to the 1970s or so. While the presentations are a bit crowded and rustic, there are explanations in English. Much of the art is outstanding, although you won't really see any works of an innovative or controversial nature. Entire rooms are devoted to the Vietnamese style of lacquer and silk painting, woodblock, and folk art. Techniques are explained—a nice touch. Interesting also are the modern works of wood statuary interspersed among the exhibits. Some are patriotic in nature, depicting daily life or events during the war or done in Soviet-influenced caricature with heavy-limbed peasants striking triumphant poses or depictions of the brotherhood of the army and the working class. The top floors are devoted to prehistoric artifacts and Buddhist sculptures, some of which are huge and impressive. Don't miss the famous 11th-century goddess of mercy (Kouan Yin), with her thousand arms and eyes, in the far-left room on the second floor. Best of all, the museum itself is in an old colonial, and, unless there's a tour group milling around, you can stroll around in relative serenity and rest on one of the many benches provided (no napping). The gift shop has some modern works of well-known artists for sale and will also sell works displayed in thematic exhibitions. The museum will then register and grant a certificate for the piece.

66 Nguyen Thai Hoc. ✆ **04/3733-2136.** Admission 20,000 VND. Daily 8:30am–5pm.

West Lake ★★ Covering a broad area north and west of central Hanoi, West Lake is home to lots of recent housing developments. In fact, the east shore of West Lake is more or less the "Beverly Hills" of Hanoi, where the best and brightest young Hanoians and expats call home. The lake is also steeped in legend and is bordered by several significant pagodas. Vietnam's oldest pagoda, **Tran Quoc,** was built in the 6th century and is located on Cayang Island in the middle of the lake, a beautiful setting. An actual fragment of the Boddhi tree under which Buddha achieved Enlightenment was given as a gift from the prime minister of India in 1959 and now grows proudly in the main courtyard. Constructed by an early Zen sect and a famous center for Dharma study, and later as an imperial feasting grounds, the temple has a visitor's hall, two corridors, and a bell tower; it still houses a group of diligent monks who carry out elaborate rituals for the dead on auspicious days (if a ceremony is underway, be conscientious and keep a distance, but visitors are welcome to observe). They recommend not wearing shorts here, but it is not enforced. All around the little peninsula that the island temple and its man-made walkway has created, you'll see fishermen busy with long bamboo poles and oversize hand reels; they essentially twirl a large spool by hand, something that's fun to watch, especially if they pull in something big.

Farther along the lake, **Quan Thanh Temple,** by the northern gate, was built during the reign of Le Thai To King (1010–28). It's dedicated to Huyen Thien Tran Vo, the god who reigned over Vietnam's northern regions. Renovated in the 19th century, the impressive temple has a triple gate and courtyard, and features a 3.6m (12-ft.) bronze statue of the god. West Lake is also a hub of local activity, particularly on weekends, when families go paddle-boating on it.

Bordered by Thuy Khue and Thanh Nien sts. No fee. Park is always open.

Dong Da District

Temple of Literature and National University (Van Mieu–Quoc Tu Giam) ★★

If Vietnam has a seat of learning, this is it. There are two entities here: Van Mieu, a temple built in 1070 to worship Chinese philosopher Confucius; and Quoc Tu Giam, literally "Temple of the King Who Distinguished Literature," an elite institute established in 1076 to teach the doctrines of Confucius and his disciples. It existed for more than 700 years as a center for Confucian learning. Moreover, it is a powerful symbol for the Vietnamese, having been established after the country emerged from a period of Chinese colonialism that lasted from 179 B.C. to A.D. 938. It is a testament to the strong cultural heritage of the Mandarins. As such, it stands for independence and a solidifying of national culture and values.

What exists today is a series of four courtyards that served as an entrance to the university. Architecturally, it is a fine example of classic Chinese with Vietnamese influences. Still present are 82 stone stelae—stone diplomas, really—erected between 1484 and 1780, bearing the names and birthplaces of 1,306 doctor laureates who managed to pass the university's rigorous examinations. Beyond the final building, known as the sanctuary, the real university began. Damaged in the French war, it is currently being restored.

Quoc Tu Giam St. ✆ **04/3845-2917.** Admission 5,000 VND and 3,000 VND for an English brochure. Daily 7:30am–5:30pm.

Hoan Kiem District

Hanoi Opera House This gorgeous, historic Art Nouveau building was built near the turn of the 20th century. Unfortunately, to get inside, you'll have to attend a performance, which are usually enjoyable (p. 123) but few and far between. The steps out front are a popular local hangout to sit and watch the world go by, and the fountain of the nearby Hilton Hanoi Opera, a building that fits like a jigsaw puzzle piece around the old opera, is, more than the opera building itself, a popular place for domestic tourists to get their photos snapped.

1 Trang Tien St. (intersection of Le Thanh Tong and Trang Tien sts., District 1). ✆ **04/3933-0113.**

Hoa Lo Prison (Hanoi Hilton) ★★ For sheer gruesome atmosphere alone, this ranks near the top of the must-see list. It was constructed by the French in 1896 mainly to house political prisoners, and the Vietnamese took it over in 1954. It was subsequently used to house prisoners of war. From 1964 to 1973, it was a major POW detention facility. U.S. Sen. John McCain was a particularly famous inmate, as was Pete Peterson, the ambassador to Vietnam, and Lt. Everett Alvarez, officially the first American pilot to be shot down over Vietnam. Their stories are told from the Vietnamese perspective in photographs and writings grouped in one small room. To the west is the guillotine room, still with its original equipment, and the female and Vietnamese political prisoners' quarters. The courtyard linking the two has parts of original tunnels once used by a hundred intrepid Vietnamese revolutionaries to escape in 1945. Only part of the original complex is left; the rest of the original site was razed and is ironically occupied by a tall, gleaming office complex popular with foreign investors. There are basic English explanations, but this is a good spot to have a guide, who is certain to be armed with a tale or two.

1 Hoa Lo St., off Quan Su St. ✆ **04/3824-6358.** Admission 10,000 VND. Daily 8am–5pm.

Hoan Kiem Lake ★★★ Hoan Kiem Lake is the center of the city, both literally and figuratively. The lake is the city's most popular strolling ground and a lovers' lane at night, with couples locked in embrace on benches or parked motorbikes looking out over the placid waters, the shadows of overhanging willows cast by moonlight. In the morning, the lake area is crowded with folks out for their morning exercise—running or walking in a circle around the lake or joining in with the many tai chi, martial arts, calisthenics, aerobics, and even ballroom dancing groups that meet in the open areas at water's edge. Hoan Kiem Lake is also the site of the city's own creation myth: the Legend of the Lake of the Recovered Sword. In the mid–15th century, the gods gave emperor Le Thai To a magical sword to defeat Chinese invaders. While the emperor was boating on the lake one day, a giant tortoise reared up and snatched the sword, returning it to its rightful owners and ushering peace into the kingdom. Stroll around the lake in the early morning or evening to savor local life among the willow trees and see elders playing chess or practicing tai chi. In the center of the lake is the Tortoise Pagoda; on the northern part is **Ngoc Son** pagoda, reachable only by the stunning **Bridge of the Rising Sun,** a long, red arch typical of Chinese temple compounds. Ngoc Son is a working temple, meaning that you might walk into a local ceremony of chanting monks and kneeling supplicants. The temple grounds offer great views of the surrounding lake, and the little lakeside park on the island is a popular place for elderly men to enjoy a game of Chinese chess. Don't miss the friendly calligrapher just inside the temple (on the left as you enter). For a nominal fee, have your and your friends' names done in Chinese characters, complete with the meanings of each symbol in English on the back (I'm "Wheat Love Machine") or have a scroll done of significant Chinese characters such as "Heart," "Love," or "Determination" (whatever you think you might need).

Hoan Kiem is a useful locator for navigating the city; for addresses downtown, people generally give directions in relation to it. It's good to know how to get from the lake to your hotel. The lake is also the jumping-off point for exploring the Old Quarter, Hanoi's labyrinth of traditional craft streets in a sprawling maze on the north end of the lake (see the walking tour in the Old Quarter, p. 103). Lakeside is also a good place to find a bench and rest your toes after trundling around town, and you can find some good little cafes, particularly on the north end. Grab an ice cream and take time to stroll, or stop and watch the moon reflect off the surface of this magical lake. You might even spot one of the giant turtles that took back the sword of Le Thai To to herald peace in Vietnam; sightings of this rare breed of turtles are quite common. Willows hang over the lake and reflect in the rippling light of dusk.

Thap Rua is the small stupa that was built in 1886 by an obscure Mandarin official. The temple was at first despised and involved in a scandal in which the official tried to have his father's bones laid to rest at the pagoda base. But over time, tiny Thap Rua, which sits on a small island at the very center of the pond, has become something of the city's Leaning Tower of Pisa, Statue of Liberty, and Eiffel Tower all rolled into one. Just two tiers of window galleries crowned by a short tapered roof, the temple commands great respect despite its recent construction, and it's a popular focal point for swooning lovers at lakeside in Hanoi's "Central Park"—the lungs of the city. The turtles that can be seen basking at the temple's base are said to be up to 500 years old and the very species that stole the sword and founded the fair city. Hanoians love their stupa of peace; in fact, recent initiatives to have the aging pagoda painted and restored—the small stupa is covered in moss and is overgrown with weeds—were met with staunch disapproval from Hanoi citizens. And so it is as it always was.

At city center, bordered by Tran Nhat Duat and Phung Hung sts. Entrance fee 12,000 VND. Temples daily 8am–5pm.

National Museum of Vietnamese History This is an exhaustive repository of Vietnamese ancient and historical relics nicely displayed with some bare-bones explanations in English. Housed in a building that was the French consulate until 1910 and a museum in various incarnations since, this collection walks you from prehistoric artifacts and carvings to funerary jars and some very fine examples of Dong Son drums from the north, excavations of Han tombs, Buddhist statuary, and everyday items of early history. It's the kind of place where schoolchildren are forced to go (and be careful if you see buses out front), and for anyone but history buffs, you might feel just as bored as the kids. For those on any kind of historical mission in Vietnam, I recommend contacting a tour agency and booking a knowledgeable guide for an excellent overview and a good beginning to any trip.

1 Trang Tien St. (just east of the opera). ✆ **04/3825-3518.** Admission 20,000 VND. Daily 8–11:30am and 1:30–4:30pm.

Quan Su Pagoda ★ Quan Su is one of the most important temples in the country. Constructed in the 15th century along with a small house for visiting Buddhist ambassadors, in 1934 it became the headquarters of the Tonkin Buddhist Association, and today it is headquarters for the Vietnam Central Buddhist Congregation. It's an active pagoda and usually thronged with worshipers; the interior is dim and smoky with incense. To the rear is a school of Buddhist doctrine. For good luck (or for fun), visitors of any stripe are welcome to buy sticks of incense and make offerings at the various altars and sand urns. It's easy to just follow suit, and folks will be glad to show you what to do.

73 Quan Su St., as it intersects Tran Hung Da, Hoan Kiem District. Free admission. Daily 8–11am and 1–4pm.

Revolutionary Museum The revolution will not be televised; however, afterward we'll have lots of old beat-up museums that celebrate the ongoing class struggle and inevitable triumph of a unified proletariat over the running dog bourgeoisie capitalists and their elitist, oppressive schemes to keep the common man in chains. Or so runs the old party line. What is best about the Revolutionary Museum is that it's a little rundown, a telling sign of where the nation's revolutionary zeal has gone in the wake of a booming capitalist economy. Uncle Ho's ideas were quickly lost in the shuffle when affordable motorbikes and TVs came on the scene. But to the elder generation of Vietnamese, the 50% who were born before 1975 and experienced Vietnam's great struggle, places like the Revolutionary Museum are important reminders of the legacy. The revolution that started with Ho Chi Minh is celebrated now less with socialism in mind than with celebrating the nation's hard-fought autonomy. The museum houses an interesting collection of photos and memorabilia not only chronicling the life and ascendancy of Nguyen Tat Tanh, otherwise known as Ho Chi Minh, but of the many early revolutions at the turn of the 20th century. Oil paintings retell the struggles and, literally, paint a grisly picture of life in colonial jails on Con Dao Island or Phu Quoc Island in the south. The museum route starts on the first floor with the 1945 August Revolution, photos and relics of victory at Dien Bien Phu, good background on the conflict with the United States, and the obligatory color photos of a prosperous Communist Vietnam as the revolutionaries envisioned. Party rhetoric is heavy here, and a big part of the allure of trundling around these big halls (once a French administrative building) is looking for words like "running dog" and finding artifacts like an old Budweiser can that was bent into a lantern for Viet Cong troops. Fun if you're a war buff.

26 Tran Quang Khai St., Hoan Kiem (east of the lake near the ring road and just adjacent to the old Opera Building). ✆ **04/3825-4151.** Admission 10,000 VND. Daily 8–11:45am and 2–4:15pm.

Women's Museum *Note:* This museum is closed for renovation and, at press time, was scheduled to reopen in 2009. Communism of the Ho Chi Minh variety was an egalitarian movement where all men and women were created equal, and revolutionary women were on the front lines throughout Vietnam's long conflicts with foreign powers. Whether pushing overladen bicycles along the Ho Chi Minh Trail Network or packing a pistol through the cave complexes outside of Saigon, Vietnamese women were a little more proactive than America's "Rosy the Riveter" of World War II fame, and Hanoi's Women's Museum celebrates their pivotal contribution to the war effort and to the growth of a modern, stable Vietnam. Western women visiting the museum have mixed reactions, as some find the collection and presentation a bit sexist: Women are often portrayed as victims or as unlikely sources of sanity and strength (stress "unlikely"), and emphasis is placed on women's abilities in the cottage industry and work at home (and there are lots of dull exhibits to that effect), but it should be stressed that the spirit of the museum is to celebrate women's contributions, though the sexist slant is a bit unfortunate. It's interesting to go and deconstruct it for yourself. The entrance is a large rotunda with a great golden statue of the oversize and overmuscled Soviet school of propaganda depicting a triumphant woman facing a great wind with a small child balanced on her shoulder. The first and second floors are "up the revolution" images and artifacts of women at war, winning the war, and winning the peace. Fascinating is the section of the many initiatives of women abroad (in the U.S. and Europe), suing for peace during conflict with the French and later Americans: Find long petitions to the U.S. government, flags and peace banners from the West, and photos of marches and protests (including images of Angela Davis and a contingent of overseas Vietnamese marching). The top floor features detailed displays of women's dress, from traditional *ao dai* to the intricate variations among ethnic hilltribe women in the Central Highlands and the far north. A popular coffee shop is just outside the entrance to the museum, a good place to chat and connect with locals.

36 Ly Thuong Kiet St., Hoan Kiem District. ✆ **04/325-9935.** Admission 10,000 VND. Tues–Sun 8am–4pm.

SIGHTS OUTSIDE THE CITY CENTER

Ho Chi Minh Trail Museum A museum dedicated to the war of inches and supplies along the borders of Vietnam, Laos, and Cambodia. The museum is far out of town but worth the trip for war buffs. Three floors are crowded with exhibits of photography, as well as lots of war machinery. The trucks, complete with leafy camouflage, that traveled parts of the Ho Chi Minh Trail are parked in a shaded area in the courtyard out front. The revolutionary rhetoric is heavy at this museum, and the focus is on the sacrifice of the many who shoveled, dug, fought, and scraped by to get supplies of rice and ammunition to North Vietnam's frontline forces. There is an important stress on the efforts of women to keep the supply lines open. The collection of weaponry and heavy machinery used throughout the war is enough to make it worth the visit, but, again, it's just for war buffs, as it is a long drive along traffic-choked roads south of town to get here.

14km (8¾ miles) southwest of Hanoi along Rte. 6 (heading toward Hoa Binh). Admission 10,000 VND. Daily 8–11:30am and 1:30–4pm.

Vietnam Ethnology Museum ★★ If you're interested in learning more about the 53 ethnic minorities populating Vietnam's hinterlands, make the jaunt out to this sprawling compound (go by cab). Vietnam's different ethnic groups, their history, and customs are explained in photos, videos, and displays of clothing and daily implements. Out back are a number of re-creations of the village homes, from a low Cham house to the towering peak of a thatched Banhar communal home. You come away with a good historical perspective on the many groups you meet in the far north and in parts of neighboring Laos and Thailand.

Nguyen Van Huyen, 6km (3¾ miles) west of town. ✆ **04/3756-2193.** Admission 25,000 VND. Tues–Sun 8:30am–4:30pm.

6 OUTDOOR ACTIVITIES & OTHER FITNESS PURSUITS

HOAN KIEM LAKE

Along with being the cultural center of Hanoi, from predawn until about 6 to 7am, the lake becomes something like an Olympic training camp. Going along the walking paths and wide road that circles the lake, hoards of locals work up a sweat, taking advantage of the morning cool and greeting the day with, as a Vietnamese friend put it, "a breath of fire." Groups doing calisthenics and light aerobics to loud taped music stand next to ranks of white-clad, slow-moving tai chi practitioners, martial arts groups, and even ballroom-dancing clubs. Joggers and speed-walkers circle the lake, and you'll spot solo exercisers doing all kinds of strange contortions or practicing meditation.

Join in! It's a great way to start the day and get into the rhythm of Hanoi life (you'll be wanting a siesta after lunch, like most locals), and it's a unique time when you can travel anonymously, unharried by sellers in the park. You always find someone going your speed, and if solo at the beginning, you're sure to meet up with friendly locals along the way. Hoan Kiem at dawn is a real scene and a great place for people-watching and a little morning wake-up. It's a similar scene near the Botanical Gardens and in Thong Nhat Park (formerly Lenin Park) overlooking Bay Mau Lake in the south end of town. Get your run in before 6:30am, though, when traffic starts to snarl.

Bicycles are easily rented from almost any hotel for about $1 a day, and though Hanoi motorbike traffic is chaos defined, you can pick your way through traffic and see more of town with your own wheels. Take extreme caution.

SPAS & FITNESS

The fitness center at **Metropole Hotel** (✆ **04/3826-6919**), has top-end equipment, a sauna, and a Jacuzzi, with day rates for nonguests.

Vietnam hasn't quite run with the ball in Asia's current spa revolution, but most hotels offer basic massage services, and the larger upmarket properties have deluxe spas. Try the Metropole, the Caravelle, the New World, or the Sheraton.

Small massage storefronts (the nonseedy variety) are all over town. Affordable and convenient to the town center for a rest while shopping or exploring the city is the second-floor **Thanh Gia** (38 Le Thai To St.; ✆ **04/3828-8196**), where a 30-minute neck and shoulder massage costs just $5. It's open daily from 11am to 11pm.

QT Salon and Spa offers good massage and beauty services from its two locations: 26–28 Le Thai To, on the western edge of Hoan Kiem lake (✆ **04/3928-6116**), and on the second floor of the Hilton Hotel.

For hair and nail treatments for ladies, look for Andre at the **Y-Not? Salon,** near Nha Tho Cathedral (1A Nha Chung St.; ✆ **04/3928-5198**).

GOLF

King's Island Golf Resort and Country Club is just 35km (22 miles) north of Hanoi and offers your best chance to hit the links near Vietnam's capital. A fine international course is set among the Ba Vi Mountains, and the club (open to visitors) has a whole range of services, from bungalow rentals to good pro services, equipment rentals, and dining. The course is in the town of Son Tay in Ha Tay Province. Call for reservations in Hanoi at ✆ **034/686-555** or 04/3772-3160.

Chi Linh Star Golf and Country Club is just east of King's Island, some 68km (42 miles) from Hanoi, on the road to Haiphong. The club recently hosted the Carlsberg Masters Open. With two fine courses, Chi Linh also offers a host of services and welcomes day guests. It costs just $55 for 18 holes on a weekday and $75 on the weekend. Contact the office in Hanoi at ✆ **04/3771-9006,** or book through the useful website www.chilinhstargolf.com.vn.

7 SHOPPING

Hanoi is like Bangkok for the sport shopper: a good choice for the last destination before flying home, if you want to easily buy and fill an extra suitcase in just a few days. Note that affordable, knockoff bags are for sale on the northeast end of Hoan Kiem Lake (where Lo Su St. terminates at lakeside). Most airlines on long-haul flights have high weight limits for each of your two check-in bags (some airlines allow as much as 36kg/79 lb. per bag), but do note that regional flights, particularly on Vietnam Airlines, impose more strict limits; you might be able to bring just two 20-kilogram (44-lb.) bags with you to Bangkok, while it's double that if you go on directly to Frankfurt. Just be sure to check.

WHAT TO BUY

Hanoi is a fine place to shop for silk, silver, lacquerware, embroidered goods, and ethnic-minority crafts. Silk is good quality and an easy buy. (If you're unsure of the quality, pluck a few strands and burn the fibers; if it smells like burned hair, it's silk.) Shops will tailor a suit in as little 24 hours, but allow extra time for alterations. Many of the shops are clustered along Hang Gai Street, whose name translates as Hemp Rope Street. It once housed ship-rigging shops but is now unofficially called Silk Street. A silk suit here will run from about $35 to $75, depending on the silk, and a blouse or shirt will cost $15 to $20. Virtually every shop takes credit cards (MasterCard and Visa). Bargain hard for all but the silk; offer 50% of the asking price and end up paying 70% or so.

Silk & Embroidery

In addition to the shops mentioned below, also consider **Thanh Ha Silk,** 114 Hang Gai St. (✆ **04/3928-5348**), and **Mavena Hanoi,** 28 Nha Chung (✆ **04/3828-5542**).

Craft Link Put your money to a good cause. This not-for-profit store has a nice collection of silk notebooks, accessories, minority art and clothing, and lacquer plates and bowls. The store is spread out over two floors of a charming, restored colonial building. The Clintons visited Craft Link during their tour through Vietnam, and there's a blown-up photo on the second floor to prove it. 43 Van Mieu St. ✆ **04/3843-7710.**

Hanoi Silk Hanoi Silk has a collection comparable to Khai Silk (see below) and carries good ready-to-wear as well as tailors' silk garments. Open daily 8am to 8pm. Sheraton Hotel at 11 Xuan Dieu Rd. ✆ **04/3719-2434.** www.hanoisilkvn.com.

Khai Silk With branches and small outlet corners in various hotel lobbies around town—also in Saigon—Khai Silk is the largest retail silk outlet in Vietnam and offers a good, high standard of silk ready-to-wear and bespoke tailored clothing. You might find better deals, but Khai Silk is justly famous for its selection, silk quality, and chic store layout. Main store is at 96 Hang Gai St. ✆ **04/3825-4237.** 26 Nguyen Thai Hoc St.: ✆ **04/3733-3866.** 113 Hang Gai: ✆ **04/3928-9883.**

New Collection: Hoa Sua Embroidery and Sewing Showroom Like their affiliated restaurants and cafes in Hanoi (and in Sapa), the folks at the Hoa Sua Showroom are an outlet for disadvantaged children, many of whom are hearing-impaired, to receive on-the-job training and placement in a career. The shop here carries a nice collection of daily-use items, tablecloths, and slipcovers, as well as made-to-order goods. An expat favorite, and your money goes to a good cause. 21D Ha Hoi, Hoan Kiem District. ✆ **04/3822-6912.**

Tips Antique Regulations

Note that the sale of antiques is a simple matter, but carrying them out of the country is another question, and many tourists have gone smiling through Customs to declare their Buddha—only to discover that they can't bring Siddhartha home with them. Dealers are not always forthcoming because they're more concerned with making the sale, but for larger, more expensive purchases, a dealer will get involved and help with the process.

Tan My ★★ This shop states they are the oldest store in Hanoi. History claims aside, it stocks some of the finest threads in this overcrowded shopping district. Come here to buy beautiful cotton or linen pieces with subtle or quirky embroidery. I love their simple white pieces marked with a single flower in a corner, and their adorable children's wear makes perfect pint-size gifts. You can also bring in photos or a design you fancy, and the shop can reproduce them into a woven picture or a motif for tablecloths and accompanying dinner napkins ($25–$40). There are several locations of Tan My shops around town, but the best selection is at their flagship on Han Gai Street. Open daily 9am to 7pm. 66 Han Gai St. ✆ **04/3825-1579.** Fax 04/3824-7522. www.tanmyembroidery.com.vn.

Traditional Items, Antiques & Souvenirs

For silver, antique oddities, and traditional crafts, try **Hong Hoa,** on 18 Ngo Quyen St. (✆ **04/3826-8341**). **Giai Dieu,** 82 Hang Gai St. (✆ **04/3826-0222;** also at 93 Ba Trieu St.), has interesting lacquer paintings and decorative items.

For fine ceramics, look to **Quang's Ceramics,** at 95 Ba Trieu St. (✆ **04/3945-4235**), in the Old Quarter.

For decorative items and souvenirs, look to the streets surrounding Hoan Kiem Lake. A good place to start is **Nha Tho Street,** also called "Church Street," as it terminates in the town's largest cathedral. Here you'll find silk and housewares designers in and among quiet cafes. **Delta Deco** (12 Nha Tho St.; ✆ **04/3828-9616**), a large dealer of lacquerware and fine furnishings, is a popular choice. Its Chinese-influenced modern designs are especially attractive. The area all around the lake is lined with budget souvenir shops offering the likes of lacquer painting of the French cartoon character Tin Tin and carvings and trinkets. Other outlets are listed below.

Hanoi Moment ★ A small selection of porcelain and lacquer flatware is sold in this smartly laid-out store. Rather than leaving you to dig through assorted stacks of plates and bowls, Hanoi Moment displays a small selection of pieces arranged in eye-pleasing display areas. Open daily 8:30am to 8:30pm. 101 Han Gai St. ✆ **04/3928-7170.** www.nishinjsc.com.

La Casa This store uses traditional Vietnamese crafts and combines local materials with a modern edge. It's an excellent place to scope out little gifts to bring back home that people will actually like. Open daily 9am to 7:30pm. 12 Nha Tho St. ✆ **04/3828-9616.** www.lacasavietnam.com.

Van Hoa Viet (Viet Culture) This hard-to-find little storefront on the southeastern edge of Hoan Kiem carries a cool collection of authentic hilltribe weavings, mostly from the Jarrai people in nearby Nam Ding, as well as copies of Christian statuary from the same region (near Ninh Binh and Phat Diem Cathedral; see chapter 8). Open daily 8am to 9pm. 1 Trang Thi St. ✆ **04/3934-7417.**

Van Loi You'll enter past one of Hanoi's classic banyan trees along Hang Gai (see the walking tour of Hanoi, p. 103) into the interior of Van Loi, which centers around a large circular staircase and open gallery space filled with fine furnishings and handicrafts, mostly in wood. 87 Hang Gai. ✆ **04/3828-6758.** Also at 43 Phan Dinh Phung. ✆ **04/3734-7377.** www.vanloi.com.

Vietnamese House A good little collection of gems, handicrafts, small ceramics, jewelry, and antiques. Open daily 8am to 7:30pm. 92 Hang Bac St. ✆ **04/3826-2455.** www.vietnamesehouse.com.

Style: Clothing, Accessories & Decor

For luxury foreign goods, and/or for a glimpse of Vietnam's burgeoning mall culture, check out **Trang Tien Plaza,** a large, three-story complex on the southeast corner of Hoan Kiem Lake. The top floor features budget clothing, and lower floors are all real name-brand fashion and electronic goods, the likes of Levi's and Sony.

Hang Dau Street, on the northeast corner of Hoan Kiem Lake (near the intersection Lo Su), is positively **"shoe heaven"** and carries a wide selection of men's and ladies' shoes. The lads will be sad to note that you won't find many sizes over 43 centimeters (about an American size 9), and the sneakers and tennis shoes are often "pleather" and not the best quality, but ladies, particularly those ascribing to the Imelda Marcos school of shoe acquisition, are in heaven with these underpriced (bargain hard) creative outlets. Most are good knockoffs or rejects of goods made in factories east of Hanoi. Also throughout the area, especially where Lo Su Street meets the lake, you'll find **bag sellers** with loads of medium- to good-quality reproductions of your favorite brands, like North Face or Adidas. Five dollars gets you a reasonable copy of a bag that might cost $100 or more at home, but the zippers give out pretty quickly.

Little Hanoi, once a bastion of hard-line Communism and rigid control over a corrupt free market, is now giving way to fashion. Led by its pop-culture benefactors—nearby South Korea and Hong Kong—Vietnam is growing its own base for pop culture alongside a burgeoning (Uncle Ho wouldn't like it) middle class of consumers, and areas like Hanoi's **Nha Tho Street** are leading the way. Close on its heels, in the expat district near West Lake and popular Vine restaurant (p. 89), is **Xuan Dieu Street,** which has quirky, Western-friendly stores. Meanwhile, high-end flagship stores like **Burberry** (oddly enough, across the street from midrange San Francisco chain **Esprit**) are congregating at the corner of Ly Thai To, between the Metropole and the Hilton. Here's a rundown of the city's best:

Galerie Royal ★ This small boutique is sandwiched between the Hilton and the Metropole and caters to high-end shoppers. They carry three lines only, Kenzo, Korloff, and La Perla. The La Perla lingerie and swimsuit selection is top-notch. Open daily 9:30am to 7:30pm. 60 Ly Thai To St. ✆ **04/3936-6672.**

Ipa Nima and Tina Sparkle You've come to the right place for gaudy little Zakka fashion bags and accouterments for the ladies. Run by jet-setting Hong Kong lawyer-turned-designer Christina Yu, the place is popular with Japanese and Singaporean ladies and has managed to cause a small stir in other international markets. Celebrities Jamie Lee Curtis and Kelly Osbourne (admittedly, not your typical fashion icons) have been known to sport an Ipa Nima creation or two. Yu herself admits that you either love it or you hate it. Her bags are creative, glitzy affairs adorned with rhinestones, metal grommets, and contrasting materials. They have two stores: a flagship Ipa Nima store in the south end of town, and Tina Sparkle, in the heart of the popular Church Street cafe area. Open daily 9am to 7pm. Ipa Nima: 34 Han Thuyen St., Hai Ba Trung District. ✆ **04/3933-4000.** www.ipa-nima.com. Tina Sparkle: 17 Nha Tho St., Hoan Kiem District. ✆ **04/3928-7616.**

Mirror Mirror ★ Young designer Ha Truong's creations are, according to her slogan, "understated, artful, contradictory." As the founder of Mirror Mirror, she has made some small waves on the international scene. Truong freely mixes and matches (for example, a wraparound dress made in multicolored lace paired with solid-colored, netted silk sleeves) and creates interesting cuts that work well on many body types. At the time of this writing, Truong was in a temporary location on the southern edge of Hoan Kiem District, but she should be opening a flagship store in the Old Quarter soon. Check her website for updates. No fixed store hours. 1 Truong Han Sieu. ✆ **04/3944-6529.** www.mirror-design.com.

Mosaique Here is a popular little boutique and a great place to pick up some designer silver jewelry, silk hangings, or ready-to-wear items, as well as home goods from furnishings to lamps. Major credit cards are accepted. Open daily 9am to 8:30pm. 22 Nha Tho St., the heart of chic "Church St." ✆ **04/3928-6181.** mosaique@fpt.vn.

Nagu Think cute gifts, like passport holders and notebooks in linens and silk. Nagu also carries a small selection of clothing (modern with a Vietnamese touch) at the back. The changing room appears by unfolding strips of cloth from a high wire—not a lot of privacy for trying on the goods. Open daily 8am to 9pm. 20 Nha Tho St. ✆ **04/3928-8020.** www.zantoc.com.

Song ★ This boutique (whose name means "life" in Vietnamese) carries original designs offering a modern twist on classic Vietnamese styles. They are a bit on the pricey side, but the clothing is thoughtful and well cut. Everything is a creation of established designer Valerie Gregori McKenzie, who first began designing in France and continued her trade in California. Her clothing and home collections are a mix of Vietnamese classical styles and a tropical bohemian chic look. Open daily 8am to 8pm. 27 Nha Tho St. ✆ **04/3928-8733.**

Tan My Design This new store showcases work from talented local designers, both expat and Vietnamese. Expect modern twists on styles of the past—mandarin collars mixed with contemporary silks or fine embroidery in quirky designs. Open daily 8:30am to 8pm. 61–65 Hang Gai St. ✆ **04/3938-1154.** www.tanmyembroidery.com.vn.

Things of Substance ★ An excellent place to find original designs, and all reasonably priced. The store has a lovely sense of humor, as evidenced by their motto: "Western sizes . . . Vietnamese prices" and their small selection of souvenir T-shirts ("Vietnam, One Party since 1975"). Things of Substance sells mostly women's cotton and linen separates with a touch of Eastern influence—the type of clothing that is perfect for the hot weather and could transfer easily to an office setting. They also have a small handful of funky accessories, like canvas yoga bags embroidered with a big dragon or boho-style leather shoulder bags made of pigskin. Open daily 8am to 8pm. 5 Nha Tho. ✆ **04/3928-5368.**

Three Trees ★ This specialty store showcases original jewelry designs by a Belgian expat. Showpieces in the front display cases are oversize but still delicate. Designs often feature floral motifs (which balance out the chunkier shapes and sizes) in gold, interlaced with well-placed, small-cut diamonds. Open daily 9am to 9pm. 15 Nha Tho St. ✆ **04/3928-8725.** Also has boutiques at the Hilton and the Sheraton.

Art

Vietnam has a flourishing art scene, and Hanoi has many galleries of oil, silk, water, and lacquer paintings. Don't forget to bargain, and know that, in most cases, the paintings you buy are not originals, but copies of well-known Vietnamese artists. Even places that like to offer a "certificate of originality" are selling you a line of bull along with the certificate and a copy of a work by a famous Vietnamese artist. The good news is that the better galleries do carry the originals, and Vietnam is now home to some international names. Try to meet the artist, if you can, and stick with the larger dealers, who are less likely to pull a fast one. All galleries will ship from door to door at a cost of about $150 for a medium-size canvas. Listed below are a few reliable stops. Galleries are mainly in the Old Quarter and along the shores of central Hoan Kiem.

Apricot Gallery This large, well-lit, air-conditioned space holds some works by Vietnam's most well-known contemporary lacquer painter, Dinh Quan, as well as other artists of the current vanguard (all priced accordingly, of course). Apricot Gallery carries 80% famous artists and 20% upcoming artists. See if you can spot which paintings fall into which categories. The gallery has hosted several international customers, including former President Bill Clinton, who purchased a landscape piece by Hoang Hai Anh. Hoang, naturally, falls into the 80% group. Open daily 8am to 8pm. 40B Hang Bong St. ✆ **04/3828-8965.** www.apricot-artvietnam.com.

Art Vietnam One of the city's premier galleries, Art Vietnam is set in a classic tube house in the Old Quarter and run by a longtime expat, collector, and steward of Vietnamese art, Suzanne Lecht. Find Suzanne at the gallery most days, and take any opportunity to chat with her and pick her brain about art in Vietnam—she also has some good tales to tell. Open daily 10am to 6pm. 7 Nguyen Khac Nhu ✆ **04/3927-2349.** www.artvietnamgallery.com.

54 Traditions Gallery ★★ This gallery is more like an ethnographic museum, library, and gallery all rolled into one. The space is divided into five theme rooms (such as "Functional Objects" and "Shamanism"), and co-owner Mark S. Rapport is more than happy to play guide for a day. Rapport is a self-described collector: baseball cards when he was a kid, African art while living in New York, and then Vietnamese minority art when he moved to Hanoi. Rapport has a natural gift for bringing the artifacts to life, and given the range of affordable pieces (small mounted prints made from antique stamps or seals go for less than $10) and exquisite antique artifacts, few people walk away empty-handed. Open daily 8am to 6pm. 30 Hang Bun St. ✆ **04/3715-0194.** www.54traditions.com.

Hanoi Gallery Different from all the rest, by virtue of the fact that this little open-air storefront sells only old Communist propaganda posters, mostly artful copies that are "worried" to look old (the difference is obvious), but the stark images are quite appealing. Open daily 9am to 9:30pm. 42 Cau Go St. (directly north of the lake). ✆ **04/3824-1854.**

Mai Gallery ★ Like the Apricot Gallery and Art Vietnam, this gallery carries a good deal of work by well-known and established Vietnamese artists. It also has a handful of exclusive artists, whose works are available only at their gallery. These include the latest darling of Vietnamese landscapes, Phan Thu Trang, a young painter (born in 1981) who has been with Mai Gallery since 2004. Staff here is helpful and the gallery has an excellent layout, with good lighting for easy viewing. Open daily 9:30am to 8pm. 113 Hong Bong St. ✆ **04/3828-5854.** www.maigallery-vietnam.com.

Viet Fine Arts Gallery Just north and east of the church area is this high-end collection of works bearing the authentic stamp of local painters. The gallery has an imposing storefront and an extensive collection. Open daily 8:30am to 8pm. 96 Hang Trong St. ✆ **04/3928-6667.** www.vietfinearts.com.

Also look for **Thanh Mai,** 64 Hang Gai St. (✆ **04/3825-1618**); **Orient Gallery,** 46 Le Thai To St. (✆ **04/3928-5747**); and **Thang Long,** 41 Hang Gai St. (✆ **04/3825-0740**), in the Old Quarter.

Trang Tien Street, the heart of the French Quarter just east of the southern end of Hoan Kiem, is full of galleries and showrooms. The road was once home to the French colonial administration buildings, and these grand facades have long been places for commerce in foreign goods (thus the many English-language bookstores and galleries). **Van Gallery,** the sister shop of Linh Gallery in the Old Quarter, is at 25–27 Trang Tien, near the Dan Chu Hotel. Below are just a few others.

Hanoi Art Contemporary Gallery This large corner space carries a large collection. The friendly staff greets you with smiles. Here you'll find standard copies and some very unique pieces. Open daily 8am to 8pm. 36–38 Trang Tien St. ✆ **04/3934-7192.** www.hanoi-artgallery.com.

Life Photo Gallery This gallery carries the works of two prominent Hanoian photographers whose color prints of the Vietnamese hinterlands, including some of the finest portraits and scenes from the hilltribes of the far north and Central Highlands region, have been published widely. You'll find some of their best prints here, framed and at prices unheard of in the West. Pick up a great souvenir or get some inspiration for your own snapshots. The eccentric photographers themselves, Mr. Le Quang Chau and Mr. Do Anh Tuan, are often on hand and happy to chat. Open daily 9am to 9pm. 39 Trang Tien St. ✆ **04/3936-3886.**

Oriental Gallery On the corner of Trang Tien and lakeside Dinh Tien Hoang, this is one of the city's biggest gallery spaces, and home to works of some of Hanoi's finest artists. The effusive dealer comes out and tells you things like, "It's crap, darling. Boring. Unoriginal. You want this one over here." Refreshing honesty. Open daily 8am to 8pm. 93 Dinh Tien Hoang. ✆ **04/3936-1428.** nguyetbmhn@yahoo.com.

Books

For foreign books in Hanoi, check out one of the many shops lining **Trang Tien Street,** the only place where you could find a book, even a simple English or French grammar, during the years of austere Communist control. Nowadays there are a few large state-sponsored bookstores, each with a simple collection of English-language books, a few shelves of the classics, and a useful section with books about travel and the culture of Vietnam, as well as a selection of coffee-table books and language-learning texts that are geared to the local market.

The **Bookworm** ★ (15A Ngo Van So, south of the lake; ✆ **04/3943-7226**) is a longtime expat favorite and carries a good collection of international bestsellers, classics, and books on culture and travel. It's your best bet for unique finds (short of swapping with fellow travelers). They do trades of the two-for-one variety, and the expat staff is friendly and helpful (there's also a useful bulletin board of local events and things for sale).

In the Old Quarter on **Ba Be Street,** you'll find backpacker book repositories; it's a good place if you're looking to trade books (especially if you find another traveler there doing the same and can make a private deal; otherwise, it's usually two-for-one at the store counters). Try **Love Planet Tours and Books,** 25 Hang Bac (✆ **04/3828-4864**), a longtime traveler favorite (they'll try to sell you all kinds of tours along with your tome, too). Also try one of the similar budget shops on **Bao Khan Street,** a popular nightlife area on the northeast corner of the lake.

Infostones (41 Trang Tien St.; © **04/3826-2993;** www.infostones.com.vn) has a great selection of cooking books and the latest international magazines.

Note that most high-end hotels (see the Sofitel Metropole, the Hilton Hanoi Opera, and the Daewoo, earlier in this chapter) have lobby book nooks with some palatable volumes and international news sources.

Also note that **Hanoi's wandering booksellers,** once the plague of the city, especially near Hoan Kiem Lake, where the hassle of tourists was legendary, are less in evidence these days. These lads sell the likes of *The Sorrow of War,* by Bao Khanh, as well as popular phrase books, guidebooks, and the obligatory *Quiet American,* or now the popular *In Retrospect,* by the Vietnam War's architect, Robert McNamara. Just $2 gets you a photocopied edition (some are rife with mistakes), and the biggest fun of all is bantering with these kids, all of whom have a good, funny line or two to get your money out of your pockets. If you haven't read these classics on Vietnam, this is a good place to pick one up (or a map or a postcard). It's almost obligatory, or at least your savvy salesman will make you feel like it is.

TRADITIONAL MARKETS

Dong Xuan Market is the city's largest traditional market and a highlight of a visit to the Old Quarter. A massive indoor pavilion is surrounded by streets teeming with sellers day and night (early morning is best to visit). Find lots of Chinese knockoff goods, produce, and stuff for everyday use in homes—but there are plenty of neat trinket shops tucked down the narrow lanes of this maze of commerce, and just the experience of walking around (or photographing the chaos) is a reason to visit.

Cho 19–12 (the **19–12 Market**) is one of Hanoi's most interesting markets. Just west and in the shadow of the Melia hotel, you'll find this labyrinth of local goods, produce, and oddities. On the south end of the market, near the main entrance, is the "whole roasted dog" aisle, with crispy Fidos stacked one atop the other. A bit of a shock, really. In the heart of the market are all kinds of *che* (Vietnamese custard) shops and local food stalls, as well as meat and produce stands. You won't be able to get over all the dogs here.

PHOTO STORES

Got a memory card full of images that you want to print or back up on CD? Looking for good film cheap, or good processing equally cheap? Hanoi's many photo stores can do it all. Try any of the following, all within a baseball throw from the lake: **A Dong Photo Company** (128 Hang Trong St.; © **04/3826-0732**), **Konica Digital Photo Center** (3B Le Thai To St.; © **04/3825-8517**), or **Nguyen Cau Digital Camera Lab** (1 Ba Trieu St.; © **04/3936-1516**).

CONVENIENCE

To pick up good snacks for a long train or bus ride, check out **Intimex** (© **04/3825-6148**), down a small alley at 22–23 Le Thai To St., on the west side of Hoan Kiem Lake. With groceries on the first floor and a small department store on the second level, you can find what you need and pay prices that are fair and marked (no bargaining). The joys of retail.

For Western wines and canned products from home, try the aptly named **Western Canned Foods** (66 Ba Trieu; © **04/3822-9217**), just south of Hoan Kiem. For fine wines from the choicest regions of the world, as well as any kind of liquor or aperitif, stop in at **La Cave** (35–37 Trang Thi St.; ✆ **04/3934-4083**). In the heart of the Old Quarter, the **Warehouse** ★ (59 Hang Trong St.; ✆ **04/3928-7666;** www.warehouse-asia.com) also has an extensive wine selection. The **Gourmand Shop** (56 Ly Thai To; ✆ **04/3826-6919,** ext. 8702) is located on the first-floor area on the east side of the grand Sofitel Metropole hotel (p. 81) and carries a fine collection of wines, cheeses, treats, and gifts. It's open from 7am to 9pm, and whatever they don't have, they can point you in the right direction to find.

8 HANOI AFTER DARK

Hanoi hosts a variety of pleasant little watering holes and even a few rowdy dance spots that stay open far past when the Communist cadres deem decent (thank goodness for kickbacks and corruption). **Apocalypse Now,** the city's notoriously seedy nightspot is back open (for now). A growing number of expat residents means that options abound. You have your pick of the real-deal Irish pub or local draft beer for pennies a pitcher at the popular streetside *bia hoi* stalls, where patrons hunker down on squat stools for the long night of boozing and chat (this is the top choice for connecting with local folks).

Hanoi is the best place in Vietnam to experience **traditional Vietnamese arts** such as opera, theater, and water puppet shows. Invented during the **Ly Dynasty** (1009–1225), the art of water puppetry is unique to Vietnam and a highlight of any visit to the city. The puppets are made of wood and really do dance on water. The shows feature traditional Vietnamese music and depict folklore and myth. Book tickets for the popular puppets at least 5 hours ahead. Check the listing below for more information.

THEATER & PERFORMANCE

The **Hanoi Opera House** (Hanoi Municipal Theatre), 1 Trang Tien St., Hoan Kiem District (✆ **04/3933-0113**), hosts performances by local and international artists. Check with any hotel concierge to see if any performances coincide with your stay, and be sure to book in advance. The **Hanoi Traditional Opera,** 15 Nguyen Dinh Chieu, Ba Dinh District (✆ **04/3943-7361**), has shows on Monday, Wednesday, and Friday at 8pm.

Central Circus, on the north end of Thong Nhat Park (formerly Lenin Park), across from the Nikko Hotel, Hai Ba Trung District (✆ **04/3822-0277**), has shows at 8pm Tuesday through Sunday. It's a real circus done on a small scale, so see it only if you're desperate to entertain the kids. As in so many isolated Communist blocks in the world, the circus was once the only game in town. But now, with the proliferation of televisions in homes, online gaming, and movies, young Hanoians have myriad options in the entertainment realm, so visiting Russian troupes don't draw a crowd. It's sad that the art is dying (be sure to check with your concierge to see if shows are running), but many foreign visitors to this circus report being saddened by the rather brutal treatment of trained animals.

Thang Long Water Puppet Theater ★★★ (Finds) Shows are thrice daily, at 5:15, 6:30, and 8pm. This might sound like one for the kids, but there is something enchanting about the lighthearted comedy and intricately skilled puppetry of this troupe. They perform numerous vignettes of daily life in the countryside and ancient tales, including the legend of Hoan Kiem Lake and the peaceful founding of the city of Hanoi. Puppeteers use bamboo poles to extend their puppets from behind the proscenium and up through the surface of a small pond that forms the stage. You will be amazed at their ingenuity, and it doesn't take much to suspend disbelief and get caught up in a magical hour of escape. The kids will like it, too. Buy tickets early in the high season. The theater is poorly raked, and that means that, though seats in the front cost a bit more, you'll have a better view—and not look at the back of someone's head—from the middle or the back (pick from a seating chart at the ticket office). You also get a better effect of verisimilitude from the back (it looks more real).

57B Dinh Tien Hoang St., Hoan Kiem District. ✆ **04/3825-5450.** Fax 04/3824-9494. thanglong.wpt@fpt.vn. Admission 60,000 VND.

CINEMA

Who knew you'd be watching a Spanish film and chatting with an elite group of cineastes in a courtyard cafe in the middle of Hanoi? Life is a mystery. This little theater is more or less kept a secret—not for long, though. Popular with expats, the tiny screen of the **Hanoi Cinematique** imports some interesting work from all over the world and holds showings nightly. It's down a little alley and is kind of a secret; to see a film here, you have to follow some funny rules. The government forbids charging money to see foreign titles (information that is beyond the censor's grasp), so the theater is, in fact, classified as a club and part of the adjacent cafe. Tickets aren't bought; they're invitations that come with a suggested donation of 50,000 VND. The best part about the Hanoi Cinematique is meeting up with Hanoi's growing bevy of wild-eyed artists and the likes of hotel general managers all mingling in one space—all for the love of the cinema. And very good cinema, indeed. Showtimes vary. Call ✆ **04/3936-2648** or just stop by the cafe, which is at the end of a long, narrow alley off of 22A Hai Ba Trung (in the area south of Hoan Kiem Lake).

BIA HOI, BARS & PUBS

Nightlife in Hanoi is more raucous than you might imagine of a town known as an austere Communist outpost. Midnight is the generally held strict closing time, but a few choice places rock until dawn. Traveler cafes in the Old Quarter are known to burst out in wild parties (I once enjoyed a rollicking Christmas Eve dinner and dance party in a travel agent's office), and there are lots of little restaurants and bars open late.

One good way to connect with local expats and be guaranteed a swilling good time is to contact the **Hash House Harriers** (www.hhhh.wso.net), a drinking fraternity for folks who like to work up a bit of a sweat before hitting the suds. The Hanoi group is quite family friendly, however, and they have fun runs every Saturday.

The best place to have a wild night—local style—is to pull up a little plastic squat stool on a street corner or in one of the many open-air bars serving the local brew, *bia hoi,* translated as "fresh beer" and otherwise known as draft beer. The kegs flow as long as folks are drinking, and sitting among locals in these cozy little joints is an infusion of local culture, where you can make friends and get close to Hanoi street life. You'll find *bia hoi* just about anywhere in Vietnam, in even the tiniest hamlet, but in Hanoi your best bet is on **the corner of Ta Hien Street and Luong Ngoc Quyen,** in the heart of the Old Quarter. Try the stalls where you see foreigners frequenting, and you're most likely to meet willing English speakers, both staff and patrons. One glass costs just a few thousand dong, so why not have another? How about one more? Stay away from the local rice whiskey unless you have an iron gut.

Bao Khanh Street ★ For nightlife geared to the expat or tourist, busy little Bao Khanh Street is a good place to start. Tucked behind a block of buildings down a short lane in the northwest corner of Hoan Kiem Lake (look for Le Café des Arts on the map of Hanoi, p. 78), the street is home to lots of popular bars and late-night spots. Some are a bit seedy, but there are a few comfortable laid-back places, and the street is lined with lots of open-air eateries, cafes, and bars geared to locals.

Most popular on Bao Khanh Street is the **Funky Monkey** at 31 Hang Thung (✆ **04/3928-6113**); they have music, pool tables, pizzas, and a cool black-light menu. Also check out **Polite Pub,** at 5 Bao Khanh (✆ **04/3825-0959;** open 5pm–2 or 3am), a popular gay men's hangout, but pretty "straight friendly," too. All of these spots are open late, and the street's always hoppin'. There are lots of nearby dining options as well (see Pepperoni's, p. 100, and Le Café des Arts, p. 95).

Eté This place lures a diverse expat crowd for its labor-intensive fresh fruit cocktails, tasty pub food, and impromptu dance parties. The spacious alfresco areas make this one of the best bars outside of the Old Quarter. Open daily 8am to midnight 95 Giang Van Minh St. ✆ **04/3722-4714.**

Highway 4 If you're getting ready to head out on the highway (in the proverbial "Born to Be Wild" sense), Highway 4 is your first stop. It's the unofficial meeting point for the Minsk Club of Vietnam (a Minsk is the rugged Russian motorbike especially popular for travel in the north of Vietnam; see "The Minsk: A Guide to Renting & Enjoying Your Big Honkin' Soviet Motorbike," in chapter 6). A visit to this bar/restaurant is all about hard drinking and tall-tale-telling about motorbike adventures up north. They even brew their own particularly potent rice whiskey, the Son Tinh brand, which will cross your eyes and make you believe any story. Softening up their image a little, the restaurant is now offering cooking classes. Open daily 9am to 2am. 5 Hang Tre, Hoan Kiem (on the eastern edge of the Old Quarter near the city ring road and the many motorbike mechanic shops). ✆ **04/3926-0639.** Also at 54 Mai Hac De in Hai Ba Trung District, ✆ **04/3976-2647;** and 575 Kim Ma St., Ba Danh District, ✆ **04/3212-8998.** www.highway4.com.

Le Pub Just a friendly little storefront bar in the heart of the backpacker area, Le Pub is a good vantage point on street life in the Old Quarter and a good meeting point when exploring town. There's also an I Love Vietnam in-house tour operation upstairs (p. 69), and the staff is quite helpful. Open daily 7am to 11pm. 25 Hang Be St. ✆ **04/3926-2104.** www.lepub.org. Daily 7am–11pm.

Nha Tho (Church Street) Nightlife along Hanoi's Church Street, Nha Tho, which extends from the town's largest Catholic cathedral, is quite inviting and laid-back. The area is lined with boutique shops and galleries, and there are a few popular restaurants, such as Mediterraneo (p. 96), as well as Paris Deli (p. 99) and Moca Café (p. 98), which attract tourists and expats. A good place to meet up before going out is **La Salsa,** which serves fine cocktails in a chic streetside overlook. 25 Nha Tho. ✆ **04/3828-9052.** Nha Tho (Church St.) extends from Vietnam's largest Catholic cathedral, St. Joseph's, on the west side of Hoan Kiem Lake.

Press Club Don't be put off by the seeming exclusivity of this old-boys' club; nothing could be further from the truth. Press Club is a cozy bar and upscale eatery, but with all kinds of affordable snacks and dishes. Both the snazzy bar area and laid-back patio seating area are anything but stuffy. You'll find regular events and live music here, and it's a good place to connect with "connected" expats to find what's going on in town. The first Friday of every month, the terrace buzzes with some big event, be it a huge outdoor barbecue or an all-out dance party. Don't miss it if you're in town. Open daily 11am to 3pm and 5pm till late. 59A Ly Thai To. ✆ **04/3934-0888.**

R & R Tavern ★★ American-owned R & R Tavern is the best place in town for a taste of classic rock and a chance to meet up with expats who dig it. They have live music Thursday to Saturday and draw a big crowd. They're located just northwest of Hoan Kiem Lake on Lo Su, just a short walk east of the busy shoe-sellers area at lakeside. Open daily 7:30am till late. 47 Lo Su St. ✆ **04/3934-4109.**

Red Beer Hanoi's newest brewpub—with two-story vats at the back of a cavernous, brick interior space like an old Boston brewpub—Red Beer is popular with locals, and tables fill up nightly. You'll hear "Yo!" ("Cheers!") all night, and you're sure to make friends. Open daily 9am to 11pm. 97 Ma May St. (in the Old Quarter). ✆ **04/3826-0247.**

The Spotted Cow Just next to Al Fresco's (p. 92), the Spotted Cow is a good choice for a night out with the boys: It's just drinkin', darts, and English Premiere League Soccer or Rugby on the telly. Open daily 11:30am till late. 23C Hai Ba Trung. ✆ **04/3824-1028.**

Studio ★ This is a hip little joint in the midst of Hanoi's budget travel agency ghetto. The two-story interior is set up with plush black cushions against minimalist white plastic furniture—it's been done before, but it still looks great. Bartenders can fix you a proper cocktail, and the lounge music will set you up for a chill evening. Open daily 10am to midnight. 32 Ma May. ✆ **04/3926 3882.**

Sunset Bar ★ Overlooking tranquil West Lake, Sunset Bar is an absolute gem. Rattan couches and cozy daybeds run the circumference of the bar's fabulous wooden deck. It's a popular hangout with hip locals and expats. Open daily 4:30pm to midnight 1A Nghi Tam St. ✆ **04/6270-8888.**

CLUBS & DISCOS

Cau Lac Bo Nhac Jazz Club In the heart of the Old Quarter, Mr. Quyen Van Minh has been churning out jazz just about as long as he's been allowed. There's no cover charge, and Minh showcases some of the best local talent. Acts vary daily. 31 Luong Van Can St. (just a short walk directly north of the traffic circle on the north end of Hoan Kiem Lake). ✆ **04/3828-7890.** Daily 9am–midnight. Music 8–11pm or so, depending on the crowd. Call ahead for schedule of events.

Solace When everything else closes, head out to sea (okay, the river) to dance until sunrise on Solace. This place used to be the Titanic, and they have inherited the old bar's reputation as the final stop before the stumble home. House and techno music blasts on the weekends. On weekdays, patrons often jump behind the turntables to try their hand at playing DJ. End of Chuong Duong Do, Hoan Kiem Lake. ✆ **0912/174-730.**

9 DAY TRIPS FROM HANOI

Hanoi is a good base for longer explorations of the north and northeast. **Halong Bay** is by far the most popular day trip, or overnight trip, for visitors to Vietnam's capital, and detailed information about boat trips there and to nearby **Cat Ba Island** can be found in chapter 7. For other destinations farther afield, see chapters 6 and 8. Below are the most convenient trips from Hanoi.

CRUISE THE RED RIVER

Ask the friendly folks at **Buffalo Tours** (94 Ma May; ✆ **04/3828-0702;** www.buffalotours.com) about their popular ***Jewel of the Delta,*** a small but cozy river cruiser that takes you from Hanoi along the busy flood plain of this life-giving river. The Red River Delta is a very productive rice-growing region, and the riverside fields are lush with green. The day tour starts early, stopping to explore **But Thap Pagoda** by bicycle (double-check to make sure they have a bicycle for your height before leaving Hanoi), then on to various handicraft villages, and cycling to small off-the-beaten-path villages connected by narrow paddy dikes. On board the boat, enjoy a nice lunch and some time to rest before hitting the village of **Bat Trang,** an important commercial hub as early as the 15th century, and now a center for the production of fine pottery. You'll have plenty of time to rest and enjoy the sun on the boat's spacious sun deck before returning to Hanoi in the late afternoon.

PERFUME PAGODA

Just 60km (37 miles) south of Hanoi is this stunning area of limestone peaks surrounding a lowland waterway through the rice fields. Visitors in groups of three and four board low rowboats for a short river ride to the temple area. The river trip is a highlight, a relaxing ride where you can take it all in and snap photos to your heart's content, or even get a chance to try the funky forward stroke of the typical Vietnamese small boat. The area looks a lot like the dynamic Tam Coc grottoes near Ninh Binh; if you've been there, don't bother with the Perfume Pagoda—Tam Coc is more beautiful.

The best part about visiting the Perfume Pagoda is the hearty climb, some 30 minutes of scrambling up to the stadium-size mouth of the mountain's holy cave. The site is home to a number of important temples and shrines, and the area is worth a wander. Tours leave early in the morning for the 2-hour drive to My Duc.

NINH BINH AREA

Just a few hours south and east of Hanoi, you'll find the town of Ninh Binh—a good home base for some interesting day trips (you might make it an overnight). But the town isn't much, and touring the sights is really best done on good organized tours based out of Hanoi. For detailed information, check out chapter 8.

The area is home to **Cuc Phuong National Park,** the nation's first park (from 1964) and a vast expanse of wilderness. The park also supports an important primate rescue and reintroduction program. Ninh Binh's popular **Tam Coc (The Three Grottoes),** with its towering limestone karst towers, is considered the "Halong Bay of the Rice Fields." Visitors can see the sight from small local rowboats. **Hoa Lu,** the ancient capital area, connects with Tam Coc via a scenic little back road; the temples themselves are 17th-century re-creations of the originals but are quite lavishly decorated. **Kenh Ga** is another scenic area—but for its busy riverside market that's very much unlike Tam Coc's peaceful charm. Just south of Ninh Binh Town is **Phat Diem,** once home to a large population of French missionaries. The town's famous cathedral is a highlight.

6

The Northern Highlands

The far north is where the rubber meets the road for hard-core adventure junkies. If you were born to be wild, take your own Minsk motorbike; if you weren't, go with a jeep and driver.

This chapter is broken into two sections: the **Northwest Highlands,** which include Lao Cai, Sapa, and the Dien Bien Phu Loop; and the **North-Central Highlands,** a shorter route including Ba Be Park and the small towns of Cao Bang and Lang Son.

In addition to breathtaking landscapes of the **Tonkinese Alps** and off-the-map destinations like **Dien Bien Phu,** one of the main attractions in the region is the **villages of the ethnic minority hilltribes.** The weather is much cooler here than in Vietnam's often sultry lowlands and coastal plains, so bring some layers, and be ready for some good adventures.

The region's most accessible and popular choice for luxury travelers, backpackers, and tour groups, **Sapa** can be reached by overnight train from Hanoi. With a range of good accommodations and dining, Sapa is a good base for trekking to hilltribe villages or as the first or last destination on a rugged highland adventure.

Below I've outlined the long loop starting in Hanoi and including the towns of **Hoa Binh, Mai Chau, Son La, Dien Bien Phu** (where the French forces in Indochina fell), and **Lai Chau** before crossing the high pass to **Sapa.** The trip is a real hoot and takes from 4 days to 1 week of adventurous road travel along some treacherous tracks through beautiful mountain scenery in the heart of the Tonkinese Alps. A trip around the loop is a great chance to experience Vietnam "off the track" and have contact with ethnic hilltribe culture.

Another route included in this chapter leaves Hanoi and heads directly north via the town of **Thai Nguyen** to the **Ba Be Lake National Park,** then to the riverside town of **Cao Bang,** where rural day trips take you to a stunning waterfall and to hilltribe markets, and finally to **Lang Son,** a provincial outpost, before returning to Hanoi. Different hilltribe groups call this region home, and weekend markets abound.

1 LAO CAI

300km (186 miles) NW of Hanoi

The access town for visitors to Sapa and Bac Ha, Lao Cai is really just a stopover, a place to catch the bus to the hills or to catch the train back to Hanoi. You won't find much to see or do, but you should know a few things in case you get stuck here for a while. The **train station** is in the heart of the town, and you can buy onward tickets here easily, though it's best to book sleeper berths a day in advance. There's one helpful tour office in Sapa, the **ET Pumpkin Tours** (Quang Truong Ga, Lao Cai City, Vietnam; ✆ **020/383-6074;** fax 020/383-6074; www.et-pumpkin.com), across the main square at the train station.

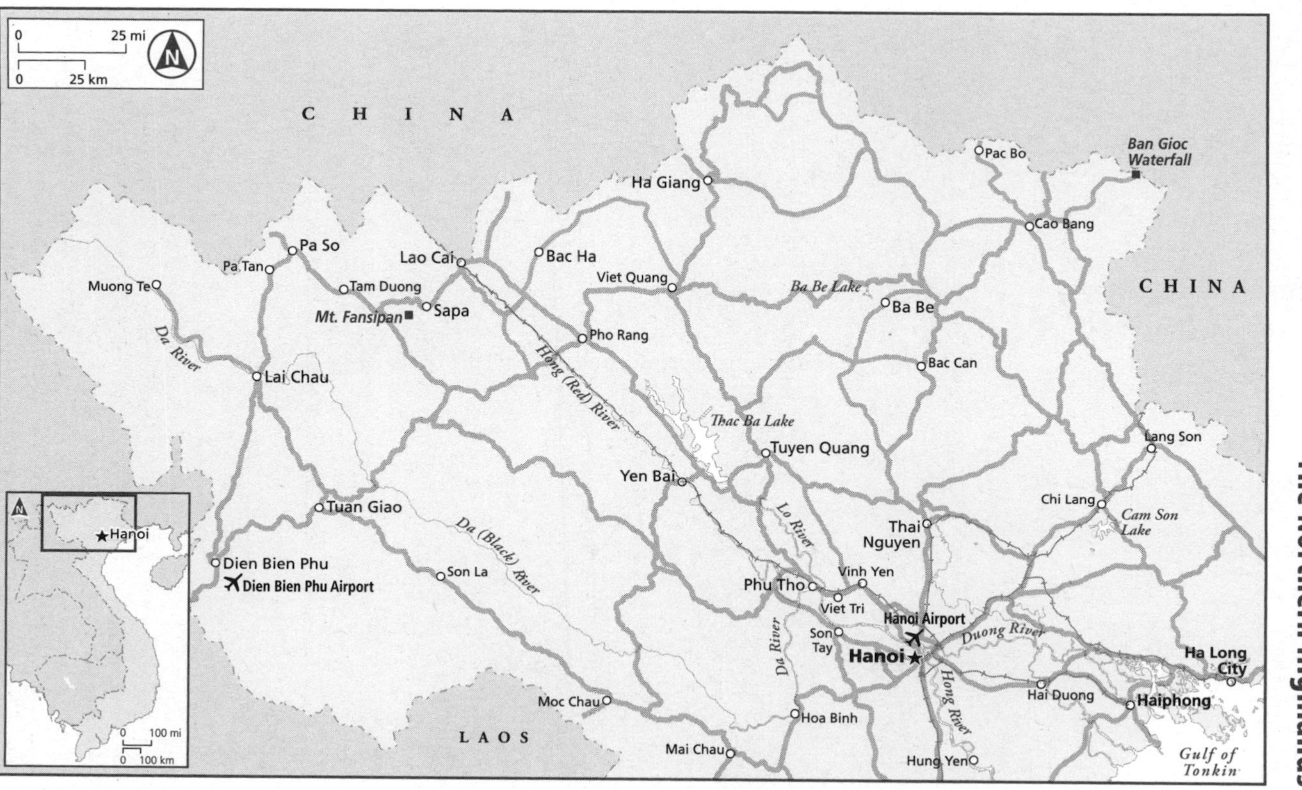
0
25 mi
0
25 km
CHINA
CHINA
LAOS
Ban Gioc Waterfall
Pac Bo
Cao Bang
Ha Giang
Pa So
Pa Tan
Lao Cai
Bac Ha
Muong Te
Tam Duong
Viet Quang
Ba Be Lake
Ba Be
Sapa
Mt. Fansipan
Pho Rang
Bac Can
Da River
Lai Chau
Hong (Red) River
Thac Ba Lake
Lang Son
Tuyen Quang
Yen Bai
Chi Lang
Cam Son Lake
Tuan Giao
Da (Black) River
Lo River
Thai Nguyen
Hanoi
Dien Bien Phu
Dien Bien Phu Airport
Son La
Vinh Yen
Phu Tho
Viet Tri
Hanoi Airport
Son Tay
Da River
Duong River
Hanoi
Ha Long City
Hong River
Hai Duong
Haiphong
Moc Chau
Hoa Binh
Mai Chau
Hung Yen
Gulf of Tonkin
0
100 mi
0
100 km

Hilltribes in Northern Vietnam

Population estimates of the diverse groups of ethnic minorities in the far north of Vietnam range widely, mainly because these independent and often elusive minority groups defy census takers' clipboards. Including disparate groups in the Central Highlands (see chapter 10), the current estimate is around nine million, or 10% of the population.

Vietnam's hilltribe ethnic minority groups originally came from Tibet and near Burma, and arrived in Vietnam via China, though a few groups in the Central Highlands are of ancient Indonesian descent. Some hilltribe groups have been in Vietnam for thousands of years, but others migrated as recently as 100 years ago or as a result of Chinese political pressure in the last 50 years.

Under the rule of the 19th-century Nguyen dynasty, the majority ethnic Vietnamese were given districts, and in exchange for paying some obeisance to the king, hilltribe groups were given near autonomy. Since the fight for independence in 1955, the Hanoi government has sought fruitlessly to portray its ethnic groups as a vanguard of the ongoing agrarian revolution. Vietnam's ethnic minorities played a major role as converts and allies of the French missionaries and colonialists, and later as foot soldiers for the American military and CIA. These groups could fight in Vietnam and then flee to safety behind the mountainous Laos border. Though considered backward and unsophisticated by the lowland majority, hilltribe people are courted by Hanoi for fear of dissent or insurgency. On a trip to the far north, you'll see lots of flimsy posters showing models of "cooperation" between Vietnamese military and northern ethnic groups, but hilltribe villages tell a tale of self-reliance and autonomy, even in the face of poverty and segregation or "enforced primitivism" as a show for tourists.

The groups of the far northwest have more in common than anything, and many do business together and intermarry (particularly the Hmong and the Dao [Zao]). Most hilltribe groups farm small hillside slash-and-burn plots and wet rice terraces in the valleys and tend domestic animals. Groups use **central marketplaces** (like the famed market of Sapa or Bac Ha) not just as opportunities for commerce, but for forming friendships and alliances, courting, and building a shared culture. Be sure to catch a market day in the north. Each group has a distinct **language.** Some groups fight to keep alive ancient traditions of transcribing their native phonemes into Chinese characters, but the practice is dying out in favor of learning Vietnamese and, increasingly, English.

Northwestern hilltribe people are mostly **animist,** except for the groups that fell under the sway of French missionaries. Hilltribe religion honors the natural world by building small shrines and carving totems. **Important note:** When out in the country, **do not photograph** or touch any carved bamboo totems and sculptures, especially near village gates, and always ask before taking someone's portrait.

A first visit to this region excites a certain awe in travelers, and photo-clicking tourists usually flip at the seeming exoticism of ethnic minority folks, especially in and around Sapa. It's important to remember that these are people, not circus sideshow acts. Do not pay anyone to take their photo. Do not give gifts. Should you find something interesting, buy souvenirs at a fair price. Go with a good guide who can make introductions and explain the subtle differences in these distinct cultures. Below is a short breakdown:

Dao (Zao) Mostly in the regions around Sapa and Lao Cai, Dao people are similar to the Hmong and notable for their elaborate dress, including the massive red headdresses and silver jewelry worn by women.

Hmong The Hmong came from China some 500 years ago, and many settled in the area around Sapa. Hmong women are distinguishable by their indigo-dyed clothing with elaborate embroidery, copious silver jewelry, and high headdresses (Hmong men commonly wear Western clothes). The most savvy of hilltribe businessmen, Hmong people lead the pack in selling trinkets and souvenirs to tourists—the friendly English speakers who sidle up to your table in Sapa and Bac Ha are most likely Hmong.

Nung Populous along the Ba Be–to–Cao Bang route, Nung people have much in common with their Tay neighbors, practicing wet rice cultivation and growing vegetables and other crops with the aid of water-wheel irrigation (some of these wheels are quite dynamic). Nung live in mud huts instead of stilt houses and are Buddhists.

Tay Similar to Kinh people, Vietnam's ethnic majority, with an estimate of more than one million people, Tay live in the most prime turf: the fertile lowland areas of the far north (Tay were some of the earliest settlers in the region). Successful wet rice cultivators and growers of cinnamon and tobacco, Tay people are much like ethnic Vietnamese, practicing the standard mix of Buddhism and Confucianism, and enjoying the benefits of progress like improved irrigation and even some luxury items (look for TV antennas in villages). Few Tay men still wear their characteristic indigo-dyed pajama-like clothes, although Tay women commonly wear the traditional headscarf and silver jewelry. Tay villages are getting wealthier, with concrete and brick structures displacing the traditional wood stilt houses. The Tay have their own written language and strong literary traditions. **Muong** people are much like the Tay people.

Thai Totaling over 60 million people in Southeast Asia, mostly in Thailand and nearby Laos, the Thai ethnic group in Vietnam is second only to the Tay in population (also at an estimate of more than one million people) and can be divided into three distinct subgroups: the Black Thai, the White Thai, and the Red Thai. The Black Thai are characteristically all in black, the White Thai have small white swatches hanging from their belts, and the Red Thai are similar to Dao groups, with red headdresses. Black Thai range as far as Son La, with large populations around Dien Bien Phu. White Thai populations are largest in and around Lai Chau. And Red Thai are in Son La.

A few basic minihotels are also near the station, if you miss your train or want to get a jump on travel to Bac Ha from Sapa for the weekend market there. Stay near the Chinese border at **Hoa Lan** (82 Nguyen Hue; ✆ **020/383-0126**). Don't expect anything fancy, but you can be reassured everything is neat and tidy. Ask for a room with a view of the river. For dining and information, the best place to visit is the family-run **Hai Nhi Restaurant** (337 Nguyen Hue St.; ✆ **020/383-5901**), which is on the left just as you exit the station. This is the town's traveler central, where shuttle buses drop off groups of tourists waiting to board the night trains back to Hanoi. If you're passing through, stop in for a good meal; the friendly young proprietor and his family can help out with any detail (they helped me empty the gas out of my motorbike, and even took me to their house for dinner).

Lao Cai is also a gateway to China, and many travelers make this their last stop before going on to the Middle Kingdom. ***Important note:*** You must have a **prearranged visa** for China before crossing at the checkpoint. (For more about obtaining visas, see "Visas," under "Entry Requirements," in chapter 3.) From Lao Cai, it's a short walk or ride on a motorbike taxi to the border area and on to China. Once across the border in China, you can catch an onward train or bus into the heart of the country (but that's another story for another guidebook).

Onward transport to Sapa leaves regularly from just outside the station. When the train arrives from Hanoi in the morning, you have your pick of transport, and friendly touts will tug and pull you to their rickety shuttle buses. The 1-hour trip costs just $2. Buses to Bac Ha are a little trickier, and it's best to arrange your way to Bac Ha Market with a tour company. Contact Topas or Handspan in Sapa, or make arrangements with a tour operator in Hanoi before boarding the train for Lao Cai.

2 SAPA

337km (209 miles) NW of Hanoi; 37km (23 miles) E of Lao Cai

Sapa is a small market town that has been a gathering spot for many local hilltribes for nearly 200 years. Hmong and Dao people, among others, still come here to conduct trade, socialize, and attend an ephemeral **"love market,"** where young men and women choose one another for marriage (these days, it's unlikely you'll see anything more than a staged re-creation of it). But seeing this as early as 1860, French missionaries said *"Mon Dieu!"* and set up camp to save souls; their stone church still stands sentinel and is well attended at the center of town. Sapa, with its mercifully cool climate, became a holiday escape for French colonists, complete with rail connection, upscale hotels, and a tourist bureau as early as 1917. The outpost was retaken by the Vietnamese in 1950, attacked and destroyed later by the French, and left in ruin, only briefly occupied by Chinese troops in 1979. The town reopened for tourism in the 1990s.

Now connected by luxury train with Hanoi, Sapa boasts good accommodations and is a great jumping-off point for trekking and eco-tours. Even a 1- or 2-day trip, bracketed by overnight train journeys from Hanoi, will give you a unique glimpse of local hilltribe culture. Trek out to nearby villages with a guide (it's actually illegal to trek without a licensed guide, and you may find yourself a very unwelcome guest in a village that does

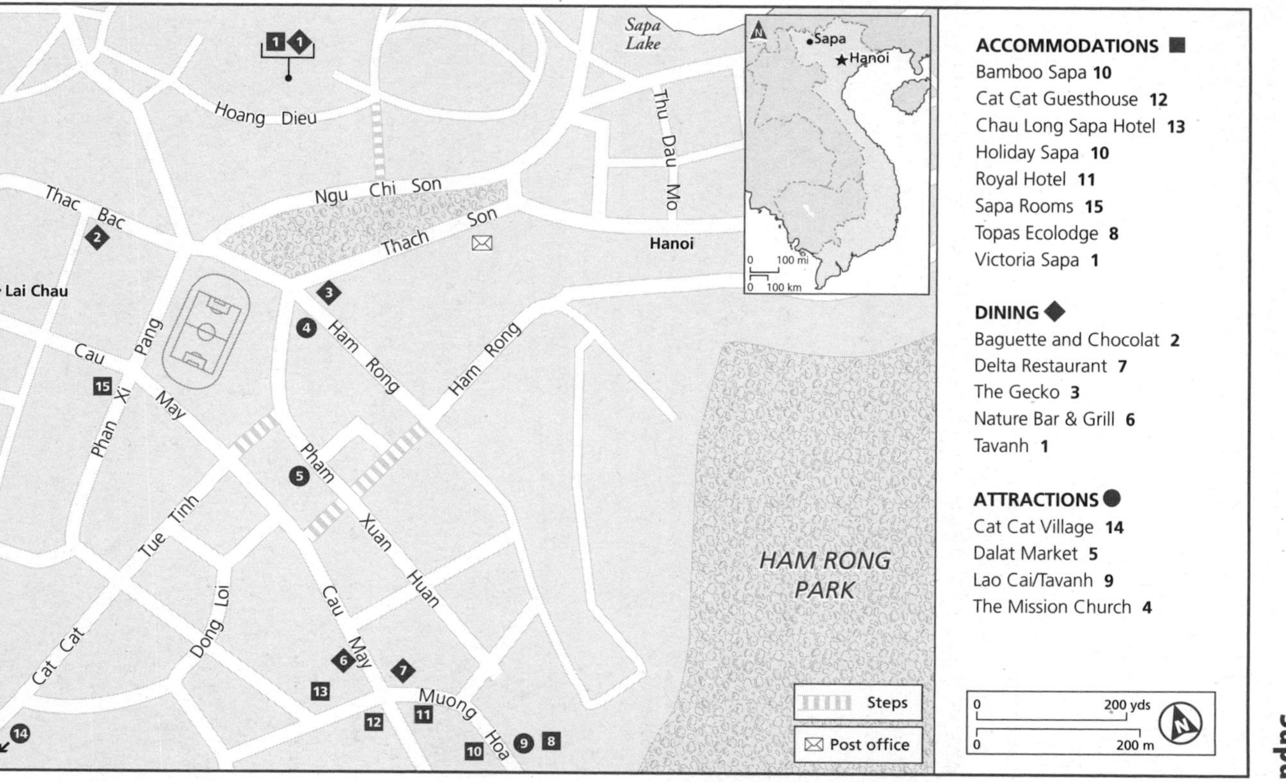
ACCOMMODATIONS
Bamboo Sapa 10
Cat Cat Guesthouse 12
Chau Long Sapa Hotel 13
Holiday Sapa 10
Royal Hotel 11
Sapa Rooms 15
Topas Ecolodge 8
Victoria Sapa 1
DINING
Baguette and Chocolat 2
Delta Restaurant 7
The Gecko 3
Nature Bar & Grill 6
Tavanh 1
ATTRACTIONS
Cat Cat Village 14
Dalat Market 5
Lao Cai/Tavanh 9
The Mission Church 4
0
200 yds
0
200 m
N
Steps
Post office
HAM RONG PARK
Sapa
Hanoi
0
100 mi
0
100 km
Sapa Lake
Hoang Dieu
Thu Dau Mo
Ngu Chi Son
Thach Son
Hanoi
Thac Bac
Lai Chau
Cau May
Pang
Phan Xi
Ham Rong
Ham Rong
Pham Xuan Huan
Tue Tinh
Dong Loi
Cau May
Cat Cat
Muong Hoa

Tips **Harvest Time**

If you can, time your trip to Sapa right before or during rice harvesting (Sept–Nov). Rice terraces are planted at intervals, allowing farmers to reap the fields over a period of several months. During the fall season, the valley will be painted various shades of green. The colors signal to farmers when a field is ready to be harvested. Along with the vibrant green colors, the valley will be dotted with bright colors of red or indigo, as many female farmers still wear their traditional ethnic minority clothing while working the land.

not accept tourists), or meet with the many hilltribe people who come to town to sell their wares.

The Tonkinese Alps are a feast for the eyes; hills striated by terraced rice farms in vast, green valleys are like a stairway up to **Mount Fansipan,** which is Southeast Asia's tallest mountain, at 3,143m (10,309 ft.). Climbing Fansipan is a multiday trip, requiring a guide and gear—best arranged through one of the tour operators listed, and only for the hearty. ***Note:*** Bring a few layers; it can get quite chilly here, especially in the winter months.

Sapa has gotten busy, and 2004 saw nearly 70,000 visitors (up from just 20,000 in 1996). Concerns are even coming from Hanoi that the growth in tourism is unsustainable and does not benefit local people, but instead lines the pockets of slick financiers. Steps are underway to ensure that the lives and customs of people here are not devastated, and you can do your part by educating yourself about some hilltribe traditions—be very cautious around any animistic totems, ask before taking photos, be careful where your money goes, and try not to encourage a culture of begging.

GETTING THERE

BY TRAIN Don't miss a chance to ride **Victoria's Orient Express** train from Hanoi to Lao Cai (from there, it is a 1½-hour ride to Sapa). With wood-paneled luxury sleeping cars and a restaurant billed as the finest dining between Hanoi and Sapa, this is an exciting option. The Victoria group replaced their cars with five new ones (including two sleeper cars and one dining car) in October 2006 and increased services to the area. Trains now run daily, except for Saturday, when cars are closed for maintenance and service. A four-course meal is offered aboard their dining cars (available on a rotational basis) for an additional $22. Menus are designed by Victoria Sapa Hotel's resident executive chef, and a la carte options are also available. The train's soft duvets, fluffy pillows, and hand-knit bags containing towel, toothbrush, and bottled water make the deflated pillows and thin comforters of the standard tourist trains look second-rate indeed. Round-trip prices range from $182 to $250. ***Note:*** You must have at least one overnight stay at the Victoria Sapa resort to ride the Victoria Orient Express. Also, if you want to book one of the train's few two-berth sleepers, book at least 6 months in advance. Contact Victoria Sapa (✆ **020/387-1522;** www.victoriahotels-asia.com) for details and reservations.

A number of standard and tourist trains also make the overnight run from Hanoi. You can make arrangements with any travel agent for a small fee, or do it yourself at the Hanoi Railway Station (where the western edge of Hoan Kiem district meets Dong Da district at 120 Le Duan; ✆ **04/394-23949**). Prices range from 299,000 VND for a hard sleeper in a six-bed berth with air-conditioning to 2,050,000 VND for a soft sleeper in a two-bed berth with air-conditioning. Trains passing through Lao Cai also continue north and make connections in China. (***Important reminder:*** You'll need a prearranged visa to enter China.) **Tulico Trains** (✆ **04/382-87806**) is another good bet, just one notch above the regular sleeper cars. All cars have four-sleeper berths in a pretty cramped space. If you like your privacy, buy yourself your own private car (and some breathing room) by purchasing all four beds and using only two of them.

To get to Sapa from the train station in Lao Cai, you'll need to transfer by bus for the 1½- to 2-hour ride from Lao Cai station. This can mean anything from a 25,000 VND fare in a rattletrap Russian castoff, or a price of $60 for a ride in a Japanese Pajero Mini (SUV) arranged through the Victoria Hotel. The road is cut into the hillside and is bumpy and windy, but the views of the terraced rice farms of the valley are beautiful as you ascend (ride on the left side).

Note: All trains to Lao Cai leave from the **Hanoi Railway Station** at 120 Le Duan St., which is often confused with Hanoi's other station. Be sure to show any taxi driver the address.

BY BUS Hanoi's tourist cafes all run frequent buses to Sapa for 300,000 VND one-way. Some include Sapa as a stop on a seat-in-coach tour around the Dien Bien Phu loop (usually a 4- or 5-day adventure stopping in Lao Cai, Son La, Dien Bien Phu, or Lai Chau and Sapa before returning to Hanoi). The train is, however, the best option if just connecting from Hanoi.

BY CAR Any tourist cafe or travel agent in Hanoi can arrange trips by private jeep or a combo jeep-and-train tour. Apart from Sapa, the vast tracts of the north are best visited through a tour company. **Ann Tourist Co., Buffalo Tours,** and **Handspan** all offer comprehensive itineraries. Especially for areas off the beaten track, avoid the temptation to book budget tours with the tourist cafes. In addition to the following section, see "Visitor Information & Tours" in chapter 5 for more information and options.

VISITOR INFORMATION & TOURS

For tours and trekking in the region, the Danish outfit **Topas Adventure Travel** (24 Hmuong Hoa, Sapa; ✆ **020/387-1331;** fax 020/387-2405; www.topasvietnam.com), with offices worldwide and experienced guides, is one of your best options (with Handspan being your other best choice). Office managers are usually tour leaders with regional experience who have been dispatched from Denmark and have worked with Topas for several years. Whether it's a day trek to nearby villages, an extended tour with homestays in villages, or the 5-day push to the top of Fansipan, these guys cover it.

Handspan—a large eco-tour outfit based in Hanoi with a good branch office overlooking the valley—is the most consistent choice for arranging day treks and transport. Find them just downhill from the Royal Hotel, at 8 Cau May St. (✆ **020/387-2110;** www.handspan.com).

Small budget-trekking offices line busy Cau May Street in Sapa, and you have your pick of guides and guided tours at budget prices. Just about anyone can hook you up with a Minsk motorbike for a 1-day rental or connect you with a guide. One of long standing and with a good reputation is **Dan Trung Auberge** (7 Muong Hoa St.; ✆ **020/387-1243**). Francophones mostly, there is also a good contingent of English speakers, and they can arrange the standard itineraries at midrange prices from their busy little guesthouse, restaurant, and tour center (long a Sapa fixture).

New is the **Tourist Information Center** (2 Fansipan St., in the center of town; ✆ **020/387-1975;** fax 020/387-1976), which can arrange an affordable guide ($10) for 1-day treks. And you'll support local villagers by booking through this center: Guides are local ethnic-minority members, few of whom speak English, but all of whom can take you on the classic day treks around the valley. The agency supports sustainable tourism in the valley and works with large international relief agencies to minimize the impact of tourists on the surrounding hilltribe cultures and customs.

BANKS & COMMUNICATION The post office is on Cau May Street (✆ **020/382-1206**), but most hotels can send postcards and letters and have stamps for sale. There are a few storefront Internet cafes, but service is slow and unreliable. All hotels provide exchange service for traveler's checks and even credit card cash advances. There is a local **bank** on Ma May where you can cash traveler's checks for the same 2% fee as at your hotel. There are two reliable ATMs in town, one in front of the Royal Hotel and another one 500m (1,640 ft.) north of the hotel on Cau May street.

WHERE TO STAY

Expensive

Topas Ecolodge ★★ For people who really want to get away from it all, Topas Ecolodge offers a clean break from TVs, telephones, and all the hustle and bustle of modern life. The beds and pillows are cozier here than at Victoria Sapa. The lodge is made up of 25 individual bungalows encircling a hilltop in the heart of Sapa Valley. The silence and breathtaking mountain and valley views are unrivaled. The lodge bills itself as an eco-tourism experience; heating and light are provided by solar panels placed behind each bungalow, and it uses a wastewater facility that ensures no or minimal pollution of the local area. Stone paths snake out from the main building (paved with stones from local stonemasons), and picturesque greenery with bright blue hydrangeas marks the way to each bungalow. Large windows in each room let in plenty of sunlight, and the design is a simple affair of wicker furniture, red-tile flooring, and whitewashed stone-cut walls. Because it is an eco-tourism destination, you will be in an up-close encounter with certain elements of nature. And while you may enjoy the company of the quiet resident dog, the occasional bug that wanders into your bungalow may be a less than welcome visitor. For those who begin to miss the haggling of sellers and the sounds of honking motorbikes, the lodge offers shuttles into town three times a day.

Located 18km (11 miles) from Sapa town. Shuttles to the lodge depart from Topas Adventure Travel's office, at 24 Muong Hoa, Sapa, Lao Cai Province. ✆ **020/387-1331.** Fax 020/387-1596. www.topasecolodge.com. 25 units. $115 double (including train to Sapa and SUV transport to and from resort). AE, MC, V. **Amenities:** Restaurant (all meals are inclusive and are set menus). *In room:* Fridge, no phone.

Victoria Sapa ★ Kids This is Sapa town's crème de la crème. Situated around a cozy courtyard, all rooms have balconies with wood-spindled railings and, inside, deep-toned wood floors offset by saturated wall colors, cane and fine wooden finish work, and local weavings and art. Unfortunately, the rural resort is a bit dated. Beds and bathrooms are beginning to show their age, mattresses are a bit lumpy, and water spots dot the white tile floor. If you're here with the kids, family rooms are huge, with up to six beds (they can be rearranged), and are a great option. For a luxe local encounter, the hotel can arrange an overnight Victoria-style homestay package (complete with the hotel's housekeeping services, mattresses, slippers, and a morning croissant) in nearby Muong Hum village. If you want rooms with a view, head to Topas Ecolodge (see above); new budget hotels and ongoing town construction have blocked the once-clear view to Mount Fansipan.

At the top of the hill overlooking town, Sapa district, Lao Cai Province. ✆ **020/3871-522.** Fax 020/3871-539. www.victoriahotels-asia.com. 77 units. $185 double; $260 suite (promotional rates available). AE, MC, V. **Amenities:** Restaurant; bar; children's playroom; fitness center; indoor heated pool; sauna; smoke-free rooms; tennis court. *In room:* Satellite TV and movie library, TV/DVD (in suites), fridge, hair dryer, minibar, Wi-Fi.

Moderate

Bamboo Sapa This large concrete block suspended over the valley near the town center is a good standby. Rooms are clean and large, and the royal blue trim is a nice change from the dingy pink at nearby Holiday Sapa. Most have balconies (sadly, too small to fit chairs), and all are oriented to the valley view. Bathrooms contain showers and are large and clean; mattresses are sturdy, hard foam; the staff is quite friendly; and the hotel has a good in-house tour operator **(Sapa Trekking Tour)** that can plan any trip. There is an open-air restaurant under the lobby, and they hold frequent, fun cultural dance shows.

18 Muong Hoa St. ✆ **020/387-1076.** Fax 020/387-1945. www.sapatravel.com. 45 units. $39–$59 double. No credit cards. **Amenities:** Restaurant; bar; motorbikes. *In room:* TV, fridge.

Chau Long Sapa Hotel ★ A tour-group favorite, the Chau Long has the look of an old hilltop castle in Europe, but that's just the facade. Down a quaint alley near the main road, rooms aren't overly special, but they're cleanly crafted in dark wood with small, tidy bathrooms. Most have balconies with good views, but many of those views are blocked in part by a new minihotel (and a larger hotel under construction next door), so be sure to ask to see the room before checking in. The friendly staff will bend over backward to make your stay fun. Be sure to say hello to their Dalmatian and their other dog, whose fur has been carefully shaved, leaving a mane which is dyed bright orange: the techno-colored lion-dog of Sapa.

24 Dong Loi. ✆ **020/387-1245.** Fax 020/387-1844. www.chaulonghotel.com. 87 units. $35–$120 double; $150 suite MC, V. **Amenities:** Restaurant; bar; bike and motorbikes; Internet; room service. *In room:* Satellite TV, fridge, hair dryer.

Holiday Sapa ★ This year-old hotel is a nice addition to Muong Hoa Street. Most rooms are clean and spacious, though you should avoid the standard rooms, which are tiny and have no view. The best deal is the superior corner room on the sixth floor, which is spacious, has a fantastic view, and features a gigantic corner balcony fitted with a cozy wooden bench. The only drawback is the bathroom, which is the all-in-one kind with no separate tub or shower cubicle. Deluxe rooms and up have separate tubs. Staff here is very friendly and speaks English better than at neighboring Bamboo Sapa.

16 Muong Hoa St. ✆ **020/387-3874.** Fax 020/387-2788. www.holidaysapa.com. 43 units. $30–$70 double; $100 suite. AE, MC, V. **Amenities:** Restaurant; babysitting; gym; pool; room service; Wi-Fi. *In room:* TV, fridge, hair dryer, minibar.

Sapa Rooms ★ This place's self-description as a boutique hotel is a bit generous, but it definitely wins for being the most contemporary and stylish option in town. Rooms are a good size, with plush, brightly colored rugs thrown over marble floors, as well as colonial-era wood furniture. If you're a small group, book yourself into the triple room, which is quite spacious and goes for the same price as a double. Bathrooms are luxurious for this price, with a stylish shower lined with wooden floors. Rooms also come with dehumidifiers, a major plus in a place as damp as Sapa. The ground-floor restaurant is a Thai-inspired area with dark-colored walls and cozy seats. There's a Segafredo cafe attached, serving coffee that rivals that of Baguette and Chocolat (see "Where to Dine," below).

18 Phan Si Pang. ✆ **020/387-2130.** Fax 020/387-2131. www.saparooms.com. 6 units. $44 double or triple; $65 suite. MC, V. **Amenities:** Restaurant; bar; bike and motorbike; Internet; room service. *In room:* TV, hair dryer, Wi-Fi.

Inexpensive

Cat Cat Guesthouse The view—that's what it's all about here. At this basic guesthouse, buildings are stacked like an unlikely pile of children's blocks against a steeply sloping hill. It's a bit of a hike up a long flight of steps, past the more eccentric rooms to the large guesthouse block and popular restaurant at the top of the hill (best views and comfort). Rooms are concrete and plain, a backpacker standard, but most have big windows and balconies. Owner Mrs. Loan will make you feel at home, and you're sure to meet other travelers who'll be saying, "Did you check out the view from the top?" Stop by for a coffee even if you don't stay.

Cat Cat Rd. (at the base of the town on the way down to the Cat Cat Village). ✆ **020/3871-946** or 387-1387. Fax 020/387-1133. catcatht@hn.vnn.vn. 40 units. $25–$60 double. No credit cards. **Amenities:** Restaurant; bar (w/best view in town); Internet. *In room*: TV.

Royal Hotel ★ It's backpacker central at this picturesque five-story tower in the heart of town, the very terminus of central Cau May Street. With just the right blend of comfort and affordability, this hotel is a real budget-traveler favorite; if you aren't a real budget traveler, you might be a bit turned off by the sparse tile-and-concrete decor, busy hallways, and hit-or-miss service. The hotel's Friendly Café is aptly named: Waitstaff here seem to be chosen for their desire (read: not ability) to speak English, and the food is basic, affordable traveler fare (fried rice, fried noodles, and beer). Every room has a balcony, and some even have a fireplace. The Royal also has its own train service, kind of a scaled-down version of Victoria's trains.

54B Cau May St. ✆/fax **020/387-1313.** Fax 020/387-1788. 30 units. $10–$15 double. AE, MC, V. **Amenities:** Restaurant; bar; Internet. *In room:* TV, fridge.

WHERE TO DINE

Baguette and Chocolat ★ FRENCH The folks from **Hoa Sua** (p. 93), a popular restaurant designed as a training center for disadvantaged youth, have done an excellent job with this cozy cafe. Open sandwiches, pizzas, salads, and omelets top a fine menu heavy on good French cuisine. Seating is in a cool "no shoe" area with rattan couches and white pillows (be sure to tidy up if coming from a day in the hills) or you can sit outside. The sandwiches here are okay, but accompanying french fries are excellent. What really attracts folks to this little cafe are the pastries and good, strong coffee; you won't find espresso and cappuccino like this elsewhere in town. They serve good, inexpensive breakfasts: a pastry and coffee will set you back only 38,000 VND, and a European breakfast costs 65,000 VND. The friendly folks at Baguette and Chocolat can also arrange picnic lunches that you can take while trekking, even for large groups if you contact them in advance.

Thac Bac St., near the hilltop terminus of central Cau May St. ✆ **020/387-1766.** www.hoasuaschool.com. Main courses 50,000 VND–160,000 VND. No credit cards. Daily 7am–9pm.

Delta Restaurant ★ ITALIAN Come here for the post-trek or post-long-haul-to-Sapa pizza. Right in the center of town on the corner across from the Royal Hotel, this place has wide glass doors that they can close on windy or foggy nights. Upstairs is a chic little wine bar with booths: cozy and romantic. The menu features the likes of gazpacho, bruschetta, good fresh salads, pasta, lasagna, ravioli, Australian steaks, and chicken dishes, but the pizza reigns supreme. Thin crust topped with light and fresh ingredients and real cheese. The Cappriciosa pizza I ordered was topped with tomato, eggplant, mushroom, olive oil, and gobs of good mozzarella. Prices are high for this little backpacker town, but that just keeps the backpackers out.

33 Cau May St. (just cater-cornered to the Royal Hotel). ✆ **020/387-1799.** Main courses $6–$12. MC, V. Daily 7:30am–10pm.

The Gecko FRENCH This small restaurant just west of the old church serves hearty but forgettable French food. Staff members speak little to no English, and the atmosphere is a bit on the bland side. They have a sister restaurant called Le Petit Gecko serving similar fare just across the street.

4 Ham Rong St. (east of the old church). ✆ **020/387-1504.** Main courses $5–$10. No credit cards. Daily 7am–10pm.

Nature Bar & Grill ★★ VIETNAMESE This is the best restaurant on Cau May Street. The specialty here is fresh, tasty Vietnamese dishes served piping hot on stone plates. The grilled beef is a good bet, as is the deer, if you like gamier meat. Vietnamese staples like fried rice, *pho,* and spring rolls round out the menu. The ambience is a cross between a country lodge and a backpacker haunt, with a giant brick fireplace in one corner and Bob Marley tunes piped in over the speakers.

24 Cau May St. ✆ **020/387-2094.** Main courses 39,000 VND–85,000 VND. No credit cards. Daily 7am–11pm.

Tavan Overrated FRENCH/VIETNAMESE The most elegant dining in the Tonkinese Alps comes with high prices and average food. You are essentially paying New York prices for small portions of underwhelming fare. The menu is rich with imports: everything from lamb, to filet, to salmon steaks. There are Vietnamese specials on an evolving menu, but I actually prefer the local specialties at Nature Bar & Grill. The pastas are a good bet—homemade and filling. The dining room is dimly lit and romantic, done up with burgundy walls and rich wood floors and local hangings surrounding a central fireplace. They do make a mean cocktail here, so do indulge in predinner drinks.

At the Victoria Sapa Hotel. ✆ **020/387-1522.** Main courses $15–$45. AE, MC, V. Daily 6:30am–10pm.

ATTRACTIONS

The town itself is the attraction here. **Cau May Street,** the main drag, and the **central market area** (all very close together) are, on any given day, teeming with hilltribe folks in their spangled finest, putting on and practicing the hard sell with some great weaving, fine silver work, and interesting trinkets like mouth harps and flutes. Especially on the weekend, it can be quite a scene. The small alleys and streets of the town are extremely wanderable, and a short walk in any direction offers great views.

Bac Ha Market ★★ Some 100km (62 miles) from Sapa, this is the most famous market in the region and more along the lines of what Sapa was once like. Here, various hilltribes converge every Sunday morning to conduct commerce. As a visitor, you're part of the trade here because folks are keen to sell you their wares, but this market isn't as much about the tourist buck (yet) as it is about small-time business and fellowship. Bring a camera. Sunday morning from dawn to late morning is prime time, but the market continues until about noon. Most visitors make the 3-hour drive from Sapa in the early morning.

By jeep/land cruiser from Sapa for $60–$70 (contact hotels for a guide). Also can be arranged from nearby Lao Cai (contact Hanoi travel agents).

Cat Cat Village ★ At the base of the hill below the town of Sapa, this Hmong village is accessible by rough-paved road most of the way, and cement path for the rest. The small waterfall here is a good spot to kick back and rest—quite dynamic in rainy season. From there, follow the narrow cement walkway up a long set of steps until the path terminates in another part of Cat Cat Village. From there you can hop on a waiting motorbike taxi for the ride back up to Sapa (20,000 VND). The trip can be made in just a few hours and offers a unique glimpse of rural life. Some travelers walk the whole valley top to bottom and back—a good way to get your lungs up to speed for later treks in the valley.

Entrance fee (paid at the top of the hill) 15,000 VND. You can walk all the way down or hire a motorbike/car taxi to pick up and drop off.

Coc Ly Market Also some 100km (62 miles) from Sapa, this is a lesser-known market than Bac Ha (see above), which means it attracts fewer tourists. It runs Tuesday mornings. However, because it is about a third the size, it also attracts few locals and is much less varied and lively than Bac Ha. It is worth a visit if you have already missed the Bac Ha market or if it coincides with your trip to or from the Lao Cai train station.

By jeep/land cruiser from Sapa for $60–$70 (contact hotels for a guide). Also can be arranged from nearby Lao Cai (contact Hanoi travel agents).

Ta Phin Village and Cave Okay, so this one is a bit canned. You'll be mobbed at the entrance to the village by young Dao women in their elaborate regalia, high red head-dresses and all, selling weavings and other wares. The ladies will keep an eye on your motorbike or car for you and offer to take you on a guided tour "for free," with only the hope that you'll perhaps look at some of their items for sale at the end of the tour. The ladies of Ta Phin are nice enough—some speak English well and can provide some useful insight into Dao and Hmong culture—but the whole experience is a bit pushy. At the end of it, you're expected to drop a big wad of dough on some pretty pathetic-looking weavings. Not worth it. Best to just say "No, thank you" to offers of a village tour.

The cave at the apex of the town requires a guide with a lantern to lead you through, but one is rarely available. Bring your own flashlight to explore deep in the cave.

Trekking & Hiking Hiking in Sapa's picturesque landscape and among Vietnam's traditional ethnic minorities is one of the main reasons visitors flock to this northern region. Convenient to the town center, the **Lao Cai–to–Ta Van** day trip from Sapa is a chance to traipse around the rice terraces and experience a bit of rural village life. Unfortunately, the convenience also means there are many tourists around. Visitors are often assaulted by (mostly Hmong) villagers trying to sell their handicrafts and wares, and many do not accept "no" for an answer. This is a tour to do only if you are pressed for time. Hire a car or motorbike for the 9km (5½-mile) road down the valley from Sapa to the Hmong village of Lao Cai (some folks even walk it); it's a nice ride in itself, with great views of the lush terraces. From there, just follow the valley for a few miles to the next town of Ta Van. Along the way, you'll walk through terraced rice fields and among some picturesque villages, and experience a bit of rural life. (Entrance fee is 5,000 VND. Drop-off at Lao Cai and later pickup at Ta Van is about $4 with a motorbike taxi and $25 for a jeep.)

As you **walk through different hilltribe villages (Hmong and Dao people),** it's helpful to have a guide to explain customs or practices to you and perhaps translate.

Farther afield, I found hikes 2 to 3 hours **north of Sapa,** among the **Tay villages,** to be less traveled; the Tay people were more shy and respectful of passersby (that is, no trinket sellers following you mercifully for hours on end). You'll still be greeted with a hearty *"Hello! Allo!"* wherever you go.

Ask at your hotel front desk, or contact Topas Adventure Travel (p. 135) for longer, less touristy treks. It is, in fact, illegal to hike without a guide, and you may find yourself a very unwelcome visitor in a village that does not accept tourists. Besides, local guides are knowledgeable about levels of difficulty and which hikes are more secluded and less touristy.

SHOPPING

The streets of Sapa are lined with small, local boutiques, and more are setting up each day. But the real shopping and good bargains come from roving groups of ethnic hilltribe ladies, many just young girls, who are sure to find you—some are true polyglots and masters of the hard sell. The best boutique in town is **Indigo ★** (12 Duong Muong Hoa; **© 020/387-2568;** daily 7am–9pm), a store run by Tanh, a local Hmoung minority, and her Japanese expat husband (they met and fell in love while he was visiting to look into the textile industry). Indigo offers simple, modern takes on traditional ethnic clothing. Most pieces are solid-colored cotton or linen, and dyed using natural vegetable dyes. Unlike many pieces sold at markets or by street sellers, Indigo's pieces are properly dyed to ensure colors won't run when thrown in the washing machine. The boutique is a fair trade company that orders fabric and various motifs from local villages, and employs local disadvantaged workers (deaf-mute graduates of the Hoa Sua school in Hanoi) to sew and embroider their clothing and wares. The Indigo line is also sold at the Victoria Sapa Hotel gift shop.

3 THE DIEN BIEN PHU LOOP

Tired of tourist trails? Here's a great opportunity to get off the track and into rugged terrain that is little affected by tourism or the world economy. In an area along the border of China and Laos, rugged roads traverse high mountain passes, cling to the side of steep mountains prone to landslide, and peer down over deep river gorges. The major thoroughfares are paved and in good condition in the dry season, but do keep an ear to the ground before setting out during or just after the summer rains (check in at **Highway 4,** a popular bar and meeting spot in Hanoi, for the most updated information; for the bar's location, see p. 125).

Travel in this region offers the best opportunity to meet and greet people of ethnic-minority hilltribe groups, from the timid White Thai to the gregarious Hmong. But remember that responsible tourism is crucial; our collective interaction with isolated ethnic minorities lays the groundwork for their future survival (or demise). Hire guides if you are going off into the boonies or out among ethnic groups. Your impact, especially if your travels take you to real rural parts, is important. (See the "Responsible Tourism" sidebar, p. 34.)

Give yourself **5 or 6 days** for the loop from **Hanoi to Sapa;** anything shorter means you'll spend all of your time on the road, with little respite or time to explore.

The best way to do this loop is by motorbike, as two wheels will take you to small villages and off the main road—places that are off-limits to a jeep. But jeeps are also a good—and certainly safer—option. A few good outfitters can arrange tours by motorbike, with or

Tips When Traveling in the Northern Highlands . . .

Bring cash. You can find local banks in each of these little towns to exchange U.S. greenbacks, but usually at a much less favorable rate. Apart from in Sapa and Lao Cai, there are **no ATMs** in the region. Just bring enough Vietnam dong to cover expenses (on your own, plan to bring about 375,000 VND). Even the smallest hamlet in Vietnam has good postal service, you can make calls via an international phone, and the Internet is accessible in the smallest town (you might even catch sight of the proverbial "thatched-roof Internet cafe"), but service is very slow, even in Sapa. **Medical services** are not up to par, even for Vietnam. You can fly yourself out of Dien Bien Phu if you're in real trouble, but you're more or less on your own out on the roads. Bring a good first-aid kit for incidental cuts and scrapes, and be sure to carry stomach medicine, bug spray, and sunscreen.

without guides, or jeep (see information on renting a Minsk below). All of the traveler cafes in Hanoi run trips up this way, but it's worth it to go with a midrange or high-quality tour provider (see Handspan, p. 135, or Buffalo Tours, p. 68); you'll get more individual attention, follow more-out-of-the-way routes, and enjoy unique itineraries with professional guides.

BETWEEN HANOI & MAI CHAU

The hardest part of the trip is getting out of Hanoi. From the city center, one-way streets actually abut one another and the traffic must disperse in either direction—it's very strange. The roads out of town going southwest, either Ton That Tung or Tay Son, are a sea of motorbikes; crossing traffic is heavy and unpredictable. If you're going over 30kmph (19 mph), you're going too fast. At the farthest edge of the city, traffic thins out, and once you pass the Ho Chi Minh Trail Museum (p. 114) some 14km (8¾ miles) south and west on Route 6, you're in the clear. (The museum is a good rest stop after the long road of city traffic.) From here, you're in the boonies and the fun begins. You can drive up to 70kmph (43 mph), but about 50kmph (31 mph) is best.

Before you reach the town of **Hoa Binh,** you'll pass through an area of towering limestone peaks; the road is lined with cafes that are popular local rest stops to relax and enjoy the mountainous views (in the evening, a kind of "Blueberry Hill" vibe pervades). The town of Hoa Binh is not worth a stop—it's just a typical Vietnamese city of cement row houses and honking motorbikes—but it's the dropping-off point for trips on the large **Da River,** or *Song Da,* reservoir, which powers the town's large hydroelectric plant. Past Hoa Binh, you'll enter the landscape typical to this region, with large hills cut by streams and lined with terrace rice farms.

Most stunning is the high pass you cross on the way to Mai Chau. The road is chiseled into the mountain's rock face, and the debris that resulted from the blasting forms a wide skirt at the foot of the mountain.

MAI CHAU

150km (93 miles) W of Hanoi; 170km (105 miles) E of Son La

Mai Chau makes a good overnight after the shakedown cruise from Hanoi (about a 5-hr. ride). The town center is a rather dull strip of small shops and a few *pho* and *com* stands (noodle soup or rice), but there are two White Thai villages just outside of town where both solo travelers and group tours commonly stay. You can take short boat trips on the **Da River Reservoir** from the pier just near the turnoff road to Mai Chau (best arranged through a tour).

Where to Stay

In addition to the recommendation below, the other option in town is to stay at one of the nearby **White Thai villages** of **Ban Lac** of **Pom Coong.** If you travel through this way on tour, you will most likely be spending the night at one of these local homestays, sleeping under a thatch roof on bamboo woven floors. Tourists have been staying here a while, and some folks even hang signs to invite visitors in. Most homestays have electric lights and TVs. You'll pay a flat fee and dine with a family. Just walk or ride to the villages sometime well before sunset. Just before you arrive at the Mai Chau Guesthouse, which is at the farthest end of Mai Chau town, you'll see a little booth where they charge a few thousand dong to enter this hilltribe area, but no one has been manning it lately. Just before the guesthouse and right in front of the booth, there is a small path through the rice fields to Ban Lac, and the path to Pom Coong is past the guesthouse a few hundred meters and to the right. The people of these villages are White Thai, and most of the women still wear traditional dress. A stay or a brief visit is a good glimpse into White Thai culture, and a rustic overnight in the village is certainly more interesting than the plain-Jane Mai Chau Guesthouse.

Mai Chau Guesthouse This plain building with dull rooms is the only tourist hotel of any sort for miles. The staff is friendly and can direct you to hikes in the villages, but it's a pretty basic affair. And the nearby karaoke bars, most on floats or suspended on a nearby pond, are a major drawback to staying here. If you check into the guesthouse in the early evening, you can enjoy a calm sunset, but not long after, the crooners arrive; get ready for some noisy racket until about 10pm.

At the farthest end of town, Mai Chau, Hoa Binh. ✆ **0218/386-7262.** 20 units. 100,000 VND double. No credit cards. *In room:* No phone.

Where to Dine

Dinner in Mai Chau (or "Your Chow," as my punny travel companion pointed out) is offered at just a few small local storefront restaurants. Ask at the front desk of the Mai Chau Guesthouse for a recommendation, and be armed with a few phrases on food like *com trung* (fried egg with rice), *rau xau* (mixed vegetables), or *pho bo* (noodle soup with beef). For more language help, see chapter 16. A few Internet outposts are in the town, but service is very slow.

Attractions

The surrounding villages of **Ban Lac** and **Pom Coong** are great for a morning wander, whether you spent the night in a village homestay or at the Mai Chau Guesthouse. The villages are touristed-out, meaning that the little dusty streets are now paved, and that though the hospitality is genuine, the folks here lead with handfuls of souvenir items for sale and not a handshake. The surrounding valley is green with rice fields and laced with fun little tracks. Bring a camera and your sense of adventure, and get lost out on the paddies for a few hours before heading on to Son La. Local guides can be hired from the Mai Chau Guesthouse for trekking farther afield.

The Minsk: A Guide to Renting & Enjoying Your Big Honkin' Soviet Motorbike

So you want to really get out and see the far north on your own? Well, one way to do it is to get yourself a Minsk. Built in Minsk, Belarus, by the Motovelo corporation, these sturdy 100cc machines come in two different models: 1) the older **classic Minsk,** which is a model of Soviet-style "function, not form" design principles; and 2) the **sport Minsk,** a higher-profile bike with better suspension, something like a standard motocross bike, but with the same engine as the classic Minsk.

A Minsk is still your best bet for reliability, durability, and easy fixability, as just about everyone up this way has one and can help you with even major repairs. Hairpins and bailing wire often suffice as replacement parts, and even the smallest little country repair shop is staffed with someone who can tap apart the crank case and fix major problems. Locals appreciate your adventurous spirit (or call you crazy) for striking out on these old hunks of metal to explore their country. Once a security guard at a hotel gave my bike a full tune-up just for the love of the bike and to ensure I'd have a safe trip. And these bikes will make a mechanic out of you: The principles of the internal-combustion engine couldn't be clearer than if Fred Flintstone himself designed it.

Be sure to learn the phrase *Xang Fa Dao* (sounds like "Sang Fa Zow"), which means "gas with oil," and *Nam Fa Jam,* which means "5%." Minsks are two-stroke, or two-cycle, motors (something like your lawn mower, weed whacker, or go-kart back home), and you need to mix 5% oil with the gas. In the countryside, folks at gas stations are very adept at this because they're used to dealing with Minsks and other two-stroke machines, but be careful in cities, where gas station attendants know only scooters. When filling up with gas, be sure to turn off the fuel line connecting to the engine, and help the attendant, who will either measure a cup of oil and then thin it out by adding gas directly to the cup, suspended over a funnel into your tank, or mix the oil and gas in a separate can. In either case, watch closely and see that the bike gets oil. When you start off, keep the fuel line closed and make some slow, swerving turns to mix the gas; then open the fuel line to the normal setting.

There are two good **rental** agencies in Hanoi:

- **Mr. Cuong's Motorbike Adventure** (1 Luong Ngoc Quyen St., on the east side of the Old Quarter near the city's major ring road; ✆ **04/3926-1534**) is the best place for straight-up rental. Cuong is a mechanic and keeps a large stable of Minsks in good condition. Each bike is nearly rebuilt after every rental. You'll pay the standard $7 per day, which includes a good helmet, but that's where service stops. Mr. Cuong's place is open daily from 8am to 6pm, and he's a very understanding man, cutting you little breaks like charging for a half-day if you bring it back early and lending extras at no cost to you.
- **Mr. Hung's Vietnam Adventure Tour,** on the other hand, provides motorbike rentals as well as comprehensive guide services. For just $30 per day,

you can hire a bike and an accompanying guide with his own bike. Choose from a number of well-planned routes around the north, enjoying ease of navigation and easier connection to locals. If you're considering going it alone, some folks have reported that Hung's bikes aren't quite as well maintained as those at Cuong's (see above), but if you're looking for more of a tour, Mr. Hung's is the place to start. Find him at his small storefront travel agent just north of Hoan Kiem Lake at 5A Dinh Liet St. (✆ **04/3926-0938**), and someone there can take you to his repair shop on the city ring road at 162 Tran Quang Khai St. (just around the corner from Mr. Cuong's).

When renting a Minsk, you'll have to leave your **yellow paper,** a rather valuable little Customs certificate that you'll need (or face a fine and some bureaucratic hassles) when leaving the country. Most shops ask that you pay in advance and sign a contract that gives you complete responsibility (to the tune of $350–$500, depending on the bike) for the bike's well-being. Demand a lock and use it when leaving the bike for long intervals (most Minsks do not have key ignitions and therefore are easily started by anyone).

Safety Demand a helmet and wear it; go slow; and honk to alert other vehicles when passing. Stay alert! Vietnamese roads are chaotic, and something or somebody is always leaping out onto the roadway or veering into your lane. The hardest part about any trip in the north is navigating Hanoi's crazy traffic and finding your way out of the city; in fact, both Mr. Hung and Mr. Cuong are given to leading their more inexperienced clients out of the city center to more sane open roads.

What to Bring In the little metal storage cases on the side of the bike (for older models) or under the seat, pack an extra tube, a patch kit, a few spark plugs, a spark-plug wrench, and a crescent wrench; most rental shops will provide it all, but be sure to ask. Minsks leak oil—in fact, just getting close to the bike usually means you get a few smudges on you—so bring two sets of clothes: one grungy pair of long pants, T-shirt, and light jacket that you won't mind getting covered in oil and road splatter during the day, as well as a clean set of dry clothes, including something warm like a sweatshirt or fleece for those chilly highland nights. Minsks can be outfitted with handy saddlebags, or else you can bungee your gear onto the rack at the back of the bike.Then keep a light day pack of daily-use items (camera, journal, wallet, and so on) on your back or at the top of the saddlebags. A "dry bag" is good to have at the ready should you hit some rain and want to just tuck away readily used items and valuables (I also drop my money belt into the dry bag if the rain starts). Be sure to bring bug repellent, a flashlight, and a hat for day hikes and cave exploring. Wear long pants, preferably jeans, when riding, and wear boots, if possible, and at least shoes or sneakers, if not (no sandals), but bring something light like flip-flops for the evening.

FROM MAI CHAU TO SON LA

Take a detour near Mai Chau and hop a ride on the **Da River Reservoir.** In fact, many tours include a long boat ride between Mai Chau and Hoa Binh, but if you just want to catch a glimpse of the water, pull off where the signs indicate just past Mai Chau. The road from Mai Chau to Son La is lined with Montagnard villages and some fine areas of karst limestone outcroppings.

SON LA

320km (199 miles) NW of Hanoi; 170km (106 miles) W of Mai Chau

Son La is a small city set in a narrow valley at the foot of low hills. A short walk up to the town's famous hilltop prison or to one of the viewpoints in the hills above gives you a good perspective on the two busy streets that make up downtown. Both accommodations and dining are rather limited, but this is a popular (pretty much essential) stop on any tour of the northeast.

A testament to the wily French colonists and their love of brutal prisons (also see Con Dao and Phu Quoc Island in the far south; between the American and the French prisons, you can, in fact, tour a prison in just about every province), Son La was home to one of the country's worst facilities, the end of the line for Vietnam's early-20th-century dissidents. A letter from French brass talking of Son La Prison's brutal effectiveness says, "The malaria and toil here would break the revolutionary zeal of any man."

FAST FACTS There's no ATM service in Son La, but the **Bank of Agriculture and Rural Development** (8 Chu Van Thinh St.) can cash traveler's checks. You'll find a few Internet terminals around town, but they're all very slow. Try the few along To Hieu Street, near the corner where Route 6 enters the town of Son La. The post office is on To Hieu in the center of town.

Where to Stay

All accommodations in Son La are basically of the same low-end minihotel standard.

The Trade Union Hotel (Cong Doan) This is where it's at. The Trade Union hotel has simple white-tile rooms with cool canopy beds fixed with mosquito nets (though they're not necessary) and ornate ceilings of white plaster, rimmed with heavy ornamental trim. The place is always busy with Vietnamese tour groups. The staff speaks English well, but they use it to press you into using their services—"You rent car? You eat here?"—though all done a bit tongue-in-cheek. The folks at Trade Union Hotel take good care of your car or motorbike—they even give it a free power-wash. The restaurant is bland but the best choice for the familiar.

04 Son Thuy, Son La. ✆ **022/385-2804.** Fax 022/385-5312. 100 units. $20–$40 double. No credit cards. **Amenities:** Restaurant; bar. *In room:* A/C, TV, fridge, minibar.

Where to Dine

At Duong Truong Chinh Road, near the intersection of To Hieu Street and on the corner where Route 6 enters the town of Son La, you'll find a number of **small storefront eateries,** most of which are cafeteria style, where you can put together a meal by pointing to what appeals to you, usually a choice of boiled eggs, vegetables, pork in broth, fried fish, or tofu fried in lemon grass, all accompanied with rice. These same shops can cook to order the likes of fried noodles or omelets upon request, but suffice it to say that dining in little Son La is far from gourmet; think of it more as a place to just fill your tummy before heading off on the road the next day. Your best bet for being understood and getting a reasonable meal is at the hotel of your choice. Resist the temptation to try the goat meat, called *thit da,* at the hilltop restaurant that some folks might point you to. The meat is gamy, and the experience appeals only to folks looking to cross off items on the "strange food I once ate" list.

Attractions

Son La Prison Hilltop **Son La Prison** is an important historical vestige. Some parts were destroyed by the French, and later by the Americans, but many of the ramparts have been rebuilt, and some interiors have been done over so that visitors get the full effect. The museum at the back tells—in cases of artifacts, translated documents, pictures, and creative renderings—the story of how prisoners marched in chains for over 220km (137 miles) and then were entombed here. (Having just gone over it by car or motorbike, think of walking the same route in chains over a 2-week period.) Expressive plaster statuary and oil paintings of scenes inside the prison express the prisoners' plight. Like many war sites or prisons in Vietnam, Vietnamese visit here as a way of remembrance, to honor and give thanks to those who have sacrificed. Find displays of prisoner shackles, photos of prison life, and weapons used by prisoners during the many uprisings, including the 1945 revolt that shut down the prison for good. The museum has a model of the prison rooms as they were, with slat beds and floor toilets. Out back, don't miss the tree of **To Hieu,** a survivor and the namesake of the town's main thoroughfare who returned in the 1950s and planted a small peach tree to celebrate peace. The tiny, gnarled tree is behind a wall just to the right of the entry to the main prison compound. The basement of the main prison building houses eerie solitary-confinement chambers and rebuilt "Tiger Cage" cells. Don't go alone unless you can handle the chill.

Adjacent to the prison area, there is a two-story museum in a more modern compound. You'll find rather tatty but organized displays on local hilltribe culture, a room dedicated to the life and legacy of Ho Chi Minh, and ubiquitous sun-bleached photos of industrial projects indicating Vietnam's victorious rise of the working man and progress into the next century (seen one, seen 'em all). There's also a room of stone and ancient artifacts, including some fine examples of Dong Son drums, evidence of Vietnam's earliest Bronze Age culture. ***Note:*** The promenade near the museum is more or less the city's "inspiration point" in the evening.

BETWEEN SON LA & DIEN BIEN PHU

The road gets more mountainous and curvy as it traces vast river valleys and brings you among more Montagnard groups. In fact, a stop just about anywhere brings you into some *National Geographic*–like moments. Be sensitive when taking pictures of hilltribe people; some groups have superstitions about photo taking. Be sure to ask first, and honor the wishes of anyone who declines to have their photo taken, however front-page-worthy. Do not offer money to take someone's photo. The road traces some high ridges, which also means some hard climbing, with jeeps and motorbikes digging down into second gear, but you're rewarded along the way with stunning viewpoints over broad valleys of terraced rice farms.

Route 6 terminates at the town of Tuan Giao, itself just a place for a little coffee or a local lunch of rice or noodles; from here, a right turn takes you some 98km (61 miles) to Lai Chau along a stunning stretch of Route 6, and a left is just 80km (50 miles) to Dien Bien Phu. Most tours take you to Dien Bien Phu, but should you be so lucky/brave/foolish to be on a motorbike, I recommend you skip a visit to Dien Bien Phu,

Finds On Route 6

Route 6 cuts across a stunning mountainous patch, a narrow ribbon of paved and broken-paved road that is more often just a shelf cut into the rock. Overlooking broad valley scenery, you'll pass through quaint hilltribe villages all along the path. The road terminates in **Mai Chau** (p.142), where you can easily find lodging for the night before pushing on to Sapa. ***Note:*** Even if you decide to go to Dien Bien Phu, see if you can find the time to travel the head of this stunning road for at least a few kilometers, to get a taste of the stunning scenery (drive up from either Tuan Giao or, on the other side, Mai Chau).

which, short of its historical significance, is just a dusty border outpost, and head over Route 6 to Lai Chau on one of Vietnam's most beautiful roads.

DIEN BIEN PHU

475km (295 miles) W of Hanoi; 150km (93 miles) W of Son La; 80km (50 miles) S of Lai Chau

Toward the end of World War II—after the withdrawal of all Japanese forces from Vietnam, and the August 1945 reading of the Vietnamese Declaration of Independence and the resultant August Revolution—the French colonial mission in Vietnam was nearly over. French forces were down to a skeleton crew after years of attrition under Japanese rule in Indochina, but despite international pressure, Charles De Gaulle sent a force of 70,000 to old Indochina under the command of General LeClerc in the 1950s. Efforts at building a French-Vietnamese coalition including Ho Chi Minh were ill-fated and failed as soon as they were implemented. Guerilla fighting and terrorist attacks by the Viet Minh forces throughout the north soon led to the full-scale Indochina War.

First, a massive French bombing campaign of northern supply lines in Haiphong, attacks that killed thousands of innocents, gave way to a long succession of bloody battles and many casualties on both sides. Nearing some truce in the conflict in 1953, the French put all of their eggs (or most of them) in one basket and chose Dien Bien Phu as the best place to intercept supply lines to rebel groups. Hoping to provoke a classic pitched battle instead of hunting terrorists, the garrison at Dien Bien Phu was surrounded by fire stations, or fortified outposts, in the hills above, supported by heavy air transport and, by 1954, manned by some 16,000 seasoned French Foreign Legion fighters. The impoverished Vietnamese guerrilla forces looked cut off, and the French expected to go to the bargaining tables with some real leverage. How wrong they were.

The battle lasted from March 13 until May 8, 1954, with Vietnamese forces surrounding the valley and pummeling French forces with artillery dragged, by hook or crook, over hill and dale from China. The French were completely surprised. Though French expeditionary troops fought valiantly, with some truly fearless French units parachuting into the crippled encampment long after the runway was destroyed, supply lines were cut and all looked lost. Strategists likened the battle to a fight between a jungle tiger and an elephant, where the Vietnamese tiger strikes at intervals and leaves its larger, stronger prey to bleed to death. Without any official surrender, the French laid down their arms and were completely overrun. The first Indochina War was over, and Dien Bien Phu would forever be a rallying cry for Vietnamese sovereignty.

The town of Dien Bien Phu itself is just a wide avenue lined with Soviet-era construction. There are a few decent hotels, but mainstream tourism is far from overrunning Dien Bien, a town whose greatest moment in history was, in fact, when it was overrun. War memorials, including a good museum, are what attract mostly war buffs and French tour groups to this outpost on the Lao border. The highlights can be seen in a casual afternoon before pressing on to Lai Chau or Sapa the following day.

Getting There by Air

There are regular flights on Vietnam Airlines that connect Dien Bien Phu with Hanoi. The small airport is just north of town on the road to Lai Chau. **Vietnam Airlines** has a booking office at the airport (✆ **0230/382-4692**) or in town on Street 5 (✆ **0230/382-4692**).

Orientation

The city center lies on the eastern shore of the Nam Rom River. The road from Son La and Tuan Giao, Route 12, enters to the north of the city (some of the better accommodations are along it), and the central avenues of Le Trong Tan and Nguyen Chi Thanh make up the busy downtown. The history museum and A-1 hill are on the south end of town, and a few important military sites—bunkers and abandoned artillery and tanks—are on the west shore. The airport is just north of town on the west bank of the river, along the road to Lai Chau.

FAST FACTS Bring cash. There are no ATMs in Dien Bien Phu. You can exchange money at **Bank for Investment and Development of Vietnam** (3 Duong 7–5; ✆ **0230/382-5774**). There are lots of local Internet storefronts along the main drag. Slow connection is the rule. Better to wait until Sapa unless you're in a pinch. The main post office is on Street no. 3 in the town center.

Where to Stay & Dine

There are no **dining** venues geared to tourists in Dien Bien Phu; you're left to your own devices among the town's rice and noodle shops. But assuming you've come this far over land, you'll be an expert with the basics in local cuisine (for a few pointers, look in chapters 16 and 17). The best shops are near the main intersection in town. The Dien Bien Phu Hanoi Hotel (see below) serves good one-dish meals at their cozy little coffee shop on the first floor, and the Muong Thanh Hotel (see below) has a basic in-house restaurant.

Dien Bien Phu Hanoi Hotel Plain, clean, and large, the Dien Bien Phu Hanoi Hotel is a big government-run beauty that's quite similar to all the others in the center of town, but the nicest one of the lot. There's a downstairs coffee shop, in-house restaurant, and massage parlor (wink-wink), all popular for regional businessmen. A good standard of basic, carpeted rooms with air-conditioning and simple wannabe-luxe decor. I recommend the Muong Thanh (see below) over this one.

849 7–5 Rd., Street 6, Dien Bien Phu. ✆ **0230/382-5103.** Fax 0230/382-6290. 39 units. 350,000 VND–450,000 VND double. No credit cards. **Amenities:** Restaurant; cafe; sauna. *In room:* A/C, TV, fridge, minibar.

Muong Thanh Hotel About 1km (½ mile) outside of town on the road from Son La, this minihotel is popular with group tours and is a comfortable little outpost. Rooms are small but clean and air-conditioned. The courtyard is always full of minivans, jeeps, and motorbikes from small tour groups and individual travelers, and the staff takes good care of your transport for the night. There's a pool, but it's more a showpiece than anything (needs a cleaning). The pool area is surrounded by cement zoo animals, and the hotel's decent restaurant overlooks the little cement pond. The staff speaks English and is quite helpful.

514 Group 21, Him Lam Commune (on the road outside of town). ✆ **0230/381-0043.** Fax 0230/381-0713. 60 units. $15–$20 double. No credit cards. **Amenities:** Restaurant; bar; small courtyard pool (a bit grungy). *In room:* A/C, TV, fridge.

Attractions

The sites in Dien Bien Phu require a lot of imagination, really. Visualize, if you will, the French dug in all around town, completely cut off from the rest of the world. Bolstered by their surprise battery of Chinese artillery, and seemingly eager to endure casualties, Vietnamese troops come in waves. Losses were devastating on both sides. The story of this important moment in history is told in the many monuments and museums and the town cemetery—but the modern concretized trade town of Dien Bien Phu is not so interesting. Take a ride across the small bridge at the southern end of town and look for the rusting gun emplacements and a re-creation of the **Bunker of Colonel Christian De Castries,** who killed himself when he finally realized that all was indeed lost.

A-1 Hill and the Dien Bien Phu Cemetery This highest point at the center of town was a holdout of French troops and a hill that was hard-fought for. Today you'll find a memorial and a quiet park that makes a good perch to get the lay of the land. Just south, at the foot of the hill, is the **Dien Bien Phu Cemetery,** with mostly unmarked graves of the fallen. A grand compound at the entrance is the Vietnamese version of the Wall in Washington, but here are the names of soldiers who died at Dien Bien.

Admission 5,000 VND to climb A-1 Hill. The cemetery is free. Daily 7–11am and 1:30–5pm.

Dien Bien Phu Museum This long, low building is a bit beat-up (and could use a weed whacker out front), but the Dien Bien Phu Museum houses important relics, photos, and displays that chronicle the long struggle of revolution and the big Vietnamese victory over the French in 1954. There are photos of tanks that were airlifted in pieces, as well as grinning American advisors and confident French troops. The artifacts tell a story of massive artillery sledges designed to carry the big guns in pieces over the mountains from China. You'll see shoulder slings, the very shovels that dug the trenches or cleared the paths, and even the smudged clothes and field maps of troops. The Vietnamese win was the genius of North Vietnam's eminent strategist, Gen. Vo Nguyen Giap, and his life and works are celebrated at the museum.

At the town center. Admission 5,000 VND. Daily 7–11am and 1:30–5pm.

BETWEEN DIEN BIEN PHU & LAI CHAU

Except for some construction spots, the road is in fairly good shape up to Lai Chau. About 300km (186 miles) from Dien Bien Phu to Sapa, many travelers make the trip in 1 day, but it's actually a bit much, considering the big climbs and descents along the way. Also, if you go from Dien Bien Phu to Sapa in 1 day, you pass through the **Tram Ton** pass to Sapa in the evening (assuming you make lunch and photo stops along the way); this pass is one of the highlights of any trip in the north, and it's a shame to get there too late in the day, when the towering peaks are in clouds. Stay the night in Lai Chau if you can spare the time, so you'll get to the pass and to Sapa at midday; the little town of Lai Chau is also a good place to do a bit of wandering or day-trekking on your own and is thus worth the overnight.

LAI CHAU

180km (112 miles) N of Dien Bien Phu; 45km (28 miles) SW of Sapa

Just a short, low-lying commercial strip off the main road between Dien Bien Phu and Sapa, Lai Chau is set in the valley of the Dong Da River and is surrounded by large communities of mostly White Thai people. The town is the terminus of Route 6 from Tuan Giao, a shortcut over the mountains from Son La and one of the loveliest stretches of mountain road in Vietnam; travelers along the stretch usually call Lai Chau home for the night. It's also a logical stop if you're coming from Dien Bien Phu and don't want to bust all the way to Sapa in 1 day. (***Note:*** If you cross the Tram Ton pass to Sapa too late in the evening, you will likely miss the most spectacular scenery. Many therefore opt to stay in Lai Chau and cross to Sapa the next day.) The little Lan Anh Hotel is your only choice for a home away from home here.

There are **no banks** or **Internet cafes** in Lai Chau. You can exchange currency at the front desk of the **Lan Anh Hotel** in a pinch, but plan to bring cash. The local post office is near the main intersection heading toward Sapa.

Where to Stay

Lan Anh Hotel This is the closest thing to an eco-lodge in the highlands. Accommodations are simple, with narrow rooms done in wood with canopy beds. There's a good central restaurant with an English menu. But the real attraction to this rural stop on the Dong Da River is a chance to meet up with young **Mr. Trang,** the owner and manager of the hotel who organizes local treks and offers helpful advice and information for onward travel. Friendly staff can help out with any eventuality during your visit, and the shaded compound with a few hammocks will draw you in. Many travelers find themselves budgeting another day, taking good day treks and enjoying meeting fellow travelers in this rustic, homey spot.

Mr. Trang runs good trips to villages in the surrounding countryside. He's produced a helpful map, and if he's not around, you can make the circuits yourself. Some routes require that you have your own transport, preferably a motorbike, and others are just short day hikes along the Dong Da River valley to local White Thai villages, returning by way of bridge crossings and down the other side of the valley.

Central Lai Chau near the riverside (about 1km/½ mile west of the main road; large signs point the way). ✆ **0230/385-2370.** Fax 0230/385-2290. www.lananhhotel.com. 58 units. $15–$20 double; $35 suite. No credit cards. **Amenities:** Restaurant/bar w/good English menu; Internet (spotty); motorbike. *In room:* A/C (in some—mostly fan only), minibar, no phone.

FROM LAI CHAU TO SAPA

The road out of Lai Chau follows the **Dong Da River Valley** as the water widens in broad valleys and narrows to small rapids through precipitous gorges. The road is well paved and not as steep as other spots on the route, but it's not straight.

One possible detour on the route north to Sapa is the village of **Sin Ho.** Some 30km (19 miles) up a dirt track just east of the main road, Sin Ho is a quiet, isolated Thai village well worth the visit for an amateur ethnologist or an adventurer looking to see what their motorbike can "really do." ***Warning:*** This is well off the beaten track, so be sure you have all the requisite gear to fix any flats or major problems; there won't be any helpful strangers wandering down this rugged road. From Sin Ho, there's a "new road" that connects to the north and with the town of **Pa So** on the way to Sapa, but note that "new road" means "not finished"; it's more or less a rutted track.

Most travelers pass Sin Ho and opt to follow the Dong Da River in a picturesque climb toward Sapa. In this case, you'll pass through **Pa So,** which has one little riverside hotel run by the same folks as Lan Anh Hotel in Lai Chau (see above), and then hit **Tam Duong,** a town where you can get your first glimpse of colorful Hmong and Dao people at roadside. There are a few little guesthouses in Tam Duong, but it is so close to Sapa that you might as well press on. From Tam Duong, you climb among stunning peaks on one of the most beautiful stretches of road before hitting the massive switchback of the **Tram Ton Pass,** which brings you up and over to the town of Sapa.

Note: Many travelers who do this route by motorbike opt to ride the short stretch from Sapa to Lao Cai, and then put their **motorbike on the train** for the overnight back to Hanoi. The road from Lao Cai to Hanoi via **Yen Bai** is rural and quite pretty, but nothing compared with the mountain roads of the highland area. It's worth saving the gas, exhaustion, and hassle to just toss it on the train for little more than $10. In Lao Cai, stop in to see the friendly folks at **Nha Nhi Restaurant** (Nguyen Hue St.; ✆ **020/835-901**), who can help you out with the details. ***Important note for Minskers:*** You have to remove all of the gasoline from your motorbike, so find a local with a Minsk motorbike and make his day by donating your gas to him.

4 THE NORTHEASTERN HIGHLANDS LOOP

Less popular than the rural regions of the far northwest, the mountainous area north of Hanoi is attractive because of its paucity of other travelers—though this also means a matching paucity of decent hotels, restaurants, and services. Roads are rough and prone to landslide, and many are under construction. It's best to hit this loop on a Minsk motorbike (for the adventurous only) or a jeep. To start the most popular route, go north from Hanoi, past the airport, and to the rather uninteresting burg of **Thai Nguyen;** then follow Route 3 farther north to **Bac Can** (168km/104 miles north of Hanoi) and onto a small side road that takes you to **Ba Be National Park,** a cache of protected land around a large lake and inland waterway. Ba Be, and the nearby town of Cho Ra, are both good places to stay overnight. From there, explore the park, and then return to the main road north and head to **Cao Bang,** a riverside provincial center that is a good base for exploration to surrounding hilltribe villages. Outside of Cao Bang, you can visit the **caves** where **Ho Chi Minh** holed up after returning from China, as well as one of the region's most stunning waterfalls, **Ban Gioc.** From Cao Bang, return directly to Hanoi, or set out east to the unremarkable city of **Lang Son,** a journey that is "about the journey, not the destination." The ride itself, dotted with ethnic hilltribe villages, is what's worth seeing, not provincial Lang Son. The road between Lang Son and Hanoi is a superhighway and a good choice back to the capital (there is also train service).

BA BE LAKE & CHO RA TOWN

270km (168 miles) north of Hanoi

About a 6-hour ride past the Hanoi airport north on Route 3, and north of **Thai Nguyen,** you'll pass through some areas of terraced rice farming that are a harbinger of the stunning mountainous scenery to come. From the town of Bac Can, you'll take the western road (a left) toward Ba Be Lake, and from there the track is a winding path carved into the side of a mountain range. As the road climbs toward the park, you experience increasingly picturesque views of the valley among hilltribe villages—a left or a right off the main track brings you to terraced rice fields and likely to invitations for tea and friendly chats with locals.

Cho Ra is the small town servicing **Ba Be National Park,** just 14km (8¾ miles) to the west. Cho Ra is the best place to overnight before a day tour in the park and an afternoon ride on to Cao Bang (or back to Hanoi). **Cho Ra** is just a quiet little outpost, one busy main street surrounded by rice fields and mountains. Surrounded by diverse ethnic hill-tribes, mostly Thai, the town's central market is very busy on weekends, when rural villagers trek to town to sell produce, as well as weaving and needlework. **Ba Be Park** is a great place to enjoy an all-day boat ride and trekking to remote villages in the surrounding hills.

Come prepared for self-sufficiency: There's no bank, post office, or Internet in tiny Cho Ra. You can usually pay with U.S. dollars at the hotels, but be sure to also carry Vietnamese dong.

Getting There

Go by car or motorbike north from Hanoi some 200km (124 miles), and then follow signs to Cho Ra.

Where to Stay & Dine

Dining is pretty minimal in this area. If you stay in the park, there's a canteen with basic, overpriced grub, but it's rarely busy, so it's kind of an ad hoc operation. You're on your own in Cho Ra Town, really, and any Vietnamese-language basics (*"com trung"* for rice and eggs, for example) or knack for charades will help out at the few little *com* (rice) and *pho* (noodle soup) stands along the main drag near the central market (at the corner where the road splits north to Cao Bang, west to Ba Be Lake, and south to Bac Can).

Ba Be Guesthouse This is the most popular guesthouse in town and the most likely address if you come here on a tour. If the place is full, lots of copycats are nearby (try the **Hai Yen,** about 1km/½ mile down the road heading toward the park), but Ba Be is your best chance to meet up with other travelers and arrange day tours on the river and lake.

In Central Cho Ra. ✆ **0281/387-6115.** 10 units. $15 double. No credit cards. **Amenities:** Restaurant (w/ English menu). *In room:* A/C, no phone.

Attractions

Ba Be National Park Just 10,000 VND to enter—plus an additional 1,000 VND for a motorbike—Ba Be National Park surrounds central Ba Be Lake, the starting point for adventurous trips to the park's more far-flung destinations. Best if organized through a tour company, you'll find many options for rugged travel here. Some start near the town of Cho Ra in a little area called **Pak Kaw,** and then spend all day on **long-tail boats** exploring the small river as it snakes among hilltribe villages before emptying into the lake. The remote caves and far-flung villages are all best visited with a guide. Standard group tours commonly hop a boat just past the park entrance (half-day trips are $10 and full-day trips are $20).

CAO BANG

285km (177 miles) N of Hanoi

This provincial outpost lies in a picturesque crook in the Bang Giang River. Few foreigners get up this far, and the state of hotels and services might indicate why, but rugged travelers are in their element. The city alone is worth a wander, especially its large riverside market, and sunset in Cao Bang is an event, best viewed from the bridge or walking along the riverside promenade. From here, you can watch water buffalos grazing and locals paddling low skiffs to bring their produce to market. What brings people to Cao Bang, apart from the call of the fun rural roads in the region, is the famed **Ban Gioc Waterfall** northwest of town, one of the most photographed waterfalls in the world. Northwest of Cao Bang are the **Pac Bo Caves** where Ho Chi Minh hid out upon returning from China. On designated days, usually on weekend mornings, you are sure to come across **hilltribe markets** in the towns outside of Cao Bang (on your way to Pac Bo or Ban Gioc)—a photographer's dream.

The **Bank for Agricultural and Rural Development** (Hoang Dinh Giong St.; ✆ **026/385-2932**) can exchange currency, as can most small hotels, but it's best to bring U.S. greenbacks or dong with you from Hanoi. There are a few Internet corners, including one very good storefront right next to the Hotel Hoang Anh. The post office is on central Hoang Dinh Gong Street.

Getting There

Cao Bang connects directly north of Hanoi on Route 3. Local buses leave from the Long Bien Station and are pretty uncomfortable. Best to go by motorbike or hired car. The road from Ba Be is quite spectacular.

Where to Stay

Cao Bang's **Thanh Loan Hotel** used to be the top dog, commanding the most prime real estate overlooking the river at the very center of town (near the bridge), but this big government-run calamity has fallen into disrepair. Some tours will try to stick you here. Don't buy it.

Dining is limited in Cao Bang. Go for "point-and-shoot"–style dining at the little local buffet at riverside, **Huong Sen Restaurant.** "Point" at what you want and say "Shoot!" when they charge you double for it. But even at double the price, it's still a bargain. They've got fried egg, tofu dishes, vegetables, fried river fish, and rice.

On the main drag, there are lots of good local coffee joints, the best of which is the **Trung Nguyen Coffee Shop** at town center. For a good, familiar snack, look for **89 Kim Dong St.,** where there is a good little stand selling *banh mi* (bread) and pâté. They'll make you a great little savory sandwich from just 8,000 VND.

Attractions

Both the journey *and* the destination in Cao Bang offer attractions. The caves at **Pac Bo** are of little interest to foreign visitors, but the waterfall at **Ban Gioc** is quite a stunning sight and worth the effort to see. The best part is that the roads to both sights pass through beautiful mountain landscapes among **ethnic hilltribe villages.** Especially on weekends, you are likely to pass through seemingly impromptu **hilltribe markets,** the roads lined for miles with Tai and Nung people in traditional wear marching their product to market. Ask at your hotel about any scheduled markets (they are often held on auspicious days in the lunar calendar).

Ban Gioc Some 85km (53 miles) of mountain road—more than a 4-hour drive one-way—east of Cao Bang brings you to one of the most well-known waterfalls in Asia. People don't know it by name, but once you tick this sight off your list, you'll be able to spot glossy photos of it in Chinese restaurants and hotel lobbies everywhere. The multi-tiered falls are fueled by the Quay Son River spilling into Vietnam from China. The French originally built small villas on the banks at the base of the falls. Vietnamese tourists now come to this beautiful place in big groups, especially on weekends, and the place is crowded with happy picnics, drinking, and chatter. Sit for a while and you might be invited to join in. **Nguom Ngao Cave** (admission 5,000 VND) is just a few kilometers past the falls, and the cavernous space is well worth the visit.

Important: You have to arrange a **special permit** (just a bit of a bureaucratic hang-up) to get to the falls. Don't try to do it yourself—a waste of time, really—just arrive in Cao Bang the night before you plan to see the falls and have your hotel make arrangements (for a small fee). The cost for the permit is $10 per group, whether the group is of one or 20.

Pac Bo (Ho Chi Minh's Hide-Out) Most sights dedicated to Ho Chi Minh are geared to Vietnamese tourists and are of little interest to Westerners. Pac Bo follows the party line. Pac Bo is the site where, returning to Vietnam after more than 30 years of exile, a fired-up Ho Chi Minh began planning the revolution in 1941, living in caves and protected by local people. The approach to the site is lined with big concrete pavilions and walkways. An open parking area gives way to paved paths along the picturesque **Lenin River** at the foot of the **Karl Marx Mountain** (Ho Chi Minh named them himself). Paths take you to some small cave sites, and signs lead the way to places where Ho wrote, slept, and ate; but the real business at Pac Bo is family swimming and picnicking. It's a great place to meet Vietnamese tourists.

LANG SON

150km (93 miles) N of Hanoi

The city of Lang Son is connected to Hanoi by a broad, flat highway, and is more or less a sleepover stop after the stunning ride from Cao Bang, before you make your way back to the capital. Dining and accommodations options are many, but only the few that are acceptable are listed below. The city is known for being overrun, repeatedly, by the Chinese over the centuries—most recently in 1979 as retribution for Vietnam's invasion of Cambodia. Things are quiet now—so quiet, in fact, that you'll just use this as an overnight, whether going back to Hanoi or to the border town of **Dong Dan** and on to China. (***Important:*** You must have a prearranged Chinese visa to travel to China; see "Visas," under "Entry Requirements," in chapter 3, for more information.)

There is **no ATM** service in Lang Son, but the **Bank for Agriculture and Rural Development** (1 Tran Hung Dao St.; ✆ **025/371-7246**) can exchange money. You'll find Internet storefronts throughout the city. The **post office** is at 49 Le Loi St.

Getting There

The road from Cao Bang, Route 4A (though never marked as such) is a stunning drive. Route 1 is a wide highway that runs straight north from Hanoi (better to trade with China, my pretty).

There are two **trains** connecting Lang Son with Hanoi daily. The train station is on Le Loi Street. Most go by the highway, however.

Onward connection to or from China is via the town of **Dong Da,** some 3km (1¾ miles) north of Lang Son. A motorbike taxi will run you there for about 25,000 VND.

Where to Stay & Dine

Next best to Van Xuan (see below), and a similar standard, is **Hoang Son Hai Hotel,** near the town's central square (57 Duong Tam Thanh; ✆ **025/371-0479**). Rooms are priced the same, but they don't see many foreign visitors here and have no services.

New Century VIETNAMESE At the very center of town, just across the market area, is this hulking restaurant that's full of comings and goings. On a small island in the river—connected by a walkway—the place hops in the evenings, with karaoke rooms, a beer hall area, and large banquet-style dining. Quieter tables at the riverside sit under the twinkling lights hanging from trees. An English-language menu presents the standard Vietnamese fare of stir-fries, noodle dishes, and rice. Cute beer hostesses in miniskirt outfits emblazoned with local beer logos sling the suds, and the waitstaff is friendly, but nobody savvies much English—just point to menu items and smile. The place is adjacent to the Van Xuan (see below).

On a small island just off the quay at the center of town. ✆ **025/389-8000.** Main courses 30,000 VND–150,000 VND. No credit cards. Daily 7:30am–10pm.

Van Xuan Of the slim pickin's in Lang Son, Van Xuan is top of the heap. This five-story riverside complex has a friendly(ish) front-desk staff and an elevator (unique in this category) that connects you with their large, clean, basic tiled rooms. It uniquely offers movie channels on TV, and the rooms are cozy (though the foam beds are kind of a drag). Compared with others in town, this is far and away the best.

147 Tran Dang Ninh St. ✆ **025/371-0440.** Fax 025/371-0436. 29 units. 200,000 VND–320,000 VND. No credit cards. **Amenities:** Restaurant; bar. *In room:* A/C, satellite TV, fridge, minibar.

7

Northeastern Coast

Named by French colonists, the stunning Tonkin coast—which extends from Haiphong and Halong Bay all the way to central Vietnam—will forever be associated with the disputed artillery exchange between U.S. and Vietnamese ships that took place in the Gulf of Tonkin. The altercation ultimately led to the Tonkin Resolution and opened the door on the whole Vietnam shootin' match. What puts this region on the map now, though, is the likelihood that the sneakers or sandals you're wearing, or the shirt on your back, were put together in one of the large factories that line the road between Hanoi and the sea.

Boat tours of the UNESCO World Heritage Site **Halong Bay,** with its legendary limestone peaks and miles of calm waters, are the highlight. The small city of **Haiphong** has its own colonial-throwback kind of charm, and little **Cat Ba Island,** with its national park, is commonly included in itineraries with Halong Bay. You can also now reach Cat Ba by high-speed ferry from Hanoi.

There are also some good "off the map" destinations in this region, including **Bai Thu Long Bay,** just north of Halong (best visited on an organized tour), and **Do Son Beach,** just south of Haiphong. The Tonkin Coast area is just a few short hours by good road from Hanoi, and an overnight should suffice to experience any of these stops. Just about anybody in Hanoi sells tours to Halong and Cat Ba, with service ranging from Hanoi's ultrabudget-traveler cafe trips on old, beat-up junk boats, to luxurious packages such as the *Jewel of the Bay* (p. 165) and the *Emeraude,* a replica of an old colonial steamer.

1 HAIPHONG

100km (62 miles) E of Hanoi

With its wide avenues and grand parks lined with colonnaded buildings of a yellowed, aging stucco, Haiphong is like a smaller, more manageable version of Hanoi. You won't find jaw-dropping sights, but the town is worth a wander and not a bad stop on the way to, or from, the likes of Cat Ba or Halong Bay. Architectural sights include the classic old city theater, the town's large cathedral (Nha Tho Lon), an eclectic museum of history, and a museum of the navy. Central An Bien Park is also worth a wander, and the town boasts a few good hotels, one rather high-end as well as affordable midrange and low-end haunts. Do Son Beach is just 21km (13 miles) southeast of Haiphong and a popular getaway for locals or Hanoi weekenders; the beach town hosts the annual Do Son Buffalo Fighting Festival, which is more or less a gory game of bull-baiting, but with lots of pomp and circumstance.

On your way to Haiphong from Hanoi, you'll pass through Binh Duyen, the industrial district east of Hanoi, where you'll find big, belching factories churning out Nike and Adidas shoes or name-brand shirts. There's an enormous Ford factory and other automotive and technical production facilities as well. Nearby, farmers use manual scoops to "cup" water from one rice terrace to the next, true manual irrigation, while just a stone's throw away, intricate pumps for automotive engines are manufactured by the thousands. It's a mad world.

GETTING THERE

BY BUS Buses make the 2-hour connection frequently throughout the day from Hanoi's Kim Ma Station (to the east) to Haiphong. Haiphong also connects by bus with Halong City. The Haiphong bus station, Tam Bac, is just an 8,000 VND ride from the city center—the usual tout circus. One way to avoid the hassles is to book with the unique **Hoang Long Bus Company** (in Hanoi, 28 Tran Nhat Duat, ✆ **04/3928-2828;** in Haiphong, 3 Tran Nguyen Han, ✆ **0313/700-778;** on Cat Ba Island, 217 Duong 1/4, ✆ **0313/887-224**), which runs very fast service by bus and high-speed boat four times daily from Cat Ba back to the mainland at Haiphong and on to Hanoi. Call directly or talk with your hotel front desk to arrange pickup.

BY TRAIN The **Haiphong Railway Station** is at 75 Luong Khanh Thien St. (✆ **0313/920-025**) and is the terminus of the eastern spur from Hanoi. Daily connections leave from the Hanoi station in the morning and in the evening. Because good roads now connect with Haiphong, this trip is more or less for the train buff.

BY BOAT Boats regularly connect with Cat Ba Island from Haiphong's ferry pier on the northernmost tip of the town peninsula. You can book at any hotel front desk with the likes of the new boat and bus trip with **Hoang Long Bus Company** (3 Tran Nguyen Han; ✆ **0313/700-778**) or with local high-speed ferries exemplified by **Thuong Nhat Transport Cooperative,** among the many. Just hop on whichever boat is heading out next.

FAST FACTS You'll find **ATM service** and a place to cash traveler's checks at **Vietcombank** in Haiphong (11 Hoang Dieu St.; ✆ **0313/842-658**). Open Monday to Saturday from 8am to 4pm, but closed for lunch 11:30am to 1:30pm. You'll find lots of budget **Internet** outfits throughout the city. The main **post office** is at 5 Nguyen Tri Phuong St. (✆ **0313/823-789**).

WHERE TO STAY

Moderate

Harbour View Hotel ★★ Done in a cool retro French-colonial style, Harbour View is the town's most impressive address. The hotel is set up to meet and greet foreign business dignitaries—the folks who come over to check on the works of their nearby textile, shoe, and auto-part factories—and as such, the staff are practiced at rolling out the red carpet. This place has a certain panache without being pretentious. Elegant wooden entries give way to large rooms, conservatively decorated in a plain chain-hotel fashion with rich green carpets, matching drapes, and fine wood furnishings. Bathrooms are large and clean, with granite. The lobby is elegantly decorated with black-and-white diamond tiles and oversize rattan chairs. It houses a mellow piano bar and a gift shop. Don't miss the classic car out front, which is not just the hotel's mascot, but can be rented for transfers and city tours at just $25 per day.

4 Tran Phu St., Haiphong. ✆ **0313/827-827.** Fax 0313/827-828. www.harbourviewvietnam.com. 122 units. $115–$166 double; $185–$230 suite. AE, MC, V. **Amenities:** 2 restaurants; bar; fitness center; small outdoor pool; room service. *In room:* A/C, TV, fridge, hair dryer, Internet, minibar.

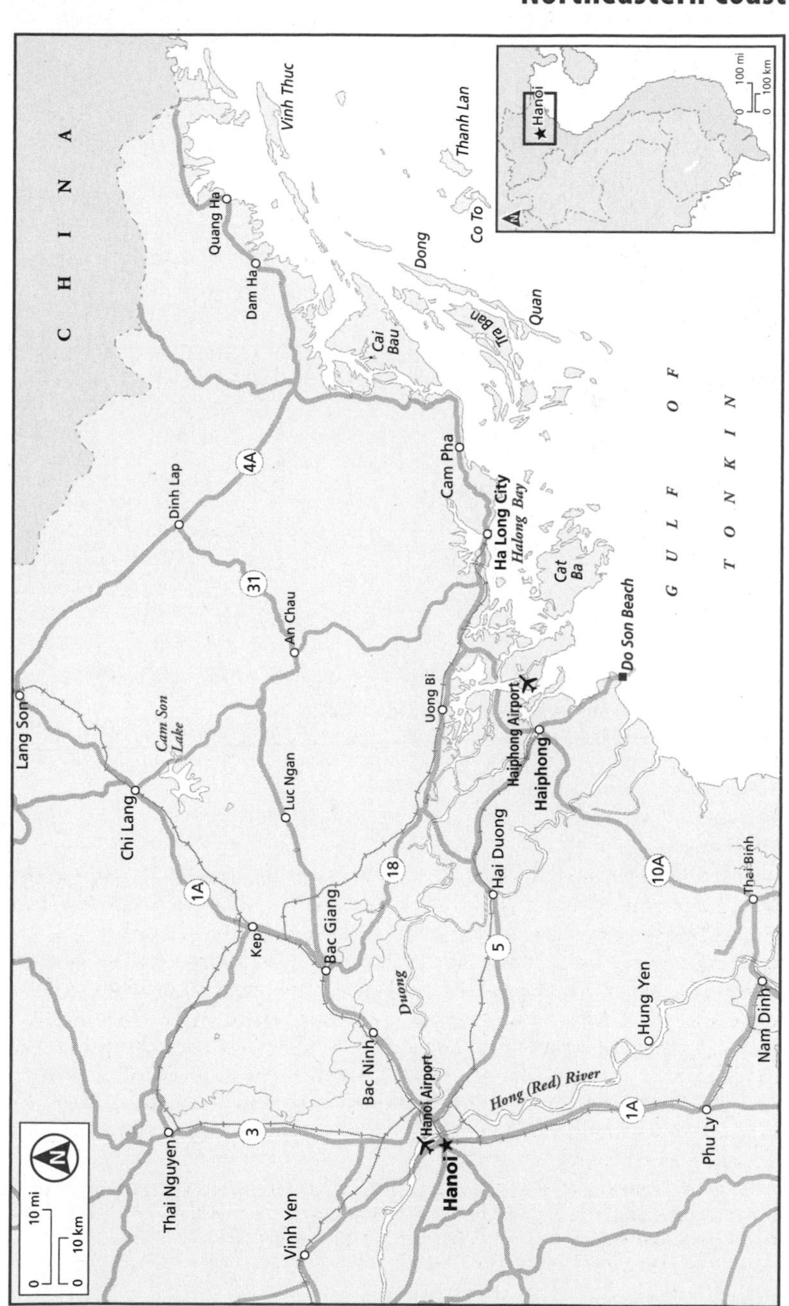
CHINA
Vinh Thuc
Thanh Lan
Co To
Dong
Quan
Ta Ban
Cai Bau
Quang Ha
Dam Ha
Dinh Lap
4A
31
An Chau
Lang Son
Cam Son Lake
Chi Lang
Luc Ngan
1A
Kep
Bac Giang
18
Uong Bi
Cam Pha
Ha Long City
Halong Bay
Cat Ba
GULF OF TONKIN
Do Son Beach
Haiphong Airport
Haiphong
Hai Duong
10A
Thai Binh
5
Duong
Bac Ninh
Hanoi Airport
Hanoi
Hong (Red) River
Hung Yen
Nam Dinh
Phu Ly
Thai Nguyen
3
Vinh Yen
0 10 mi
0 10 km
N
0 100 mi
0 100 km

Inexpensive

If you're in a pinch and the two hotels below are closed, try **Hotel (Kach San) Kim Thanh** (67 Dien Bien Phu; ✆ **0313/745-264**), which is a rabbit warren of less-than-average rooms starting at $17.

Bach Dang Hotel One of the best of the town's hotels in this category, Bach Dang is set on a busy corner of Dien Bien Phu Street, just adjacent to the town's popular Maxim's Restaurant (see below). Old but clean rooms come in all shapes and sizes. Be sure to have a look first. The hotel was a proud supporter of athletes during the Asia Games, and the staff speaks English and can help sort out any travel arrangements. A large restaurant and massage parlor (kind of sleazy) are just around the corner.

40 Dien Bien Phu St., Haiphong. ✆ **0313/842-444.** Fax 0313/841-625. bachdanghotelhp@hn.vnn.vn. 34 units. 250,000 VND–450,000 VND double. MC, V. **Amenities:** Restaurant; bar. *In room:* A/C, TV, fridge, minibar, Wi-Fi.

Maxim Hotel Maxim is the best minihotel in town. For my money, it's a far better choice than the beat-up old business hotels at the town center that charge more than double the price for musty rooms. Maxim also hosts one of the town's best restaurants on its second floor, as well as the popular Maxim's Restaurant (run by the same owner) just down the street. Rooms are small but have good modern conveniences like satellite TV and clean bathrooms done in designer tile.

3K Ly Tu Trong St., Haiphong City. ✆ **0313/746-540.** maxim@vnn.vn. 30 units. 250,000 VND–850,000 VND double. No credit cards. **Amenities:** Restaurant and bar (see review of Truc Lam, below). *In room:* A/C, TV, fridge, minibar, Wi-Fi.

WHERE TO DINE

For a taste of local fare in "real" local atmosphere, head to tiny **Hoa Dai Do**—just north of the park at 40 Le Dai Hanh St. (✆ **0313/810-452**)—which slings hash Vietnamese style, the likes of good stir-fries, noodle soups, roasted dinners, fried rice, and noodles. They march out an English menu when you arrive, but you can also have a peek in the kitchen to see what looks familiar or appetizing.

In the park adjacent to the high-end **Harbour View Hotel** (see "Where to Stay," above), find **Van Tue Restaurant** (1A Hoang Dieu; ✆ **0313/746-338;** www.vantue.com). This oversize garden restaurant caters mainly to big wedding parties and other special events, but they do have some private rooms and serve delicious fresh seafood (by the pound) from a limited English menu. It's a bit pricey but good, especially with a group.

Maxim's Restaurant and Bar ★ Try this place for a familiar Western meal in a casual coffee-shop setting. Little extras like linen tablecloths and flowers on the table add to an old-school diner feel—surly waiters and all. The menu features Vietnamese versions of Western favorites—the likes of good sandwiches, pizza, and steaks—as well as a host of affordable Vietnamese fare. Breakfasts are hearty, the coffee is strong, and they change the TV to CNN when foreign visitors don the doorstep.

49 Dien Bien Phu St. ✆ **0313/822-934.** Set menu 45,000 VND–100,000 VND. MC, V. Daily 6:30am–11:30pm.

Truc Lam *Truc Lam* means "Bamboo Forest" and refers to an old Chinese legend about travelers lost in the woods (the owner will patch the story together for you). On the second floor of the Maxim minihotel (see above), Truc Lam serves up classic Vietnamese cuisine and offers special imports on occasion, like salmon from Norway or beef from New Zealand. Meals are tastefully presented on oversize crockery and tables are

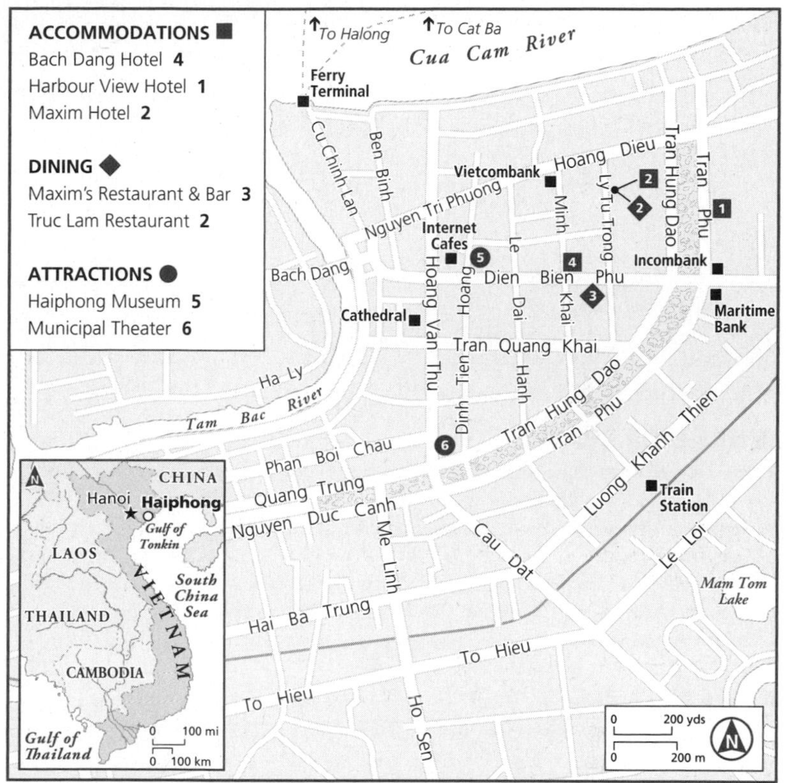

draped in linen. The narrow interior's dark red walls are bisected by heavy shelves displaying oversize pottery, and some fine examples of local painters hang here and there. Just opened and moved from their old address, this restaurant is always full and seems to attract a unique mix of expats and locals—a slick mafia set, but don't let them know I told you. The only drawback to the dining experience at Truc Lam is the secondhand smoke, so go for a seat near the veranda (and certainly not back near the small bar). They regularly feature live music, too.

36 Le Dai Hanh St. ✆ **0313/842-487.** Main courses 45,000 VND–180,000 VND. MC, V. Daily 6am–midnight.

2 HALONG CITY

160km (99 miles) NE of Hanoi

Just a jumping-off point for trips to the bay, really, Halong City has grown in direct proportion to increased tourism, and you'll find a number of fine hotels to choose from. Many visitors choose to overnight on one of the cruisers in the bay (see section 3,

"Halong Bay," below) or take a full-day boat trip that ends at Cat Ba Island. But if you're not keen on sleeping on the ocean blue or overnighting in a little island outpost, Halong City might be just the ticket. Most visitors here are part of Vietnamese and Chinese tour groups, especially in the summertime, when Hanoians want to get out of the humid capital.

The town is divided into **Bai Chay,** the main tourist strip of hotels and boat piers for trips to the bay, and **Hong Gai,** a more local area that's reachable by ferry from the north end of town (a bridge is currently under construction that will speed up that connection). Hong Gai has just a few minihotels and local restaurants geared mainly to Chinese tour groups. The local Halong City culinary specialty is *gio,* a minced pork dish popular with Chinese tourists.

FAST FACTS A **Vietcombank** branch in Bai Chay along Halong Road near the main pier (✆ **033/381-1099**) offers **ATM service** and can cash traveler's checks. Open Monday to Saturday 8am to 4pm, but closed for lunch 11:30am to 1:30pm. The outlet adjacent to the post office offers the best **Internet** service. The main Halong **post office** is at the intersection of Vuon Dao and Halong Street at seaside.

WHERE TO STAY

Below I've listed the three best hotels of many in Halong City. Because few tour groups stay in town (most opt for overnights on boats in the bay), the city attracts more regional tourists and larger Chinese tour groups. There isn't much to see in town—but the hotels are good.

If you're looking for something a little lighter on the wallet, check out **Sunlight Hotel** (88 Hung Thang, Group 8 Section 9A Bai Chay; ✆ **033/384-4479**), just around the corner from the Mithrin (reviewed below). It has clean, basic rooms—not to mention a helpful tour desk—from as low as $21 per night.

Halong Dream Hotel ★ Near the boat pier for Saigon tourists, the Halong Dream is the last decent hotel option before you get to the town's northern terminus and ferry, and the soon-to-be-complete bridge. The hotel has a vaulted lobby area with columns and lots of marble and glass. The large rooms have fluffy duvets and marble bathrooms and are tidy, if a bit boring. Suites are much larger versions of the same chain-hotel-style decor. There's a small spa and fitness center, and the midsize pool is not bad for kicking back one afternoon. Good views from the upper floors showcase the busy bay and distant Halong.

10 Halong Rd., Bai Chay Ward, Halong City. ✆ **033/384-9009.** Fax 033/384-4855. www.halongdreamhotel.com.vn. 184 units. $108–$178 double; $198–$278 suite. MC, V. **Amenities:** International restaurant; bar; lobby lounge; health club; Jacuzzi; outdoor pool; room service; sauna; small spa. *In room:* A/C, TV, fridge, minibar, Wi-Fi.

Mithrin Hotel Sticking out like a sore thumb over the undeveloped southern end of the Halong City strip, Mithrin was built with unflagging optimism that this town will boom and the hotel will be the center of a little skyscraper village (for now, it's still a barren salt flat). Managed by Swiss-Belhotel International, a company of good reputation in the region (see the Hanoi Horison, p. 82, and the Golden Sand in Hoi An, p. 218), the Mithrin covers all the bases: It has a small pool, salon, gym, small spa with sauna and Jacuzzi, and a very helpful and accommodating staff. Rooms are large and rather dull, a typical businessman's hotel with lots of disinfectant sprayed about, but they're clean and pleasant enough, with cable and standard in-room amenities. Bathrooms are smallish. The standard is a bit compact, and I'd recommend bumping it up one notch to superior if you can swing it.

Hoang Quoc Viet Rd., Halong City. ✆ **033/384-8090.** Fax 033/384-1770. www.mithrinhotelhalong.com.vn. 88 units. $85–$95 double; $160 superior. MC, V. **Amenities:** Restaurant; bar; Jacuzzi; outdoor pool; room service; sauna; tennis. *In room:* A/C, TV, fridge, minibar, Wi-Fi.

Saigon Ha Long Hotel ★ A massive hotel on a hill above the bay (and across from a private jetty for Saigon tourist boats), Saigon Ha Long Hotel is government owned—usually a bad thing—but, in this case, covers all the bases and is quite cozy. The hotel attracts huge groups and the front-desk staff at times has to work like soldiers in a trench when the onslaught hits, but they seem to handle it with aplomb. Deluxe rooms have large balconies and good views (go for the 14th floor, which is the highest one here). The pool in a small courtyard is near an outdoor restaurant that overlooks the street below.

168 Halong Rd., Bai Chay Ward, Halong City. ✆ **033/384-5845.** Fax 033/384-5849. www.saigonhalonghotel.com. 228 units. $95–$125 double; $225 suite. MC, V. **Amenities:** 2 restaurants; 3 bars; babysitting; small health club; Jacuzzi; outdoor pool; room service; sauna; tennis courts. *In room:* A/C, TV, fridge, minibar, Wi-Fi.

3 HALONG BAY

175km (109 miles) E of Hanoi; 55km (34 miles) NE of Haiphong

The light playing on the arching rock formations of Halong Bay is never the same, painting rich colors on a stunning landscape, and the bay attracts many artists and photographers. A Vietnamese fable says that the towering limestone-karst rock formations at Halong were formed with the crash landing of a dragon sent by the prehistoric gods of early Vietnamese animism to protect the country from an invading navy. The picturesque area did, in fact, play host to some important Vietnamese naval victories against Chinese forces, but the bay is most famous for its UNESCO World Heritage status, its emerald green water, and the 3,000 islands of towering limestone in the Gulf of Tonkin.

The total area of the bay is 1,553 sq. km (606 sq. miles), but only 434 sq. km (169 sq. miles) are part of the UNESCO World Heritage Site (designated as such in 1994). Of the more than 700 islands and islets in this area, only a few are habitable. Some islands were originally named by local fisherman, usually based on their shape. You'll find the likes of Tea Pot Island, Mother and Child Island, and Stone Dog Island.

The bay's topography developed over 250,000 years, from when Earth's crust was unstable. Originally deep under a prehistoric ocean, the area formed layers of limestone sediments that slowly weathered and receded. Limestone being porous, it created mountains that look a bit like Swiss cheese, laced with hundreds of caves. More than 20 caves in the bay are open to visitors.

Tran Hung Dao had his great standoff with the Chinese in this area. Anticipating the Chinese attack, so the story goes, wily Tran Hung Dao had his men place long bamboo stakes in the bay, and when the Chinese ships arrived at low tide, they were pierced and thus easily attacked by the fearless Vietnamese hero and his men. You'll see Tran Hung Dao's statue in nearly every town in Vietnam, and the story of his clever foiling of the Chinese (not, of course, their subsequent return and rule of Vietnam for nearly 1,000 years) is the stuff of real glory. ***Do Go,*** or the Cave of Stakes (see "Attractions," below), is the reputed resting place of the stakes that foiled the Chinese.

Hundreds of thousands of visitors have climbed aboard the tour boats making the rounds of the sights. The crowds at the overstuffed ferry pier in Halong City are a bit

How Halong Got Its Karst

Karst—a name derived from a limestone plateau in Slovenia—refers to outcroppings of readily soluble rock, commonly limestone, that are eaten away by chemical reactions catalyzed by dripping water. The karst outcroppings in Halong—and in places like Guilin in China or Krabi in Thailand—are made of this porous sedimentary rock and tend to develop dynamic caves that drip minerals and form stalactites and stalagmites. Other features of limestone karst deposits and erosion are wide fissures and underground streams—in short, a constantly changing, dynamic landscape caused by chemical erosion. Some of Halong's many caves are actually "dead," meaning that the leaching process is over, but others are constantly changing.

much (you're never alone out on the bay), but the water is flat, great for kayaking and swimming, and a visit here is a real highlight of any tour of Vietnam.

A visit to Halong Bay—about a 4-hour drive from Hanoi—usually includes an overnight stay (though it can be done in one very long day). Given the logistics, the trip is best done through an agent or with a group. When you book a tour with an overnight stay, you'll probably cruise on a junk for 4 to 6 hours along the bay, stopping to explore two or more grottoes and other sights along the way. You might pause for swimming or kayaking, depending on the operator (some offer just cruising; others have extensive adventure agendas). Overnight trips can cost anywhere from $16 to upward of $150. It depends on whether you hire a bus or a private driver, where you stay, and what you eat. Sinh Café does a fine job on the low end, but don't expect much more than the ride and a surly guide. Good luxury options abound (see below).

The best time to visit is from May to October. Though the weather's at its hottest, it's your best chance for good visibility. Note that entrance to the park (usually included in day tours) costs 30,000 VND.

As Halong gets more and more crowded with tourist junks, some companies are branching out with tours by boat to **Bai Tu Long Bay,** just north and east of Halong. The area is a busy fishing zone, and the scenery is not quite as dynamic as in Halong, but many visitors appreciate the absence of huge tour groups. Contact a tour agency in Hanoi for information.

Eco-tourism is taking off here: The steep karst outcrops of the bay are not only beautiful, but ideal for **rock climbing.** Two- or 3-day **sea-kayaking** adventures are also becoming popular. Contact Buffalo Tours or Handspan (see below) for exciting multiday trip packages starting from $180.

THE BOATS OF HALONG BAY

Halong Ginger ★★ **(Finds)** For a stellar experience on the water, look no further than the *Halong Ginger.* Unlike the *Emeraude* (see below), *Halong Ginger* is a small, intimate affair, equipped with only 10 cabins all pushed to either side of a central deck to ensure each room has a private, unobstructed view of the ocean. Deluxe rooms come with three large windows, letting in plenty of light and ocean sounds. Rooms have huge bathrooms, especially for a boat, and marble countertops.

Halong Ginger's cruising route moves away from the traffic of Halong Bay, and unlike other junks in the bay, it doesn't retrace its path. Passengers board the boat between

11:30am and noon, with staff on hand to carry suitcases to your cabin so that you can enjoy a welcome drink on deck. The boat sets off at 12:30pm and a set menu of local seafood is served for lunch half an hour later. The boat docks at Soi Sim, an island in the heart of Halong Bay, where you either take a dip or go for a trek. Then it's off to Lan Ha Bay, south of Halong Bay, where you are taken into a traditional fishing village. If you opt for kayaking, you can kayak yourself through the village. From here, it's time to board bamboo boats to maneuver through narrow waterways into a secluded cave.

Dinner aboard the boat is a sumptuous set seafood menu. Finish your evening with drinks on the upper deck. Then it's a dreamy sleep in your luxe cabin before the early morning tai chi class. The second day is a simple, relaxing cruise back to the hectic pace of land life. The price of *Halong Ginger*'s overnight cruise is hefty, ranging from $419 to $493. Book through their website at www.cruisehalong.com or call their offices at ✆ **04/3984-5085** (fax 04/3984-4538). Look out for their junks, the ***Halong Jasmine*** and the ***Halong Violet,*** both of which will be smaller, more exclusive, and (incredibly enough) more expensive than the ***Halong Ginger.***

The Emeraude ★★ For a unique high-end experience, book passage aboard the *Emeraude*—a copy of a French steamer that once plied these waters in the early 20th century. Certainly the largest boat, at 55m (180 ft.), the elegant *Emeraude* has 38 cabins, a fine-dining outlet, and plenty of room to stretch your legs. The luxury trip comes with a price tag, of course, but the 2-day, 1-night cruise is well worth it.

Leaving Hanoi at 8am, you'll check in at the private *Emeraude* pier and be walked to the boat. Compact, as ship cabins always are, onboard rooms are decked out in hardwood, with nice fixtures such as air-conditioning, a private reading lamp, slippers for shuffling about the decks, and a tidy, compact bathroom area with toilet, shower, and a separate room for a small sink stand. Everything on board is retro, which means pleasing hardwood, brass, and fine linens. The oversize wicker chairs on the top deck are cozy, and you'll find shaded areas as well as sun-worshiping space. A casual, friendly atmosphere pervades, especially when the corks start popping.

Dining on board is a delicious buffet, and most guests find themselves sharing a meal with new friends. Lunch on day 1 is followed by a stop at the Surprise Cave (see "Attractions," below), then an afternoon of cruising and great views of the islands. The boat docks in a quiet harbor, and guests have an opportunity to, on their own or with a guide, explore nearby Trinh Nu and Hang Trong, the Virgin Cave and the Cave of the Winds, or take a dip in the bay. Dinner is a sumptuous affair of fine local cuisine (heavy on seafood) and good Western options. Enjoy drinks on the upper deck as you watch the moonlight glisten off the bay.

Day 2 starts with tai chi classes on the sun deck as a brilliant sunrise paints its colors on the arching canvas of high limestone peaks jutting from the glassy waters. Blissful. After your exercise, tuck in to a hearty Western-style breakfast. The boat returns to the dock by 9:30am, and a direct transfer finds you back in Hanoi by lunchtime. The trip is quite memorable, and a ride on this retro ship, outfitted to the nines, is unique to Halong Bay. The price for the overnight cruise is $281 for a luxury cabin for two and $479 for the one-suite room, but discounts for larger groups are available. Shuttle bus transfer from Hanoi costs $35. Check the website at www.emeraude-cruises.com or call the offices at the Press Club in Hanoi (✆ **04/3934-0888;** fax 04/3825-5342).

The Jewel of the Bay ★ Another highly recommended luxury boat (just a step down from the *Emeraude*), the *Jewel of the Bay* runs overnight trips concentrating on eco-tourism that include kayaking, touring, and fine dining. For more information or to book a trip, contact **Buffalo Tours** (✆ **04/3828-0702;** www.buffalotours.com/jewel). The company runs varying itineraries, including a trip that loops out as far as Cat Ba. Buffalo's boat now has a companion vessel.

The Dragon's Pearl Run by the people at **Handspan** (✆ **04/3926-2828;** www.handspan.com), the very popular *Dragon's Pearl* has a high standard comparable to the *Jewel of the Bay,* and the focus is similarly on hearty eco-tourism and getting away from the crowds.

ATTRACTIONS

The caves and attractions are listed in the order that you'll reach them on tour from Halong City. All boat trips will point out the prescribed route on a detailed map of Halong Bay or provide a map. Most day trips include stops at one or two of the major caves (but not all). Entrance to the caves is usually included in a tour itinerary, but be sure to specify when booking.

Thien Cung Grotto (Heavenly Cave) One of the most popular caves for day trips, a visit to Thien Cung starts from the crowded dock area where wooden walkways lead to steep stairs going up to the mouth of the cave—just a short walk. The interior is a cavernous space, with hokey circus lighting, lots of big rock formations, and the usual interpretive names. This is considered the Cave of the Dragon, where the dragon who created Halong sought refuge, and guides are quick to point out one elaborate stalactite that looks like a dragon (or maybe a hoagie, depending on your interpretation). There's a legend surrounding the cave about a young girl who, in order to end years of oppressive drought, married the presiding dragon in the cave, and their wedding was attended by all in the animal kingdom. Brave girl. It is a "dead cave" in that, unlike many limestone caves, it is no longer dripping water and growing formations of additional deposits or creating new fissures and caves. Lit like a Vegas casino, this is the first cave most visitors reach on the way to Cat Ba Island.

4km (2½ miles) directly east off the shore of Halong City. Admission 30,000 VND. Daily 8am–5pm.

Do Go (The Cave of Stakes) Reputed resting place of the long stakes that Tran Hung Dao used to sink the Chinese fleet that came to attack Halong and Haiphong, Do Go is a massive cave with three chambers, not far from the Thien Cung Grotto (see above).

Included with entrance to the Thien Cung Grotto (see above). Daily 8am–5pm.

Surprise Cave ★★ What's the surprise? The French arrived and said, "*Mon dieu!* Why, it is a cave!" Discovered in 1901, this very large grotto was used by Viet Cong as a hide-out during the war with the United States. A short, steep climb up paved steps leads you to three chambers, the last being the largest. In 1999, the Chinese cooperated to install lights and a safe pathway through the cave. A tour of the cave usually involves a guide leading you on an interpretive stalagmite hunt. Guides like to point out a large phallic formation glowing under a bright red spotlight—Freudian interpretations of the rock formations abound. Also look for tiger, dragon, and penguin formations, as well as unique "melon ball" stalactites. Toward the top of the cave are viewing platforms overlooking the sprawling bay, with its myriad junks, far below.

Admission 30,000 VND. Daily 8am–5pm.

Drum and Virgin Cave Adjoining the most popular place for overnights in Halong Bay, this stunning and quiet nook in the bay is a place where you might be able to interact with some local fisherman if you can get out on the water in a kayak. The caves are on opposite sides of the calm bay, and each is but a shallow area. Some tours even set up fully catered meals with banquet tables in the caves.

Free admission. Daily dawn–dusk.

Ba Hung Informally called the Indochine Cave ever since the film starring Catherine Deneuve was shot here, this short grotto leads to a hollowed island lagoon with steep walls of jungle surrounding shallow salty waters. On budget trips to Cat Ba Island, boats stop at the entrance and small shuttle boats will take you to the cave through low openings. The cost is 20,000 VND for the short ride, but the proceeds allegedly go to help the small floating school in the nearby floating village (you pass the school on the way).

Free admission. Boat ride is 20,000 VND. Daily dawn–dusk.

4 CAT BA ISLAND

I first came to Cat Ba in 1998 on an overnight tour by boat from Halong City. At the time, the little bay of Cat Ba was choked with beat-up old fishing junks, and the quiet little oceanside strip had but a few budget hotels. A sturdy Russian Minsk motorbike was the main mode of transport. Oh, but the times they are a-changin'.

The population of little Cat Ba Island is now over 30,000, the bay has been cleared of junks (all fishing vessels must park a few hundred meters offshore), and the main seaside avenue has been widened. There are a number of midrange high-rise hotels, and even a luxury resort on the Cat Co III beach just north of town. Direct high-speed boat service runs from Hanoi via Haiphong, or, even better, try the direct bus that goes from the town center, rides on a ferry, and delivers you to the center of Haiphong or on to Hanoi. The town is very busy with Hanoi weekenders, especially in the summer, and thus best avoided then (the hotel prices are often nearly double on summer weekends). Most travelers zip through on 1-night package tours, but it's best to arrange your own transport to this area. Tours to Cat Ba limit you to dinner with the group and a strict schedule. I recommend booking a tour with a group for *transport only* or making Cat Ba your last stop on a budget tour of Halong Bay, and then arranging your own hotel and making your own schedule for your time in Cat Ba. The Cat Ba National Park has some good trails to explore, and the interior of the island and the rocky eastern coast are great places to get off the map (contact any hotel tour desk for an all-day tour of the island). You might want to check out the April 1 festival that commemorates Ho Chi Minh's visit to the island: It's quite a grand fete, with dragon-boat races and a big fashion show.

GETTING THERE & GETTING AROUND

BY BOAT/BUS Most visitors get to Cat Ba on tours through Hanoi's budget cafes. The typical boat journey includes an exploration of Halong Bay and an overnight on the island, but more and more folks are now booking their boat journey through Halong with a tour company, then ending the trip in Cat Ba and taking the reigns from there. You might even arrange a stop in Haiphong or onward to Ninh Binh.

New on the scene, with a very fast bus-to-boat service, **Hoang Long Bus Company** (in Hanoi, 28 Tran Nhat Duat, ✆ **04/3928-3720;** in Haiphong, 11 Tran Nguyen Han, ✆ **0313/700-778;** on Cat Ba Island, ✆ **0313/887-224**) runs four times daily from Cat Ba back to the mainland at Haiphong and on to Hanoi. They have air-conditioned buses that pick you up and whisk you to the dock of a high-speed ferry. Departure times from Hanoi start at 4:50am and run every 30 minutes; the last departure is at 9pm. From

Haiphong, boats start at 6:05am and the last one leaves at 9:05pm. Return tickets will set you back 60,000 VND.

A high-speed ferry also leaves from the pier at the town center every half-hour between 7am and 5pm. The cost is 90,000 VND. Contact **Thuong Nhat Transport Cooperative** (cosponsored by Vietnamese and Japanese) through the folks at the **Sunflower Hotel** (Nui Ngoc Rd., just 20m/66 ft. off the seaside boulevard; ✆ **0313/888-429**), where they can arrange a ticket.

WHERE TO STAY

Cat Ba Sunrise Resort This new small resort sets a whole new standard on little Cat Ba. On a strip of reclaimed land between mountain and beach, the resort is set in a small protected cove called Cat Co III beach. To get to the cove, you have to walk up a flight of steps from the road, then down steps to the narrow beachside strip. Cat Co Beach III connects with the other Cat Co beaches by a high walkway carved into the rocks along the shore. The resort has a midsize central pool overlooking a thin stretch of beach lined with tidy lawn chairs and thatch umbrellas. The space is tight, hemmed in by the dark rocky shore and cliffs that surround the little enclave, but the rooms are of a high standard and the place has enough amenities to cover all the bases. Clean, tiled rooms have beds draped with burgundy covers, matching heavy drape curtains, and dark-wood built-in cabinets. Suites are large and luxurious, with redwood trimmings, and unique are the top-floor family suites—great for parents traveling with kids. All units have sea views, and most have balconies. The place is just getting going and glitches abound—unfortunate is the piped-in Vietnamese pop music at poolside. But you'll find good dining options in a spacious and lively open-air bar. Beach parties with bonfires are held for special groups.

Cat Co III Beach, Cat Ba Island. ✆ **0313/887-360.** Fax 0313/887-365. catba-sunriseresort@vnn.vn. 39 units. $120–$132 double; $205 suite. MC, V. **Amenities:** Restaurant; bar; small health club w/sauna and Jacuzzi; outdoor pool in courtyard; room service. *In room:* A/C, TV, fridge, minibar, Wi-Fi.

Holiday View Hotel ★ Holiday View, the only international-standard hotel on Cat Ba, has raised the bar along the busy shorefront. The 13-story tower, on the north end of the main Cat Ba strip, offers new and neat accommodations, though not particularly luxurious ones. Owned by Vinaconex, a Vietnamese manufacturer and retailer, the hotel is strangely empty. Rumor has it that the building was put up just about as fast as you can say "money laundering," and the hotel is just getting going. Standard rooms are somewhat compact but offer cool wood floors and tidy coverlets on beds. Everything is clean and not musty (yet). Bathrooms have granite counters but are the guesthouse variety, with shower nozzles that open to the toilet and sink area (kind of a disappointment for this category). Better are the large corner rooms, especially on higher floors with good views of the busy bay out front. Deluxe rooms have bathtubs and a lot more space—they're worth the upgrade. The Holiday View caters mainly to regional businessmen and small conventions, but it's also a good choice for an individual traveler.

Zone 4, Cat Ba Town (north end of the main strip, on the way to the beaches). ✆ **0313/887-200.** Fax 0313/887-209. holidayviewhotel@vnn.vn. 120 units. $50–$74 double. MC, V. **Amenities:** Restaurant; bar. *In room:* A/C, TV, fridge, minibar, Wi-Fi.

Prince Hotel Just a few meters off the main street, Prince Hotel is an old standby. The staff is still friendly as can be, happily accommodating any wish—from hiring guides, to renting motorbikes, to purchasing onward transport—but the place is pretty beat up. Don't miss a chance to talk with the helpful and effusive front-office manager.

(*Note:* His name tag really reads "Elton John," and if you chat with him long enough, he'll be singing; he's a very kind young man, a "candle in the wind" even.) Set in a towering courtyard, the rooms are best on the top floor with views over surrounding buildings to the bay; otherwise, expect to look at concrete walls.

303 Nui Ngoc Rd., Cat Ba Town (just 20m/66 ft. up a side road off the seaside boulevard). ✆ **0313/888-899.** Fax 0313/888-7666. www.catbatravel.com. 80 units. $25–$40 double. MC, V. **Amenities:** 2 restaurants; bar; health club w/Jacuzzi. *In room:* A/C, TV, fridge, minibar, Wi-Fi.

Sunflower One Hotel A brightly lit lobby of crayon yellow greets you at this popular hotel among tour groups. If only the staff were so bright and cheery—but with the many tours coming through, they hear many complaints from budget tourists who'd expected more. The clean rooms are comparable to what you'll find at nearby Prince Hotel (see above), but the greeting and service at the Prince is far more kind and genuine. Still, Sunflower One remains the pick for Sinh Café tours, which means folks will keep coming.

Nui Ngoc Rd., Cat Ba Town (just 20m/66 ft. up a side road off the seaside boulevard). ✆ **0313/888-429.** Fax 0313/888-451. sunflowerhotel@hn.vnn.vn. 72 units. $25–$90 double. No credit cards. **Amenities:** Restaurant; bar; room service. *In room:* A/C, TV, fridge, minibar, Wi-Fi.

Yen Thanh Hotel Typical of the budget hotels in Cat Ba, the Van Anh is a standard minihotel, but its friendly staff and central location raise it one notch above the rest. Rooms are big and clean but rather basic. Best are the rooms overlooking the oceanside fountain and the busy bay. The hotel is owned by the mayor of Cat Ba, who, like it or not, is responsible for the growth of tourism along the Cat Ba town strip. This hotel is named for his daughter.

220 Zone 1/4, Cat Ba Town (right across from the high-speed ferry landing on the town's main drag). ✆ **0313/888-201.** 22 units. 500,000 VND double. No credit cards. **Amenities:** Restaurant. *In room:* A/C, TV, fridge, Wi-Fi.

WHERE TO DINE

Seafood dining on the bay is not what it once was. Petrol spills abound, and I was paddled out to a seafood joint similar to one I'd visited years ago, and what was brought up from their live well was just a handful of dead shrimp. Cooking conditions are not real hygienic, and these folks weigh your catch when wet, then just chop it all up with a cleaver, and cook it. These restaurants are not really atmospheric, and they provide neither good value nor good quality. Stick to dining on the mainland. (***Note:*** One floating restaurant that you can reach by a walkway from shore serves good fresh fish and seafood from clean live tanks; see Bien Xanh, below).

The main drag of Cat Ba is chockablock with small storefront eateries. Young hostesses stand out front and try to get your attention, drag you in, and fill you up with seafood by the pound. Prices are reasonable. These places are nothing spectacular but are a good value for local seafood. Try **My Ngoc** (see below). I had a meal of deep-fried squid that was positively succulent and cost less than a McDonald's Happy Meal.

Just offshore, **Bien Xanh** (at the north end on the way to the beaches; ✆ **0313/887-529;** daily 6–11pm) is Cat Ba's only quality floating restaurant. In an entirely different school from the little floating restaurants in the bay, Bien Xanh is connected to shore by a walkway and gangplanks; inside, find a fine-dining area and good fresh fish and seafood much like the town's other oceanside restaurants, but here you're in a quieter and more romantic setting.

Flightless Bird Cafe INTERNATIONAL Aussie owner Graeme offers a friendly welcome, a pint, or a coffee, and can dispense good information about the area. Flightless Bird is a cozy little streetside cafe and bar in the southern end of the town's main strip. It fills up on weekends with expats and locals.

Zone 4 1/4 Rd. (oceanside on the southern end of town), Cat Ba Town. ✆ **0313/888-517.** 10,000 VND–15,000 VND. No credit cards. Daily 5pm–12:30am.

Green Mango ★ CONTINENTAL/ASIAN Fine dining comes to little Cat Ba via the borrowed style of one of Hanoi's coolest cafes, Bobby Chin's. Green Mango is your best bet for a sophisticated meal on the island. Young Chef Hai sidles up to your table and gives you the lowdown on the night's specials in a way that makes you feel like you've just heard about a new club opening up or about the latest new fashion trend. It's a cool, open-air, terra-cotta-tiled, candlelit space on the north end of the main strip, but the hip vibe is kind of cooled by the presence of local Mafiosi barking on their cellphones and wandering in and out of a seedy little pool hall next door. The food, from a great tapas menu with lots of daily specials, is presented on cool white plates. I especially like the fresh spring rolls, red snapper spaghetti, and a fresh filet cooked with Thai green curry on a bed of linguine. For dessert, try the delicious crepe with rich pudding. This is a good place to hook up with a good bottle of something imported and enjoy a leisurely evening in an intimate booth.

Group 19 Zone 4 (oceanside in the north end of town). ✆ **0313/887-151.** Main courses 80,000 VND–180,000 VND. MC, V. Daily 6:30am–late.

My Ngoc Of the fairly typical Cat Ba riverside restaurants, this place is my pick for fresh seafood that's affordable. ***Warning:*** Service is terrible and you might see lots of unhappy groups fighting for scraps or counting every spring roll in their portion to make sure it matches up with what they agreed on when booking their budget trip. The favorite dishes change daily.

212 Duong 1/4 (south end of the strip). ✆ **0313/888-199.** 50,000 VND–120,000 VND. No credit cards. Daily 5am–11pm.

Noble House ★ CONTINENTAL Noble indeed is this three-story stylish house. The open-air, first-floor dining is done in a cool mix of rough-hewn timber and stone masonry. The second floor has low tables and floor cushions, and the top is a rockin' bar with a pool table and raised platform seating. Australian owner Peter rules the roost and can share good local information about the town or touring the surrounding area. The food is a savory mix of the familiar. Good "fry-up" breakfasts for the homesick or hungover (often from a night spent on the same stool) are served all day, and the likes of a cheese omelet are done with real cheese, just like at a good ol' U.S. diner. There are also good local stir-fries, lots of grilled or steamed fish dishes, and a popular beefsteak, fries, and salad entree. The steamed crab with ginger is a favorite. You're sure to meet lots of expats and fellow travelers here. (Start with happy hour 6–9pm and go from there.)

Next to Van Anh hotel on the main oceanside strip. ✆ **0313/888-363.** Main courses 100,000 VND–120,000 VND. No credit cards. Daily 6am–late.

CAT BA NATIONAL PARK

The Cat Ba National Park, established on March 31, 1986, takes up some 50% (15,200 hectares/37,544 acres) of the island's mountain and coastal areas, with vast tracts set aside for "primary care and stringent protection" of endangered species. The park's low peaks—the highest is Cao Vang, at just 322m (1,056 ft.)—are a dynamic, verdant setting. Cat

Ba is cool year-round, with an average temperature of 73/74°F (23/24°C). In July, it can get up to 82/83°F (28/29°C), and in January and February, it can go as low as 61/62°F (16/17°C). Rainy season is from April to November. The park is comprised of limestone evergreen forests, upland flooded forests, coastal mangrove forests, inshore coral reefs, and extensive areas of limestone outcroppings laced with caves. All is evergreen tropical monsoon forest.

The park supports a veritable Noah's Ark of diversity, with drought-resistant lizards and herbivores, and over 30 mammals, including langurs, civets, leopards, rhesus macaques, and barking deer. Many species in the park are rare or endangered, especially the **golden-headed langur,** which is unique to this area but has a fragile population of an estimated 100 individuals. Ongoing efforts try to prevent hunting in the park. You might also see pythons, vipers, and water snakes, but your only real chance of catching sight of something unique is to take a full-day hike through the park with a guide.

Coastal bird life is astounding, and on any journey along the island's coast, you can see some of Cat Ba's nearly 70 bird species, both tropical monsoon birds and migrants. Water birds, like the sea eagle, kingfisher, and teal, can be spotted along the island coast. Inland, find the likes of the great hornbill, the thrush, and the woodpecker.

This park is geared to domestic tourists, but the scenery is fine and there are a few good hikes. The Educational Center, just on the right after the entry, has one large panel with information (in English) about the park's many rare species, as well as advice about nearby trails. No English speakers are on staff, though, so you're more or less on your own here, which is fine because navigating the park's few trails is a piece of cake.

From the park entrance, walk about 1km (½ mile) straight back along the wide, clearly marked path, past the rather uninspired zoo with just a few unhappy barking deer in a small field, to the beginning of a good steep grade and signs for the **Kim Giao Forest.** Covering some 20 hectares (49 acres), the forest is of a unique hardwood prized for furniture making. The trees are not remarkable, however—just squat little things about 5m (16 ft.) high. From here the path gets treacherous, but just 1.5km (1 mile) of hiking gets you to the **Kim Giao Peak.** To get to the peak, just pass the turn (on your right) to the Kim Giao Forest and follow the proverbial middle road (the fork to the far left is a steep muddy slope) to the top of the peak. The tiptop requires a good bit of rock scrambling, although there are a few ladders and metal steps set up to make things slightly easier.

Good hikes also go to **Trung Trang Cave** (along the road from Cat Ba Town just before the park entrance), as well as farther into the depth of the park and the Ao-Ech village route to a freshwater reservoir or to the Viet Hai village. Longer routes require a good guide; ask in town about all-day hikes with a boat ride back to Cat Ba Town.

Entrance to the park is just 15,000 VND, and 2,000 VND for motorbike parking. Hiring a guide, if you can find somebody willing, costs about 150,000 VND to go up the peak.

OTHER ATTRACTIONS

Cat Co Beaches Just thin strips of hard sand on isolated little bays at the base of Cat Ba's cliffs, the Cat Co beaches aren't a bad place to put your feet up for an afternoon—especially after a long boat trip or for the morning before heading back to Hanoi. The more mellow members of your crew can opt out on hiking Cat Ba National Park and instead rest here and dig into a novel. Cat Co III has just seen the building of the new Cat Ba Sunrise Resort, making that beach exclusive for anything but walking by and taking a dip. (In other words, you can't use the thatched umbrellas, but nobody owns the water. A small bribe, though, might earn you a seat in the shade at Cat Ba's new resort.)

Cat Co I and II are open to the public (with a charge of just 5,000 VND), and you can get there easily on your motorbike, by motorbike taxi for about 10,000 VND, or by foot. From the Sunrise Resort on Cat Co III, you can follow the high-cliff walks heading north and enjoy stunning views of the bay on your way to the other beaches.

Hospital Cave ★ On the road leading north from Cat Ba—on your way from Cat Ba town to the Cat Ba National Park—you'll crest a small hill and spy first a small cave entrance and ladder off to your right. Then you'll likely spot him: one of Vietnam's greatest treasures. Wearing his finest dress brown drabs and stiff officer's hat, 74-year-old Mr. Khoi will likely be out on the road waving you down. You see, these are his caves, more or less. Mr. Khoi is originally from the area, but the war against the United States took him far and wide as an artilleryman in the Viet Cong. Upon his retirement, the kindly Mr. Khoi took it upon himself to be the steward of this cave complex. The labyrinth of well-designed underground buildings once housed a large hospital and recovery rooms, as well as offices and planning rooms, ammunition storage, recreation rooms, a theater, and a small swimming pool. The caves are important vestiges of the war: In fact, this is the spot where Everett Alvarez, the first American pilot shot down in combat operations in Vietnam (on Aug 5, 1964), was originally held. The complex of concrete reinforced walls set deep in the cave was built from 1960 to 1965. But Mr. Khoi himself is the most memorable part of a visit here. He lines up visitors at the entrance and gives a bellowing North Vietnamese salute before entering the cave, where he hales forth with a constant stream of information while waving his flashlight from room to room. Be sure to go with a translator, or his voice will be lost. He has a wonderful message of peace and of how visitors to the cave take part in the healing and reconciliation process between Vietnam and the world and can move to the future. He even sings a rip-roaring military ballad for you. He'll ask you to sign his book and make comments, and you'll come away with a memory of his cherubic smile and a good feeling about life, peace, and possibilities.

On the road to Cat Ba National Park just a few clicks north of Cat Ba Town. No phone. 20,000 VND. Daily 8am–5pm (or whenever Mr. Khoi is there).

North-Central Vietnam

8

Most travelers fly over this region between Hue and Hanoi (or take the overnight train), and towns like Vinh are rarely visited by Westerners (though admirers of Ho Chi Minh go to his birthplace like Elvis fans flock to Graceland). North-Central Vietnam does have some treasures, especially in and around Ninh Binh—a popular place for a day trip or overnight from Hanoi.

1 NINH BINH

90km (56 miles) S of Hanoi; 110km (68 miles) N of Vinh

The many sights in and around Ninh Binh—just an hour-and-a-half ride south of Hanoi on Hwy. 1—are often visited as a day trip or with an overnight on a planned tour from Hanoi. Independent travelers arriving in Ninh Binh find themselves in a cluster of shops along busy Hwy. 1, with little in the way of good food and just one hotel that even passes muster. And, in fact, you'll probably end up paying more to do the trip independently. I recommend taking a good, private tour to the area; just choose the sights that most interest you (you can't really do them all in a day) and find a tour operator that makes the trip. Any of the tour operators in Hanoi will do. The exception to this, and the only place that really merits an overnight—but for nature buffs only—is Cuc Phuong National Park; if you visit Cuc Phuong on a day trip from Hanoi, you get there at the wrong time of day, when any wildlife is hiding out, so it's worth an overnight. Otherwise, go with a tour.

GETTING THERE

BY CAR This is your best bet. Contact Hanoi travel agents to hire your own vehicle with a driver for the 1-day trip, or overnight, and return. It's just over an hour's drive.

BY BUS There's a regular connection between Hanoi's Giap Bat (Southern Bus Station) and a small station stop just adjacent to the central train station—although some buses will drop you off right on Hwy. 1. Keep an eye out for the hotel of your choosing, best at the Thuy Anh Hotel (see below), and buses will stop for you. You can also connect with Vinh or with Hanoi by minibuses.

BY TRAIN The Reunification Express makes a stop in Ninh Binh, but if you're just making the short trip from Hanoi, it's more of a hassle than going by road.

VISITOR INFORMATION & TOURS

Check with the many tour operators in Hanoi for arranging quality tours of the scenic Ninh Binh area. Go with **Sinh Café** for peanuts and you'll cover all the bases (for as little as $15 per day); if you book a high-end tour with a company like **Buffalo Tours,** you'll get the best view of local culture and natural sites.

FAST FACTS There's a branch of the **Industrial and Commercial Bank of Vietnam** on Hwy. 1 at the center of town (Tran Hung Dao; ✆ **030/387-2614**). All hotels provide slow **Internet** connections in lobby terminals, but best is a small Internet nook just across

Hwy. 1 from Thuy Anh Hotel; a small sign leads you down a narrow alley. Cost is just 5,000 VND per hour. The main **post office** is in the south end of town (look for the high radio tower). Open daily 7am to 9pm.

WHERE TO STAY & DINE

In addition to the recommendation below, **Khachsan Hoa Lu** (Tran Hung Dao St.; ✆ **030/387-1217**) has rooms from $25 and is in the north end of Ninh Binh along Hwy. 1. Some budget tours may book you here, but it's mostly a businessmen's hotel—and a rather gritty one, at that. **Thanh Thuy's Guesthouse** (at 128 Le Hong Phong St.; ✆ **030/387-1811**) is a bare-bones operation off the main road, but rooms start at $10 and they have a helpful tour desk with reasonable rates. **Queen Mini Hotel** (21 Hoang Hoa Tham St.; ✆ **030/387-1874;** fax 030/387-3005) is a basic but popular backpacker haunt outside the train station entrance. Rooms, which are a bit tattered, go from $5 to $15. The hotel offers good basic tour services—the staff will help you hire a guide and rent a motorbike or car—and a little restaurant with good one-dish meals.

Dining in Ninh Binh is only at local storefront restaurants, none more interesting or sanitary than the other. Most group tours include meals at Thuy Anh Hotel in their courtyard dining hall or rooftop restaurant (dull but not bad), and the little budget backpacker joints near the train station (see Queen Mini Hotel, above) also serve good, affordable one-plate meals. Just outside the Thuy Anh Hotel and farther down the road away from busy Hwy. 1, find the town's busiest local restaurant. There is no sign and no English menu, and they'll be amazed to see you, but the place is always packed with locals. Though you don't know what you'll get, the food's good.

Thuy Anh Hotel This place is by far the best in town, but everyone knows it. Thuy Anh is always booked with tour groups, and though the standard is high—for the low price—they don't necessarily court the individual traveler, as tour groups account for most bookings. They do, however, have a helpful front-desk staff and can arrange for motorcycle rentals or a guide for the day. Large rooms are rather plain, with clean white-tile and dark-wood furnishings. Bathrooms are the all-in-one guesthouse variety, but they are clean and have hot water. Dining is a communal affair in the hotel's large courtyard or at the rooftop restaurant.

55A Truong Han Sieu (just a few meters east of Hwy. 1 at the center of Ninh Binh). ✆ **030/387-1602.** Fax 030/3876-934. www.thuyanhhotel.com. 37 units. $15–$40 double. MC, V. **Amenities:** Restaurant; bar; Internet. *In room:* A/C, TV (no satellite service), fridge, minibar.

ATTRACTIONS

The sights of Ninh Binh are scattered outside the city, too many to see all in one day. Most travelers visit Ninh Binh on a tour from Hanoi, so it's a good idea to look closely at the sights below before joining a set itinerary. Private tours give you lots of flexibility, and an overnight for some is preferable (especially if you want to visit Cuc Phuong National Park). A **typical 1-day itinerary** might be either of the following: Tam Coc (the three grottoes), nearby Bich Dong Temple, Hoa Lu (the old capital), and Phat Diem Cathedral; or Kenh Ga (chicken village), Hoa Lu, and Cuc Phuong. ***Note:*** Tam Coc and Kenh Ga require boat rides, and visitors usually find one or the other—but not both—to be plenty of floating for one day; Tam Coc is more interesting.

Tam Coc (The Three Grottoes)

Located near the village of Van Lam, 7km (4¼ miles) southwest of Ninh Binh, the Tam Coc area is a highlight of any visit to Vietnam. Called "The Halong Bay of the Rice

Fields" after the UNESCO World Heritage Site north of Hanoi, the stunning limestone karst towers hearken to the famed landscape of the bay, as well as Guilin in southern China—a landscape that has inspired poets for centuries.

The karst towers of Tam Coc are set in wide lowland fields of wet rice, and visitors can experience a 1-hour boat ride along a meandering river. Take in the stunning scenery as you listen to the hypnotic clacking of the oars against the side of the boat and enjoy the meditative progress of the boat along the winding river.

Tam Coc means "Three Grottoes," after the three caves you pass through on the backtracking route. The caves transport you through a seeming portal in time, ever farther from the familiar into the misty mountain valley along this meandering stream; there is Hang Ca, Cave One, which is over 100m (328 ft.) long; then Hang Hai, Cave Two, at 70m (230 ft.); and lastly the smaller Hang Ba, Cave Three.

At the large gated entrance, you can buy your ticket (cost is 40,000 VND), which entitles you to visit the caves, enjoy a boat ride (you must present your coupon to the rower), and see a few adjoining temple sites. The wooden rowboats leave from a village whose main street is lined with very local linen and embroidery shops—a good selection at very low prices. The rowers are a friendly lot and are happy to chat; some speak English, others smile, and everybody sings as they row, often in unison. Your new friend turns into salesman by the end of the ride, though—kind of a drag. The item up for bid is embroidery, which they'll tell you was executed by the shaking hand of an ailing grandmother, anything to get you to fork over a few dong. Your rower has a tacit agreement with other sellers along the route to bump your boat against anyone with even a few bananas for sale. In these cases, if you whip out your wallet, you might as well shout "Free for all! Come and get 'em!" Best to just quietly decline. In lieu of a purchase, a small tip to your rower at the end of the ride is a better bargain, but know (and accept) that there's no way to fend off the sellers at Tam Coc. Tourists are like ducks on a pond. The most important thing is not to let it get you down, keep it light—but say "no"—and keep your eyes on the passing scenery.

The time to go to Tam Coc is after 10am (the morning fog obscures the shape of the precipitous peaks). If you arrive too early and the place is still foggy, take a ride by road out to **Bich Dong Temple,** and then come back for the boat trip when things have burned off. By midday, though, the sun is blistering and the open boats offer no shade. Local hucksters are quick to make the most of your misery and sell (or rent) umbrellas to ward off the sun, but it's best to just bring a good hat and cover up with sunscreen. Along the route you'll see shy kingfishers flitting about, as well as cranes padding around the paddies and floating weeds. Local fishermen, quite used to the steady stream of tourists, are busy setting nets and paddling about in boats the size of snow saucers. Some fishermen row with their feet, while others use the unique standing technique of leaning forward and pushing the oars in a heaving forward lunge; the stroke is beautiful to watch, but try doing it and see how difficult it is.

Bich Dong is a stunning temple complex at the base of high cliffs about 2km (1¼ miles) past the starting point for boat rides to Tam Coc. A pond is near the entry, and the main temple courtyard gives way to a series of pagodas along the short path up the high rocky hillside: a good vantage point over the surrounding countryside. ***Note:*** At this sacred place, as at other temple sites, it's best to be well behaved and stay covered up (no shorts), even though no one officially checks or enforces a dress code.

Hoa Lu: The Ancient Capital

For a short period at the end of the first millennium (A.D. 968–1009), Hoa Lu was the capital of Vietnam under the Dinh dynasty and the first part of the Le dynasty. The area was chosen because the limestone formations surrounding the site—the same ones that attract tourists by the thousands—were a stalwart natural defense against the Chinese. The temples of Hoa Lu are worth a visit and part of most itineraries out of Ninh Binh. The two temples, both dedicated to respective Le and Dinh kings, are ornate 17th-century re-creations on the site of some ancient ramparts and walls, but what makes the trip interesting is the beautiful scenery of the area, especially along the rural road connecting the site with nearby Tam Coc (see above). The whole valley is hemmed in with high limestone walls of karst, much like the dynamic setting of Tam Coc. One temple honors Dinh Tien Hoang with an imposing statue. The other temple, farther from the road across a large field often used for large festivals, is dedicated to Le Dai Hanh, one of Dinh's generals and the first king of the Le dynasty, who grabbed power in A.D. 980 after Dinh was mysteriously assassinated. Hoa Lu can easily be seen on a day trip from Hanoi. The temples are 113km (70 miles) south of Hanoi.

Kenh Ga: Chicken Village

Here, tour among floating villages teeming with life, where local oarsmen (and women) row with their feet. Photographers delight. Reach the site by motorbike, either your own rented machine or on the back of a bike with a driver. The village is more than 10km (6¼ miles) west of Hwy. 1 starting at a juncture 11km (6¾ miles) north of central Ninh Binh. Expect to pay at least 50,000 VND per person for a few hours exploring this beautiful waterside town and floating village.

Cuc Phuong National Park

Ho Chi Minh established Cuc Phuong in 1962 as Vietnam's first national park, and it remains a source of national pride. The park is a lush mountain rainforest with more than 300 bird and 100 mammal species, including tigers, leopards, and the unique red-bellied squirrel. But the park's many visitors—mostly large domestic tour groups, especially on the weekends—might keep you from the kind of wildlife experience you expect in the brush.

Cuc Phuong is just 120km (75 miles) south of Hanoi and a 30-minute ride from Ninh Binh. A little town with very basic services (food stall, gasoline stand) is outside the park's first gate. Once in the park, you'll pass first the visitor center, a small museum on your right, and then the park's popular Primate Resource Center (see below) on your left before reaching the main gate. There, check in at the main information booth, pay the 40,000 VND entry fee (children 20,000 VND), and connect with the park's able guides and rangers (ask to talk with a guide named Mr. Som). Your entrance fee includes a guide who will accompany you on a visit to the Primate Resource Center and who can be hired for $15 a day to take you on hikes in the park.

A well-paved road runs through the length of the park, and trails and roadside sites are all well marked. Cuc Phuong hosts good hikes, including ones to the park's 1,000-year-old tree, a waterfall, and Con Moong Cave, where prehistoric human remains have been discovered. The park holds 117 species of mammals, 307 types of birds, 110 reptiles and amphibians, 65 species of fish, and 2,000 kinds of insects. The rare Asian black bear and the golden leopard live here.

Cuc Phuong National Park Endangered Primate Resource Center ★★★ (✆ 030/384-8002; www.primatecenter.org) is the highlight of a visit to the park. Run by an international team of primate experts, mostly from the Frankfurt Zoological Society and supported by zoos worldwide, the project houses some 150 animals in cages, large monkey-houses with swinging bars, and, at the back, a sprawling semiwild jungle enclosure (good for the animals, not great for viewing them). Find many species of gibbon, multicolored langurs, including the very rare, protected Catba golden-hair langur and the endangered Delacour's langur, and the teacup-size slow loris. Animals are lovingly cared for, in the best situation possible, and they put on quite a show—hopping, hollering, and swinging from ropes in large enclosures. ***Note:*** Though you pass the Primate Center on your way to the main gate, you must still check in at the park's main entrance and backtrack, with a guide, to visit the animals; this policy ensures some measure of control over the number of visitors and their impact on these very intelligent, sensitive creatures.

The goal of the center is to create stable captive populations of endangered animals and eventually through socialization and acclimatization in the semiwild habitat, reintroduce animals to the wild. If you visit the park on a day tour from Hanoi, you'll come at the wrong time: midday, when animals are listless and resting in the heat. Folks with an interest in primates will want to spend the night and might even have a chance to meet up with staff or researchers who can provide more in-depth information. A small civet-breeding program is next door.

The **1,000-year-old tree** is at the end of a good loop hike that starts at the park's interior visitor center, some 30 minutes' ride past the gate. The path is well marked, mostly paved, and set up with convenient walkways, but the jungle scenery is dense and, if you walk quietly, you might catch a glimpse of some wildlife (especially in the morning or evening).

The **Cave of the Prehistoric Man** is just a roadside attraction, a short hike off the main drag up a hillside with a wide cave. The cave was discovered in 1966, and the remains of an early man along with his stone tools and relics are said to date back as far as 12,000 years ago. The walkway to the site is a good place to sit still and see what kinds of wild things you can spot.

Cuc Phuong is a good day trip from Hanoi, and some tourist cafes offer programs for as little as $30 (if you have four people in your group); but a day trip means arriving in the middle of the day, when jungle animals are fast asleep and when the heat and humidity, especially in the spring hot season, can be too much. It is also possible to overnight in the park headquarters or at the visitor information center. They offer basic rooms in a block building at the entrance. Doubles go for $15 to $25. One of the most pleasant aspects of visiting Cuc Phuong is the possibility of connecting with visiting naturalists and scientists (when I was there, I met a large contingent from the Philippines), and the overnight accommodations, though rustic, make for a fun evening—especially with a gaggle of scientists in the canteen. There's a lake just inside the park, which is set up like a small summer camp for large groups, usually Vietnamese school kids, and the site echoes with good Vietnamese campfire songs.

Foreigners comprise only a small percentage of the 70,000 people or so who visit the park annually, and the large groups of Vietnamese tourists—and many school groups—are not yet well versed in eco-tourism practices. (I kept coming across a group of more than 50 school kids, all dressed in the same bright yellow T-shirts and wearing oversize straw hats, led by a guide with a bullhorn blaring instructions and information—so much for animal spotting.) Talk to guides about good night-spotting trips and rigorous overnights in the jungle.

Phat Diem

Popular in conjunction with a visit to the ancient city of Hoa Lu, a visit to Phat Diem cathedral is an important pilgrimage for the faithful or the architecture buff. Nowhere will you find such a unique melding of contemporary Christian motifs with Asian-style architecture.

The site is 121km (75 miles) southeast of Hanoi and about 25km (16 miles) south and east of the town of Ninh Binh. The road passes through beautiful areas of lush lowland rice fields and past many lesser cathedrals and Christian burial sites: Note that **Ton Dao Church,** just outside of town, is a particularly imposing edifice with high stone spires, intricate carvings on lintels and facade, and reliefs of St. Francis ministering to the sick and impoverished. The town of Phat Diem is just a little commercial strip—not much to see, really.

Follow signs to Phat Diem from the main road, down a narrow street that spills onto a broad courtyard at the end of its length. At the center of the courtyard is a pond with an expressive statue of Jesus, and beyond that is your first glimpse of the cathedral.

Enter to the right, but be sure to go back and experience the temple starting at the large Chinese-style gate. The church and grounds uniquely blend East and West. The main cathedral, an imposing wooden structure, has Chinese-influenced parapets, the roofline upturned at the corners, and out front are elaborate lintel bas-reliefs of saints that would elsewhere be Buddhas. All of the structures are decked out in Chinese roofs of terra-cotta tile, and small Chinese pagodas pepper the grounds around the main cathedral. The building stands flanked by a number of small chapels.

The **Cathedral of Saint Joseph**—the first building you reach when making a clockwise circuit around the main temple—was built in 1896 and is made of wood and covered in elaborate engravings and carvings. Behind it is the **Chapel of St. Pierre,** also built in 1896. Usually the interior is closed to the public (most chapels here are), but if you peak along the sides of the altar, which is a 1-ton block of stone, in the back you can see reliefs of the Twelve Apostles and their names in Chinese letters.

Far back on the left is the diminutive **Stone Chapel (Legise de Pierre),** a very refined structure of glossy marble. The chapel is dedicated to the Virgin Mary, and out front is an engraving (in four languages) that reads, "Immaculate Heart of Mary Pray for Us." Relief works on the cornices of the building depict mythical beasts.

Completing the circuit, and near the entrance of the cathedral grounds, the temple to St. John the Baptist is where locals once came during a cholera epidemic to invoke the help of St. Roch and, when miraculously healed, renamed the building **Roch Chapel.**

The interior of the main chapel is like any Chinese temple, with thick wooden pillars supporting a raised gallery. Red and gold filigree at the altar would be more familiar in a small city temple in Hanoi or Ho Chi Minh City, which makes this cathedral unique. Statues of Mary and Jesus take the place of an expected Buddha, and stained glass depicts both European and Vietnamese martyrs. The main altar was cut from stone block and was consecrated on October 6, 1991, on the 100th anniversary of the temple that was originally built in 1891.

Phat Diem is a working cathedral, and services are ongoing throughout the day.

2 VINH

300km (186 miles) S of Hanoi; 370km (230 miles) N of Hue

An important bastion of revolutionary thought, the town of Vinh was the scene of a large-scale rebellion led by Le Hong Phong in the 1930s. Bombed beyond recognition during the war with the United States, Vinh was rebuilt with an East German flair, which means that large concrete-block compounds line broad boulevards. Drab and depressing, there isn't much for foreign tourists to see here. What attracts most, and mainly Vietnamese tourists, are the sites dedicated to the city's most famous inhabitant: Ho Chi Minh. Born here in 1890, Ho Chi Minh lived in a small village just 14km (8¾ miles) outside of the city center. A visit to Ho's birthplace in the adjoining village where his father was a local official, and to the large central square with his statue, are the only real sights. Nearby **Cua Lo Beach** is a popular local escape lined with minihotels and beachside coffee shops. Vinh is also a popular way station for those going to or coming from Laos.

FAST FACTS **Vietcombank** has a branch at 9 Nguyen Sy Sach St. (✆ **038/384-4044**) that's open daily from 8am to 5pm (closed for lunch 11:30am–1:30pm). They offer **ATM service** and can cash traveler's checks. There is reliable **Internet** service next to the post office. The main post office is at 2 Nguyen Thi Minh Khai St.

WHERE TO STAY & DINE

For **dining** along the Cua Lo strip, the best choice is **Thuy Hang** (✆ **038/395-1125**), at the center of town across the road from the beach. It serves crab, shrimp, squid, and the whole fish as you like. It's the kind of place where you need a bib, but the beauty of it, like most seafood joints in Vietnam, is you can dig in and get your hands dirty, spit shells on the floor, and then wash your hands in the big bucket of water with lemon.

Who Was "Uncle Ho"?

Ho Chi Minh, Vietnam's greatest revolutionary and patriot, was demonized in the West during the Vietnam War and at the same time canonized as a saint by the Vietnamese, especially after his greatest dream of an independent, united Vietnam was achieved. His martyred image is just as skewed as his vilification in the West. So who was Uncle Ho?

Ho Chi Minh's life is an allegory of the Marxist struggle in Vietnam, or so young Vietnamese school kids are taught: the ultimate "hero's journey out," where Ho left his homeland, picked up socialist ideals, and returned to raise the flag of revolution. The truth is a bit more complex.

Born **Nguyen Tat Thanh** on May 19, 1890, in the village of Hoang Tru near Vinh, just north of Hue in central Vietnam, Ho spent his young life looking over his father's shoulder as Dad studied to be a mandarin (high government official). While living in Hue, he saw his mother and sister die—experiences that steeled him for a harsh later life. Ho's father was a thinker and had many friends who were active in radical politics, and from an early age Ho was exposed to lots of revolutionary talk. Ho studied only briefly at university before setting out on his own, walking the length of Vietnam and working as a teacher here and there from 1906 to 1911. He spent time in Nge An, Hue, Quy Nhon, Phan Thiet, and Saigon (all places with "Ho Slept Here" tour spots). Like Che Guevara's motorcycle trip around South America, Ho Chi Minh's formative wanderings in Vietnam were a major part of his identity. He developed his compassion and understanding of the Vietnamese people and also saw up close their struggles under a colonial yoke.

Leaving from Saigon in 1911, Ho set sail as a cook on a ship. Reputedly, this was the time when he gained his worldly perspective and began to understand notions of the world as a class struggle, a kind of Darwinian fight that can have only one solution: an ongoing peasant/proletariat revolution. He connected with other free thinkers abroad, working in kitchens in London, and then moved to Paris, where he changed his name to **Nguyen Ai Quoc** ("Nguyen the Patriot"). His ideas began to gain clout among fellow dissidents, and he became involved in underground print journalism while building a Rolodex of fellow revolutionaries.

Green Hotel Owned by the conglomerate that owns Maximart, Vietnam's burgeoning version of 7-Eleven, the Green Hotel is your best choice along Cua Lo Beach (all around are minihotels that fill up in the summer season). Rooms are clean but a bit musty. Deluxe rooms have spacious sitting areas and good views (usually on upper floors) of the long, muddy stretch of beach outside. More affordable rooms are at the back, with showers only; these are clean, if rather spartan, with guesthouse-style bathrooms. The hotel has lots of services, but most go unused. This is the top choice of the many Vietnamese honeymooners who visit from surrounding provinces.

Binh Minh St., Cua Lo Town, Nghe An Province. ✆ **038/394-9949.** Fax 038/394-9949. 183 units. Winter 350,000 VND–800,000 VND double; summer 500,000 VND–1,100,000 VND double. MC, V. **Amenities:** 2 restaurants; bar; disco; small pool; sauna. *In room:* A/C, satellite TV, fridge, hair dryer, Internet, minibar.

He traveled between Moscow and China, a revolutionary peripatetic, for most of the 1930s, and grew a large following. As a founder of the Indochinese Communist Party (ICP), he was under constant suspicion and surveillance, at one point fleeing to Hong Kong and then on to the south of China, where he formed the League for an Independent Vietnam, whose members, later soldiers, were called the Viet Minh, and then Viet Cong in the war with the United States. Imprisoned by Chiang Kai-shek in 1940, Ho changed his name to **Ho Chi Minh** ("Enlightened One") and returned to Vietnam via surreptitious border crossings and long stays in hide-out caves in the far north (near Cao Bang).

On August 19, 1945, after the surrender of the Japanese in World War II, Ho Chi Minh made his "Declaration of Independence" that borrowed language from U.S. and French documents of freedom. Thus began the armed revolution.

Outwardly an ascetic, Ho was reputedly a ladies' man, and stories of his nighttime dalliances, real or imagined, pepper more recent histories. He is even said to have taken up with a French woman and to have fathered a number of children. Diminutive and delicate, Ho was a leader who lived a spartan existence, upholding the ideals of egalitarian revolution, living in a simple two-room building on the grounds of the former imperial palace (you can see his home near the mausoleum in Hanoi).

Ho Chi Minh died from natural causes in 1969, just 6 years short of seeing his dream of a unified Communist Vietnam. Nearing death, Ho was explicit about his wishes to be cremated, his ashes divided into three separate portions and distributed at sites in the north, center, and south to celebrate the reunification of the country. He asked for no pomp or circumstance, no grand tomb or homage to his remains. The hulking mausoleum, set on the site where he declared independence in 1941, would have him turning in his grave if he weren't, in fact, embalmed and set on a palanquin for general public viewing. A visit to the mausoleum is a quirky highlight of any trip to Hanoi.

Following a long tradition of deifying war heroes, Ho Chi Minh's image is everywhere: on cabs, in shrines, and in long rows of portraits hung in family rooms, sanctified in the family pantheon as one of the great immortals.

Phuong Dong Hotel Adjacent to the central park and statue of Ho Chi Minh in the city center, the Phuong Dong is the finest hotel in town, but that's not saying much. The rooms are pretty beat-up, and the service isn't great. But if you're coming to Vinh, it's your best bet. It's a popular stop for Thai tour groups that are coming in increasing numbers on overland jaunts across Laos—if a Thai group is in residence, the whole place kind of cheers up; otherwise, it can be pretty gloomy. The hotel covers all the bases, though, and can get you a car rental for trips out to Uncle Ho's birthplace or to Cua Lo Beach. Prices listed below are more or less fictitious points of departure for haggling (pay as low as $20 for a single).

2 Truong Thi St., Vinh City. ✆ **038/356-2299.** Fax 038/356-2562. 177 units. $48 double; $69 suite. MC, V. **Amenities:** 2 restaurants; bar; small swimming pool; sauna; steam room. *In room:* A/C, satellite TV, fridge, hair dryer, Internet, minibar.

To truly honor the memory of Ho Chi Minh, visitors to these sights are obliged to buy a bouquet of flowers to lay at three separate places: 1) at the foot of his statue in the central square in the city of Vinh, 2) at his birthplace, and 3) in the nearby village of Kim Lien, where he lived for many years (see listing, below). It costs 20,000 VND per bouquet, and to do the full obeisance costs 60,000 VND. Worth it? Your call. Going without flowers is, of course, okay, but foreign visitors who follow the tradition get much more respect from the Vietnamese groups. A visit to these sights is a somber one, and foreign visitors should refrain from goofing around. Docents at each sight speak Vietnamese only, but some will hand you an information card printed in English. ***Note:*** Especially if you're with Vietnamese friends or tagging along with a group, pretend you're listening; walking away while the docent is speaking is considered rude.

Statue of Ho Chi Minh In the center of Vinh (and also adjacent to the town's best hotel, the Phuong Dong), the massive square in front of this statue is the city's most popular strolling ground. Western visitors are bombarded by young students eager to practice their English and who want to have their photograph taken with a bona fide Westerner (put on your best "materialistic and indulgent" grin). The massive statue of Ho at one end of the square is surrounded by a faux mountain range to depict the land of Vietnam, and Ho himself looks downright jaunty, one hand raised as he strides forward, a "revolutionary winning" grin on his bright, silver visage. The steps leading up to the statue are guarded by some surly, jack-booted soldiers who growl at anyone who goes near. The only exception is if you've come with a bouquet for the fallen leader and, leaving your shoes at the bottom of the steps, humbly pad to the foot of the statue and lay your wreath in obeisance (you can stop for a photo on the way down, but don't linger or the lads will bark at you).

At the center of town in Vinh. Free admission. The park and entrance to the statue are open daily dawn–dusk.

Hoang Tru Village The house where Ho Chi Minh was born belonged to his paternal grandfather and lies in Hoang Tru Village. It's a pilgrimage sight for Vietnamese tourists who come by the busload, especially on weekends and national holidays. Souvenir stalls out front sell busts of Ho, books (some good volumes in English), and bouquets of flowers for placing on the small family altar in Ho's home. The home is the original, but the furnishings are re-creations—except for the bed, which is the actual one in which Ho was born. What strikes any visitor, and is something that Vietnamese almost worship, is the rugged simplicity of these dirt-floored, thatch-wall rooms in which the country's greatest leader sprang from obscurity to spurn a revolution. Ho's father was involved in government, and it was in this house, as well as his second home nearby (see below), that Ho first heard the rumblings of discontent from local officials and revolutionary friends of his father. In fact, the likes of Phan Boi Chau, Phan Chu Trinh, and Phan Dinh Phung (names familiar from major city thoroughfares throughout Vietnam) graced the family hearth, and much of Ho's passion for politics came from overhearing these conversations. He was immersed in the cause of peasant revolution. Ho Chi Minh was descended from two generations of teachers, and his studious father endured much to attain the rank of mandarin. Study was therefore a focus for young Ho, too, and his desk and study area are enshrined here, almost like places of worship for Vietnamese, who are so grateful for the high ideals the man held and lived by.

Hoang Tru is 14km (8¾ miles) south of Vinh. Most visitors come by bus or car and then walk to nearby Kim Lien, Ho Chi Minh's second place of residence during his father's shifting career in government.

Free admission. The sights are open daily 8–11am and 1–5pm.

Kim Lien Village Walking here—it's just 1km (½ mile) from Hoang Tru, along a flat road flanking lush green rice fields—is part of the experience of getting in touch with Ho the man, who, as a young teacher, walked the length of Vietnam going from job to job and searching for a purpose. His journey is chronicled in Vietnamese schools and celebrated in many "Ho Chi Minh Slept Here" sights around the country.

The village of Kim Lien features an imposing series of museums and monuments. Display areas with photos of Ho's life and the rise of the revolution grace the walls of two buildings that flank the courtyard entry, and at the back there's a unique building—its interior decorated in red with a great golden bust of Ho Chi Minh—where you're meant to lay another bouquet of flowers. It's all strangely like a Buddhist temple, and the vibe is a bit eerie if you're not into worshiping false idols and such (I was with a group of Vietnamese and more or less obliged to offer flowers and make an obeisant nod to the bust, however uncomfortable I felt about it). Behind this large compound is the house where Ho Chi Minh's father, Nguyen Sinh Sac, lived after his first appointment as a local mandarin official. The house is just as humble as the family's first one, but here you'll see the plaque of the mandarin hanging in Ho's father's office area and a more elaborate family altar. Also on the museum grounds, there are quiet lotus ponds and a large pavilion with souvenirs (a ceramic Ho Chi Minh bust costs just 10,000 VND) and books, many in English.

Free admission. The sights are open daily 8–11am and 1–5pm.

Cua Lo Beach The other grand attraction in this region is Cua Lo Beach—wide and wind-swept, with many services along its length that cater mostly to the Vietnamese holiday crowd (the place is packed on weekends and in the summer). You'll find some great little seafood places on Cua Lo and a few affordable hotels. The beach is just 16km (10 miles) east and south of Vinh.

The last emperor of Vietnam, the "Playboy King" Bao Dai, had a villa here. Now, with lots of little local coffee outlets and romantic picnic areas, the beach is best for strolling (rather than swimming and lying out in the sun). It's a nice escape; don't expect to see other foreign tourists here. Just off the coast, you can see Hon Mat Island in the distance, and tiny Lan Chu Island can be reached on foot at low tide.

Cua Lo Beach is 16km (10 miles) southeast of Vinh.

Phong Nha—Ke Bang National Park A visit to this national park in Quang Binh Province—which has been designated as a UNESCO World Heritage Site—makes for a good day trip from Vinh. Famous for its massive grottoes, the Phong Nha cave system is 40km (25 miles) long, starting from Ruc Ca Roong Cave to Vom Cave, descending some 300m (984 ft.) before the cave water spills into the sea. The main grotto, and the highlight of a tour here, has 14 "rooms" covering over a kilometer-long (half-mile) corridor. Boats travel its length upstream. Contact tour operators in Hue or Hanoi to visit this stunning natural site. There's no public transportation to the caves.

Nearly 500km (311 miles) south of Hanoi and 55km (34 miles) northeast of Dong Hoi. Admission is 20,000 VND. Caves are open daily 6am–4pm.

9

Central Vietnam

Many of Vietnam's most significant historical sites and some of its best beaches are clustered along its central coast. This is the country's narrowest region; in some places, there's just over 50km (31 miles) of land between the sea and nearby Laos. Coming from the north, after having passed through (or over) minor cities such as Ninh Binh and Vinh (see chapter 8), the most significant place to visit along the coast is the former Vietnamese capital, **Hue.** With its **Imperial City** and emperors' tombs, it's an important stop for any historical tour of Vietnam and a UNESCO World Heritage Site.

The next-most important area as you head south is **Hoi An,** another UNESCO World Heritage Site and a historic trading town that had its heyday in the 17th century. Hoi An boasts more than 800 perfectly preserved classic Chinese and Vietnamese houses and temples laid out in a rabbit warren of streets, preserved as they were hundreds of years ago, thanks to the protection of UNESCO. Formerly the seat of the Cham kingdom from the 2nd through 14th centuries, the central coast also has the greatest concentration of Cham relics and art. Be sure to visit the Cham Museum at **Danang** and the nearby Cham temple site at **My Son.**

Sample the Vietnamese beach scene in its youthful stages at **China Beach** and **Cua Dai,** where luxury resorts are beginning to crowd out fishermen and attract the world's well-heeled. The proximity and convenient transportation among the main tour stops in central Vietnam means you'll be able to cover ground efficiently. Danang and Hoi An, for example, are so close (about half an hour by car) that you can easily stay in one and make day trips to the other.

1 HUE

Hue (pronounced *Hway*) is culturally and historically significant. It was once Vietnam's Imperial City and later the country's capital under the Nguyen dynasty (1802–1945).

The **Thua Thien–Hue** region was a political football during hundreds of years of early Vietnamese dynastic turf wars with the Cham people in the south and the Chinese in the north. It wasn't until the late 18th century that the leaders of the **Tay Son Rebellion** and Emperor Quang Trung, having routed the Chinese out of the north, established a capital at Hue. Later, the Nguyen dynasty leaders, beginning with powerful Gia Long, made Hue the capital that served the Vietnamese puppets of the French until the end of World War II. The first citadel and Imperial City was built by Gia Long in 1803 on a former royal site; many of the city walls still stand, battle scarred from fighting with the French as far back as 1873, and later with the Americans during the notorious Battle of Hue in 1968.

Although much of Hue—tragically, including most of Vietnam's walled Citadel and Imperial City—was decimated during wars with the French and the Americans, there's still much to see. And because of the damaged buildings, you'll want to hit the temples with a good English-speaking guide who can bring the place back to life and offer some good background (otherwise, you might see just walls and rubble).

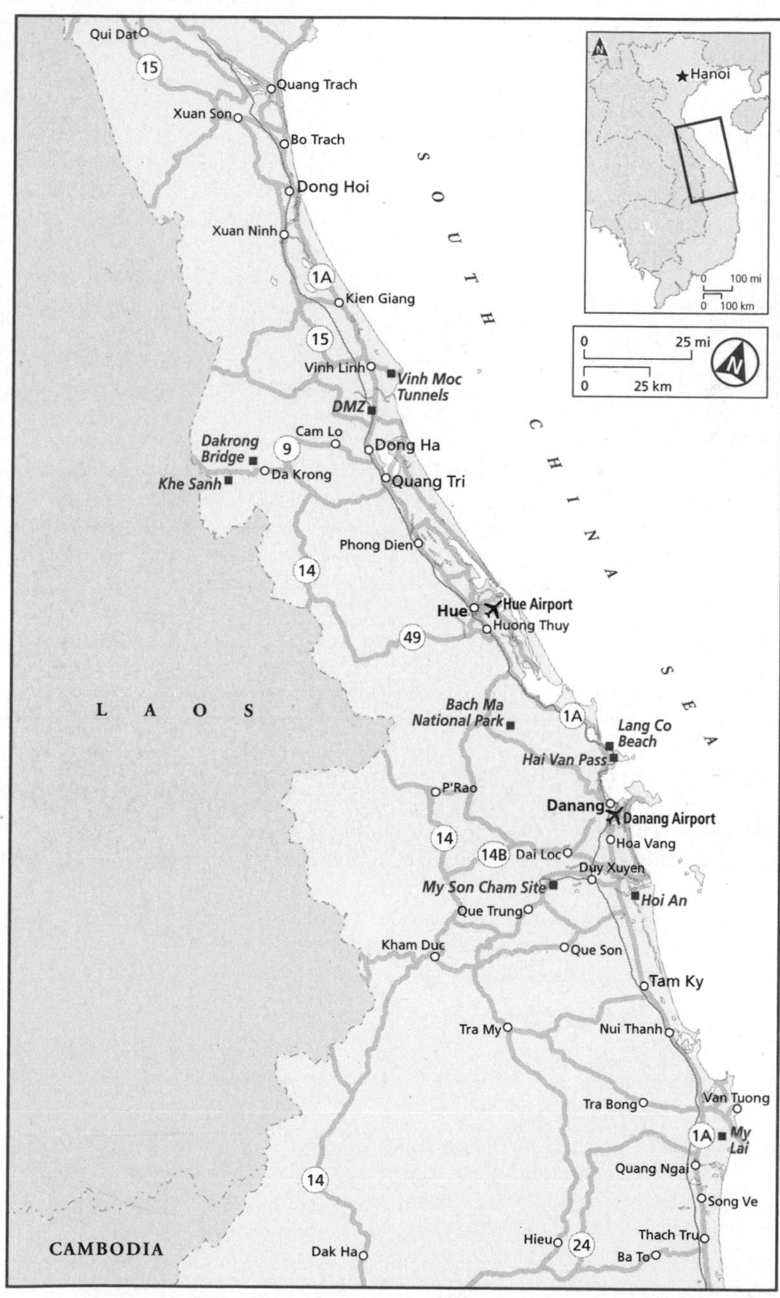
Qui Dat
15
Quang Trach
Xuan Son
Bo Trach
Dong Hoi
Xuan Ninh
1A
Kien Giang
15
Vinh Linh
Vinh Moc Tunnels
DMZ
Cam Lo
Dakrong Bridge
9
Dong Ha
Da Krong
Khe Sanh
Quang Tri
Phong Dien
14
Hue
Hue Airport
Huong Thuy
49
SOUTH CHINA SEA
LAOS
Bach Ma National Park
1A
Lang Co Beach
Hai Van Pass
P'Rao
Danang
Danang Airport
Hoa Vang
14
14B
Dai Loc
Duy Xuyen
My Son Cham Site
Hoi An
Que Trung
Kham Duc
Que Son
Tam Ky
Tra My
Nui Thanh
Tra Bong
Van Tuong
1A
My Lai
Quang Ngai
14
Song Ve
Thach Tru
Hieu
24
Ba To
CAMBODIA
Dak Ha
Hanoi
0 100 mi
0 100 km
0 25 mi
0 25 km
N

Perhaps most captivating is the daily life on **Perfume River,** with its many dragon boats, houseboats, and long-tail vessels dredging for sand. You can visit many of the attractions, including the tombs of the rather flamboyant and megalomaniacal **Nguyen dynasty emperors,** by boat. The enjoyable town features low-slung, colorful colonial-style buildings, and strings of lights at outdoor cafes at night are like the flame for the many tourist-moths that quickly flit through here. Try to sample some of the many local cuisine specialties; you'll find fine-dining establishments that specialize in tempering the cuisine to foreign tastes (with varying degrees of success). The **Trang Tien Bridge,** which connects the citadel area with the new town across the Perfume River, is itself a major attraction, a lovers' lane of sorts and a national symbol. You'll see local photographers selling their services in the little riverside park on the new-town side. The bridge is lit up at night with constantly changing bulbs, and lovers stroll the promenade, taking in all of the good Technicolor glistening off the river below. Vendors line the riverside promenade and it's a good place to buy something sugary (they even have cotton candy).

You may want to plan a full-day excursion to the nearby demilitarized zone (DMZ), the beginning of the Ho Chi Minh Trail, and the underground tunnels at Vinh Moc.

GETTING THERE

BY PLANE Hue connects from both Hanoi and Saigon with Vietnam Airlines (in Hue, ✆ **054/824-709**). A taxi from the airport costs 170,000 VND. There's also an airport bus that will drop you off or pick you up at your hotel and covers the half-hour trip to the airport for 30,000 VND. You can buy tickets at a stand in the airport's arrival area, or book through your hotel's front desk or any tour operator.

BY TRAIN Trains depart daily from both Hanoi and Saigon to the station in Hue (✆ **054/382-2686**); there are two nightly departures, at 7 and 11pm. A trip from Hanoi to Hue takes 14 hours on an express train and costs about 462,000 VND in a soft-berth compartment with air-conditioning. From Saigon, in a soft-berth compartment with air-conditioning, it's about $50.

BY CAR If you're coming from the south, contact any of the tour operators listed below or in section 5 of this chapter, and they can arrange a car for the 3½-hour ride from Danang to Hue for about $40.

BY BUS Many travelers take a nerve-rattling overnight bus or minivan from Hanoi to Hue. Tickets are $9 through one of Hanoi's tourist cafes (see chapter 5), and the trip takes an excruciating 17 hours. Hue is a major stop on any "open tour" ticket, and open-tour-cafe buses connect with Danang and Hoi An for just 50,000 VND, or Nha Trang for $6. (The latter is a long, bumpy trail, but it is cheap and convenient.)

GETTING AROUND

You can easily get around on foot in the main tourist area along the southern bank of the Perfume River (though the many cyclo and taxi touts would have you think otherwise), but to hit the main sites, you'll need some wheels.

BY TAXI/CAR Taxis are much cheaper here than in Hanoi: 10,000 VND starting out and 10,000 VND for each kilometer after. Flag 'em down or call **Gili** at ✆ **054/382-8282** or **ThanhDo** at ✆ **054/385-8585.** Any hotel front desk can arrange a car and driver for the day.

BY CYCLO Because Hue is relatively small, renting a cyclo by the hour for 16,000 VND to 20,000 VND works well, but not to the imperial tomb sites outside of town.

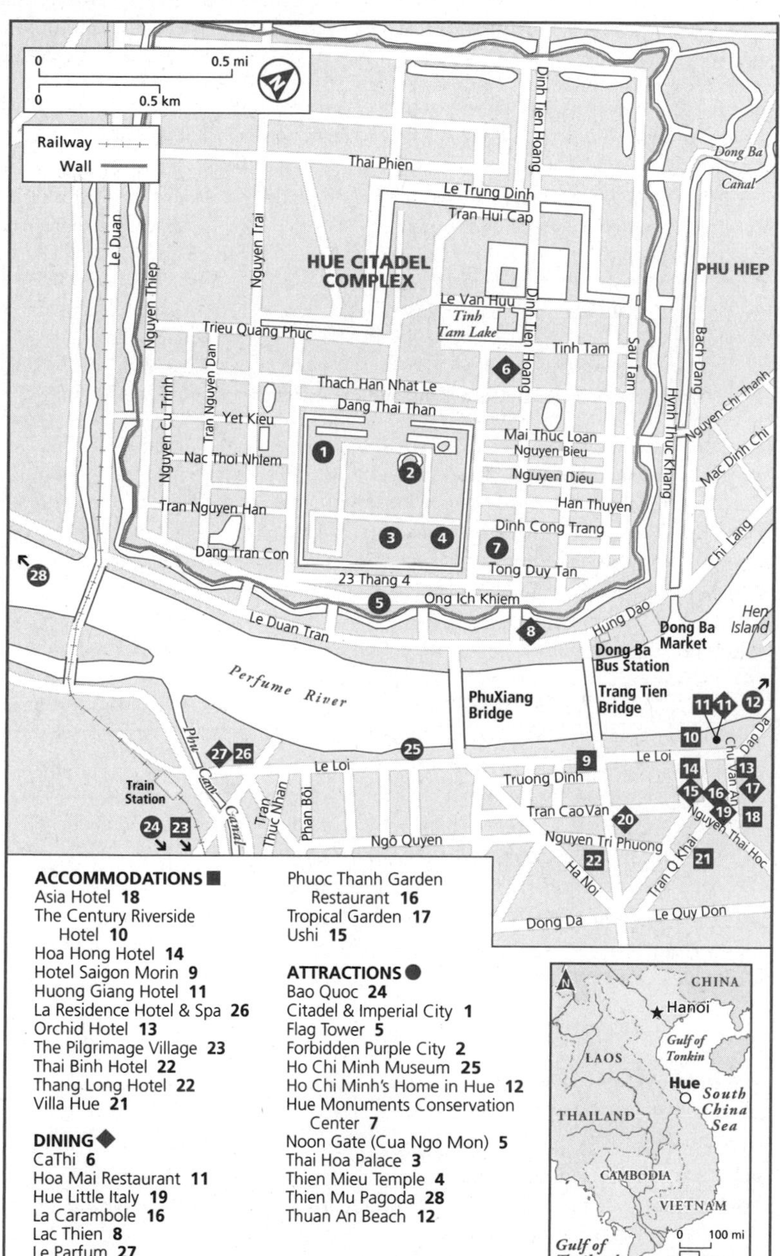
0 0.5 mi
0 0.5 km
N
Railway
Wall
HUE CITADEL COMPLEX
Thai Phien
Le Trung Dinh
Tran Hui Cap
Dinh Tien Hoang
Le Duan
Nguyen Thiep
Nguyen Trai
Le Van Huu
Tinh Tam Lake
Trieu Quang Phuc
Tinh Tam
Sau Tam
Thach Han Nhat Le
Dang Thai Than
Nguyen Cu Trinh
Tran Nguyen Dan
Yet Kieu
Nac Thoi Nhlem
Mai Thuc Loan
Nguyen Bieu
Nguyen Dieu
Han Thuyen
Tran Nguyen Han
Dinh Cong Trang
Dang Tran Con
Tong Duy Tan
23 Thang 4
Ong Ich Khiem
Le Duan Tran
Hung Dao
Dong Ba Canal
PHU HIEP
Bach Dang
Hynh Thuc Khang
Nguyen Chi Thanh
Mac Dinh Chi
Chi Lang
Hen Island
Dong Ba Market
Dong Ba Bus Station
Perfume River
PhuXiang Bridge
Trang Tien Bridge
Phu Cam Canal
Train Station
Le Loi
Truong Dinh
Tran Thuc Nhan
Phan Bôi
Ngô Quyen
Tran Cao Van
Nguyen Tri Phuong
Dap Da
Chu Van An
Nguyen Thai Hoc
Ha Noi
Tran Q Khai
Dong Da
Le Quy Don
ACCOMMODATIONS
Asia Hotel 18
The Century Riverside Hotel 10
Hoa Hong Hotel 14
Hotel Saigon Morin 9
Huong Giang Hotel 11
La Residence Hotel & Spa 26
Orchid Hotel 13
The Pilgrimage Village 23
Thai Binh Hotel 22
Thang Long Hotel 22
Villa Hue 21
DINING
CaThi 6
Hoa Mai Restaurant 11
Hue Little Italy 19
La Carambole 16
Lac Thien 8
Le Parfum 27
Mandarin Café 20
Phuoc Thanh Garden Restaurant 16
Tropical Garden 17
Ushi 15
ATTRACTIONS
Bao Quoc 24
Citadel & Imperial City 1
Flag Tower 5
Forbidden Purple City 2
Ho Chi Minh Museum 25
Ho Chi Minh's Home in Hue 12
Hue Monuments Conservation Center 7
Noon Gate (Cua Ngo Mon) 5
Thai Hoa Palace 3
Thien Mieu Temple 4
Thien Mu Pagoda 28
Thuan An Beach 12
CHINA
Hanoi
Gulf of Tonkin
LAOS
Hue
South China Sea
THAILAND
CAMBODIA
VIETNAM
Gulf of Thailand
0 100 mi
0 100 km

BY MOTORBIKE/BICYCLE Even the tiniest hotel provides motorbike rentals at $3 to $5 per day and bicycles for $1—both great ways to get out in the countryside and visit the sites. Cycling the Hue riverside areas is particularly memorable.

VISITOR INFORMATION & TOURS

You can book boat trips and visits to the DMZ through one of the tour companies in Hue. Every hotel will also be able to assist you, but the tour companies are more affordable, especially for transport.

Huong Giang Tourist Company, 17 Le Loi St. (✆ **054/383-2220;** www.charming vietnam.com), organizes personalized tours to the tombs and the DMZ at a premium, or you can join one of their group tours. This is Hue's most upscale and efficient group, and also the most expensive. A half-day tour by car and boat, with guide, to the Citadel and Thien Mu Pagoda is $25 for one, $30 for two. A private boat up the Perfume River will cost $29.

On the budget end, **Sinh Café** (7 Nguyen Tri Phuong or 12 Hung Vuong St.; ✆ **054/384-5022;** www.sinhcafevn.com) rents boats for $20 per day and has very reasonable junkets to the DMZ or around town.

An Phu Tourist (11 Nguyen Tri Phuong St. or 54 Le Loi St.; ✆ **054/383-3897** or 382-0058) arranges reasonable group tours (100,000 VND per person) visiting most of the major tombs; tours run daily from 8am to 4:30pm.

Fast Facts Hue

Banks & Currency Exchange Most hotels in Hue change currency. **Vietcombank** is at 78 Hung Vuong St. (✆ **054/384-6058**). Vietinde, the foreign-exchange bank, has an office at 41 Hung Vuong St. (on the roundabout at the terminus of the main tourist drag); a Western Union representative, it can provide cash advances. An Incombank ATM is on your left as you exit the airport.

Internet **Sinh Café,** at 07 Nguyen Tri Phuong, has good service for 10,000 VND per hour, and good spots are on Hung Vuong (the main tourist street south of the river), Pham Ngu Lao Street, and Doi Cung Street.

Post Office The Century and Huong Giang hotels have mini–post offices. The main post office, at 8 Hoang Hoa Tham St., is open from 7am to 9pm.

Telephone The city code for Hue is 54. You can place international calls at the post office and from most hotels.

WHERE TO STAY

For the volume of tourists coming through this town, there isn't much in the way of quality accommodations. Even the best options are bland, with lots of package tourists arriving to disappointing drab cells ("Honey, it doesn't look like the picture at all!"). Always ask to see your room first. Hotel services in the town's minihotels are limited, but all stops have basic tour services and include breakfast. Prices are flexible, so press for a discount.

Expensive

The Century Riverside Hotel ★ Rooms are bland and show their age, but this hotel is centrally located, clean, and fairly comfortable, with newer tile and marble bathrooms

Tips Party On at the Hue Festival!

Local holidays and events abound in Vietnam. But the annual **Hue Festival** is arguably the largest and most colorful event. Celebrating ancient Vietnam's richest cultural traditions of dance and theater, the festival has drawn visitors from throughout Vietnam since its inception in 2000. To witness the spectacle, you'll have to book your hotel far in advance—and expect to pay at least double the usual tariff—but you'll enjoy a wild show of floats, dance, and cultural events. **Hue's Imperial Dance** was in fact named a UNESCO World Heritage vestige of vital "Intangible Culture."

(be sure to ask for a recently renovated room). It's very popular with big tour groups. Standard rooms are rather small, with older carved-wood furniture and an impersonal layout that leaves guests feeling rather cold. The river-view rooms are more than worth the extra outlay (usually about $10), and there are great views from upper floors of the busy river: long-tail boats puttering by or fishermen paddling small dugouts. The pool is in a prime spot by the river, and the Riverside Restaurant offers nice views along with good, familiar fare, if a bit bland.

49 Le Loi St., Hue. ✆ **054/382-3390** or 382-3391. Fax 054/382-3394. www.centuryhotels.com. 133 units. $70 double; $100–$120 suite. AE, MC, V. **Amenities:** 5 restaurants; bar; bikes/motorbikes; concierge; gym; outdoor pool overlooking river; room service; 2 tennis courts. *In room:* A/C, TV, fridge, hair dryer, Internet, minibar.

Hotel Saigon Morin ★ The Saigon Morin is a government-run, refurbished colonial block near the main bridge in town. The addition of an executive floor raised their room standard somewhat, but they are no match for nearby La Residence (see below), despite having similar prices. "Junior Deluxe" rooms have large, stylish bathrooms with separate tubs and glass standing showers, and they're connected to the bedroom via a fun "peekaboo" shuttered opening. The lower-standard rooms are still the same Chinese business-hotel basic, with old laminated furniture and threadbare carpeting dotted with cigarette burns. The hotel forms a large courtyard around a central garden and pool area with dining. Over 100 years old, the Morin was originally the colonists' address of note, and photos line the halls of this bygone era. The street in front of the Morin was where a young Ho Chi Minh carried his first placard in protest of foreign occupation. If he could only see the place now. The exterior maintains some of that old colonial charm, but common areas are brash and busy, neon lit, and cluttered with souvenir stalls. Service is a bit hit-or-miss but usually friendly.

30 Le Loi St., Hue. ✆ **054/382-3526.** Fax 054/382-5155. www.morinhotel.com.vn. 184 units. $120–$160 double; $250–$500 suite. AE, MC, V. **Amenities:** Outdoor buffet area; lobby restaurant; 2 bars/cafe (1 on the roof w/good views); concierge; gym; Internet; outdoor pool; room service; sauna. *In room:* A/C, TV, fridge, hair dryer, Jacuzzi (in executive suites), minibar.

Huong Giang Hotel ★★ This hotel is a veritable Asian wonderland, enamored with carved wood and bamboo furnishings in a faux "Imperial" style. Tacky? Yes. But it's also kind of fun. Standard rooms are clean and comfortable, in basic bamboo, but the bathrooms are a disappointing dormitory style, with plastic shower curtains and no counter space. Try to get a good deal on one of the Royal Suites, with carved-wood walls, grandiose furniture with inlaid mother-of-pearl, and a massive wooden room divider—sort of a mini pagoda right in your room. The words *emperor* and *bordello* both leap to mind. The Royal Restaurant, worth a photo just for its gaudy gold-and-red-everything design alone, is for prearranged group dinners, during which the costumed staff serves a fancy traditional dinner at a hefty price. The River Front Terrace Bar is the best place in Hue to have a drink and watch life on the river. Splurge for a river-view room and enjoy a fine meal at the Hoa Mai restaurant.

51 Le Loi St., Hue. ✆ **054/3822-122** or 3823-958. Fax 054/3823-102. 165 units. $55 gardenview double; $60 river-view double; $100–$250 suite. AE, MC, V. **Amenities:** 3 restaurants; 2 bars; concierge; health club; pool; sauna. *In room:* A/C, cable TV, fridge, hair dryer, Internet, minibar.

La Residence Hotel & Spa ★★ This hotel has set the standard of luxury for the ancient city of Hue. Set on the banks of the Perfume River, the main building was the former residence of the French government and is the centerpiece of the hotel. In the lobby, you can take in the Art Deco antique tiles and mounted black-and-white photos depicting colonial life in Indochine in the early 20th century—copies of photos from a museum in France. The rest of the hotel's rooms are found in two separate wings that flank the main building and form an arch around the deep saltwater swimming pool. Doubles have spacious, ceramic tiled bathrooms, with retro sink taps marked by *Froid* and *Chaud*—yet another reminder of the hotel's French roots. Most rooms face west and have a small balcony. The unobstructed view of the Perfume River and the outer gate of the Imperial city makes for fantastic sunset views. If you can spring for a suite, I recommend the utterly charming Voyageen Chine. Like the other suites, it has a private balcony and large four-poster bed draped in a mosquito net to give the feeling of bygone years, before the invention of pesticides.

5 Le Loi St., Hue. ✆ **054/3837-475.** Fax 054/3830-822. www.la-residence-hue.com. 122 units. $139–$324 double. MC, V. **Amenities:** Restaurant; bar; bikes; concierge; health club/fitness center; outdoor pool; room service; spa w/Jacuzzi, sauna, and massage; tennis court; Wi-Fi. *In room:* A/C, TV, fridge, minibar.

The Pilgrimage Village ★★ If you are looking for a secluded, tropical getaway, this is your best choice in Hue. The resort offers spacious rooms and private villas in a garden setting surrounding a fine-dining pavilion. Some 5km (3 miles) southeast of the town center on the way to the royal tombs and temples, Pilgrimage Village is one of the only independently owned and operated hotels in the area, which explains the laid-back feel and high service standard. Rooms are large with oversize, modern, dark-wood furnishings and exposed brick walls. For a real treat, book one of the three Vietnamese pool houses, huge villas with terra-cotta floors and beautiful wooden pillars. It comes with a small private pool and 2 hours of free spa treatments. All rooms have balconies and faux fireplaces, creating a cozy lodgelike ambience. The tastefully decorated restaurant, Junrei, is the largest traditional wooden house in central Vietnam and serves fine Vietnamese fare. A garden area at the resort's entry is lined with traditional buildings housing craftspeople at work producing fine embroidery, ceramics, and woodcarving that's for sale in some fun little shops. Regular shuttles run to the downtown area, and the very friendly staff can help arrange thoughtful, informative tours to nearby temples and imperial tombs.

130 Minh Mang Rd., Hue. ✆ **054/388-5461.** Fax 054/388-7057. www.pilgrimagevillage.com. 109 units. May–Sept $148 double, $611 Vietnamese pool house; Aug–Apr $179 double, $663 Vietnamese pool house. MC, V. **Amenities:** Restaurant; bar; bikes; fitness center; nice-sized outdoor pool and kiddie pool; room service. *In room:* A/C, TV, fridge, hair dryer, minibar, Wi-Fi.

Moderate

Asia Hotel ★ Just next to La Carambole Restaurant, this oversize minihotel is popular among regional visitors (mostly Thai). It's near the city center's many shops and restaurants, and just a short walk to the river. Rooms are newer, tidy, and clean (though not luxurious), with cheap fuzzy hotel blankets and drapes that are already beginning to look old and ugly. There's a cool top-floor restaurant with great views (this is the tallest building away from the river), and some of the rooms have good river views as well. The pool is like an oversize bathtub in a raised area near the rooftop restaurant, but not a bad place to escape with a book on a hot day.

17 Pham Ngu Lao St., Hue. ✆ **054/383-0283.** Fax 054/382-8972. www.asiahotel.com.vn. 60 units. $45 double; $80–$120 suite. MC, V. **Amenities:** 2 restaurants (1 lobby, 1 rooftop); babysitting; top-floor tiny pool; room service. *In room:* A/C, TV, fridge, hair dryer, Internet, minibar.

Hoa Hong Hotel ★ Though showing its age, the Hoa Hong has bargain rates and is still popular, especially among tour groups. Rooms are nondescript—think navy and beige, with ugly polyester spreads—but all are comfortable, with good, firm beds. The nice-size bathrooms are tidy and have bathtubs. Ask for a city view rather than a noisy street view. The suites are worth it and have authentic Asian furniture. There are two restaurants, one of which specializes in the popular "royal dinner" theme evenings, when both staff and guests dress like emperors and empresses. The lobby has a fun little bar and serves flowery "umbrella drinks." Tour and car-rental services are available, as is round-the-clock room service. Book early; rooms tend to fill up.

1 Pham Ngu Lao St., Hue. ✆ **054/382-4377** or 382-6943. Fax 054/382-6949. hoahonghotel@dng.vnn.vn. 52 units. $25–$80 double. Rates include breakfast. AE, MC, V. **Amenities:** Large restaurant; bar; 24-hr. room service; Internet in reception. *In room:* A/C, TV, fridge, Internet, minibar.

Orchid Hotel ★ This popular minihotel is good value for the money. Rooms are comfortable and the beds are done up nicely, with charming textiles and accent pillows. There are a few things that veer to the tacky side—faux-wood-finish floors, armchairs made of that uncomfortable pleather material, and leopard-print silk bathrobes, for example—but on balance, this place is clean and cozy. Family rooms, or triple rooms, are an excellent value; they are about double the size of standard rooms and come with small balconies. Rooms come with free afternoon fruit and cake.

30A Chu Van An St., Hue. ✆ **054/383-1177.** Fax 054/383-1213. info@orchidhotel.com.vn. 18 units. $35–$40 double; $49 family room. Rates include breakfast. MC, V. **Amenities:** Cafe. *In room:* A/C, TV/DVD, fridge, minibar.

Villa Hue ★ This is Hue's best choice in this price range. Villa Hue is run and operated out of the Hue School of Tourism; the rotating management team is made up of teachers, and the hotel staff is comprised of second-year students. The hotel occupies one length of a courtyard, and all rooms face into the central area overlooking the rest of the school. Everyone is friendly, and the teachers/managers are quick to jump in and help when staff stumbles on service (which they do now and again). Deluxe rooms come with cozy beds and overstuffed chairs. Unlike the minihotels in this price category that litter too much into too small of a room, everything here is quite spacious; rooms come with comfy, overstuffed furniture, but there's still plenty of wide spaces left to move around. The bathrooms are similarly huge, with slate-colored granite floors, a good-sized tub, and separate shower cubicle in deluxe rooms. Little extras, such as evening chocolates and handmade beaded DND (Do Not Disturb) signs, make this a charming choice.

4 Tran Quang Khai St., Hue. ✆ **054/383-1628.** Fax 054/383-1627. 12 units. $59 deluxe; $71 superior. $15 surcharge Dec 22–Jan 9. Rates include breakfast. AE, MC, V. **Amenities:** Cafe; Internet. *In room:* TV, A/C, fridge, minibar.

Budget

Thai Binh Hotel (02 Luong The Vinh St.; ✆ **054/382-7561;** ksanthaibinh@hotmail.com; 34 units; $20–$35 double) is good in a pinch, with tidy, basic rooms in a quiet location. **Thang Long Hotel** (18 Hung Vuong St.; ✆ **054/382-6462;** dinhxuanlong@dng.vnn.vn; 20 units; $12–$18 double) is a beat-up, old budget choice that's been around for a while, but it has air-conditioned rooms (from $8) and a good little in-house tour company manned by a friendly and helpful staff.

WHERE TO DINE

Hue cuisine is unique, featuring light ingredients in popular fresh spring rolls, or try *bun bo Hue,* a noodle soup with pork, beef, and shredded green onions; or *banh khoi,* a thin, crispy pancake filled with ground meat and crispy vegetables. Local dishes are best at streetside, and there are a few good spots with English menus along the river and in the backpacker area, along Hung Vuong.

Moderate

CaThi ★★ VIETNAMESE This tiny, hush-hush restaurant—just opening at press time—is a good place to enjoy a special lunch after visiting the Citadel and Imperial City. In a tranquil courtyard garden, alfresco dining takes place on cool, shaded patio areas surrounded by restored, low, open pavilions that are held up by ornate carved pillars and covered with terra-cotta tile roofs. It all overlooks a tranquil pond filled with hearty Japanese koi.

24 Tran Thuc Nhan St., Hue. ✆ **054/384-5924.** cafecathi@yahoo.com. Set menus 80,000 VND–150,000 VND. MC, V. Daily 9am–10pm.

Hoa Mai Restaurant ★★ VIETNAMESE Hoa Mai is decked out in kitschy bamboo furnishings in an open area on the top floor of the Huong Giang Hotel. Atmosphere aside, the Vietnamese fare is good and you'll have great views of the Perfume River. Try *banh rom Hue,* triangular fried rolls stuffed with ground meat, shrimp, and vegetables. Daily special set menus are good; mine featured a unique fried cuttlefish with grapefruit, crab soup, and shrimp with fig and rice cake. Be sure to choose a table near the riverside window and away from any banquet-size setups that say RESERVED.

51 Le Loi St., 3rd floor, Huong Giang Hotel. ✆ **054/382-2122.** Main courses 24,000 VND–120,000 VND; set menus 180,000 VND–270,000 VND. AE, MC, V. Daily 6am–11pm.

Le Parfum ★ ASIAN FUSION Though the restaurant bills itself as offering Vietnamese cuisine, the menu features a lot of European fare. The Fiesta Summer Salad was a tasty mix of grilled eggplant, green and yellow zucchini, and red peppers over a bed of lettuce, topped with feta cheese and sun-dried tomatoes. Pastas are served in appetizer and main sizes. Old standbys like spaghetti carbonara and even hamburgers and fries are available. The outdoor seating is a quiet setting overlooking the Perfume River and lit by retro gas lamps placed on each table. It's an excellent place to unwind after a day of temple- and tomb-hopping.

Inside La Residence Hotel & Spa, Hue. ✆ **054/383-7475.** Main courses $5–$30. AE, MC, V. Daily 6am–11pm.

Phuoc Thanh Garden Restaurant VIETNAMESE Among lots of budget stops, this large, open-front restaurant borrows its style from the mandarins and temple compounds outside of Hue, but it's thoroughly modern and tidy, and caters mostly to large groups. They ask your nationality when you arrive and deliver your country's flag to your table when you sit down. Phuoc Thanh is a good choice for hygienic versions of local specialties like *bun bo Hue* (local noodle soup), *nem ran* (fresh spring rolls), or *banh khoi* (pancakes). A long list of tasty stir-fries, as well as delicious hot pots, rounds out the menu. Set menus include a gourmand's succession of soup, appetizers, and main courses. There's also a small selection of "European dishes" with fish and chips or other familiar eats for the kids.

30 Pham Ngu Lao St., Hue City. ✆ **054/383-0989.** Main courses 30,000 VND–120,000 VND; set menus 100,000 VND–400,000 VND. MC, V. Daily 8am–10pm.

Tropical Garden ★★ VIETNAMESE Though a popular tour-bus stop, Tropical Garden has a good laid-back feel. The restaurant, with a sister location called **Club Garden** just down the road (08 Vo Thi Sau St.; ✆ **054/382-6327**), serves fine Vietnamese fare from a good English menu, and there is live music nightly. Even when it's packed here, there are enough intimate corners that you'll feel comfortable. The place specializes in "embarrassing entrees," the kind of flaming dishes and multitiered platters that would impress that eccentric uncle of yours. It's all good fun, so just go with it. The food is good but a bit overpriced for a la carte items. Set menus are quite reasonable and walk you through some house specialties, like the banana flower soup and the steamed crab with beer. As an appetizer, don't miss the grilled minced shrimp with sugar cane wrapped in rice paper and served with peanut sauce: unique and delicious. Service is a bit hit or miss, either fawning or forgetful.

27 Chu Van An St. ✆ **054/384-7143.** Fax 054/382-8074. Main courses 56,000 VND–100,000 VND; set menus 126,000 VND–350,000 VND. MC, V. Daily 7:30am–10:30pm.

Inexpensive

Hue Little Italy ITALIAN The place to get your pizza and pasta cravings in order. This was opened by the same folks who brought you the DMZ Café (see "Cafes, Bars & Nightlife," below). The interior is small and cozy, with some tables near the window overlooking their small backyard garden. The pizzas have meat, cheese, and a crust, but they are nothing to write home about.

2A Vo Thi Sau St. ✆ **054/382-6928.** www.littleitalyhue.com. Main courses 45,000 VND–95,000 VND. No credit cards. Daily 8:30am–11pm.

La Carambole ★★ VIETNAMESE/CONTINENTAL Good music is the first thing you notice at La Carambole. The decor is cheerful: cool indirect lighting, red tablecloths, and playful mobiles hanging from the ceiling, all as welcoming as the kind waitstaff. The gregarious French proprietor, Christian, and his wife, Ha, will certainly make you feel at home, and the good "comfort items" on the menu, like spaghetti, burgers, pizzas, and various French-style meat-and-potatoes specials, will stick to your ribs. The set menus are a good deal (salad and beefsteak at $5, for example), and portions are ample. There's a game table, and you're sure to meet lots of other travelers.

19 Pham Ngu Lao St. ✆ **054/381-0491.** Fax 054/382-6234. Main courses 30,000 VND–140,000 VND; set menus $6–$10. No credit cards. Daily 7am–11pm.

Lac Thien ★ VIETNAMESE This is one a trio of small restaurants run by extended family members, several of whom are deaf. The neighboring two eateries serve similar fare, but I am partial to Lac Thien for the owner's incredibly friendly personality. The owner also makes simple bottle openers, consisting of a piece of wood and a corkscrew, which are presented to customers as free mini souvenirs. There's a small mural of photographs on the wall showing customers cracking open beers around the world.

6 Dinh Tien Hoang St. ✆ **054/352-4674.** Main courses 10,000 VND–50,000 VND. No credit cards. Daily 8am–10pm.

Mandarin Café ★ VIETNAMESE/CONTINENTAL In a busy storefront a short walk from the riverside (near the Saigon Morin), Mandarin is always full of young backpackers, and for a reason: good, affordable Vietnamese fare, predominantly one-dish items like fried rice or noodles on top of a roster of comfort foods. Try this place for a casual meal and likely conversation with fellow travelers. Have a banana pancake. The owner, Mr. Cu (pronounced *Coo*), is a practiced photographer and his works—classic images of rural Vietnam—line the walls and are for sale as postcards or prints. For the amateur shutterbug, the images are inspiring, and the best part is that Mr. Cu is more than happy to share secrets and talk shop.

24 Tran Cao Van St., Hue City. ✆ **054/382-1281.** mandarin@dng.vnn.vn. Main courses 15,000 VND–50,000 VND. No credit cards. Daily 6:30am–10:30pm.

Ushi ★ VIETNAMESE/GERMAN When owner Thanh Huong opened the restaurant, it was originally called Hien's Canteen. Dutch tourists would wander in and told her she looked like Ushi, who was the creation of a politically incorrect Dutch talk show host who would don a long black wig and buck teeth to take on a Japanese persona and bellow out "Ushi, say hi!" Huong quickly took up on the marketing potential, dubbed herself "the real Ushi," and renamed the restaurant. The menu has hearty German dishes like bratwurst, alongside Vietnamese noodle soup standbys. If you have some time to kill, I highly recommend striking up a conversation with Huong/Ushi. She is a fantastic character who will tell you tales of her 6-month motorcycle ride through Europe, or her previous life growing up during Vietnam's closed-economy era. She is frank and friendly and always has a smile at the ready.

Across from La Carambole, 42 Pham Ngu Lao St., Hue City. ✆ **054/382-1143.** ushivietnam@yahoo.com.vn. Main courses 55,000 VND–85,000 VND; set menus $5–$12. No credit cards. Daily 8am–10pm.

CAFES, BARS & NIGHTLIFE

Across from the major riverside hotels is the **DMZ Café** (60 Le Loi St.; ✆ **054/382-3414**), which stays up late in a sort of beer-swilling frat-party style, and along Hung Vuong you'll find a few backpacker bars open 'til midnight, but this is a pretty sleepy town. **Pomten's Bar** (22 Pham Ngu Lao; ✆ **054/381-0310**) has a pool table and a chic bistro bar setup, with a gallery space next door. **Brown Eyes** (56 Chu Van An; ✆ **054/382-7494**) is a late-night bar and cafe that's a short taxi ride from the town center.

SHOPPING

All along Le Loi Street, you'll find souvenir stalls that vary from the cute to the kitschy. You can find good deals on commemorative spoons and velvet Ho Chi Minhs here, but nothing too traditional or authentic. There are, however, a few good silversmiths and some little gems on sale in the glass cases of even the most kitschy tourist boutique.

A few tailors are in and among the souvenir shops. You might stop by **Seductive** (40 Le Loi St.; ✆ **054/382-9794**), a small ready-to-wear-silk boutique. Riverside Le Loi, just across from the town's best hotels (Huong Giang and Century Riverside), is also a good place for affordable silk tailors. Try **Viet Silk** at 68 Le Loi (✆ **054/382-5219**), or just around the corner at 8 Pham Ngu Lao St. (✆ **054/384-6090**). Both stores are open daily from 7am to 10:30pm.

Bambou Company (21 Pham Ngu Lao St., next to La Carambole) produces unique T-shirts of local theme and design, all Western size.

ATTRACTIONS

Hue's **Citadel and Imperial City** are the main attractions, but a visit here is usually done in conjunction with half-day trips to outlying temples and the many **imperial tombs.** You might want to bicycle to the Citadel itself, then along the riverside to **Thien Mu Pagoda,** back to town for lunch, and then out to the tombs (distances are long, but it's a relatively flat ride). You can also hit the sites on a self-guided tour in the comfort of a cyclo ("Pedal on, James!"). But hiring a guide—see any hotel front desk—is a good idea and offers useful background on the rich history of the town.

The Citadel & Imperial City ★★★ The **Citadel** is often used as a catchall term for Hue's Imperial City, built by Emperor Gia Long beginning in 1804 for the exclusive use of the emperor and his household, much like Beijing's Forbidden City. Most of the site is comprised of crumbling stone buildings and walls overtaken by trees and plants. The natural disrepair gives the place an authentic, ancient feeling. Unfortunately, restoration is happening fast, and inner palaces and buildings are being reconstructed and given a fresh coat of paint. The result is rather kitschy, and a theater toward the north end of the city has been set up for scheduled, somewhat cheesy evening dining and entertainment (250,000 VND per person; ✆ **054/352-9857;** www.hueworldheritage.org.vn). The city actually encompasses three walled enclosures: the Exterior Enclosure, or Citadel; the Yellow Enclosure, or Imperial City, within that; and, in the very center, the Forbidden Purple City, where the emperor actually lived.

The Citadel is a square 2km (1¼-mile) wall, 7m (23 ft.) high and 20m (66 ft.) thick, with 10 gates. Although the complex was constructed by a French military architect, it was actually the French who destroyed it many years later. Get a ticket and enter the main entrance to the Imperial City through the southwest gate, the Ngo Mon, more often called the Noon Gate.

See the Imperial City with a good English-speaking guide. The site is not spectacular in itself, but the history and traditions are rich, and a good guide can give you a breakdown of what things once looked like and what life was like at the Imperial court, and connect you with a dance show of the Imperial Dance Troupe. The breakdown below is a short overview.

Admission 55,000 VND. Daily 7am–5:30pm.

Sites Within the Imperial City

The Flag Tower ★★ The focal point of the Imperial City, a large rampart to the south of the Noon Gate, this tower was built in 1807 during Gia Long's reign. The yellow flag of royalty was the first to fly here and was exchanged and replaced by many others in Vietnam's turbulent history. It's a national symbol.

The Forbidden Purple City ★ Once the actual home of the emperor and his concubines, this second sanctum within the Citadel is a large open area dotted with what's left of the king's court. Almost completely razed in a fire in 1947, a few buildings are left among the rubble. The new **Royal Theater** behind the square, a look-alike of the razed original, is under construction. The partially restored **Thai Binh Reading Pavilion,** to the left of it as you head north, is notable mostly for its beautifully landscaped surroundings, including a small lake with stone sculpture, and the ceramic and glass mosaic detailing on the roof and pillars, favored by flamboyant emperor Khai Dinh.

Catch a performance of the **Royal Traditional Theater** at the Hue Monuments Conservation Center. Eight performances daily, from 9am to 4pm, highlight the ancient art of *nha nhac,* courtly dance, at a cost of 20,000 VND.

Hue Monuments Conservation Center ★ Set in an old picturesque Chinese temple (you're asked to wear shoe covers at the entry in order to preserve the wood), the Hue Monuments Conservation Center is the Imperial Museum of the old capital, displaying all the treasures (or what's left over) from the Nguyen kings. Precious coins, stone carvings, and Ming dynasty pottery from China are just a few of the gifts in this repository of courtly finery presented to Vietnam's 19th-century leaders by visiting dignitaries. Unique is the lacquer-framed gong made of stone from China. At the back you'll find lacquered palanquins and furnishings for the royal court and procession, and farther back look for the very embroidered finery donned by Nguyen kings on parade.

Next door is the **Exhibition of the Resistance Against the American Invader,** which doesn't mince words. The courtyard out front displays some captured war machines. Inside is a rhetorical parade of faded photos and artifacts that tell the story of American aggression from the July 1954 Geneva Agreement to the North Vietnamese Army's jubilant liberation of Saigon, with images of the hard fighting in Hue city in 1968. The exhibition is propagandistic, with captions telling of the "lackey" government of "puppet" rulers in the south, and selections of photos depicting Americans as torturers who disemboweled their North Vietnamese prisoners, but that very rhetoric is what's so interesting. History is told by the victors, and the Vietnamese are proud of their victory and of what they had to endure to survive as a sovereign nation. Elsewhere, as with the War Museum in Saigon, which changed its name from "Museum of the American War Crimes," Vietnamese rhetoric about their own recent history is softening, or disappearing altogether.

On the southeast corner of the main citadel entrance. Admission 22,000 VND. Daily 7am–5:30pm.

The Noon Gate (Cua Ngo Mon) ★★ One of 10 entrances to the city, this southern entrance is the most dynamic. It was the royal entrance, in fact, and was built by Emperor Gia Long in 1823. It was used for important proclamations, such as announcements of the names of successful doctoral candidates (a list still hangs on the wall on the upper floor) and, most memorably, the announcement of the abdication of the last emperor, Bao Dai, on August 13, 1945, to Ho Chi Minh. The structure, like most here, was damaged by war but is now nicely restored, with classic Chinese roofs covering the ritual space, complete with large drums and an altar. Be sure to climb to the top and have a look at the view.

Thai Hoa Palace Otherwise known as the Palace of Supreme Harmony, it was built in 1833 and is the first structure you'll approach at the entrance. It was used as the throne room, a ceremonial hall where the emperor celebrated festivals and received courtiers; the original throne still stands. The mandarins sat outside. In front are two mythical *ky lin* animals, which walk without their claws ever touching ground and have piercing eyesight for watching the emperor, tracking all good and evil he does. Note the statues of the heron and turtle inside the palace's ornate lacquered interior: The heron represents nobility, and the turtle represents the working person. Folklore has it that the two took turns saving each other's lives during a fire, symbolizing that the power of the emperor rests with his people, and vice versa.

Thien Mieu Temple ★★ Constructed from 1921 to 1922 by Emperor Minh Mang, this temple has funeral altars paying tribute to 10 of the last Nguyen dynasty emperors, omitting two who reigned for only days, with photos of each emperor and his empress(es) and various small offerings and knickknacks. The two empty glass containers to the side of each photo should contain bars of gold, probably an impractical idea today.

Across from Thien Mieu you'll see Hien Lam, or the Glorious Pavilion, to the far right, with the **Nine Dynastic Urns** in front. Cast from 1835 to 1837, each urn represents a

Nguyen emperor and is richly embellished with all the flora, fauna, and material goods that Vietnam has to offer, mythical or otherwise.

Imperial Tombs

As befits its history as an Imperial City, Hue's environs are studded with tombs of past emperors. Because they're spread out over a distance, the best way to see them is to hire a car for a half-day or take one of the many organized boat tours up the Perfume River. All together, there were 13 kings of the Nguyen dynasty, although only 7 reigned until their deaths. As befits an emperor, each had a tomb of stature, some as large as a small town. Most tomb complexes usually consist of a courtyard, a stele (a large stone tablet with a biography of the emperor), a temple for worship, and a pond. You can visit the tombs on an all-day boat trip, best if arranged with one of the small tour companies (see "Visitor Information & Tours," earlier in this chapter), but also possible with a little haggling at the riverside. Expect to pay as little as $2 for the boat trip, and note that each tomb has a stiff (for Vietnam) entry fee. If going by boat, note that some tombs are far from the riverside and may require a short trip by motorbike, which sometimes doubles the entry fee but saves your muscles for clambering around the sites.

Khai Dinh's Tomb ★★ Completed in 1931, this tomb is one of Hue's wonders. The emperor himself wasn't particularly revered, being overly extravagant and flamboyant (reportedly he wore a belt studded with lights that he flicked on at opportune public moments). His tomb, a gaudy mix of Gothic, baroque, Hindu, and Chinese Qing dynasty architecture at the top of 127 steep steps, is a reflection of the man. Inside, the two main rooms are completely covered with fabulous, intricate glass and ceramic mosaics in designs reminiscent of Tiffany and Art Deco. The workmanship is astounding. The outer room's ceiling was done by a fellow who used both his feet and his hands to paint, in what some say was a sly mark of disrespect for the emperor. ***Also noteworthy:*** In most tombs, the location of the emperor's actual remains are a secret, but Khai Minh boldly placed his under his de facto tomb itself.

Admission 55,000 VND. Summer daily 6:30am–5:30pm; winter daily 7am–5pm.

Tomb of Minh Mang ★ One of the most popular Nguyen emperors and the father of last emperor Bao Dai built a restrained, serene, classical temple, much like Hue's Imperial City, located at the confluence of two Perfume River tributaries. Stone sculptures surround a long walkway, lined with flowers, leading up to the main buildings.

Admission 55,000 VND. Summer daily 6:30am–5:30pm; winter daily 7am–5pm.

Tomb of Tu Duc ★★ With the longest reign of any Nguyen dynasty emperor, from 1848 to 1883, Tu Duc was a philosopher and scholar of history and literature. His reign was unfortunate: His kingdom unsuccessfully struggled against French colonialism, he fought a coup d'état by members of his own family, and although he had 104 wives, he left no heir. The "tomb" was constructed from 1864 to 1867 and also served as recreation grounds for the king, having been completed 16 years before his death. He actually engraved his own stele, in fact. The largest in Vietnam, at 20 tons, it has its own pavilion in the tomb. The highlight of the grounds is the lotus-filled lake ringed by frangipani trees, with a large pavilion in the center. The main cluster of buildings includes Hoa Khiem (Harmony Modesty) Pavilion, where the king worked and which still contains items of furniture and ornaments. Minh Khiem Duong, constructed in 1866, is said to be the country's oldest surviving theater. It's great fun to poke around in the wings. There are also pieces of original furniture lying here and there, as well as a cabinet with household objects:

Tips Taking a Boat to the Tombs

Expect to pay between $2 and $4 for a shared boat ride to the temples (depending on which agent you use), *plus* 55,000 VND for *each* tomb. Be prepared for when the boat pulls to shore at the tombs: You'll have to hire one of the motorcycle taxis at the bank to shuttle you to and from the site. You will not have enough time to walk there and back, so you're basically at their mercy. Haggle as best you can—about 10,000 VND one-way is a good starting point.

the queen's slippers, ornate chests, and bronze and silver books. The raised box on the wall is for the actors who played emperors; the real emperor was at the platform to the left.

Admission 55,000 VND. Summer daily 6:30am–5:30pm; winter daily 7am–5pm.

Temples

The **Thien Mu Pagoda** (see below) is a popular stop on riverboat trips along the Perfume River's north bank and is also easily reached by bicycle or motorbike. The road leading to the imperial tombs south of town affords you a great glimpse of a few working temples—the likes of **Bao Quoc** and **Tu Hieu**—with busy monks, groups of students rushing between classes, and lots of workshops that you can observe.

Bao Quoc Just past the train station on your way south toward the imperial tombs, little Bao Quoc temple is a Buddhist temple dating back to the 17th century. At the top of the steps leading to the main temple square, you'll see the grand arched entry of a classic Chinese school.

Just south of the train station (away from the river) on Dien Bien Phu St. Daily dawn–dusk.

Thien Mu Pagoda ★★ Often called the symbol of Hue, Thien Mu is one of the oldest and loveliest religious structures in Vietnam. It was constructed beginning in 1601. The Phuoc Dien Tower in front was added in 1864 by Emperor Thieu Tri. Each of its seven tiers is dedicated to either one of the human forms taken by Buddha or the seven steps to enlightenment, depending upon whom you ask. There are also two buildings housing a bell reportedly weighing 2 tons, and a stele inscribed with a biography of Lord Nguyen Hoang, founder of the temple.

Once past the front gate, observe the 12 huge wooden sculptures of fearsome temple "guardians"—note the real facial hair. A complex of monastic buildings lies in the center, offering glimpses of the monks' daily routines: cooking, stacking wood, and whacking weeds. Stroll all the way to the rear of the complex to look at the large graveyard at the base of the Truong Son mountains, and wander through the well-kept garden of pine trees. Try not to go between the hours of 11:30am and 2pm, when the monks are at lunch, because the rear half of the complex will be closed.

On the northern bank (same side as the Citadel) of the Perfume River. About 5km (3 miles) southwest of the Citadel entrance. Daily 8am–5pm.

Tu Hieu At this working Buddhist temple, the many monks and novices clad in brown robes are always busily padding about from class to class and to meditation and worship. Wooden gongs clock the activities of the day. Monks are friendly, and if you time it right (btw. class time or before or after lunch), you are sure to meet up with these cherubic lads, who are all eager to practice their English. I even got some Vietnamese singing lessons. The surrounding ponds and gardens are immaculate, real-deal Zen living, and the temple was just recently graced with a visit by Vietnam's most well-known expatriate teacher—whose writings are so popular in the West—Thich Nhat Hahn. Next door is a nunnery, busier than the monastery and with a small Bannar house adjoining. The approach road to the temple continues on to hilly farmland.

Just past the Nam Giao Esplanade, a large tiered area used by emperors for performances and ceremony, stay to the right at the intersection and follow the road a few clicks to the ornate gated entry to Tu Hieu, a large Buddhist monastery and school. No phone. Free admission. Daily dawn–dusk.

Other Sites

Ho Chi Minh Museum Every city's got one, an homage point for Vietnam's national hero, and this one is actually kind of interesting. In a large rotunda on the road heading from the new town toward the train station, the Ho Chi Minh Museum in Hue is the usual collection of photos and memorabilia telling the story of Ho's early life of poverty in Vinh, here with a stress on the years he spent in Hue during his father's tenure in the university (see Ho Chi Minh's Home in Hue, below). There are images and a reproduction of the boat he sailed on as a galley hand, as well as a unique picture of Ho working in the kitchen of the Castleton Hotel in London in 1914, a time when his ideas about Marxism and revolution began to flower. The museum tells the history of Hue, from capital to revolution and the aftermath, in photos. Also find some interesting political cartoons parodying French rule, as well as extensive copies and basic translations of Ho's writings—the likes of the *8 Requirements of Society,* which Ho presented at the Versailles Conference in Paris in 1919.

On the way to the train station at 7 Le Loi. Free admission. Tues–Sun 8–11am and 1:30–4:30pm.

Ho Chi Minh's Home in Hue On the way to Thuan An Beach, a narrow lane leads over a small bridge off of the main road at a curve some 6km (3¾ miles) north of Hue. An immediate right after the bridge brings you along the small river area where Ho bathed during his time here, and just about 100m (328 ft.) farther brings you to the humble home, a reconstruction, and new temple that mark the site where the leader spent formative years during his father's study for examinations to become a mandarin (government official).

6km (3¾ miles) north on Le Loi heading toward Thuan An Beach. Free admission. Daily 8–11am and 2–4pm.

THUAN AN BEACH

At this local beach site, 12km (7½ miles) north of Hue, the turbulent waves make Thuan An less popular for swimming and more popular for hanging in a hammock and taking it all in. To get here, just follow riverside Le Loi Street east and then north. The place fills up on weekends with young domestic vacationers from the big cities. You pay for parking and are pretty much obliged to buy some snacks or baubles from sellers, and then you can plan to hang out with the young "boy racer" crowd as you look over a picturesque windswept stretch of coast. You can also sample some fresh seafood.

2 THE DEMILITARIZED ZONE (DMZ)

If you're old enough to remember the Vietnam War from television, you'll know **Hue** from the large-scale battles waged here. The 1968 **Battle of Hue,** which heralded the Tet

Offensive in the far south, was one of the most gruesome and well-documented battles, and scenes of the fray were depicted in the film *Full Metal Jacket.*

Starting from Hue, a day trip to the nearby DMZ and Vinh Moc Tunnels is a sobering reminder of the tumultuous wartime, and crossing the invisible line of demarcation between north and south is an important part of bringing things full circle for returning veterans and folks who lived through the war years. All of Quang Tri Province is a vestige of the war years really, as this was the site of some of the heaviest shelling and artillery exchanges during the war.

Under the Geneva Accords of 1954, an agreement brought peace to Indochina after its struggle with French colonists. Vietnam was divided into north and south along the **17th Parallel.** What was meant to be a short-term political fix became a battle line known as the **DMZ** (demilitarized zone), a tangle of barbed wire and land mines bombed and defoliated into a wasteland. The famous American fence, what was called the "million-dollar eye"—a folly of U.S. Defense Secretary Robert McNamara—was an elaborate system of barbed wire tangle laced with electronic sensors that the United States built along the border's length; when sensors in the DMZ were tripped, they triggered American bombers into action. The North Vietnamese regularly foiled U.S. efforts, playing cat-and-mouse with the sensors and sending livestock into No Man's Land to draw fire. The perimeter was overrun in 1975.

The once-scorched earth of the DMZ is now green with growth again and completely unremarkable except for its history. Nearby are strategic sites with names you may recognize: the **Rockpile, Hamburger Hill, Camp Carroll,** and **Khe San,** a former U.S. Marine base that was the site of some of the war's most vicious and deadly fighting. If you take a tour of the area, you'll also visit **Dakrong Bridge,** an official entryway into the Ho Chi Minh Trail region near where the trail begins. The **tunnels of Vinh Moc,** where border troops along with whole families burrowed underground, effectively creating their own underground city, is a testament to the determination and motivation of Viet Cong forces at the north end of the DMZ. A visit here is likely the highlight of any DMZ tour.

Important: If you're interested in tours to the DMZ, your best bet is to pay a little extra and find a knowledgeable guide who can paint a vivid portrait. Except for a few memorial sites and preserved relics, the physical battle scars on the landscape have healed. To make this trip engaging, you'll want to go with someone who knows about the history of the area and can take you to out-of-the-way bunkers and battle sites. Budget tours of the DMZ are often just a full day riding around on a bus, with little time to visit sites and scant information about scheduled stops. "Lots of people fighting here long time ago," your guide might say, pointing to a farmer's field no different than the farmer's field adjoining. It's important to note that the heavy plant growth is only recent, and that this area was the hardest hit of anywhere in Vietnam by the U.S. defoliation campaign Operation Ranch Hand.

The many sites in the DMV are some 60km (37 miles) north of Hue. Visitors with a serious interest in the history of the area could certainly make it a multiple-day operation; in such instances, but only in such instances, it makes sense to overnight in the town of **Dong Ha,** the jumping-off point to the DMZ and for onward travel to Laos. Most budget tours stop in Dong Ha for lack of options, but this one-stoplight burg is not the kind of place you want to be stranded in for too long. The best local hotel is little more than a concrete block of the older Soviet style. Near Dong Ha, you will cross the Ben Hai River, and most trips stop briefly to take in the old French guard towers and old denuded battlegrounds.

For tours, contact Hue tourist cafes: The best is Sinh Café on the budget end, or Huong Giang Tourist for a good private tour. See "Visitor Information & Tours," earlier in this chapter. Tours leave early in the morning and trace Route 1 north of Hue into Quang Tri Province. The coastal highway passes some lovely stretches of natural inland sand dunes lined with colorful Chinese tombs, some like small temples in themselves, before reaching the town of Dong Ha. From here, there are two routes to follow, one up north to the Vinh Moc Tunnels and the other north and then west toward Laos and a number of deserted American bases; most day tours follow both tracks. Some opt to just visit the tunnels of Vinh Moc and a few sites near Dong Ha, making this a half-day tour.

Camp Fuller and the Rockpile These significant mountain outposts were American strongholds throughout the war that came under constant barrage from North Vietnamese regulars. This is the highest ground in the region along a high ridge, so it was valuable turf for artillery units and snipers. The area is now green with foliage (apart from the most heavily bombed mountaintops), but it's a far cry from what was once dense jungle. Operation Ranch Hand, the U.S. defoliation campaign, was relentless in this area.

The Dakrong Bridge and the Ho Chi Minh Trail The current incarnation of the Dakrong Bridge was built in 1975 after reunification. Just west of the main DMZ zone, the bridge was considered the beginning of the Ho Chi Minh Trail network, and during the years of conflict with the United States, this access point was hotly contested. The Dakrong Bridge fell many times. Now it's a grand suspension bridge, a proud thumbed nose as if to say, "You can't knock down my bridge anymore." The road to the bridge leads to the border with Laos, and even the overnight buses that take intrepid travelers over this route will stop for a good look at the bridge, which heads south (buses continue on the main road west to Laos). Across the bridge is a small village that's a popular stop for tour groups, and where most buses turn around and head back to the main highway. The stunning scenery all along Hwy. 9 is worth the ride.

Note: The **Ho Chi Minh Trail** is a concept, not a road. The trail was a vast network, spread across hundreds of miles of terrain extending far into the interior of Laos, a broad avenue of hundreds of kilometers of trails that brought supplies to North Vietnamese troops, by hook or by crook, usually on the backs of porters or with giant loads precariously perched on overlaid bicycles. You might call it "the path of least resistance," or the "road less bombed or occupied," really. The trail starts in Quang Tri Province, basically anything from the Dakrong Bridge south, and the Americans were constantly trying to foil the Viet Cong and Gen. Vo Nguyen Giap's relentless end-run around the front line to stage attacks in the south.

Hamburger Hill Many know the name from the Clint Eastwood film depicting the events of May 10 to May 21, 1969, when U.S. Airborne Troops stood toe-to-toe with heavily dug-in Vietnamese forces in order to stop North Vietnamese movement through the A Shau valley and south. You would only really go to Hamburger Hill if you had some connection with the battle that took place here. The denuded slope is some 100km (62 miles) to the interior from the main DMZ area. To arrange special tours, returning veterans should contact **Huong Giang Tourist Company,** 17 Le Loi St. (✆ **054/383-2220;** www.huonggiangtourist.com).

Khe San ★ If most of the former battle sites in the area require more imagination than many visitors can muster, the base at Khe San is worth the trip for its informative museum and some tangible evidence of American presence and the years of strife in the region. Khe San is where, in January 1968, Viet Cong forces launched a massive attack.

It was a diversion to keep U.S. Gen. William Westmoreland comfortable in his illusion that the war was being fought on a single front, and only a few months later the real might of the Tet Offensive landed in the south after skirting the heavily guarded DMZ, but nobody told the two divisions of North Vietnamese troops that it was a diversion. The January 21 attack at Khe San left big numbers of casualties on both sides. The Tet Offensive nearly broke the back of Vietnam's fighting capability (they lost more than 10-to-1 in casualties), but it also broke the back of world and U.S. opinion about the conflict, and it was the beginning of the end for support of the war. After the offensive, U.S. forces pulled back to Camp Carol near Dong Ha town.

The large **museum compound** at Khe San is home to a collection of war detritus: an abandoned Huey helicopter, the remains of crashed recon planes, the hulking shell of an M41 tank, a massive CH47 helicopter, and disarmed bombs and shells arranged like a piece of modern art. Inside the museum, a concrete building on stilts, find a good collection of photos and effects that chronicle the events of U.S. buildup, conflict, and withdrawal from this Khe San base. Exhibits have good English descriptions, but captions are as didactic as they are informative. Under one photo of wounded U.S. troops struggling for cover, the caption reads, "What was Johnson thinking?" Exhibits make much of the cooperation of local ethnic hilltribe people, a general fabrication, really, as most hilltribe groups supported U.S. efforts to oust ethnic Vietnamese. Ho Chi Minh and later Vietnamese administrators worked hard to bring hilltribe minorities into line, but to this day there is general suspicion in Hanoi about these offshoot groups, many of whom know no borders and move freely from Laos and even as far as Burma or China. An entry ticket is included with most tours, but if not, entrance into the museum costs 25,000 VND.

Vinh Moc Tunnels ★★ The tunnels at Vinh Moc are a testament to human tenacity. Like the tunnels in the south at Cu Chi (see chapter 12), soldiers and civilians took to the underground, literally, digging over a mile of tunnels from 1965 to 1966 to support Viet Cong troops and confound U.S. battalions at this strategic position near the line of north-south demarcation. People lived here from 1966 until 1972. An estimated 7 tons of bombs were dropped per person living in the Vinh Moc Tunnels. The initial complex took 18 months to excavate some 6,000 sq. m (64,583 sq. ft.) of red soil that had to be carefully dispersed, usually at night to avoid surveillance, and buried in the nearby sand of the beach. Up to 20m (about 66 ft.) below the surface, multilevel tunnels formed a real community haven, with "living rooms" for families, a conference and performance room, a small cinema, a field hospital, clean facilities, and kitchens complete with elaborate systems to dissipate the smoke of cooking fires. All tunnels also have ingenious exit points inland and along the coast, providing some cross-ventilation. Visitors walk through about 300m (984 ft.) of the tunnels in a main artery that is 1.6m high by 1.2m wide (5⅓ ft. high by 4 ft. wide), going down three stages. Wear your play clothes, because it's dirty, clammy, and a bit claustrophobic. There's a museum at the entrance with survivors' photos and testimonies. The museum houses photos of life among the tunnel families, as well as maps of their labyrinth (including a map that shows where the day's tour will lead) and tools from excavation of the site. Admission is 25,000 VND, but the price is usually included in DMZ tour prices.

FARTHER AFIELD FROM HUE

Hai Van Pass Towering Hai Van Pass has been an inspiration to Vietnamese artists and poets for centuries. Straddling the highest point on the steep terrain between Danang and

Hue, it was a natural defense post during Vietnam's lengthy conflicts, and the large "pill box" fortifications are still in evidence at the peak just above the road. Tour buses, and even local buses, take a quick pit stop here, and the local vendors descend like their own invading army, but a cloudless day means stunning views north and south. Before crossing the pass from the north, you pass the entrance to Bach Ma National Park and trace the thin strip of land along Lang Co Beach (see listings below) before zigzagging up the slope.

3 BACH MA NATIONAL PARK

Bach Ma—with more than 20,000 hectares (49,400 acres) of high mountain trails and sweeping valleys—was once a playground for the French, who built villas on these mountaintops to stay cool when on holiday from Hue. You'll see a number of ruin sites, mostly the remnants of small French resorts and secluded cabins. The park is humid and rainy year-round, but the high elevation (1,712m/5,617 ft. at its peak) makes for cooler temperatures (bring a light windbreaker). The best time to go is in March and April, when the rhododendrons bloom (see "Hiking Trails," below). Entrance to the park is just 10,500 VND, 5,500 VND for students, and fees for hiring a jeep to take up the rocky track to the park's pinnacle start at 350,000 VND. There's a network of well-marked trails (though nobody has a map), and some cozy lodging at the top. You can hire a guide at the park office for hiking. The park is on the road between Lang Co Beach (at the northern end of the Hai Van Pass) and the town of Hue. Many make this a full afternoon before carrying on to Hue, with an overnight in Lang Co (see the next section), or heading over the hump to Danang or Hoi An. For details, contact (or show up at) the Ecotourism and Environmental Education Center at the base of the hill (the entrance is well marked from Hwy. 1; ✆ **054/3871-330;** fax 054/3871-329; www.bachma.vnn.vn). The park office is open daily from dawn to dusk.

WHERE TO STAY

There are a number of budget choices in the park, including a small guesthouse at the base. The **National Park Guesthouse** (✆ **054/387-1330**) or the **Phong Lan Villas** (✆ **054/387-1801**) can both be found on the road leading to the top but are quite basic. Stick with the Morin, if you can.

Bach Ma Morin Hotel Owned by the same folks who bring you the grand Saigon Morin in Hue, the Bach Ma Morin might sound grand, but this mountaintop hotel is just a basic collection of simple, fan-cooled rooms in an old, restored, concrete colonial at the park's peak—just adjacent to the fun Summit Trail (see "Hiking Trails," below). Rooms are large and clean, with guesthouse-style shower and tub. They can muster up some grub in their little canteen and connect you with a guide, but little else. The hotel commonly hosts budget or adventure groups, and fewer individual travelers, but this is your best bet for an overnight in Bach Ma.

At the top of the mountain. ✆ **054/387-1199.** 12 units. $20 double. No credit cards. **Amenities:** Restaurant; bar. *In room:* Fan (high altitude, so A/C not needed), fridge, minibar.

HIKING TRAILS

Bring lots of water, bug repellent, a swimsuit, a waterproof bag for your camera or other valuables, and another bag for your garbage (always try to be a good example of ecotourism). Wandering Bach Ma makes for a good full day or a few hours to kick the pollution out of your lungs on a stop as you head up the coast.

The trails of Bach Ma are lined with medicinal plants. Ask your guide and look for the Nhe Den (or Curcuma Zedoraria), which is a yellow tuberous root that grows a few meters high and is commonly used to treat cancers of the womb and skin, as well as indigestion. Also keep an eye out for some stunning orchid varieties; in particular, growing out of the trunks of trees high up in the spring is the Vani orchid, with lovely fragrant yellow flowers used as an expectorant.

Keep an eye out for Sambar deer tracks, and you might even spot the shy animals in the dense wood if you're very quiet. You'll also see the crumbling remains of old colonial villas and homes of Vietnamese who came to work on the area's small farms.

The short **Summit Trail** takes you a few kilometers past the Bach Ma Morin at the terminus of the park road and brings you to a pavilion with 360-degree views of the surrounding area, usually mist shrouded and above the clouds. Quite stunning and an easy, paved walk.

Five Lakes Trail starts just a few short clicks back from the park's highest point (near the Bach Ma Morin); the trail is a stunning descent from the road following a small waterfall—the five "lakes" are quaint catch basins along the waterfall's cascade. It's slippery in spots and even technical, with guide wires and ladders as needed. Go with a guide.

The **Rhododendron Trail** is a great walk. In spring, around March and April when the heat on the coast is at its worst—this was also the busiest time for the old French colonials to visit the high forests at Bach Ma—the rhododendrons bloom, sending explosions of red and clouds of fragrance onto the trails of the park. The trail begins near the National Park Guesthouse.

Just over 2km (1¼ miles) of trail hiking brings you to the terminus of the Five Lakes Trail (see above) and to the top of a 300m (984-ft.) waterfall. It's a gradual pitch at the top, and you can test your mettle by looking over the waterfall's edge—yikes! Just next to the falls is a set of steep stone stairs, and if you've got the chutzpah, the 1-hour hike down (and, more important, back up—it's a dead-end trail) brings you to the bottom of the fall. The 689 steps are a killer on the knees: Though there is a good handrail (be careful, because it's slippery), the steps are large, so the descent is bone jarring and each step of the ascent is a haul. But the stunning view from the bottom of the cascade is well worth it.

There are a number of other tracks through the park, and you can hire a local guide at a cost of just $10. Check at the park headquarters.

4 LANG CO BEACH

A good day stop along Route 1A between Hue and Danang/Hoi An, Lang Co Beach is a sweeping expanse of sand good for dipping your toes and taking a rest. The absence of group tours and touts is the main draw, and options for overnight stays are growing.

The beach lies at the northern end of Hai Van Pass, and the sands of Lang Co begin just where the mountain switchbacks end. Behind the long stretch of beach is a large lagoon, and the lightly populated town area is just a narrow strip of land between sea and lagoon, with most Lang Co villagers in homes along Hwy. 1. The beach is most popular for fishing and for boat repairs, used more as a garbage dump or as a local latrine than for sun-loving tourists, but the southern section of beach near the resorts gets cleaned up on occasion, and this windswept stretch at the base of Hai Van Pass is quite stunning.

Starting with the Lang Co Beach Resort, there's a small clutch of cozy budget warrens of bungalows, and more development is slated.

A tunnel will soon connect Lang Co directly with Hue, but tourists will still likely make the pilgrimage up to Hai Van Pass. The town has no good dining to speak of, just a few little backpacker places that are popular among passing truck drivers; and where there are passing truck drivers, there are brothels—which seem to be the town's only real industry. The beach is pretty hassle-free, but plan to pack your own lunch and drinks. There are no services on the sands.

Bach Ma National Park (see above) is just a short motorbike taxi ride from Lang Co, and the beach makes a good overnight before a day of hiking and onward travel to Hue, or Lang Co could be your overnight rest after the park and before crossing the pass to Danang and Hoi An.

WHERE TO STAY

Lang Co Beach Resort takes credit cards (and will cash traveler's checks for a hefty percentage), but note that you should come to Lang Co prepared to be self-sufficient. There are no services outside of the basic lodgings listed below.

Lang Co Beach Resort ★ This place always seems to be rather empty, so bring a friend. Lang Co Beach Resort is run by Huong Giang Tourist Company, a large government firm. They do a great job with large package junkets looking to step off the more obvious stops on Vietnam's north-south route, and Lang Co certainly fits this bill. Rooms are all quite large, with wide glass windows and doors facing the sea. The resort stands over a stunning area of windswept beach, and all rooms have large glass sliders that open onto porch areas, some right on the water. Terra-cotta tile floors and dark-wood furnishings make a stay here cozy but not particularly luxurious. The pool is in disuse. They have a good restaurant and aim to please.

On the north end of Lang Co Beach, Phu Loc District. ✆ **054/387-3555.** www.langcobeachresort.com.vn. 87 units. $40 double; $70–$160 villa. MC, V. **Amenities:** 2 restaurants; bar; bikes; outdoor pool; room service. *In room:* A/C, TV, fridge, Internet, minibar.

Thanh Tam Hotel This little seaside stop is constantly growing, with new amenities and bungalows every year, but the place is still pretty rustic. Best are the free-standing bungalows. The small hotel block at the back isn't really worth it. They're building like mad here though, erecting hokey cement statuaries of Vietnamese legends as quickly as they are the new bungalows. There's a cozy little grove of seaside pines for lounging, too. Dining is in a small open-air area. Service is limited, and nobody speaks much English, but you can mime a motorbike-revving wrist twist and get some wheels, and there's a useful list of tour options in English.

Central Lang Co Beach, Phu Loc District. ✆ **054/387-4456.** Fax 054/387-3762. 42 units. $43–$60 double. No credit cards. **Amenities:** Restaurant. *In room:* A/C, fridge, hair dryer.

5 DANANG

Danang, the fourth-largest city in Vietnam, is one of the most important seaports in the central region, and the current booming Vietnamese economy has seen an economic growth (GDP) rate in busy Danang as high as 14%. As the most convenient deepwater port in the region, Danang is now greeting more and more international cruise ships, along with the glut of trade vessels.

Who Are the Cham?

There is little written history of the Cham. What we do know comes mainly from Chinese written history and from splendid religious artwork the empire created in its prime.

The Cham are of Indonesian descent, and records of their civilization go as far back as the 2nd century A.D. in Tuong Lam, along the central coast of Vietnam, when the Cham fought Chinese incursion. The Cham declared a new land, dubbed the Lin Yi by the Chinese, which extended from Quang Binh to present-day Danang Province. The center of the civilization for most of its existence was in what the Cham called Indrapura, or Tra Kieu, near present-day Danang.

The Cham belong to the Malayo-Polynesian language family, same as Hawaiian islanders and the Maori people near New Zealand and Australia. Traditionally, Cham lived by rice farming; fishing; and trading pepper, cinnamon bark, ivory, and wood with neighboring nations, using Hoi An as a base. Hinduism was their dominant religion, with Buddhist influences and an infusion of Islam starting in the 14th century.

In the middle of the 10th century, internal warfare, as well as battles against both the Khmer to the south and the ethnic Vietnamese, or Dai Viet, to the north, began to erode the Cham kingdom. By the mid–15th century, Cham territories had been almost entirely absorbed into Vietnam. By the early 1800s, there was no longer a separate Cham nation.

Today the Cham are still a distinct ethnic group in Vietnam, and despite years of pressure to assimilate, Cham culture and traditions survive. Cham people have their own language, with a written text derived from Sanskrit, and many of their traditions remain, in ancient Hinduism or in Islam, to which many have converted.

The city played a prominent historical role in the Vietnam War. It was the landing site for the first U.S. troops officially sent to Vietnam on March 8, 1965. On that day, 3,500 soldiers in beach assault vehicles joined more than 23,000 U.S. advisors who were already in the country.

Danang has nothing in the way of charm, and there aren't any major attractions except for the **Cham Museum,** which has become just a quick stop on the tourist-cafe buses between Hoi An and Hue. But **Furama Resort,** a short ride from the city center, is one of the finest high-end resorts in Indochina, and there are some excellent-value hotels in town (some use this as a budget base to explore nearby Hoi An).

China Beach, and also nearby **My Khe Beach,** are worth a stop. This former U.S. recreation base has a light-sand coast with excellent views of the nearby Marble Mountains, and it's beginning to draw more and more international tourists, as well as weekend visits by Danang's growing expat community.

GETTING THERE

BY PLANE You can fly to Danang from both Hanoi and Ho Chi Minh City. The Vietnam Airlines office is at 35 Tran Phu St. (© **0511/382-1130**). A taxi to or from the airport costs about 60,000 VND.

BY BUS If you're traveling on the "open tour" ticket, Danang is not a specified stop anymore, but the budget tourist cafes can drop you off at the Cham Museum on the southern end of the city. You'll have to call the office in either Hue or Hoi An for pickup when you're ready to leave, or contact **An Phu Tourist** (20 Dong Da St. in the far north end of town; ✆ **0511/381-8366;** anphu_cndn@yahoo.com), which is the only traveler cafe with an office in town. Catch local buses at the **Interprovince Bus Station** at 33 Nguyen Luong Bang, which is not a bad option for a short hop to Hoi An or Hue (note that these local buses have hourly departures as opposed to traveler-cafe buses, which leave only twice a day). Travelers planning to take the rigorous bus journey onward to **Laos** should say a little prayer and contact **An Phu Tourist** for buses to **Savannakhet.** Expect to pay about $25 and expect a long, harrowing journey (honestly, fly if you can).

BY CAR Danang is about 3½ hours by car from Hue, and the route passes Lang Co Beach (good for a stop and a rest) and crosses the very scenic **Hai Van Pass** (p. 202). You'll pay $40 to take the trip by rented car with driver. From Hoi An, it's about an hour and costs $25. This ride makes a good day trip along with the **Marble Mountains** (p. 211). From either Hoi An or Hue, contact local traveler cafes or travel agents; from Danang, contact An Phu Tourist, or your hotel can make arrangements.

BY TRAIN All trains stop at the **Danang Railway Station,** at 202 Hai Phong St. (✆ **0511/382-1175**).

GETTING AROUND

Danang has the usual contingent of **motorbike taxis** and **cyclos** whose operators are quicker to find you than vice versa. Haggle and expect to pay as little as 5,000 VND for trips in town and about $1 for a ride out to Furama Resort or My Khe Beach. **Taxis** can be called or hailed anywhere, and the initial cost is 10,000 VND, with 6,000 VND for every kilometer after that. Contact the following: **Airport Taxi** at ✆ **0511/382-5555,** or **Dana Taxi** at ✆ **0511/381-5815.**

VISITOR INFORMATION & TOURS

There are few tour offices in Danang because most major tour operations are based out of nearby Hoi An or Hue. Any hotel can help with onward travel, either by private car, by minivan, or through budget cafes. Tours can also be booked with any concierge.

An Phu Tourist (20 Dong Da St., in the far north end of town; ✆ **0511/381-8366;** anphu_cndn@yahoo.com) is the local budget tourist cafe and can arrange any low-budget connections (they also have offices in Hoi An). Their office is in the north end of Danang near the Saigon Tourane Hotel, but they can arrange pickup from your hotel and are generally pretty accommodating.

Fast Facts Danang

Banks & Currency Exchange **Vietcombank** is at 140 Le Loi St. (✆ **0511/382-1955**).

Hospital The **Family Medical Clinic** of Danang offers high-end emergency and general medical services to expatriates and travelers. Their office is at 50–52 Nguyen Van Linh St., Hai Chau District (✆ **0511/358-2699;** danang@vietnammedicalpractice.com).

Post Office The post office is at 47 Tran Phu St. (✆ **0511/382-1134**). At the time of writing, they had temporarily relocated to 38 Yen Bai St., but they should be back at their old location by the time you read this. Call ahead just in case.

Telephone The city code for Danang is 0511. You can make international calls from the post office. Danang hosts the usual contingent of budget dial-up Internet shops. Look along Dong Da Street adjacent to the An Phu Tourist office (9 Dong Da St.).

WHERE TO STAY

Keep your eyes out for new hotels from well-known names, as Danang has been attracting some attention lately. Raffles has already broken ground on a new property, but high-end luxury takes time. The 150-room resort is scheduled to open in 2011. Inter-Continental also recently signed on to build their third property in Vietnam (the other two being in Hanoi and Ho Chi Minh) in this up-and-coming beach town.

Expensive

Furama Resort Danang ★★★ Just a short ride southwest of Danang and elegantly situated near a beautiful sand beach, this popular upscale gem greets you in style with a grand lobby that is more or less the gilded frame to beautiful scenery: sand, sun, and sky. Whether you're a sailor, a beach bum, or a comfort junky, you'll find what you want here. There are two gorgeous swimming pools: one a multitiered minimalist still life overlooking the open beach, and the other a faux lagoon, complete with small waterfall and bridge, a romantic hideaway. The hotel offers local tours, yoga, tai chi, a spa, and a full aesthetic salon. Rooms are large and comfortable, with wood floors, Vietnamese-style furniture, and sliding doors to balconies that overlook the ocean or pool. Large marble bathrooms have all the amenities. Small suites are a great option, with large double beds on raised areas and a sunken sitting area with a large, cushy white couch overlooking balconies and the sea beyond. Dining choices are great, and their restaurants flank a large, central area with a small reflecting pool in the center—quite peaceful. There are shuttles to the city.

68 Ho Xuan Huong St. (oceanside 11km/6¾ miles south and west of Danang). ✆ **0511/384-7333.** Fax 0511/384-7220. www.furamavietnam.com. 198 units. $200–$220 garden view; $280–$300 ocean view; $600–$700 suite. AE, MC, V. **Amenities:** 3 restaurants; 3 bars; concierge; diving; health club; Internet; kayaks; 2 outdoor pools (1 in courtyard, 1 multilevel w/ocean view); room service; sailboat (Laser); spa; 2 tennis courts. *In room:* A/C, TV, fridge, hair dryer, minibar.

Moderate

Bamboo Green Hotel ★★ The best choice in Danang proper, Bamboo Green is operated by Vietnamtourism—this one's the best of its three properties in town (Bamboo Green II and III are comparable but less luxurious). Rooms are large, with clean beige carpets, and are well furnished (except for the hideous polyester bedspreads). The good-size marble bathrooms with hair dryers look brand-new, and rooms are as cozy as at any midrange U.S. chain. Ask for a room on the top floor for a good city view. There's a big restaurant with decent Asian/Vietnamese fare and good tour services. The staff is friendly.

158 Phan Chau Trinh St., Danang. ✆ **0511/382-2996** or 382-2997. Fax 0511/382-2998. 42 units. $55 superior; $70 deluxe; $100 suite. AE, MC, V. **Amenities:** 2 restaurants; bar; room service; sauna. *In room:* A/C, TV, fridge, hair dryer, Internet, minibar.

Saigon Tourane Hotel ★ This hotel is popular with European tour groups; you can expect comfort at a low cost in this nondescript, friendly hotel on the north end of town. Carpeted rooms are clean, with tidy, good-size bathrooms; some have good city views from upper floors. But it's certainly not luxurious: The general atmosphere is marked by failing neon signs and worn carpets that speak of the volumes that pass through. Saigontourist owns this hotel and can make any necessary arrangements with little hassle. The staff couldn't be any kinder. Be sure to ask for a room away from the karaoke—far away from the karaoke. Right next door is the **Danang Hotel** (01–03 Dong Da St.; ✆ **0511/383-4662**), with budget rooms from $16 if you're in a pinch.

5 Dong Da St., Danang. ✆ **0511/3821-021.** Fax 0511/3895-285. 82 units. $50–$70 double; $80 suite. MC, V. **Amenities:** 2 restaurants; bar; basic gym; sauna; smoke-free rooms; karaoke. *In room:* A/C, TV, fridge, hair dryer, Internet, minibar.

Inexpensive

Bach Dang Riverside Hotel This big riverside hotel that's long been a popular expat address has already fought its battles and is pretty beat-up. But rooms are tidy and there are lots of amenities that are well maintained. Staff is quite helpful, and you'll find lots of shops and local dining options in the esplanade out front. Nothing to write home about, though.

50 Bach Dang St., Danang. ✆ **0511/382-3649.** Fax 0511/382-1659. bdhotel@dng.vnn.vn. 100 units. $35–$80 double. MC, V. **Amenities:** Restaurant; bikes; midsize swimming pool; tennis court. *In room:* A/C, TV, fridge, Internet, minibar.

At My Khe Beach

Just 3km (1¾ miles) from town across the large lagoon bridge, you'll find a few quiet, little hotels worth the escape on My Khe Beach. This stretch of sand is most popular as a local hangout, but it's got quite affordable accommodations.

Tourane Hotel This hotel is currently undergoing renovations, which is good because rooms here are a bit beat-up. The villas of this popular old hotel, when complete, will be a good midrange standard—not luxurious, but cozy, with wood floors and high ceilings. The Tourane is a big government hotel, which means it's drab and bare throughout, but the villas are across the road from the beach and the best choice along this strip.

My Khe, Phuoc My Ward, Danang City. ✆ **0511/393-2666.** Fax 0511/384-4328. 70 units. $40–$90 double. MC, V. **Amenities:** Restaurant; pool; 2 tennis courts. *In room:* A/C, TV, fridge, Internet, minibar.

WHERE TO DINE

If you're at Furama, that's where you'll find the best fine dining, but beachside seafood shacks adjacent to the resort also serve good barbecue for a fraction of resort prices. In Danang proper, choices are few—mostly small storefront restaurants. **Bread of Life** (215 Tran Phu St.; ✆ **0511/389-3446**) is a wonderful new cafe/restaurant serving tasty Western fare such as savory burgers and homemade pies. The owners employ deaf Vietnamese youth, teaching them American Sign Language (quite similar to Vietnamese Sign, both derived from French Sign) and life skills to encourage self-sustainability. **Kim Do Restaurant** (180 Tran Phu St.; ✆ **0511/382-1846**) is a Chinese restaurant of long standing, with good stir-fries and steamed Cantonese specials. **Bamboo Restaurant** (70 Xuan Dieu; ✆ **0511/353-7831**) is a mellow place for tasty Vietnamese fare and a popular choice among locals. The small storefronts adjacent to the Cham Museum are a good find; they serve tasty duck and rice dishes.

ATTRACTIONS

In addition to the listings below, Danang hosts a small enclave of the **Cao Dai sect,** a contemporary Vietnamese denomination incorporating aspects of all religions, including science (for more information, see "Day Trips from Ho Chi Minh," in chapter 12). Most practitioners of Cao Daism are in the far south, but this Cao Dai temple is one of the largest outside of Tay Ninh, home of the Cao Dai Holy See. The **Cao Dai Temple** in Danang is at 63 Hai Phung, open daily dawn to dusk. You might have to wake somebody up to get inside, but someone is usually on-site with a key.

The Cham Museum ★★ The Cham Museum was established in 1936 (originally the Ecole Française d'Extrème Orient) to house the relics of the powerful Hindu culture that once ruled vast tracts of central Vietnam. The museum has the largest collection of Cham sculpture in the world, in works ranging from the 4th to 14th centuries, presented in a rough outdoor setting that suits the evocative, sensual sculptures well. The more than 300 pieces of sandstone artwork and temple decorations were largely influenced by Hindu and, later, Mahayana Buddhism. Among the cast of characters, you'll see symbols of Uroja, or "goddess mother," usually breasts or nipples; the linga, the phallic structure representing the god Shiva; the holy bird Garuda; the dancing girl Kinnari; the snake god Naga; and Ganesha, child of the god Shiva, with the head of an elephant. The sculptures are arranged by period, which are, in turn, named after the geographic regions where the sculptures were found. Note the masterpiece Tra Kieu altar of the late 7th century, with carved scenes telling the story of the Asian epic *Ramayana.* The story is of the wedding of Princess Sita. Side one tells of Prince Rama, who broke a holy vow to obtain Sita's hand. Side two tells of ambassadors sent to King Dasaratha, Prince Rama's father, to bring him the glad tidings. Side three is the actual ceremony, and side four depicts the celebrations after the ceremony. There is a permanent photo exhibition of the many Cham relics *in situ* at various locations throughout Vietnam.

1 Bach Dang (at Tran Phu and Le Dinh Duong sts.). No phone. Admission 30,000 VND. Daily 7am–5pm.

The Marble Mountains **Overrated** The "mountains" are actually a series of five marble and limestone formations, which the locals liken to the shape of a dragon at rest. For the Vietnamese, it is a place of significance, which means you are often climbing with loud tour groups who are trying to elbow past you. The hills are interlaced with caves, some of which are important Buddhist sanctuaries. The caves at the Marble Mountains, like so many in the country, served as sanctuaries for the Viet Cong during the Vietnam War. Each peak is named for an element: Hoa Son, or fire; Mo Son, or wood; Kim Son, or gold; and Tho Son, or earth. The highest mountain, Tho Son, is climbable via a series of metal ladders beginning inside the cave and extending to the surface at the top. Ling Ong Pagoda, a shrine within a cave, is a highlight. The quarries in Non Nuoc village, at the bottom of the mountains, are as interesting as the caves are. Fantastic animals and fanciful statues of folk tales and Buddhist figures are carved from the rock. Try to get a good look before you are set upon by flocks of hawkers. What's more, even if you're interested in the items they hawk—incredibly cheap mortar and pestle sets, some very nice chess sets, turtles, and small animals—any amount of marble adds considerable weight to luggage. When someone asks, "Is your bag full of rocks," you don't want the answer to be "Yes." You can easily see the mountains as part of your trip en route either to or from Hoi An; most cafe tour buses stop here.

11km (6¾ miles) south of Danang and 9.5km (6 miles) north of Hoi An along Hwy. 1. All tours stop here. Admission 30,000 VND. Daily 7am–6pm.

6 HOI AN

Hoi An was designated a UNESCO World Heritage Site in 1999, and a visit to this old-world gem is a sure cultural highlight of any tour in Vietnam. From the 16th to the 18th century, the city was Vietnam's most important port and trading post, particularly of ceramics with nearby China. Today it is a quaint old town of some 844 structures protected as historical landmarks, and the unique influence of Chinese and Japanese traders who passed through (or settled) can still be felt. It's a picturesque town, small enough to cover easily on foot, with lots of good nooks and crannies, shops, and gastronomic delights to discover.

Wander among historic homes and temples, perhaps stop to lounge in an open-air cafe, gaze at the oddities and exotic foods in the market, or take a **sampan ride** down the lazy river. In the afternoons when school is out, the streets are thronged with skipping children in spotless white shirts and girls in their *ao dai* uniforms, and you can still see local craftsmen at work in some parts of the city.

During the full moon of every month, local shop owners turn off the electricity and hang lanterns bearing their shops' names, and a candlelight lantern procession, complete with a few small floats, makes its way through the Old Town and along the riverfront. It's well worth timing a visit to enjoy the spectacle and the post-processional festivities.

GETTING THERE

BY PLANE OR TRAIN Major transport connections go through Danang. From there, you can take a car to Hoi An for between $8 and $25.

BY BUS Hoi An is a major stop on all open-tour-cafe buses. Connection with Danang is just $3.

GETTING AROUND

Hoi An is so small that you'll memorize the map in an hour or two. Most hotels and guesthouses rent out bicycles for 5,000 VND to 7,000 VND a day, a great way to explore the outer regions of the city or head out to Cua Dai Beach. Motorbikes are 45,000 VND to 75,000 VND per day and are not difficult to drive in this tiny city or out busy Cua Dai Road to the beach, but going by foot or on a bicycle is the best, quietest option for touring this historic town, and increasingly the streets in the heart of the old city are forbidding motorbike traffic (not that anyone follows the rules). **Cyclos** are here and there; 10,000 VND or so should get you anywhere within the city. Car rental is available anywhere. Try **Faifoo Travel** for a car by the hour or for the day (✆ **0510/391-4580**), or contact **Mai Linh Taxi** at ✆ **0510/391-4914.**

VISITOR INFORMATION & TOURS

- **Hoi An Tourist Guiding Office,** with offices at 01 Nguyen Truong To (✆ **0510/386-1327**) and at 12 Phan Chu Trinh St. (✆ **0510/386-2715**), sells the entrance ticket to the Hoi An World Cultural Heritage Organization attractions. A one-ticket purchase offers limited admission to all of the town's museums, old houses, and Chinese assembly halls. For more information about the ticket, see "Attractions," later in this chapter, or visit www.hoianworldheritage.org.
- **Hoi An Tourist Service Company,** inside the Hoi An Hotel, 10 Tran Hung Dao St. (✆ **0510/386-1373;** fax 0510/386-1636), books every type of tour of the city and surrounding areas, including China Beach and the Marble Mountains, and is a reliable operation.
- **Sinh Café IV,** 18B Hai Ba Trung St. (✆ **0510/386-3948;** www.sinhcafevn.com), provides bus tours and tickets onward.
- **An Phu Tourist** has scaled down its office at 722 Hai Ba Trung St. (✆ **0510/386-2643;** www.anphutouristhoian.com), but the skeleton crew can do the same work (book onward bus connection or local trips) as at their new location in the **An Phu Hotel,** just out of the town center toward Cua Dai (288 Nguyen Duy Hieu St., away from town toward Cua Dai Beach; ✆ **0510/391-4345;** fax 0510/391-4054; www.anphutouristhoian.com).

Fast Facts Hoi An

Banks & Currency Exchange The **Vietcombank** branch at 4 Huong Dieu St. has an ATM, exchanges most major currencies, and does credit card cash-withdrawal transactions. Hours are Monday to Saturday 7:30am to 7pm. Hoi An **Incombank** has offices with exchange services at 09 Le Loio St. At 4 Hoang Diet St., **Exchange Bureau #1,** across from the Hoi An Hotel at 37 Tran Hung Dao, has exchange services and an ATM. There is also an ATM at the post office (see below). You'll find a **Western Union** outlet at Vinh Tours (26 Tran Hung Dao).

Internet Along Le Loi you'll find service at prices of about 100 VND per minute (50¢ per hour), but access is generally slow. **Min's Computer,** at 125 Nguyen Duy Hieu, on the northern end of town (✆ **0510/391-4323**), is as good as it gets and so popular now that if they are full, just pop into one of the copycat shops that has opened up on the same street (try **123 Internet** next door). There's also good Internet service right next to the post office at 4B Tran Hung Dao (✆ **0510/386-1635**).

Post Office The post office is at the corner of Trang Hong Dao and Huong Dieu streets, and is open Monday to Saturday from 6am to 9:30pm.

Telephone The city code for Hoi An is 0510. You can place international phone calls from the post office listed above and from most hotels.

WHERE TO STAY

Hoi An has seen a recent boom in upscale resorts, and there are more on the way along Cua Dai Beach. Large-scale new construction in Hoi An proper is prohibited by UNESCO, but smaller hotels are getting nicer and there are a few new options closer to town. The hotels listed below are broken into four sections: at China Beach, in Hoi An town proper, along Cua Dai Road, and at Cua Dai Beach. With so much competition and so many new resorts going up and posting promotional rates, you can find some great deals for very fine rooms and, with some good bargaining, real steals on a room in the heart of the old city.

At China Beach

Very Expensive

The Nam Hai ★★★ This is the best resort in Hoi An, and certainly one of the best luxury destinations in all of Vietnam. Individual villas are discreetly laid out over an immaculately tended 35 hectares (86 acres). Staff is incredibly friendly and quick to be of service at the first sign of a furrowed brow. The one-bedroom hotel villa is a chic affair of granite stone floors, earthy colors, and dark local wood. The centerpiece is a dark-wood, six-column, raised platform topped with lattice woodwork and draped in silk curtains. This is where you'll find the elevated, plush bed facing a huge oceanview window. Behind it are the daybed and a bathtub done in traditional crushed eggshell lacquer, and if baths aren't your thing, there are both indoor and outdoor rain shower cubicles. For in-room entertainment, a flatscreen TV swivels out to face the bed, or there's the iPod loaded with tunes hooked up to a Bose sound system. New to the resort are in-house activities like Vietnamese cooking demonstrations or tennis tournaments, a nice touch, as sometimes you want to do more than just lounge poolside.

Pool villas are styled like traditional Vietnamese courtyard houses. An elevated dining and living room occupies the center of the courtyard and looks out onto the backyard swimming pool and nearby ocean. Multi-bedroom pool villas are fantastic value if you're a group of four or more, as they come with super-luxurious "club benefits" like return airport limousine transfer, a personal butler, complimentary minibar, and evening cocktails and canapés with free-flowing champagne and wine.

Hamlet 1, Dien Duong village, Dien Ban District, Quang Nam Province. ✆ **0510/394-0000.** Fax 0510/394-0999. www.ghmhotels.com. 100 units. $830–$935 1-bedroom villa; $1,500–$4,300 1- to 5-bedroom pool villa. AE, DC, MC, V. **Amenities:** 2 restaurants; bar; badminton court; basketball court; bikes; health club; library; 3 outdoor pools; spa; room service; 4 tennis courts. *In room:* A/C, TV, movie library, iPod/MP3 docking station, fridge, hair dryer, minibar, Wi-Fi.

In Hoi An Town

Expensive

Life Resort Hoi An ★★ What a difference a renovation makes! Life Resort closed down for about 6 months in 2008 after a sizeable chunk of it was damaged in the worst Hoi An flood in recent history. Room layouts are the same, but all the furniture, floors, and beds are brand spanking new. The decoration is a cool look of warm browns and whites, offset with organza and black textiles and pillows. It is stylish and contemporary and makes this resort your top choice in Hoi An town. Raised sleeping areas are done in cool cream tile floors with dark-wood trim. Bathrooms are tucked behind wide doors that slide open to reveal a slick and modern space with large sink stands and spacious central showers. (You can request a room with a cozy granite tub if you are partial to baths.) Request rooms that face the river or spill out into the central pool area; they have the best views and ambience. All rooms come with private verandas lined with a pair of daybeds. The new Heritage Bar out front is a great place to mingle with other guests and chill out with a glass of wine (it's got the most extensive wine list in Hoi An) or cocktail. Certain staff members are outstanding here and can help you out with virtually anything—from scheduling a torturous Vietnamese language lesson, to recommending a fabulous tailor in town.

1 Pham Hong Thai St. ✆ **0510/391-4555.** Fax 0510/391-4515. www.life-resorts.com. 94 units. $120 double; $154–$170 suite. AE, MC, V. **Amenities:** Restaurant; 2 bars; cafe; outdoor pool; room service; new spa. *In room:* A/C, TV, fridge, minibar, Wi-Fi.

Moderate

Hoi An Hotel ★ Still the most convenient in-town address, the Hoi An Hotel was the first high-end hotel in Hoi An, and it works hard to keep its reputation. As a result, it stays busy with lots of tour groups. The friendly staff does a great job and handles large numbers with a modicum of grace. Don't expect anything fancy, but rooms are unusually large and impeccably clean, with tile floors and comfortable beds—older rooms are just as good for the money. Basic tile bathrooms are in good condition. The newest building has upscale rooms with dark-wood floors and a fun, contemporary Chinese theme. The central pool is large, though often overcrowded. Their casual open-air dining facilities are good, and the folks at their tour desk are very helpful. Convenient to downtown sites.

10 Tran Hung Dao St. ✆ **0510/386-1373.** Fax 0510/386-1636. www.hoiantourist.com. 160 units. $92–$120 double; $217 suite. AE, MC, V. **Amenities:** Restaurant; garden bar; babysitting; concierge; Jacuzzi; nice courtyard pool; tennis court. *In room:* A/C, TV, fridge, hair dryer, minibar, Wi-Fi.

Vinh Hung Resort ★ The folks at Vinh Hung have followed a Chinese style of entrepreneurship with the model "Start small; go big." (See also Vinh Hung I, II, and III, below.) Their small in-town properties have been popular, and they've turned the income from them into this latest project: a self-contained, midlevel resort on Hoi An Island that is just getting up and running. The area, slated for further development in coming years, is just a 10- or 15-minute walk from the canal bridge at Hoi An center. Deluxe rooms

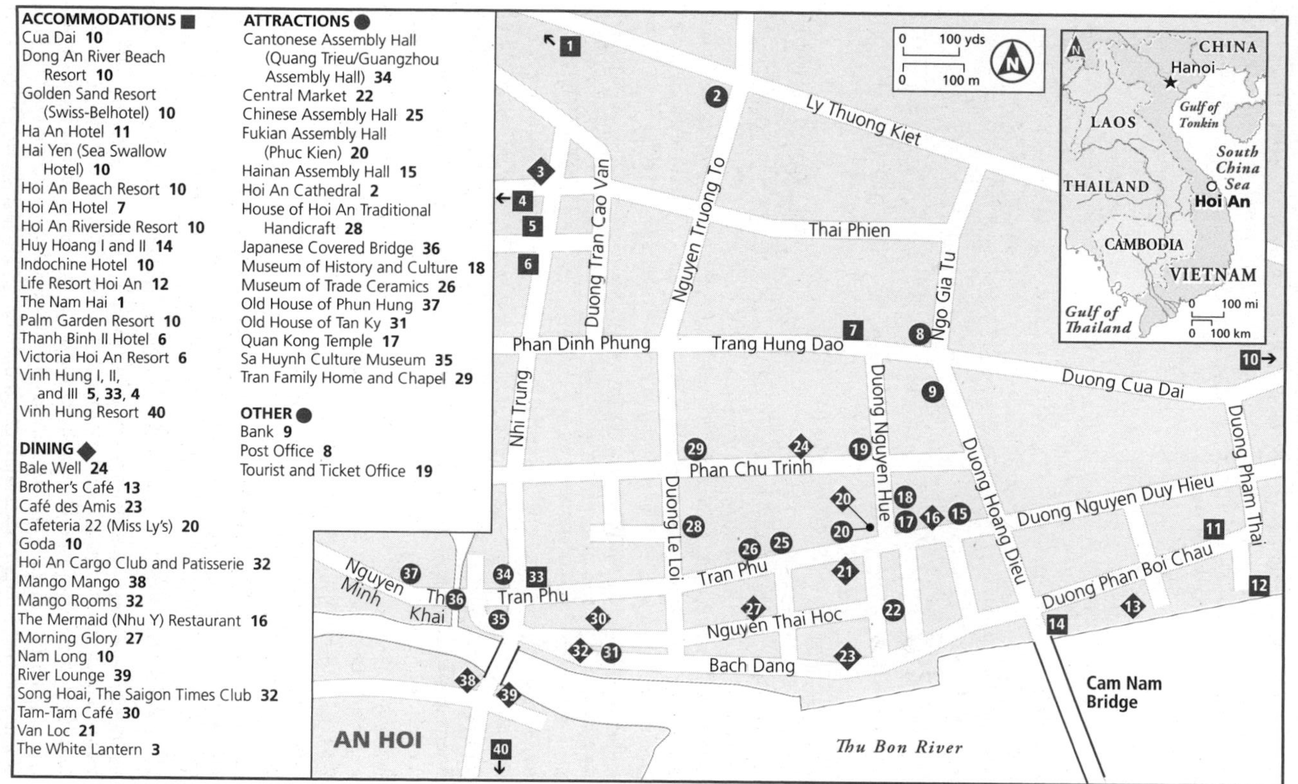
ACCOMMODATIONS ■
Cua Dai 10
Dong An River Beach Resort 10
Golden Sand Resort (Swiss-Belhotel) 10
Ha An Hotel 11
Hai Yen (Sea Swallow Hotel) 10
Hoi An Beach Resort 10
Hoi An Hotel 7
Hoi An Riverside Resort 10
Huy Hoang I and II 14
Indochine Hotel 10
Life Resort Hoi An 12
The Nam Hai 1
Palm Garden Resort 10
Thanh Binh II Hotel 6
Victoria Hoi An Resort 6
Vinh Hung I, II, and III 5, 33, 4
Vinh Hung Resort 40
DINING ◆
Bale Well 24
Brother's Café 13
Café des Amis 23
Cafeteria 22 (Miss Ly's) 20
Goda 10
Hoi An Cargo Club and Patisserie 32
Mango Mango 38
Mango Rooms 32
The Mermaid (Nhu Y) Restaurant 16
Morning Glory 27
Nam Long 10
River Lounge 39
Song Hoai, The Saigon Times Club 32
Tam-Tam Café 30
Van Loc 21
The White Lantern 3
ATTRACTIONS ●
Cantonese Assembly Hall (Quang Trieu/Guangzhou Assembly Hall) 34
Central Market 22
Chinese Assembly Hall 25
Fukian Assembly Hall (Phuc Kien) 20
Hainan Assembly Hall 15
Hoi An Cathedral 2
House of Hoi An Traditional Handicraft 28
Japanese Covered Bridge 36
Museum of History and Culture 18
Museum of Trade Ceramics 26
Old House of Phun Hung 37
Old House of Tan Ky 31
Quan Kong Temple 17
Sa Huynh Culture Museum 35
Tran Family Home and Chapel 29
OTHER ●
Bank 9
Post Office 8
Tourist and Ticket Office 19
0 100 yds
0 100 m
N
CHINA
Hanoi
Gulf of Tonkin
LAOS
South China Sea
THAILAND
Hoi An
CAMBODIA
VIETNAM
Gulf of Thailand
0 100 mi
0 100 km
Ly Thuong Kiet
Thai Phien
Duong Tran Cao Van
Nguyen Truong To
Ngo Gia Tu
Phan Dinh Phung
Trang Hung Dao
Duong Cua Dai
Nhi Trung
Duong Nguyen Hue
Duong Hoang Dieu
Duong Pham Thai
Phan Chu Trinh
Duong Le Loi
Duong Nguyen Duy Hieu
Tran Phu
Duong Phan Boi Chau
Nguyen Minh Khai
Nguyen Thai Hoc
Bach Dang
Cam Nam Bridge
AN HOI
Thu Bon River

are the best—large and tidy, with wooden floors, Chinese tapestries, and carpeted sitting areas. High-end rooms are enormous, some with Jacuzzis. Rooms encircle a pool area and, though resort services are limited and everything is a bit compact, Vinh Hung Resort is an affordable and convenient getaway. Some rooms overlook the wide river—a good choice. They have kayaks for rent, a unique commute to the town center, and they cover all basic amenities.

111 Ngo Quyen (on Hoi Island, across the small bridge connecting to Hoi An near Bach Dang St., and a short ride to the opposite end of the island). ✆ **0510/391-0577.** Fax 0510/386-4094. www.vinhhung resort.com. 82 units. $70–$90 double; $125 suite. AE, MC, V. **Amenities:** Restaurant; bar; babysitting; bikes; small fitness center; Jacuzzi; kayaks (can paddle to town); outdoor pool; room service; sauna; tennis court. *In room:* A/C, TV, fridge, Internet, minibar.

Inexpensive

Ha An Hotel ★ This colonial-style place with a courtyard entry is just a short walk from town. Rooms in the faux colonial–style building are compact but tidy and comfortable. The Ha An is basically like minihotels elsewhere, but slightly more spacious and with nice touches such as rattan furniture and nice wall hangings. Unique are the DVD players and videos available to borrow. The hotel restaurant is cozy and the staff aims to please. It's a good choice, out of the in-town tourist jumble, and a nice alternative if you can't afford to splash out at neighboring Life Resort.

06–08 Phan Boi Chau St. (just outside the entrance to Life Resort). ✆ **0510/386-3126.** Fax 0510/391-4280. www.haanhotel.com. 24 units. $45–$70. MC, V. **Amenities:** Small courtyard restaurant and bar; bikes; Internet; outdoor pool table. *In room:* A/C, TV, DVD, fridge, minibar.

Huy Hoang I and II ★ The original of this growing local chain is a good bargain option set in a yellow-and-white faux-colonial close to the Central Market. Tidy, basic tile-floor rooms are just $15. There are no phones or other amenities, and only the few $45 rooms are of any substantial size (and also have bathtubs). Breakfast is served in a patio in the back, with views of the river. The staff is exceedingly friendly. The second property, on the opposite edge of town, is a similar low-end workhorse of a place.

Huy Hoang I: 73 Phan Boi Chau St. ✆ **0510/386-2211.** Fax 0510/386-3722. kshuyhoang@dgn.vnn.vn. 26 units. $15–$45 double. No credit cards. **Amenities:** Restaurant; bar. *In room:* A/C, TV. **Huy Hoang II:** 87 Hung Vuong St. ✆ **0510/3916-233.** Fax 0510/3862-126. 28 units. $12–$20 double.

Thanh Binh II Hotel ★ The Thanh Binh II hotel is newer and nicer than its sister property, the Thanh Bin I on Le Loi Street. The three-story building has a Chinese-inspired lobby, with carved dark-wood furnishings and cafe tables. Upstairs, the very clean and basic rooms are spacious. The decor is a color-coordinated mishmash. There's not a musty smell to be found, bathrooms are tidy, and the staff is friendly. For fun, ask about one of the suites: a huge room with wooden paneling, carved Chinese-style furnishings (plus a mosquito net over the bed), a nice balcony with beaded curtains, and, in the center of the room, a large wooden carving of a fat, happy Buddha.

712 Hai Ba Trung St. ✆ **0510/386-3715.** vothihong@dng.vnn.vn. $18–$35 double. AE, MC, V. *In room:* A/C, TV, fridge, minibar. **Thanh Binh I** is at 01 Le Loi St. ✆ **0510/386-1740.** Fax 0510/391-6777. **Thanh Binh III** is at 98 Ba Trieu St. ✆ **0510/391-6777.** Fax 0510/391-6779. Total 88 units.

Vinh Hung I, II, and III ★ Vinh Hung I, a downtown property set in an old wooden Chinese house, is a Hoi An institution: Its two signature rooms are almost museum pieces—alone worth a visit—but they're not especially luxurious or comfortable. Standard rooms in both Vinh Hung I and II are large, with wooden appointments and cool retro features like mosquito nets and Chinese latticework on wood balconies. Vinh Hung

II is a tour-group favorite and is often full, but for good reason (the central pool is unique in this price category). However, its popularity means the place is getting a bit rough around the edges. The new Vinh Hung Resort (see above) is an improvement.

Vinh Hung 1: 143 Tran Phu St. ✆ **0510/386-1621.** Fax 0510/386-1893. **Vinh Hung II:** Nhi Trung St. ✆ **0510/386-3717.** Fax 0510/386-4094. **Vinh Hung III:** 96 Ba Trieu St. ✆ **0510/391-6277.** Fax 0510/391-6359. www.vinhhungresort.com. Total 119 units. $35–$120 double. AE, MC, V. **Amenities:** Restaurant; small outdoor pool. *In room:* A/C, TV, fridge, Wi-Fi.

Along Cua Dai Road

Busy little Cua Dai doesn't offer the most spectacular accommodations, but you can find some small hotels along its length, a few with a pool and popular with large groups. Discounts abound, and the prices listed here are just a point of departure for negotiating. If calling for reservations, ask about a "contract rate" or a current discount policy, and begin bargaining for a price for 1 day and ask for less for 2 or more. The **Hoi An Riverside** is an exception: It's a fine high-end property.

Expensive

Hoi An Riverside Resort ★★ For upscale, tranquil, and intimate surroundings, you'll find no better than this lush little resort between road and river outside of Hoi An (just 3km/1¾ miles). The place has a cozy feel, as if guest rooms kind of grew around the winding path of the garden and tranquil courtyard pool. Vietnamese- or Japanese-theme rooms have smallish but immaculate bathrooms and nice wood appointments throughout. The staff is invisible, meaning that this place carries on like an immaculately trimmed golf course that gets a once-over each night. The Song Do restaurant serves fine Vietnamese and Continental fare, and a visit to their Faifo bar hearkens back to another era. The staff is very professional and informative.

175 Cua Dai Rd., 3km (1¾ miles) from Hoi An. ✆ **0510/386-4800.** Fax 0510/386-4900. www.hoianriverresort.com. 60 units. $110–$175 double. AE, DC, MC, V. **Amenities:** 3 restaurants; bar; babysitting; health club; Internet; outdoor pool; room service; snooker/billiards room. *In room:* A/C, TV, fridge, minibar.

Moderate

Cua Dai ★★ A good budget gem on the beach road just out of town (like nearby Hai Yen, reviewed below), the Cua Dai is a good marriage of affordability and comfort. It's easy to settle in here, with its open sitting areas and basic but comfy rooms. The kind staff will make you feel right at home. The only drawback is the busy road out front, but all rooms have double glass and are relatively quiet. Rooms in the newer wing in back have fine wooden appointments and creative local decorations; older rooms in the main building are quite large. Cua Dai is a good base for exploring, and a sure bet for meeting some expats and long-stay travelers here on cultural or humanitarian missions.

544 Cua Dai St. ✆ **0510/386-2231** or 386-4604. Fax 0510/386-2232. 27 units. $40–$75 double. MC, V. **Amenities:** 3 restaurants; bikes and motorbikes; pool; room service. *In room:* A/C, TV, fridge, minibar.

Hai Yen (Sea Swallow Hotel) ★ On the edge of the old town (a short walk or ride toward the beach), Hai Yen is a popular choice for big budget-tour groups. Slick diagonal black-and-white (or blue-and-white) tile decorates throughout, and rooms are big but have funky Chinese relief carvings, overly fancy curtains, and shiny polyester spreads. I'd give it an A for effort, but the general effect is kind of unsettling. The small pool is a surprise luxury in this price range. It's all a bit rough around the edges, but the staff is friendly and can help with any detail.

568 Cua Dai St., Hoi An. ✆ **0510/386-2445** or 386-2446. 41 units. $20–$40 double. AE, MC, V. **Amenities:** Restaurant; motorbikes; small outdoor pool. *In room:* A/C, TV, fridge, minibar, Wi-Fi.

Indochine Hotel ★ This one attracts hoards of French tourists and is always booked. A midrange choice (prices listed below are just a starting point for negotiation), the hotel is a faux-colonial set at a bend in the river about 1km (½ mile) from Cua Dai Beach. You'll have to arrange transport anywhere you go, but it's a cozy place with a big U-shaped courtyard. The basic rooms are large and clean, a good deal for the money, with pricing based on a room's view of the river or garden. There's a fun spirit of camaraderie if you catch the right group, and the rooftop restaurant is a casual evening escape.

87 Cua Dai St., Cam Chau Village (about 1km/½ mile back from the beach). ✆ **0510/392-3601.** Fax 0510/392-3400. 60 units. $35–$59 double; $65–$80 suite. MC, V. **Amenities:** 2 restaurants (lobby and top floor); bikes; Internet; room service. *In room:* A/C, TV, fridge, minibar.

At Cua Dai Beach

The Cua Dai Beach area is lined with hotels, and surveyors are already lining up for future development. There's some decent swimming and a few very good, affordable accommodations.

Expensive

Golden Sand Resort (Swiss-Belhotel) ★ Kids During the day, sunshine floods into this hotel's gigantic, vaulted-ceiling lobby through big windows with lattice woodwork frames. The big fountain and oversized Chinese statues are less intimidating with all that sunshine. The resort is a large open campus on a cleared beach, and all rooms are set in big, square, three-story pavilions. I prefer Victoria Hoi An (see below), which has similar prices but where you are less likely to be sharing your vacation with a big, noisy tour group. Superior rooms are compact and far from the beach, with limited views (mostly of other superior blocks), but they are done in a clean light-wood interior with lots of good amenities. Deluxe rooms are larger versions of the same, with smart redwood consoles at the head of each bed and silk-lined lamps, like Bauhaus architecture trying to look Asian. Oceanside suites are absurdly luxurious, with Jacuzzis surrounded by granite tile and a bidet. The oceanside pool is enormous, 150m (490 ft.) long with funky little bridges spanning narrow channels and a good poolside bar and dining. Next to it is a mini–water park, with several slides and a big wading area, where all the ankle-biters happily splash about while Mom or Dad looks on from a chaise longue.

Thanh Nien Rd., Cua Dai Beach, Hoi An. ✆ **0510/392-7555.** Fax 0510/392-7560. www.swiss-belhotel.com. 212 units. $160 superior double; $210 deluxe double; $480 suite. AE, MC, V. **Amenities:** 2 restaurants (oceanside and in a large block near the lobby); babysitting; bikes; children's center; health club; Jacuzzi; 2 pools; room service; spa; tennis courts; watersports rentals. *In room:* A/C, TV, fridge, minibar, Wi-Fi.

Hoi An Beach Resort ★ Opened in 2000, this is the flagship of Hoi An Tourist, a government-owned company, and it's their answer to recent upscale development in town. The resort is across the road from Cua Dai Beach and close to the small restaurant row and popular tourist sunbathing area. Everything from the casual open-air restaurant to the more expensive rooms and suites faces the De Vong River as it approaches the sea, offering a unique glimpse of everyday riverside life. The hotel recently opened a bar and an upscale access point to the beach, where you can sit in private chairs without harassment from beachside sellers. All rooms here are nice, but the villas are certainly worth the extra few bucks: They're quite large, with high ceilings and large private balconies. Villas and suites have vaulted ceilings, and some have separate entrances with a shower area for cleanup after the beach. Service and general standards are comparable to the high-end competition in town. It's a popular choice for large European tours and can get a bit wild in the busy season, but it's all good fun. The pools are large, dining is good, and frequent shuttles run to town.

1 Cua Dai Beach. ✆ **0510/392-7011** or 392-7015. Fax 0510/392-7019. www.hoiantourist.com. 85 111 units. $148–$180 single/double garden deluxe; $215 oceanview and river-view villas; $280 suite. AE, MC, V. **Amenities:** Restaurant; bar; small health club; Internet; Jacuzzi; 2 outdoor pools; room service; sauna; spa; steam bath. *In room:* A/C, TV, fridge, hair dryer, minibar, Wi-Fi.

Palm Garden Resort ★ This large resort is much like the others (see the reviews for the Victoria, below, or the Golden Sand Resort/Swiss-Belhotel, above) along this open stretch of beach, but it has a bit more charm and thatch. Bungalows on the beach are the best bet and have cool Zen rock gardens at each entry and some laterite stone detail. Beach bungalows have air-conditioned bedrooms and open-air bathrooms with tubs. All rooms have balconies facing the beach—though in varying degrees of proximity. Deluxe rooms are set in four-unit hotel blocks and have no outdoor bathroom. The resort sits on wide, manicured lawns. The lobby is in a high open-air space with lots of light. Staff is as friendly as can be. They offer a host of good services and fine dining. The large pool is very inviting.

Lac Long Quan Rd., Cua Dai Beach (just 500m/1,640 ft. north of Cua Dai Beach, reached through a warren of streets). ✆ **0510/392-7927.** Fax 0510/392-7928. www.palmgardenresort.com.vn. 166 units. $90 standard double; $105–$135 superior; $180–$205 bungalow; $390–$500 suite. MC, V. **Amenities:** 3 restaurants; 2 bars; babysitting; bikes; children's center; health club; Internet; Jacuzzi; enormous outdoor pool; room service; spa sponsored by Shiseido; 2 tennis courts; watersports equipment. *In room:* A/C, TV, fridge, minibar, Wi-Fi.

Victoria Hoi An Resort ★★ The Victoria offers peace and palm trees, just a short ride (4.8km/3 miles) from ancient Hoi An. The resort has all the amenities and lots of activities, and begs for at least a few days' stay. Rooms are either the bungalow variety, in low-slung beachside buildings, or set in parallel two-story rows to mimic Hoi An's ancient streets—the latter are not displeasing, but a bit like a theme park. Prices reflect beachside proximity. Design and layout vary widely from room to room; some are decorated in French country style, with canopy beds and wicker furniture, and others are unique Japanese rooms, with open-timber construction, bamboo floors, and tearooms hidden behind sliding doors. Bathrooms are large and spacious, except for those in superior rooms, which are a bit crowded and have no tubs. My Japanese-style bungalow was done in warm tones of pale green and maroon, and came with an outdoor rain shower set in an enclosed central courtyard. There's a certain flow to the public spaces here—from beach to garden and from rooms to common spaces (including a small billiards room with gaming tables and reading nooks)—that invites guests to wander; it's all connected by stone paths. Convenient shuttles connect to town frequently, or you can rent a motorcycle with sidecar.

Cua Dai Beach, 5km (3 miles) from Hoi An. ✆ **0510/392-7040.** Fax 0510/392-7041. www.victoriahotels-asia.com. 109 units. $170–$225 double; $300–$305 suite. MC, V. **Amenities:** Restaurant; 3 bars; babysitting; children's play area; health club; Internet; Jacuzzi; small library; outdoor pool (beachside); room service; spa; 2 tennis courts. *In room:* A/C, TV/DVD (in suites), movie library (in suites), fridge, minibar, Wi-Fi.

Moderate

Dong An River Beach Resort ★ If you're looking for beach access at a budget rate, Dong An might be your best choice. It attracts large groups at cut-rate prices; if you contact the hotel directly, you might get a good contract rate. Rooms are set in a large U shape around a central courtyard with a smallish pool. The staff is surly, but it's understandable, considering the daily plague of locusts ascending. Though not spectacular, rooms are tidy and you're just a stone's throw from the Cua Dai Beach. This is like a high-end minihotel set in a larger-hotel atmosphere. Plan to use the services—travel agents, car rental, and dining—elsewhere, but this is a fine place to lay your head near the beach.

5 Cua Dai Beach (4km/2½ miles from Hoi An Old Town), Hoi An. ✆ **0510/392-7888.** Fax 0510/392-7777. www.donganbeachhotel.com.vn. 88 units. $110–$160 double; $180–$285 suite. MC, V. **Amenities:** Restaurant/bar; bike; small central pool. *In room:* A/C, TV, fridge, minibar, Wi-Fi.

WHERE TO DINE

Hoi An is a feast for the stomach as well as the eyes. Local specialties include *cao lau* (rice noodles with fresh greens, rice crackers, and croutons), white rose dumplings of shrimp in clear rice dough, and large, savory fried won tons. Good, fresh seafood is available everywhere (don't miss the morning market). There are some new high-end options in town alongside some popular standbys, and each of the resorts has its own fine dining (see above). The riverfront road, Bach Dang, has become the de facto "restaurant row," and below are listed a few good spots, but if you take a stroll down here any time in the day, you're sure to be besieged by some friendly but persistent touts who'll drag you bodily into their restaurants. All the places along Bach Dang are comparable in price and cuisine (fried rice and noodles), and it's sometimes fun to let the restaurant choose you.

Note: If you do eat on Bach Dang, choose a table a bit off the street and say a consistent and calm "No" to the many young Tiger Balm and chewing-gum salesman if you'd like a quiet meal.

Expensive

Brother's Café ★★ VIETNAMESE Serving similar fine Vietnamese fare as its sister restaurant in Hanoi (but here it's a la carte, not buffet), Brother's Café is a great choice for cuisine and atmosphere. A bland streetside facade gives way to the lush garden sanctuary formed by this grand U-shape colonial by the river. Indoor seating is upscale Indochina of a bygone era, and the courtyard is dotted with canvas umbrellas to while away a balmy afternoon or enjoy a candlelit evening riverside. The fare is gourmet Vietnamese at its finest, with great specials; be sure to ask for a recommendation. It's a good place to try local items like the white rose, a light Vietnamese ravioli, or *cao lao* noodles. Set menus are great here and change daily. With a group, this is a great spot to order up family style and sample it all. They also feature a cooking school (just ask the staff). Everything's good, the atmosphere is great, and the staff couldn't be friendlier.

27 Phan Boi Chau St. ✆ **0510/391-4150.** Main courses $6–$15; set menu $30. AE, MC, V. Daily 10am–11pm.

Nam Long ★ VIETNAMESE The owners of Brother's Café (see above) stake out a claim on Cua Dai Road. This is the place to come for a secluded, riverside view. A hostess greets you out front and leads you through the front garden, past wild lilies, palm trees, and orchids floating in water vessels. The indoor seating is nicer than at Brother's, with dark wooden chairs with double happiness symbols carved into the back, and subdued lighting throughout. However, it's better to stake out a table on the outdoor patio. Food and staff are as fabulous and friendly as at Brother's.

103 Cua Dai St. ✆ **0510/392-3723.** Main courses $6–$18. AE, MC, V. Daily 10am–10pm.

Song Hoai, The Saigon Times Club ★★ VIETNAMESE Set in the most picturesque period building in town, on a corner overlooking riverside Bach Dang, this Saigon-managed restaurant is as much about atmosphere as it is about dining. Rivaled only by Brother's (see above), the two open floors here reflect true old Hoi An elegance. The second floor has great views of the river and is dramatic, with a high, exposed-tile ceiling and languid ceiling fans. I had the Vietnamese-style ravioli and the local white rose specialty, and enjoyed fresh pan-fried shrimp. They serve regional dishes like Hanoi *cha ca* and *mi quang* wide noodles. Presentation is arguably the classiest in town, with fine china, stemware, and lacquered dishes on linen, and the service is professional, if a bit hovering. A good choice for a romantic evening of fine dining, Hoi An style.

119–121 Nguyen Thai Hoc (riverside). ✆ **0510/391-0369.** Fax 0510/391-0436. Main courses 50,000 VND–300,000 VND. AE, MC, V. Daily 10am–10pm.

Tam-Tam Café ★★ ITALIAN/CONTINENTAL Tam-Tam is the place to be in Hoi An. The brainchild of three French expats, it is historic and laid-back, serving good, familiar food. The decor is authentic local style, with hanging bamboo lamps, a high wooden ceiling, and fantastic wooden figurines. The dinner menu, served in a separate restaurant room with checkered tablecloths, is simple—featuring generous portions of homemade pastas, steaks, and salads—but the food is delicious. The dessert menu includes flambéed crepes, sorbet, and hot chocolate. There are two barrooms: The bigger one to the left of the entry has a pool table, a book-swap shelf, comfortable lounge chairs, and sofas, and is the place to hang out in Hoi An. The extensive drink menu features all kinds of bang-for-the-buck rum specials, and there's even a small counter on the balcony where you can sip a cocktail and watch life go by on the street below. Even if just for a coffee, don't miss this place.

110 Nguyen Thai Hoc St. (on the 2nd floor). ✆ **0510/386-2212.** Main courses 25,000 VND–170,000 VND. AE, MC, V. Daily 8am–2am.

Moderate

Café des Amis ★★ VIETNAMESE What's on the menu? There isn't one. It's your choice of a set menu, either seafood or vegetarian, and the details are, well, a surprise. And the surprise is always good, one of the best meals in Vietnam, if you ask me. But don't ask me. Read the straight dope from the many guests who come and sign their endorsements in Mr. Kim's lengthy guest book (you'll be asked to sign, too, of course). I enjoyed a leisurely meal starting with a savory clear soup, fried won tons with shrimp, broiled fish, stuffed calamari, and scallops on the half shell. Sit back and surrender yourself to the surprises of the effusive Mr. Kim and his attentive staff. He is careful to explain the intricacies of each dish and even demonstrates how to eat some of the more unique entrees. A meal here makes for a memorable evening.

52 Bach Dang. ✆ **0510/386-1616.** Set menu 120,000 VND. No credit cards. Daily 8am–10pm.

Cafeteria 22 (Miss Ly's) ★ The menu here is limited, but that means everything is always available and fresh in this little hole-in-the wall cafe in the heart of the old town. Cafeteria 22 is the best place in Hoi An to try the town's famous fried won tons, a rice pastry stuffed with meat, shrimp, and onion and topped with Ly's special sauce, onion, and tomato—messy and delicious. Ly has been at it for over 10 years now and has just the right formula. There's nothing fancy here, and that is the appeal for folks who tire easily of trumped-up atmosphere and overpriced, altered versions of local fare. Come meet Ly and try the real deal.

22 Nguyen Hue St., Hoi An. ✆ **0510/386-1603.** Main courses 20,000 VND–90,000 VND. No credit cards. Daily 8:30am–10pm.

Goda ★ FUSION A crossroads of Vietnam and the West, this locally owned cafe offers a good host of specials: papaya salad, hot pots, local stews, and stir-fries, as well as burgers, pasta, and pizza. But because it's Vietnamese-owned and -run, it's best to stick with local dishes (though locals who come here all eat the very average pizza). The place is a contemporary, chic, two-story cafe with a big winding staircase and good jazz music piped in. Located on Cua Dai Street about halfway between the town and the beach, it's a good stop on the way back from the beach for coffee. Bad English writing on the menu about the philosophy of the place, with far too many adjectives, begs for editing. Offer to do it and they'll buy you a drink. Goda is a good laid-back place to meet locals.

308 Cua Dai St., Cam Chau Ward. ✆ **0510/392-3644.** www.goda.biz. Main courses $3–$15. No credit cards. Daily 8am–11pm.

Hoi An Cargo Club and Patisserie ★★ INTERNATIONAL This stylish storefront serves light meals in a lounge bar on the first floor and, upstairs, is a refined restaurant specializing in contemporary Vietnamese cuisine. There are good seafood dishes like the crab in five spices or jumbo shrimp with tamarind sauce. Sandwiches, soups, and salads are served with fine fresh bread that's baked on-site. Upstairs seating is on a cool balcony overlooking the river or a chic indoor space, and the first floor offers casual bar or lounge seating. Curries and good veggie dishes round out a good, affordable menu. They also have the best pastries in southern Vietnam. Cargo Club is a good place to reconnoiter if traveling in a group or to meet other travelers.

107–109 Nguyen Thai Hoc. ✆ **0510/391-0489.** www.hoianhospitality.com. Main courses 75,000 VND–195,000 VND. MC, V. Daily 8am–11pm.

Mango Mango ★★ Finds VIETNAMESE/FUSION North of the Thu Bon River is *so* done. This new restaurant, from lively owner Duc of Mango Rooms fame (see below), is a gem of an addition to Hoi An's dining scene. It has fantastic views of the Japanese Bridge and the river, but without the persistent hawkers that can disrupt your dining experience along Bach Dang Street. Mango Mango's whitewashed walls and orange trim give the place a cool hacienda vibe. The menu's sandwich options make it a good option for lunch. For larger mains, try "keeping flower ly," prawns seasoned in a savory sauce of white wine, passion fruit, butter, and garlic with a hint of chocolate. The dish is an homage to Duc's lovely wife. Come after dark to indulge in cocktails, good music, and the great view.

45 Nguyen Phuc Chu (across the river from the Japanese Bridge). ✆ **0510/391-1863.** Main courses 60,000 VND–220,000 VND. No credit cards. Daily 8am–midnight.

Mango Rooms ★★ VIETNAMESE/FUSION This is the hippest little restaurant between Ho Chi Minh and Hanoi. Owner and chef Duc spent his formative years in Texas before earning his stripes in hotels and fine-dining establishments. He brings to Hoi An his own blend of cuisines, putting words like *salsa* and Vietnamese *nuoc mam* (fish sauce) in jarring juxtaposition, and serving up cool combinations of California cuisine, down-home barbecue, and Pacific Rim—all stylishly presented in a fashion that would make the grade among the finest bistros of New York or San Francisco (he calls it "Vietnamese with a twist served California-style"). Duc runs the show from an open central kitchen and greets guests with a flamboyant, "Oh man, we're rockin' tonight!" as he steps out from behind the grill to see if he can help you find a seat and tempt you with some new idea. Try the likes of La Tropicana, a chicken breast with lemon grass and garlic; the "Asian Sins" of rice noodles pan-fried with vegetables, garlic, onion, and sweet basil; or seared tuna in rice paper. There are fresh-fish specials daily. The drink list is long and the cocktails divine. Try the delicious sticky rice with mango for dessert.

111 Nguyen Thai Hoc (with an entrance on riverside Bach Dang next to the Saigon Times Club and just across from Tam-Tam Café). ✆ **0510/391-0839.** Main courses 175,000 VND–300,000 VND. No credit cards. Daily 8am–midnight.

The Mermaid (Nhu Y) Restaurant ★★ VIETNAMESE This quiet spot in the heart of downtown is an ivy-draped, unassuming storefront that serves some of the best authentic Vietnamese food in town (for next to nothing). If you like what you eat, stick around and take a **cooking class** in the large adjoining kitchen that's open to the street: Here's a unique chance to bring some of Vietnam home to your kitchen. I had a scrumptious tuna filet cooked in a banana leaf with turmeric. The spring rolls are light and fresh, with a whole jumbo shrimp in each, and they serve the most unique dish, called white eggplant: It's eggplant covered in spring onion, garlic, and chili, and then pressed, sliced, and served in a light oil. Everything is good. The staff members also teach the class and are very friendly and can explain it all.

2 Tran Phu St. ✆ **0510/386-1527.** www.hoianhospitality.com. Main courses 32,000 VND–78,000 VND. No credit cards. Daily 10am–10pm.

Morning Glory ★★ VIETNAMESE This is crown jewel of local restaurateur Ms. Vy's empire (owner of the Mermaid, White Lantern, and Hoi An Cargo Club). The two-story restaurant is housed in an old colonial building in the heart of Hoi An's old district. It features an open kitchen on the ground floor, large dining areas on both floors, and a trio of tables on the balcony upstairs. The menu is a delightful selection of Vietnamese street food; it includes tips and recommendations from Ms. Vy on the health properties of ingredients (for example, for cooling the body in hot weather, try the traditional dessert *Che,* made with soft tofu and ginger syrup). Order the morning glory sautéed with garlic for a healthy boost of leafy greens. For mains, I highly recommend the caramelized fish in a clay pot—the portion is a bit small, so if you don't want to share, order two—and the *banh xeo* (crepe-style pancakes stuffed with shrimp, bean sprouts, and other veggies). This restaurant is an absolute must-visit.

106 Nguyen Thai Hoc St. ✆ **0510/324-1555.** Main courses 45,000 VND–195,000 VND. MC, V. Daily 9am–10pm.

River Lounge ★ Finds FUSION A menu designed and implemented by a Michelin-star chef? Yes, please! River Lounge is part of the new crop of hip places cropping up north of the river. Where its neighbor Mango Mango (see above) is all casual riverside eatery, River Lounge is channeling a Café Ibiza–meets–James Blunt kind of atmosphere. The interior is minimalist white, with turquoise scrawlings on the walls and overstuffed daybeds and lounge chairs upstairs. For dinner, the three-course set menu featuring Hoi An's lovely seafood is a steal at 110,000 VND. The menu is fusion with a healthy representation of Vietnamese influences. The owners are a pair of Austrian brothers, so it should come as no surprise that they also serve excellent Euro fare such as Wiener schnitzel, linzer cake, and the best Italian coffee in town.

35 Nguyen Phuc Chu. ✆ **0510/391-1700.** Main courses 75,000 VND–158,000 VND; set menu 110,000 VND. No credit cards. Daily 8:30am–midnight.

The White Lantern ★★ VIETNAMESE This is a very popular tour group stop, so try to get there early (or late); if you see buses parked out front, head for the hills. Everyone's here for good reason, though: delicious, affordable Vietnamese cuisine and a mellow atmosphere. Strumming guitarists roam the tables playing old Beatles melodies and some nice local numbers, and the large open area on the first floor, with long tables for groups, and the second-floor balcony space are dimly lit and romantic. Owned by the same folks that run the Mermaid (Nhu Y), discussed above, this is a slightly upscale version. Set menus are a great bet; I had a fine meal of a delicate won-ton soup, spring rolls, and chicken in a light curry. It's a good find just north of the town center.

710 Hai Ba Trung St. ✆ **0510/386-3023.** Main courses 28,000 VND–145,000 VND; set menu 80,000 VND. MC, V. Daily 7am–10pm.

Inexpensive

Bale Well ★★ VIETNAMESE Bale Well is the epitome of local dining, but they're quite used to foreign visitors and make you feel right at home. This is your chance to experience squat stools and dining at streetside, but with a good standard of cleanliness ensured. The meal is simple: a set menu of *nem nuong,* the kind of spring rolls that you make yourself, rolling chicken, beef, or pork with fresh greens and condiments into sheets of rice paper. You might also want to try the good pork satay, savory *banh xeo* (pancakes), or good fried spring rolls. The restaurant is in a little alley just off of Tran Hung Dao Street. The sign is more or less hidden, as if to say, "If you know where you're going, you're here."

45–51 Tran Hung Dao St. ✆ **0510/386-4443.** Set menu 50,000 VND. No credit cards. Daily 9am–9pm.

Van Loc ★ VIETNAMESE Pull up a chair and try the special, *cao lau,* a thick but tender white noodle in light soy with fresh vegetables, garnish, and croutons. This is where the locals eat it. It's an open-air place, and the atmosphere is a little rough, but they serve a nice selection of local favorites, too, all for next to nothing. The portions are big and everything's authentic, right down to the kindness in this little mom-and-pop. There are no touts here—it's the food that brings 'em in.

27 Tran Phu. ✆ **0510/386-1212.** Main courses 25,000 VND–50,000 VND. No credit cards. Daily 8am–8pm.

ATTRACTIONS

The whole town is an attraction, its narrow streets comprised of lovely historic buildings buzzing with open-air craft shops, woodworkers, and carvers. Tran Phu and Nguyen Thai Hoc streets are crowded with the shops of the original Chinese merchants and clan associations. Most Hoi An buildings have been lovingly restored and transformed into cafes, art galleries, and silk and souvenir shops, while still retaining their historical dignity. If you're an artist, bring your sketch pad and watercolors; photographers, bring plenty of film or an extra memory card.

The Hoi An World Cultural Heritage Organization (www.hoianworldheritage.org) has the dilemma of financing the restorations and maintaining the old portions of the town. They sell a 75,000 VND ticket that allows limited admission to the sights within the old town, each of which is listed below. "Limited" means a "one from column A, one from column B" formula. One ticket gets you one of the three museums, one of the three assembly halls, and one of the four old houses; entrance to a handicraft workshop and traditional music concert (10:15am and 3:15pm, respectively, Tues–Sun); plus a choice of either the Japanese Bridge, the Quan Kong Temple, or the local handicraft workshop.

So to see everything, you'll have to purchase three tickets. The three-star choices in each category are your best bet if you don't have time to see it all.

Museums

Museum of History and Culture ★ This tottering building erected in 1653 houses works that cross 2,000 years of Hoi An history from Cham relics to ancient ceramics and photos of local architecture. There are English explanations, but they are scanty. If you're seeing only one museum, make it the Museum of Trade Ceramics (see below). One interesting tidbit: The name Hoi An literally means "Water Convergence" and "Peace."

7 Nguyen Hue St. (7 is the official address, but it's actually the building on the south side of 11 Nguyen Hue St.). Daily 8am–5pm.

Museum of Trade Ceramics ★★★ Located in a traditional house, this museum describes the origins of Hoi An as a trade port and displays its most prominent trade item. Objects are from the 13th through 17th centuries and include Chinese and Thai works as well. While many of the exhibits are in fragments, the real beauty of the place is that the very thorough descriptions are in English, giving you a real sense of the town's origins and history. Furthermore, the architecture and renovations of the old house are thoroughly explained, and you're free to wander through its two floors, courtyard, and anteroom. After all the scattered explanations at the other historic houses, you'll finally get a sense of what Hoi An architecture is all about.

80 Tran Phu St. Daily 8am–5pm.

The Sa Huynh Culture Museum ★ After local farmers around Hoi An dug up some strange-looking pottery, archaeologists identified 53 sites where a pre-Cham people, called the Sa Huynh, buried their dead in ceramic jars. The two-room display here includes some of the burial jars, beaded ornaments, pottery vessels, and iron tools and weapons that have been uncovered. English descriptions are sketchy. Upstairs, the little-visited Museum of the Revolution includes such intriguing items as the umbrella "which Mr. Truong Munh Luong used for acting a fortune-teller to act revolution from 1965 to 1967." Huh? This is for connoisseurs only.

149 Tran Phu St. Daily 8am–6pm.

The Old Houses

The Old House of Phun Hung ★ This private house, constructed in 1780, is two floors of combined architectural influences. The first floor's central roof is four-sided, showing Japanese influence, and the upstairs balcony has a Chinese rounded "turtle shell" roof with carved beam supports. The house has weathered many floods. In 1964, during a particularly bad bout, its third floor served as a refuge for other town families. The upstairs is outfitted with a trapdoor for moving furniture rapidly to safety. You might be shown around by Ms. Anh, who claims to be an eighth-generation member of the family. Tour guides at every house make such claims; however, like at many of Hoi An's old houses, the family really does seem to live here.

4 Nguyen Thi Minh Khai St. Daily 8am–5pm.

The Old House of Tan Ky ★ There have been either five or seven generations of Tans living here, depending on whom you speak with. Built over 200 years ago, the four small rooms are crammed with dark-wood antiques. The room closest to the street is for greeting visiting merchants. Farther in is the living room, then the courtyard, and, to the back, the bedroom. The first three are open to the public. A guide who will greet you at the door will hasten to explain how the house is a perfect melding of three architectural styles: ornate Chinese detailing on some curved roof beams, a Japanese peaked roof, and a simple Vietnamese cross-hatch roof support. The mosaic decorations on the wall and furniture are aged, intricate, and amazing. Take your time looking around.

101 Nguyen Thai Hoc St. Daily 8am–5pm.

The Tran Family Home and Chapel ★★ In 1802, a civil service mandarin named Tran Tu Nhuc built a family home and chapel to worship his ancestors. A favorite of Viet Emperor Gia Long, he was sent to China as an ambassador, and his home reflects his high status. Elegantly designed with original Chinese antiques and royal gifts such as swords, two parts of the home are open to the public: a drawing room and an ancestral chapel. One roof tile has been replaced with transparent glass, allowing a single shaft of light to slice through the chapel and onto the altar in the morning. The house does a splendid job of conveying all that is exotic and interesting about these people and their period. The drawing room has three sections of sliding doors: the left for men, the right for women, and the center, open only at Tet and other festivals, for dead ancestors to return home. The ancestral altar in the inner room has small boxes behind it containing relics and a biography of the deceased; their pictures hang, a little spookily, to the right of the altar. A 250-year-old book with the family history resides on a table to the right of the altar. Beside it is a small bowl, containing yin and yang coins, meant to bring good luck. Give them a toss, and if they land one yin and one yang side up, you are on your way to prosperity. I got it on my first try, but the guide will give you three chances. In back of the house are a row of plants, each buried with the placenta and umbilical cord of a family child, so that the child will never forget its home. As if it could.

21 Le Loi (on the corner of Le Loi and Phan Chu Trinh sts.). Daily 8am–5pm.

The Assembly Halls

Cantonese Assembly Hall (Quang Trieu/Guangzhou Assembly Hall) Built in 1885, this hall is quite ornate and colorful. All of the building materials were completed in China, brought here, and then reassembled. The center garden sports a fountain with a dragon made of chipped pottery, the centerpiece. Inside, look for the statues depicting scenes from famous Cantonese operas and, in the rooms to each side, the ancestral tablets of generations past.

176 Tran Phu St. Daily 8am–6pm.

Fukian Assembly Hall (Phuc Kien) This is the grandest of the assembly halls, built in 1697 by Chinese merchants from Fukian Province. It is a showpiece of classical Chinese architecture, at least after you pass the first gate, which was added in 1975. It's loaded with animal themes: The fish in the mosaic fountain symbolizes scholarly achievement, the unicorn flanking the ascending stairs symbolizes wisdom, the dragon symbolizes power, the turtle symbolizes longevity, and the phoenix symbolizes nobility. The main temple is dedicated to Thien Hau, goddess of the sea, on the main altar. To the left of her is Thuan Phong Nhi, a goddess who can hear ships in a range of thousands of miles, and on the right is Thien Ly Nhan, who can see them. Go around the altar for a view of a fantastic detailed miniature boat. There are two altars to the rear of the temple: the one on the left honoring a god of prosperity and the one on the right honoring a goddess of fertility. The goddess of fertility is often visited by local couples hoping for children. She is flanked by 12 fairies or midwives, one responsible for each of a baby's functions: smiling, sleeping, eating, and so forth.

46 Tran Phu St. Daily 7am–6pm.

Other Sites

Japanese Covered Bridge ★★★ The name of this bridge in Vietnamese, Lai Vien Kieu, means "Pagoda in Japan." No one is exactly sure who first built it in the early 1600s (it has since been renovated several times), but it is usually attributed to Hoi An's Japanese community. The dog flanking one end and the monkey at the other are considered to be sacred animals to the ancient Japanese, and my guide claimed the reasoning is that most Japanese emperors were born in the year of either the monkey or the dog by the Asian zodiac. Later I read something else that claimed maybe it meant construction began in the year of the dog and was completed in the year of the monkey. I'm sure there are many other interesting dog and monkey stories going around. Pick your favorite. The small temple inside is dedicated to Tran Vo Bac De, god of the north, beloved (or cursed) by sailors because he controls the weather.

At the west end of Tran Phu St.

Quan Kong Temple ★ This temple was built in the early 1600s to honor a famous Chin dynasty general. Highlights inside are two gargantuan 3m-high (9¾-ft.) wooden statues flanking the main altar, one of Quan Kong's protector and one of his adopted son. They are fearsome and impressive. Reportedly the temple was a stop for merchants who came in from the nearby river to pay their respects and pray for the general's attributes of loyalty, bravery, and virtue.

168 Tran Phu St. (on the corner of Nguyen Hue). Daily 8am–5pm.

Attractions Not on the World Cultural Heritage Ticket

Central Market ★★ If you see one Vietnamese market, make it this one, by the river on the southeast side of the city. There are endless stalls of exotic foodstuffs and services, and a special big shed for silk tailoring at the east end (these tailors charge much less than the ones along Le Loi). Check out the ladies selling spices—curries, chili powders, cinnamon, peppercorns, and especially saffron—at prices that are a steal in the West. But don't buy from the first woman you see; the stuff gets cheaper and cheaper the deeper you go into the market. Walk out to the docks to see activity there (best early in the morning), but be careful of fish flying through the air, and stand back from the furious bargaining (best before 7am).

At Nguyen Hue and Tran Phu sts. along the Thu Bon River.

Hoi An Cathedral The only spectacular thing about this Catholic cathedral is its resilience. Originally built in 1903, the structure was rebuilt in 1964 with the influx of greater numbers of Catholics seeking refuge from persecution in the North. There's a small orphanage out back, and this stalwart working cathedral ministers to more than an estimated 1,000 patricians in the area. Sunday Mass—delivered in Vietnamese—is a well-attended affair. If you go, have a look at the cool contemporary stained glass depicting the early French missionaries alighting in Hoi An.

Just north of the town center on the corner of Le Hong Phong and Nguyen Trung To. Services Mon–Sat 5am and 5pm; Sun 5:30am and 4pm.

House of Hoi An Traditional Handicraft ★★ This is basically a silk shop with an interesting gimmick: On the first floor you can see both a 17th-century silk loom and a working, machine-powered cotton one. On the second, you can see where silk comes from: There are trays of silkworms feeding, then a rack of worms incubating, and then a tub of hot water where the pupae's downy covering is rinsed off and then pulled, strand by strand, onto a large skein. They have the best selection of silks, both fine and raw, in many colors and weights good for clothing and for home interiors.

41 Le Loi St. Daily 8am–5pm.

HITTING THE BEACH

Cua Dai Beach ★★ is a 25-minute bicycle ride from Hoi An on a busy road with vistas of lagoons, rice paddies, and stilt houses. Simply follow Tran Hung Dao Street to Cua Dai Street to the east of town and follow for 3km (1¾ miles). The beach is thin and crowded with hawkers, but there are cozy deck chairs (for a small fee), and the sand, surf, and setting, with views of the nearby Cham Islands, are worth the trip. Tour companies tout boat excursions in season (Mar–Sept) to the Cham Islands, a group of seven islands about 13km (8 miles) east of Hoi An; prices vary, but expect to pay about 30,000 VND. Contact the traveler cafes in town. There are also boat trips on the Thu Bon River from town; just walk along central Bach Dang near the river, and the boatmen will find you.

CHAM ISLAND TOUR

Just 5km (3 miles) off the shore of Cua Dai Beach (see above), Cham Island is a quiet little fishing area populated by ethnic Cham people, an Austro-Asiatic group that fought the north Vietnamese for this territory for centuries (see the box "Who Are the Cham?" on p. 206). A tour to Cham Island costs just peanuts and takes half a day; you can make arrangements with sign-waving touts on Cua Dai Beach who will putt-putt you out on tour boats, and some travelers start their trip on the river right in the center of Hoi An and travel by boat to the sea before transferring out into the bay. Contact any hotel front desk or talk with the boatmen themselves at riverside along Bach Dang in Hoi An town. Expect to pay about $10 for one person from town to the beach.

For a bit of an adventure, contact the effusive Mr. Lodovico, an Italian expat of 10 years in Hoi An and the owner and operator of **LaoCham Sailing Club Hoi An.** His office is at 98 Bach Dang St. (✆ **0510/391-0782**), near the Saigon Times Restaurant. For trips starting at $30 per person for an all-day excursion, you can explore, with a knowledgeable English-speaking guide, the high seas off the coast of Cua Dai, visit with a Cham family for a brief homestay, and snorkel on remote island areas. The trip can be done as an overnight, staying either in LaoCham's simple but cozy guesthouse on Cham Island or with a family, and Lodovico even runs special sailing trips on small local sailers for the adventurous.

AN EXCURSION TO MY SON ★★

My Son, some 40km (25 miles) from Hoi An (and 71km/44 miles from Danang), is an important temple ruin of the Cham people, a once powerful Hindu empire. The temples were constructed as a religious center for citizens of the Cham capital, Danang, from the 7th through 12th centuries during the height of Cham supremacy. My Son (pronounced *Mee sun*) might also have been used as a burial site for Cham kings after cremation. Originally there were over 70 towers and monuments at the site, but bombing during the war with America (the Viet Cong used My Son as a munitions warehouse) has sadly reduced many to rubble. Additionally, many of the smaller structures and most decorative carvings have been removed to the Cham Museum in Danang. The complex is a very serene and spiritual setting, however, and what does remain is powerful and evocative. It's not hard to imagine what a wonder My Son must once have been. The site is deep in the Truong Son Cordillera, and the main temples overlook the 350m (1,148-ft.) Mount Chua, "Mountain of the Gods." My Son is a designated UNESCO World Heritage Site.

The earliest temple constructions are from the 4th century A.D., but much of what remains today are structures built or renovated during the 10th century A.D., when the cult of Shiva, founder and protector of the kingdom, was predominant in the Cham court. Each group had at least the following structures: a **kalan,** or main tower; a gate tower in front of that, with two entrances; a **mandapa,** or meditation hall; and a repository building for offerings. Some have towers sheltering stele with kingly epitaphs. A brick wall encircles the compound.

Architecturally, the temple complex shows Indian influences. Each temple grouping is a microcosm of the world. The foundations are Earth, the square bases are the temple itself, and the pointed roofs symbolize the heavens. The entrance of the main tower faces east, and surrounding smaller towers represent each continent. A trench, representing the oceans, surrounds each group. Vietnamese architecture is represented in decorative patterns and boat-shape roofs. The temple compound is divided into a number of "Groups" built by successive Cham kings and designated by French archaeologist Henri Parmentier with letters of the alphabet. Group A is the most dynamic.

Group A originally had 13 towers. A-1, the main tower, was a 21m-tall (69-ft.) masterpiece before it was destroyed in 1969. Group B bears the marks of Indian and Indonesian influence. Note that B-6 holds a water repository for statue-washing ceremonies. Its roof is carved with an image of the god Vishnu sitting beneath a 13-headed snake god, or **naga.** Group C generally followed an earlier architectural style called Hoa Lai, which predominated from the 8th century to the beginning of the 9th. Groups G and H were the last to be built, at around the end of the 13th century.

Arrange a half-day trip to My Son with any tourist agent in Hoi An (p. 212). Entrance to the site is 50,000 VND, and a private half-day tour with a guide is $35 for a car and $43 for a van. The half-day seat-in-coach tour by Sinh Café costs $2 per person and is nothing more than a ride there, without any explanations. Less frequent tours also depart from Danang (70km/43 miles from the site).

SHOPPING

Southeast Asia is packed with would-be Buddhists, travelers on a real spiritual mission espousing lives of detachment from material desires. These folks usually walk away with just the "one suit, two shirts, trousers, and a tie" package when they leave Hoi An. Shopaholics wander the streets in a daze.

Hoi An is a silk mecca. The quality and selection are the best in the country, and you'll have more peace and quiet here during a fitting than in Hanoi. **Silk suits** are made to order within 24 hours for about $35; **cashmere wool** is $45. There are countless shops, and the tailoring is all about the same quality and fast. A good way to choose a shop is by what you see out front—if you see a style you like, it'll help with ordering. Make sure you take the time to specify your style, down to the stitch (it can come back looking pretty cheap without specifics). Try any of the shops along Le Loi; to recommend one in particular would be like recommending one snowflake over another. The tailoring is very fast but not always great, so plan to have two or three fittings. Be choosy about your cloth, or go to the market and buy it yourself (**Hoi An Cloth Market** is at 01 Tran Phu St.), and haggle. It's not a bad idea to bring an actual suit or piece of clothing that you'd like a copy of. Get measurements from friends and relatives for good gifts.

There are also skilled cobblers who make custom shoes at affordable rates. Find them near the market on Tran Phu Street.

Tran Phu Street is lined with **art galleries** and good **pottery** and **woodcarving** vendors. Along the river, lots of places sell blue-and-white **ceramics.** However cumbersome your finds are, such as those lovely **Chinese lanterns,** shopkeepers are masters at packing for travel and to fit in your luggage, and will do so before you've even agreed on a price or decided to buy. Haggle hard.

Hand-painted **Chinese scrolls** make a great souvenir, and down the street from the Hung Long Art Gallery (see below), Mr. Ly Si Binh (21 Nguyen Thai Hoc St.; ✆ **0510/391-0721**) can script anything from *peace* or *determination* to your best buddy's name in Chinese (if it's wrong, he won't know the difference anyway). And it's fun to watch cheery Mr. Binh at work.

Note: Unless otherwise noted, most stores listed below are open from 8am to late evening (around 9pm), but hours can and do vary.

Bambou Company Bambou produces their own unique T-shirts with local themes and designs, all in real cotton with big Western sizes available. They also have cool Asian-inspired clothes, like string-button Chinese shirts and loose travel togs like fishermen's pants and loose shirts. 96 Nguyen Thai Hoc St.

Hanh Hung This is one of the best of the town's many budget tailor shops. Ms. Hung is friendly, speaks English well, and cuts good budget deals or can do higher-quality work with better materials for just a hitch more. You can't miss this two-story, neon-lit place on the corner of Phan Dinh Phung and Nhi Trung, or at 02 Le Loi (also near Phan Dinh Phung). It's open daily from 8:30am to 10pm. 103 Tran Hung Dao St. ✆ **0510/391-0456.**

Hung Long Art Gallery This popular gallery features fine lacquer-works by artist Nguyen Trung Viet. These stylized images, mostly of young women, are quite appealing. Prices are affordable and they can ship anywhere on the globe. 105 Nguyen Thai Hoc St. ✆ **0510/386-1524.**

Yaly Couture If you're confused by the glut of small tailor storefronts and wonder about the quality of the work, Yaly Couture is your answer. Yes, the prices are higher, but quality comes with more of a guarantee and the same efficient service (12-hr. turnaround for a new suit). Also try their many ready-to-wear items in the small showroom at the town center. Good track record. 47 Nguyen Thai Hoc: ✆ **0510/391-0474.** 47 Tran Phu: ✆ **0510/386-1119.** 358 Nguyen Duy Hieu: **0510/391-5999.**

COOKING COURSES

Miss Vy's School of Cooking Recently relocated to Morning Glory restaurant, the cookery school is just your chance to meet Hoi An's diva, the stylish and effusive Ms. Vy, who nearly has the market cornered on good dining in Hoi An. Come find out her secrets. The tour starts early with a visit to the market and then returns to the restaurant by cyclo for a morning of cooking. The payoff is eating your creations.

109 Nguyen Thai Hoc. ✆ **0510/3910-489.** http://hoianhospitality.com. Call or contact them through their website for advance booking.

Red Bridge Cooking School This half-day morning cooking class from Hai Scout Café starts with a trip to the market and then takes you by boat (25 min.) back to the cafe, where you spend the rest of your time cooking and eating a big lunch. The course finishes at 1pm and requires a minimum of two students.

Thon 4, Cam Thanh, Hoi An. ✆ **0510/3933-222.** www.visithoian.com.

HOI AN AFTER DARK

For the most part, Hoi An is a town that sleeps early, but you can find a few good night-spots. **Tam-Tam Café** (see "Where to Dine," earlier in this section) has long been a popular spot for travelers, expats, and locals. **Hai Scout Cafe** (98 Nguyen Thai Hoc St.; ✆ **0510/386-3210**) is a popular late-night hangout for travelers, offering standard bar drinks as well as cappuccino and espresso and some great baked treats. Friendly Hai runs the show at this long-popular courtyard bar and cafe, where, as the Beastie Boys say, "The candlelight is just right, the hi-fi is in the background, and the wine is delicious." **Treat's Same Same Café** (158 Tran Phu St., at the intersection with Le Loi; ✆ **0510/386-1125**) is also usually hopping as late as it can and has a pool table and a guillotine (for show, of course). Also check out **Treat's Same Same Not Different Bar** at 93 Tran Hung Dao St. (✆ **0510/386-2278**), which is, in a word, similar. **ChamPa** (75 Nguyen Thai Hoc; ✆ **0510/386-2974**) has comfy chairs, good wine, and a cozy, late-night atmosphere with frequent cultural dance performances. **Mango Rooms** (111 Nguyen Thai Hoc; ✆ **0510/391-0839**) is the town's most popular little bistro and gathering point for local expats and visiting literati.

10 The Central Highlands

The mountainous Central Highlands are a few hundred very hilly kilometers inland from Nha Trang, a bumpy ride north from Ho Chi Minh City, or over the paved and very scenic Ho Chi Minh Trail south from Hoi An. The area saw its share of fighting during the war; names like the **La Drang Valley, Pleiku,** and **Kontum** will ring a bell with veterans or those who watched Walter Cronkite every night. But the scorched earth has grown again, and the region prospers as one of the most productive agricultural areas for produce, and one of the most prosperous for coffee growing.

Called **Tay Nguyen** in Vietnamese, the Central Highlands of five provinces—Kontum, Gia Lai, Dak Lak, Dak Nong, and Lam Dong—stretch along the high ridge of the **Trong Son Mountain Range** of the **Annamese Cordillera** that serves as a natural border between Vietnam and Laos and Cambodia. With the increase in altitude, the temperature is cool—from 64°F to 77°F (18°C to 25°C).

The most accessible city is **Dalat,** a former French colonial outpost nestled among the hills; it retains a serene, formal air of another time, though with some eccentric modern twists. The cooler weather in Dalat is a welcome respite from Vietnam's year-round coastal heat, and the town is full of fun, with hokey local tourist sights, most geared to young Vietnamese honeymooners. Dalat also seems to attract (or create) eccentric local residents, and many Vietnamese artists call this "Petite Paris" their home.

Dalat is also a good jumping-off point for the less-visited towns of the highlands, areas that are still under close watch for ethnic minority insurgents (suspicion that was founded in hilltribe complicity with American forces). The roads of this rugged region are now open to all and bring you into Vietnam's green and picturesque coffee-growing hills, among diverse hilltribe cultures, and along portions of the old Ho Chi Minh Trail that skirts the border between Laos and Cambodia and was pivotal to Viet Cong supplies and mobility over the decade-long war.

Outside of Dalat, tourist services are limited, and towns like **Buon Ma Thuot, Pleiku,** and **Kontum** support only barebones hotels and dining choices. Riding local buses is just short of masochism; it's best to arrange your own transport or go by tour. Many options, including the fun Easy Riders motorbike trips, start from Dalat, and various options depart from Ho Chi Minh City and Nha Trang.

1 DALAT

Known as "Le Petit Paris" by the early builders and residents of this hillside resort town, Dalat is still a luxury retreat for city dwellers and tourists tired out from trudging along sultry coastal Vietnam. In Dalat you can play golf on one of the finest courses in Indochina, visit beautiful temples, and enjoy the town's honeymoon atmosphere with delightfully hokey tourist sights.

At 1,500m (4,920 ft.), Dalat is mercifully cool year-round—there's no need for airconditioning. The town is a unique blend of pastoral hillside Vietnam and European

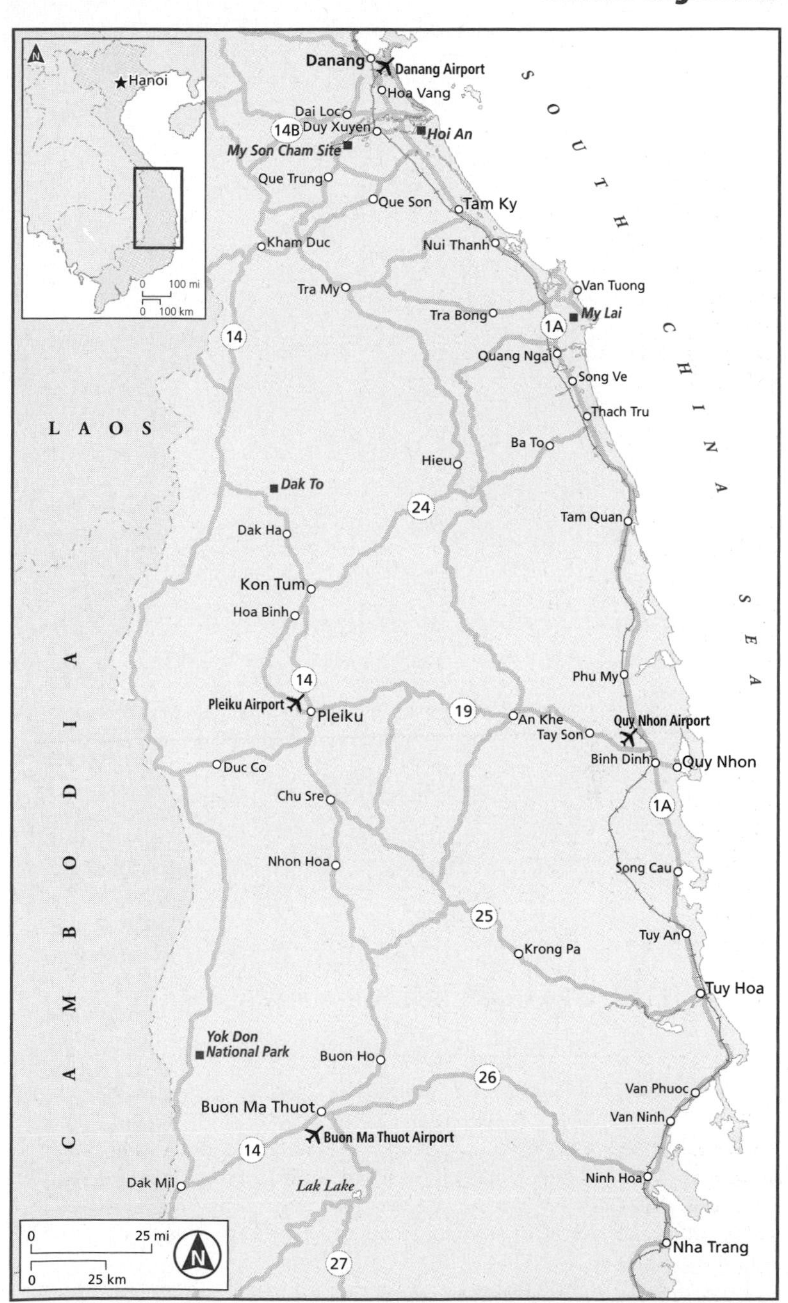
Hanoi
0 100 mi
0 100 km
Danang
Danang Airport
Hoa Vang
Dai Loc
14B
Duy Xuyen
Hoi An
My Son Cham Site
Que Trung
Que Son
Tam Ky
Kham Duc
Nui Thanh
Tra My
Van Tuong
Tra Bong
My Lai
1A
14
Quang Ngai
Song Ve
Thach Tru
LAOS
Ba To
Hieu
Dak To
24
Tam Quan
Dak Ha
Kon Tum
Hoa Binh
SOUTH CHINA SEA
14
Phu My
Pleiku Airport
Pleiku
19
An Khe
Quy Nhon Airport
Tay Son
Binh Dinh
Quy Nhon
Duc Co
1A
Chu Sre
Nhon Hoa
Song Cau
CAMBODIA
25
Tuy An
Krong Pa
Tuy Hoa
Yok Don National Park
Buon Ho
26
Van Phuoc
Buon Ma Thuot
Van Ninh
Buon Ma Thuot Airport
14
Dak Mil
Lak Lake
Ninh Hoa
0 25 mi
0 25 km
Nha Trang
27

Central Highland Ethnic Minority Hilltribes

The French called them Montagnards, or "people of the mountains," and these groups have long suffered under more powerful central governments. Hilltribe people paid dues to early Vietnamese kings and later achieved some autonomy under the French, who converted them to Catholicism and then conscripted them into labor on roads and bridges in the region. Alliances with American or North Vietnamese forces were just another form of conscription.

The Northern Highland groups—see chapter 6—are known for their more colorful traditional dress, while Central Highland hilltribe people, particularly the men in their Western attire, are often indistinguishable from lowland Vietnamese. But having endured so much for some measure of autonomy, these feisty highlanders still cling to tradition.

The ethnic minorities of the Central Highlands—the M'nong, the Ede, and the Bannar, among others—have as much in common as they do differences from one another. Most villages are of thatched single-family houses arranged around a central communal **longhouse** (called a *nha rang* in Vietnamese) raised on stilts at the center of town, where all ceremony and governance take place. Each group has a particular style of *nha rang,* the most dynamic being the Bannar style of a peak of thatch over three stories high, but each kind of *nha rang* is an important symbol of community-respective groups and the center of worship and colorful ceremony. Many hilltribe groups celebrate harvest time or auspicious occasions with the ritual slaughtering of a buffalo, a frenetic event soaked in local whiskey and accompanied by wild dance. Music is important to each group, and each has strong traditions—like the Jarai, who woo their brides by serenading, and the M'nong, famed for their drumming.

Many hilltribe groups are matrilineal, where names and even fortunes are passed from generation to generation from mother to child, and almost all practice some kind of animist religion, in which gods are the hills themselves or the natural forces that made them. Funeral ceremonies vary, but all of the Central Highland groups practice elaborate graveside rights, where bodies are interred in elaborate spirit houses decorated with ceremonial carvings and paintings, and later feted and celebrated to the funeral pyre or grave. Musical traditions among hilltribes are elaborate, with gongs, drums, and bamboo flute music integral parts of any ceremony.

Catholic missionaries had varied success bringing the good word to these remote, autonomous groups, and the legacy of their efforts still stands in the many churches, orphanages, and missions throughout the region (check out the Mission School in Kontum). Ede and Bannar people are among the most commonly converted. Minority groups in the region retain their ethnic traditions and some territorial autonomy, though investments from the Hanoi government have focused more on "enforced primitivism" programs and segregated villages (many open for tour-group visits). Opportunities to visit with these minority groups are many, and below is just a short breakdown of each group.

Important: Be very careful when photographing ethnic minorities. Few in the region are at all used to tourists, and there are many taboos about photography and collecting images of people. Always ask and respect an answer of "No." Often patient persistence pays off—stay and talk to people and explain where you're from and what you're doing. I've often been asked to take a photo by someone after I was initially denied the shot.

Jarai With an estimated population over 300,000, the Jarai are the largest group in the highlands. Villages are situated around a central longhouse where village elders hold court over local policy. Jarai people are animistic, with powerful gods of the wind, water, and the mountains. Complex Jarai funeral practices start with interring a body in a small spirit house surrounded by a person's effects and ritual statues, followed by cremation. Jarai society follows a matrilineal succession, meaning that family names are passed on from mother to child, and there's a kind of egalitarianism to cooperative villages of hunter-gatherers, river fishermen (villages are usually near water), and subsistence farmers. Jarai people are rumored to have migrated from the central coast long before the "Chinese millennium" some 2,000 years ago, and settled near Pleiku and Kontum, where most Jarai people are found today. Jarai musical talents are renowned (see a whole set of Jarai drums and gongs in the small Hilltribe Museum in Buon Ma Thuot).

Ede The second-largest group in the highlands, Ede have a society quite similar to the Jarai (see above), which centers around a village longhouse on stilts, with one window per family and a large section set aside for communal work and governance. Ede are matrilineal and follow rich animistic traditions like the Jarai. Find Ede villages on the outskirts of Buon Ma Thuot, mostly in situations of "enforced primitivism" under the watchful eye of the party.

Sedang Sedang are notorious warriors. Once known to practice human sacrifice, the Sedang were heavily conscripted as fighters by all sides: the French, the U.S., and North Vietnam. Sedang people follow a model of pure egalitarianism in village governance and duties. Find Sedang settlements in and around Kontum, with settlements as far as the Quy Nhon coastal area.

M'nong You will likely meet M'nong people, the elephant hunters and wranglers of the region, at Lak Lake when you get ferried out across the water by elephant. M'nong are matrilineal and known for their fine small-craft production and distinct percussion music. The M'nong practice elaborate funeral rituals—placing a coffin in a funeral house decorated with wooden statues before burial.

Bru & Taoi Two related groups living in the northern end of the highlands, the Bru and Taoi originally inhabited lands near the 17th Parallel, which meant that villages were swallowed in the destruction, and those that didn't flee farther south or to Laos (mostly Bru) were caught up as conscripts of the North Vietnamese (mostly Taoi) and played an important role in keeping the Ho Chi Minh supply line moving. Find Bru peoples in and around Khe Sanh.

alpine resort. Alexander Yersin, the Swiss geologist who first traipsed across this pass, established the town in 1897 as a resort for French commanders weary of the Vietnamese tropics. In and around town are still scattered the relics of colonial mansions, as well as some serene pagodas in a lovely natural setting; you've escaped from big-city Vietnam for real. A few ethnic minorities, including the Lat and the Koho, live in and around the picturesque hills surrounding Dalat, and you can visit a number of rural villages on local tours.

Dalat is a top resort destination for Vietnamese couples getting married or honeymooning. If the lunar astrological signs are particularly good, it's not unusual to see 10 or so wedding parties in a single day. Many of the local scenic spots, like the Valley of Love and Lake of Sighs, pander to the giddy couples. The waterfalls are swarming with vendors, men costumed as bears, and "cowboys" complete with sad-looking horses and fake pistols. A carnival air prevails. It's a "so bad that it's good" kind of tacky that is definitely worth the trip. There are also some picturesque temples and hillsides lined with the crumbling weekend homes of French colonials. Emperor Bao Dai, the last in Vietnam, had three large homes here, one of which is now the Sofitel Hotel; the other two can be visited on tours.

GETTING THERE

BY PLANE The only direct flights to Dalat are from Ho Chi Minh City (flight time: 50 min.). In Dalat, call Vietnam Airlines (✆ **063/383-3499** or 382-2898) to confirm your ticket or with any flight inquiries. Dalat's **Lien Khuong Airport** is 30km (19 miles) south of town. A taxi from the airport to the city is $3 and takes 30 minutes.

BY BUS Dalat is the first stop on the **"Open Tour" tickets** from Ho Chi Minh City's budget traveler cafes. Buses from both north and south first stop at Phan Rang, an old Cham temple site, where the road turns inland for the hills of Dalat. The ride to Dalat from the coast is winding and spectacular, at one point following hairpin turns underneath a large hydroelectric project. From Nha Trang (to the east) or Ho Chi Minh City (to the south), it's a 7-hour trip and costs $5 at any tourist cafe. Hire a private car for the trip and save about an hour. You can make arrangements at your hotel or with one of the tour providers listed below in the "Visitor Information & Tours" section.

Local buses connect Dalat with Nha Trang and Ho Chi Minh City, as well as Buon Ma Thuot, the next town north of Dalat along the highlands ridge—a grueling all-day ride. Buses leave from the Express Bus Station southwest of the city center (get there by motorbike taxi for about 16,000 VND); be prepared to haggle for your ticket.

BY CAR/MOTORBIKE Take the new highway through the mountains via hired transport in a minivan or car. The trip is just 3½ hours. Also popular are the unique motorbike trips with Dalat's "Easy Riders" (see the "Get Your Motor Running!" box, below). Check the listings below or in Saigon and Nha Trang (a few agents from Nha Trang specialize in tours of the highlands) for more options.

GETTING AROUND

There are no cyclos in Dalat, but walking is very pleasant in the cool air. You can catch most of the city sights, like the market and the lake, **on foot.** For sights outside of town, it's best to rent a motorbike or join a tour. On weekends, the busy streets of the central city are closed to motorbike and auto traffic.

BY TAXI For taxis in town, try **Dalat Taxi,** at ✆ **063/383-0830,** or **Mai Linh Taxi,** at ✆ **063/351-1511.**

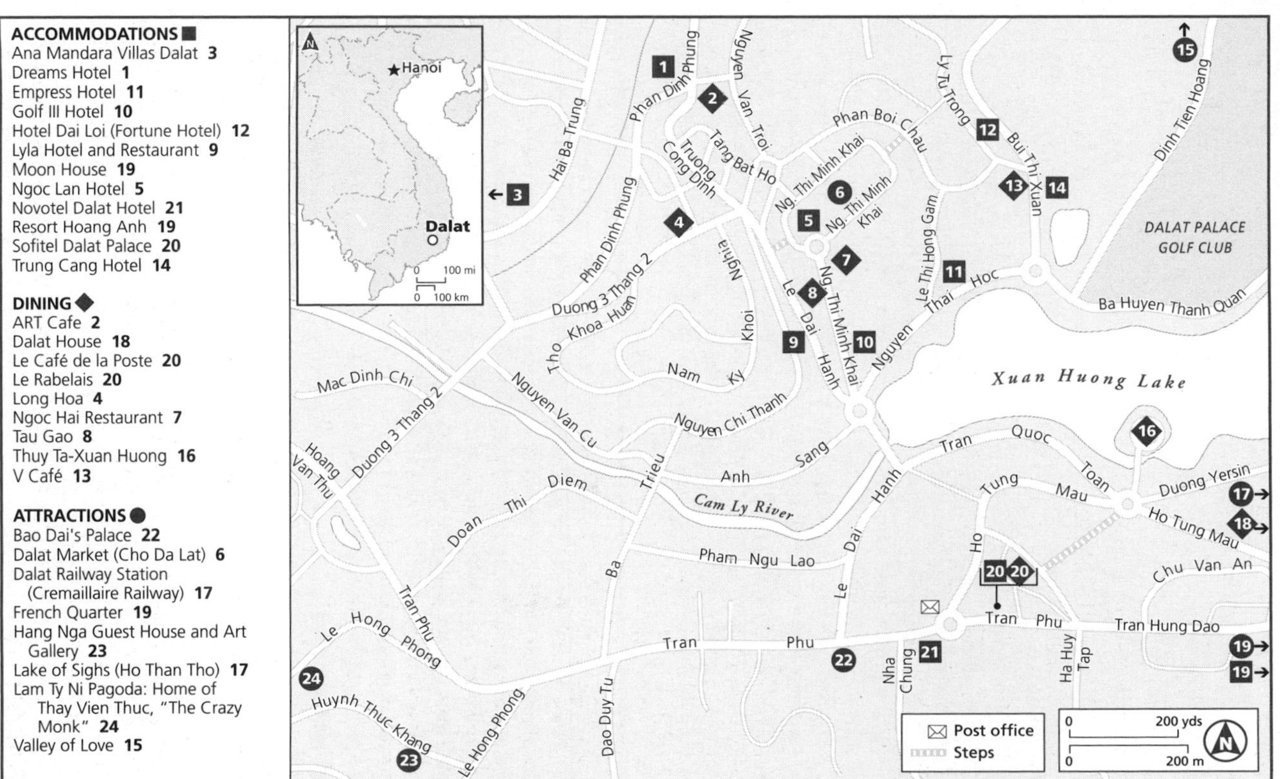
ACCOMMODATIONS
Ana Mandara Villas Dalat 3
Dreams Hotel 1
Empress Hotel 11
Golf III Hotel 10
Hotel Dai Loi (Fortune Hotel) 12
Lyla Hotel and Restaurant 9
Moon House 19
Ngoc Lan Hotel 5
Novotel Dalat Hotel 21
Resort Hoang Anh 19
Sofitel Dalat Palace 20
Trung Cang Hotel 14
DINING
ART Cafe 2
Dalat House 18
Le Café de la Poste 20
Le Rabelais 20
Long Hoa 4
Ngoc Hai Restaurant 7
Tau Gao 8
Thuy Ta-Xuan Huong 16
V Café 13
ATTRACTIONS
Bao Dai's Palace 22
Dalat Market (Cho Da Lat) 6
Dalat Railway Station (Cremaillaire Railway) 17
French Quarter 19
Hang Nga Guest House and Art Gallery 23
Lake of Sighs (Ho Than Tho) 17
Lam Ty Ni Pagoda: Home of Thay Vien Thuc, "The Crazy Monk" 24
Valley of Love 15
Hanoi
Dalat
100 mi
100 km
Xuan Huong Lake
Cam Ly River
DALAT PALACE GOLF CLUB
Phan Dinh Phung
Nguyen Van Troi
Ly Tu Trong
Phan Boi Chau
Bui Thi Xuan
Dinh Tien Hoang
Hai Ba Trung
Truong Cong Dinh
Tang Bat Ho
Ng. Thi Minh Khai
Le Thi Hong Gam
Nguyen Thai Hoc
Ba Huyen Thanh Quan
Duong 3 Thang 2
Tho Khoa Huan
Nghia
Khoi
Nam Ky
Le Dai Hanh
Mac Dinh Chi
Nguyen Van Cu
Nguyen Chi Thanh
Tran Quoc Toan
Anh Sang
Trieu
Hoang Van Thu
Doan Thi Diem
Tung Mau
Duong Yersin
Ho Tung Mau
Pham Ngu Lao
Ba
Chu Van An
Tran Phu
Tran Hung Dao
Le Hong Phong
Huynh Thuc Khang
Dao Duy Tu
Nha Chung
Ha Huy Tap
Post office
Steps
200 yds
200 m

Get Your Motor Running!

Do you wish you were "Born to Be Wild," as the song goes, but fear that so far your life has been "Born to Be Responsible"? No experience on motorcycles, but want to make the leap out on the open road and get some proverbial "bugs in your teeth"? Well, here's your chance to have a taste of the open road, and none of the road rash or traffic hassles that riding a motorbike yourself brings. Hire the services of an **Easy Rider,** Dalat's now-famous motorbike taxi drivers who haul all over tarnation on 125cc Honda Bonus motorcycles. You can find the Easy Riders at the **Peace Cafe** in the backpacker district at 64 Truong Cong Dinh St. (✆ **063/382-2787**). ***Tips:*** Beware of imitations! Other riders want in on the action and have copied Easy Rider's jackets and certificates. The real team can be found at Peace Cafe. Their bikes have good suspension and plenty of room for two. Most of these guys are retired after careers in the South Vietnamese Army and come to Dalat after years of struggle in the "New Vietnam" and now in the "Global Marketplace." These gentlemen have tuned in, turned on, and dropped out, in a sense, and all have great stories to tell and speak enough English after years working with American forces to tell it. A guidebook writer, having heard of them through many letters from readers, encouraged the guys to find a name and to form an affiliation. Being an easygoing bunch, they took on Easy Riders and are, in fact, just so. Easy Riders can take you on anything from day trips around Dalat for $12, to longer trips around the region for about $50 per day, all-inclusive, riding the whole ridge of the highlands up through Buon Ma Thuot, Pleiku, and Kontum, and on to Hoi An over the newly paved Ho Chi Minh Trail, or even farther up or down the coast. Memorable.

BY BUS Because most sights are outside city limits, one good option is to take a **half- or full-day tour** through your hotel or a **tourist cafe,** which hits many of the main sights. Some spots, like homes in the weaving villages or at the "Crazy Monk," require some kind of introduction, so going with a guide or following a tour is smart.

BY CAR You can **rent a car** with a driver for about $35 per day for a four-seater, or $40 for a seven-seater, with most tour companies. Contact any hotel front desk or the folks at **Dalattourist** (01 Nguyen Thi Minh Khai St.; ✆ **063/351-0104**), just south of the market area in the very center of town.

BY MOTORCYCLE Dalat is a good place to **rent your own motorbike.** The cheapest options are with the streetside places on Nguyen Thi Minh Khai St. (btw. the market and the lake), for about $5 per day ($6 from hotels and cafes). Be sure to check the brakes, and be sure the horn is working, because you should beep-beep all the way, especially when passing or on curves. The hillside, windy roads will have you feeling like a Hell's Angel if you can forget that you're riding the motorcycle equivalent of a hair dryer. This is a good, adventurous way to get to all the funky sights outside the city, but you may find it hard to get "into" places such as the Chicken Village or to the closed door of the "Crazy Monk"—some attractions are best visited on tours.

Another option is to get a **motorbike with a driver** for the day (about $1–$2 per hour, or fix a rate for the day and the destinations) or hook up with Dalat's famous **Easy Riders,** a group of motorbike taxi drivers that are more than your average motorbike taxi (for more information, see the "Get Your Motor Running!" box, above). Meet up with them at the **Peace Cafe** in the backpacker district at 64 Truong Cong Dinh St. (✆ **063/382-2787**). These guys speak English well, and a day spent with an Easy Rider is fun and educational. You'll hear of their experiences in the war years and benefit from their knowledge of the country, not to mention their driving skills. They ride sturdy bikes, the real deal from Japan, and charge $12 to $20 for a 1-day tour of the sights around Dalat. For about $50 per day, including gas, guiding, and budget accommodations, saddle up with an Easy Rider for trips far afield—up to Buon Me Thuot, farther north to Pleiku, and even along the Ho Chi Minh Trail as far as Hoi An. These guys are real adventurers. "The world is round," my driver said when I parted. "I know I'll see you again."

VISITOR INFORMATION & TOURS

The *Dalat Traveler,* a bimonthly English- and Vietnamese-language publication, has local happenings, festivals, and new developments in hotels and restaurants, as well as some basic maps and information about the city and surrounding sights.

- **Dalattourist,** 01 Nguyen Thi Minh Khai St. (✆ **063/351-0104;** fax 063/383-4144; www.dalattourist.com.vn), is located right in the center of Dalat with a small kiosk south of the main market. They book classic tours to anywhere in the region and offer good day trips and affordable car rentals. Quite unique, they'll book you tours with other companies if they don't have the services or prices that fit your needs. In fact, they have a booklet filled with pamphlets and fliers from local budget operators, making this a reliable one-stop shop for a traveler on any budget.
- **Phat Tire Ventures,** 73 Truong Cong Dinh (✆ **063/382-9422;** fax 063/382-0331; www.phattireventures.com), offers a unique eco-tourist option in Dalat. Contact Brian and Kim (young U.S. expats), who can arrange anything from day treks to jungle expeditions, mountain biking (they have a stable of top-quality bikes and hold daily clinics), rock climbing, repelling, or canyoning. Daily rates for activities are priced between $20 and $70 and include lunch, transport, and a knowledgeable guide. Safety and environmental stewardship are their trademarks. They also book classic tours through their affiliate, **Dalat Tours,** which shares space with Phat Tire Ventures and has the same contact information.

Budget Tours

- **An Phu Tourist Co.,** 07 Hai Thuong St. (✆ **063/382-3631**), provides the same budget buses and tour services here as in its Hoi An and Ho Chi Minh City offices.
- **Groovy Gecko Tours,** 65 Truong Cong Dinh (✆ **063/383-6521**), is a groovy, albeit unoriginal, outfitter providing basic eco-tours in the area.
- **Sinh Café,** 4A Bui Thi Xuan St. (✆ **063/383-6702**), has an information and tour office adjacent to Trung Cang, its budget hotel (p. 243). The standard services include arrangements for the open tour and some budget countryside and city tours.
- **TM Brothers,** 58 Truong Cong Dinh St. (✆ **063/382-8383**), books standard budget tours from its office on "cafe street" (overlooking the market). They'll pick you up at your hotel and are very professional, especially for their prices.

Fast Facts Dalat

Banks & Currency Exchange **Vietcombank** is at 6 Nguyen Thi Minh Khai St. (✆ **063/351-0479;** open daily 7:30–11am and 1:30–4:30pm). You can exchange traveler's checks here, and you'll also find an ATM that accepts most cards. There's also an ATM just outside the **Novotel,** at 12 Tran Phu St., and at the top of the hill near the central market stalls (just up the street from the Lyla Hotel and Restaurant).

Internet Reliable Internet connections can be found at the **Sofitel Dalat Palace** (below).

Post Office The main office is located at 14 Tran Phu St., across from the Novotel, and it's open Monday to Saturday from 6:30am to 9:30pm.

Telephone The area code for Dalat is 063.

WHERE TO STAY

With its long history as a popular resort area for both foreigners and Vietnamese, Dalat offers some choice lodgings. You'll find plenty of good minihotels, many geared toward Vietnamese weekenders escaping the summer heat in the big cities, and all quite easy on the budget. ***Note:*** No hotel in Dalat has air-conditioning, but with the year-round temperate weather, none is needed.

Very Expensive

Ana Mandara Villas Dalat ★★★ At the risk of sounding hokey, this place is magical. The views are spectacular during the day, with the sun shining on the nearby Langbian Mountains and illuminating the town below. Villas are two or three stories high, and each has a common dining area, living room, and kitchen. Families should head straight to Villa 15, which has an attic and lodge tucked under a slanted ceiling—a perfect play area for kids. Floors and furniture are a rustic, dark-brown wood, and everything else is creamy white. There are working stone fireplaces in most bedrooms and living rooms. A retro Art Deco heater whirs away in the corners. Fuzzy loafers are on hand for roaming around the room, and fleece bathrobes are a bundle of warmth after a hot bath. All the different elements come together for a rustic, cozy ambience that leaves you feeling warm and fuzzy.

Le Lai St. ✆ **063/355-5888.** Fax 063/355-5666. www.anamandara-resort.com. 65 units. $234–$593 villa. AE, DC, MC, V. **Amenities:** Restaurant; cafe; bar; concierge; vintage car rentals; heated outdoor pool; room service; spa. *In room:* TV, heating, fridge, hair dryer, minibar, Wi-Fi.

Sofitel Dalat Palace ★★★ Built in 1922 as the address of choice for French colonists on holiday, and once the home of Emperor Bao Dai, this recently renovated beauty, with its understated old-world opulence, is one of the finest five-star choices in all of Indochina. From the huge fireplace and mosaic floor in the lobby to the hanging tapestries, 500 oil reproductions of classic European art, and thick swag curtains, it's a French country château with a Southeast Asian colonial flair. The large rooms, with glossy original wood floors, are finished with fine fabrics and throw rugs, and all beds are crowned with an ornate wooden housing for a mosquito net (purely for decoration). The bathrooms feature hand-painted tiles and large claw-foot bathtubs with antique-style fixtures. Genuine antique French clocks and working reproduction telephones complete the picture, yet nothing feels overdone. All deluxe rooms and suites have a foyer and a fireplace. Lake-view rooms open to a huge veranda with deck chairs. The high, high ceilings and huge corridors with hanging lamps contribute to the palatial feeling. Service is superb. All in all, this is an exquisite place that should not be missed. Their in-house dining is unrivaled (see "Where to Dine," below).

12 Tran Phu St. ✆ **063/382-5444.** Fax 063/382-5666. www.sofitel.com. 43 units. $169–$214 double; $319–$414 suite. Prices vary by day, so check the website for discounts. AE, DC, MC, V. **Amenities:** 3 restaurants; 3 bars; children's playroom and outdoor playground; concierge; horseback riding; motorbikes; room service; spa; tennis. *In room:* TV, fridge, hair dryer, minibar, Wi-Fi.

Expensive

Ngoc Lan Hotel ★ This hotel was still scrambling to finish everything up in time for their soft opening in mid-2007. From the outside, it's a gleaming white building that towers over the action on Nguyen Chi Thanh Street. There's a purple-and-white theme throughout the building, so it feels a little bit like being in an oversized dollhouse. Deluxe rooms are spacious and come with a balcony that has a good view of the lake. Bathrooms have marblelike countertops, big bathtubs, and separate showers. The furniture is a little chintzy, but the whole thing is neat, tidy, and centrally located.

42 Nguyen Chi Thah St. ✆ **063/382-2136.** Fax 063/382-4032. www.ngoclanhotel.vn. 91 units. $85–$145 deluxe rooms; $385 suite. AE, MC, V. **Amenities:** Restaurant; bar; concierge; small fitness center. *In room:* TV, fridge, hair dryer, minibar, Wi-Fi.

Novotel Dalat Hotel ★ This is the scaled-down companion hotel to the Sofitel Dalat Palace. It was renovated in 1997 from a 1932 building that was originally the Du Parc hotel, and a lovely job was done of it. The best thing at this hotel is the unique wrought-iron lift. It's a relic and so much fun to ride. The smallish rooms have attractive historical touches: glossy wood floors, tastefully understated wood furniture, and molded high ceilings. All the rooms are pretty cramped, with very little walking space between the bed and the walls. Thankfully, long-overdue plans are in place to reduce the hotel's capacity (to 80 units) and expand room sizes. Everything is tidy and convenient, with nice local artwork throughout and homey warmth in tone and atmosphere. The bathrooms are a nice size, efficient, and spotless, with sleek granite and dark wooden trim. The staff is businesslike and abrupt, but can be persuaded to be friendly if you persist in your smiles. The hotel shares fine amenities with neighboring Sofitel Dalat Palace (see above).

7 Tran Phu St. ✆ **800/221-4542** or 063/382-5777. Fax 063/382-5888. www.accorhotels-asia.com. 139 units. $61–$91 double; $111 suite. Prices vary by day, so check the website for discounts. AE, MC, V. **Amenities:** 2 restaurants; 2 bars; concierge; motorbikes; tennis. *In room:* TV, fridge, minibar.

Resort Hoang Anh This hotel took an old French villa and buried it under gray tiles. It's sparklingly clean and very popular with the Vietnamese tourists. The hotel resort consists of 10 separate villas and is spread out over a decent lot of land. Rooms are quite spacious, and bathrooms have big bathtubs and separate showers. Cheesy replica period furniture adorns each room.

2 Nguyen Du St. ✆ **063/381-0826.** Fax 063/354-9036. 122 units. www.hoanganhotelgroup.com. $80–$95 double; $120–$150 suite. AE, MC, V. **Amenities:** 4 restaurants; bar; concierge; fitness center; Internet; tennis court. *In room:* TV, fridge, hair dryer, minibar.

Moderate

Empress Hotel ★ This Hong Kong/Vietnamese joint venture is a good, upscale, but affordable oasis just a stone's throw from the lake and close to all the action. Tucked into the side of a hill, the hotel has rooms that form a courtyard, with the steep gable of a European lodge–style reception and restaurant on one side and two floors of rooms all facing the courtyard on the other. Comfortable rooms have dark-wood walls, terra-cotta tile floors, rattan furniture, good indirect lighting, nice local artwork, and elegant cotton and silk bedspreads. Bathrooms are large, with granite counters and nice fixtures, some with bathtubs and others with an open arrangement with a combined shower/toilet area (like a guesthouse, but spotless). The suites are large and luxe, with a sunken tub and large sitting area, but for my money, I'll take a deluxe room, which is a larger version of a standard and has views of the stone courtyard and lake below. However, if you're looking at this price range, you are better off booking yourself into a room at Ana Mandara or a double at the Sofitel (see above). There's a nice restaurant serving good local and Continental fare; if the staff is slightly cool, it's almost refreshingly real of them. Go for a room on the second floor (first-floor rooms are getting a bit musty).

5 Nguyen Thai Hoc St. ✆ **063/383-3888.** Fax 063/382-9399. expresdl@hcm.vnn.vn. 19 units. $45–$60 double (superior/deluxe); $90–$150 suite. AE, MC, V. **Amenities:** Restaurant. *In room:* TV w/in-house movies, fridge, hair dryer, minibar, Wi-Fi.

Golf III Hotel The Golf is a three-star chain hotel and a good choice in Dalat (local Golf I and II are low-end versions). Large rooms are upholstered in purple with gaudy carved-wood details. Some rooms are a bit frayed around the edges. It's worth springing for a deluxe room, a Vietnamese honeymooner favorite, with parquet floors rather than carpet and larger bathrooms with big sunken tubs. The constant stream of Vietnamese wedding parties in and out lends a welcome festive air to the place, and this hotel is at its best when trying to be a little more than it is; blooming bonsais, overstuffed chairs, and a glitzy sheen over the lobby area stand testament. Golf III is right in the center of the busy market area, but set back far enough from the road that rooms are relatively quiet. Amenities are basic, like a rooftop steam, sauna, and massage area (a little seedy), and the lobby restaurant, which serves a fine breakfast.

4 Nguyen Thi Minh Khai St. (near the market). ✆ **063/382-6042** or 382-6049. Fax 063/383-0396. www.vinagolf.vn. 78 units. $50–$55 double; $75–$105 suite. AE, MC, V. **Amenities:** Restaurant; bar; room service; sauna; steam. *In room:* TV, fridge, minibar, Wi-Fi.

Inexpensive

Dreams Hotel ★★ Budget tourists rave about this one, and for good reason. Dreams Hotel offers large, clean rooms with cable TV and hot water starting at just $15 for a single, including a sumptuous breakfast and free Internet access. The owner, Ms. Dung, and her son are very helpful, and this is a good budget base and a place to connect with other travelers. Just at the bottom of the hill from a street with many budget options, this hotel is also close to local tour providers like Phat Tire (see "Visitor Information & Tours," above), as well as to the friendly Easy Riders (see "Getting Around," above), who can take you on fun motorbike trips. Be sure to book ahead, best by e-mail, as Dreams is always fully booked.

151 and 164B Phan Dinh Phung St. ✆ **063/383-3748.** Fax 063/383-7108. dreams@hcm.vnn.vn. 20 units. $15–$20 single; $20–$25 double. Rates include breakfast. MC, V. **Amenities:** Restaurant (breakfast only); free Internet. *In room:* TV, fridge, Wi-Fi.

Hotel Dai Loi (Fortune Hotel) ★ If you want value for your money, look no further. It's affordable, comfortable, and still looks fresh. Most other places in this category have musty smells and dingy decor, but not the Fortune. The place is spotless, the location is far enough from the center of town for quiet, yet close enough for access, and the price is right. More expensive rooms have two double beds and nice, large bathtubs, and most have balconies. The second-floor restaurant is open and inviting. The small lobby bar has white walls and white plastic chairs, and could be airlifted to a museum as a "minimalist installation," but there is nice black-and-white tile throughout to give it a nice, crisp look. The staff members speak little English but are nonetheless quite helpful.

3A Bui Thi Xuan. ✆ **063/383-7333.** Fax 063/383-7474. 39 units. 400,000 VND–700,000 VND double. AE, MC, V. **Amenities:** Restaurant; bar; motorbikes. *In room:* TV, fridge, minibar, Wi-Fi.

Moon House The exterior of this government-renovated French villa is exquisite, with a round driveway, crumbling stone, and picturesque cone rooftops. The interior, however, disappoints. Rooms are furnished with lacquered wood furniture, and beds are covered in floral-patterned velour bedspreads. Bathrooms in basic rooms are a bit cramped and do not have separate showers or shower curtains, so spring for a suite, which comes with a bathtub. The friendly staff, though, is a plus.

16 Hung Vuong St. ✆ **063/382-2417.** Fax 063/381-2109. 6 units. 250,000 VND–400,000 VND double. No credit cards. **Amenities:** Restaurant; cafe; free Internet. *In room:* TV, fridge (in some).

Trung Cang Hotel ★ The Sinh Café expands its monopoly on budget-traveler amenities here with this centrally located little gem. Rooms have clean tile floors and basic amenities. Any lack of design (hello, pink ceramic bathrooms) is compensated by their clean, airy rooms for next to nothing, though some even have nice filigreed ceilings and cool, subdued lighting. The hotel does get its share of groups, and things can get pretty noisy. This is a good budget option, and the folks at Sinh Café are always accommodating when arranging tours or getting you around town. Service is friendly but not always effective.

4A Bui Thi Xuan St. ✆ **063/382-2663.** Fax 063/383-6701. 27 units. 350,000 VND–540,000 VND double. Rates include breakfast. MC, V. **Amenities:** Restaurant; Wi-Fi. *In room:* TV, fridge, minibar.

WHERE TO DINE

Dalat dining is pretty basic. Meals are simply prepared and heavily influenced by Chinese cuisine. The huge variety of local ingredients, particularly fruit and vegetables, makes for fresh food. Many small restaurants are located at Phan Dinh Phung Street, but some of the best dining, according to locals, is at the many stalls in the central market. Try the artichoke tea and strawberry jam, two local specialties (and good souvenirs to take home from the market). In the evenings, look for the small stalls selling delicious-flavored soy drinks on the main road near the central market.

Expensive

Le Rabelais ★★ FRENCH Dining here is an experience in genuine fine dining, French colonial style. Prices are high for this region, but so is the standard of preparation and service. The Sofitel people work closely with local organic farms, and all dishes are prepared with the finest fresh produce. In the tradition of the original 1922 Langbian Palace Hotel, Le Rabelais serves from a limited menu, which ensures that everything is done just right. Dinner is a slow progression of delicious courses. I had a divine crab flower that was crisped to perfection. The wine list is long and, unique in the region, the staff knows the right suggestions for any given meal—in fact, the staff here is uniquely efficient and professional, attentive without either fawning or hovering. Certain things do get missed, but overall, a great place to take that special someone for an evening of candlelit opulence.

12 Tran Phu St. (adjoining the lobby of the Sofitel Dalat Palace Hotel). ✆ **063/382-5444.** Main courses $25–$47; set menus $65–$85 dinner, $22 lunch. MC, V. Daily 6am–10pm.

Moderate/Inexpensive

ART Cafe ★ VIETNAMESE In the heart of the backpacker area along Truong Cong Dinh, ART Cafe serves up local cuisine at prices just a tick above the local standard, but in an intimate, semiformal dining room with white linen tablecloths and rattan tables and chairs. The owner (the artist himself) is very friendly and a good source of local information. They serve great stir-fries and have excellent vegetarian options. I had delicious fresh spring rolls and an order of savory tofu cooked in lemon grass with a side of steamed vegetables. Portions are large and ingredients fresh. Packed with young travelers nightly.

70 Truong Cong Dinh St. (near the Peace Cafe at the bottom of the hill of "Backpacker St."). ✆ **063/351-0089.** Main courses 39,000 VND–50,000 VND. No credit cards. Daily 10am–11pm.

Dalat House ★ ASIAN/WESTERN It's out of the town center, so you'll have to take a cab, but that somehow adds to the experience of this dolled-up Western restaurant, a place where local businessmen go to impress clients—it evokes the theme to *The Godfather.* It's a mix of Asian and Western cuisine served on fine white china on candlelit, linen-draped tables. The best local choices are the good stews that take the chill out of a cool Dalat evening: hot-pot dishes great for sharing, or baked clay-pot specials. Western meals are all country-club standbys: meat and potatoes, fish filet, and pasta.

34 Nguyen Du, Dalat (about 4km/2½ miles east of town, past the railway station). ✆ **063/381-1577.** Main courses 60,000 VND–140,000 VND. No credit cards. Daily 6am–10pm.

Le Café de la Poste ★★ CONTINENTAL This cozy, colonial gem, part of the Dalat Palace Hotel, is located in an open, airy corner building across from the post office (go figure). It's more a restaurant than cafe, really, and has a great selection of light choices, sandwiches, and desserts, in addition to hearty entrees like spareribs, T-bone steak, and fresh pasta. The salads are big and fresh, and they have a great French onion soup. Don't miss the cheesecake for dessert. It's slightly pricey for Dalat, but it's worth it in a way that the Dalat Palace's fine-dining venue, Les Rabelais, is not.

12 Tran Phu St. ✆ **063/382-5444.** Main courses $9.50–$30. MC, V. Daily 6am–10pm.

Long Hoa ★★ VIETNAMESE/CONTINENTAL On a busy street just opposite the hilltop cinema, this small bistro is a Dalat institution. The Long Hoa is bright and tidy but sacrifices none of the old charm. The cozy dining room has checkered tablecloths and an atmosphere that attracts passersby. The owner, a vivacious, self-taught speaker of many languages, is very welcoming and will walk you through any menu choices, travel recommendations, or local lore in the language of your choice. You'll feel like a regular or will become one even if you are in Dalat for only a few days. The menu is categorized by ingredient (chicken, beef, fish, and so on), and they have various sautéed or steamed dishes, as well as a variety of hot-pot dishes and soups that are great on cold Dalat nights. It's inexpensive, excellent local fare with a French flair.

6 Duong 3 Thang 2 (Duy Tan) Dalat. ✆ **063/382-2934.** Main courses 40,000 VND–110,000 VND. No credit cards. Daily 11:30am–2:30pm and 5:30–9:30pm.

Ngoc Hai Restaurant ★ VIETNAMESE/CHINESE Just down the street from the market, this local spot is two floors of bright, clean, indoor/outdoor dining. It's nothing spectacular, but the staff at Ngoc Hai is friendly and the menu is ambitious; ask for anything, and you'll hear hearty replies of, "Have. Have." Selections from the Western end of the spectrum include roasted chicken with potatoes and a mock-up of British fish and chips, but go for the Chinese-influenced Vietnamese stir-fries, one-dish meals, and soups. Reasonable set menus vary daily and are a good bet. Good veggie selections, too.

6 Nguyen Thi Minh Khai St. ✆ **063/382-5252.** Main courses 60,000 VND–150,000 VND; set menus 120,000 VND–200,000 VND. V. Daily 6am–10pm.

Tau Cao ★ CHINESE/VIETNAMESE This is a friendly hole-in-the-wall restaurant serving one great dish: noodle soup. Thin yellow noodles are topped with a couple won tons, minced pork, barbecue pork, and spring onions, all in a tasty broth.

217 Phan Dinh Phung St. (next to Drems Hotel). ✆ **063/382-0104.** Bowl of soup 20,000 VND. No credit cards. Daily 6am–10pm.

Thuy Ta—Xuan Huong ★ VIETNAMESE Two restaurants sponsored by Dalattourist have entered the dining scene: one on a little island over central Xuan Huong Lake, the other just opposite on the shore, and both serving good Vietnamese grub. The lake site is a particularly picturesque pick, even if just for an evening drink. The place gets overrun with wedding parties, so keep an eye on the horizon, lest you get dragged into the proceedings.

01 Yersin St. and 02–04 Tran Quoc Toan St. ✆ **063/382-2288.** Main courses 55,000 VND–80,000 VND. No credit cards. Daily 6:30am–10pm.

V Cafe ★ VIETNAMESE/WESTERN This place is cozy and affordable. The chairs are mismatched and the decoration is eclectic. Amateur photography adorns the walls, along with plenty of paper lanterns. Lights with conical hat lampshades are suspended over each table. The food is good and filling; try their BBQ Pork Banh Uot Dalat, a dish of barbecue pork over a bed of mushroom-stuffed wide rice noodles. Service is very friendly. If you're an early bird, they've got some comfort breakfast options, like "French Toast—Oh La La." Looks like they've got a sense of humor, too.

1/1 Bui Thi Xuan (across the street from Trung Cang Hotel). ✆ **063/352-0215.** Main courses 59,000 VND–90,000 VND. AE, MC, V. Daily 11am–10pm.

Cafes

Nguyen Chi Thanh Street is lined with cafes, one indistinguishable from another in many ways. Each building hangs over the main market street, and all serve ice cream, tea, and beer to cuddling couples and backpackers. Try **Artista Cafe,** at 9 Nguyen Chi Thanh St. (✆ **063/382-1749**), for some good ice cream, classic rock, and friendly folks. A couple doors down is **Café Galy,** which pretty much has the same menu, but has a fun purple exterior and stained-glass windows.

Peace Cafe, 64 Truong Cong Dinh St. (✆ **063/382-2787**), is the heart of backpacker Dalat—an institution, really. Surrounded by the town's most popular budget guesthouses and minihotels, Peace Cafe is where to go to meet Dalat's **Easy Riders** for tours of the countryside and beyond (see the "Get Your Motor Running!" box, earlier in this chapter).

For a peek into the local **art scene,** see if you can find Mr. **MPK** (you have to ask him what it means). He makes his home at the back of a little villa guesthouse overlooking a beautiful valley (Khach San Van Khanh; 11/8 Khoi Nghia Bac Son, up in the hills near the Bao Dai Palace II). MPK is an inspired photographer, best when he's up close to his subject. He shoots with an old rusty camera and turns the lens backwards, shooting through a rough-hewn tube to get incredible macro close-ups. Have a coffee, peruse his photos, and buy something (if he's selling), for a unique visit.

ATTRACTIONS

Much of what there is to see in Dalat is natural sights: Lakes, waterfalls, and dams dominate the tourist trail. Things are spread over quite some distance, so consider booking a tour or renting your own car or motorbike.

If touring on your own, remember to avoid visiting pagodas between 11:30am and 2pm, when nuns and monks will be having their lunch. You might disturb them and also miss a valuable opportunity for a chat. It's also correct to leave 1,000 VND or 2,000 VND in the donation box near the altar.

Typical 1-day itineraries by minivan to sights outside the city include a visit to one of the falls, either Prenn Falls or Pongour Falls south of Dalat, followed by a stop at Truc Lam Monastery, the Lat (Chicken) Village, the Valley of Love, Crazy House, and a visit with the Crazy Monk, and ending with a stop at Bao Dai's summer palace or the old train station. Most tours make stops at small silk-weaving villages where you can watch the whole process from worm to wear, as well as incense-making workshops, vegetable-growing terraces, and coffee plantations.

Bao Dai's Palace ★ Completed in 1938, this monument to bad taste provided Bao Dai, Vietnam's last emperor, with a place of rest and respite with his family. It has never been restored and, indeed, looks veritably untouched since the emperor's ousting and hasty exile. On a busy weekend in high season, you might get a rush by imagining you're there to liberate the place and are part of the looting masses—that's not hard to imagine, with the crowds ignoring any velvet ropes and posing for pictures in the aging velvet furniture. You'll be asked to go in stockinged feet or wear loose shoe covers, which makes it fun for sliding around the home's 26 rooms, including Bao Dai's office and the bedrooms of the royal family. You can still see the grease stains on Bao Dai's hammock pillow and the ancient steam bath in which he soaked. The explanations are in English, and most concern Bao Dai's family. There is pathos in reading them and piecing together the mundane fate of the former royals: This prince has a "technical" job, while that one is a manager for an insurance company. There are three other Bao Dai palaces in town, the Sofitel Dalat Palace Hotel among them, but this is the most choice.

South of Xuan Huong Lake, up the hill behind "Crazy House." Admission 15,000 VND. Daily 7–11am and 1:30–4pm.

Dalat Market (Cho Da Lat) ★★★ Huge, crowded, and stuffed with produce of all varieties, this is the top stroll-through destination in Dalat. Here's where you can see all the local specialties—and even have a try! Some of the vendors will be happy to give you a sample of some local wine or a few candied strawberries. Dalat in general is low on the hassling tourist touts that plague the big towns and tourist sights in Vietnam, and entreaties from the merchants are friendly; you can walk around without too much hassle here because the locals are doing all the shopping. The top floor of the market now houses a high-end embroidery studio, and shops catering to tourists are on the rise, but mostly what's for sale are good local wines, preserves, and produce. Just outside the market, a number of vendors sell anything from sweetened soy milk to affordable dinners. The place is busy night and day, mostly with domestic tourists wandering the town. A fun vibe pervades it.

Central Dalat.

Dalat Railway Station (Cremaillaire Railway) Built in 1943, the Dalat station offers an atmospheric slice of Dalat's colonial history. You can see an authentic old wood-burning steamer train on the tracks to the rear, and stroll around inside looking at the iron-grilled ticket windows, which are now empty. Although the steamer train no longer makes tourist runs, a newer Japanese train makes a trip to Trai Mat Street and the Linh Phuoc Pagoda (see below). A ride costs $5 and leaves when full.

Near Xuan Huong Lake, off Nguyen Trai St. Daily 8am–5pm.

The French Quarter ★★ The whole town has the look and feel of a French replica, but on the ridge-running road, Tran Hung Dao, don't miss the derelict shells of the many

French colonial summer homes once populated and popular; it's where the connected and successful came to escape the Saigon heat in summer. Most are owned by the folks at Sofitel, and who's to say what will become of them in years to come, but they are a beautiful and eerie reminder of the recent colonial past. The road itself, one you'll take to many of the sights outside of town, offers panoramic views.

Best visited by motorbike or in a car with driver. Follow Tran Hung Dao Rd. a few kilometers southeast from town. Some of the houses are on private roads at the end of promontories.

Hang Nga Guest House and Art Gallery ★★ Otherwise known as the "Crazy House," this Gaudí–meets–Sesame Street theme park is one not to miss. It's a wild mass of wood and wire fashioned into the shape of a giant treehouse and smoothed over in concrete. It sounds simple, but there's a vision to this chaos; just ask the eccentric owner/proprietor and chief architect, Ms. Dang Viet Nga. Daughter of aristocracy, Ms. Nga is well heeled after early schooling in China and has a degree in architecture from the university in Moscow. In Dalat, she has been inspired to undertake this shrine to the curved line, what she calls an essential mingling of nature and people. The locals deem her eccentric for some reason, but she's just misunderstood; don't pass up any opportunity to have a chat with the architect herself. On a visit here, you'll follow a helpful guide and are sure to have fun clambering around the concrete ladders, tunnels, hollowed-out nooks, and unique "theme" rooms of this huge fantasy tree trunk. It's an actual guesthouse, too, but it offers more theme than comfort. It's better just to visit than to stay. There's a small family shrine in a large common area at the back. It all spoke to me about Vietnam's refreshingly lax zoning laws, but to many it's an interesting, evolving piece of pop art. This is a fun visit.

3 Huynh Thuc Khang St. ✆ **063/382-2070.** Admission 16,000 VND. Daily 7am–6pm.

Lake of Sighs (Ho Than Tho) ★ This lake has such romantic connotations for the Vietnamese that you would think it was created by a fairy godmother rather than French dam work. Legend has it that a 15-year-old girl named Thuy drowned herself after her boyfriend of the same age, Tam, fell in love with another. Her gravestone still exists on the side of the lake, marked with the incense and flowers left by other similarly heartbroken souls, even though the name on the headstone reads "Thao," not "Thuy." The place is crammed with honeymooners in paddle boats and motorboats.

Northeast of town, along Ho Xuan Huong Rd. Admission 8,000 VND. Daily 7am–5pm.

Lam Ty Ni Pagoda: Home of Thay Vien Thuc, "The Crazy Monk" A visit with the man is a highlight for some and just plain creepy for others. The temple itself is nothing special, though the immaculate garden in the back is nice; the attraction here is Mr. Thuc's large studio. Thuc, a Vietnamese Zen practitioner, seems to be painting, drawing, and scribbling his way to Nirvana. It's a unique glimpse into the inner sanctum of a true eccentric, and though locals say that he's not a real monk, just a painter and salesman, it's an interesting visit. Perhaps a polyglot afflicted with graphophilia (a language genius who can't stop drawing), Mr. Thuc has a message of "peace and connectedness" characteristic of the Zen sect, and he conveys that message in Vietnamese, Chinese, French, English, Japanese, German, and Swedish as he continually cranks out poems with small stylized drawings when you talk with him. Your part in the plan is that, for $1 (a bargain), he'll scribble an original before your eyes and pose for a photo; he has tentative plans to visit everyone who buys one of his paintings and bring us all together. Hmmm.

You're free to ask him questions, browse his stacks of finished works in the studio, and sign the guest book. This is a standard stop on city/country tours.

2 Thien My, Dalat. ✆ **063/382-1775.** Free admission, but most feel obliged (or compelled) to buy one of his paintings.

Lat Village (Chicken Village) A village of the Co Ho minority people, the Lat, or "Chicken," Village is usually part of the all-day tours in the hills around Dalat. Why chicken? Well, there is an enormous cement statue of a chicken at the entry to town—the bird has to do with a village legend (ask your guide—I've heard about four different versions of the story, and each is a hoot). The Co Ho people are very used to the many foreign visitors who come here every day; trinket sellers are not pushy, and you are free to walk about this rustic little town at your own pace.

About 16km (10 miles) south of Dalat.

Linh Phuoc Pagoda ★ Here is another example of one of Vietnam's fantasyland glass-and-ceramic mosaic structures. Refurbished in 1996, this modern temple features a huge golden Buddha in the main hall, and three floors of walls and ceilings painted with fanciful murals. Go to the top floor for the eye-boggling Bodhisattva room and views of the surrounding countryside. In the garden to the right, there is a 3m-high (10-ft.) dragon climbing in and out of a small lake. You'll find very cool little nooks and crannies to explore.

At the end of Trai Mat St. (20 min. by car/bike). Daily 8am–5pm.

Prenn Falls ★ The falls are actually quite impressive, especially after a good rain. You can ride a rattletrap little cable car over them if you're brave or follow a stone path behind the falling water (prepare to get your feet wet). That's a little thrill, of course, but the true Prenn experience is all about staged photos for Vietnamese tourists: couples preening, boys looking macho, and girls looking wan and forlorn. Professional photographers run the show and pose their willing actors on a small wooden bridge, on the back of a costumed horse, with an arm around a guy in a bear suit, on a small inflatable raft in front of the falls, or perched in one of the cool treehouses high above (be careful of the loose rungs when climbing up). Come here to have a laugh and observe until you find out that, as a foreign tourist, it's you that's being observed; in that case, say *"Xin chao"* (pronounced *sin chow*) or return a few "hellos" and go from there (you'll be getting your photo snapped, for sure). You might walk away with some new chums, not to mention some souvenirs (plastic samurai sword, anyone?). Other falls in the area include the **Gougah Falls,** some 40km (25 miles) south of Dalat, as well as **Pongour Falls,** 55km (34 miles) south.

At the foot of Prenn Mountain pass, 10km (6¼ miles) south of Dalat. Admission 15,000 VND. Daily 7am–5pm.

Thien Vuong Pagoda ★ Otherwise known as the "Chinese Pagoda," built as it was by the local Chinese population, this structure (ca. 1958) is unremarkable except for its serene setting among the hills of Dalat and the very friendly nuns who inhabit it. It does have three awe-inspiring sandalwood Buddhist statues that have been dated to the 16th century. Each statue is 4m (13 ft.) high and weighs 1½ tons. Left to right, they are Dai The Chi Bo Tat, god of power; Amithaba or Sakyamuni, Buddha; and Am Bo Tat, god of mercy.

3km (1¾ miles) southeast of town at the end of Khe Sanh St. Daily 9am–5pm.

Truc Lam (Bamboo Forest) Zen Monastery ★★ What's refreshing is that you can walk around Truc Lam with no harassment, unlike many other temples and most pagodas in Vietnam. This is a working temple, and though it's packed with tourists at certain times of the day, you'll be wandering amid meditation halls and classrooms that are utilitarian, not museum pieces. You'll get to see monks at work and have an informative glimpse into the daily rhythms of temple life. The complex was completed in 1994 with the aim of giving new life to the Truc Lam Yen Tu Zen sect, a uniquely Vietnamese form of Zen founded during the Tran dynasty (1225–1400). Adherents practice self-reliance and realization through meditation. The shrine, the main building, is notable mainly for its simple structure and peaceful air, and there is a large relief sculpture of Boddhidarma, Zen's wild-eyed Indian heir, at the rear of the main temple. The scenery around the monastery, with views of the nearby man-made lake, Tuyen Lam Lake, and surrounding mountains, is breathtaking. Truc Lam can now be reached by a scenic **tram ride** from a hilltop overlooking Dalat; a motorbike or taxi to the tram station costs little, and the round-trip is 50,000 VND.

Near Tuyen Lam Lake, 6km (3¾ miles) from Dalat. A popular spot on any countryside tour. Daily 7am–5pm.

Valley of Love ★★ The Valley is scenic headquarters in Dalat and a popular stopover for honeymooners. It's a good place to find some really bizarre kitsch, the kind whose precedent can only be roadside America; here, I mean guys in bear suits and huge-headed cowboys with guns that spout "bang" flags. There are a few nice walking paths among the rolling hills and quaint little lakes, and everyone enjoys the antics of Vietnamese honeymooners zipping around on motorboats and posing for pictures with guys in fuzzy jumpsuits. Don't miss it.

Phu Dong Thien Vuong St., about 3.2km (2 miles) north of town center. Admission 10,000 VND. Daily 6am–5pm.

Xuan Huong Lake ★★ Dalat's centerpiece, Xuan Huong, was created from a dam project that was finished in 1923, demolished by a storm in 1932, and reconstructed and rebuilt (with heavier stone) in 1935. The water originates as a trickle in the faraway Lat (Chicken) Village. You can rent windsurfing boards and swan-shape paddle boats, but I've never seen anyone out on the lake (only in the brochures). This is Dalat's other prime strolling territory (you walk here from the nearby market), and you're sure to see newlyweds, some wearing full wedding regalia, posing for pictures or staring longingly into one another's eyes as their life together begins. You'll see saddled horses and horse carts that Vietnamese tourists rent for staged photos. It's about 5 short kilometers (3 miles) around the perimeter, a nice walk in the early evening, and closer to town are some cool little local cafes over the water where you can stop for a *Cafe Sua* (a robust coffee made of locally grown beans and dripping with ultrasweet condensed milk).

Central Dalat.

2 BUON MA THUOT

350km (217 miles) N of Ho Chi Minh City; 200km (124 miles) N of Dalat; 200km (124 miles) S of Pleiku; 180km (112 miles) W of Nha Trang

There isn't much to this little provincial capital, just a maze of busy streets surrounding the center Thang Loi (Victory) Monument, with its high arch and a statue of the first tank to enter the town during liberation in 1975. Services in Buon Ma Thuot are basic, and the few hotels with any oomph cater mostly to local coffee growers' expatriate managers and folks (mostly Swiss) visiting the highlands on agricultural aid projects. The sleepy town has a few beat-up old museums hardly worth seeing, but Buon Ma Thuot is a good base for day trips out into the broad-reaching hill areas. Rolling hills covered with the ordered striations of row upon row of coffee plants bring you to far-flung ethnic minority villages of the Ede and the M'nong people. You can organize all kinds of trekking and tours in town that include canoeing, hiking, and elephant riding, as well as some great options for overnights and homestays in rural villages, or visit **Yok Don National Park** just north of town. You can also visit a working coffee plantation. In town, expect little more than local souvenir shopping, mostly for good, fresh coffee and jars of locally brewed whiskey in fired pots of the M'nong people.

Note: This part of the highlands was more or less "off the map" for tourism until recent years, not for want of sights or natural beauty, but because the Vietnamese government still suspects subterfuge among ethnic minority groups. The local cadres are really pretty relentless. I met a young traveler putt-putting all around the region on his own rented motorbike out of Ho Chi Minh City; for his troubles, he was made *persona non grata* in the provinces of Gia Lai and Dak Lak for traveling without a passport (he had a photocopy, which is usually okay because you often need to leave a passport at the rental office), and the poor guy had to endure lengthy interviews with a paranoid party member who thought he might be a spy. Spying for whom? Juan Valdez? Take care and avoid the men in uniform.

GETTING THERE

BY PLANE There are direct connections between Buon Ma Thuot and Ho Chi Minh City, and Buon Ma Thuot and Danang. The airport in Buon Ma Thuot is 10km (6¼ miles) from the town center. The office of **Vietnam Airlines** is at 67 Nguyen Tat Thanh St. (✆ **0500/395-4442** or 395-5055). Flight schedules vary, and you should book your flights to and from here in advance (possible from any Vietnam Airlines office countrywide).

BY CAR/MOTORBIKE Probably the best way to arrange transport to Buon Ma Thuot is to hire your own vehicle. The town is a popular stop for the many adventurous travelers who saddle up on a motorbike with one of the highland area's Easy Riders (see the section on Dalat, earlier in this chapter), and there are also good options for private accommodations in a car or van—at premium prices of about $60 per day—from Nha Trang (try to split the cost with other travelers, or join a larger tour).

BY BUS Local buses to or from Nha Trang leave at 7am and cost 50,000 VND for the 5-hour ride. Onward travel to Pleiku and Kontum, or south to Dalat, leaves in the early morning as well. The public bus station in Buon Ma Thuot is on Nguyen Tat Than Street (an artery that originates at the large tank and traffic circle at the city center). Between the station and hotels in town, expect to pay about 10,000 VND for a motorbike taxi.

GETTING AROUND

BY CAR Contact **Damsan Tourist** (✆ **0500/385-0123**) or **Daklak Tourist** (✆ **0500/385-2108**) for rentals with drivers. Expect to pay about $50 per day. (For more information, see their listings in the section "Visitor Information & Tours," below.) Also ask at any hotel front desk about rentals or shared vehicles for day trips.

BY MOTORBIKE You'll pay about $10 per day for rental from your hotel. Best to go on a bike with driver and guide. Pay between $10 and $15, depending on where you plan to go. To Yok Don National Park, for example, pay about $10 for the 1-day round-trip. For Lak Lake, some 55km (34 miles) south, expect to pay $12, and for a combo trip including Dray Sap Waterfall, pay a total of $15. For a reliable and helpful driver, contact **Mr. Tam Nguyen** at ✆ **0932/474-242** (23 Nguyen Cong Tru St.).

VISITOR INFORMATION & TOURS

The local government agency, **Daklak Tourist,** 53 Ly Thuong Kiet St. (✆ **0500/385-2108;** fax 0500/385-2865; travel@daklaktourist.com.vn), has an office just north of the Thang Loi (Victory) Hotel near the central monument. Housed in an old wooden house, the company's helpful staff can arrange good trips to just about anywhere in the province, with services comparable to those of Damsan, below. These guys are expensive (car rental is from about $50 per day, depending on where you go), but this office is convenient and a good place to pick up information. They sell a useful local map for 10,000 VND. It's open daily from 7:30 to 11am and 1:30 to 5pm.

Damsan Tours (212–214 Nguyen Cong Tru St.; ✆ **0500/385-0123**) is a very helpful little outfit, and a good place to just pick up information (or a map, at a cost of 10,000 VND) before hiring a motorbike guide yourself. Their prices match those of Daklak Tourist (see above). It's open daily from 7 to 11am and 2 to 5pm.

FAST FACTS **Vietcombank** has a branch at 6 Tran Hung Dao (✆ **0500/385-7899**), and you'll find a 24-hour ATM at **Vietcombank ATM,** located just west of the Victory Monument in front of the Thang Loi (Victory) Hotel. The **Agricultural and Rural Development Bank** at 37 Phan Boi Chau (✆ **0500/385-2433**) can cash traveler's checks, as can most hotel front desks.

WHERE TO STAY

Damsan Hotel ★ The Damsan is about 1km (½ mile) east of the town center and overlooks a quiet valley with coffee fields out front. The location might sound like a drawback, but the hotel's very helpful in-house tour company and good dining make this place quite self-contained. Just arrive, and you can plan all of your travels from here. The hotel is comparable to the White Horse but is more convenient. Ask for a room on a higher floor with views of the coffee plantation. They've recently replaced the tennis courts and even upgraded suites and deluxe rooms—it's worth paying the extra $5 for a bigger, newer room. The pool has also been cleaned out (goodbye, algae) and is a nice place to relax in the afternoon. Arrange any kind of trek here, perhaps a long day trip by bus or motorbike that includes canoeing or elephant rides, or spend a night in a hilltribe village, leaving your bag with the kind folks at Damsan in anticipation of a nice shower and air-conditioning; funny how our perspective on luxury changes when we meet with people living under thatch with no walls.

212–214 Nguyen Cong Tru St., Buon Ma Thuot. ✆ **0500/385-1234.** Fax 0500/385-2309. damsanhotel@dng.vnn.vn. 68 units. $30–$40 double; $60 suite. AE, MC, V. **Amenities:** 2 restaurants; bar; Internet; outdoor swimming pool; tennis court. *In room:* A/C, TV, fridge, minibar.

White Horse Hotel (Bach Ma) ★ Newly built and popular, the Bach Ma is a good, clean place with friendly front-desk service and good support for trips to the countryside or businesses in the area—many of the expatriate coffee buyers stay here for want of anything better—but nothing about the place is luxurious. The lobby's attempt at grandiosity starts and ends with a towering marble statue of an ancient Greek woman greeting you in the lobby and open elevators with views of the town. Double rooms are downright bedilicious, with two large double beds dominating the space, but in just a large, plain, white-tile room. VIP rooms are not worth the extra bucks. They may come with a computer and the bonus of a shower curtain, but the carpets are stained and the sitting room is a separate room dominated by cheap leather couches.

09–11 Nguyen Duc Canh St., Buon Ma Thuot. ✆ **0500/381-5656.** Fax 0500/381-5588. www.bachmahotel.com. 70 units. $30–$40 double; $50 VIP room. AE, MC, V. **Amenities:** Restaurant; bar; sauna; steam. *In room:* A/C, TV, fridge, minibar, Wi-Fi.

WHERE TO DINE

Quan Ngon ★ VIETNAMESE A big, bright, flashy joint at night, this is the place locals drive by and say, "Expensive," before taking you to their favorite little place around the corner (at half the price). But by Western standards, Quan Ngon is cheap and serves good local fare, the usual stir-fries, rice and noodle dishes, and hot pots, as well as seafood brought in regularly from the coast and kept in tanks (I'd stick to land animals, though). The place is always packed for lunch and dinner, and you might even catch a coffee-plantation business lunch at this open-air, tin-roofed eatery. The restaurant is about a 5-minute walk east of the central square. The small attached coffee-and-liquor shop sells the local finest, as well as a funky collection of herbs and traditional medicines.

72–74 Ba Trieu. ✆ **0500/385-1909.** Main courses 50,000 VND–230,000 VND. No credit cards. Daily 10am–10pm.

Thanh Van's Nem Nuong (Spring Rolls) ★★ VIETNAMESE A meal here is as cheap as it comes—and it's a tasty meal among locals. This shop is just one among about four on this little street just west of the Victory Monument, and right in the heart of the town's most choice budget accommodations. Here's the drill: Sit down and say "one" or just hold up a finger, and your table will be covered with dishes such as grilled pork and thin pork rind, white rice noodles, pickles, lettuce, a few sauces, and a plate of rice paper. You build 'em yourself, good fresh spring rolls. If you've never done it before and you struggle for a minute—while everyone is watching and laughing—someone will come over to show you how to do it. Lots of variations (keep an eye on techniques at adjacent tables), and the only way to do it wrong is to miss getting it in your mouth.

20 Ly Thuong Kiet, Buon Ma Thuot. ✆ **0500/385-9561** or 0914/093-990. Spring roll set for 1 17,000 VND. No credit cards. Daily 8am–10pm.

ATTRACTIONS

Museums

The Ethnographic Museum The museum—in a beat-up old colonial-style building adjoining a park and old administration buildings—is hardly organized, but it showcases a good collection of the effects of local hilltribe peoples: the Ede, M'nong, Ra-glai, Jarai, Bannar, and Cham. You'll find an interesting array of traditional dress for each group and displays of everyday items such as the large M'nong whiskey jars, rattan backpacks, wooden mortar and pestles for grinding grain, elaborate musical instruments, and lots of farming and weaving implements. There's a small model of a Rong House and a few interesting examples of the unique pillars used to mark graves, as well as various items of ritual statuary. One room features a hauda (a large, multiperson elephant saddle), elephant riding gear, and photos of local elephant culture. Sadly, there are few English explanations, but much is self-explanatory. This is the most interesting of the town's three museums.

182 Nguyen Du St. ✆ **0500/385-0426.** Admission 10,000 VND. Daily 7:30–11:30am and 2–5pm.

Revolutionary Museum For war buffs and history freaks, this faded collection of photos is worth a visit—if just for another chance to see the Vietnamese side of the story. You'll find reproductions of classic images from the war, such as the "Girl in the Picture" or "Crossing the River," as well as more obscure shots of early U.S. advisors in the region and ethnic minority actions during the war years. The Hanoi government is still waging a hard-fought—and failing—PR campaign to win hearts and minds of the ethnic minorities in the region, and images in this museum are heavy on the "local heroes," or the hilltribe folks who supported the North during the revolution. The whole story of the revolution is told in the museum's three rooms, and though there are few English signs (other than recognizable names), the clockwise progression through the museum is a good story and, as always, ends with faded glossies of the happy, fully functioning factories and farms of the present day. The nearby **Historical Museum** (18 Than Thuot St.) was under a major renovation at press time.

01 Le Duan St. ✆ **0500/385-2527.** Admission 10,000 VND. Daily 7:30–11:30am and 2–5pm.

Sights Outside of Town

Originating in the high peaks deep inside the highlands' long ridge, the **Serepok River** falls from on high, gouging dynamic ravines in layers of sediment and bedrock to form stunning falls before emptying into the wide, lazy Lak Lake to the far south. All of Buon Ma Thuot's sights are along the river's length. The best way to see the sights is to hire a motorbike on your own (from any hotel front desk) or arrange a tour with the town's two tour agencies (see "Visitor Information & Tours," above). Check the places below to create your day-trip itinerary. Typical 1-day trips include one of the following: Lak Lake, Yok Don, or Dray Sap Falls. Follow with a visit to the Ede village just outside of town.

Ede Village Just 15km (9¼ miles) south of town, this tiny parcel is an ethnic enclave set up by the Vietnamese government, something like their own "Strategic Hamlet Program," to deal with the perceived threat of splinter factions among ethnic minorities. The first house you come to in the village is the town's English-speaking family, and you'll certainly want to see if anyone's home. One of the younger kids gave me a quick tour of the village, explaining how extended families live in segregated longhouses on stilts and that you can tell how many nuclear families are in one household by the number of windows. Folks are friendly, even if seeming shy, and it's okay to take pictures if you ask first. With my guide, I was able to talk with some of the lads—they wanted to know how much my camera cost and if I had a car. It feels like the village is set up for tourism, and it is (older ladies march out a few weavings they have on sale), but not too many tourists make it out this way, and the village is quite a welcoming place. Do not bring gifts or donations: However, if you plan to be in the area for any amount of time, find out what kind of needs there are and, with the help of a guide, offer some useful supplies (usually medicine or school supplies), but passing out bonbons or pens is not encouraged (even the village head himself asks visitors not to).

Dray Sap and Gia Long Waterfalls These two stunning waterfalls are some 30km (19 miles) south of Buon Ma Thuot. Down opposite forks of the same entrance road (pay just 8,000 VND to enter), they're a good day trip from Buon Ma Thuot. ***Note:*** Lak Lake and the falls, though both to the south, are separate day trips—it's too much driving for 1 day.

First, **Dray Sap Falls** has a shaded kiosk area at the entry, a good place to buy a cool beverage after the long, dusty ride. Two paths connect to the falls from the kiosk, the lower road tracing the water's edge up to the falls (don't cross the bridge, as that path just leads to cotton fields and a less picturesque falls view) and the upper path of uneven cobble leading to the top of the falls. Take the low road and have a dip at the base of this stunning high waterfall created by a massive granite shelf. There are some good shaded areas, thanks to some massive, overhanging banyans and willows. The view from the top of the falls is great, and the rocky path is a fun climb that connects with the cobbled trail leading high above the bank back to the kiosk. Nearby **Gia Long Waterfall** is just a few clicks down a well-maintained service road, and this waterfall is even more dynamic, not so much for the falling water—which is just a trickle in the dry season—but for its steep rock formations. The whole area around the Gia Long Waterfall is eminently climbable.

Yok Don National Park North of Buon Ma Thuot, this park is a great place to travel among small communities of ethnic minorities, including skilled M'nong elephant mahouts. In this park—Vietnam's largest, at over 100,000 hectares (247,000 acres)—you'll find more than 60 species of mammals, including deer, monkeys, and even wild elephants, as well as a number of rare and endangered animals. You can take an elephant ride with a M'nong mahout, swim in the Serepok River, or take a good day hike to **Ban Don,** a small village set up for tourists. Yok Don is not only the largest park in Vietnam, but the most temperate, with average temperatures in the mid-70s (mid-20s Celsius) and lots of rainfall. The park is 40km (25 miles) north of Buon Ma Thuot, and a trip here—whether a day trip or an overnight in a homestay—is best arranged through one of Buon Ma Thuot's travel agents, Damsan or Daklak Tourist (see "Visitor Information & Tours," above). Overnight tours stay either in the very drab concrete-block guesthouse near the park entry or in Ban Don village at a longhouse set up for foreigner visitors. An overnight gives you a chance to spot animals in the early morning, but most folks do this as a day trip (start early for a chance to see some wildlife).

Lak Lake The 1½-hour bumpy ride south of Buon Ma Thuot to Lak Lake is a worthwhile day trip and a good access point to visit hilltribe villages. There are many groups of M'nong people, small splinter groups with disparate languages even, represented in the enclaves surrounding the lake. You enter the Lak Lake area via the **Jun Village** and can go by boat or on elephant back across the shallow waters to the adjacent **M'Lieng Village.** More adventurous tours take you by boat and then on foot farther back into the bush. When you visit the villages, note the large mounds outside of any enclave: When M'nong die, they put all effects and the body in a raised grave for 1 year, and then cremate it.

If you're visiting the lake on your own, whether by hired motorbike or car, you'll park in busy little Jun Village, alone worth a stroll to see what rural life along the lake is like, and from here exploration is best by boat. For a 1-hour boat ride on Lak Lake and across to the M'Lieng village, expect to pay about $10 for an hour. You can do the same trip by elephant for $30. These trips are included if you book a tour, but you can also arrange them at the water's edge with a bit of casual coffee drinking and shooting the breeze (and these figures are just points of departure for a bit of bargaining). Look for Mr. Duc, who speaks all of three English words ("You go boat"), at the first little coffee shop near the TOURIST INFORMATION sign. He's a real hoot, and his wife, Mai, cooks the best eats in town. Reach him by phone at ✆ **0500/358-6280** or 0905/371-633, and use a translator (or say "I go boat").

Note: On a hilltop above the Jun Village area of Lak Lake is the little Hotel Biet Dien, operated by Daklak Tourist. The hotel offers great views, and there's a fun "lodge" feel to the place, with old wood floors throughout. Large units are clean, if a bit sparse, but are more stylish than anything near the lake. For just $30, you can sleep in Emperor Bao Dai's actual former room, with great views of the north end of the lake. The six units here range from $20 to $30. Because you're really out in the sticks, this is more or less just a rural slumber party, but the place has a good restaurant, and the mostly French-speaking staff is kind and accommodating. The place is run by Daklak Tourist (see "Visitor Information & Tours," above), and they can make all necessary arrangements for transport there and staying overnight. Be sure to contact them beforehand, because the place gets booked with big French tour groups. Another good option is **Lak Resort** (✆ **0500/358-6184;** Lien Son Townlet, southeast bank of Lak Lake), also run by Daklak Tourist. They have small 1950s-style bungalows in white and pastel green at the southeast end of the lake. They're spacious and clean, and a good bargain at $25. They also have a small outdoor pool on-site. Serious budget travelers can stay in a longhouse for $8. For more information, contact Daklak Tourist in Buon Ma Thuot at Lien Son Street, Lak District, Daklak (✆ **0500/358-6767**).

SHOPPING

Coffee is the name of the shopping game in Buon Ma Thuot, and just about everyone sells **Trung Nguyen,** the Vietnamese Coca-Cola of coffee (you can buy it or drink it in coffee shops just about anywhere). Trung Nguyen's headquarters are in Buon Ma Thuot (268 Nguyen Tat Thanh St.; ✆ **0500/386-5116;** www.trungnguyen.com.vn), and this company sponsors just about every other storefront. You'll find vendors all along the streets around the market or the central Victory Monument. Also look for smaller outlets with lesser-known brands, the likes of **Nam Nguyen** (30 Tran Quang Khai St., near the White Horse Hotel; ✆ **0500/395-5255**).

All of Buon Ma Thuot's souvenir shops are geared toward Vietnamese domestic weekenders from the larger cities, and large **M'nong-style jugs of whiskey,** a smaller replica of the hilltribe's whiskey containers, are for sale along with the long straws that you use to get the stuff in ya (some real fire water). The cool ceramic jugs are a nuisance to carry home on the bus/car/plane, but they're not a bad gift if you plan to visit Vietnamese friends.

3 PLEIKU & KONTUM

Kontum is 50km (31 miles) N of Pleiku; 245km (152 miles) N of Buon Ma Thuot; 198km (123 miles) W of Quy Nhon

The town of Pleiku, capital of Gia Lai Province, is easily recognizable to those who lived through the Vietnam War era: The American Seventh Cavalry, an air brigade and the unit featured in the film *Apocalypse Now* as the Wagner-blaring helicopter squadron that rains terror in its path, touched down south of Pleiku near famed Camp X-Ray in the La Drang Valley on November 14, 1965, for what would be the first open combat between American and North Vietnamese regulars after full American deployment at Danang. The bloody battle pitted 450 U.S. ground forces against nearly 2,000 North Vietnamese regulars, and the 48-hour fight caused many casualties before a tentative U.S. victory. It's not a famous battle of scale, but of legend, because it was where warriors on both sides really cut their teeth and sized each other up for what would be 8 more years of war. The clash was also important because it made the war look "winnable" to Americans, but it didn't actually prove to be a model in the war, in which the hit-and-run North Vietnamese enemy was rarely in sight, and in which engaged pitch battles were only of their choosing. The area is hallowed ground to the veterans of both sides who fought here, and hosts many returnees.

Most visitors give Pleiku a pass and move on to the quieter town of Kontum, which played its own important part in the Vietnam War and has a number of interesting sights outside of the city.

Kontum, and the hills surrounding the provincial city, were home to some of the heaviest fighting at the war's end in 1972, and again after the "Vietnamization" of fighting, when the last holdout units of South Vietnamese soldiers were pummeled into submission along rocky ridges north of town. A motorbike or car ride north of Kontum brings you to the likes of **Charlie Hill** and **Dak To,** now denuded peaks, and a short ride up the now-paved Ho Chi Minh Trail takes you among some great mountain scenery and ethnic villages. Good tours can be arranged out of Kontum. The city itself has just basic services and, apart from the few interesting in-town sights, is as dull as—though less busy than—Pleiku. Do take a walk out along the **Dakbla River.**

Kontum is the last jumping-off point before many travelers hop on the newly built Ho Chi Minh Highway—where the Ho Chi Minh Trail once ran. The road, also known as Hwy. 14, connects Kontum with Danang and Hoi An along the coast. The route is popular for travelers riding along with Easy Riders on motorbike tours out of Dalat (see the "Get Your Motor Running!" box, earlier in this chapter).

The area around Kontum is home to a number of ethnic minorities: Large populations of Bannar people (famed for their high-peaked roof houses) live near the city center, and there are Sedang and Bo villages here, too. Accommodations and dining options are spartan, but the interesting sights are worth the journey.

GETTING THERE

Kontum is 50km (31 miles) north of Pleiku and 245km (152 miles) from Buon Ma Thuot. Coastal Quy Nhon can be reached by road, via Pleiku (about 5 hr.), and the new Ho Chi Minh Trail, Hwy. 14, connects with Danang, far to the north and down along the coast—a 12-hour ride (some Easy Rider tours overnight along the way). All of these routes can be done by local bus—a very uncomfortable, slow option. Going by **private car, motorbike** for the adventurous, or **preplanned tour** are your best options (see "Visitor Information & Tours" in the Dalat section, earlier in this chapter).

Warning: If braving the local buses out of Kontum, know that the bus-station folks will take you for a real ride of resentment. Ticket prices are posted, but they don't sell tickets to foreigners at booths (Kontum is still considered "off-limits" to independent travelers). This means that foreign visitors have to haggle with the surly busmen for a reasonable fare, and these guys start with ridiculous prices like $20. Avoid the hassle and come with your own wheels. Or smile and pantomime that you won't get on the bus for that price, buy yourself a coffee, and let your amateur thespian take over (you can whittle them down to $7).

GETTING AROUND

The sights in both Pleiku and Kontum are all far out in the hills, so you'll have to arrange some kind of transport or tour. This is popular turf for the Easy Riders from Dalat (see "Getting Around" in the Dalat section, earlier in this chapter), and, in fact, you'll be grateful you have a guide here: Most of what you'll want to see in the countryside, whether coffee plantations or rural homes and workplaces, requires some kind of introduction or an ability with the Vietnamese language. You're sure to meet a few cycling tours in these parts, and if you've got the legs for the hills or can afford a support van, cycling these roads is memorable. You can rent rickety little city bicycles in Kontum and hit the few sights around town, or even go out to the Konkoitu Village some 5km (3 miles) out of town, but otherwise you'll need some good, reliable wheels. Motorbikes can be rented at about $7 per day from the hotels listed below, and all hotels can arrange tours to outlying areas, as can the folks at **Kontum Tourist** (see "Visitor Information & Tours," below).

VISITOR INFORMATION & TOURS

Kontum Tourist is the name of the game in Kontum. Find their office on the bottom floor of the Dakbla Hotel at 02 Phan Dinh Phung (✆ **060/386-1626**). It's open daily from 7 to 11am and 2 to 5pm. I couldn't find anyone who speaks much English, but they knew what I was there for and had good maps and menus of tours. Transport is a bit pricey. Expect to pay $20 per day for a motorbike driver/guide, or from $60 for a car. If you haven't come with your own transport, these folks are the best bet, but if you're traveling on the cheap, get your own wheels elsewhere (try the folks at Family Hotel; see below).

FAST FACTS Bring cash to Kontum. There's the **Investment and Development Bank,** 1 Tran Phu St., near the town center (✆ **060/386-2339**), but their services are limited. In Pleiku, try the **Investment and Development Bank,** at 112 Le Loi St. (✆ **059/382-4310**), or the **Vietcombank Bank,** with ATM service at 12 Tran Hung Dao.

WHERE TO STAY

Should you decide to overnight in Pleiku, look for the **Pleiku Hotel,** at 124 Le Loi St. (✆ **059/382-7778**), with basic rooms starting at $19. For a splurge, nicer digs (from $40) and friendly staff can be found at Hoang Anh Gia Lai Hotel, at 1 Phu Dong Sq. (✆ **059/351-8459**).

Dakbla Hotel Named for the river it's located next to, but oriented to a busy intersection, the Dakbla was once all there was in town and packed in miserable group tours for years. In recent years, it had fallen into serious disrepair, but the hotel is in the midst of a renovation, so hopefully that means no more overpriced, musty rooms. The hotel has only one thing going for it: the Dakbla Tourist office on the first floor, which can arrange good visits to ethnic minority villages and to sights around Kontum.

02 Phan Dinh Phung St. (riverside). ✆ **060/386-3333.** Fax 060/386-3336. 20 units. $24 double. MC, V. **Amenities:** Restaurant; bar. *In room:* A/C, TV, fridge, minibar.

Family Hotel The Family Hotel is your standard budget choice. The folks here are, as the name suggests, friendly and inviting, and can help out with any eventuality in your stay in Kontum, including bicycle and motorbike rentals. Husband-and-wife team Phong and Minh and their kids always wear smiles. The same gang of rugged travelers you meet here will all be hanging out at the Dakbla Restaurant later (see below), and you're sure to make friends. If they're full—and in high season they're likely to be—check out **Tay Nguyen** (53 Tran Hung Dao St.; ✆ **060/386-9484**), which has a similar standard of rooms but downright surly service that will make you long for the Family (just next door).

55 Tran Hung Dao St. ✆ **060/386-2448.** Fax 060/386-5748. 20 units. $12–$18 double. No credit cards. **Amenities:** Restaurant (breakfast only); bikes and motorbikes. *In room:* A/C, TV (no satellite), fridge, minibar, Wi-Fi.

WHERE TO DINE

Other than Dakbla (below), the little storefront places geared to backpackers in Kontum (there are a few near the Family Hotel) aren't worth it, and you're better off at a local *pho* (noodle soup) stand. **Hoan Vu Restaurant** (81 Nguyen Hue St., along the riverside road; © **060/386-2792**) is a large, empty place glowing with neon lights, the kind of joint that's popular with big wedding parties and Vietnamese groups, but not very inviting for individual diners. This one's really basic—okay, it's downright grungy—but look for **Huong Hue,** a little open-air place across from the Dakbla Restaurant along Nguyen Hue; they serve rice meals for next to nothing (about 50¢ a plate).

Dakbla Restaurant ★ VIETNAMESE/WESTERN This place is traveler central. Named for the nearby river and unaffiliated with the beat-up Dakbla Hotel around the corner, the Dakbla Restaurant is a cozy storefront. The friendly English-speaking staff greets you heartily, and the place serves up good, affordable one-plate meals, including Vietnamese stir-fries and rice dishes. They offer a few Western specials, including good sandwiches and fry-up breakfasts. A stop at Dakbla's is also your best bet for hooking up with other travelers in the area and splitting the cost of day tours or onward connection by hired car. The atmosphere is laid-back, and the restaurant is a good place to kick back in the midday heat and take up a game of backgammon or chess. They sell all kinds of local hilltribe wear and paraphernalia, all of which decorates the walls. They also rent bikes.

168 Nguyen Hue St., Kontum. © **060/386-2584.** Main courses 30,000 VND–80,000 VND. No credit cards. Daily 8am–9pm.

Eva Coffee ★★ Finds COFFEE SHOP/VIETNAMESE Mr. An, with his wife, Cam, and three kids, brings a bit of the art world to the little city of Kontum. This quiet coffee corner on the far edge of town (on the way to or from the Bannar Rong House to the east) is overflowing with Mr. An's shrapnel sculpture and pieces made of war fallout, as well as his unique rough-hewn and weathered wooden carvings of contorted human faces, a medium inspired by the hilltribe custom of making funerary statues over a grave and leaving the wooden pieces to decay. All kinds of cool stuff are scattered all about this quiet little garden. An grew up in Kontum and later wrote a thesis about hilltribe gardens, his inspiration for designing this quiet hideaway. Grab a cool drink, put your feet up, and prepare for a long talk with the man himself, and maybe you'll discover the soul of the garden (or be inspired to plant your own). You'll find a simple menu of snacks and one-plate meals, along with their roster of good coffees, teas, and desserts.

01 Phan Chu Trinh St. (on the eastern end of town near the Kontum Village and Bannar Rong House). © **060/386-2944.** evacoffee2002@yahoo.com. No credit cards. Daily 6am–11pm.

ATTRACTIONS IN TOWN

Old Wooden Church and Orphanage Built in 1932 on the site of an earlier, more humble structure, Kontum's main church is still a busy place, and on Sunday ministers to a large population of the converted, mostly ethnic hilltribe villagers from the surrounding hills. Check out the intricately carved mantles over the main entrances and the cool, contemporary stained glass featuring modern saints—the likes of French missionaries wearing cravats. A model of a Bannar house is in the courtyard, as is a glowing white statue of Mary and child. The **orphanage** at the back of the main church building is a wild, cacophonous experience. Prepare yourself. A short walk down the steps, and you're attacked by groups of youngsters eager and well accustomed to talking and goofing with foreign visitors (also keen for the sweets and gifts that many visitors bring with them). These children, most orphaned by disease, are cared for by nuns, and visitors are welcome to volunteer their services. In fact, I met a small contingent of Americans doing relief work at the school.

Along the river at the town center. Free admission. Dawn–dusk.

Seminary and Ethnic Hilltribe Museum This massive wooden structure of timber and frame was left by aggressive French missionaries who, from a humble skeleton crew in 1848, grew steadily in numbers as they sought to bring the seemingly heathen hilltribe folks into the fold. This seminary was built in 1935 and was at its heyday under **Martial Jasmin,** the first Catholic bishop of the area until 1940. The French were forced to skedaddle as fighting flared up from the 1950s, and activities at the seminary died down. But from the time of reunification in 1975, a Vietnamese bishop was installed at the head, and the seminary now ministers to the needs, both humanitarian and spiritual, of great numbers of hilltribe villagers, all of whom wait in long queues outside the many offices and the clinic here.

The **Ethnic Hilltribe Museum** tells as much about the story of the monastery as it does about hilltribe culture, listing the lineage of bishops with photos of the seminary's many projects over the years—for improved irrigation, agriculture, health, and education. The museum springs from the more modern, post–Vatican II notion of spreading the faith without completely squelching rich local traditions. For instance, some practices, such as the making of large wooden representations of human figures to don graves (the statues decay over time into the most stunning expressionistic pieces), were accepted as part of local Christian practices. You need to visit the museum with a docent, a kind and informative tour guide.

Along Tran Hung Dao heading east of town. Check in at the main desk to contact a docent. Donations accepted. Mon–Sat 8–11am and 2–4pm.

OUTSIDE OF KONTUM

An All-Day Ride North of Kontum

Rent a motorbike (for the adventurous) or join a tour for this all-day ride around the picturesque hills north of little Kontum. Many follow this route with an Easy Rider motorbike guide and carry on to Danang or Hoi An.

From Kontum, head north on Phan Dinh Phung past the bus station on the outskirts of town. Concrete storefronts give way to curving roads along mountain tracks and into the hilly expanse that once was the stamping ground of legions of jolly green American giants and sandal-clad Vietnamese forces, a major battleground during the war. Sights up this way include **Dak To,** some 50km (31 miles) north. Centered around a model *nha rong,* a Bannar longhouse, the town of Dak To is quite well developed. Follow signs from here to nearby **Charlie Hill,** the famous battleground where so many gave their lives. Use this place as a reference point to the south of the road leading toward the Laos border; all that even the best guide can do is to tell of the valiant fighting that took place here and of the massive loss of life, especially among the last holdout South Vietnamese forces late in the war.

Continue on the **Ho Chi Minh Trail** through this area. Just recently, on September 2, 2004 (National Day), the ribbon was cut and Hwy. 14, also known as the Ho Chi Minh Trail Road, was opened. The highway follows a scenic path of the vital wartime supply line, and the road's completion was an act of national unity as much as a route for traffic and commerce. Starting all the way in Quang Tri Province, just south of the demilitarized zone (DMZ) near Hue, the road runs the long ridge of the Central Highlands through Kontum,

Pleiku, and Buon Ma Thuot. The section north of Kontum is particularly lovely, with rolling hills and quiet villages.

Past Dak To and Charlie Hill—tour guides usually take you to a select few villages along the way—you'll come to the crossroads in the town of Ngoc Hoi, some 60km (37 miles) out of Kontum. From Ngoc Hoi, a right turn on the Ho Chi Minh Trail (Hwy. 14) carries you to the north—a left from the crossroads of Ngoc Hoi brings you to a checkpoint where you'll be turned back; carrying on straight brings you along some 20km (12 miles) of picturesque mountain road among little-visited villages leading up to the **Indochina Corner,** where the border of Laos, Cambodia, and Vietnam meet. You can find the point on a map, but short of the interesting ride through some beautiful mountain landscape, the Indochina Corner is a heavily guarded area and nationals of most Western nations are forbidden from crossing any of these borders, so expect a swift turnabout before a checkpoint—but at least you can say you were there.

Konkoitu and the Villages East of Kontum Accessible by a long but worthwhile bike ride, this little village is a model of "enforced primitivism"—the folks from government-run Dakbla Tourism even come out to monitor and assist with preparations for festivals in the village (really just to ensure that the busloads of tourists they bring out this way will be entertained). When I arrived, a large contingent of shifty-eyed government guys were milling about, and the local people busied themselves decorating long bamboo poles that would be erected for a ceremony. When the officials left, it was like the teacher walked out of the room. The craftsmen made a few jokes and everyone laughed; then they invited me over to chat with them—many learned to speak English having served as guides and scouts for U.S. forces during the war.

Most ethnic hilltribes in the region are situated along a river—much like villages in nearby Laos—and Konkoitu overlooks a wide bend in the Dakbla (a good place to go dip your toes and meet with people swimming, bathing, and doing laundry). At the village center is the high-peaked Bannar Rong House (or *nha rong*), home to the community center, a temple, and government offices. A number of other Bannar communities are along the road—all easily recognizable by their high-peaked *nha rong.* To get to Konkoitu, follow central Tran Hung Dao Street heading east out of Kontum. Stay straight, past one *nha rong* on the right, and cross the bridge over the Dakbla. From there, stay left and follow the curving riverside road a few clicks until you come to a large settlement, where you'll see the high roof on your left. Ask to take a photo. The people of Konkoitu are used to foreign visitors, and most are glad to pose for a frame or two, but always be sure to ask. Contact Kontum Tourist (see "Visitor Information & Tours," above) to inquire about festivals and tours to more far-reaching Bannar and Sedang villages.

11

South-Central Vietnam

South-Central Vietnam is a stunning sweep of coastal beaches—some of Vietnam's most popular places to put your toes in the sand and have a big, embarrassing drink with an umbrella poking out the top. The area is flanked on the west by the **Trong Son Mountains** of the Central Highlands (see chapter 10). Traveling south from Danang and Hoi An, you'll first reach the town of **Quy Nhon,** a little deepwater port famed for its fine shipbuilding trade. Just outside of town are a number of cool beach areas. You'll find just one luxury resort—the Life Resort Quy Nhon—and a few fun budget stops in town.

Heading farther south, you'll pass mile after mile of fishing villages and open beach areas before arriving in thriving **Nha Trang.** Once geared only to Vietnamese tourists on beach holiday in the summer months, some of the finest resorts in all of Vietnam have found a home in Nha Trang. And now the area draws many international tourists who can easily connect from any major city (Hanoi, Ho Chi Minh, or Danang) by daily flights on Vietnam Airlines. With good day-trip options, booze cruises, snorkeling, diving, or sailing, Nha Trang has something for everyone. The town also hops late into the night with a fun, friendly bar scene—mostly young backpackers. More far-flung resorts on outlying islands and peninsulas mean more and better options for escaping the busy, central backpacker party area of Nha Trang—but that's what lots of folks come for.

Between Nha Trang and Ho Chi Minh City (Saigon) in the far south, you'll pass the small town of **Phan Rang** (or Thap Cham), with its high Cham Towers—really just a crossroads for trips up into Dalat (see chapter 10)—before arriving in **Phan Thiet** and the nearby beaches of **Mui Ne.** Just a 3-hour drive from Ho Chi Minh City, the beaches at Mui Ne have become a popular escape for the city's expats, with a growing set of kite-surfing devotees, as well as golf enthusiasts for Nick Faldo's famed course. From here, day trips are easy to giant sand dunes and a remote lake. Before hitting Saigon (farther south), one of these sights is a good spot for some rest and relaxation.

1 QUY NHON

320km (198 miles) S of Danang; 230km (143 miles) north of Nha Trang

A popular saying goes, "It is not the north, it is not the south; nobody trusts the center." Historically fiercely independent, folks in this part of Vietnam enjoyed their moment in history when two brothers, most notably **Nguyen Hue,** incited what became the **Tay Son Rebellion** in 1772, an uprising against the Nguyen rulers. The rebels marched to Hanoi and struck a crushing blow to a vastly superior Chinese force at Dong Da, and Nguyen Hue became **Emperor Quang Trung**—only briefly, though. He died and rule passed to Gia Long, the first king of the last Vietnamese monarchy. Quang Trung's feisty spirit is celebrated during the Tet holiday nationwide—his great victory came during the Lunar New Year—and in Quy Nhon with an annual festival and at the local museum. Quy Nhon is Vietnam's Texas—as in, "Don't Mess With . . . ."

The small peninsula city of Quy Nhon is sheltered by outlying islands and a curved spit of land like a "cap," which makes this a very effective deepwater port, the most important in a long stretch between Danang and Nha Trang. As a result of this strategic importance, the town was hotly contested over for centuries, first by the Chinese and later by the French and the Americans (some of the largest U.S. troop deployments, including the famed "Air Cav" unit, came ashore here at Quy Nhon in 1968).

Although it's long been—and continues to be—more of a fishing port than a tourist destination, Quy Nhon's long central beach is beginning to attract new developments for tourists.

GETTING THERE

BY PLANE **Vietnam Airlines** flies between Quy Nhon and Ho Chi Minh City daily, and connects with Hanoi 3 days a week (Mon, Wed, and Sat). Contact the airline through your hotel front desk or through their local office (55 Le Hong Phong St.; ✆ **056/382-5313**). Quy Nhon's **Phu Cat Airport** is 35km (22 miles) north of the port area.

BY BUS **Local buses** will get you anywhere in the region: to the Central Highlands via Kontum (about 6 hr.), to the north via Danang (6 hr.), and to the south via Nha Trang (about 5 hr.). **Mai Linh Taxi** (✆ **0510/391-4914**) runs daily shuttle buses from Hoi An for 90,000 VND (5½ hr.). Apart from the overnight buses between Nha Trang and Hoi An that sometimes pick up passengers in Quy Nhon at around 4am, the **"Open Tour" buses do not make regular stops here,** so you'll have to use local buses or hire a car for overland travel. The **bus station** in Quy Nhon is about a kilometer (half a mile) from the beach at the far south end of town (about 10,000 VND by motorbike taxi from most points in the city).

BY TRAIN Local trains as well as the Reunification Express connect Quy Nhon with Nha Trang to the south and Danang to the north. The passenger station is far from the city center, and messing around arranging tickets is time-consuming (and frustrating), but most hotels or **Barbara's Backpackers** (see "Visitor Information & Tours," below) can arrange it for you for as little as 7,000 VND commission.

GETTING AROUND

If you're arriving by plane, contact your resort of choice for a transfer (which is usually included, but specify when booking). **Quy Nhon Taxi** (✆ **056/381-5815**) can get you around the peninsula in style for just 10,000 VND per kilometer. **Motorbike taxi drivers** are less pushy in Quy Nhon, and in fact, you'll have to hunt them down a bit, which is refreshing; a ride around town starts from 5,000 VND. There are no set places to **rent a motorbike,** but contact your hotel front desk or stop by **Barbara's Backpackers** (see "Visitor Information & Tours," below) to get yourself a set of wheels (expect to pay about 80,000 VND). Barbara's also rents bicycles for $1 a day, as do many of the town's hotels. Biking to the sights in town is doable, but the beaches require a short hill ride, and visiting the Cham towers means navigating city traffic.

ORIENTATION Quy Nhon is a V-shaped peninsula that, at its narrowest point, is an important deepwater port protected from the stormy seas by outlying islands and a long curve of landmass. Riverside Nguyen Hue Street in the central and northern end of town turns into An Duong as it passes to the south. Quy Nhon is just off the main north-south highway, Route 1, along a newly constructed spur road, Route 1A. The best beaches in the area are south of Quy Nhon center.

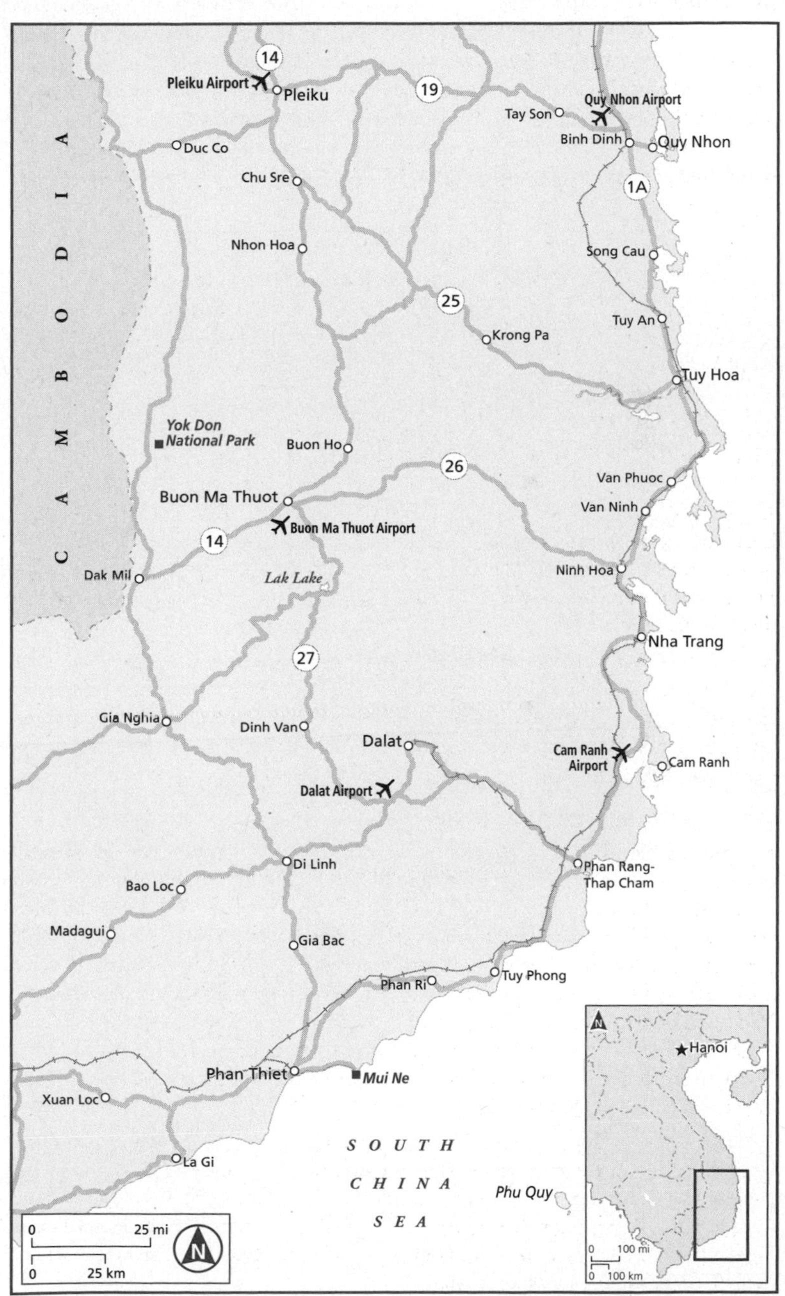
CAMBODIA
14
Pleiku Airport
Pleiku
19
Quy Nhon Airport
Tay Son
Binh Dinh
Quy Nhon
Duc Co
Chu Sre
1A
Nhon Hoa
Song Cau
25
Tuy An
Krong Pa
Tuy Hoa
Yok Don
National Park
Buon Ho
26
Van Phuoc
Buon Ma Thuot
Van Ninh
Buon Ma Thuot Airport
14
Ninh Hoa
Dak Mil
Lak Lake
Nha Trang
27
Gia Nghia
Dinh Van
Dalat
Cam Ranh
Airport
Cam Ranh
Dalat Airport
Di Linh
Phan Rang-
Thap Cham
Bao Loc
Madagui
Gia Bac
Tuy Phong
Phan Ri
Phan Thiet
Mui Ne
Xuan Loc
La Gi
SOUTH
CHINA
SEA
Phu Quy
0 25 mi
0 25 km
N
Hanoi
0 100 mi
0 100 km

VISITOR INFORMATION & TOURS

Barbara's Backpackers (18 Nguyen Hue St.; ✆ **056/389-2921;** nzbarb@yahoo.com) and Kiwi Restaurant are pretty much *it* in town; they're basically expat and traveler information central. Barbara is a very friendly New Zealander who has been in Quy Nhon for 10 years and helps coordinate the many aid projects coming into the area; she or one of her very helpful staff members can help with any eventuality, arrange tours, find you a motorbike to rent, and give good advice about local happenings (and the food is good, too—see Barbara's Backpackers under "Where to Dine," below).

Fast Facts Quy Nhon

Banks & Currency Exchange **Vietcombank** has a branch with all services (including ATM) at the corner of Le Loi and Tran Hung Dao (✆ **056/382-2408;** open daily 8–11am and 1:30–5pm, Sat in the morning only).

Internet **Internet cafes** are just about everywhere in town, but service is slow and not so reliable (try early in the morning or late at night if the place stays open).

Post Office The **Central Post Office (Buu Dien)** is at 197 Phan Boi Chau St. (✆ **056/382-1441;** open daily 6:30am–10pm).

WHERE TO STAY

In a pinch? **Quy Nhon Hotel** is run by Saigontourist and is kind of a mess but offers lots of services and is located in the middle of town (08 Nguyen Hue St.; ✆ **056/389-2401;** fax 056/389-1162; www.quynhonhotel.binhdinh.com.vn).

Expensive

Life Wellness Resort Quy Nhon ★★ This resort is a real find, a self-contained hideaway far from the wicked world. Guest rooms are huge, and top-floor rooms have peaked tile roofs. Everyone gets a spacious balcony and unobstructed views of the grand sweep of rocky bay. Most bathrooms have corner shower units that look out over the sea from a floor-to-ceiling plate-glass window (there's a curtain, if you're shy); if you would prefer a small tub, request a ground-floor suite. The cool open plan of the rooms is quite cozy, especially when the ocean breezes blow. The resort has a fine spa, with luxurious treatment centers set on a cliff-top area amid lush gardens. The smallish central pool offers great views of the bay, but I suggest taking up residence on the resort's private beach. This is the perfect place to sit and watch the small basket boats, which are just big enough for one or two people and used as tenders to carry a catch or supplies ashore, riding the dangerous surf just north of the resort—take a walk and you might get to talking with these friendly locals. Dining at the resort is excellent—try the sea bass seasoned with ginger and lemon grass and steamed in a banana leaf. The resort does have one drawback: its remote location some 16km (10 miles) south of Quy Nhon town. There are, however, plenty of in-house activities (free yoga, tai chi, snorkeling trips to a nearby island, and even beginner Vietnamese lessons) to keep you busy in this idyllic resort.

Ghenh Rang, Bai Dai Beach, Quy Nhon City, Binh Dinh Province (16km/10 miles south of town along the coastal road, Rte. 1A). ✆ **056/384-0132.** Fax 056/384-0138. 63 units. $116–$132 double; $162 suite.

MC, V. **Amenities:** Restaurant; bar and lounge; outdoor pool (oceanview); babysitting; free bike; children's center; Jacuzzi; room service; sauna; spa w/natural outdoor pool; watersports equipment rentals and scuba center.

Moderate/Inexpensive

Hai Au (Seagull Hotel) This government hotel was one of the first along this stretch. A recent expansion means that rooms are modern and comfortable, if lacking in style. Rooms have plush maroon or orange carpet lines, which, despite the fleur de lis pattern, are distinctly Asian in decor. Double rooms come with small balconies and compact, tidy bathrooms with tubs only. Full ocean views are available with suites only, which also come with a spacious separate shower cubicle and brand-new flatscreen TVs.

489 An Duong St. ✆ **056/384-6473.** Fax 056/384-6926. www.seagullhotel.com.vn. 169 units. $65–$85 double; $200–$300 suite. MC, V. **Amenities:** 6 restaurants; room service; sauna; steam. *In room:* A/C, TV, fridge, minibar, Wi-Fi.

Hoang Anh Quy Nhon Resort ★ South of central Quy Nhon, just before climbing the hill out of town, Hoang Anh Resort is tidy and affordable. It's especially popular with Vietnamese tourists and businesspeople (lots of local conventions). At portside, the resort has a nice sandy beach out front. Wooden boardwalks connect four-unit building blocks, some of which face the sea. The resort owner is a Vietnamese wood-and-granite magnate—and owns Pleiku's professional soccer team, to boot—so the fine raw materials (wood and stone, go figure) make the resort's rooms rather sumptuous affairs, especially for the price. Bathrooms are large and have proper tubs and decent amenities. Rooms are the best in town, and sea views of the busy port area are good. They have two pools (the larger pool is quite picturesque and cozy), and unlike other in-town hotels, this resort's beach is kept clean and has shaded lounges. The hotel has two good restaurants: one a Thai restaurant set in a faux boat at the resort center, and the other a large Chinese affair away from the beach.

01 Han Mac Tu St. (on the farthest end of Quy Nhon's main bay). ✆ **056/374-7100.** Fax 056/374-7111. 133 units. $46 city view; $60 sea view. MC, V. **Amenities:** 2 restaurants; bar; small fitness center; Internet; 2 pools; small spa; 2 outdoor tennis courts. *In room:* A/C, TV, fridge, minibar, Wi-Fi.

WHERE TO DINE

Barbara's Backpackers ★ WESTERN/VIETNAMESE While many storefront restaurants catering to budget tourists try to do too much, the more limited menu here means that they actually *have* everything they list and, more important, do it right. The sandwiches on local baguettes are good. Salads are ample. Breakfasts are hearty, and you can get good pizza and pasta. Check the blackboard for daily specials. And at least pop in for a drink and a chat with Barbara herself or the many young travelers and NGO folks who call the place home (at least for dinner).

18 Nguyen Hue St., Quy Nhon. ✆ **056/389-2921.** Main courses 20,000 VND–80,000 VND. No credit cards. Daily 7am–9pm.

Dong SEAFOOD Set in a little warren of streets not far from the central market and port area of Quy Nhon, Dong is just one of many little seafood places (also check out **2000** at 3 Tran Doc St., ✆ **056/381-4503,** just around the corner). Dong is a two-floor open-air restaurant, low luxe but done in tile and quite clean. The fare is seafood as you like it. Yes, there's rice, and you can order some vegetables to go with it, but this is more or less a seafood meal. There's an English section toward the back of the menu. There's one guy who knows the words "fried, steamed, or grilled," and you'll be sure to learn the words for lobster and crab.

26 Nguyen Lac, Quy Nhon. ✆ **056/382-4877.** Main courses are market price. Expect to pay $4–$6.50 per plate for small items like shrimp or squid, $20–$30 per kg for fish and lobster. No credit cards. Daily 8am–11pm.

ATTRACTIONS

If you have time for only one attraction here, be sure to check out the huge **boatbuilding** operation on Phan Chu Trinh Street. Up to 10 large oceangoing boats are in production at any given time, and visitors are free to wander around at their own peril. The whole place is a great photo opportunity. Craftsmen start with chain saws and hand planers on rough-hewn planks, light fires to heat and bend the sections that make the curved prows of the boats, and assemble the large frames under a large tin-roof warehouse, a track leading from the shop to the sea. You'll see some serious heaving and hauling by large gangs of young workers, and can get up close with the more skilled craftsmen or chat with grinning septuagenarians marking planks with neon paint. A memorable visit and the kind of place that eats up rolls of film and fills up memory cards.

Binh Dinh Museum This small museum has a few good examples of Cham sculpture and pre-Cham Bronze Age pieces. More for school trips than international tourists, but you can expect signs in Vietnamese and English. If you want to continue exploring after this museum, you might check out the **Quang Trung Museum** some 40km-plus (more than 25 miles) south of Quy Nhon—on the site of the original Tay Son Rebellion—but it's mostly for history buffs or as the second leg on a school trip including the Binh Dinh Museum. (Are we there yet?)

Oceanside at 26 Nguyen Hue St. Free admission. Daily 8am–5pm.

Queen's Beach and Quy Hoa Leper Colony This half-day jaunt starts at **Ghenh Rang Landscape Park** just south of the Hoang Anh Quy Nhon Resort (see "Where to Stay," above). Take the first left after the resort up the hill. You'll pay 4,000 VND for entry and an additional 2,000 VND for a motorbike to get into the park. The road from there winds its way high above the coast and affords great views back to the busy port and peninsula of Quy Nhon. Stop for a coffee and chat with locals in one of the little roadside stops along the way.

The road through Ghenh Rang leads over a hump of seaside land directly to the **Queen's Beach** and **Quy Hoa Leper Colony** (2.5km/1½ miles south of the main beach road, either through Ghenh Rang Park or off of Rte. 1A). The beach out front, named for the wife of Bao Dai, the last emperor of Vietnam, is quite inviting, and a good place (albeit no lounge chairs) to put your feet up. It's refreshingly free of touts and sellers, but actually you'll find that the lack of them means you have to bring all the stuff—lunch, snacks, an umbrella—yourself. The leper colony is a tidy set of buildings all fenced in, yet surrounded by the homes of former patients who now live quite full lives. The seaside promenade just in front of the leper colony is picturesque; you'll see a small grove of trees and a gallery of busts of famous scientists and great medical innovators from Greece, England, France, and Vietnam (just one woman, a Vietnamese lady). Look for the bust of Marie De La Passion (1839–1904) near the center of the park; she was a longtime French missionary at the colony. Because of the hard work of colony residents, the whole area is refreshingly free of garbage. You're likely to run into Vietnamese school tours on weekdays, and the *"Hello! Wha choo nay?"* are fast and thick. Say *"Xin chao"* (hello) right back.

Just a few kilometers up and over the hill on the south end of town (best by rented motorcycle or taxi). Entrance to the park is 4,000 VND plus 2,000 VND with motorbike. Daily 8am–4pm.

Revisit the My Lai Massacre

March 16, 1968: Chasing an elusive enemy and beleaguered by gruesome casualties from anti-personnel mines and booby traps set by wily North Vietnamese soldiers, the 11th Brigade of Charlie Company led by Lt. William Calley marched into the village of **My Lai,** a subdivision of larger **Son My.** Eschewing strict protocol, motivated by hate, and incited by Calley, U.S. troops were given free reign to "search and destroy" in the village as retaliation for the many U.S. casualties. Reports were conflicting, and it was some months after the incident that anything was reported—and even then, only by members of the press—but more than 300 victims (some estimates say more than 500), mostly women and children, died that day in a flurry of disorder and mayhem. Calley himself supposedly sequestered a group of villagers and executed them in a ditch.

The incident was a sharp thorn in the side of U.S. military policymakers and fuel for fires of dissent and division in the United States. The My Lai Massacre, as it became called, was the beginning of the end of the war at home; the incident incited shouts of "baby killers" from antiwar protesters and brought the brutal reality of the war in Indochina to the attention of the U.S. public. The whole world began to question what many people asked from the start: "Is the U.S. doing more harm than good in Vietnam?" Calley was charged and convicted of murder, but he served only a few years before a successful appeal.

Today a large stone monument marks the ground where the atrocities occurred, and a number of small stelae stand in front of specific family homes. The sight is 10km (6¼ miles) northeast of **Quang Ngai,** capital of Nghia Binh Province, which is about halfway between Hoi An and Quy Nhon. There's a small museum with photographs. Many veterans groups and former war protestors make the pilgrimage here. You can arrange a tour from Hoi An or hire private transport out of Quy Nhon. Most trips visit the sight as a halfway stop between Hoi An and Quy Nhon, or make it a long day trip out of Hoi An (about 4 hr. round-trip). If spending the night in Quang Ngai, try the **Petro-Song Tra Hotel** (2 Quang Trung St.; ✆ **055/382-2665**) or the **Central Hotel** (784 Quang Trung St.; ✆ **055/382-9999**).

Thap Doi Cham Towers There are many Cham sights outside of the city. In fact, you'll see some of the most dynamic on the ride in from the airport or from the Central Highlands, but Thap Doi is right in town, just off of Tran Hung Dao Street. The two towers are unique, in that there are two (Cham towers usually come in groups of odd numbers) and that they're in town (usually on hilltops). The sight is actually less spectacular than the walk through this quiet little neighborhood to a sea inlet where you'll find a few local seafood places. The relief work on the tower sculptures is in good shape, particularly the floral lintels, and the little park area around the towers is a place to rest (but you won't be alone long; folks down this way are friendly).

Just off of Tran Hung Dao on the edge of town. Free admission. Daily 8am–5pm.

2 NHA TRANG

Welcome to Vietnam's ocean city! The capital of Khanh Hoa Province, Nha Trang sees a heavy local and international tourist influx, especially in the summer. The central beachside city area is quite busy and full of cheap guesthouses and small restaurants. The beach and its outlying islands have sprouted some fine new resorts. The surf isn't bad (for frolic, not for surfing) along the vast crescent-shaped beach in Nha Trang's central city, and the bright-blue vista is dotted by more than 20 surrounding islands. There are many good high-end hotels and resorts to choose from, and the high-rises in the town center hearken almost to a large beach town in Florida. Good budget options abound, too. Dining is all about fresh seafood.

Nha Trang is a very popular vacation spot for Vietnamese. In the summer months, the town is chockablock with tourists and young kids out "cruisin' the strip" on the main seaside avenue. The beaches of Nha Trang are a great place to spend 2 or 3 days playing in the surf, snorkeling and diving, or taking a cruise to the nearby islands. And Nha Trang's nightlife is thumping. Centering around the busy backpacker area along Biet Thu Street, the bars hop until late. In fact, the party often starts out on the boats by day and then continues at the bars until late. Prepare to shake thy booty at the beach.

Culturally, the **Pasteur Institute** offers a glimpse into the life and work of one of Vietnam's most famous expats. Both the **Long Son Pagoda** and the well-preserved **Po Nagar Cham Temple** are interesting sights.

In the winter, the surf can be quite rough, making swimming and watersports less than desirable, but daylong boat trips are always a go. Nha Trang is a good place for **diving** to soft coral sites brimming with reef fish, and a number of very professional dive outfitters can take you there (quite inexpensive by Western standards). Also note the newly developed **Whale Island,** just a few hours north, as well as new developments near the airport.

Because Nha Trang expects an increase in regional and international flights, the airport moved to Cam Ranh Bay, 30 minutes south of town. The logic of the new airport is clear—longer runways for bigger planes—but the old in-town airport is now home to a bevy of military jets, which take off in a deafening roar over the south end of the beach throughout the day. It's kind of cool if you like jets, but not so cool if you like peace and quiet.

GETTING THERE

BY PLANE Nha Trang is 1,350km (839 miles) from Hanoi and 450km (280 miles) from Saigon. Vietnam Airlines makes daily connections with Vietnam's urban centers and nearby Dalat. The **Vietnam Airlines Office** in Nha Trang is at 91 Nguyen Thien Thuat St. (✆ **058/352-6768**); storefront travel agents can make any reservations for a small fee. The Nha Trang airport, once in the center of town, has traded places with a larger military facility, is now called **Cam Ranh Airport,** and is some 35km (22 miles) south of town. The 30-minute ride costs 170,000 VND for a taxi, 200,000 VND for a minivan/SUV taxi. Buses will drop you off at your hotel for 35,000 VND. The larger resorts offer more affordable group connections or limousine service, and some include free transfers.

BY TRAIN Nha Trang is a stop on the Reunification Express and is 12 hours from Ho Chi Minh City on a soft sleeper for 340,000 VND, and 20 hours to Hanoi for 954,000 VND. Buy your ticket at least 1 day in advance at the Nha Trang train station, 17 Thai Nguyen St. (✆ **058/382-2113**), or from any travel agent. The overnight connection with Ho Chi Minh City is the most convenient route.

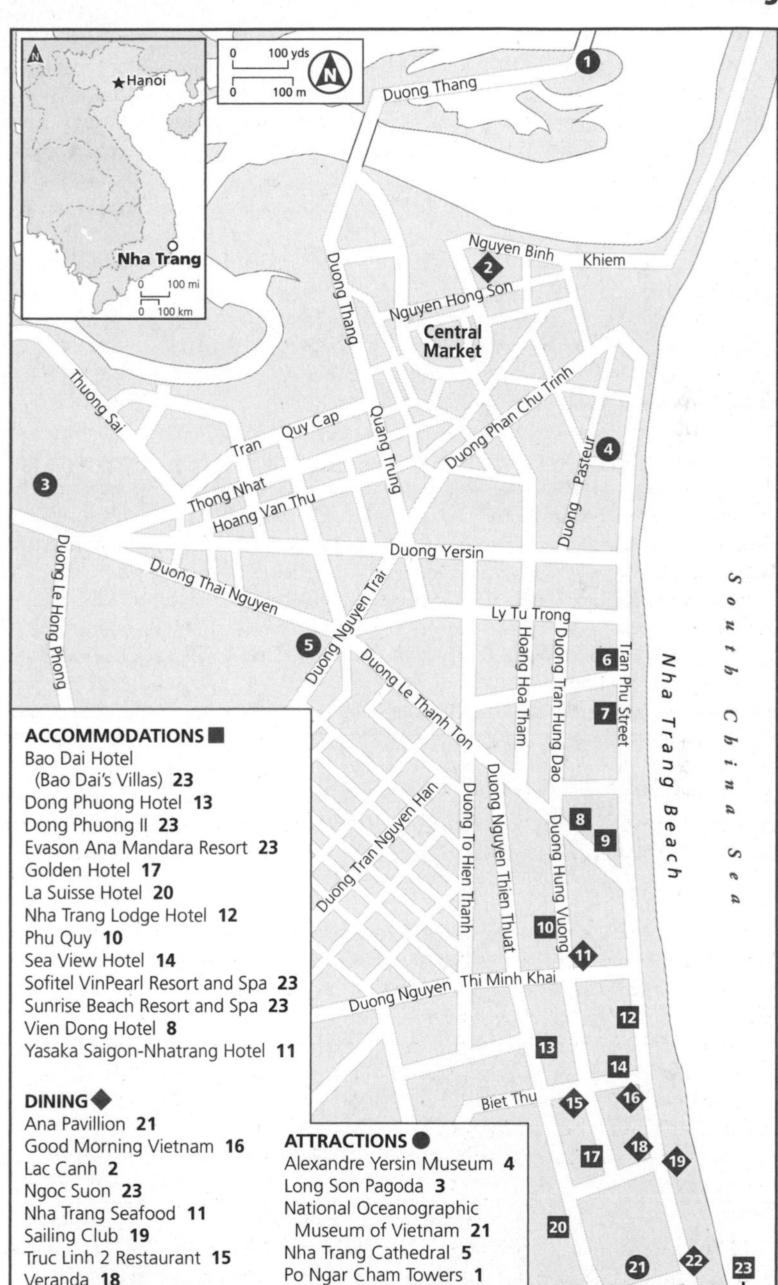
Hanoi
Nha Trang
0 100 mi
0 100 km
0 100 yds
0 100 m
N
Duong Thang
Nguyen Binh Khiem
Nguyen Hong Son
Central Market
Thuong Sai
Tran Quy Cap
Quang Trung
Duong Phan Chu Trinh
Duong Pasteur
Thong Nhat
Hoang Van Thu
Duong Yersin
Duong Le Hong Phong
Duong Thai Nguyen
Duong Nguyen Trai
Ly Tu Trong
Hoang Hoa Tham
Duong Tran Hung Dao
Tran Phu Street
Duong Le Thanh Ton
Nha Trang Beach
South China Sea
Duong Tran Nguyen Han
Duong To Hien Thanh
Duong Nguyen Thien Thuat
Duong Hung Vuong
Duong Nguyen Thi Minh Khai
Biet Thu
ACCOMMODATIONS
Bao Dai Hotel (Bao Dai's Villas) 23
Dong Phuong Hotel 13
Dong Phuong II 23
Evason Ana Mandara Resort 23
Golden Hotel 17
La Suisse Hotel 20
Nha Trang Lodge Hotel 12
Phu Quy 10
Sea View Hotel 14
Sofitel VinPearl Resort and Spa 23
Sunrise Beach Resort and Spa 23
Vien Dong Hotel 8
Yasaka Saigon-Nhatrang Hotel 11
DINING
Ana Pavillion 21
Good Morning Vietnam 16
Lac Canh 2
Ngoc Suon 23
Nha Trang Seafood 11
Sailing Club 19
Truc Linh 2 Restaurant 15
Veranda 18
ATTRACTIONS
Alexandre Yersin Museum 4
Long Son Pagoda 3
National Oceanographic Museum of Vietnam 21
Nha Trang Cathedral 5
Po Ngar Cham Towers 1

BY CAR If you choose to drive from Hoi An to Nha Trang, it's a 10-hour trip and will cost you about $120 by car.

BY BUS "Open tour" buses connect you with Hoi An (530km/329 miles; 10 hr.; every day at 7am or 7pm) or Ho Chi Minh City (450km/280 miles; 8 hr.; every day at 7:30am and 8pm) for about $8 (less if you book multiple trips with the same company). The overnight schedules to Ho Chi Minh City and Hoi An are long and tiring rides, but a good option if you're short on time and don't want to waste your precious daylight hours looking out the window of a tour coach. Daytime routes connect to both towns as well. Open tour buses also connect with Dalat (214km/133 miles; 6 hr.; every day at 7am) and the beaches at Mui Ne (6 hr.; every day at 7am).

The **local bus station** is the **Lien Tinh Bus Station** at 23/10 Street, about a 16,000 VND taxi or 10,000 VND motorbike taxi ride from the town center. Buses connect with all points north and south, as well as to towns in the interior Central Highlands (closest is Ban Ma Thuot).

GETTING AROUND

The main street in Nha Trang, **Tran Phu,** runs along a 4km (2½-mile) beach lined with the myriad minihotels and beach attractions that make up the town center. **Biet Thu Street** runs perpendicular to Tran Phu and is where you'll find lots of smaller restaurants and budget tour operators, as well as the city's most affordable accommodations. **Taxis** congregate around the major hotels; most meters start at 15,000 VND for the first 2km (1¼ miles), 10,000 VND for each additional kilometer. **Mai Linh** is a reputable taxi company (✆ **058/381-7817**). Renting **a bike** from your hotel for $1 to $2 a day is a good option, as are cyclos, which you can rent for $3 per hour from your hotel. A **cyclo** across town will cost about 10,000 VND. In addition, **motorbike taxis** cost 20,000 VND per hour. All of these prices come with only a bit of friendly bargaining. Note the glut of empty cyclos, and keep walking until you get a reasonable price (and then, as I always do, give a large tip).

VISITOR INFORMATION & TOURS

All hotels in Nha Trang can book city tours, day-boat trips, or onward travel to your next destination. One-day city or countryside tours are worth it, as are the town's popular 1-day boat trips (for more information, see "Attractions" and "1-Day Boat Cruises" at the end of this section).

City tours can be booked anywhere, at the budget "open tour" companies listed below or at any hotel front desk. One-day boat tours can be booked just about anywhere from hotels to Internet shops. The cost is $6.

Warning! Crime in Nha Trang

With droves of tourists wandering about, Nha Trang is notorious for petty crime, particularly the motorbike "snatch and run." Perps cruise the beach and grab bags from the unsuspecting, so be careful on the road, whether walking or in a cyclo. Go by taxi at night. Also, be aware on the beach because, unless you're at a private resort, you'll be hassled by sellers all day; say no, keep an eye on valuables, and leave what you can in a hotel safe.

For onward tours to the Central Highlands area, trips that connect you from Nha Trang to Ban Me Thuot, and either on to Dalat or north to Kontum, contact the friendly folks at **Highlands Tour** (54G Nguyen Thien Thuat St.; ✆ **058/352-4045;** daily 7am–9:30pm; free Internet in an air-conditioned room in the back). These guys help consolidate groups or individuals with similar goals and craft the most economical trip possible. This option is preferable to lighting out to the Central Highlands by local bus.

For bus tickets and connections to Dalat, contact any of the following tourist cafe branches. **Sinh Café III** is the best of the lot, with offices in every town in Vietnam. Find it in Nha Trang at 10 Biet Thu St. (✆ **058/352-1981**). Sinh's competition in town comes from **TM Brother's Café,** at 34 Nguyen Thien Thuat St. (✆ **058/352-3556**), and **An Phu Tourist,** 1/24 Tran Quang Khai St. (✆ **058/352-4471**); both companies have offices in points south and in Ho Chi Minh City.

Fast Facts Nha Trang

Banks & Currency Exchange **Vietcombank**'s local branch is located at 17 Quang Trung St. (✆ **058/382-5120**). Hours are 7:30 to 11am and 1:30 to 4pm. It offers the usual currency and traveler's check exchange and credit card cash-withdrawal services. Along Biet Thu, some of the tour operators will cash traveler's checks and change money—rates are the same as at the bank (except for a small service fee), and they're open longer hours.

Internet & E-Mail Biet Thu has a cluster of Internet cafes for between 200 VND and 300 VND (a couple cents) per minute.

Post Office & Mail The main branch is at 4 Le Loi St. (✆ **058/382-1271**). Hours are 6:30am to 10pm Monday to Saturday. DHL express mail services and Internet access are available. There is another branch at 50 Le Thanh Ton.

Telephone The city code for Nha Trang is 058.

WHERE TO STAY

There are hundreds of minihotels in Nha Trang, most quite basic and geared to the summer influx of Vietnamese vacationers; these places are quite easy on the budget. On the luxury end, Ana Mandara and its sister, Evason Hideaway Ana Mandara, stand in a class all their own.

Very Expensive

Evason Ana Mandara Resort ★★★ Your luxury stay starts the moment you step off the plane. A Six Senses booth is immediately to your left when you enter the airport. Drop off your tag and staff will retrieve your baggage while you're ushered out of the small, cramped airport and into an air-conditioned van where comfy leather seats, bottled water, and a cool face towel are waiting. Neck pillows and daily newspapers and magazines make it an enjoyable 30-minute ride to the resort. ***Note:*** You have to book the airport transfer service prior to arrival. It's well worth the $14. The resort itself is on the busy main beach street in Nha Trang. In the afternoons, the lobby is filled with the peaceful sounds of the zither and *to rung* (a percussion instrument made of bamboo rods) being played by two local musicians. You can still hear outside traffic when walking through the resort, but it's nothing but ocean sounds inside your villa. The rooms are beautifully decorated with bamboo-accented wooden furniture. Bathrooms are spacious and large doors lead to the Jacuzzi bathtub in a private outdoor enclave. If you can, spring for a beach villa so that you can almost fall from your balcony onto the sand and surf. It's the little things that make this resort special: native art and handiwork all about, the bowl with floating flowers in the bathroom, the basin of rainwater on your private veranda for rinsing sandy feet, the burning incense in the open-air lobby. The staff is excellent at meeting your every needs, from helping set up in-room Internet connections, to sending a driver out to buy a new mobile phone card. You won't want, or need, to leave this luxury oasis.

Beachside, Tran Phu Blvd. ✆ **058/352-2222.** Fax 058/352-5828. www.sixsenses.com. 78 units. Low season $266–$409 double/villa, $515 suite villa; high season (minimum 5-night stay) $301–$460 double/villa, $564 suite villa. AE, DC, MC, V. **Amenities:** 2 restaurants; 2 bars; concierge; health club; Internet; Jacuzzi; 2 large outdoor pools w/hot tub; room service; smoke-free rooms; tennis court. *In room:* A/C, TV, fridge, hair dryer, Internet, minibar.

Evason Hideaway Ana Mandara ★★★ If you aren't someone who is used to the life of luxury, this is the kind of place where, after your butler leaves you alone in your room, you do a little dance of glee. In fact, other hotels in Nha Trang do not hold a candle to this place. The attention to detail here is impeccable. Staff wave you off as the boat pulls away for the 20-minute ride to the resort and are waiting to greet you when you arrive at Hideaway's jetty. Then it's off to your villa for a tour and private check-in. The villas are sanctuaries of cool, off-white stone and blond wood. The main floor has a bathroom the size of a standard living room. A large wooden bathtub sits between the his-and-her vanities, and the tropical rain shower is outside, under the bamboo roof. Upstairs is the spacious living room, with gorgeous ocean views. Back downstairs is the bedroom, which also faces the ocean; you can take in the view from the window seat big enough for two, the four-poster bamboo bed, or the outdoor lounge chairs next to your private infinity pool. Decisions, decisions.

Dining is lovely in a two-story, open-air pavilion at seaside, with great views of the sunset and romantic nooks. On low-tide evenings, diners can enjoy a meal near the surf under the stars. The area is completely secluded, nary a motorbike or car to be found. At night, the skies are so clear it feels like you could reach out and tuck a star into you pocket.

Note: The resort also runs a private beach located two bays over with only one booking per day, great for honeymoon getaways.

Ninh Van Bay, Ninh Hoa, Khanh Hoa. ✆ **058/372-8222.** Fax 058/372-8223. www.sixsenses.com. 58 units. $800–$1,200 villas; $2,300 presidential villa. AE, MC, V. **Amenities:** 3 restaurants; bar; concierge; dive center; health club; Jacuzzi; library; outdoor pool; room service; spa; watersports rentals (snorkeling, sailboats, water-skiing, and runabouts); 1 villa available for those w/limited mobility. *In room:* A/C, TV/DVD, fridge, hair dryer, high-speed Internet, minibar, private pool.

Expensive

Sofitel VinPearl Resort and Spa ★ This enormous newer resort (500 rooms when complete) on Bamboo Island, a 10-minute boat ride from coastal Nha Trang, gets an A for effort. Visitors familiar with the Sofitel standard, however, may be disappointed with this property. It veers on kitsch. That much is evident as you approach the island and view the word VINPEARL placed in the hills like the famous Hollywood sign. It lights up at night. You'll be away from the main Nha Trang drag (cable car or speedboat connections to the mainland are 100,000 VND round-trip), but the hotel is pretty self-contained. Everything on the island, from construction materials to the very water that comes out of the taps, is transported by large tankers—an incredible undertaking. Public spaces, like the double-height marble lobby rotunda, are grand in scale but rather uninteresting. Rooms are similarly large and comfortable, with all the amenities, but plain. The resort is designed in an arc around the vast acreage of the central pool, reputedly the largest in the region, with lots of fun slides, meandering river areas, and bridges, all overlooking a secluded bay. Dining is familiar but uninspired. VinPearl is so far a favorite with wealthy Vietnamese weekenders and Korean group tours, but time will tell.

Phu Quy Port, South Cau Da Port, Vinh Nguyen, Nha Trang (connect by boat from the pier on beachside Tran Phu just south of Ana Mandara). ✆ **058/359-8188.** Fax 058/359-8147. www.vinpearlland.com. 485 units. $206–$255 double; $327–$404 suite. AE, MC, V. **Amenities:** 2 restaurants; 3 bars; babysitting; children's center; concierge; health club; Jacuzzi; outdoor pool; room service; tennis courts; watersports rentals. *In room:* A/C, TV, fridge, hair dryer, minibar, Wi-Fi.

Sunrise Beach Resort Nha Trang ★ This grand edifice is all polished marble and white columns, with 10 floors of pomp. Everything about the place is shiny, new, and grand. They bill themselves as a beach resort, but you have to cross a very busy street to get to the sand and waves. Rooms are decorated with light-colored furniture made of particleboard wood, and sofas have removable Velcro covers. Most have great views of oceanside Tran Phu Street and the beach. The executive suites are on the 10th floor. Elevator doors open to a huge, six-column Greek/Roman entrance to the private bar. Rooms are spacious and decidedly sensual—a frosted-glass divider bears silhouette images of seminude ancient Cham dancers, and a Jacuzzi is set up on the balcony with a gorgeous private view of the ocean. The layout of the hotel is a bit confusing. Reputable spa chain Qi Spa is attached to the hotel, next to the Shiseido boutique, but you have to navigate through hallways to a separate wing to get to it. The pool is one floor above the lobby, but you have to walk through a big, empty room to get to it. It feels like you're walking through someone's basement or storage room. Not a top choice for your beach vacation.

12 Tran Phu St., Nha Trang. ✆ **058/392-0999.** Fax 058/382-2866. www.sunrisenhatrang.com. 123 units. $210–$450 double; from $535 suite. AE, MC, V. **Amenities:** 3 restaurants; 5 bars (1 rooftop); babysitting; health club & spa; Jacuzzi; outdoor pool; room service. *In room:* A/C, TV, fridge, minibar, Wi-Fi.

Yasaka Saigon-Nhatrang Hotel ★★ On the main strip overlooking Tran Phu and the ocean blue, this hotel bridges the gap between the ultraluxe resorts and low-end minihotels—a good compromise. All rooms have good, basic amenities, as cozy as your favorite highway hotel chain back home. Upper-level rooms have good views of the sea, some with balconies, and the view from corner suites is quite spectacular and worth the upgrade. The lowest standard, the superior, is quite comfortable and large, if bland; the deluxe room, an upgraded version of the superior and on higher floors, is your best bet for atmosphere, comfort, and price. Everything is done in cream or tan carpet, and rooms have flower-print spreads (no shiny polyester). Large, clean tile bathrooms are homey. Service is friendly, there are lots of good dining options on-site (the Red Onion is a local favorite), the rooftop pool is small but inviting, and it's just a short hop across busy Tran Phu Street to the beach. A good breakfast buffet is included.

18 Tran Phu St., Nha Trang. ✆ **058/382-0090** or 382-5227. Fax 058/382-0000. www.yasanhatrang.com. 204 units. $152–$198 double; $250–$350 suite. Rates include breakfast buffet. AE, MC, V. **Amenities:** 2 restaurants; bar; nightclub; karaoke; motorbikes; health club; Jacuzzi; rooftop pool w/ocean view; room service; sauna; rooftop tennis court. *In room:* A/C, TV w/in-house movies, fridge, minibar, Wi-Fi.

Moderate

Bao Dai Hotel (Bao Dai's Villas) ★★ Built in 1923 as a seaside resort for then-emperor Bao Dai, the hotel is a cluster of plain colonial-style buildings set high on an oceanside hill south of Nha Trang, so far south that you're in the next town really. There's an interesting Gothic quality to the place, and one could certainly imagine a king wandering the promontory at night, watching the hotel's lighthouse scan the sea and sky, and worrying about the loss of his kingdom, which was, in fact, the case. Bao Dai's very room is the master suite and makes for a memorable stay. The less expensive rooms are musty monks' cells, but the villa-style rooms have high ceilings and large, shuttered windows overlooking the coast—a good bet. The more top-end rooms vary, but all are palatial in size even if they're wanting in amenities (the furniture can't keep up with the space). The bathrooms are nothing special but are sizable and clean, with bathtubs. Some of the buildings have creaky old winding wooden staircases and rooftop access.

Cau Da, Vinh Nguyen/Nha Trang. ✆ **058/359-0147** or 359-0148. Fax 058/359-0146. www.vngold.com/nt/baodai. 18 units. $25–$50 standard; $70 superior; $80 suite. MC, V. **Amenities:** Restaurant; bikes and motorbikes; Internet; room service. *In room:* A/C, TV, fridge, hair dryer, minibar, Wi-Fi.

Nha Trang Lodge Hotel ★ The 5-year-old lodge calls itself a "business hotel," and indeed it's a well-run and accommodating 12-story high-rise. Average-size rooms are chain-hotel style, with clean carpets, floral bedspreads, and tidy, modern furnishings. The bathrooms are a fine size, with marble finishes. If you can, spring for an oceanview room with balcony (on an upper floor away from street noise, if possible). The staff is professional, and this comfortable seaside address covers all the bases with amenities and services. It's a nice, uninspired, affordable place and a bit like the younger, less-accomplished brother of the Yasaka (see above). Don't miss a meal in the popular outdoor seafood barbecue area.

42 Tran Phu St. ✆ **058/3521-452** or 381-0900. Fax 058/352-1800. www.nt-lodge.com. 125 units. $55 standard; $90 superior; $110 suite. AE, MC, V. **Amenities:** 2 restaurants; bar; fitness center; pool; room service; sauna; tennis court. *In room:* A/C, TV, fridge, minibar, Wi-Fi.

Vien Dong Hotel Connected with Hai Yen hotel, another large government tour-agency hotel, the Vien Dong is showing its age after years of heavy tour-group use, but it's a relatively comfortable three-star with all the amenities. The large pool is a highlight. Smallish rooms have tatty carpet, simple wood furnishings, and sturdy foam mattresses. Bathrooms are clean but bare. A college dorm room comes to mind. Suites are not worth it. There's an inviting outdoor restaurant featuring nightly music and a cultural dance show. You're sure to meet other travelers here, and the general atmosphere is friendly, which helps. It's just one row back from the beach. The staff, though taxed by the many large groups coming and going, is kind and helpful.

1 Tran Hung Dao St. ✆ **058/352-3608** or 382-1608. Fax 058/352-1912. 103 units. $20–$40 double; $40 suite. AE, MC, V. **Amenities:** 2 restaurants; bar; outdoor pool w/slide; room service; tennis. *In room:* A/C, TV, fridge, hair dryer, minibar, Wi-Fi.

Inexpensive

Dong Phuong Hotel ★ It's function, not form, in this motel-style block that typifies the budget accommodations in town (this is one of three properties of the same name and standard in Nha Trang). Rooms are bright but spartan, with spotless tile and not much more than a bed and a good-size, shower-in-room-style bathroom. Some rooms have a good city view, and if you're lucky, you'll be blessed with a classy nude done in painted tile mosaic in the bathroom (the only decoration I could find throughout). Family rooms are large and a good value, and their penthouse room adjoins a huge rooftop area with 365-degree views of town. It's your standard minihotel service, though: just rooms.

103 Nguyen Thien Thuat St., Nha Trang. ✆ **058/352-6247.** Fax 058/382-5986. dongphuongnt@dng.vnn.vn. 47 units. $15–$20 double; $30–$40 deluxe (family). MC, V. **Amenities:** Restaurant; outdoor pool. *In room:* A/C, TV, fridge, hair dryer, Wi-Fi.

Dong Phuong II Just reaching the end of its construction at press time, this companion to the popular Dong Phuong in the town center (see above) is typical of the many affordable minihotels along this busy section of Tran Phu south of the town center. The lobby is a big, open tile area where buses and cars park, and the hotel looks to be a real workhorse already, with many budget groups calling this home even before it was complete. Rooms are simple affairs, best out front with balconies and views of the ocean, although many of these are pretty noisy because they're near the street. Don't expect style or special services here, but it is convenient, affordable, and away from the busy backpacker party scene along Biet Thu.

96A4 Tran Phu St. (on the south end of the Nha Trang strip across from Ana Mandara). ✆ **058/381-4580.** Fax 058/382-5986. dongphuong2@dng.vnn.vn. 140 units. 300,000 VND–1,200,000 VND double. MC, V. **Amenities:** Restaurant; motorbikes; laundry service. *In room:* A/C, TV, fridge, minibar.

Golden Hotel It's little more than a surly welcome and room, but with no other expectations than these, you can't go too wrong. Private spaces in this oversize minihotel are, in fact, quite nice, done with dark-wood trim, crown molding, and filigree, and more cozy than basic minihotels in the area. Amenities are bare-bones: just good tour services and a lobby safety box.

1K–2K Hung Vuong, Nha Trang. ✆ **058/352-4496.** Fax 058/352-4498. 31 units. $20–$60 double. MC, V. **Amenities:** Internet. *In room:* A/C, TV, fridge.

La Suisse Hotel ★ Here's one of the friendliest little minihotels in town. Tucked down a quiet(ish) lane just south of the backpacker area, bright and colorful La Suisse Hotel offers new, clean, and cozy rooms with air-conditioning and TV. Decor includes snazzy checked bedspreads and large headboards. Bathrooms are the guesthouse variety but have decorator tile. More high-end rooms have large black faux-granite sink stands. There's nothing Swiss about the place except a hokey painting in the lobby of mountain-climbing, horn-blowing Swiss in lederhosen. Upper-floor suites have large curved balconies, and one has a raised wooden platform with a funky shag rug. Staff is extremely friendly and helpful, with genuine sentiment despite an inability to communicate. They can book tours, too.

34 Tran Quang Khai St. (just south of the central backpacker area). ✆ **058/352-4353.** Fax 058/352-4564. lasuissehotelnt@dng.vnn.vn. 30 units. $15–$25 double; $40 suite. MC, V. **Amenities:** Internet. *In room:* A/C, TV, fridge, minibar, Wi-Fi.

Phu Quy ★ The Phu Quy is an interesting conglomeration of three properties, so rooms vary (and some of the passages btw. buildings require you to duck through the most unlikely doors). Ask for something nice, and be sure to bargain a bit. All of the buildings sport small, bright, and very clean rooms with newer plastic furniture. The beds are comfortable and bathrooms are small, with shower-in-room facilities. There are no views, to speak of, but go for one of the top floors to escape street noise. Of course, that means climbing lots of stairs. This place has no amenities whatsoever, but breakfasts are good and cheap, and, of course, the hotel will book tickets. This is backpacker central and an anthill of activity, and that, along with the price, makes it worth a stay. The large, shaded penthouse area has hammocks and lawn chairs, and is a good place to relax (they'll deliver food to you there, too). It's family run, and owner Mr. Quy is as nice as they come.

54 Hung Vuong St. ✆ **058/352-6444.** Fax 058/381-2954. phuquyhotel@dng.vnn.vn. 45 units. $8–$16 double with fan; $12–$25 with A/C. Visa accepted with a 4% commission. **Amenities:** Restaurant/bar. *In room:* A/C (in some), fan (in some), TV (in some), no phone (in some), Wi-Fi.

Sea View Hotel Here's a very good, relatively new, and clean oversize minihotel with an elevator. The Sea View is right in the heart of the busy backpacker area, and you'll have to be on higher floors to garner any actual sea view, but rooms are large, simple, and tidy, with tile floors and shower-in-room-style bathrooms, some with balconies. Amenities are few, but the hotel is convenient to the busy downtown and the very helpful staff can arrange anything from rentals to transfers and onward travel. Being close to downtown means that, especially with street-facing rooms, you get up-close and personal with rowdy revelers who take to the streets when the bars shut down. The shallow pool on the first floor is tepid and cloudy (I've never seen anyone in it), but it's tempting to jump into from surrounding balconies. Don't think about it.

4B Biet Thu St. ✆ **058/352-4333.** Fax 058/352-4335. seaviewhotel@dng.vnn.vn. 59 units. $15–$25 double. MC, V. **Amenities:** Outdoor pool. *In room:* A/C, TV, fridge, Wi-Fi.

WHERE TO DINE

Expensive

Ana Pavilion ★★★ ASIAN/CONTINENTAL Without question the finest dining on this beautiful stretch of coast, the Ana Pavilion is the jewel in the crown of the Ana Mandara Resort and serves exquisite food in elegant natural surroundings. Whether you're on the oceanfront veranda, under a canvas umbrella in the courtyard, or eating by candlelight over the open ocean on the seaside jetty, the location alone is breathtaking. The food is creatively prepared and beautifully presented, and portions are healthy. Chef David Thai serves from an ever-evolving roster of local and seasonal specials, fine East-West fusion, with anything from sandwiches made with bread baked on-site and imported cheese or imported Aussie steaks to local favorites such as banana flower salads and even sushi done to a T for the many Japanese guests. Don't miss the seafood hot pot served in a large, coal-fired crock and brimming with the catch of the day delicately stewed with vegetables. There's an excellent daily lunch buffet, and evening set menus are a great value. This is the best choice for romantic ambience and fine dining.

Tran Phu Blvd. (at the Ana Mandara Resort). ✆ **058/352-2222.** Main courses $7–$19; prix-fixe menus $35–$52. AE, MC, V. Daily 6am–11pm.

Moderate

Good Morning Vietnam ★ ITALIAN This little Vietnamese chain might seem a little out of place (and kind of redundant, with six locations in tour centers nationwide), but with an Italian manager ensuring good quality, this outlet, the first of the chain, serves familiar Italian fare. It's a nice break after many meals of noodle soup and local beer. Affordable by any standard, everything is cooked fresh and ingredients are of the highest quality. All pastas are homemade. Try the gnocchi dumplings with pesto or Gorgonzola, or the ravioli filled with braised meat. The *fritto misto* of deep-fried squid, shrimp, and sea bass served on the pasta of your choice is a house specialty. The place is not luxurious, by any means—just another storefront in and among the town's most popular bars, such as Crazy Kim's and Guava (see "Nha Trang After Dark," later)—but Good Morning Vietnam has a nice "grotto" feel and is a cozy respite from the noonday heat, as well as a good spot to watch travelers on Biet Thu as the evening's nightlife lights up.

19B Biet Thu St., Nha Trang. ✆ **058/352-2071.** www.goodmorningviet.com. Main courses 90,000 VND–170,000 VND. No credit cards. Daily 10am–11pm.

Ngoc Suong ★★ SEAFOOD Nha Trang has dozens of good seafood restaurants, but this one leads the pack. Whether in the very pleasant thatched outdoor pavilion or the vaguely nautical, softly lit interior, it's "seafood as you like it" served by a helpful, friendly staff. Whole fish and crustaceans can be chosen by pointing in the large tank and smiling greedily; the day's catch, including shrimp and crab, is ordered by the pound, grilled, fried, or boiled with basic spices like tamarind or pepper and lemon. The oysters, if they have them, are small but succulent. The name of the restaurant refers to a delicate marinated whitefish salad, one of the specialties and a great appetizer. This is a popular local and expat favorite.

96A Tran Phu (south of the town center at beachside). ✆ **058/352-5677.** Main courses 70,000 VND–450,000 VND. AE, MC, V. Daily 10am–10pm.

Nha Trang Seafood ★★ SEAFOOD/VIETNAMESE Popular with Japanese groups (or local fat cats out to impress their mistresses), Nha Trang Seafood serves it fresh and delicious as you like it: grilled, steamed, or fried. Viet-style preparation is sweet, sour, and/or spicy; grilled items are good, and the shrimp in coconut, clay-pot dishes, and hot pots are affordable and delicious. The atmosphere is plain, best by candlelight on the second floor when the place is crowded (dull by the light of day). The staff is fun-loving and friendly.

46 Nguyen Thi Minh Khai St. ✆ **058/352-2664.** Main courses 80,000 VND–500,000 VND. No credit cards. Daily 10am–10pm.

Sailing Club ★★ ITALIAN/INDIAN/INTERNATIONAL Sailing Club is a great base for days at the beach. You can rent a chair, order lunch and snacks, and have drinks delivered all day. The prices are a little higher than if you were to rent a chair elsewhere and buy from locals, but the service is good and you can be sure of quality. You have three separate menus from which to choose, along with three seating areas: to your right is Casa Italia, left is Taj Mahal, and Sandal Restaurant is in the back toward the beach. Head to Sandal if you want a mix of everything. The place turns into a bar in the late evening, and just as the Sailing Club has been exempted from local building codes, they're also the only bar able to stay open until the wee hours. The place has seen constant upgrades over the years and is a very stylish seaside pavilion of thatched-roof indoor seating, low beachside outdoor seating, and a private thatch lounge area on the beach. Nha Trang Sailing Club is also home to an office of **Rainbow Divers,** and you can also rent boats for the day from here.

72–74 Tran Phu St. ✆ **058/352-4628.** www.sailingclubvietnam.com. Main courses 100,000 VND–300,000 VND. AE, MC, V. Daily 7am–11pm. Bar noon–3am.

Inexpensive

Lac Canh ★★ CHINESE/VIETNAMESE Two words: grilled shrimp. The Chinese-influenced Vietnamese cuisine here is all about its ingredients, so go for the basics. Try the fresh seafood in a light marinade that you cook yourself on a rustic, cast-iron brazier frill. The place is packed with locals and tourists. Try to sit outdoors, because the atmosphere is smoky. They don't speak English as well as staff at Truc Linh 2 (see below), but the food is better—and cheaper. This is definitely the local "greasy spoon," and it makes for a fun evening.

44 Nguyen Binh Khiem St. ✆ **058/382-1391.** Main courses 16,000 VND–140,000 VND. No credit cards. Daily 9:30am–10pm.

Truc Linh 2 Restaurant ★ VIETNAMESE An eclectic menu here has anything from the backpacker standbys of fried rice and noodles to sirloin steak and T-bone: It runs the gamut. There's a seafood smorgasbord out front from which you can choose your own jumbo shrimp, crab, squid, or fresh fish of the day and then have it weighed and cooked to your taste. They've got fondue and clay-pot specials, barbecued beef on clay tile, and rice-paper spring rolls with shrimp that are delicious. Truc Linh has become one of the hottest spots in Nha Trang, and even folks from the big resorts make it here for a meal at least once. Cover the table in seafood to share. Waiters in smart Nero jackets do the "Hurry, hurry, step right up" act out front, but they're hawking good, fresh seafood at budget prices, so let yourself get dragged in. Don't confuse this place with little Truc Linh 1, also on Biet Thu, closer to the beach, which serves simple Viet and Western cuisine (not a bad spot for an afternoon snack or coffee, though).

18A Biet Thu St., Nha Trang. ✆ **058/352-1089.** Main courses 50,000 VND–180,000 VND. No credit cards. Daily 7am–10pm.

Veranda Restaurant SEAFOOD/VIETNAMESE A great location and standard seafood dishes. The decor is cozy contemporary, and a nice respite from the hustle and bustle of the main street.

66 Tran Phu St. ✆ **058/352-7492.** Main courses $1.50–$6.50. No credit cards. Daily 9:30am–10pm.

CAFES

Louisiane This seaside pavilion unfortunately cranks out the loud Asia pop tunes, which destroys the atmosphere. They serve good salads, sandwiches, snacks, and rich French fare at reasonable prices. And the view is still tops, so see if you can persuade them to turn down the music.

Lot 29, Tran Phu St. (south of city center at beachside). ✆ **058/352-1948.** Main courses 60,000 VND–180,000 VND. No credit cards. Daily 7:30am–midnight.

Rainbow Bar ★★ A cool, dimly lit little bar and cafe area just off of Biet Thu, the Rainbow Bar is a good place to plan your dive trip over a pint with the professionals, or just enjoy some good basic pub grub, pasta, pizza, and steaks for little money, and wash it down with imported ales and wine.

90A Hung Vuong St. ✆ **058/352-4351.** www.divevietnam.com. Main courses 80,000 VND–160,000 VND. No credit cards. Daily 7am–10pm.

Romy's Ice Cream and Coffee Bar ★ Look no further if you are an ice cream buff. German owner Fridtjof Rommeley is a trained cook and chef who left the kitchen for the ice cream freezer 2 decades ago. He has run an ice creamery for 16 years in his hometown and now brings his much-needed expertise to Nha Trang. Almost everything, including the waffle cones and garnishes, is homemade, with ingredients imported from Italy. The "Special Dalat" is their bestseller, a huge affair of mostly local fruits and ice cream topped with a healthy dollop of whipped cream. The ice cream was the creamiest I've ever had in Vietnam.

1C Biet Thu St. ✆ **058/352-7677.** Ice cream dishes 25,000 VND–90,000 VND. No credit cards. Daily 10am till last customer.

ATTRACTIONS

One-day city tours visit Long Son Pagoda, Bao Dai's Villa, the Oceanographic Institute, and the Po Cham Tower. Country tours take you to Ba Ho Waterfall and secluded Doc Let Beach far to the north, or to Thap Ba Hotspring. If you get a group together yourself, you can arrange custom trips for very little with any tourist cafe. ***Important note:*** No matter what anyone tells you, Monkey Island is not worth the trip, especially if you like animals and don't like wasting your time (you can just buy a "monkeys on bikes" postcard and be done with it).

Alexandre Yersin Museum ★★ Here you can get an inkling of the work of one of Vietnam's greatest heroes. Swiss doctor Yersin founded Dalat, isolated an important plague-causing bacterium, and researched agricultural methods and meteorological forecasting, all to the great benefit of the Vietnamese. Yersin arrived in Nha Trang in 1891 and dedicated the better part of his life to scientific discovery from his busy laboratory here, until his passing in 1943. He founded the Pasteur Institute in 1895. On display are his desk, overflowing library, and scientific instruments.

In the Pasteur Institute, 10 Tran Phu St. ✆ **058/382-2355.** Admission 26,000 VND. Mon–Sat 8–11am and 2–4:30pm.

Long Son Pagoda ★ The main attraction at this pagoda (ca. 1930s) is the huge white Buddha on the hillside behind the main compound; the 24m-high (79-ft.) statue is an important symbol of Nha Trang. Around the base of the Buddha are portraits of monks who immolated themselves to protest against the corrupt Diem regime; each monk's portrait, carved in relief on a paneled side of the statue, is framed in flames. After climbing the numerous flights of stairs, you'll also be rewarded with a bird's-eye view of Nha Trang.

Thai Nguyen St. Free admission. Daily 8am–5pm.

National Oceanographic Museum of Vietnam ★ Established on September 14, 1922, the Oceanographic Center south of Nha Trang (at the foot of the outcrop where Bao Dai built his villa) is a fun visit for kids and popular with large groups of domestic tourists. The place is a bit run-down, with outdoor aquarium areas that could use a good scrub and a coat of paint. Despite some rather lackluster presentation—the shark tank, for example, is a big cement pond that you look over from above and from one window on the side—there is an exacting collection of the kinds of fish you would find in the sea near Nha Trang, and all are labeled in English. The best are the smaller aquariums in the back. Find reef sharks, turtles, living coral, anemones, puffers, lionfish, clownfish, sea horses, and a whole array of colorful reef species, some quite rare. The big turtles out back live in pretty cramped quarters, as do the crocs, but the kids delight at being close-up to these big boys, and particularly the aquarium area is a fun visit alongside the many Vietnamese tour groups who don't see too many Westerners in their day-to-day lives (you're as much on display as the fish). The museum area holds 20,000 specimens collected over its long history, some full skeletons and others preserved in formaldehyde solution. The institute sponsors ongoing research and community projects, ranging from monitoring aquatic life to developing captive breeding programs and encouraging preservation and regeneration of local coral reefs.

01 Cau Da, Nha Trang (at the southern base of the small hilltop on which Bao Dai's Villa sits). ✆ **058/359-0037.** www.vnio.org. Admission 15,000 VND. Daily 7am–4pm (closed for lunch).

Po Ngar Cham Towers ★ Starting in the 8th century, the Cham people, an early Hindu empire in central Vietnam (see the box "Who Are the Cham?" in chapter 9), built the Po Ngar Cham temple complex to honor Yang Ino Po Ngar, mother of the kingdom. Set on the site of an earlier wooden temple burned by the Japanese in A.D. 774, there were originally 10 structures here, of which just 3 remain. The main tower, or Po Ngar Kalan, is one of the tallest Cham structures anywhere, and its square tower and three-story cone roof are exemplary of Cham style. The towers of Po Ngar have retained structural integrity, giving you a good idea of how it might have looked in all its glory. Two pillars of carved epitaphs of Cham kings are in the vestibule, and two original carved doors are in the sanctuary. The statue inside is of the goddess Bharagati, aka Po Ngar, on her lotus throne. It was carved in A.D. 1050. The Po Ngar temples are still used by local Buddhists who have adopted the site as their own, and the altars and smoking incense add to the intrigue of the architecture. Detracting from the whole experience are kitsch stands and lots of hawkers. To get there, you cross an expansive bridge spanning the mouth of the Cai River as it flows to the sea. There's a small fish market along the river—take a left to the riverside as you approach the temples—a great place to visit in the early morning, when boats are just bringing in their catch. The wide river, with its many bright blue and red fishing boats, is a picture.

2km (1¼ miles) out of the city center at 2 Thang 4, at the end of Xom Bong Bridge. Admission 10,000 VND. Daily 7:30am–5pm.

THE BEACH

What brings everyone to Nha Trang is the big pond out front, better known as the Pacific. The waves are more or less a tumbling beachfront break on the best of days, and sea winds can whip up a real chop in the November-to-February monsoon season, but otherwise the beach is a great place for a dip or for lounging in the sun and forgetting it all. Beachside facilities abound, as the long 6km (3¾-mile) park area gets more and more developed with concrete paths and gardens. Nha Trang is a good place to grab a pay-by-the-day beach chair—usually something like 30,000 VND or a promise to buy lunch works from smaller vendors. Also, the few large beachside places rent out chairs. Best is the **Nha Trang Sailing Club** (72–74 Tran Phu St.; ✆ **058/352-4628**), where you can order a delicious lunch or have drinks delivered all day. Just a hitch farther south is **La Louisiane** (Tran Phu; ✆ **058/381-2948**), which has a tidy little central pool and cafe area, rents shaded lounges for the day, and can arrange any kind of trip. The options below are good for getting out, stretching your legs, and earning some beach time, but don't feel bad about falling into a good novel and relaxing in Nha Trang—that's what it's all about in this sprawling ocean city.

Diving & Snorkeling

Diving is big in Nha Trang. The best season for weather and visibility is from March to September. There are a number of professional operations, mostly staffed by expatriate divers and all certified with PADI. Whether you're a beginner or an expert, make your choice based on safety more than anything.

Because of years of large-scale dynamite fishing and bottom dragging, most of the best coral sites are long gone. Most dive trips head straight for **Islands of the Hon Mun Marine Park.** In fact, all of the dive companies surround just a few tiny islands, and it can get quite crowded (a drawback). Underwater life is a colorful mix of hard and soft coral and lots of aquatic life and Technicolor reef fish (for a close-up glimpse of Nha Trang's colorful undersea life without all the bulky gear and expense, head to the National Oceanographic Museum of Vietnam; see p. 279). Angelfish, clownfish, puffers, and all kinds of shellfish are in abundance. For less crowded dive sites, ask at Jeremy Stein's Rainbow Divers (see below) about their trips to Whale Island (see "Outside Nha Trang," below).

Expect to pay about $50 for a trial dive, and from $200 for a multiple-day open-water course. All operators listed below are open from 8am to 8pm.

Blue Diving Club If you've got a good thing, copy it, says Blue Diving Club's philosophy. The result is that this copycat is a high-quality, safe, and completely secure operator—like the others listed here.

66 Tran Phu St. ✆ **058/352-7034.** www.vietnamdivers.com.

Jeremy Stein's Rainbow Divers The folks at Rainbow were the first in the area, and in the years since have taken advertising to the level of pollution in Nha Trang, with seemingly every storefront claiming a connection. But whatever your belief is in truth in advertising (or quantity of advertising), these guys are the best in town and you can book just about anywhere. Rainbow also has dive centers throughout Vietnam: on nearby Whale Island, on Phu Quoc Island (south of the Mekong Delta), and on Con Dao Island (east of Saigon).

Visit their useful website for comprehensive information: www.divevietnam.com. Try their shop at the entrance to the **Nha Trang Sailing Club** (✆ **058/352-4628;** see "Where to Dine," above), or call ✆ **058/382-9946.** They run the Rainbow Bar (90A Hung Vuong St.; ✆ **058/352-4351**), but you can also find them or book trips with them in many locations around town, such as at **La Louisiane** (Tran Phu south of Sailing Club; ✆ **058/381-2948**).

Vietnam Explorer One of the newer players on the scene, Explorer targets mostly the Vietnamese market, but they can do anything the others can and also run good 1-day boat trips.

02 Tran Quang Khai. ✆ **058/352-4490.** Daily 8am–8pm.

1-Day Boat Cruises

One-day **boat cruises** to some of Nha Trang's 20 surrounding islands are very popular. For years, Nha Trang was famed for rowdy trips that were more like daytime raves. **Hahn's Green Hat Boat Tour** (2C Biet Thu St.; ✆ **058/382-4494**) is the old favorite, a remnant of the old "Mama Hahn" trips—Mama Hahn was famous for saying, "Smoke and drink! Don't be lazy!" but is now doing a stint in jail for her industriousness. Though the trips have toned down significantly, you will want to ask details first and maybe leave the kids at home or opt for a private trip without all the "floating bars" and free mulberry wine. A number of other small agents offer similar tours (you can book these trips anywhere). The going rate is $7 per day, including a 9am hotel pickup and afternoon drop-off.

Expect a mellow day of motoring through some lovely bays. First, you'll hit **Mun Island,** where you're guaranteed some snorkeling, and then **Mot Island,** where you can enjoy a big feast for lunch and a floating bar (this is where the headache juice—some bad grape wine—comes into the picture). Beer and drinks are available all day. The next is **Tam Island,** where you can visit tiny Tam Resort and enjoy some free time for swimming and sunbathing, followed by a visit to **Mieu Island,** where you can rent a bamboo basket, those odd doughnut-shaped boats you see bobbing around fishing ports, and paddle around the bay with local fishermen. This last stop includes a visit to some large floating fish farms and information about the growing industry in Vietnam. ***Note:*** Just about everyone in town will want to book you on one of these tours, so ask at any hotel front desk and be sure to nail down all specifics (meals, transport included, and the like).

Other Water Activities

For **sailing,** contact the **Nha Trang Sailing Club** (✆ **058/352-4628**), **La Louisiane** (Tran Phu south of Sailing Club; ✆ **058/381-2948**), or the **Ana Mandara** (✆ **058/352-2222**). Go for a Hobie Cat, if it's available (about $30 per hour), and hire a captain if you're inexperienced. The strong ocean breezes and choppy waters make for a memorable sail. **Runabouts** and **jet skis** are also available at the same locations. **Parasailing** happens just south of La Louisiane.

The popular **Thapba Mud Bath and Hotspring Resort** is just outside town. Hire a car, ask at any front desk, or call them directly at ✆ **058/383-4939.**

SHOPPING

Jean Lou Coiffure De Paris, a French hairstylist and designer, has a little storefront at 13 Biet Thu (✆ **058/352-4159**) and not only does hair and nails, but also serves drinks and does laundry, too. It's open daily from 8am to midnight.

Groove Shack, at 17 Hung Vuong St. (✆ **058/352-4738**), has lots of copycats, but owner Zac has this business down. The business provides good pirated CDs and media loaded onto your iPod or personal computer. Ethical? Not really. Convenient? Yes. And you can fill up on good new tunes (or DVDs) for kicking back at the beach. Zac also sells T-shirts and beach clothes. Open daily from 8am to 10pm.

Bambou (15 Biet Thu; ✆ **058/352-3616;** daily 8am–9:30pm) is a popular T-shirt shop in the heart of the backpacker area of Biet Thu. These shirts are becoming like the "Black Dog" shirts of Martha's Vineyard for Vietnam.

At 17A Biet Thu, the heart of the busy traveler street in Nha Trang, you can't miss bright **Tashunco** (17A Biet Thu; ✆ **058/352-3035;** daily 7am–10pm), a little grocer that carries familiar Western goods, ranging from Diet Coke to good cheese.

NHA TRANG AFTER DARK

Nha Trang has a few lively beachfront bars where tourists congregate to swap stories, and it gets pretty raucous sometimes, especially when boatloads of booze-cruising day-trippers bring the party to the mainland. Bars and restaurants in the city center, and particularly along Biet Thu, are forbidden from staying open much past midnight (though a few do), but beachside Nha Trang Sailing Club (see below) picks up the slack.

Crazy Kim Bar In the heart of the backpacker area, Crazy Kim is the meeting point for the young and wild. Their motto is "Be hot. Be cool. Be crazy. Just be." There are many personified versions of that motto walking around this place. It's especially popular with the diving crowd and the few expats in town. Open until 1am. 19 Biet Thu St. ✆ **058/352-3072.**

Guava Just next door to popular Crazy Kim (see above), Guava is a similar young scene. They often have good live music acts. Open until 1am. 17 Biet Thu. No phone.

Nha Trang Sailing Club The Sailing Club is the only bar/restaurant on the beach (all others are across the main road) and is extremely popular. This is the only place that stays open much past midnight, but it gets a little seedy after that. They have open-air bamboo huts by the beach, and a large central pavilion with pool table and a dance floor. Open till late. 72–74 Tran Phu St., across from the Hai Yen Hotel. ✆ **058/352-4628.**

Why Not Bar This one seems to skirt the midnight rule. A large brick pavilion, the place stays up later, thanks to reputed "special" local connections. Live bands and dancing. Just south of the Biet Thu area. Open till late. 24 Tran Quang Khai St. ✆ **058/352-2652.**

SIDE TRIPS & OVERNIGHTS FROM NHA TRANG

Cam Ranh Bay ★ Go. Someday, you'll be able to say, "I went to Cam Ranh before it was touristy." It won't be for long. It's adjacent to the airport, so you can't miss this stunning sweep of sand if you're on your way to or from a flight. The high, winding road offers stunning views, and I'm not the first to think so; developers are lining up to have at it with pick and shovel. There's a bit of a hold on it now, but not for long. There's nothing to the beach but sand and a few local hammock-swinging joints. Cam Ranh is 30km (19 miles) south of Nha Trang and can be reached by car for about 150,000 VND each way (same as the airport), or by motorbike taxi for about 70,000 VND round-trip. 30km (19 miles) south of Nha Trang.

Doc Let Beach ★ More or less geared toward regional tourists—chairs and tables line the surf instead of beach loungers, and affordable guesthouses are nearby instead of pricey resorts—Doc Let is a good place to meet locals and get away from the backpacker factory that busy Nha Trang has become. Doc Let is 45km (28 miles) north of Nha Trang. You can get there easily on a rented motorbike (for something like 60,000 VND–70,000 VND). By rented car, expect to pay about 450,000 VND one-way. Once there, the choices of accommodations are slim. Doc Let makes a good day trip rather than an overnight.
45km (28 miles) north of Nha Trang.

3 OUTSIDE NHA TRANG

JUNGLE BEACH

Budget tourists rave about **Jungle Beach.** Run by a Canadian expat, the place is eco-friendly, basic living at beachside. Jungle Beach—a quiet, rustic **homestay**—is located 60km (37 miles) north of Nha Trang by road. There are three rooms in a longhouse and nine basic cabanas made of bamboo catay and thatch (lots of guests even sleep out in the hotel looking up at the open sky—under a mosquito net, of course). This is for folks who like living close to the land—real close to the land—in a low-luxe alternative to the more comfortable Whale Island (see below). Rooms have shared bathrooms. Food, included in the affordable rate, is home-cooked and all you can eat (though not drink; you have to pay for your own booze). They offer trekking trips right from the cabana site, or you can just hang out in a hammock or on the beach. Rooms, including meals, are 250,000 VND per day/night. Contact them by phone at ✆ **058/362-2384** (mobile phone ✆ **091/429-144**) or e-mail Syl at syl@dng.vnn.vn. Make a reservation and they can help you get to the beach. On your own, expect to pay about 300,000 VND by car from Nha Trang (100,000 VND by motorbike). You can also ask tourist or local buses from Hoi An or Nha Trang to drop you off at Doc Let, and from there get a ride with a motorbike taxi driver for just 50,000 VND.

WHALE ISLAND

If you ever wanted to be a castaway on a little coconut island, here's your chance. Thanks to great roads, **Whale Island ★★** is just a few hours' drive north from Nha Trang and a 10-minute boat ride offshore. Set in the crook of a long peninsula, not far from the easternmost point in Vietnam, Whale Island is surrounded by tranquil waters year-round, and but for a few small fishing villages, you have the place to yourself. The island has just one all-inclusive resort (✆ **058/384-0501;** fax 058/393-9031; www.iledelabaleine.com), the brainchild of a longtime French expatriate and his Vietnamese wife who've been attracting their own small contingent of mostly expatriate clientele for some 7 years now. (With 32 units, rates are $39 double and $57 suite; meals are $22 per person.) The idea is to get away from it all, and to frolic on the beach or explore the underwater life on good scuba trips sponsored by the island's exclusive operator, Rainbow Divers. You can also take good hikes around the island, and there are sailboats and canoes for rent.

Word has it that Whale Island was the auspicious site where scuba co-inventor and famous aquanaut Jacques Cousteau, while on assignment as part of a scientific mapping expedition, witnessed pearl divers staying underwater for what seemed an eternity and saw that they were using tubes from the surface. This experience inspired him to create, along with a team of scientists and engineers, the self-contained underwater breathing apparatus system that we rely on now. Maybe you'll find your own inspirations on Whale Island.

Leaving Nha Trang early in the morning on one of the resort's shuttles (included in the package), the road north takes you through some scenic areas, along low-lying rice lands spotted with Chinese tombs and white egrets flying overhead. Near the coast, pass by miles and miles of fish farms and rows of rickety stilt houses lining salt flats. As the road approaches the end of the peninsula adjacent to Whale Island, you pass along a spit of high windswept dunes and a high beach buffeted by massive crashing waves—very dynamic.

The short ferry ride to the resort is covered in a zippy oversize runabout (the same boat they use for diving), and there's a speedboat on hand for emergencies. The resort area is just a thin strip of bungalows along a narrow beach. Rooms are simple, rustic affairs, with no air-conditioning but with 24-hour power for fans and good mosquito nets for nighttime. Bathrooms are small guesthouse affairs but clean. All rooms have small balconies and little garden areas out front. There is also a small area farther back from the sea with one dorm unit and a few cozy, quiet units. A stay at Whale Island is about getting out into nature, and the rustic accommodations are part of that.

Dining is in a cozy little open-air area overlooking the tranquil bay. In the midst of a small community here, you're sure to meet your neighbors, and guests normally share meals, all from a set menu of delicious local fare—heavy on the good fish dishes. Drinks at the bar afterward or in all-night billiard matches in the enclosed library area can cement those friendships for a lifetime.

Diving is shallow coral diving, and visibility is not spectacular but comparable to areas off of Nha Trang. The area has been ravaged by dynamite fishermen, but isolated dive sites, most near Hon Mun Island, mean you won't be crowded by big groups, and there are good chances of seeing big fish, sting rays, and even whale sharks in the right season. Dive season is from November to February.

The nearby fishing villages are also worth a visit when snorkeling, and there are some great little trails all over the island that lead to secluded beaches, all well marked with signs and paint splotches on the exposed rock areas.

The transfer to the island costs $40, which is taken off your rack rates if you arrive with your own wheels. In addition to the numbers listed above, you may contact the main office on the mainland (2 Me Le Linh St.; ✆ **058/381-1607;** fax 058/351-3873). The resort takes MasterCard and Visa.

4 PHAN THIET TOWN & MUI NE BEACH

This is one of the best laid-back getaways in Vietnam. The town of Phan Thiet itself is a bustling little fishing port—quite picturesque and good for a day's visit—but you'll want to get out to the long, sprawling, sandy stretch of beach to the east: Mui Ne. This is a popular weekend getaway from nearby Saigon, and development in recent years has been rapid. You'll find some very nice upscale resorts and comfy little boutique bungalow properties.

Nick Faldo's golf course at the Novotel in Phan Thiet is a big draw, and the consistent winds of Mui Ne Bay bring windsurfers and kite surfers from all over the world. Farther east and north along the coast, there are vast sand dunes, like a beachside Sahara, and inland there's the famous and strangely verdant Silver Lake amid the towering, shifting sands—a good day trip. These spots, as well as other small fishing villages, make for great day trips. There are also some local Cham ruins, and the town of Phan Thiet, famous for a brand of fish sauce *(nuoc mam)* made here, is worth exploring (especially the market). Phan Thiet is a good getaway from Saigon or a good place to take a break as you make your way down the coast.

GETTING THERE

BY BUS OR CAR Phan Thiet is just 3 hours from Saigon. The tourist cafe buses connect here from Nha Trang and Dalat, as well as Saigon, and **Sinh Café** covers all the bases from their **Mui Ne Resort** (144 Nguyen Dinh Chieu St., Ham Tien; ✆ **062/384-7542;** www.sinhcafevn.com), or just ask at any hotel front desk for car rentals or return bus tickets. A private car can be hired for around $80 each way. **Vietnam Vespa Adventures** (168 De Tham St., District 1, Ho Chi Minh City; ✆ **08/3920-3897**) is an excellent new company running multiday tours to Mui Ne from Ho Chi Minh City. Book with them to roll into town in style on lovingly restored vintage Vespa scooters.

GETTING AROUND

BY TAXI/MOTORCYCLE TAXI There are two reliable companies. The nationwide **Mai Linh** taxi company (✆ **062/389-8989**) has new cars and minivans with meters that start at 12,000 VND for the first 2km (1¼ miles). **Duy Sang Taxi** (✆ **062/383-3833**) has slightly older four-door sedans, and the meter starts at 10,000 VND. There are also plenty of drivers on motorbikes ready to shuttle you to your destination. Expect to pay 10,000 VND to 20,000 VND for a ride of 2 to 3km (1¼–1¾ miles).

Fast Facts Phan Thiet & Mui Ne

Banks & Currency Exchange **Vietcombank** has a branch with all services (including ATM) at 87 Duong 19/4 (✆ **062/373-9065;** open daily 8–11am and 1:30–5pm,

Sat in the morning only). In Mui Ne, there is a 24-hour **Vietcombank ATM** beside the Saigon Mui Ne Resort.

Internet There are several places offering Internet services on the main street of Mui Ne, Nguyen Dinh Chieu Street. Expect to pay around 5,000 VND per hour. Most resorts offer free Internet access. Service is faster and more reliable at newer places like Terracotta.

Post Office The **Government Post Office** is at the corner of Nguyen Hue and Tran Phu in Phan Thiet (open daily 6:30am–10pm). In Mui Ne, there's a post office at the **Swiss Village** (44 Nguyen Dinh Chieu St.; ✆ **062/374-1015;** open daily 7:30am–8pm)

WHERE TO STAY

In addition to the recommendations in the section below, the **Novotel** offers the only international standard in the town of Phan Thiet, but most people are heading to the main beaches farther along. Along the beach at Mui Ne, about 9km (5½ miles) to the east, you'll find a growing clutch of luxury resorts that cover all the bases. Many folks find that they plan to stay only a short time and end up in a hammock for a few extra days.

Budget accommodations line the main drag in Mui Ne. The scene is constantly changing, but expect to pay $8 to $20 for basic guesthouse accommodations. If you come by cafe bus, they'll take you around to shop for the spot you'd like (though expect certain hotels to be recommended/pushed upon you more than others). It gets cheaper and more rustic the farther east you go on the main road.

Sinh Café, ever expanding their monopoly on the budget tourist market in Vietnam (they run all the buses), has just opened the **Mui Ne Resort** (144 Nguyen Dinh Chieu St., Ham Tien, Mui Ne; ✆ **062/384-7542;** www.sinhcafevn.com), a 48-room budget hotel on the farthest end of Mui Ne. If you come by one of their buses, they'll strand you there as long as they can in the hopes that you'll stay. Rooms start at $20 and aren't a bad bet. There's a pool and all the basics. A festive atmosphere pervades, with lots of young partyers here.

Another good choice in the budget department is **Full Moon Beach** (84 Nguyen Dinh Chieu, Ham Tien, Phan Thiet; contact Phuong or Pascal at ✆ **062/384-7008;** fax 062/384-7160; www.windsurf-vietnam.com), a popular spot for kite surfers and windsurfers. Rooms vary from wood perches overlooking the beach to midrange comfort in the newest building.

Note: Most addresses are listed by their distance from Phan Thiet. You'll find **Internet service** at most resorts at inflated prices.

Very Expensive

Princess D'Annam ★★★ This new resort sets the luxury standard for Phan Thiet. I highly recommend ending your Vietnam vacation here. Most travelers start Vietnam journeys in the north, working their way south via cultural sites and hikes through rice paddies. By the time you get to Ho Chi Minh City, you are exhausted and need a serious recharge—the Princess D'Annam is the perfect place to indulge and toast yourself for all your hard travels. Standard suites are spacious, with raised wraparound wooden foundations for the king-size bed and daybed. The bathroom is equally large, with separate rain showers and a deep tub shaped like an inverted trapezoid. Everything is white or cream, with silk textiles in shades of gold and pale blue throughout. Life-size sepia photographs of Vietnam life adorn the walls. Villas are connected via a narrow stone path, surrounded by a lush tropical garden that is home to a rainbow of butterflies. The stand-alone two-story villas house a couple rooms, are luxurious, and come with an open minibar, but if you can splurge on only one destination in Vietnam, the multiroom pool villas at the Nam Hai (p. 213) are better value.

Hon Lan, Tan Thanh Commune, Ham Thuan Nam District. ✆ **062/368-2222.** Fax 062/368-2333. www.princessannam.com. 57 units. $465 suite; $675–$1,370 villa. AE, MC, V. **Amenities:** Restaurant; 2 bars; babysitting; spacious children's playroom; concierge; health club; 3 outdoor pools; 2 tennis courts. *In room:* A/C, TV, fridge, hair dryer, minibar, Wi-Fi.

Expensive

Novotel Coralia Ocean Dunes Phan Thiet ★ Kids "Fore!" Sandwiched between Nick Faldo's golf course and an open lawn and sandy beach, the Novotel is a popular choice for golfers and Saigon expats on holiday. Rooms are decorated with nondescript carpets and floral prints. There are a few nicks and cracks in the furniture, showing the resort's age. The original hotel is an old Soviet-era resort, and concrete-block rooms are limited by their original build—small and not particularly luxe, but comfy. The two villas on the western part of the resort are only a couple years old, and I highly recommend a villa stay. Where the hotel has a cold, generic Holiday Inn feeling, the villas are warm and charming. Villa rooms have wooden floors, and all the furniture is dark wood with bamboo accents. Bathrooms have partially outdoor showers with rock and stone floors. Each villa has a shared common room with a lounge area and bar. The resort is 9km (5½ miles) from the popular beaches of Mui Ne. The beach is narrow and rocky, but the pool area and surrounding yard is expansive, great for kids (there's even a small jungle gym). The hotel has lots of activities and children's programs and rents jet skis and sailboats.

1 Ton Duc Than St., Phan Thiet. ✆ **062/382-2393.** Fax 062/382-5682. www.accorhotels-asia.com. 135 units. $118–$148 golf/sea villa; $300 villa suite. AE, MC, V. **Amenities:** Restaurant; 2 bars; babysitting; children's playground; concierge; golf; health club; Internet; 2 pools; smoke-free rooms; 2 tennis courts; watersports rentals. *In room:* A/C, TV, fridge, hair dryer, minibar, Wi-Fi.

Romana Resort & Spa ★ The Romana has a beautiful layout. Villas are dotted along a small hill so everyone has a bit of privacy and a good ocean view. Unlike other resorts in Phan Thiet, the rooms in the hotel section are still quite charming, decorated in dark wood with contrasting bright light-gray tiles. The balconies are on the small side and can fit only one lounge chair. Villa rooms are larger, with a raised entryway, dark stone tile floors, a larger balcony, and a private pool, which is slightly larger than a bathtub. The outdoor bathroom comes with a tiny bathtub that has an awkwardly placed shower head that isn't high enough for anyone over 4-foot-11.

Km 8, Mui Ne, Phan Thiet. ✆ **062/374-1289.** Fax 062/374-1281. www.romanaresort.com.vn. 96 units. $65–$125 double (hotel and villa); $275 suite. AE, MC, V. **Amenities:** Restaurant; bar; babysitting; gym; library; 2 pools; smoke-free rooms; spa; tennis court. *In room:* A/C, TV, fridge, hair dryer, minibar, Wi-Fi.

Victoria Phan Thiet Resort ★★ The Victoria is located away from the main drag and stands on a quiet little knoll overlooking the sea. It's a grass-and-garden campus traced by pathways that connect tidy, upscale bungalows. It's a unique layout, with pebble stone catwalks lined with sweet-smelling orchids and tropical flowers connecting the main buildings. The atmosphere is comfortable, laid-back, and private. The pool areas are great places to while away the day, and they have a good massage facility in a seaside grove. Guest rooms are large, private bungalows, some with two tiers and all done in terra cotta, bamboo catay, red earth brick, and dark wood; it's refined comfort with nice touches like stylish indirect lighting, large ceiling fans, and local artwork. Family bungalows have multiple sleeping areas and a pullout couch. Bathrooms have big bathtubs and partially outdoor rain showers with rock and stone floors. A couple deluxe villas have their own private Jacuzzi. Their newer rooms are farther from the beach but are very close to the infinity pool. The beach is rocky, but the resort overlooks its own quiet cove and there are beachside thatch awnings. Service is good, and the resort has all the amenities of a much larger property, only here done in intimate and friendly miniature. Come for the weekend, and you'll stay for the week.

Km 9, Phu Hai, Phan Thiet. ✆ **062/381-3000.** Fax 062/381-3007. www.victoriahotels-asia.com. 59 units. $150–$240 bungalow; $650 villa. AE, MC, V. **Amenities:** 2 restaurants; bar; motorbikes; children's play area; exercise room; Internet; 2 outdoor pools; tennis court. *In room:* A/C, TV, fridge, minibar, Wi-Fi.

Moderate

Blue Ocean Resort ★★ This is one of the best resorts in Mui Ne. The entire place was given a much-needed makeover in 2008 and is now managed by Life Resorts. Staff is incredibly friendly, much more so than at nearby Sailing Club. Skip the standard rooms, if you can, as they are quite small (you have to negotiate your way around the bed) and have tiny bathrooms. Superior rooms have a spacious open-style layout with large bathrooms. Bungalows are your best bet; they come with his-and-hers sinks and a private outdoor area big enough for the stone tub and rain shower. All units come with private balconies and a pair of daybeds. The entire resort is channeling a breezy Mediterranean decor, with whitewashed buildings livened up with bright orange cushions on the daybeds and colorful accent pillows.

54 Nguyen Dinh Chieu, 200 Ham Tien, Phan Thiet. ✆ **062/384-7322.** Fax 062/384-7351. www.blueoceanresort.com. 84 units. $70–$100 double; $110–$165 bungalow; $225–$265 family bungalow. AE, MC, V. **Amenities:** Restaurant; bar; babysitting; outdoor pool; room service; spa. *In room:* A/C, TV, fridge, minibar, Wi-Fi.

Coco Beach Resort ★ Coco Beach doesn't look like much from the road—just an ugly pink wall to keep out the noise—but it's a real seaside garden oasis. They were the first to build along the strip at Mui Ne. Rooms are wooden bungalows on stilts, each with a comfy balcony area with a couch and table. It's a nice standard, intimate and tidy, and the real wood and thatch gives it an authentic 1970s rustic atmosphere. Spacious bungalows—the best are the oceanside villas—have high vaulted ceilings, dark beams, exposed thatch roofs, bamboo catay lanterns, mosquito nets, and subdued, indirect lighting. Service is attentive and genuine, the best along the main strip of Mui Ne. Coco Beach has two restaurants that are the best in town: Paradise Beach Club, the resort's laid-back oceanside seafood venue, and the more upscale Champa (see "Where to Dine," below). A great open-air massage facility is here, too.

58 Nguyen Dinh Chieu, Phan Thiet. ✆ **062/384-7111.** Fax 062/384-7115. 31 units. $90–$110 bungalow; $170–$210 2-room villa. MC, V. **Amenities:** 2 restaurants; bar; Jacuzzi; motorboat and sailboat rental; pool; room service. *In room:* A/C, fridge, minibar, Wi-Fi.

Mui Ne Sailing Club ★ This seaside spot is owned by the same Aussie folks who run the popular Sailing Club in Nha Trang. All rooms have terra-cotta tile with bamboo matting, cloth hangings, and bamboo floor lamps. There is an American Southwest feel in the artful beveled edges of the plaster walls and in the similarly rounded built-in nightstands. Large bathrooms are nicely appointed in tile and dark-wood trim, and are separated from the bedroom by only a hanging cloth, a nice touch. The high-end bungalows with private balconies are the best choice and certainly worth the upgrade. The pool is small, but in a picturesque seaside courtyard adjoining the open-air colonial-style restaurant. This is a popular stop for windsurfers and kite surfers; you can rent equipment and take lessons.

24 Nguyen Dinh Chieu St., Ham Tien Ward, Phan Thiet. ✆ **062/384-7440.** Fax 062/384-7441. www.sailingclubvietnam.com. 30 units. $77 double; $105–$143 bungalow. AE, MC, V. **Amenities:** Restaurant; bar; babysitting; motorbikes; Internet; outdoor pool; room service. *In room:* A/C, TV, minibar, Wi-Fi.

Terracotta ★ (Kids) This resort has a fun, childlike look and feel to it, even down to its block-lettering logo, which would be right at home in a playschool, and a bright yellow-and-blond-wood reception area. Large unfinished terra-cotta jugs and vases are everywhere, molded with daisies or flowers and the resort's logo. The garden lawns are decorated with tiny pottery statues of little people in pondering poses. A see-saw made from a varnished log resides on a patch of grass. There's also an activity center set up where you can paint and bake your own ceramic mug and saucer. This is a place to bring the kids. Rooms in the hotel section have blond furniture and small bathrooms with shower curtains but no cubicles. However, they are also too close to the main road, and you can easily hear the honking and revving of passing cars and motorbikes. For a quieter stay, spring for the bungalow rooms that are closer to the beach. Rooms are spacious and have gray-stone tile floors and a small roof ledge displaying terra-cotta vases.

28 Nguyen Dinh Chieu, Ham Tienm, Phan Thiet. ✆ **062/384-7610.** Fax 062/384-7611. www.terracottaresort.com. 59 units. $70–$120 double; $132–$151 bungalow; $230–$260 suite. AE, MC, V. **Amenities:** Restaurant; 2 bars; gym; Jacuzzi; pool; room service; sauna. *In room:* A/C, TV, fridge, minibar, Wi-Fi.

WHERE TO DINE

In addition to the reviewed Paradise Beach Club below, you may wish to try the **Mui Ne Sailing Club** (24 Nguyen Dinh Chieu St., Han Tien Ward, Phan Thiet; ✆ **062/384-7440**), which serves good, basic Western fare in an open-air building at poolside overlooking the ocean. Farther east, **Full Moon Beach** (84 Nguyen Dinh Chieu, Ham Tien, Phan Thiet; ✆ **062/384-7008**) is a good stop for coffee or breakfast on your way to Silver Lake or the big dunes north of town.

Thatched-roof eateries line the main beachside road in Mui Ne. **Luna d' Autuno** (Km 12, 51A Nguyen Dinh Chieu, Ham Tien; ✆ **062/384-7591**), a popular Saigon pizzeria, has a cool restaurant serving excellent Italian food and offering an extensive wine list under a high thatched roof. A couple doors down is **Gecko Mui Ne** (✆ **062/374-1033**), serving French food and some familiar Western dishes. There's also a **Good Morning Vietnam Restaurant** (Km 11.8, Ham Tien; ✆ **091/802-2760**), Vietnam's pizza and pasta franchise that serves good, affordable, familiar meals for little money.

The **Hot Rock** (77A Nguyen Dinh Chieu, across from Bien Xanh Resort; ✆ **062/384-7608**) is a casual watering hole with good, basic Western fare. Plans are afoot to beautify Hot Rock by replacing the plastic chairs and whitewashing the colorful walls. **Jibe's Bar** (90 Nguyen Dinh Chieu; ✆ **062/384-7405**) is a lively place with a terrace overlooking the ocean. It's a favorite late-night hangout.

Paradise Beach Club ★ SEAFOOD Set in a soothing seaside pavilion at the popular Coco Beach Resort (see "Where to Stay," above), the Paradise Beach Club is the place for fine fresh seafood and barbecue. Choose from a raw bar and have your meal cooked to order, as you like it. The long roster of a menu covers anything from light snacks and sandwiches to hearty Western meals. For dessert, they make the most unique sundaes I've ever seen. Check it out. The resort's more upscale restaurant, **Champa,** is also a great choice.

At the Coco Beach Resort (58 Nguyen Dinh Chieu, Ham Tien, Phan Thiet). ✆ **062/384-7111.** Main courses $2–$18. MC, V. Daily 6:30am–11pm.

ATTRACTIONS

Some 20km (12 miles) northeast of town are **Cape Mui Ne**'s ★★ sprawling sand dunes, and a trip out this way brings you through lots of quaint seaside villages that are well worth a wander. Coming from Mui Ne Beach, you'll first reach a small fishing town and can explore its fine little rural market—great in the early morning. Heading inland away from the beach, you'll first come to the towering **Red Dunes** ★★. A walk to the top offers great views of the town and surrounding countryside, and you're sure to be followed by a gaggle of friendly kids trying to sell you on the idea of renting one of their plastic sleds for the ride down the steep dune slopes. It's kind of fun; pay anywhere between 5,000 VND and 10,000 VND for a few runs. From the Red Dunes, if you have time, the unique **Silver Lake** ★★ is reached only after a long, bumpy ride, but the views of the coast are dynamic and this unique little verdant lake in the large, parched silver dune makes the trip worth it. It's a long day, though. Ask at any hotel or resort for tours. Expect to pay $10 per person for two or more to go to the tip of the cape and the Red Dunes, and more to go inland.

At the highest point on the road between Phan Thiet Town and Mui Ne Beach, you won't miss **Cham Tower,** an impressive spire of crumbling brick. The tower dates from the end of the 13th century and is worth a stop if you weren't able to catch any of the Cham sites near Hoi An and Danang. Any taxi will be happy to make a brief stop on the way. There are also Cham sites some 2 hours' drive inland near Phan Rang, and all hotels and resorts can arrange tours.

OUTDOOR ACTIVITIES

The wind conditions in Mui Ne are steady and strong in the dry season (Oct–May), and the beach is becoming a real kite-surfing and windsurfing mecca (it has over-12-knot winds for two-thirds of the year). **Jibe's** (90 Nguyen Dinh Chieu, Ham Tien, Mui Ne; ✆ **062/384-7405;** www.windsurf-vietnam.com), a popular rental shop, windsurfer club, and bar, is a good place to check in or rent a board, and a great opportunity for first-time kite surfers. A day with an IKO-certified instructor starts at just $85; the focus is on safety, of course, and the savings are significant (similar lessons elsewhere cost a mint).

Sailors will want to contact the folks at the **Mui Ne Sailing Club** (24 Nguyen Dinh Chieu St., Han Tien Ward, Phan Thiet; ✆ **062/384-7440**) or at any hotel or resort about renting Hobie Cat and Laser sailboats, windsurfers, jet skis, or runabouts.

The outstanding Nick Faldo–designed **Ocean Dunes Golf Course** (1 Ton Duc Thang St., Phan Thiet; ✆ **062/382-3366**) is a big draw here in town, for both domestic golf buffs and international players.

Ho Chi Minh City (Saigon)

Ho Chi Minh City (Saigon) is Vietnam's commercial headquarters—brash and busy—with a keen sense of its own importance as Vietnam emerges from years of austerity to claim a place in the "Asian Tiger" economic slugfest. Located on the Saigon River, Ho Chi Minh City is Vietnam's major port and largest city, with an estimated population of over eight million people, most of whom cruise the town's clogged arteries on an estimated three million motorbikes. True to its reputation, the city is noisy, crowded, and dirty, but the central business district is rapidly developing in steel-and-glass precision to rival any city on the globe. The old Saigon still survives in wide downtown avenues flanked by pristine colonials. Hectic and eclectic, Ho Chi Minh City has an attitude all its own.

But what are you supposed to call it? Is it Istanbul or Constantinople? Ho Chi Minh City or Saigon? After North Vietnamese victory in 1975, the first piece of legislation at the first National Assembly in 1976 saw the name change to honor the country's greatest nationalist leader. Foreign visitors, especially folks who knew the city of old or during the war years, have a hard time making the change to Ho Chi Minh City, and you'll notice that most Vietnamese people, apart from crusty cadres, usually use the old name: Saigon. To set the record straight, "Ho Chi Minh City" refers to the larger metropolitan area comprised of some 19 districts of sprawl, while "Saigon" is the name of the main commercial center—districts 1, 3, and 5—and people still refer to the town as such—like referring to New York as Manhattan.

Saigon is a relatively young Asian city, founded in the 18th century, but its history tells the story of Vietnam's recent struggles. Settled mainly by civil-war refugees from north Vietnam along with Chinese merchants, Saigon quickly became a major commercial center in the late 1800s. With a very convenient protected port along the Saigon River, the city became a confluence in Indochina for goods passing from China and India to Europe. Places like today's popular tourist stop Ben Thanh Market were abuzz with activity. When the French took over the region about that time—in the 1880s—they called the south "Cochin China," Annam being central Vietnam and Tonkin the north. Saigon became the capital. We owe the wide boulevards and grand colonial facades of central District 1 to years of French control and influence. After the French left in 1954, Saigon remained the capital of South Vietnam until reunification in 1975.

As the logistical base for American operations during the Vietnam War time, the city is all too familiar to the many American servicemen and women who spent time in Vietnam. Saigon is perhaps best known for its "fall," a pell-mell evacuation from the rooftop of the U.S. Embassy and the desperate last-ditch efforts of helicopter pilots to get just one more person out to the offshore U.S. carriers. The stories of that day, of divided families and the ones left behind, are heart-wrenching.

The years that followed were even bleaker, with a country feeding itself on ideology, not rice, but the progressive Doi Moi economic reforms, which opened Vietnam to foreign investment, aid, and

A Veteran's Trip Back

Our flight from Honolulu to Vietnam in July 2002 was an hour late. After takeoff, I smiled to myself because it took 30 years to return to my adopted second home—late indeed. From May 1967 until March 1972, I was flying into Vietnam or Thailand on support missions, or serving one of three combat tours in Vietnam, Laos, or Thailand. The culture, the food, the language, and the people became part of my heart and soul. Vietnam got a bad rap, in my opinion, in the American psyche from the dark messages of *Apocalypse Now* and *Deer Hunter.* My experiences were quite different; I remembered a beautiful country and great loving people.

On the long flight, I read a book my sister had given me titled *Soul Retrieval,* by Sandra Ingerman. From it, I realized the source of my longing. Part of me was still there, and I felt incomplete. The mission we were sent to complete had no ending—no welcome home. The war had been waged in my head day after day ever since I left.

When I landed at Tan Son Nhat Airport (the name was never changed!) in Saigon, the years were bridged in minutes. All of our old aircraft revetments and bunkers were still there, and the landmarks had not changed. My heart was pounding with excitement. Ahhh, the hot, humid air hit my face as soon as the door opened, a familiar aroma filled my nostrils, and the high-pitched voices of intense Vietnamese conversation told me I was home. Why had I waited so long? What was I afraid of? The first stop was passport control, facing uniforms of my former enemy, red star and all. What if they kept an "Enemies List"? They could whisk me off and nobody would ever know. The man processing my visa did not react to my Vietnamese greeting, and he seemed to take a long time. I later realized there was simply a lot of information to enter into his computer. My bags were waiting in the baggage claim, Customs waved me through, and 15 minutes after we landed, I was inside the country, free to find my way. There was a crowd of Vietnamese waiting for arriving passengers. As I wheeled my cart down the gauntlet of people, I stopped and raised my arms Rocky style and shouted "Vietnam, Vietnam!" Six young men saw me and thought it was the funniest thing they had ever seen and mimicked me. We exchanged smiles and hearty laughs.

The logistics of getting downtown were painless. There was a choice of a van for $10 or a metered taxi for about $5. Armed with Vietnamese dong, I chose

cooperation, set the town on its feet. The city boomed for a little while in the 1990s until foreign investors were choked and bullied by bureaucracy—many companies pulling out lock, stock, and barrel—but FDI (Foreign Direct Investment) is returning, led mostly by Asian investors (from Japan, Korea, and China). Now the future looks bright for this burgeoning Tiger capital.

There are two distinct seasons in Saigon: The always hot (average 82°F/28°C) and rainy season lasts from May to November, the dry season from December to April.

Some of Saigon's tourism highlights include the **Vietnam History Museum;**

the taxi and was soon at the Palace Hotel. All of the major accommodations are in the District 1 area. I found a minihotel much more suited to my taste—cozy, friendly, and away from the hustle and bustle, plus one-third of the cost. I hired a van to drive me to the places where I had flown and lived. I went to Long Xuyen, in the Mekong Delta, where I had spent a year. In a stroke of luck, as I was showing 30-year-old photos of my former residence, "Marie House," to people in the old neighborhood, one 70-year-old man exclaimed, "That was my mother-in-law's house until 1975! It's right over here." The front yard where we parked our jeeps was now a pharmacy and our beloved house was a government insurance building. It broke my heart. It wasn't my house anymore, it wasn't anybody's house, but I would never have found it without the gracious help of this gray-haired gentleman half my height. He ran into his nearby house to put on long pants for the photo I took of the two of us, and he hugged me like a son.

After my nostalgic trip through the delta, I went to Dalat, in the hill country. It took about 5 enjoyable hours on the road. A lake in the center of town is the crown jewel of a beautiful Shangri La. I made friends with the family who owned my favorite Internet cafe. They brought me as the guest of honor to their house for lunch. It was a great time, with lots of laughs, 10 scrumptious dishes, and family love from all 22 family members. Suddenly it hit me: The war is over, and I'm no longer the enemy. We're fellow earth travelers with a common bond.

It was a spiritual journey for me, and much healing took place. My tours in Southeast Asia were the centerpiece of my 28-year career in the United States Air Force, and now Asia has again become part of my life. I have been back 4 more times to Vietnam, 4 times to Laos, and 10 to Thailand, which I use as my home base. I'm a different person for having made the trip. It allowed me to recapture my soul and end my war.

—by Mike Cavanaugh

The author of this story retired from the USAF as a full colonel and has resided in Honolulu for over 20 years. He now splits his time among Hawaii, Thailand, Laos, and Vietnam. Mike also served as the Air Attaché to Afghanistan from 1978 to 1979. He holds the Silver Star and 50 other combat decorations. Half of his 4,000 flying hours were in combat.

the grisly **War Remnants Museum;** and **Cholon, the Chinese District,** with its pagodas and exotic stores. **Dong Khoi Street**—formerly fashionable Rue Catinat during the French era and Tu Do, or Freedom Street, during the Vietnam War—is once again a strip of grand hotels, some dating from the colonial era, new chic shops and boutiques, and lots of fine dining and cafes. Saigon's food is some of the best Vietnam has to offer, its nightlife sparkles, and the shopping here is fast and furious. The city is also a logical jumping-off point for excursions to southern destinations, including the **Mekong Delta,** the **Cu Chi Tunnels,** and **Phan Thiet beach.**

1 ORIENTATION

GETTING THERE & AWAY

BY PLANE Most regional airlines connect with Ho Chi Minh City, including Malaysian Airlines, Thai Airways, Bangkok Airways, Silk Air/Singapore Airlines, Lao Aviation, Garuda Indonesia, Philippine Airlines, United, and Cathay Pacific (from Hong Kong). Vietnam Airlines usually has the best fare, thanks to government controls. If you're flying to Vietnam directly from North America, check with United flights or with Cathay Pacific for good fares and itineraries. Domestically, Saigon is linked by Vietnam Airlines flights from Hanoi, Hue, Danang, Hoi An, Nha Trang, and Dalat.

At the airport in Saigon, you can change foreign currency for VND, but taxi drivers to town don't mind payment in U.S. dollars. Arranging a hotel limousine to greet you will certainly make life a bit easier, but taxis are aplenty outside the arrivals hall. You can also book a taxi at the airport taxi booth just beyond the baggage claim area; the trip to town is around 180,000 VND for a regular taxi or 200,000 VND for an SUV/van taxi. There is a small tourist information booth near the airport exit, but for now it has just a scant few hotel pamphlets. You can contact the **airport lost and found** at ✆ **08/3844-6665,** ext. 7461.

In town, the **Vietnam Airlines office** is at 116 Nguyen Hue, District 1 (✆ **08/3824-4482**), or call their reservations office, which is at 49 Truong Son St., Tan Binh District (✆ **08/3832-0320**). Just about everyone in town, from the many traveler cafes to hotel front-desk staff or concierge, can book your onward domestic flights on Vietnam Airlines.

To get to town from the **Tan Son Nhat** airport, taxis wait in front of the arrivals area. If you didn't book a taxi at the taxi booth (see above), stick with established companies (see "Scam Alert," below). For a fun ride in style, look around at the airport for the few old white Peugeot taxis that still roll around town; the price is the same, but the ride is slow and you'll feel like a khaki-clad colonial. The ride to most locations in District 1 should be no more than 90,000 VND. To get to the airport from town, contact any hotel front desk to arrange the fixed 80,000 VND fare from most locations in District 1. Departure taxes are included in the price of air tickets. Below is the contact information for all airlines in Ho Chi Minh City: **Air France,** 130 Dong Khoi, District 1 (✆ 08/3829-0981); **Asiana Airlines,** 34 Le Duan, District 1 (✆ 08/3822-2622); **Austrian Airlines,** 9 Dong Khoi, District 1 (✆ 08/3829-7117); **British Airways,** 170–172 Nam Ky Khoi Nghia, District 1 (✆ 08/3822-2262); **Cathay Pacific Airways,** 115 Nguyen Hue, District 1 (✆ 08/3822-3203); **China Airlines,** 37 Ton Duc Thanag, District 1 (✆ 08/3911-1591); **China Southern Airlines,** 21–23 Nguyen Thi Minh Khai, District 1 (✆ 08/3823-5588); **Eva Air,** 19 Nguyen Hue, District 1 (✆ 08/3822-4488); **KLM Royal Dutch Airlines,** 130 Dong Khoi St., District 1 (✆ 08/3823-1990); **Korean Airlines,** 34 Le Duan, District 1 (✆ 08/3824-2878); **Lufthansa,** 14/F 19–25 Nguyen Hue, District 1 (✆ 08/3829-8529); **Malaysia Airlines,** 37 Ton Duc Thang, District 1 (✆ 08/3829-2529); **Qantas,** 170-172 Nam Ky Khoi Nghia, District 1 (✆ 08/3930-2944); **Singapore Airlines,** Ste. 101, Saigon Tower Building, 29 Le Duan, District 1 (✆ 08/3823-1588); **Thai Airways,** 29 Le Duan, District 1 (✆ 08/3829-2810); **United Airlines,** 29 Le Duan District 1 (✆ 08/3823-4755); and **Vietnam Airlines,** 116 Nguyen Hue, District 1 (✆ 08/3832-0320).

Warning! Scam Alert

If you go with a taxi driver, even a metered one, from the airport in Saigon, watch out for the hotel bait-and-switch scam. Drivers get commissions for leading tourists to one hotel or another, and they commonly insist that the hotel you're going to is full, has closed, or has some other problem. The driver will pull a dour face and even sound pretty convincing as he tries to take you to his friend's hotel. Sit tight until you're at your intended destination. It might help for you to agree in writing where you're going before setting out. ***Important:*** Go with established companies when going by metered taxi (choose yellow Vina Taxi, red Saigon Tourist Taxi, or white Mai Linh Taxi), as many small operators have rigged meters.

BY BUS/MINIVAN Saigon is the hub of transport in the south, and all bus lines pass through here. Saigon is the terminus of the "Open Tour" Ticket for budget bus tours, and Saigon's many **traveler cafes** that line the streets of the Pham Ngu Lao budget travel area are your best bet for convenient onward travel by road, whether by air-conditioned bus or minivan. See the tour information below for listings.

Tourist buses also connect Saigon by road via the Moc Bai **border crossing** with nearby **Cambodia.** The all-day ride leaves daily in either a minibus or a large air-conditioned coach from the De Tham–area tourist cafes (see "Visitor Information & Tours," below). From Cambodia to Saigon, contact the likes of Capitol Tours in Phnom Penh (or any other budget tour office).

Local buses are, as anywhere in Vietnam, a bit harrowing, but Saigon's bus stations are the most organized and offer myriad routes out from this central hub. See chapter 3 for more information about local buses. Also be sure to leave from the correct bus station (there are three) for your destination.

Mien Dong Bus Station (292 Dinh Bo Linh Rd., Binh Thanh District; www.vexe24h.com) has services to the north of Vietnam, including to the Central Highlands and Phan Thiet. **Mien Tay Bus Station** (395 Kinh Duong Vuong Rd., Binh Tan District; **✆ 08/3877-6594**) serves the Mekong Delta to the south. **Cholon Bus Station** (84 Trang Tu Rd., District 5) connects with nearby towns in the Mekong Delta, as well as west toward Cambodia and the town of Tay Ninh.

BY CAR For safety reasons alone, if you're renting a car, I suggest that you book a minivan with a tour or arrange a car with driver. Self-driving is possible, but chaotic roads and shoddy insurance can mean some major hassles. Contact any hotel front desk for arrangements. Many of Saigon's hotels are run by the massive government-run Saigontourist, and they offer lots of affordable in-town and regional tour options by private car (see their listing in "Visitor Information & Tours," below).

BY TRAIN Saigon is the southern terminus of the Reunification Express, Vietnam's north-south rail connection. **Ga Saigon,** or the Saigon station, is in District 3 at 1 Nguyen Thong St. Bookings can be made at the convenient **Saigon Railway Tourist Service Co.** in the backpacker area at 275C Pham Ngu Lao St. (**✆ 08/3931-2828**). The office is open from 7:30am to 8pm, and they're a pretty surly bunch, but you should find English-speakers in the group. Most popular from Saigon is Nha Trang (about 6½ hr.; 316,000 VND), Danang (13 hr.; 665,000 VND), Hue (14½ hr.; 753,000 VND), or all the way to Hanoi (31 hr.; 1,125,000 VND). Prices above are for the fastest trains and comfortable, air-conditioned sleeper berths; budget options are the hard-berth sleepers with six to a car or the masochistic hard seat. Vietnamese trains are quite efficient and a good way to meet locals.

BY BOAT Check out the unique options to connect by boat from **Phnom Penh** or **Chau Doc** in the Mekong Delta. One option is the weeklong cruise between **Angkor Wat** and either **Can Tho** or **My Tho** in the Mekong Delta aboard one of the luxury, shallow-draft **Pandaw Cruise Boats** (www.pandaw.com). Shared rooms on the vessel start at $1,034. Check with budget tour cafes in your departure city.

GETTING AROUND

BY TAXI Taxis are clustered around the bigger hotels and restaurants. They cost 10,000 VND to 15,000 VND at flag fall and 6,000 VND or so for every kilometer thereafter. Call **Mai Linh Taxi** (© **08/3925-0250**), **Vina Taxi** (© **08/3815-5145**), or **Vinasun** (© **08/3272-727**). Stick with the larger companies listed here, as others (many with copycat names that sound similar) are famous for doctoring the meter and charging far more than the accepted price.

BY CAR You can simplify your sightseeing efforts if you hire a car and driver for the day. Contact Ann Tours, Saigontourist, or any hotel concierge. Expect to pay about $30 for a day's rental with driver.

BY MOTORCYCLE TAXI If you can't beat 'em, join 'em. Saigon's crazy motorbike traffic is maddening in a car, which feels something like an elephant in a forest of buzzing mosquitoes, so a motorbike is a great way to weave through the chaos—a quick trip is 10,000 VND for the savvy haggler (usually closer to 15,000 VND), while hourly booking can be in the ballpark of $1 per hour (don't bother with the English-speaking drivers in the Dong Khoi area who tell you that they'll be your guide for 50,000 VND per hour). A bit hair-raising sometimes, but it is a good way to get around. Ask for a helmet; most city drivers carry one in a plastic bag on the side of their bike for safety-conscious clients. Keep your knees in, and many drivers will appreciate if, when merging in traffic, you help out looking back and signaling your turn with a wave to oncoming traffic. You'll come back caked in city grime, with some good stories for friends back home.

BY CYCLO Cyclos are available for an hourly rental of about 20,000 VND, but they're simply not a good option in Saigon, especially outside District 1. First, drivers have an odd habit of not speaking English (or, indeed, any other language) halfway through your trip and taking you to places you never asked to see, or simply driving around in circles pretending to be confused. Second, riding in a slow, open conveyance amid thousands of motorbikes and cars is unpleasant and dangerous, and cyclo passengers are low to the ground and in the front, something like a bumper. A short jaunt around the Dong Khoi area or for hops between some of the city sights is memorable, but all-day cyclo tours are not recommended.

BY BICYCLE & MOTORBIKE Saigon traffic is chaos, so you might want to think twice before renting a motorbike or bicycle to get around the city on your own. Any hotel front desk can arrange rental at an inflated fee, or try the many little storefronts on Pham Ngu Lao, just west of the intersection with De Tham, where a full-day bike rental starts at $1 and a motorbike is from $5. Wear a helmet and drive slowly, staying in the middle of the herd.

Saigon's Districts

Metropolitan Ho Chi Minh City is divided into 19 administrative districts, numbered 1 through 12 and including Tan Binh, Bin Thanh, Phu Nhuan, Thu Duc, Go Vap, Binh Tan, and Tan Phu. Be sure to know the name or number of the district you need when looking for an address, and try to group your travels accordingly (you don't want to try to crisscross too many districts in 1 day). Most of the hotels, bars, shops, and restaurants are in **District 1,** parts of which are easily covered on foot—though you'll want to hop a motorbike taxi or cab to cross the length of a district. District 1 is home to the central **Ben Thanh Market** and includes the city's most busy commercial area, **Dong Khoi,** as well as the **backpacker district** of **Pham Ngu Lao.** District 1 is flanked to the east and south by the Saigon River, which is where Dong Khoi Street terminates and marks the boundary of the most developed part of the city. Saigon's sightseeing attractions are spread among districts 1, 3, and 5 (Cholon). **District 3** is just north and west of the central Dong Khoi area and is home to many foreign business offices and embassies. **District 5** is a fair ride west of the town center and supports the city's large ethnic Chinese population, a number of older temples, and a market area.

VISITOR INFORMATION & TOURS

Every major tourist agency has its headquarters or a branch in Saigon. They can book tours and travel throughout the city and the southern region, and usually countrywide as well. Ann Tours, Exotissimo, and Saigontourist are upper tier. Ben Thanh Tourist and Sinh Balo are a lower range. Ann Tours is a favorite of Frommer's readers and the subcontractor of choice for many of the best international tour operators.

- **Ann Tours,** 58 Ton That Tung St., District 1 (© **08/3833-2564;** fax 08/3832-3866; www.anntours.com), has a great reputation that's well deserved. Ann's specializes in custom tours for individuals or small groups. They can be relatively expensive, but that's in comparison to the seat-in-coach cattle-drive tours. These guys will help you do virtually anything you want to in Vietnam. Ask for director Tony Nong, and tell him Frommer's sent you.
- **Exotissimo,** Saigon Finance Center, 9 Dinh Tien Hoang St., District 1 (© **08/3825-1723;** fax 08/3829-5800; www.exotissimo.com), has a chic downtown office and can arrange just about any tour or international itinerary. They are a very professional outfit, and their guides are knowledgeable and speak excellent English. Like Ann Tours, they are on the pricey side, but I highly recommend Exotissimo for their attentive and thorough tours.
- **Saigontourist,** 49 Le Thanh Ton St., District 1 (© **08/3824-4554;** fax 08/3822-5516; www.saigontourist.net), is a large government-run group, but it'll get you where you want to go and is a far better choice than the budget cafes (see below). They man desks in the Majestic, Rex, and Sheraton hotels. They can arrange tours by private car, organize specialized larger group tours to places like the Cu Chi Tunnels and the Mekong Delta, or match you up with larger groups. Day rates start at $18 for a city tour and $25 to $55 per day for sights farther afield. Offices are open daily from 7:30am to 6:30pm.
- **Sinh Balo** means "Sinh the Backpacker," so-called after the company founder and budget-tour pioneer Mr. Sinh, who also gave his name to the very popular (and much copied) cafe tour company for budget tourists (see "Budget Tourist Cafes," below). In 1995, Mr. Sinh started this more high-end tour company and has attracted quite a

large following. Sinh Balo runs good classic tours as well as a host of eco-tour itineraries. Their offices are at 283/20 Pham Ngu Lao, District 1 (✆ **08/3837-6766;** fax 08/3836-7682; http://sinhbalo.com).

- **Tourist Information Center,** 4G–4H Le Loi St., District 1 (✆ **08/3822-6033;** fax 08/3822-6028; www.ticvietnam.com), is a great place to pick up cards for a lot of the good restaurants and hotels in town. An on-site currency exchange center gives standard rates for cash-only transactions and charges 3% commission. There are also computers with free Internet access.
- **Vietnam Vespa Adventure,** 169 De Tham St., District 1, inside Café Zoom (✆ **08/3920-3897;** www.vietnamvespaadventures.com), is a fantastic new tour operator running multiday trips to Mui Ne or Nha Trang aboard beautifully restored vintage Vespas. The easy-to-handle scooters, spectacular views, and friendly co-owners Steve and Patrick come together to create an unforgettable experience. They also do 1-day city tours of Ho Chi Minh City.

Budget Tourist Cafes

Saigon's budget tourist cafes, with their many options for affordable seat-in-coach tours in the south and "open tour" bus tickets that run you along the length of Vietnam, are many and all quite similar in the Pham Ngu Lao backpacker area. Sometimes you book with one and get consolidated with another tour at another company. Same prices and services are the rule. Sinh Café (below) is the über-cafe, but there are many others that offer much the same services, including TNK, 216 De Tham St. (✆ **08/3920-4766;** www.tnktravelvietnam.com).

Sinh Café, 246–248 De Tham, District 1 (✆ **08/3837-6833;** www.sinhcafevn.com), or in their newer office, **Sinh Café II** near the Dong Khoi area at 24–26 Pho Duc Chinh St. (✆ **08/3821-7421**), is the best choice for inexpensive trips and tours. On paper, the tours seem exactly the same as others offered at private tour agents. They have computerized air booking and are quite efficient, if usually overrun with the heavy volume of Western tourists.

Fast Facts Ho Chi Minh City

Banks & Currency Exchange As elsewhere in Vietnam, you can change money in banks and hotels. The exchange rate in Saigon is better than in many smaller cities.

Major banks in Saigon include **ANZ Bank,** 11 Me Linh Sq., District 1 (✆ **08/3829-9319**); **Citibank,** 115 Nguyen Hue St. (✆ **08/3824-2118**); **HSBC,** 235 Dong Khoi St., District 1 (✆ **08/3829-2288**); and **Vietcombank,** 29 Ben Chuong Duong, District 1 (✆ **08/3829-7245**). All offer international ATM services.

A good currency exchange is at 4C Le Loi St., right in the town center.

Western Union has a number of locations throughout the city. Their main office is at 104–106 Nguyen Hue St. (across from the Rex Hotel; ✆ **08/3823-9116**).

Dentists **International SOS** (see "Hospitals & International Clinics," below) has a dental clinic. Also try **Maple Healthcare Dental Clinic** (72 Vo Thi Sau, District 1; ✆ **08/3820-1999;** fax 08/3840-7286; www.maplehealthcare.net).

Doctors See "Hospitals & International Clinics," below.

Drugstores Vietnamese drugstores are on every street corner, and they're more or less the "prescribe it yourself" kind, whether you need antibiotics or stomach medicines.

Embassies & Consulates For embassies, see "Fast Facts: Hanoi" in chapter 5. Ho Chi Minh's consulates are all in District 1, as follows: **United States,** 4 Le Duan St. (✆ 08/3822-9433); **Canada,** 235 Dong Khoi St. (✆ 08/3827-9899); **Australia,** 5B Ton Duc Thang St. (✆ 08/3829-6035); **New Zealand,** 9/F 235 Dong Skhoi St. (✆ 08/3822-6908); and **United Kingdom,** 25 Le Duan St. (✆ 08/3829-8433).

Emergencies For **police,** dial ✆ **113;** for **fire,** dial ✆ **114;** and for an **ambulance,** dial ✆ **115.** Have a translator on hand, if necessary; operators don't speak English, and for any major situation you will want to contact your country's embassy or consulate. For **medical emergencies,** contact one of the clinics listed under "Hospitals & International Clinics," below). For an **international operator,** dial ✆ **110.**

Hospitals & International Clinics Saigon's large expatriate community gets sick, and when they do, they need doctoring, which means good emergency clinics are available. Any of the clinics listed below act as a general triage for emergencies and can help coordinate evacuation. They're staffed with both foreign and Vietnamese specialists.

International SOS is at 167 Nam Ky Khoi Nghia St., District 3. During office hours, call ✆ **08/3829-8520,** and in the evenings, dial their 24-hour hot line, ✆ **08/3829-8424.**

The **Family Medical Practice** is at the Diamond Plaza, 34 Le Duan, District 1 (✆ **08/3822-7848**).

The **International Medical Center** (1 Han Thuyen, District 1; ✆ **08/3827-2366** during office hours, ✆ **08/3865-4025** for emergencies) offers services similar to what you'll find at International SOS.

Internet Almost every upscale hotel provides Internet services in Saigon, but they charge a pretty penny. You won't find any service on Dong Khoi, but a short walk in any direction brings you to service for an average of 200 VND per minute. Try **Welcome Internet,** at 15B Le Thanh Ton (✆ **08/3822-0981**). Service in the Pham Ngu Lao backpacker area is fast and cheap; Internet cafes line De Tham and charge 5,000 VND to 6,000 VND per hour. **Hong Hoa** (185/28 Pham Ngu Lao St., 250 De Tham St., District 1; ✆ **08/3836-1915;** www.honghoavn.com) is exemplary of the good, affordable services on Pham Ngu Lao (dial-up, though, which makes it a little slow). Bui Vien is lined with small Internet operators (try **FTC Travel;** 74 Bui Vien St.; ✆ **09/201-228**).

Maps The **Tourist Information Center,** at 4G-4H Le Loi St., District 1 (✆ **08/3822-6033**), has free detailed city maps.

Post Office The main post office is at 2 Cong Xa Paris, District 1 (✆ **08/3827-1149**), across from Notre Dame cathedral. It's open daily from 7:30am to 8pm. Postal service is also available in most hotels and at various locations throughout the city.

Safety The biggest threat to your safety in Saigon is likely to be the street traffic. Cross the wildly busy streets at a slow, steady pace. If you're having a really hard time getting across, find a local who is crossing and stick to his heels!

Pickpocketing is a big problem in Saigon, especially motorbike drive-bys, with someone slashing the shoulder strap, grabbing the bag, and driving off. Keep your bag close and away from traffic. Hang on to your wallet, and don't wear flashy jewelry. Be especially wary in crowded places like markets. Women should avoid wandering around in the evenings alone past 11pm or so. Contact your consulate or your hotel if you have a serious problem. If you insist on going to the local police, bring a translator. But know that the Saigon police tend to throw up their hands at "minor" infractions such as purse snatching or thievery.

Telephone The city code for Saigon is 8. When dialing within Vietnam, the city code should be preceded by the 0 as indicated in the numbers listed in this guide; note that the 0 should be omitted when dialing from overseas.

Toilets There are no public toilets, per se. Seek out hotels, restaurants, and tourist attractions.

2 WHERE TO STAY

Saigon presents the best variety of hotels in Vietnam, from deluxe business and family hotels to spotless minihotels and cozy guesthouses down busy back alleys. Most hotels are clustered around Nguyen Hue Street and Dong Khoi in District 1, as are the city's best restaurants, shops, and bars.

If you're traveling on a tight budget, head for the Pham Ngu Lao area, the center of which is the intersection of Pham Ngu Lao and De Tham streets, a backpacker haven loaded with guesthouses and minihotels down little rabbit-warren alleys. Here, a fan-cooled room with a cold-water shower goes for as little as $5 per night, or an air-conditioned room with hot water for around $15. Most of these places are very basic (and a bit noisy from street traffic), but tidy, well run, and friendly. The area is also convenient to the city's many budget travel services and has lots of bars, traveler-friendly *bia hoi* (local draft beer) stands, and cafes.

Remember that prices listed here are rack rates and should be considered only a guideline. Internet, group, and standard promotional rates are the rule, and especially in the off season (Mar–Sept), you can expect discounts of up to 50%. But remember that many hotels levy a VAT of up to 20%.

Very Expensive

Caravelle Hotel ★★★ Named for a light, fast ship, this sleek downtown address gives you that very impression. A French company built the original in 1956 when it overlooked the Place Garnier, now Lam Son Square and the classic Opera House. After honeymoon years as the town's address of note, the hotel became a shabby hangout for wartime journalists—in 1964, a bomb was targeted at the many correspondents at the hotel, but the joke goes that it wasn't dropped close enough to the bar. On the day of Saigon's liberation, a tank pulled into the square out front of the hotel, aimed at the facade, but didn't fire, to the delight of the many journos in the bar. In postwar years, the hotel fell into obscurity as the Doc Lap (Independence) Hotel. The Caravelle was renovated and expanded beyond recognition in 1998, and is now an extremely attractive, efficient, and well-appointed place. I think it's the best international business hotel in

Saigon. With top-notch amenities and stylish rooms, the luxury accommodations here attract business travelers and well-heeled tourists alike.

Rooms in the old wing carry more history. Suite 610, where the aforementioned bomb landed, is a Special suite (seriously, that's the name). It's a lavish room with a small entrance hallway, a kitchen, separate dining area, and living room. Rooms in the new wing are large and plush, with neutral furnishings and firm beds; higher floors have great views of the Cathedral and Opera house. Marble bathrooms are sizable. The Caravelle is the five-star hotel in the heart of Saigon, offering free Internet and Wi-Fi—a great deal, considering that you fork over $15 to $20 per day at nearby Park Hyatt or Sheraton. Suites are luxe beyond belief. And the classic character of the old hotel lives on in the old-wing rooftop Saigon Saigon bar, an open-air colonial throwback with rattan shades, low-slung chairs, and twirling ceiling fans. If you let your imagination go, you might just see Graham Greene or a wartime correspondent sidling up to the bar.

19 Lam Son Sq., District 1. ✆ **08/3823-4999.** Fax 08/3824-3999. www.caravellehotel.com. 335 units. $230–$280 double; $330–$350 signature rooms (with separate check-in and private business lounge); $380–$1,200 suite. AE, DC, MC, V. **Amenities:** 2 restaurants; 3 bars; 24-hr. health club; Jacuzzi; motorbikes; rooftop pool; room service; sauna; spa; rooms for those w/limited mobility. *In room:* A/C, satellite TV, fax, fridge, hair dryer, minibar, Wi-Fi.

Hotel Majestic ★ This 1925 landmark on the picturesque, riverside corner of Dong Khoi Street (formerly Catinat) still has some historical charm, despite many renovations, and is a real picture-postcard colonial from the outside. The hotel is an affordable and atmospheric choice, and it's always full. The lobby is a busy affair of stained-glass windows, chandeliers, and Roman statues, but rooms and facilities here are classy and comfortable for the cost. High ceilings, original wood floors, and retro fixtures are a nice touch in all rooms. Bathrooms are large, all with tubs and old-style taps. Majestic suites have large Jacuzzis. The small central courtyard pool area is lined with picturesque shuttered windows and walkways; in fact, the best choices are the fine deluxe rooms facing this quiet spot. Suites are just larger versions of deluxe rooms, and standards are small and quite basic. The staff couldn't be nicer—they're the friendliest I've ever met at a Saigontourist-operated hotel—and have a genuine desire to make your stay memorable, whether that means explaining the eccentricities of Vietnamese cuisine or hailing you a taxi. Don't miss the great views from the rooftop Sky-Bar, a good spot to have a chat, and popular for weddings and parties.

1 Dong Khoi St., District 1. ✆ **08/3829-5514.** Fax 08/3829-5510. www.saigontourist.com. 175 units. $170–$250 single; $190–$270 double; $320–$600 suite. AE, DC, MC, V. **Amenities:** 3 restaurants; 3 bars; babysitting; fitness center; small courtyard pool; sauna. *In room:* A/C, satellite TV, fridge, hair dryer, minibar, Wi-Fi.

Legend Hotel Saigon ★ This sprawling property—always busy—along the Saigon River gets mobbed with groups on package tours or large business and incentive crowds. The professional staff is quite unflappable, though, and handles it all cheerily. This large, 17-floor Japanese joint venture is also popular for Japanese business travelers—a good sign of a consistently high standard. Rooms are spacious, if rather simple, like a chain hotel anywhere (although this is not a chain). Legend rooms are large, luxe, and just one step down from the town's best: the Caravelle and the Sheraton. In rooms, you'll find cool built-in Chinese cabinets on one wall and pastel colors throughout, which are a bit unsettling, but all done in a tasteful modern design. Bathrooms are stylish, with black granite counters and black wood trim. Views of the city and river are "legend," especially from higher floors—the hotel is far enough from the downtown clutter of buildings to

ACCOMMODATIONS ■

A & Em V **13**
Bong Sen Hotel **34**
Bong Sen Hotel Annex **26**
Caravelle Hotel **31**
Dong Phuong: Oriental Hotel **49**
Duxton Hotel Saigon **38**
Empress Hotel **1**
Grand Hotel **30**
Hotel Continental **32**
Hotel Equatorial **2**
Hotel Majestic **37**
Huong Sen Hotel **30**
Indochine **28**
Kim Do Royal City Hotel **30**
Legend Hotel Saigon **18**
May Hotel **20**
Medal Hotel—Chuong Hoang Yen **17**
Mövenpick Saigon Hotel **3**
New World Hotel Saigon **47**
Norfolk Hotel **41**
Palace Hotel **36**
Park Hyatt Saigon **23**
Que Huong—Liberty 1 **6**
Que Huong—Liberty 3 **48**
Que Huong—Liberty 4 **50**
Renaissance Riverside Hotel Saigon **29**
Rex Hotel **39**
Riverside Hotel **29**
Sheraton Saigon **31**
Sofitel Plaza Saigon **12**
Spring Hotel (Mua Xuan) **14**
Windsor Plaza Hotel **2**

DINING ◆

Allez Boo **48**
Augustin **34**
Blue Ginger **45**
Camargue **22**
Lemongrass **34**
L'Olivier **12**
Mandarin **16**
Ohan Restaurant **42**
Opera **23**
Pomodoro **19**
Quan An Ngon Restaurant **9**
The Refinery **21**
Skewers **19**
Square One **23**
Sushi Bar **15**
Tandoor **21**
Temple Club **43**
Warda **35**
Wrap and Roll **25**
Xu **26**
ZanZBar **27**

ATTRACTIONS ●

Ben Thanh Market **46**
City Hall and Nguyen Hue Plaza **33**
Emperor Jade Pagoda (Phuoc Hai) **5**
General Post Office (Buu Dien) **11**
Giac Lam Pagoda **2**
The Hoa Binh Noodle Shop **4**
Ho Chi Minh City Museum **40**
Ho Chi Minh Museum **44**
Notre Dame Cathedral **10**
Reunification Palace **8**
Saigon Opera House (Ho Chi Minh Municipal Theater) **24**
Vietnam History Museum **5**
Vinh Nghiem Pagoda **4**
War Remnants Museum **7**

Ly Chinh Thang
Nam Ki Khoi Nghia
Tran Quoc Toan
Tran Quoc Thao
Vo Thi Sau
Tu Xuong
Le Quy Don
Dien Bien Phu
Truong Dinh
Ngo Thoi Nhiem
Ba Huyen Thanh Quan
Ho Xuan Huong
Nguyen Dinh Chieu
Vo Van Tan
Nguyen Thi Minh Khai
Cach Mang Thang Tam
TAO DAN PARK
Bui Thi Xuan
Le Thi Rieng
Nguyen Trai
Nguyen Thi Nghia
Le Lai
Pham Ngu Lao
De Tham
Cong Quynh
Bui Vien
Nguyen Cu Trinh
Tran Hung Dao
Tran Dinh Xu
Co Bac
Co Giang

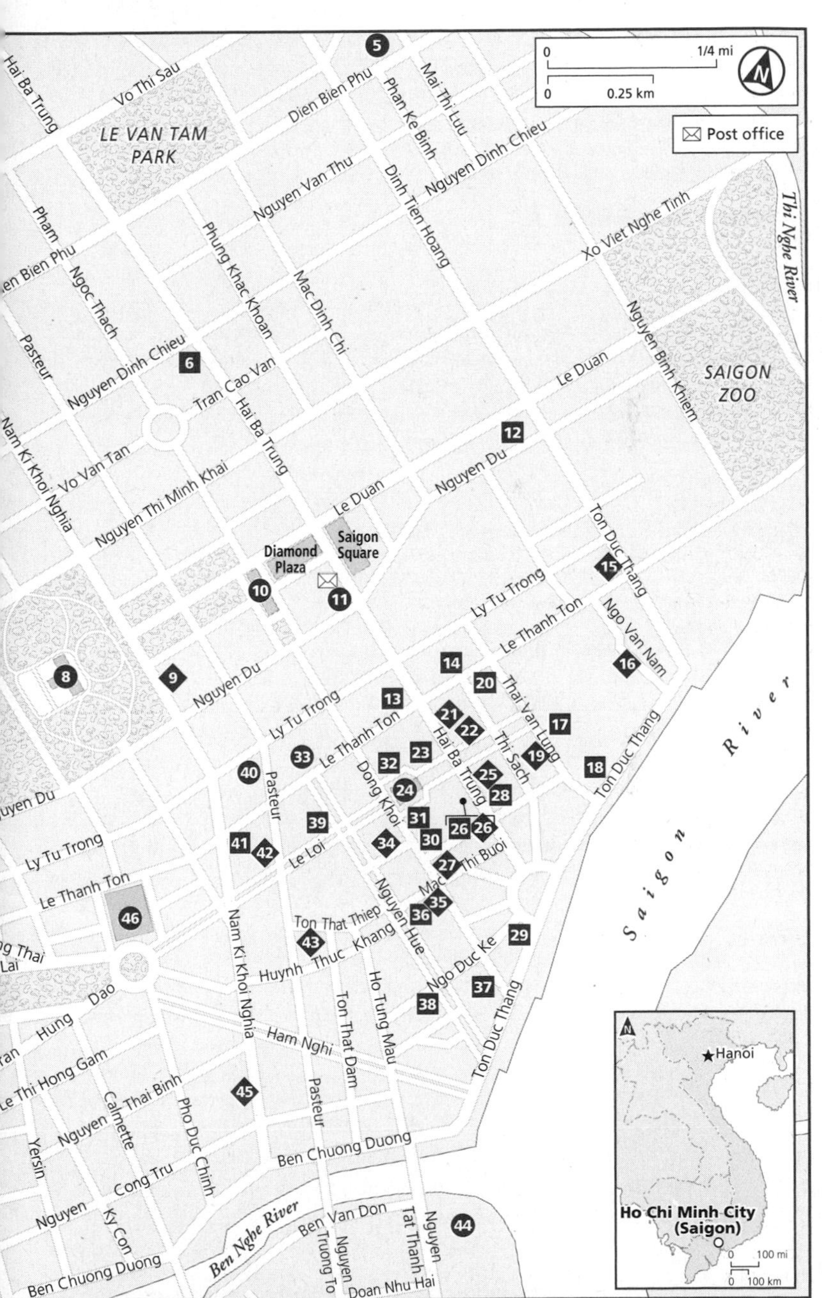

0
1/4 mi
0
0.25 km
N
Post office
LE VAN TAM PARK
SAIGON ZOO
Thi Nghe River
Saigon River
Ben Nghe River
Diamond Plaza
Saigon Square
Hai Ba Trung
Vo Thi Sau
Dien Bien Phu
Phan Ke Binh
Mai Thi Luu
Nguyen Dinh Chieu
Nguyen Van Thu
Dinh Tien Hoang
Xo Viet Nghe Tinh
Pham Ngoc Thach
Phung Khac Khoan
Mac Dinh Chi
Nguyen Binh Khiem
Pasteur
Tran Cao Van
Le Duan
Vo Van Tan
Nam Ki Khoi Nghia
Nguyen Thi Minh Khai
Nguyen Du
Ton Duc Thang
Ly Tu Trong
Le Thanh Ton
Ngo Van Nam
Thai Van Lung
Thi Sach
Dong Khoi
Le Loi
Mac Thi Buoi
Nguyen Hue
Ton That Thiep
Huynh Thuc Khang
Ngo Duc Ke
Ton That Dam
Ho Tung Mau
Ham Nghi
Le Thi Hong Gam
Calmette
Nguyen Thai Binh
Pho Duc Chinh
Yersin
Cong Tru
Ben Chuong Duong
Nguyen Ky Con
Ben Van Don
Truong To
Nguyen Tat Thanh
Doan Nhu Hai
Hung Dao
Hanoi
Ho Chi Minh City (Saigon)
100 mi
100 km

offer clear views, but close enough for convenient access to the many shops and restaurants on Don Khoi. The overall scale is large, from a double-height colonnaded lobby, all glass and marble with faux-stained-glass ceiling and large, bronze prancing horses, to the sunken dining area and nice circular pool out back. Everything is clean and neat. A fine downtown standard, and a welcome break from the city's many dull, state-owned hotels.

2A–4A Ton Duc Thang St., District 1. ✆ **08/3823-3333.** Fax 08/3823-2333. www.legendsaigon.com. 283 units. $180–$325 double; from $750 suite. AE, MC, V. **Amenities:** 2 restaurants; 2 bars; gym; health club; Jacuzzi; midsize outdoor pool; room service. *In room:* A/C, satellite TV, fridge, hair dryer, minibar, Wi-Fi.

Mövenpick Saigon Hotel ★ This hotel will be a gem once renovations are completed at the end of 2010. Swiss hotelier Mövenpick recently took over management of this former CIA and U.S. Army quarters and is responsible for the much-needed face-lift. I had a chance to see the first renovated room—the university dorm feel of current rooms will be replaced with sleek new furniture, flatscreen TVs, bathrooms fitted with marble countertops, rain shower heads, and glass partitions to lend the room a spacious feel. The lobby will retain its colonial flavor and Art Deco details. Popular Irish pub Mulligan's is still around, and the fitness center will be relocated to the rooftop. One sweet treat: Turndowns in the clubroom come with a mini Toblerone chocolate. The drawback: It's 10 minutes from the airport, but you're in District 3 and some 15 minutes from town. For now, most taxi drivers still know the hotel by its old name: Omni.

253 Nguyen Van Troi St., Phu Nhuan (District 3). ✆ **08/3844-9222.** Fax 08/3844-9198. www.moevenpick-hotels.com. 248 units. $200 double; $260–$430 suite. Long-stay rates available. AE, DC, MC, V. **Amenities:** 3 restaurants; 2 bars; babysitting; health club; Jacuzzi; outdoor patio pool; room service; spa. *In room:* A/C, TV, fridge, hair dryer, Internet, minibar.

New World Hotel Saigon ★★ President Clinton called this first-rate hotel home during his brief stay in Saigon, and, more recently, British footballer David Beckham stayed here (the hotel was nearly overrun). Everything is big, flashy, and deluxe in this 550-room hotel (the largest in Vietnam), and a stay at the New World guarantees luxury and bang for your buck. The hotel is in the center of town, far east of Dong Khoi and just a short walk from Ben Thanh Market (see "Exploring Ho Chi Minh City," later in this chapter). The impeccable, plush rooms are done in a soothing array of neutrals, and the bathrooms are a sharp contrast in black-and-gray marble. One-bedroom suites come at a great discount and, with all the extra space and good views, are worth the upgrade. The four executive floors, with an executive lounge, have an impressive list of benefits. If convenience is your game, it's well worth the bump up from a standard double room. The staff snaps to it, and service is ultra-efficient. Ask right away if you'd like a nonsmoking room. The lounge area has good jazz late into the evening, and the Hisago Japanese restaurant is one of the most popular in the city. The hotel fitness center and professional massage facility are tops, and a kids' club offers all kinds of programs.

76 Le Lai St., District 1. ✆ **08/3822-8888.** Fax 08/3823-0710. www.newworldvietnam.com. 552 units. $160–$250 double; $340–$1,600 suite. AE, DC, MC, V. **Amenities:** 2 restaurants; bar; babysitting; concierge; executive/clubrooms; health club; outdoor pool; room service; smoke-free rooms; sauna; spa; tennis court. *In room:* A/C, satellite TV, fridge, Internet, minibar.

Park Hyatt Saigon ★★ This is, hands down, the best business hotel in the city. From the modern black *ao dai* uniforms of reception staff to the nonbranded, black-top water bottles in the bathroom, everything at the Park Hyatt is sleek, modern, and sophisticated. In fact, a stylish touch of traditional Vietnamese elements resonates throughout the hotel. Original oil and lacquer paintings hang in the lobby and hallways, and bedrooms are decorated with mounted black-and-white photographs of old Saigon. Accent pillows are gold with black designs of bamboo and Chinese symbols for happiness. Standard rooms come with a high two-poster wooden bed, the kind you have to hop onto. Mattresses are luxuriously thick. A two-tone inlaid rug with a subtle fleur-de-lis pattern is spread beneath the desk and bed area, while dark wooden floors line the rest of the room. The shower and bathtub are in a separate glass enclosure, with an obscenely large mirror over the tub (ah-hem). Executive suites come with a spacious living and dining room area and a kitchenette stocked with a full set of flatware and dishes. The Park Hyatt certainly has a business hotel feel to it, but it manages to be reassuring and cozy at the same time. This is a fabulous place to return to after a hectic day in Saigon.

2 Lam Son Square, District 1. ✆ **08/3824-1234.** Fax 08/3823-7569. www.saigon.park.hyatt.com. 252 units. $290–$320 double; $620–$650 suite. AE, MC, V. **Amenities:** 2 restaurants; bar; concierge; health club; Jacuzzi; outdoor pool; 24-hr. room service; spa. *In room:* A/C, satellite TV, fridge, minibar, Wi-Fi.

Renaissance Riverside Hotel Saigon ★ Managed by Marriott, the Renaissance Riverside is a convenient downtown address. The lobby is done in a colonial theme, with a small central-domed ceiling and a grand spiral stair connecting to the mezzanine. Rooms have black-and-white tile entries, tidy carpet, and light furnishings all done in a cool eggshell and pastel. Electric control panels near the headboard are like a 1970s bachelor pad. Bathrooms have black marble countertops and an antique black-and-white tile pattern throughout. The Riverside is a popular business hotel, and that means smoking everywhere: All public spaces are a bit musty, and rooms, even on designated nonsmoking floors, smell like a bar after closing time. Be sure to ask for nonsmoking and ask to see it before checking in. This is not the hotel of choice if you are afraid of heights. There's an indoor vaulted atrium that runs from the fifth floor all the way up to the ceiling skylight. Rooms are placed around this open space, and if you're staying on one of the higher floors, there's a slight feeling of vertigo as you pass the open space en route to the elevator.

8–15 Ton Duc Thang St., District 1. ✆ **08/3822-0033.** Fax 08/3822-2900. www.renaissancehotels.com/sgnbr. 336 units. $187–$210 double; $410 suite. AE, MC, V. **Amenities:** 2 restaurants; bar; babysitting; health club; rooftop pool w/great city view; room service; smoke-free floor; spa. *In room:* A/C, satellite TV, fridge, Internet, minibar.

Sheraton Saigon ★★ This is an excellent hotel right in the middle of the city center. The rooms are not quite as cozy as those at nearby Park Hyatt, but everything is done on a grand scale, from colossal meeting rooms and top business facilities to enormous, plush guest rooms. Bathrooms are huge, with separate shower and tub. The walls are covered in striped cream-and-lavender wallpaper for a bit of French colonial flair, and textured carpet in a bamboo pattern lines the floor. Level 23 (p. 334)—a double-height rotunda space that hosts live bands on the top of the city (the 23rd floor is the highest point for now)—is a popular nightspot. All public areas are oversize and luxurious, and from the moment your car pulls up out front, you'll know you've arrived; every guest is given the quality treatment. Executive services—including a separate check-in area, lounge, and meticulous business services—create a smooth and easy transition. The hotel is often booked up, and lobby traffic can be hectic at times. Overall, though, this is still one of your top hotel choices for the city center.

88 Dong Khoi St., District 1. ✆ **08/3827-2828.** Fax 08/3827-2929. www.sheraton.com/saigon. 472 units. $280–$400 double; from $500 suite. AE, MC, V. **Amenities:** 3 restaurants; 2 bars; babysitting; concierge; health club; Jacuzzi; outdoor pool; room service; sauna; spa; tennis court. *In room:* A/C, satellite TV, fridge, hair dryer, Internet, minibar.

Sofitel Plaza Saigon ★★ The Sofitel hotel chain is famous in Southeast Asia for converting grand old colonials into the most charming hotel properties. This is not one of them. But what it lacks in colonial charm, it more than compensates for in modern luxury, convenience, and comfort. Guest rooms are handsome, with fine Art Deco touches like the curving, clean-lined desks in most rooms. You'll never be wanting for any amenity here, and the staff is helpful and professional. In a convenient spot just across from the former U.S. and French embassies, this is a popular choice for the international business crowd and long-stay executives, who enjoy the sleek executive floor with a private lounge, daily buffet, drinks, and business services. To date, this is the only high-end hotel offering free in-room ADSL and Wi-Fi services, a major bonus for business travelers. The hotel is away from the busy activity of the main shopping drag, but it is only a 5-minute walk to Lam Son Square. The bonus is, you're away from the heavy traffic and noise.

17 Le Duan Blvd., District 1. ✆ **800/221-4542** in the U.S., or 08/3824-1555. Fax 08/3824-1666. www.accorhotels-asia.com. 290 units. $210 double; $340 suite. AE, MC, V. **Amenities:** 2 restaurants; bar; babysitting; concierge; health club; rooftop pool; room service; smoke-free floors; spa. *In room:* A/C, satellite TV, fridge, minibar, Wi-Fi.

Expensive

Duxton Hotel Saigon ★ Formerly the Prince, before becoming part of the popular Australian chain, the Duxton Saigon is efficient, affordable, and stylish (if a bit studied). Beige rooms are nice size, tasteful, and comfortable, with plush beds, carpets, and coffeemakers. The bathrooms are smart black-and-white marble. The lobby, entered by swooping stairs from a circular drive and, inside, circled by a mezzanine, is classy but not overly grand. It's a good downtown meeting point. This place is popular with business travelers, especially those on an extended stay, who come here for all the comforts of home. The staff is efficient and personable. The second-floor spa offers excellent Hong Kong massage service, along with steam and Jacuzzi (ask about special midweek spa rates). Also try the authentic Japanese restaurant on the mezzanine floor. The hotel recently added a small rooftop swimming pool, which provides a nice secluded place to cool off in the afternoons.

63 Nguyen Hue Blvd., District 1. ✆ **08/3822-2999.** Fax 08/3824-1888. www.duxton.com. 196 units. $150–$270 deluxe double; $320–$370 suite. AE, DC, MC, V. **Amenities:** Restaurant; bar; concierge; small health club; Jacuzzi; outdoor pool; room service; sauna; smoke-free rooms; steam. *In room:* A/C, ADSL, satellite TV, fridge, minibar.

Grand Hotel ★★ This 1930s colonial, owned and renovated by Saigontourist, is done just right (okay, close, at least). The renovated Grand has a serene, tasteful atmosphere, and there are some choice features, like the lovingly restored iron elevator at the center. The Grand is at its best when taking advantage of its long history, and rooms in the older block are much more charming than the bland, chainlike units in the new wing. Deluxe rooms clustered in the old building near the old, wrought-iron elevator have classic high ceilings, rich wood floors, and a comfortable colonial charm. Rooms in the new wing have fallen into disrepair; the silk bedspreads are looking a bit threadbare, toilet seats are stained yellow, and the walls are in desperate need of a new coat of paint. Rooms in the old wing are big, with simple dark-wood furniture and large wardrobes, and without the musty smell that plagues the new wing. The bathrooms are small but have big counters and stylish dark tiles. The lobby is bright, the staff is friendly, and the location on Dong Khoi couldn't be better—right in the thick of it. The quiet atmosphere

here suggests tourists rather than business. The notable amenities, of many here, are the quiet sitting areas and bar, and the central courtyard's small but peaceful pool area, which offers a unique escape from busy Ho Chi Minh City.

8 Dong Khoi St., District 1. ✆ **08/3823-0163.** Fax 08/3827-3047. www.grandhotel.com.vn. 104 units. $140–$150 double; $190–$270 suite. AE, MC, V. **Amenities:** 2 restaurants; bar; small health club; Jacuzzi; outdoor pool; steam. *In room:* A/C, satellite TV, fridge, minibar, Wi-Fi.

Hotel Continental ★ This hotel is a big shame. It's not that it's so bad, really, but it could be a world-class heritage hotel, but instead it's in shambles—thanks to the shortsightedness of the folks at Saigontourist. Built in 1890, it's the preeminent historic hotel in Saigon, of Graham Greene's *The Quiet American* fame. But its last renovation was in 1980. The very heart of Saigon's downtown, its colonial facade attracts shutter-clicking tourists and admirers—yet that's where the love affair ends. The lobby is gaudy, with oversize chandeliers, Chinese vases, and that fake, semigloss shine of a low-end business hotel. Rooms are enormous, with high ceilings, but it's the red velveteen curtains, tatty red carpets, and general run-down feel that spoil the fantasy. It looks more like an aging cathouse, really, and the furniture can't seem to fill the big, empty space. Bathrooms are done plain, like a guesthouse, but are big and clean and have bathtubs. "First-class rooms" are big and comfy, with roll-top desks, ornate columns, new flatscreen TVs, and a wood archway separating a small sitting area. The hotel staff is friendly but a tad dazed and confused. If you want to stay here, you are most likely paying homage to the historical significance of the hotel. Thus, request to stay in room no. 210, the corner suite where Greene resided for almost 2 years.

132–134 Dong Khoi St., District 1. ✆ **08/3829-9201.** Fax 08/3824-1772. www.continentalvietnam.com. 86 units. $170–$190 double; $230–$420 suite. Ask about frequent discounts. AE, MC, V. **Amenities:** 2 restaurants; 2 bars; small fitness center; room service. *In room:* A/C, satellite TV w/video rental, fridge, minibar, Wi-Fi.

Hotel Equatorial This large edifice is a good distance from tourist Saigon, in the far reaches of District 5, but the Equatorial has long been a popular business address for regional and international conventioneers. It covers all the bases with good amenities and service, but nothing about it is all that luxurious or opulent—more like tidy, utilitarian, and cozy. Superior rooms are rather dull. Deluxe are larger versions of the same, with seeming acres of carpet, floral bedspreads, and plain furnishings. Ask for a nonsmoking room on one of the few designated floors. Bathrooms are done in a cool green granite and marble tile, but all are just plain tub/showers. The cozy lobby bar is always busy with foreigners, and there's a good selection of dining outlets. For the exec on the go, be sure to upgrade to enjoy their snazzy two-story executive lounge—connected by a chic winding stair. The hotel is just 10 minutes by car to the Dong Khoi area.

242 Tran Binh Trong St., District 5. ✆ **08/3839-7777.** Fax 08/3839-0011. www.equatorial.com. 333 units. $132 double; $320 suite. MC, V. **Amenities:** 2 restaurants; 2 bars; airport transfer; concierge; health club; Jacuzzi; outdoor pool w/swim-up bar; room service; smoke-free floors; spa. *In room:* A/C, satellite TV, hair dryer, limited Wi-Fi.

Kim Do Royal City Hotel If you can get a really good rate, this hotel is in a good downtown location. If not, you will be better off at the newly renovated Palace Hotel (see below) across the street. Expect a fountain misting with dry ice in the lobby, pink plastic hangers, polyurethane slippers in the closet, and shiny polyester bedspreads. There's a rooftop massage area with a hot tub surrounded by plaster reliefs of sea nymphs and electric-light blinking stars on the ceiling. The original hotel was built nearly 100 years ago and underwent a renovation in 1994, and everything is still in good shape. The lobby and hallways don't have air-conditioning, so it's not a very welcome place to return to after touring around the hot city all day. All rooms are quite large and have interesting Asian carved furniture, tidy carpeting, and rock-hard beds (you can request a soft one). Bathrooms are clean but basic (no counter space). The hotel offers great discounts if you book directly through their website.

133 Nguyen Hue Blvd., District 1. ✆ **08/3822-5914** or -5915. Fax 08/3822-5913. www.kimdohotel.com. 134 units. $190–$230 double; $290–$399 suite. AE, DC, MC, V. **Amenities:** Rooftop restaurant; bar; concierge; Internet; tiny pool; room service; smoke-free floor; steam. *In room:* A/C, TV, fridge, hair dryer, Internet, minibar, Wi-Fi.

Norfolk Hotel ★★ This snappy little business hotel has one of the highest occupancy rates in town, and for good reason: It's affordable and convenient, and covers all the bases. Rooms are large and bright, furnished in slightly mismatched chain-hotel style, but everything is like new. Carpets are still nice and plush, and the beds are soft and deluxe. Each room has a safe. The marble-finished bathrooms are small, but space has been maximized with sliding doors. Deluxe rooms have a tiny hallway entrance with a small countertop to put keys and wallets—an excellent touch that makes the room feel a bit like home. Staff is efficient and helpful. The restaurant is bright and upscale, featuring extensive breakfast and lunch buffets, as well as monthly themes and special menus. It's perfect for the business traveler or tourist seeking amenities like a good business center, health club, sauna, room service, and travel desk to cater to any need—all at reasonable prices.

117 Le Thanh Ton St., District 1. ✆ **08/3829-5368.** Fax 08/3829-3415. www.norfolkgroup.com. 104 units. $150–$200 double; $280–$310 suite. AE, MC, V. **Amenities:** Restaurant; bar/club; concierge; small health club; room service; sauna; smoke-free rooms; steam. *In room:* A/C, satellite TV, fridge, Internet, minibar.

Que Huong—Liberty 1 Liberty 1 is the best choice of the Liberty Hotel chain, which has four other properties in Saigon. Their **Hotel Metropole** (148 Tran Hung Dao; ✆ **08/3920-1937**) is the fanciest, but it's a bit smelly and really just a regional businessman's hotel. This hotel is just a short ride or long walk up busy Hai Ba Trung Street, just north of the Dong Khoi area in District 3. A bright, busy staff greets you at the door of the bright, busy lobby. Red-carpet halls give it that "old men's hotel in Brooklyn" feeling, but everything is clean, and rooms are quite large, if rather plain. All rooms have tidy tile bathrooms, all with tub/showers, and the best rooms on higher floors have decent city views—though the elevator is slow as molasses. The hotel is near a busy park and local shopping area, with lots of fruit stands, coffee shops, and bright bakeries, and the place is popular for long-stay business guests. One drawback is the chaotic traffic out front on Hai Ba Trung, a popular commute in and out of the city and noisy night and day—otherwise, a good midrange choice.

167 Hai Ba Trung St., District 3. ✆ **08/3829-4227.** Fax 08/3829-0919. www.libertyhotels.com.vn. 51 units. $120–$170 double; $210–$270 suite. MC, V. **Amenities:** Restaurant; bar; babysitting; concierge; room service. *In room:* A/C, satellite TV, fridge, minibar.

Moderate

Bong Sen Hotel The Bong Sen (also see the budget Bong Sen Hotel Annex, below) is a bland but affordable and convenient downtown operation. It always offers special rates, and especially good ones if you contact the hotel directly—you can't beat paying as little as $56 to be right in the heart of the city in and among the likes of the Sheraton and the Caravelle. The place is always busy, though, so be sure to try to book in advance.

Also be sure to ask for a nonsmoking room. Rooms are large and plain, with a standard host of amenities; everything is clean and works. The bathrooms are quite cramped, and sinks and tubs are an unappealing baby blue. The suites are not worth the extra cost, as rooms are almost the same size as the standards. If you want deluxe, book the executive Bong Sen Suite, which has a spacious bathroom (with sparkling white porcelain sink and tub!) and a gigantic balcony overlooking Dong Khoi Street. They have two good dining venues at streetside—check out the Mangosteen. Little else, really, but what more do you need? Saigon is at your fingertips from here. At press time, the hotel was undergoing a much-needed renovation, so you might want to check on its progress before booking.

119–123 Dong Khoi St., District 1. ✆ **08/3829-1516.** Fax 08/3824-6894. www.bongsencorporation.com. 127 units. $105–$154 double; $275 suite. MC, V. **Amenities:** 2 restaurants (Vietnamese and cafe); bar; gym; small health club. *In room:* A/C, satellite TV, fridge, minibar, Wi-Fi.

Huong Sen Hotel Another of the many government-owned places whose service is marked only by varying levels of indifference, but worth a look for its price and downtown location. The decor is a downer, but this hotel is a popular choice for big tour groups, and great group rates (and Internet prices) are available. Rooms are big and newly renovated, with simple, colorfully painted wood furniture and floral drapes and headboards. Nice touches include molded ceilings and marble-topped counters in the spotless bathrooms. Some rooms have balconies, and beds are ultra-comfortable. The hotel is comparable to any other in this category, but quite bland.

66–70 Dong Khoi St., District 1. ✆ **08/3829-9400.** Fax 08/3829-0916. www.vietnamtourism.com/huongsen. 76 units. $99–$149 double. AE, DC, MC, V. **Amenities:** Restaurant; bar; fitness center; Internet; Jacuzzi; rooftop pool; room service; sauna. *In room:* A/C, TV, fridge, minibar.

May Hotel ★ This brand-new hotel, just around the corner from Spring Hotel, had just opened at time of writing, and the final touches were being added to an indoor pool and bar. Despite being just a couple months into their soft opening, the hotel was almost fully booked. Rooms have pleasant, light-wood furniture and spacious bathrooms. The deluxe rooms come with a small balcony. With its excellent downtown location, the May is a nice place to stay if you want something a bit more upmarket than Spring Hotel.

28–30 Thi Sach St. ✆ **08/3823-4501.** Fax 08/3823-4502. www.mayhotel.com.vn. 117 units. $55–$80 double; $140 suite. Rates include breakfast. AE, MC, V. **Amenities:** Restaurant/bar; pool; room service; Wi-Fi. *In room:* A/C, satellite TV, fridge, Internet, minibar.

Palace Hotel ★ This downtown tower has been around for a while. In fact, it was popular for U.S. soldiers on R & R during the war years. They are in the midst of an image-changing renovation (should be done by the time you read this), and the hotel looks 10 times better. The modern Art Deco decor and new windows let in plenty of light. Carpets are done in pinstripes of red, brown, and orange, with solid-colored cushions and footstools for contrast. Just in case they fall behind schedule, make sure to ask for a renovated room. The walls have a fresh coat of cream-colored paint, the furniture is dark wood, the thin, ratty blue bedspreads of past rooms have been replaced with cozy white cotton duvets, and the bathrooms are sparkling and new.

56–66 Nguyen Hue Blvd., District 1. ✆ **08/3824-4231.** Fax 08/3824-4229. www.bongsencorporation.com. 150 units. $90–$100 double; $150 suite. AE, MC, V. **Amenities:** 2 restaurants; 2 bars; rooftop pool; room service; sauna; spa. *In room:* A/C, TV, fridge, minibar, Wi-Fi.

Que Huong—Liberty 3 As the name suggests, this hotel is part of the little Liberty chain (see Que Huong—Liberty 1 above, under "Expensive"). Liberty 3 is right in the heart of the Pham Ngu Lao backpacker area and arguably the best choice down that way.

But unlike the backpacker hotels, the lobby has air-conditioning, which is a welcome relief after a sweaty day of touring the city. Rooms have all the amenities of a proper hotel but are priced just above the average minihotel. You'll find unfortunate thin office carpets and bland decor throughout, but everything is clean. Standard rooms are a bit too small; a superior is your best bet. Be sure to request a window and ask to see the room before checking in, as some are worse than others (and many are musty from smoking guests). The adjoining **Allez Boo** bar and restaurant (p. 318) is an old backpacker standby and now managed by the hotel.

187 Pham Ngu Lao, District 1. ✆ **08/3836-9522.** Fax 08/3836-4557. www.libertyhotels.com.vn. 61 units. $110–$190 double. AE, MC, V. **Amenities:** Restaurant. *In room:* A/C, satellite TV, fridge, hair dryer, minibar, Wi-Fi.

Rex Hotel ★★ The Rex has an unorthodox history: It used to be a French garage, was expanded by the Vietnamese, and then was used by the United States Information Agency (and some say the CIA) from 1962 to 1970. The hotel was transformed in a massive renovation and opened in 1990 as the kitschy, atmospheric government-run place it is today. The hotel has a new wing with modern rooms that are nicely appointed but are not quite on par with the chic and comfortable rooms available at the Park Hyatt or Caravelle nearby. The wing is still being renovated and should be done sometime in 2010, so ask about nearby construction noise before booking here. Rooms in the old wing are large and clean, with fluffy carpets, and have dated though endearing Vietnamese details everywhere—from the bamboo and rattan furniture to the duvet throws with lotus embroidery. The hotel is in a great downtown location, across from a square that has a lively carnival atmosphere at night. It is also known for its rooftop bar, with its panoramic Saigon view.

141 Nguyen Hue Blvd., District 1. ✆ **08/3829-2185** or 3829-3115. Fax 08/3829-6536. www.rexhotel vietnam.com. 217 units. $120–$135 double old wing; $175 double new wing; $150–$315 suite old wing; $225–$255 suite new wing. AE, MC, V. **Amenities:** 3 restaurants; 2 bars; babysitting; health club; Internet; Jacuzzi; outdoor pool; room service; sauna; smoke-free rooms; tennis. *In room:* A/C, satellite TV, Wi-Fi.

Windsor Plaza Hotel ★ The massive Windsor Plaza is a good distance from the heart of the city, but it's smack in the center of Greater Ho Chi Minh City (District 5)—the developers reckon that, over time, the city center will come to them. This behemoth rises from the base of an enormous, low-end shopping compound and contains extensive food and beverage outlets, a two-story nightclub, a casino, karaoke lounges, and a massage facility fit for hundreds. The modern pleasure palace and shrine to excess is a bit much, really.

But for the hotel's current focus—regional businesspeople and investors from neighboring countries—the Windsor offers a comfortable and affordable standard. Suites are over-the-top, some quite gaudy even, but room facilities are tidy—the one red-velvet-lined Chinese suite is enough to make you giddy. Standard rooms are done in plain tile with carpet and have dull built-in cabinets and oversize lacquer painting on the walls. Regular shuttles run to the Dong Khoi area, and the hotel can gladly arrange a car or a day tour of the city.

18 An Duong Vuong St., District 5. ✆ **08/3833-6688.** Fax 08/3833-6688. www.windsorplazahotel.com. 405 units. $100 double; $150–$460 suite. MC, V. **Amenities:** 4 restaurants; babysitting; health club; Internet; Jacuzzi; small rooftop pool; room service; sauna; smoke-free rooms. *In room:* A/C, satellite TV, fridge, hair dryer, Internet, minibar.

Inexpensive

A & Em V This is the latest offering from A & Em, a local Vietnamese chain with now a handful of hotels in Ho Chi Minh City. Think of this chain as the Vietnamese version of a Best Western—but with even better prices. The rooms aren't particularly stylish, but the floral patterns and frosted glass in the bathrooms are nice touches. Beds are comfortable, with decent mattresses and cozy sheets. Public spaces have that overly bright, fluorescent lighting popular in Asian hotels and restaurants, but at least the glaring lights reveal spick-and-span environs. Bathrooms are a good size and come with deep tubs, a true luxury in this price range.

60 Le Thanh Ton St., District 1. ✆ **08/3825-8529.** Fax 08/3825-8534. www.a-emhotels.com. 30 units. $40–$50 double; $90 suite. AE, MC, V. **Amenities:** Restaurant. *In room:* A/C, TV, fridge, minibar, Wi-Fi.

Bong Sen Hotel Annex ★ This small annex to the large Saigontourist-owned Bong Sen provides many of the same amenities at a lower price. The lobby is bright and welcoming, which is a treat for a minihotel. Rooms are basic but tidy, with light-wood furniture, thin carpet, and blue-tile bathrooms. Everything is kind of on the small side, though, and the economy rooms have only one small window, next to a small balcony. Suites have big king-size beds and a separate living room decorated like a college dorm room, but if you're a group on a budget, you can easily fit two extra twin beds beside the couches. Make sure you're getting the Annex and not the main Bong Sen, which, though recently renovated, isn't much of a value. Service is indifferent, but this is a fine place to lay your head for cheap.

61–63 Hai Ba Trung St., District 1. ✆ **08/3823-5818.** Fax 08/3823-5816. www.hotelbongsen.com. 57 units. $50–$60 double; $90 suite. AE, MC, V. **Amenities:** Restaurant. *In room:* A/C, satellite TV, fridge, hair dryer, minibar, Wi-Fi.

Dong Phuong: Oriental Hotel A popular minihotel right in the heart of Pham Ngu Lao, Dong Phuong is a little more grand than others. Large and always busy with budget groups, the hotel has a friendly staff and rooms with basic amenities like air-conditioning and cable TV; it is otherwise not outstanding—just tidy, with chintzy furnishings and loud checkered bedspreads. The Oriental is a good choice if you're between trips to the Mekong Delta and onward travel to the north, as you can make your travel plans easily through the tour operators just outside on De Tham. Go for one of the good-size double or triple rooms facing the front, some with large octagonal windows or balconies facing the busy street below and the city skyline beyond. There are no amenities to speak of, but the neighborhood itself is your best budget resource.

274–276 De Tham St., Pham Ngu Lao Ward, District 1. ✆ **08/3920-3993.** Fax 08/3836-9886. orienthotel@hcm.vnn.vn. 69 units. $20–$50 double. Rates include breakfast. MC, V. **Amenities:** Restaurant. *In room:* A/C, satellite TV, fridge, minibar.

Empress Hotel ★ This popular colonial-style minihotel right in the heart of the downtown area is run by the same folks as the Empress Hotel in Dalat City. Rooms have charming sliding windows, with wooden slats and bamboo blinds. Bathrooms have separate showers but no bathtubs. Rooms are small, but they feel cozy, not cramped. The staff is quite friendly, and the entire hotel is neat and clean. The drawback is the location; they are a bit too far west to be in the center of Saigon's action.

136 Bui Thi Xuan St., District 1. ✆ **08/3832-2888.** Fax 08/3832-8215. www.empresshotelcn.com. 40 units. $40–$50 double; $57–$66 suite. MC, V. **Amenities:** Restaurant; gym; smoke-free floor. *In room:* A/C, satellite TV, fridge, hair dryer, minibar, Wi-Fi.

Indochine Location, location, location. Indochine is across the street from Xu, one of the hippest bars in town, and a couple hundred meters from the top hotels. That being said, Indochine is in the thick of all the downtown action. It's about a tenth the cost of a room at the Park Hyatt, but you get what you pay for. The lobby is a dim, unwelcoming cave. The elevator says it can hold eight people, but I would never ride in it with more than two guests (including me). Some of the rooms have a pervasive cigarette smell, and bathrooms are on the small side. But everything is neat and tidy, and you get cozy duvets rather than the flimsy bedspreads offered at other budget hotels.

40–42 Hai Ba Trung St., District 1. ✆ **08/3822-0082.** Fax 08/3822-0083. www.indochinehotel.com. 31 units. $24–$52 double. MC, V. **Amenities:** Restaurant. *In room:* A/C, satellite TV, fridge, Internet, minibar.

Medal Hotel—Chuong Hoang Yen Medal is another low-end business hotel with clean, basic rooms and limited services. You're just north of Dong Khoi and right in the heart of a good expat dining and nightlife area, which makes this a convenient choice. Just a place to rest your head, though; there's nothing fancy about it.

8A/6D2 Thai Van Lung St., District 1. ✆ **08/3823-8764.** Fax 08/3823-8761. 54 units. $45–$70 double. MC, V. **Amenities:** Restaurant (breakfast only). *In room:* A/C, satellite TV, fridge, minibar, Wi-Fi.

Que Huong—Liberty 4 ★ Very tidy, large rooms here are nicely furnished. Service is very efficient, and the staff really snaps to, even when swamped with European tour groups. You'll find lots of in-house services, and the hotel is just a skip away from De Tham Street, the busy backpacker area, but not as noisy as most. There is a cozy bar, karaoke lounge, and massage area, as befits any Asian business hotel worth its salt, and the rooftop restaurant is intimate and relaxing, with great views of the city. Standard rooms are nothing special—airless and unpleasant, really—but most superior and deluxe rooms (deluxe have just a bit more space) face the cityscape and are tidy and airy. Be sure to ask to see your room before checking in; they do vary.

265 Pham Ngu Lao St., District 1. ✆ **08/3836-4556.** Fax 08/3836-5435. www.libertyhotels.com.vn. 71 units. $70 double; $110–$150 suite. MC, V. **Amenities:** Restaurant; bar; gym; spa. *In room:* A/C, satellite TV, fridge, minibar, Wi-Fi.

Riverside Hotel Wedged into an old colonial storefront area between the hulking Renaissance Riverside and the wedding-cake Majestic, the Riverside is a standard budget stop. The public spaces are pretty banged and battered (worn carpets all around, a dark and not very welcoming lobby), but private spaces are expansive for the price and everything is clean. It's an old building, and some rooms conform to the angled footprint in unique ways. Bathrooms are huge, plain affairs with small tub/showers, a simple sink, and no counter space—but, again, tidy, if simple. Deluxe rooms are worth the upgrade; they're much larger and have newer carpet and better amenities. The leopard-skin-pattern synthetic blankets are a turnoff, but the dark wooden doors, wardrobes, and windows are a nice touch.

18–20 Ton Duc Thang St., District 1. ✆ **08/3822-4038.** Fax 08/3825-1417. www.riversidehotelsg.com. 73 units. $70–$100 double; $140–$170 suite. AE, MC, V. **Amenities:** 2 restaurants. *In room:* A/C, satellite TV, fridge, hair dryer, minibar, Wi-Fi.

Spring Hotel (Mua Xuan) ★★ If you don't care about fancy amenities and want to be downtown, look no further than the Spring, with nicer rooms than many hotels twice its price. Accommodations here are neat and clean, with comfy double and super-king-size beds, and nice, solid dark-wood or light rattan furniture. The bathrooms are on the small side—I bumped my hip on the doorknob several times because of the narrow space between the doorjamb and the bathtub. The floral motif isn't bad, and the carpeted floors are impeccably clean. Go as high up as you can, to escape street noise, which is the hotel's one failing (though the elevator's kind of slow, too). Modems are located on every floor, so in-room Wi-Fi Internet access is super fast. Lowest-priced "economy" rooms have no windows. Standard rooms on the eighth floor have good views, but the bathrooms are small and have no bathtub, and only a curtain separates the toilet from the shower area. Suites are large, with couches in large, separate sitting rooms. The Spring has an unsettling Greco-Roman motif, with statues and filigreed molding here and there. If the lobby's hanging ivy, colonnades, and grand staircase seem a bit over-the-top, at least the rooms are a bit more toned down, utilitarian, and pleasant. A short walk from Dong Khoi and the central business district, this is a popular choice for long-term business travelers. The staff couldn't be nicer or more helpful.

44–46 Le Thanh Ton St., District 1. ✆ **08/3829-7362.** Fax 08/3822-1383. www.springhotelvietnam.com. 45 units. $45–$63 double; $79 suite. Rates include breakfast. MC, V. **Amenities:** Restaurant/bar; room service. *In room:* A/C, satellite TV, fridge, minibar, Wi-Fi.

3 WHERE TO DINE

Saigon offers the widest array of restaurants in Vietnam, and virtually every world cuisine is represented. The area around Dong Khoi is home to many fine-dining choices; ask locals where to eat, though, and they'll point you to the outdoor stalls in places like the open market area that opens in the evening just adjacent to Ben Thanh Market, or to a small neighborhood storefront. Saigon's famous street stalls serve up local specials like *mien ga* (vermicelli, chicken, and mushrooms in a delicate soup), *lau hai san* (a tangy seafood soup with mustard greens), and, of course, *pho* (Vietnam's staple noodle soup, popular everywhere). See "Quest for the Perfect Noodle," p. 319, for a few good places to slurp Saigon's delectable noodle dish.

Expensive

Camargue ★ FRENCH/CONTINENTAL Camargue is two floors of enchanting renovated colonial. Choose from softly lit interior or spacious outdoor terrace seating surrounded by palm fronds. The menu changes regularly. A sampling from our visit included warm goat-cheese salad, roast pork rondalet, and venison. Camargue also seems to have given tourists the nod by adding ubiquitous, lower-priced pasta dishes. The food, alas, isn't as perfect as the surroundings, and the service is substandard, but it's a quaint, laid-back spot downtown. The first-floor bar, **Vasco's,** is very popular and open late on Friday. Call ahead before you go, as rumor has it that the restaurant's lease is up and they will be forced to move soon.

191 Hai Ba Trung St., District 3. ✆ **08/3824-3148.** Reservations recommended on weekend nights. Main courses 270,000 VND–450,000 VND. AE, DC, MC, V. Daily 6am–11pm.

L'Olivier ★★ FRENCH This hotel restaurant serves incredible French food in a charming atmosphere that feels as bright and cozy as a French countryside home. The food is innovative, with such highlights as perfectly done pan-fried sea scallops balanced over slices of turnip and a touch of mango chutney. For dessert, treat yourself to the chocolate volcano cake, which is injected with a shot of pistachio. This is a fine place to have a leisurely evening repast.

17 Le Duan Blvd., District 1. ✆ **08/3824-1555,** ext. 7731. Reservations recommended. Main courses $22–$30. AE, MC, V. Mon–Fri noon–2pm and 6:30–10:30pm; Sat 6:30–10:30pm. Closed Sun.

Mandarin ★ VIETNAMESE/CHINESE On a quiet side street between busy Le Than Thon and the river, cross the threshold at Mandarin and you enter a quaint, elegant oasis that will have you forgetting the seething city outside. Decor is an upscale Chinese motif with timber beams, fine Chinese screen paintings, and artwork on two open-plan floors. It's plush but not stuffy, and you'll feel comfortable in casual clothes or a suit. The staff is professional and attentive but doesn't hover, and it is helpful with suggestions and explanations. Ask about daily specials and set menus. I had an excellent spicy sautéed beef served in bamboo with rice. For a memorable meal, don't miss the famed duck done in a sweet "Mandarin style." The steamed lobster in garlic is as good as it sounds, and their seafood steamboat for four is a real coup. The restaurant features a live classical trio (call ahead for schedule).

11A Ngo Van Nam, District 1. ✆ **08/3822-9783.** Fax 08/3825-6185. Reservations recommended. Main courses $10–$60; set menu from $35 per person (minimum 2). AE, MC, V. Daily 11am–2pm and 5:30–10pm.

Ohan Restaurant ★★ JAPANESE Tatsuhiko Itano is one of Ho Chi Minh's best-known and most-loved expats. His smile and bellowing *"Irashaimase!"* greet you at the door of this real-deal Japanese Oshushiyasan. Key ingredients are imported, the fish is very fresh, and the presentation is unrivaled. This is the place where Saigon's many Japanese expatriates come to celebrate, and on weekend nights the place is packed. Mr. Itano serves all kinds of Japanese cuisine, along with his famous sushi, from udon noodles to Ochazuke, a dish of special herbs and spices over rice soaked in hot tea. Ohan is the town's most authentic, and Sushi Bar (see below), the most affordable.

71 Pasteur St., District 1. ✆ **08/3824-4896.** Reservations recommended on weekend nights. Main courses $6.50–$14. MC, V. Daily 11am–2pm and 6–10pm.

Opera ★ ITALIAN Excellent, fresh Italian food in a bright, contemporary setting. There's an open kitchen so you can watch them toss fresh fettuccini or linguine with mouthwatering homemade sauces. Staff is attentive and friendly. An addictive loaf of warm ciabatta bread is served with an eggplant and olive oil dip while you wait for your main dish.

1/F Park Hyatt Hotel. ✆ **08/3823-7569.** Reservations recommended. Main courses $20–$32. AE, MC, V. Daily 6–10:30am.

Pomodoro ★ ITALIAN Good large salads and tasty personal pizzas are popular at Pomodoro, a cozy little dining room with tile floors and brick walls in an arch that gives the place an Italian grotto feel. But the restaurant's actually quite light and airy, and the staff is friendly. Antipastos of bruschetta or prosciutto and melon are great, and if you bring your appetite, you can follow them up with a *primi piatti* of pasta and a rich *secondi piatti* of fish, meat, or poultry. Ingredients are generally fresh, but I ordered a pesto dish and it was delivered in all of 30 seconds, speaking of a precooked, microwave kitchen. Ask to have any pasta cooked to order. The wine menu is deep, with some fine Italian reds. The place is always full, with lots of casual international business dinners over a shared love of Italian cuisine.

79 Hai Ba Trung St., District 1. ✆ **08/3823-8998.** Reservations recommended. Main courses 140,000 VND–295,000 VND. MC, V. Daily 10am–10pm.

Skewers ★ MEDITERRANEAN The best food at this chic bistro does, in fact, come on skewers; barbecue entrees, particularly the lamb kabobs, are delicious. Also try the moussaka, baked fish and seafood, grilled Moroccan sea bass, good pastas, or barbecued entrees like vodka-flamed beef or ribs dipped in honey. All the flame-bursting barbecuing is done in an open-air kitchen at the front of the restaurant—fun to watch. The salads are large and delicious, and they serve great light meals and appetizers, with great dips like hummus and baba ghanouj. And to top it all off, they've got the best cigars and whiskey in town. The atmosphere is candlelit and cozy, a great spot for a romantic evening.

9A Thai Van Lung St., District 1. ✆ **08/3822-4798.** www.skewers-restaurant.com. Main courses $5–$18. MC, V. Mon–Fri 11:30am–2pm and 6–11pm; Sat–Sun 6–11pm.

Square One ★★ VIETNAMESE/WESTERN You don't come to Square One to eat; you come to spend an evening paying homage to good food. Dining here is like having a front-row ticket to a fancy cooking show. The cooks behind the glass partitions look confident and are constantly in motion, grilling seafood, changing charcoal, or wrapping fish in giant pandanus leaves. It's a mouthwatering show. The menu is divided into traditional Vietnamese starters and mains and Western dishes. The spring rolls, pork, bean sprouts, and mint wrapped in fresh rice paper, and then wrapped in a cabbage leaf and tied together with a strip of pandanus leaf, are light and crunchy and incredibly fresh. Vietnamese dishes are meant to be shared, so expect large portions for main courses. My red grouper—grilled to perfection and served with a chili sauce that was zesty but not spicy—was more than enough for two people. Early-evening chill lounge music segues into a funkier upbeat tempo after 9pm. Get a table facing one of the five open kitchens—it's better than people-watching.

3/F Park Hyatt Hotel. ✆ **08/3520-2357.** Reservations recommended. Main courses $10–$35. AE, MC, V. Daily noon–2:30pm and 6–10:30pm.

Sushi Bar ★★ JAPANESE The food speaks for itself (in Japanese, no less) at this friendly corner sushi bar. At the end of Le Thanh Ton, known to some as "Little Tokyo," this is one of many Japanese eateries popping up and is popular among longtime residents. It's a typical busy, big-city sushi bar, complete with a wise-cracking sushi master from Japan. Upstairs there are tatami rooms, and the place always seems full, which is a good sign. Everything's fresh, the lunch specials are a good bargain, and the good sushi and sashimi are worth the price.

2 Le Thanh Ton, District 1. ✆ **08/3823-8042.** Main courses 15,000 VND–280,000 VND. MC, V. Daily 10am–11pm. Delivery until 10pm.

Moderate

Augustin ★ FRENCH On the quaint, up-and-coming "restaurant row" Ngueyen Thiep (just off Don Khoi), this bright, lively little place is a favorite with French expats and tourists. The food is simple yet innovative French fare, including beef *pot-au-feu* and sea bass tartare with olives. Try the seafood stew, lightly seasoned with saffron and packed with fish, clams, and shrimp. The seating is quite cozy, especially because the restaurant is always full, and the Vietnamese waitstaff is exceptionally friendly, speaking both French and English. The menu is bilingual, too. A large French wine list and classic dessert menu finish off a delightful meal.

10 Nguyen Thiep. ✆ **08/3829-2941.** Main courses 90,000 VND–220,000 VND. No credit cards. Daily noon–2pm and 6–11pm.

Blue Ginger VIETNAMESE Also called the Saigon Times Club, this Vietnamese bistro is an atmospheric choice with fine local specialties; as a result, it's a tour-group favorite, but that doesn't spoil the atmosphere. It features a nightly performance of folk music, and the dulcet tones mingle nicely with clinking glasses and the low hum of conversation in the candlelit dining room; it makes for a nice, casual evening. The specialty here is a large seafood steamboat, a veritable cornucopia of seafood done like Japanese *nabe* in a large pot in front of you (for two or more). I had the caramelized pork served in a clay pot, and it was excellent. There are great set menus of up to 10 courses, and the desserts are all there: ice cream, crème caramel, and fried bananas.

37 Nam Ky Khoi Nghia, District 1. ✆ **08/3829-8676.** Main courses $2–$6; set menus 120,000 VND–450,000 VND. MC, V. Daily 7am–10:30pm.

Lemongrass VIETNAMESE The atmosphere is candlelit and intimate, very Vietnamese, with cane furniture and tile floors, yet its three floors of subdued dining are a still a nice place to duck out of the midday sun. Set lunches are an affordable and light option ($8–$10). The long menu emphasizes seafood and seasonal specials. Particularly outstanding are the deep-fried prawn in coconut batter and the crab sautéed in salt and pepper sauce. The portions are very healthful, Asian family style, so go with a group if at all possible, and sample as many delicacies as possible.

4 Nguyen Thiep St., District 1. ✆ **08/3822-4005** or 3822-0496. Main courses 80,000 VND–200,000 VND. AE, MC, V. Daily 11am–2pm and 5–10pm.

The Refinery ★ FRENCH This French bistro is built in the former headquarters of the leading Opium refinery (hence the name) of old Indochine. They've got a great selection of light and filling food that's made just right. I had the eggplant with tomato-mint sauce, goat cheese, and brown and wild rice—a perfect blend of healthy starches and cheesy indulgence. Being a bistro, they're always ready to serve a coq au vin at the drop of a hat. The understated decor makes for casual, intimate dining. Floors are retro red, white, and black tiles, and seating is that of a Paris bistro—low wooden tables and round chairs. The outdoor terrace is shrouded in plants and a mélange of leather chairs and small tables—you'll forget that you're actually sitting in a *hem* (a small street or alley).

74/7C Hai Ba Trung St. (walk through the traditional yellow gate—it's on your left after about 100m/328 ft.), District 1. ✆ **08/3823-0509.** Main courses $5–$15. MC, V. Daily 11am–11pm.

Sandals ★ MEDITERRANEAN This restaurant is owned by the same folks who run Sailing Club in Nha Trang (p. 277) and Mui Ne (p. 288), so it should come as no surprise that the food has a beachside comfort quality to it. Sandwiches are hearty and the salads filling—for a salad that packs a carbs punch, try the Lamb Kofta & Harissa (90,000 VND), a mix of Vietnamese salad and greens tossed with grilled lamb and Harissa sauce served over butter roti.

93 Hai Ba Trung St. ✆ **08/3820-3130.** Main courses 85,000 VND–125,000 VND. AE, MC, V. Daily 10am–1am.

Tandoor ★ (Finds) INDIAN Bringing north Indian and tandoori cuisine at its best to Vietnam since 1995, this luxurious little enclave a good little ride north of the Don Khoi area is set in a casual, comfortable French-style villa in District 3 (about 30,000 VND by taxi from downtown). Start with an appetizer of pakora, savory fritters, or samosas. As the name suggests, cuisine at Tandoor centers around the traditional clay oven fired at high heat with charcoal, which is great for grilling meat and browning good Indian breads. The restaurant is best known for their good kabobs of mutton, chicken, or fish. Try the chicken kabob marinated in spinach and mint before it's grilled in the tandoor oven, or the vegetarian kabob of minced vegetables with cheese. They serve all kinds of biryani, unique Kashmiri specials, a host of good curries—great creamy Korma and spicy vindaloo—and Saag dishes of spinach done with mutton, chicken, fish, or seafood. They have good side salads and yogurt dishes to cool the palate, and follow it up with a sweet lassi yogurt drink. They offer set lunches for Saigon's busy business crowd, cater events for large parties, and offer free home (or hotel) delivery.

74/6 Hai Ba Trung St., District 1. ✆ **08/3930-4839.** Main courses $5–$10. MC, V. Daily 11am–2:30pm and 5–10pm.

Temple Club ★★ VIETNAMESE For atmosphere alone, the Temple Club is a must-see in Ho Chi Minh. As the name suggests, this is an old Chinese temple (ca. 1900), with original wood and masonry. The decor is upscale, but the prices are reasonable and the food is great. The ceiling is high, and the walls are exposed brick. The floor is terra cotta draped in antique throw rugs, and there are some great Buddhist tapestries and statuary about. There's a classic old wooden bar and a formal but comfortable dining room, as well as a lounge area in the back for coffee and dessert. The cuisine is standard Vietnamese from all parts of the country. This place does a good Hanoi-style *cha ca* (fried monkfish), and the grilled fish *Long Va* style (grilled fish on a bed of spring onions and dill covered in crisp garlic and peanuts) is an excellent choice. For dessert, the homemade Hue cake in secret sauce, a steamed cake made of ground green beans served with a pandan and coconut sauce, is done just right. The coffee is the real thing; they even have cappuccino. This is one of the most atmospheric and romantic spots in town.

29–31 Ton That Thiep St., District 1. ✆ **08/3829-9244.** Main courses 90,000 VND–240,000 VND. MC, V. Daily 11:30am–midnight.

Warda ★ LEBANESE You walk into this place and get a tiny urge to break into a belly dance. The walls are painted in two-tone solid-colored (yellow downstairs, blue upstairs) horizontal stripes. Beaded turquoise curtains mark the entrance to a semicircular cave of mirrors (the bathrooms, naturally), and there is an outdoor terrace protected by a patterned awning that looks like something out of Arabian Nights. It's great decor, and the food is excellent, to boot. The fish and pear tajine, a braised sea bass marinated in olive oil, parsley, and chili, with thin pear slices, is divine. The fish falls apart at the mere touch of your fork. Drinks have a hint of Arabic style, like bitter saffron or rose martinis. If you've got a sweet tooth, you'll love the crispy phyllo pastry filled with almond paste for dessert, and for those watching the waistline, an order of apple-flavored tobacco served in a shisha pipe should round out your evening quite nicely.

71/7 Mac Thi Buoi St., District 1. ✆ **08/3823-3822.** Main courses $4–$12. MC, V. Daily 9am–midnight.

Xu ★★ VIETNAMESE Co-owner Bien Nguyen left school at 15 to work in the food and beverage industry. An old French couple took him under their wing and taught him, as he puts it, "the A to Z of F and B." Saigon is grateful to that couple and to Bien, who has created one of the finest restaurants Saigon has on offer. The food is innovative, and yet retains the traditional taste and feel of Vietnamese eats. I highly recommend the Sea Bass Taste, a sampler plate that comes with perfect, small portions of grilled sea bass over mashed potatoes, a crispy Vietnamese pancake with fresh veggies, and a sea bass rice flour roll, or *banh cuon.* The decor is modern, with retro wooden chairs fixed with deep purple velvet cushions. The lounge (p. 334) is a great place for pre- and after-dinner drinks.

71–75 Hai Ba Trung, District 1 (walk through the alleyway for about 150m/492 ft. and head up the stairs on your right). ✆ **08/3824-8468.** Main courses 80,000 VND–380,000 VND. AE, MC, V. Daily 11am–midnight.

ZanZBar ★ INTERNATIONAL This restaurant has a loyal following among Saigon's expat crowd, and for good reason. I tucked into a generous blackened prawn appetizer, served with an avocado half stuffed with cubed tomatoes and black olives. It was delectable and almost big enough to be a main course. The eatery is small and cozy, but doesn't feel crowded. There's usually a pleasant buzz of activity and energy running well into the evening.

41 Dong Du St., District 1. ✆ **08/3822-7375.** Main courses $8.20–$23. AE, MC, V. Daily 7am–2am.

Inexpensive

Allez Boo ★ VIETNAMESE/WESTERN This little corner eatery is in the very heart of the Pham Ngu Lao backpacker area. Allez Boo serves affordable one-plate meals and a good selection of Vietnamese and faux-Western in an open-air corner bar. Come for dinner and stay for drinks or a game of pool in this busy but cozy spot, all done up in a beachside bamboo-and-thatch theme. The food is good (stick to Vietnamese dishes), and it's always hoppin' till late. You're sure to meet some fellow travelers. It's pickpocket central, though, so keep an eye out at the window tables.

195 Pham Ngu Lao. No phone. Main courses $1–$3. MC, V. Open 24 hr.

Quan An Ngon Restaurant ★★★ VIETNAMESE *Ngon* means "delicious," and, for authentic Vietnamese, this restaurant lives up to its name and gets my vote for the best in Vietnam. Ngon has become a real Ho Chi Minh institution and is always packed with both locals and tourists; they've even built a new location nearby to handle the overflow. The atmosphere is chaotic: a cacophony of laughing, chattering guests, shouting waiters, and clanging pots and pans. Seating is a mix of regular table dining in the central colonial or in the balcony or courtyard out back. The main building is surrounded by cooking stations, each serving a regional specialty. The menu is a survey course in Vietnamese cooking, and the tuition is low. Go with a Vietnamese friend, if you can, or someone who can explain some of the regional specialties. If you're alone, just point and shoot. Everything is good. They have Hue-style *bun bo* (cold noodles with beef), a catalog of *pho* (noodle soup), and all kinds of seafood. Meals here are best as leisurely, many-course affairs, but go just for a snack if you're visiting the Reunification Palace or any sights downtown. Don't miss it!

Warning: Service here is getting better, but this isn't Temple Club. You'll have to flag down staff, and ordering means pointing to the menu, but restaurant service in a real Vietnamese restaurant is never doting or effusive, so think of it this way: You're not being ignored; you're just getting the real thing.

138 Nam Ky Khoi Nghia, District 1. ✆ **08/3829-9449.** Main courses 45,000 VND–200,000 VND. AE, MC, V. Daily 6:30am–11pm.

Wrap and Roll VIETNAMESE This restaurant did for the fresh Vietnamese spring roll what Pho 24 did for beef noodle soup. It's a chain restaurant that serves DIY spring rolls in a clean and friendly place. Signature dishes come with your choice of meat or seafood (I had grilled beef wrapped in grape leaves and highly recommend it), along with a big plate of assorted shrubbery like basil, mint, and lettuce, and a small pile of vermicelli noodles. Roll it all up in a rice paper wrapper and dip it in the bowl of fish sauce, and it's a perfect sampling of a Vietnamese classic.

62 Hai Ba Trung St., District 1. ✆ **08/3822-2166.** Main courses 28,000 VND–68,000 VND. MC, V. Daily 7:30am–10:30pm.

Snacks & Cafes

Local dining in the evening in the open areas around the **Ben Thanh Market** is the best opportunity to try real local dishes (from after 6pm until 10 or 11pm daily). These

Quest for the Perfect Noodle

Pho, or Vietnamese noodle soup, has become a popular dish in the West, but it's a national obsession in Vietnam, eaten any time of day. The simplicity of this dish is the attraction: beef stock with rice noodles garnished as you like, with meat and herbs, all ingredients left to speak for themselves. You can eat *pho* on any street corner and in any market, but here are a few especially good places in Saigon with English menus and a high standard of cleanliness:

Pho 2000 Set on Tran Hung Dao just cater-cornered to the Binh Thanh Market, Pho 2000 is a Saigon institution and a beehive of activity day or night. Former U.S. President Bill Clinton even made a visit here, and if Bubba liked it, it must be good.

Pho 24 The most popular outlet of this growing Vietnam chain (they have numerous shops in Saigon and Hanoi) is on Nguyen Thiep Street, a little restaurant row off of busy Don Khoi. They serve a busy crowd all day in a cool, clean storefront. Also look for Pho 24's other shops in town: at Diamond Plaza, at 67 Hai Ba Trung, and at 89 Mac Thi St., among others.

Pho Tezuka Katsuyoshi On Don Khoi, across from the Grand Hotel, look for the large **pho** sign and Japanese characters at 37 Don Khoi St.; inside, the place is covered in woodcarvings and serves great soups—popular with Japanese tourists and endorsed by a sign that reads YOU DON'T LIKE IT, YOU DON'T PAY.

The Peace Noodle Shop Otherwise known to locals, and on the sign, as **Pho Binh,** this little noodle storefront at 7 Lo Chinh Thang St., in District 3, is a good place to sample some real local *pho* while you visit a piece of Vietnam War history.

restaurants are quite clean, and most have full-size plastic chairs around large tables for those who don't jibe with squatting low at streetside. Try *pho* (**Pho 2000** restaurant is just adjacent) or *banh khoi* (Vietnamese pancakes).

Also note the many riverboat restaurants at the terminus of Dong Khoi Street, near the river ferries and high-speed boats to Vung TauTau. **Ben Nghe** (at quay-side Ben Bach Dang; ✆ **08/3823-1475**) is typical of the Christmas-light-draped live stage (or loud karaoke) riverside barges with long tables shared by big groups. The seafood and big fry-ups make for a fun night.

Note: Unless otherwise specified below, cafes in Ho Chi Minh City open at 8 or 9am and close, as does most of the city, at 9pm.

Bach Dang *Finds* A Saigon institution, Bach Dang is three floors of fun. It's always crowded and the best place in town for good ice cream and to meet local people.
26 Le Loi St., District 1. ✆ **08/3829-2707.**

Café Central Café Central is a great little international deli. Stop in for breakfast or a sandwich any time. If you come at night, you'll be rubbing elbows with the many locals who like to spend their evenings here, watching the world go by.
In the Sun Wah Tower, 115 Nguyen Hue, District 1. ✆ **08/3821-9303.**

Café l'Opera Just next to the entrance of the Caravelle hotel, Café l'Opera is a bright, upmarket coffee corner run by *illy.* They've got the best machines, proper coffee, and excellent, simple Italian food. They recently made a Starbucks-esque move and opened two near-identical locations nearby.

11–13 Cong Truong Lam Son, District 1. ✆ **08/3827-5946.** 6 Thai Van Lung St., District 1. ✆ **08/3823-5795.** Daily 8am–11:30pm.

Cafe 333 Known as Cafe "Ba-Ba-Ba" to locals, this hole in the wall on busy De Tham, the heart of the backpacker neighborhood, is a good place to put your feet up and watch the parade of travelers. You'll have to fight off the young gum, lighter, book, and trinket salesmen with a stick, but it's a good place to take it all in and enjoy an affordable breakfast or snack before boarding a budget tour bus.

201 De Tham St. ✆ **08/3836-0205.** Daily 6am–midnight.

Highland Coffee This is the best location of the popular Vietnamese chain (more or less like the Starbucks of Vietnam), with open-air seating in a cool pavilion just behind the historic central Ho Chi Minh City Opera House.

7 Cong Truong, on Lam Son Sq. just behind the Opera House. ✆ **08/3822-5017.** Daily 6:30am–midnight.

La Fenêtre Soleil Mismatched sofas, antique chairs, and unfinished wooden tables adorn this cozy cafe. A couple chandeliers reflecting the afternoon light and a Bose sound system playing classical music make it a perfect place for midday tea.

1/F 135 Le Thanh Ton St. (entrance is around the corner on Nam Ki Khoi Nghia St.; go through the alley and up the stairs on your right). ✆ **08/3822-5209.** Daily 9am–11pm.

Mojo ★ INTERNATIONAL This funky little place belongs to the Sheraton, but it doesn't have the feel of a hotel cafe. It's got simple, Scandi-style furniture, and there are loungelike sofas in the back to get cozy with your dining companions. It's a great place to do some people-watching. Hearty sandwiches are served with the crusts cut off.

88 Dong Khoi St., District 1. ✆ **08/3827-2828.** Main courses $6–$13. AE, MC, V. Mon–Fri 8am–11pm; Sat–Sun until midnight.

4 EXPLORING HO CHI MINH CITY

The museums and attractions of Ho Chi Minh City are mostly in the downtown areas of districts 1 and 3. And although the museums are interesting, the bustling city itself is the major attraction here.

TYPICAL 1-DAY ITINERARY

In the morning, start off at tranquil **Giac Lam Pagoda** and tour the city's nearby **Chinatown** and busy **Binh Te Market** in the historic Cholon area of District 5; there are a number of hidden temples among Chinese shop houses, and this is a great district to have a guide to take you around. From there, hit the large, central **Ben Thanh Market** (a good place for lunch—or you might try nearby Don Khoi).

In the afternoon, take a walk through the **Reunification Hall,** where the jig was up for the Saigon government in 1975; then walk through the square flanked by the towering **Notre Dame Cathedral** and Saigon's historic **Post Office.** From there, head toward the **War Museum,** which tells the tale of Vietnam at war with the French and Americans. The museum is a bit much for some visitors, and certain groups opt instead for a visit to the

Emperor Jade Pagoda, a large Chinese compound in the northeast of the city—also a good stop if you have time after visiting the War Museum. Afterward, enjoy a casual stroll down central **Don Khoi**—likely near your hotel—and take a rest (you'll be whipped), or enjoy a coffee or snack at one of the many restaurants or cafes along this busy strip.

Note: This is a lot to do in 1 day, especially if you take motorbike taxis and try to find your own way. If you'd rather take a tour, see the "Visitor Information & Tours" section at the beginning of this chapter. With an additional day, try to catch some of the more out-of-the-way sights, such as the **Hoa Binh (Peace) Noodle Shop** and nearby **Vinh Nghiem Pagoda,** or the sprawling **Vietnamese History Museum** or raggedy old **Ho Chi Minh City Museum.**

More than 2 full days in Saigon certainly calls for a day trip out to the **Cau Dai Temple** and/or the **Cu Chi Tunnels.**

ATTRACTIONS IN DISTRICT 1

Ben Thanh Market ★★ The clock tower over the main entrance to what was formerly known as Les Halles Centrale is the symbol of Saigon, and the market might as well be, too. Opened first in 1914, it's crowded, a boon for pickpockets with its narrow, one-way aisles, and loaded with people clamoring to sell you cheap goods (T-shirts, aluminum wares, silk, bamboo, and lacquer) and postcards. There are so many people calling out to you that you'll feel like the belle of the ball or a wallet with legs. Watch for pickpockets. Out front, near the main entrance, find lots of knockoff brand-name clothes, and farther in is a number of small souvenir stands. Toward the back are a few small cafes serving local cuisine or coffee and *che,* a popular Vietnamese dessert. The wet market at the far back, with its selection of meat, fish, produce, and flowers, is interesting and hassle free; no one will foist a fish on you. The market has cleaned itself up for the tourists over the years, which is a shame because the added hygiene comes at the cost of the market's old charm and raw authenticity. In open-air stalls surrounding the market are some nice little eateries that open just as the market itself starts closing down, and this is, in fact, one of the best place to try authentic local cuisine. The adventurous can sample good local specialties like rice dishes, noodle soup, *bun* dishes of vermicelli noodles, or ice cream and dessert for next to nothing.

Note: If you start from Ben Thanh Market and take a walk up Le Loi Street (the main east-west avenue) toward central Dong Khoi, you'll stroll past loads of tourist shops with souvenirs, booksellers with photocopy knockoffs on the street, watch-repair shops, camera stores, and T-shirt shops. As good as—maybe even better than—the sprawling market.
At the intersection of Le Loi, Ham Nghi, Tran Hung Dao, and Le Loi sts., District 1.

City Hall and Nguyen Hue Plaza Saigon's city hall was originally a French hotel constructed between 1902 and 1908, a fantastic ornate example of refined colonial architecture. Unfortunately, it's not open to the public, but there is a small walking mall out front and running the length of the behemoth Rex Hotel, itself an important vestige of the American years when it housed the CIA headquarters. The park is a great spot for a good group photo with the majestic City Hall in the background, and the people-watching here is supreme (though you're likely to be the people that are being watched).
Facing Nguyen Hue Blvd.

Ho Chi Minh City Museum ★ Formerly the Revolutionary Museum, this central behemoth attracts more newlyweds posing for photos on the front steps than anything. Originally built in 1890 by the French as a commercial museum, then a Governor's

Palace, and later committee building, the exhibits in this museum cover a broad range, from archaeology to ethnic survey, early photos of the city, and documents from its founding in the 1600s. The second floor is heavy on Vietnam's ongoing revolution, with displays of weaponry and memorabilia from the period of struggle against imperialism and many flags, placards, and dispatches from the rise of Communism, beginning with the August Revolution of 1945 all the way to the fall of Saigon. The bias is heavy, of course, and it is an important rendering of Vietnam's protracted struggle and ideologies, but it is interesting to note how the displays, not unlike socialist ideals, are a bit frayed around the edges in a land that is going pell-mell toward a market economy. The grounds are picturesque, thus the young couples posing for wedding photos, and there is an interesting collection of captured U.S. fighter planes, tanks, and artillery in the main courtyard. Underneath the building is a series of tunnels (closed to the public) leading to the Reunification Palace, once used by former President Ngo Dinh Diem as a hide-out before his execution in 1962.

65 Ly Tu Trong St. ✆ **08/3829-8250.** Admission 15,000 VND. Daily 8:30am–4:30pm.

Ho Chi Minh Museum This large museum commemorates the man this city was named for. The museum is in the "Dragon House *(Nha Long)* Wharf," a 19th-century building with a European design and stylish Chinese-style roof from which it takes its name. The location is auspicious because this is where the young Ho Chi Minh (then Nguyen Tat Thanh) left to sail for Europe. The museum tells the rags-to-equality story of a self-made revolutionary, but mostly in Vietnamese. The relics of Ho's life are many, and much can be gleaned from photos and what English descriptions you can find. The museum is south of town, just across a small canal off the Saigon River in District 4.

1 Nguyen Tat Thanh Rd., District 4. No phone. Admission 10,000 VND. Tues–Sat 8–11:30am and 2–5:30pm; Sun 8am–8pm.

Notre Dame Cathedral ★ The neo-Romanesque cathedral was constructed between 1877 and 1883 using bricks from Marseilles and stained-glass windows from Chartres. The Romanesque towers of nearly 60m (197 ft.) loom over a large white statue of the Virgin Mary and the nearby Saigon Post Office. The cathedral would pretty much be at home in any Catholic European country. The tiles are a cubic pattern done in black, white, and gray. They have a slightly disconcerting 3-D effect, but they are no match for the statue of Mary framed in neon blue lights in the first archway on your left. The atmosphere is fairly serene, and there's something calming about taking a rest on the wooden pews.

Near the intersection of Dong Khoi and Nguyen Du sts., District 1.

Reunification Palace ★ Designed as the home of former President Ngo Dinh Diem, the U.S.-backed leader of Vietnam until his assassination in 1962, this building is most notable for its symbolic role in the fall of Saigon in April 1975, when its gates were breached by North Vietnamese tanks and the victor's flag hung on the balcony; the very tanks that crashed through the gates are enshrined in the entryway, and photos and accounts of their drivers are on display. Built on the site of the French governor general's home, called the Norodom Palace, the current modern building, designed when *modern* meant "sterile," was completed in 1966—it looks something like an old elementary school to my eye now, but modern-design fans love it. Like the Bao Dai Palace in Dalat, the Reunification Palace is a series of rather empty rooms that are nevertheless interesting because they specialize in period kitsch and haven't been gussied up too much. Tour private quarters, dining rooms, entertainment lounges, and the president's office that feel like everybody just up and left one day (they did)—a tour is almost eerie, really. Most interesting is the war command room, with its huge maps and old communications equipment, as well as the basement labyrinth. There is an ongoing screening in a series of rooms in the basement—mercifully cool and a good rest while touring—of mostly propaganda about the war years (plays in French, English, Japanese, and Chinese in separate screening rooms).

The Conference Hall in the main room is still used for important national events. The carpeting you'll see on your visit is a shabby piece of cheap cloth used for display and protection purposes only. For special events, like the recent APEC summit and the signing of the WTO accord, the display rug is whisked away and the "for guests only" carpet, a plush, bright red piece with gold accents, is unveiled.

106 Nguyen Du St. Admission 15,000 VND. Daily 7:30–11am and 1–4pm.

Saigon Opera House (Ho Chi Minh Municipal Theater) This magnificent building was built at the turn of the 20th century as a classical opera house to entertain French colonists. The building was renovated in the 1940s, only to be badly damaged by bombers in 1944. A shelter for refugees after the Geneva Accord split the country at the 17th Parallel in 1954, the building would briefly house the parliament before falling under first private and, ultimately, state hands (after reunification) as an opera house and theater. There have been extensive renovations in recent years. The three-story interior houses some 1,800 seats. Today the Municipal Theater does very little in terms of performances, but it is a stalwart atmospheric holdout amid the rising steel-and-glass downtown.

At the intersection of Le Loi and Dong Khoi sts.

Vietnam History Museum ★★ Housed in a rambling concrete pagodalike structure, the museum presents a clear picture of Vietnamese history, with a focus on the south. There's an excellent selection of Cham sculpture and the best collection of ancient ceramics in Vietnam, although some of the artifacts are being held together by Scotch tape. Weaponry from the 14th century onward is on display; one yard is nothing but cannons. Room 4 (left of the main entrance) has a fascinating, slightly creepy display of an embalmed body in remarkable shape that dates back to 1869. One wing is dedicated to ethnic minorities of the south, including photographs, costumes, and household implements. Nguyen dynasty (1700–1945) clothing and housewares are also on display. There are archaeological artifacts from prehistoric Saigon. Its 19th- and early-20th-century histories are shown using photos and, curiously, a female corpse unearthed as construction teams broke ground for a recent housing project. There are even some general background explanations in English, something missing from most Vietnamese museums.

A small three-row theater inside the museum shows regular water puppet performances. It's an intimate venue, and the performance is more clever and witty than the for-the-tourists water puppet show in Hanoi. Tickets are just 32,000 VND, and performances are held every hour between 9 and 11am and 2 and 4pm Tuesday through Sunday.

Also adjacent to the History Museum is the **Ho Chi Minh City Campaign Museum,** the first address on Le Duan Street, which originates just across from the entrance to the botanical garden and zoo. In the large courtyard outside the museum, you'll find another collection of war detritus similar to what you'll see at the War Remnants Museum and the Ho Chi Minh City Museum, but here you can see the crumpled remains of an American reconnaissance plane shot down, as well as more utilitarian vehicles, troop carriers, and the construction equipment from the U.S. defoliation campaign. The museum has little in the way of English explanations—it's more or less a place for Vietnamese school field trips (there's a long block of classrooms attached)—but Vietnam War enthusiasts can find some weaponry and tools not displayed in other museums in town.

2 Nguyen Binh Kiem. ✆ **08/3829-8146** (Water Puppet Theater ✆ 08/3823-4582). Admission 15,000 VND. Tues–Sun 8–11:30am and 1:30–5pm.

ATTRACTIONS IN DISTRICT 3

Emperor Jade Pagoda (Phuoc Hai) ★★ One of the most interesting pagodas in Vietnam, the Emperor Jade is filled with smoky incense and fantastic carved figurines. It was built by the Cantonese community around the turn of the 20th century and is still buzzing with worshipers, many lounging in the front gardens. Take a moment to look at the elaborate statuary on the pagoda's roof. The dominant figure in the main hall is the Jade Emperor himself; referred to as the "god of the heavens," the emperor decides who will enter and who will be refused. He looks an awful lot like Confucius, only meaner. In an anteroom to the left, you'll find Kim Hua, a goddess of fertility, and the King of Hell in another corner with his minions, who undoubtedly gets those the Jade Emperor rejects. It's spooky.

73 Mai Thi Luu St., District 3. Daily 8am–5pm.

The Hoa Binh Noodle Shop ★ The name means "Peace Noodles," and this little shop is no different from the many others in town, except for a small red plaque above the entrance and a flag of the Communist regime. The plaque, written in Vietnamese, marks this discreet little storefront's important place in history. Its upstairs floors were the staging ground of the Tet Offensive of 1968, a surprise attack on U.S. forces region-wide during a cease-fire that, with thousands of losses, was tantamount to the Viet Cong throwing themselves on their collective sword. However, with the incursions reaching as far as the U.S. Embassy in Saigon, as well as at points throughout the city, this was a turning point in the conflict; it changed popular opinion in the United States and among troops stationed in Vietnam, creating a major diversion from later intensified fighting on northern fronts. Eighty-eight-year-old Ngo Toai, the shop owner, was the Madame Lefarge of the offensive, serving noodles by day and hosting high-level Viet Cong planners by night. The raid blew his cover, and Mr. Toai spent the rest of the war in jail, only to return to his shop in 1975 and pick up the ladle right where he left it, never once betraying the revolutionary zeal that made him a place in history. If you're lucky, you'll meet the genial Mr. Toai during your visit; if not, his sons will serve you up some good noodles and hand you their ready-made packet of information about their father, complete with photos from the war days as well as ones taken with the many tourists who visit, and a few articles from international papers. The noodles are pretty good, too. Often visited in conjunction with Vinh Nghiem Pagoda (see below).

7 Lo Chinh Thang St., District 3. Daily 7am–11pm.

Vinh Nghiem Pagoda Located to the north of town on the road to the airport, this pagoda is distinct because of its constant activities at the attached school, as well as for the daily workings of the many monks and nuns housed here. I visited when the place was in preparation for a funeral, and it was like the set of a Hollywood movie, complete with egoistic flower coordinators and a bevy of fawning assistants. Housed under large, sloping Chinese-style roofs, with upturned cornices, the temple has two floors, with a grand sanctuary on the second floor (often closed to visitors) and a more utilitarian hall on the ground floor, as well as large block of classrooms and housing for monks and nuns, some of whom may come out and greet you in the hopes of practicing their English. A visit here is popular in conjunction with the Hoa Binh Noodle Shop (see above).

Near Vinh Nghiem in District 3, you'll also find the brash pink facade of the wedding cake that is **Tan Dinh Cathedral,** a busy working Catholic church with daily services that stands out like a sore thumb (or a pink elephant) in the busy Saigon streetscape of the Tan Dinh area. The nearby **Tan Dinh Market** is notable for the absence of foreign visitors and the pushy hard sell going on in the popular Ben Thanh Market; Tan Dinh is a good glimpse at the workings of an average city market, with cloth sellers at the front, dry-goods vendors in the center, and meats, vegetables, and fish sold in the back.

On Nguyen Van Troi St., directly north of the city center in District 3. Free admission. Daily dawn–dusk.

War Remnants Museum ★★ The War Remnants Museum is a comprehensive collection of the machinery, weapons, photos, and documentation of Vietnam's wars with the both the French and Americans (though the emphasis is heavily on the latter). The museum was once called the War Crimes Museum, which should give you an idea of whose side of the story is being told here. Short of being outright recrimination, this museum is a call for peace and a hope that history is not repeated—visitors are even asked to sign a petition against the kind of aerial carpet-bombing that so devastated the people of Vietnam. The exhibit begins to the right of the entrance with a room listing war facts: troop numbers, bomb tonnage, statistics on international involvement in the conflict, and numbers of casualties on both sides. Next is a room dedicated to the journalists who were lost during the war. The exhibits are constantly evolving, and the museum is currently expanding and modernizing, improving its presentation and explanations throughout. One room is devoted to biological warfare, another to weaponry, and another to worldwide demonstrations for peace. The explanations, which include English translations, are very thorough. There is a large collection of bombs, planes, tanks, and war machinery in the main courtyard. Kids will love it, but you might want to think twice before taking them inside to see things like wall-size photos of the My Lai massacre and the bottled deformed fetus supposedly damaged by Agent Orange. There's also a model of the French colonial prisons, called the Tiger Cages, on the grounds.

28 Vo Van Tan St., District 3. ✆ **08/3930-6235.** Admission 15,000 VND. Daily 7:30am–noon and 1:30–5pm (last admission 4:30pm).

ATTRACTIONS IN DISTRICT 5

Cholon ("Chinatown" of Ho Chi Minh City) ★★ Cholon is a sizable district bordered by Hung Vuong to the north, Nguyen Van Cu to the east, the Ben Nghe Chanel to the south, and Nguyen Thi Nho to the west. Cholon is the predominately Chinese district of Saigon and probably the largest Chinatown in the world. Cholon exists in many ways as a city quite apart from Saigon. The Chinese began to settle the area in the early 1900s and never quite assimilated with the rest of Saigon, which causes a bit of resentment among the greater Vietnamese community. You'll sense the different environment immediately, and not only because of the Chinese-language signs. Cholon is where you might have found dark, exotic opium dens and brothels in the French colonial time, the same opium dens and brothels that greeted American troops. Story has it that a huge number of U.S. troops went AWOL in Cholon during the war—when the fall of Saigon was imminent, U.S. expeditionary forces advertised a period of amnesty for U.S. citizens on the lamb in the district—only one dazed and confused soldier came stumbling out.

A bustling commercial center, Cholon is a fascinating maze of temples, restaurants, jade ornaments, and medicine shops. Gone, however, are the brothels and opium dens of earlier days. You can lose yourself walking the narrow streets, but it makes sense to take a cyclo by the hour to see the sights. Many of the city tours (see "Visitor Information & Tours," earlier in the chapter) start at Giac Lam Pagoda and make a few stops in the district, including the large market.

If on your own, start with a motorbike or taxi ride to the **Binh Tay Market ★★**, on Phan Van Khoe Street, which is even more crowded than Ben Thanh and has much the same goods, but with a Chinese flavor. There's much more produce, along with medicines, spices, and cooking utensils, and you'll find plenty of hapless ducks and chickens tied in heaps. From Binh Tay, head up to Nguyen Trai, the district's main artery, to see some of the major temples on or around it. Be sure to see Quan Am, on Lao Tu Street off Luong Nhu Hoc, for its ornate exterior. Back on Nguyen Trai, Thien Hau pagoda is dedicated to the goddess of the sea and was popular with seafarers making thanks for their safe trip from China to Vietnam. Finally, as you follow Nguyen Trai Street past Ly Thuong Kiet, you'll see the Cholon Mosque, the one indication of Cholon's small Muslim community. Other sights in Cholon include the following:

Chua Quan Am Temple (12 Laoth St.) is a classic Chinese temple wafting with incense, blaring with music meant to soothe and speak of mountains—but crackling speakers at high decibels mean different things to different people. Nearly 20 resident monks and a cherubic abbot are on hand and welcome foreign visitors. In fact, they'll even take the time to show you around and allow you to take photos, but the expectation is a small donation in the alms box at the altar. Buy one of the oversize incense—the size of a large flashlight—and make a wish for your journey (in Vietnam or in life). The temple is heavily gilded in snazzy gold and red paint, and don't miss the cool mechanized rotating offering stands. This is a "working temple," and that means the place is busy day and night with visiting supplicants. Just outside the entrance, don't miss the busy cabinetmakers at work in a large collective at streetside.

Cha Tam is Cholon's small Catholic cathedral, with high vaulted ceilings and surrounded by the Stations of the Cross. A statue of Mary stands in a small grotto out front and looks like a Buddhist Bodhisattva with all of the offerings, placards, and prayer entreaties at her feet. This little cathedral is a cool place to take a break and visit an imposing white statue of Jesus or a standing statue of St. Francis of Assisi. Don't miss the large relief of the Last Supper.

Thien Hau—The Lady Temple was originally built by a Cantonese congregation in the early 19th century. The temple pays homage to a special psychic lady, Thien Hau, born A.D. 940, who was said to be able to predict the weather and protect sailors. The classic Chinese temple has a wooden entry; small central ponds flanked by heavy, bright red pillars; and elaborate carvings of gods and monsters. The place is busy all day and echoes with sounds from the adjacent schoolhouse. The huge coils of incense hanging over the central courtyard space make for great photos.

Giac Lam Pagoda ★ Giac Lam Pagoda, originally built in 1744 and remodeled in the early 1900s, is the oldest pagoda in Saigon. The garden in the front features the ornate tombs of venerated monks, as well as a rare bodhi tree. Next to the tree is a regular feature of Vietnamese Buddhist temples, a gleaming white statue of Quan The Am Bo Tat (Avalokitesvara, the goddess of mercy) standing on a lotus blossom, a symbol of purity. In the temple, there are just two simples rules: no hats and no smoking (though most do); wearing shoes is permitted. Inside the temple is a spooky funerary chamber, with photos of monks gone by, and a central chamber chock-full of statues. Notice the aged dark carved wood of the double-height hall. Walls are lined with funerary portraits, from large red-and-yellow plaques to small wallet-size photos, and there is some very elaborate statuary about and an altar with gilded figures. There are three altars at the back: The central is Ho Chi Minh, who is flanked by photos of the recently deceased. The monks are busy but quite friendly (when they're not chatting on their cellphones). For a small fee, monks don yellow prayer robes over their daily temple attire and perform beautiful chanting services, accompanied by bells, for visiting supplicants, mostly to loved ones. One well-known monk ministers to the sick and suffering (and tells fortunes) in a side room. Take a look at the outside courtyard with its many tombs of long-deceased monks and stewards of the temple, and don't miss the large outbuilding just to the right of the entrance—inside are aisles of shelves with colorful urns of ashes, Chinese pots with red lights, candles, and offerings. There are lots of older gentlemen milling about, playing checkers and chewing the fat, and a big Buddha statue rests near the entry road, as well as a nearby pagoda—quite new—dedicated to the Buddha of Compassion. You can climb the temple for a good view of town, but the real attraction is the original wooden structure.

118 Lac Long Quan St., District 5. Daily 5am–noon and 2–9pm.

DAY TRIPS FROM HO CHI MINH

Can Gio Island Best by motorbike—and the ride there is really what this little adventure is about—Can Gio is far more popular with escaping Saigoners than tourists. Rent a motorbike for a day $5 to $10 from any of the shops along Pham Ngu Lau in Saigon's backpacker district. Can Gio is a beach and mangrove area just west of the Vung Tau Peninsula and only about 1½ hours south of Saigon. The bumpy ride there crosses a number of small bridges and requires a few short ferry hops. The beach is not spectacular, nor set up for fun and frolic, but instead it's a place where Vietnamese families come to picnic—and that's the main allure. Taking a holiday alongside locals, you'll likely be dragged into a group for a good barbecue and cup after cup of rice whiskey (careful if you've driven yourself here). Heading south of Saigon, you'll first reach the Nha Be area, a wide, wet plain, followed by two ferry crossings. Next, it's on to the island's mangrove forest area and beach—*beach* being almost a euphemism for these low mudflats and hard sandy shores, but good for a long walk and to clear Saigon's pollution (and the honking traffic) out of your lungs and mind. You can get a bite at one of the local seafood shacks and enjoy a long, lazy repast before heading back to the big city.

Cao Dai Holy See Temple ★★ The Cao Dai religion is less than 100 years old and is a broad, inclusive faith that sprang from Buddhist origins to embrace Jesus, Mohammed, and other nontraditional, latter-day saints such as Louis Pasteur, Martin Luther King, and Victor Hugo. Practitioners of Cao Daism are pacifists, pray four times daily, and follow a vegetarian diet for 10 days out of every month. Cao Daism is practiced by only a small percentage of Vietnamese people, mostly in the south, but you'll see temples scattered far and wide—easily recognizable by the "all-seeing eye," which, oddly enough, looks something like the eye on the U.S. dollar. Often included with trips to the **Cu Chi Tunnels** (below), the temple at Tay Ninh is the spiritual center—the Cao Dai Vatican, if you will—and the country's largest. Visitors are welcome at any of the four daily ceremonies, but all are asked to wear trousers covering the knee, remove their shoes before entering, and act politely, quietly observing the ceremony from the balcony area. The temple interior is colorful, with bright murals and carved pillars. Cao Dai supplicants wear either white suits of clothing or colorful robes, each color denoting what root of Cao Daism they practice: Buddhist, Muslim, Christian, or Taoist.

On the way from Saigon to the Cao Dai Temple you'll pass through the town of **Trang Bang,** site of the famous photo of 9-year-old Kim Phuc who was burned by napalm and whose story is told in the popular book *The Girl in the Photo.*

The road also passes **Nui Ba Den,** the Black Virgin Mountain, which is just 11km (6¾ miles) northeast of Tay Ninh (100km/62 miles from Saigon). The story goes that a young girl was forced to marry a wealthy mandarin but, rather than do so, fell to her death from the peak. The mountain is dotted with small temples. Most tours just drive by, as your guide recounts a bit of the history. Ba Den also marks the end of the Ho Chi Minh Trial as the supply line descended from the north to reinforce the North Vietnamese guerillas, including the people of Cu Chi (see below). Despite relentless fighting throughout the war, U.S. forces were never able to clear North Vietnamese from the area.

Cu Chi Tunnels ★★ The Cu Chi Tunnels are definitely worth the day trip out of Saigon. Vietnamese are proud of their resolve in their prolonged history of struggle against invading armies, and the story of the people of Cu Chi is indicative of that spirit. Just 65km (40 miles) northwest of Saigon, the Cu Chi area lies at the end of the Ho Chi Minh Trail and was the base from which Ho Chi Minh guerillas used to attack Saigon. As a result, the whole area became a "free-fire zone" and was carpet-bombed in one of many American "scorched-earth" policies. But the residents of Cu Chi took their war underground, literally, developing a network of tunnels that, at its height, stretched as far as Cambodia and included meeting rooms, kitchens, and triage areas—an effective network for waging guerilla warfare on nearby U.S. troops. The U.S. Army's 25th Infantry Division was just next door, and there are detailed maps denoting land that was either U.S. held, Vietminh held, or in dispute.

Visitors first watch a war-era propaganda film that's so over-the-top it's fun. The sight supports a small museum of photos and artifacts, as well as an extensive outdoor exhibit of guerilla snares and reconstructions of the original tunnels and bunkers. Wear your "play clothes" if you choose to get down in the temples; the experience is dirty and claustrophobic. There is also a shooting range where, for $1 per bullet, you can try your hand at firing anything from a shotgun to an AK-47. At the end of the tour, visit the dining hall and try the steamed tapioca that was a Cu Chi staple. Souvenir hawkers abound. A half-day trip can be arranged with any tour company in Saigon, often including a visit to the Cao Dai Temple (above).

65km (40 miles) northwest of Saigon. ✆ **08/3794-6442.** Admission 70,000 VND. Daily 7am–5pm.

GOLF

There are two excellent 18-hole golf courses at the **Vietnam Golf and Country Club.** Fees are $90 during the week for nonmembers, and $120 on Saturday and Sunday. The clubhouse is at Long Thanh My Ward, District 9 (✆ **08/3280-0124;** fax 08/3280-0127; www.vietnamgolfcc.com).

Along with its two internationally accredited 18-hole courses, the Vietnam Golf and Country Club offers extensive pro services, a driving range, locker facilities, a pro shop, a swimming pool, and tennis courts. The first course was built in 1994, and the second in 1997 was designed by Lee Trevino. Just 20km (12 miles) from Saigon, the club is open to nonmembers. Reservations are required.

SPA & MASSAGE

Most of the major hotels listed have extensive spa and massage facilities, and Saigon now plays host to lots of little storefront spas. Busy Dong Khoi Street is lined with affordable foot-massage shops and manicurists; young ladies in traditional *ao dai* dress stand out front and pass out flyers. Back-alley places in the same area might offer more services than you want, but the foot-massage spots are okay and a bargain. Prices start from $10 for a bone-crunching massage. **L'Apothiquaire** (63 Le Thanh Ton St.; ✆ **08/3822-1218**) is just north of the Dong Khoi area, adjacent to City Hall, and offers a long roster of affordable pampering, from facials and scrubs to massage and manicures. Open daily 9:30am to 8pm. Call for an appointment.

Anam QT Spa (26–28 Dong Du St., District 1, near Dong Khoi; ✆ **08/3823-0242**) is sponsored by Clinique and does it all—you can get facials, manicures, waxing, body treatments, and massages ($30 for a 1-hr. oil massage). Open daily 10am to 10:30pm.

Jasmine (20 Thi Sach, District 1; ✆ **08/3827-2737**) is more like a deluxe salon than a spa, and it's especially popular with expatriate ladies. Open daily 9am to 8pm.

5 SHOPPING

Saigon has a good selection of silk, fashion, lacquer, embroidery, and housewares. Prices are higher than elsewhere, but the selection is more sophisticated, and Saigon's cosmopolitan atmosphere makes it somewhat easier to shop, meaning that shop owners, especially in more upscale boutiques, aren't immediately pushing you to buy. Stores are open 7 days a week from 8am until about 7pm. Credit cards are widely accepted (often with a charge of 3%–5%), except at local markets and streetside places.

Dong Khoi is Saigon's premier shopping street. Formerly Rue Catinat, it was a veritable Rue de la Paix in colonial times. The best blocks are the last two heading toward the river, but the whole area is loaded with shopping opportunities. With the glut of Japanese tourists, there are lots of Japanese *Zakka* shops with cute—though overpriced—jewelry, accessories, and shoes. You'll also find little watch shops, repair shops, and old camera vendors (the street adjacent to Dong Khoi, Nguyen Hue, is lined with camera shops). Good silk tailors abound. Below is just a short selection of the many choices. Explore.

SHOPPING A TO Z

Art Galleries

In addition to the galleries reviewed below, a few other popular galleries in town include the **Apricot Gallery,** 50–52 Mac Thi Buoi St., District 1, near Saigon Sakura Restaurant (✆ **08/3822-7962**); and **Particular Art Gallery,** 123 Le Loi St., District 1 (✆ **08/3821-3019**).

If these galleries pique your curiosity about contemporary Vietnamese art, pick up a copy of ***Vietnam Discovery*** or ***The Guide,*** two local happenings guides, for further listings and special shows.

Galerie Lotus Stop by this large upstairs gallery space, and the friendly staff can arrange reproductions and commission work. They also have the standard Vietnamese copies lining the walls. Open daily 8am to 9pm. Accepts MasterCard and Visa. 67 Pasteur St. ✆ **08/3829-2695.** www.lotusgallery.com.

The Ho Chi Minh Fine Arts Museum If you're truly keen on learning about "the scene" in Ho Chi Minh, this is the place to start. Three floors house an evolving modern collection, featuring new and established Vietnamese artists' works in sculpture, oil, and lacquer, as well as a nice collection of ancient Buddhist artwork and some Cham statuary. The museum offers a good glimpse into the local scene. From there, have a look at Lac Hong Art Gallery, located on the ground floor of the museum (© **08/3821-3771**), which features the works of many famous Vietnamese artists. There are galleries throughout the city, many clustered around Dong Khoi and near all the major hotels. Here you can get some great deals on reproductions of popular works (reproduction being a big industry in town), and those with deep pockets will find easy introductions to the artists or their representatives themselves. For a price, you can turn any photo into an enormous oil painting. Open Tuesday to Sunday from 9am to 5pm (closed Mon). 97A Pho Duc Chinh St., District 1. © **08/3829-4441.** Admission 10,000 VND.

Bookstores

The city's official foreign-language bookstore, **Xuan Thu,** is at 185 Dong Khoi St., across from the Continental Hotel (© **08/3822-4670**). It carries a limited selection of classics in English and French (mostly geared to Vietnamese readers), as well as some foreign-language newspapers, good regional maps, and locally published volumes for foreign students of Vietnamese. Daily 8am to 10pm.

Best are the many small bookshops on De Tham Street in the backpacker area of town. Here you'll find little hole-in-the-wall shops carrying many pirate titles and used books. Some of these places do swaps, but you're certain to come away frustrated. Just come ready to spend a few bucks, and instead of trading that old novel, pass it on to a fellow traveler.

Elsewhere in the city—pretty much anywhere tourists herd and congregate, really—you are sure to run into young booksellers or pass many streetside kiosks with the same collection of good books about Vietnam, from guidebooks to some of the more popular nonfiction writing about the Vietnam War years, as well as the current popular novels and backpacking classics, all photocopied at one of Vietnam's many reproduction factories and quite cheap (usually $2–$5).

Camera Shops

Good camera stores, the likes of **Thien Ngan** (46 Nguyen Hue St.; © **08/3822-0327;** daily 8am–10pm; MasterCard and Visa accepted), line busy Nguyen Hue Street (just parallel to Dong Khoi) and can print and develop as well as fix or replace most amateur equipment. You'll also find lots of good deals on used 35mm equipment—but be warned that much of it has been reconditioned and comes with no guarantee.

Clothing & Accessories

Gaya ★★ This store carries a beautiful selection of clothing, home decor, and furniture from one local Vietnamese and four expat designers. Everything is of serious quality. The linens are from Catherine Denoual (see below), so expect a beautiful collection. Clothing is by Cambodian-born, France-raised Romyda Keth. The dresses are beautifully cut and are often multicolored and touched with embroidery or a bit of sparkle. It can look like too much on the hanger, but more often than not looks smart and sophisticated once you put it on. The quality of material and cuts are amazing, and the staff has an excellent eye for fit. Open daily 9am to 9pm. 1 Nguyen Van Trang St., District 1 (at the corner of Le Lai St.). © **08/3925-1495.**

Ipa Nima The place to get funky, original handbags decked out in tassles, patterns, and busy prints. Their Saigon stores are not as large and expansive as their flagship in

Hanoi (p. 118), but there is still a great selection on offer. Open daily 9am to 9pm. 85 Pasteur St.: ✆ **08/3824-2701.** 1/F New World Hotel, 76 Le Lai St.: ✆ **08/3824-3652.**

La Bella Come here for a fine collection of silk, jersey, and cotton separates and dresses, as well as silk sleep and loungewear. Some designs are simple, like long, Roman-style jersey dresses, and others are eccentric, like silk wraparound halters and sequined skirts. Open daily 9am to 9pm. 85–87 Pasteur St. ✆ **08/3823-0172.**

Mi Indochine ★ This store has original, contemporary clothes that look like a cross between high-street Vietnamese fashion and Roberto Cavalli. The fabrics and cuts are of excellent quality, with prices to match. Open daily 9am to 9pm. 132–134 Dong Khoi St. ✆ **08/3827-2733.**

Daily Goods

Annam A fine selection of imported goods, with Italian and French wines, as well as European chocolates and other comfort foods. Open Monday to Saturday from 8am to 9pm, and Sunday from 9am to 8pm. 16–18 Hai Ba Trung, District 1. ✆ **08/3822-9332.**

Bacchus Corner Expat communities bring their luxury tastes with them, and this stylish storefront carries hundreds of fine vintages for the discerning, including an amazing selection of imported wines. Open Monday to Saturday from 8am to 9pm, and Sunday from 11am to 3pm. 158D Pasteur St., District 1. ✆ **08/3829-3306.** www.tankhoa.com.

Veggy's This cool little grocery caters to the most finicky expat from any country. Find fresh daikon along with expensive, imported condiments and staples from Japan; fresh cheeses, even yogurt, and wine for Westerners; and good fresh vegetables and special cuts of meat brought in fresh—not frozen—from Australia and New Zealand. It's all in a big walk-in freezer that clients are welcome to peruse. (The owners of this place also have a similar shop in Phnom Penh, Cambodia.) Open daily 7am to 9pm. 15 Thai Van Lung St., District 1. ✆ **08/3823-8526.**

Department Stores & Outlets

There are a number of newer department stores and budget outlets for fashion and footwear. Try the following:

Diamond Department Store The hulking Diamond offers an array of familiar luxury items, from appliances to fashion. More or less a museum to Western luxury for most cash-strapped Vietnamese, Diamond is a good place to pick up any essential from home that you might have forgotten. The top floor of Diamond has a large entertainment area with video games, a bowling alley, and a movie theater that often runs popular Western features (though only sometimes in English with subtitles, so be sure to check ahead). This is a good place to bring the kids for a dose of quarter-plunking, mind-numbing entertainment when tired of touring the busy city. Open daily 10am to 9:30 pm. Major credit cards accepted. In the Diamond Plaza just north of Notre Dame Cathedral, at 34 Le Duan St. ✆ **08/3822-5500.**

Saigon Square (Finds) Come here for cheap local and Chinese-imported copies of designer sportswear, anything from the latest temples for your toes to winter coats. The quality is, well, fake, but the price is right and the stuff is good and rugged. It's not a bad place to stock up on travel items or on things you'll need heading home in wintertime. The massive Saigon Square complex also houses all manner of small budget fashion boutiques, jewelry sellers, and accessories vendors (a good place to pick up copies of the latest Prada or Burberry bag). Open daily 9am to 9pm. Just east of the central post office and Notre Dame Cathedral, at the intersection of Le Duan and Hai Ba Trung.

Handicrafts, Gifts & Souvenirs

Note: Unless otherwise stated, most stores listed below open daily at 9am and close around 9pm, but regular hours aren't always (or often) followed. Be prepared for somewhat random opening and closing times, based on the whims of storekeepers.

Alphana Jewelry Gold, silver, and precious stones for all budgets. Open daily 9:30am to 7pm. Accepts MasterCard and Visa. 159 Dong Khoi St., District 1. ✆ **08/3829-7398.**

Authentique Interiors This outlet is just across from the Majestic Hotel, at the terminus of Dong Khoi Street at riverside. The place is two floors of warehouse-style shopping, with every tchotchke you could imagine. On the first floor, find unique table settings that are decidedly modern, but made from local materials and with a Vietnamese/Chinese flair. Upstairs are lots of little bins with trinkets, as well as furnishing and gifts. Prices are marked, but they offer discounts if you buy in bulk (and this might be a good place to pick up a handful of small gifts for family and friends back home). 38 Dong Khoi. ✆ **08/3822-133.**

Catherine Denoual–Maison ★ This store has exclusive linen and silk cotton blends in elegant neutral tones of white and cream. Bedding, cushions, and runners are designed with tasteful embroidery, and everything has a luxuriously high thread count. Open daily 9am to 8pm. 15C Thi Sach St. ✆ **08/3823-9394.**

Dong Duong (Comtoir De L'Indochine) Soapstone carvings and fine statuary. Open daily 9am to 9pm. 45 Dong Khoi St., District 1. ✆ **08/3827-3748.**

Les Epices A chic little air-conditioned storefront, Les Epices has a nice collection of lacquerware, as well as wooden boxes, gift items, and souvenirs. 25 Dong Khoi St. ✆ **08/3823-6795.**

MC Decoration Unique, tasteful, hand-embroidered pillows, table linens, and handwoven fabrics, as well as fine furnishings, can be found at this stylish outlet. 92C5 Le Thanh Ton, across from the Norfolk Hotel. ✆ **08/3822-6003.**

Red Door Deco Large, contemporary copies of classic Asian-theme furnishings, colonial and Chinese motifs, as well as fine modern pieces. Open daily 8am to 8pm. 31A Le Thanh Ton, District 1. ✆ **08/3825-8672.**

Saigon Crafts Lacquer crafts and gifts. Open daily 8:30am to 9:30pm. Accepts MasterCard and Visa. 74 Dong Khoi St., District 1. ✆ **08/3829-5758.** www.saigoncrafts.com.

Sapa Crafts and fashions from northern Vietnam near the China border. They have a groovy little outlet in the Pham Ngu Lao backpacker area. Open daily 7am to 10pm. 223 De Tham. ✆ **08/3836-5163.**

Tombo The best of Ho Chi Minh City's many Japanese Zakka shops. What is a Zakka shop? More or less a collection of lady's accouterments, from shoes and wraps to earrings and fine jewelry, the kind of stuff Dad brings home to Mom after a long business trip. This is one of Ho Chi Minh City's most popular—with everything short of Hello Kitty in the mix. Open daily 8:30am to 9pm. Accepts MasterCard and Visa. 145 Dong Khoi St., District 1. ✆ **08/3827-5973.**

Silk

Hoang Silk Tailor Lien can make you a lovely *ao dai* or a silk separate according to your style and design in 24 hours. If the fit comes out wrong or is off, she is excellent at tweaking and working with you until it comes out right. Open daily 8:30am to 9pm. 201 Dong Khoi St. ✆ **08/3825-6629.**

Kenly Silk A brand-name supplier with some of the best ready-to-wear silk garments in the town. Open daily 9am to 8pm. 132 Le Thanh Ton. ✆ **08/3829-3847.**

Khai Silk With outlets throughout the country, Khai Silk is one of the best places for ready-made and tailored silk in Vietnam. The signature store is right downtown at 107 Dong Khoi St., but they have shops throughout the city in some of the finer hotels. Good business sense says, "If something works, then copy it," so there are lots of Khai Silk look-alikes, but Khai is the best. Open daily 9am to 10pm. Main shop: 107 Dong Khoi St. ✆ **08/3829-1146.** www.khaisilkcorp.com. (Smaller shops are also at 38 Dong Khoi St., the Legend Hotel, the New World Hotel, and the Sheraton Saigon Hotel and Tower.)

6 SAIGON AFTER DARK

When Vietnam entered the world scene in the mid-1990s, Ho Chi Minh City quickly became one of the hippest party towns in the East. The mood has sobered somewhat, but it's still fun. Everything is clustered in District 1; ask expats in places like **Saigon Saigon** or **Level 23** about underground club happenings. All bars open in the evening and usually keep running not until last call, but until last customer. As for cultural events, Saigon is sadly devoid of anything really terrific, except for a few dinner and dance shows.

For a nonbar experience, **Bonsai Cruise** (3/F, 101 Nguyen Van Thu St., District 1; ✆ **08/3910-5095;** www.bonsaicruise.com.vn) operates dinner cruises on the Saigon River for $21 to $28. A local boat also runs a 2-hour cruise for an unbeatable price of $2. Boats depart from a pier just south of the Renaissance Riverside hotel.

BARS & CLUBS

The Pham Ngu Lao area stays up late, and there are a number of good watering holes that cater to young travelers. On De Tham Street, about 100m (328 ft.) off Pham Ngu Lao, you'll find a host of little cafes, restaurants, and bars. For a club or chilled lounge vibe, stick to the streets around the Opera House. Also see the box "Saigon Nights: *Bia Hoi* on the Sidewalk Stools," below.

Allez Boo Now a part of the Liberty 3 Hotel, Allez Boo is a popular hangout for young travelers. Set up like a little bamboo beachfront bar draped with icicle lighting, the place has seen an upgrade in recent years, and the outdoor seating area on either side of this corner bar is always full of fellow wanderers (you're sure to see a familiar face if you've taken any tours or traveled on the cafe buses). 187 Pham Ngu Lao. ✆ **08/3837-2505.**

Amber Room ★ This funky lounge is the new "it" place of Saigon. It's got a slick New York–bar feel to it, with dark wood, overstuffed sofas, and fine cocktails. By day, the music and atmosphere is relaxed and loungelike. The tunes are funkier come nightfall, but the mellow vibe remains. 59 Dong Du St., opposite the Sheraton. ✆ **08/6291-3686.**

Cafe Latin Hope you weren't expecting Latin dancing. This place is a sports bar through and through, with big TVs on hand to show the latest football matches and other international sporting events. 19–21 Dong Du St. ✆ **08/3822-6363.**

Cage A hip place that draws a steady crowd with chill vibes and Art Deco style. Weekends are popular for the regular rotation of international DJs pumping out dance tunes well into the night. 3A Ton Duc Thang (in the alley next to Legend Hotel), District 1. ✆ **09/0510-5854.**

Go² Bar ★ This bar is in the backpacker district, but you'll find everyone from backpackers to businessmen in this place. It's one of the only places serving alcohol 24 hours a day (nearby Allez Boo, above, being the other one). The terrace spills onto the street, and the party regularly rocks on until 4 or 6am. 187 De Tham St., District 1. ✆ **08/3836-9575.**

Level 23 Level 23 is a rotunda with two-story-high ceilings overlooking town that hosts an all-out disco scene on the weekends. They feature good live bands. Imagine Indochina meets the Hard Rock Cafe. The bar is pretty dead on weeknights, so opt instead for the outdoor patio, a great place to have a chat over late-night drinks. 88 Dong Khoi St. (23rd floor of the Sheraton Hotel). ✆ **08/3827-2828.**

O'Briens If it's good drinkin' and darts you be wantin', you come to the right place. This brick-walled Irish pub always packs 'em in, and if you don't know anybody when you walk in, you're sure to know somebody by the time you walk out. Also serves some great pizza. 74A Hai Ba Trung. ✆ **08/3829-3198.**

163 Cyclo Bar Just down the street from Allez Boo (see above) is this busy bar. It rocks from 4pm until late, usually to 4 or 5am. The scene is a little seedy sometimes; hang on to your valuables (or leave them in a hotel safe). 163 Pham Ngu Lao St. ✆ **08/3920-1567**).

Pacharan ★ This is a happening place in a perfect location beside the Caravelle and across the street from Park Hyatt. A flatscreen TV is tuned into sports on the first floor, live bands are often playing on the second floor, and the outdoor terrace is on the top floor. A great place to grab a beer, some Spanish wine, or (my personal favorite) a pitcher of sangria. The Spanish tapas here make for good nibbles, but check your bill before leaving, lest you be paying for baskets of bread and aioli dipping sauce that—though tasty—you didn't even order! 97 Hai Ba Trung, District 1. ✆ **08/3825-6024.**

Q Bar Set in the cool, labyrinthine basement of the central opera house is the town's hippest club. This funky catacomb has good music, cozy private nooks, and an eclectic mix of people. Bartenders aren't very good, though; if you want a proper cocktail, you're better off at Xu (see below). 7 Cong Truong Lam Son. ✆ **08/3823-3479.** www.qsaigon.com.

Saigon Saigon On the top floor of the old wing of the Caravelle Hotel, this very popular spot features live music (usually a Filipino cover band) and a terrific view from the balcony seating area. This is undoubtedly the most classic of Saigon experiences (journalists hung out here during the Vietnam War), with great views through heavy wooden shades and under slow-turning ceiling fans of Lam Son Square and the Opera House. Open daily 11am to late. 19 Lam Son. ✆ **08/3823-4999.**

Sheridan's Something like O'Briens, above, Sheridan's is a good, friendly local watering hole—Irish style. 17/13 Le Thanh Ton St. ✆ **08/3823-0793.**

Vasco's Bar This chic, open-air bar twinkles with Christmas lights and the town's elite. It's especially popular with the French crowd. Friday nights really hop. Open daily 5:30pm to midnight (later on Fri nights). 74/7D Hai Ba Trung, District 1. ✆ **08/3824-2888.**

Xu ★ This is a groovy place with big comfy couches and urban lounge tunes playing in the background. It's not so loud that you have to yell, and not so slow that you fall asleep. The cocktails are excellent—the coconut martini is near-addictive. This is the perfect evening lounge spot in the hotel district. Open daily 11am to midnight. 171–175

Finds Saigon Nights: *Bia Hoi* on the Sidewalk Stools

The best local nightlife is out on the street at the city's many *bia hoi* stands. In the Dong Khoi area, look for Saigon Bia Hoi on the first floor of a large brewery on Hai Ba Trung, near its terminus at riverside.

Best, and a much more interesting option than rubbing elbows with fellow travelers in Saigon's backpacker district, is to take a walk just around the corner from the bars on Pham Ngu Lao (away from De Tham) and along Nguyen Thai Hoc Street to its many streetside beer stalls. Vietnamese customers pull up on a motorbike, grab a stool and a table, and settle in for an evening of beers by the pitcher. You pay just pennies a glass and will likely meet some local folks. Sellers come around with trays of peanuts, robin's eggs, and fish sausages wrapped in banana leaves (the fish sausages are not recommended). All of these stalls will dust off an English-language menu, if you ask. The food is good and just about free (1,500 VND per glass).

Note: If a table is too close to the street, vendors are often harassed by police. Part of the show is watching the owners offer a bribe or make their guests lift up their tables and chairs, moving closer to the shop when the police arrive, only to move back when they leave.

Hai Ba Trung, District 1 (walk into the alleyway for about 150m/492 ft., then up the stairs on your right). ✆ **08/3824-8468.**

MUSIC & THEATER

A few hotels stage traditional music and dance shows at dinner theaters. The **Rex Hotel** (141 Nguyen Hue Blvd.; ✆ **08/3829-2185**) has regular performances as well. Call ahead of time to check the performance schedule.

7 SIDE TRIPS FROM HO CHI MINH CITY

A SIDE TRIP TO VUNG TAU

130km (81 miles) SE of Ho Chi Minh City

Just a hop, skip, and a boat ride from Ho Chi Minh City, Vung Tau is a popular playground for Saigon's expatriate community. It is sort of a low-luxe version of the usual beach resort, popular mostly for its convenience to the city. You wouldn't fly around the world to get there, but if you have an extra day or so in Ho Chi Minh and want some beach time, Vung Tau is a good choice, short of going to the more picturesque Mui Ne Beaches (about 3 hr. by car) or on to Nha Trang.

Originally called Cape Saint Jacques by French colonists who once vacationed and sailed out of here, the small peninsula and town area today is just a port, but more and more vacation villas are popping up in the beachside hills in the surrounding area. The better hotels in Vung Tau City proper are geared to serving European and regional petrochemical workers—offshore oil and gas deposits are mined, shipped to offshore refineries, and then reimported for domestic use. The town also has a thriving hostess-bar scene catering to the same set; in fact, the area is notorious for sex tourists. But there are a few fine beach developments just a short ride from the city, and you'll find good, fresh seafood here.

For some reason, the town has inspired builders of oversize sculpture. Look out for the giant statue of Jesus, a smaller version of the statue in Rio De Janeiro, and to the north of town, a grand Madonna and Child, plus a big Buddha on a lotus leaf. A sizable Christian population accounts for the Christian statuary, as well as the town's large central cathedral.

Essentials

GETTING THERE & AWAY Boat connection is your best option. The 1½-hour trip costs just $10, payable in U.S. dollars or Vietnamese dong (150,000 VND). With two companies sending out boats, there are hourly departures to or from Vung Tau. Boats are rarely full, but departures can be crowded on weekends, so buy a ticket in advance if leaving Saigon on Friday evening or returning from Vung Tau on Sunday; otherwise, you can just show up and see which company has the next departure. Contact **Vina Express** at their riverside ticketing booth, either at the dock area or across the street from the launch at 2 Ton Duc Thang St. (✆ **08/3829-7892**). They have departures starting in the morning at 6am (then at 8:30am, 10:30pm, 12:30pm, 2:30pm, and 4:40pm). Competitor **Petro Express** (20 Truong Cong Dinh St., in Vung Tau; ✆ **064/353-0775**) sells tickets at dockside. The high-speed, Soviet-built boats hydroplane across the surface. Tracing the Saigon River, you get a good look at the boom in import/export traffic from the country's largest port area. The ride is smooth until the mouth of the river, where the boat crosses a short stretch of open sea and bounces around a bit. There's a bathroom on board, and attendants provide complimentary water. Connecting by road from Ho Chi Minh is also a quick and easy trip, just 1½ hours by rented car or minivan. Local buses leave Ho Chi Minh's **Mien Dong Station** in District 3 and take about 2 hours to reach Vung Tau.

ORIENTATION The city of Vung Tau is spread out over the wide peninsular area ending to the south with hills and the town's large statue of Jesus. Distances across town are a bit far to traverse on foot, so it is a good idea to rent some wheels: bicycle, motorbike, or car. The west side of the peninsula is called **Front Beach;** the east is **Back Beach.** Hotels line the busy western port area. The large statue of Tran Hung Dao, at the terminus of the road by the same name, is a good orientation point—many restaurants and services surround this central square, and the road that originates here extends north through town. Tran Phu Street runs along the west side of the peninsula and leads to the town's good seafood restaurants and a few sights.

GETTING AROUND You'll be swamped by taxi drivers when you pull in at the port. Just get it over with and pick somebody. Metered taxis—the best is **Mai Linh taxi** (✆ **064/356-5656**)—are available all over town. Motorbikes are for rent right at the pier for 80,000 VND, and motorbike taxi drivers and cyclos are available at negotiable rates (about $1 per hour or 5,000 VND–10,000 VND for short trips in town).

FAST FACTS **Vietcombank** has a branch at 27 Tran Hung Dao St. (✆ **064/385-2309**) with ATM service and can exchange currency or traveler's checks (daily 8am–4pm, with a break for lunch). Internet connections are available in a few storefronts along central Tran Hung Dao Street. Try **Tom Tin Internet,** at 22 Tran Hund Dao (✆ **064/352-5857**), which charges 4,000 VND per hour.

Where to Stay

A few budget choices are along the western Front Beach. **Thuy Tien** is just across from the beach and adjacent to the large Madonna (84 Tran Phu St.; ✆ **064/3835-220**); they have clean, very spartan rooms in a three-story hotel block for 300,000 VND per night.

Palace Hotel The most popular and busiest of the affordable central lodgings for the town's petrochemical workers (you might feel out of place without a helmet and oily jumpsuit), the Palace has a good array of services and makes for a quick and convenient overnight in Vung Tau (quite close to the ferry pier and the town's expatriate area). It's nothing special, with large, basic, tidy rooms, something like an average U.S. motel. But there are lots of good in-house services, including a large, open pool area, a good restaurant overlooking a funky little fountain area, a big bar area, and massage services. The staff is used to international clients, and service is quite efficient for the price. The **Grand Hotel** (2 Nguyen Hue St., Vung Tau; ✆ **064/385-6888;** fax 064/385-6088; www.grand.oscvn.com) is just next door, a slightly more polished standard, with rooms from $69, and the two hotels are in negotiation to combine as one: "The Grand Palace," perhaps?

01 Nguyen Trai St., Vung Tau City. ✆ **064/385-6411.** Fax 064/385-6878. www.palace.oscvn.com. 94 units. $88–$110 double; $130 suite. MC, V. **Amenities:** Restaurant; bar; small fitness center; Internet; outdoor pool; tennis court. *In room:* A/C, satellite TV, fridge, Internet, minibar.

Paradise Resort ★ The name is pushing it, but for work-weary residents of Saigon, or tourists looking for a quick escape from steamy city touring, Paradise is something special. And who thought paradise could be just an hour and a half by boat plus a 10-minute ride on the back of a motorbike away? This resort is a collection of free-standing beachside bungalows surrounding a small central pool. Half of the units are older with rough-hewn balconies and exteriors of bamboo and wood sheathing; newer units have a stucco exterior. Both are air-conditioned and tidy, if lacking in style; shiny bedspreads and tacky drapes are kind of a shame, as is the fact that they're a bit dark. But everything is clean, they have a good little restaurant, and the resort is adjacent to the town's popular golf course (under the same ownership). The central area has fun, white-plaster Greek statues of scantily clad goddesses and a large lion presiding over the whole scene. You'll need to bring your own wheels or call cabs, but it's only 4km (2½ miles) back to Vung Tau, and you won't likely need to get there much.

On the far north end of Back Beach (in-town sales office: 01 Thy Van, Vung Tau City). ✆ **064/381-1559.** Fax 064/358-5894. 98 units. $45–$65 double. No credit cards. **Amenities:** Restaurant; bar; golf course; outdoor pool. *In room:* A/C, satellite TV, fridge, minibar.

Petro House ★ A grand circular drive and a boutique, colonial lobby greet you at busy Petro House, a popular choice of European expat workers, many on long stay with the petrochemical companies that operate in Vung Tau. Rooms are large and very clean, if a bit sparsely decorated and not quite the match of the hotel's stylish public spaces, but the mattresses are comfy, and the larger suites are great (ask for one with fine terra-cotta tile instead of the thin carpeting). Hotel staff does all they can to support their guests, even dig up information and contact support for projects. A "can-do" attitude prevails. Their La Maison restaurant serves good Continental cuisine. The courtyard pool is small but cozy, and the bar is always busy, a good place to grab a game of pool and get the lowdown on the local scene. The Petro House also has fine service apartments.

63–65 Tran Hung Dao St., Vung Tau. ✆ **064/385-2014.** Fax 064/385-2015. www.viehotel.com/petrohousehotel. 71 units. $55–$65 double; $70–$100 suite. MC, V. **Amenities:** 2 restaurants; bar; fitness center; small courtyard pool. *In room:* A/C, satellite TV, fridge, minibar, Wi-Fi.

Where to Dine

In addition to the two recommended venues below, consider **La Maison,** at the Petro House Hotel (63–65 Tran Hung Dao St., Vung Tau; ✆ **064/385-2014**), which serves fine French; or, near the pier, **Summer Wine and Mermaid,** at 20 Quang Trung St., for reputedly the best steak in town in a surprisingly posh setting.

Nightlife in little Vung Tau is pretty seedy. The places with English signs surrounding the central Tran Phu Square are hostess bars that do a brisk business with Vung Tau's many sailors in port.

Ganh Hao VIETNAMESE/SEAFOOD Serving delicious, fresh seafood from a cool oceanside promontory, Ganh Hao is the best place to dine in Vung Tau (next-door Bamboo is nearly identical, but locals tout this one as the best). Choices here include lobster with butter or tamarind, fried soft-shell crabs, crabs steamed with beer, jumbo shrimp dishes, oyster, and squid, as well as great whole-fish dishes such as goby, snake-head fish, sea bass, or red tilapia. I enjoyed a delicious "Ganh Hao Fish Salad" of whitefish lightly sautéed in butter with onions and peanuts, wrapped in a rice paper roll with coriander, basil leaves, and lettuce, and is dipped in sweet or fishy sauce. Absolutely delicious, and the view of the ocean from the terrace makes for a pleasant afternoon or evening. If it's too windy, try the large, two-story restaurant section. Take a taxi here; it's about 4km (2½ miles) up Tran Phu Street along Front Beach.

03 Tran Phu St., Vung Tau. ✆ **064/355-0909.** Main courses 30,000 VND–75,000 VND; luxe seafood can run up to 500,000 VND. No credit cards. Daily 9am–10pm.

Good Morning Vietnam ITALIAN This unoriginal chain of eateries can be found in almost all of the tourist spots in Vietnam, but each one's individually owned and managed. This is a good one, with an effusive Italian owner who hosts lots of international business clients looking for a taste of the familiar. Portions are large, ingredients are fresh, and the pizza is tops.

6 Hoang Hoa Tham St., Vung Tau. ✆ **064/385-6959.** Main courses 65,000 VND–190,000 VND. No credit cards. Daily 9am–10pm.

Attractions & Activities

Thic Ca Phat Dai is the name of the temple and large statue of the Buddha that stands high over the seaside about 5km (3 miles) north along Tran Phu Street at Front Beach. Buy a pack of incense at the bottom of the hill from the kids who will swarm you (just 2,000 VND) and climb the hill, first to the small temple, and then on up the steps to the large open area with the big Buddha overlooking the port below (burn your incense sticks here), as well as other statuary and little pavilions. One gazebo has inscriptions from the Buddhist precepts—in transliterated Pali, Vietnamese, and English—about the delights of passionless meditation, cultivating good in oneself, the impermanence of the body, and the belief that viewing the world as a fragile bubble, a mirage, fends off fear of death. Heady stuff. The Theravadan monks in vermilion don't speak much English but are welcoming and carefully guide you to the alms box. Just before reaching the big Buddha, meet the giant Madonna standing over another stretch of beach. Both sights are free, but with plenty of suggested donation boxes, and are open from dawn to dusk.

If you're interested in golf, check out the **Paradise Resort** (on the far north end of Back Beach; see "Where to Stay," above), which hosts the popular beachside **Paradise Ocean Noon Golf Club,** a recently renovated course of 27 holes with a small dining area, club rentals, and a pro shop. Contact the clubhouse directly at ✆ **062/382-3366.**

A SIDE TRIP TO LANG HAI

120km (75 miles) SE of Ho Chi Minh City; 40km (25 miles) NE of Vung Tau

Just a short trip north along the coast from Vung Tau—or a direct drive south (crossing some ferry points) from Saigon—Lang Hai is a secluded getaway along a very dynamic piece of coastline. The fancy Lang Hai Beach Resort just opened here, and it might eventually rival the area's most comfortable getaway, Anoasis Resort. There are some day hikes and nearby temples, but Lang Hai is more or less a quiet beach getaway (unless, bless you, you're there on a convention). The nearby town is a Fellini-esque barren place, but the many kids flying massive kites of sharks and dragons make it a sight (and *really* Fellini-esque).

Getting There

From Vung Tau, it's a 24km (15-mile) ride north to Baria, where you make a right (no sign) and follow the road to Lang Hai (there will be signs with mile markers on the road). The total trip is about 45km (28 miles). From Saigon, it is 120km (75 miles; follow signs at the same turnoff in Baria).

Where to Stay

Anoasis Resort ★★ This cozy resort has long been a hush-hush favorite of Saigon's expatriates. In an area where the last emperor, Bao Dai, once came to play, Anoasis Resort is run by a French expatriate and his wife, a helicopter pilot of local fame. It plays host to many meeting and incentive groups, as well as small, relaxed conventions, and it can get pretty busy on the weekends with folks fleeing the city heat. Whether in their large pavilion rooms or a smaller bungalow, the accommodations are neat, characterized by double-height thatch roofs, oversize bamboo furnishings, and lots of comfortable areas to sit back and put your feet up (bathrooms are a bit small, though). The service is impeccable. The place is arranged along a hillside overlooking a picturesque bay where the wind howls and the surf rolls in, mesmerizing in the cool of a hammock at seaside. Individual units nestle nicely into little nooks in the hills with lush, overflowing flower boxes and manicured gardens ensuring privacy and the sweet smell of tropical nectar. The central pool is large and has great shaded lounges and places for the kids to frolic—even basketball hoops. They have a kids' center and can provide babysitting, and they offer a bit of pampering in a relaxed massage area in a grove of trees. The hilltop restaurant is stunning, with French and familiar Western gourmet cuisine. Attached is a residential compound for long-stay expatriates. This place is a true escape, from Saigon or the world.

Domain Ky Van, Long Hai, Vung Tau. ✆ **064/386-8227.** Fax 064/386-8229. www.anoasisresort.com.vn. 46 units. $120–$200 pavilion room/bungalow; $275–$300 villa. MC, V. **Amenities:** Restaurant; bar; small fitness pavilion; outdoor pool; tennis courts. *In room:* A/C, satellite TV, fridge, minibar, Wi-Fi.

Long Hai Beach Resort ★ Just recently opened, sprawling Long Hai Beach Resort is a slightly more luxurious companion to the popular Anoasis Resort (see above). The setup is more "classic resort," with a large, ostentatious lobby and wide walkway leading down to oceanside colonnades and a picturesque pool perched over the rocky beach. Because it's still getting on its feet, though, it has some kinks to work out, so I'd recommend Anoasis over this one for now. Public spaces are stylish, but rooms are tacky in terra-cotta tile and faux-Chinese furnishings. The large thatched-roof restaurant is quite stunning, though, and views of the pool and shore are great. Time will tell with this one.

North of Long Hai, next to Anoasis Resort along Provincial Rd. 44, Long Hai Town, Long Dien District, Vung Tau. ✆ **064/366-1355.** Fax 064/366-1356. www.longhaibeachresort.com. 110 units. $120–$280 double; $185–$230 deluxe villa. MC, V. **Amenities:** 2 restaurants; bar; bikes; children's center and playground; small fitness center; Jacuzzi; outdoor pool at beachside; room service; spa. *In room:* A/C, satellite TV, fridge, minibar.

Thuy Duong The only comfortable budget choice along the beach, Thuy Duong is an isolated, low-luxe resort complex. Some 10 years old and popular with vacationing Vietnamese, it's got a kitschy beachside vibe (lots of little cottages, playgrounds, and busy coffee shops overlooking the sea). Rooms in the hotel block are clean and nondescript, but comfortable; best go for the $45 double rooms, which are larger and have decent furnishings, offer windows with views, and are less prone to must. The pool is a postage stamp. The hotel is in Phuoc Hai, a few kilometers north of the two fine resorts at Lang Hai; it is, however, pretty self-contained, with a host of activities, including boat and jet-ski rentals, a large nightclub with karaoke, and a massage parlor. Especially popular with Vietnamese tourists.

Phuoc Hai Village, Long Dat Do District, Vung Tau Province. ✆ **064/388-6215.** Fax 064/388-6180. www.thuyduongresort.com.vn. 113 units. $45–$165 double. No credit cards. **Amenities:** 2 restaurants; bar/nightclub; small outdoor pool; tennis; watersports rentals. *In room:* A/C, satellite TV, fridge, minibar, Wi-Fi.

Attractions

The beach is the real attraction here, and you'll likely spend all of your time at your resort; there are, however, a few fun day trips. Contact the folks at the Anoasis Resort (see above) to arrange transport and tours. The **Binh Chau Hotsprings** are a long ride east along the coast, where visitors can take a plunge in hot mud or soak in a steaming bath of soothing mineral water at the Suoi Mo, or "Dream Spring," and boil an egg for a snack over the scalding water of a geothermal opening. You might also consider a visit to Lang Hai's nearby **Chua Phap Hoa** (just 4km/2½ miles inland from the resort area), an old pagoda famed for its population of clambering monkeys, or take a day-trip hike up the rocky peak of **Minh Dam,** which offers great views of the surrounding area.

A SIDE TRIP TO CON DAO ARCHIPELAGO: CON SON ISLAND

180km (97 nautical miles) SE of Vung Tau

There's an old saying on Con Son: On days when the water surrounding this remote island's rocky cliffs is windless and still, locals say that, with the shimmering reflection in the deep blue-green water, it's as if the "birds swim in the sea and the fish fly in the clouds."

Con Son, part of the larger Con Dao Archipelago (and usually referred to as Con Dao) is the kind of out-of-the-way outcrop that inspires poetry. But the loudest voices from the island come from the memory of the hundreds of thousands who suffered in the island's notorious prisons (estimates begin at about 20,000 for the number who died here). A visit to the island is a unique glimpse into the story of the Vietnamese struggles during the colonial era and during the war with America, and also a chance to travel among Vietnamese tourists, who travel to the island to pay homage to the many who suffered here. I got caught up in a weekend of revolutionary fervor, with red-flag-waving dance performances and patriotic singing and marching in the evenings out in front of the Revolutionary Museum. It was almost like walking into Sen. Joseph McCarthy's worst nightmare around 1950.

The Portuguese first landed on Con Son, which means "Pearl Island," in 1516, the French arrived in 1686, and the British even made a pit stop with one of the East India Company ships in 1702, but the French laid claim (as in poked a flag in and claimed ownership) to the island chain from 1721. Calling it the Orleans Archipelago, the French used Con Son as a reconnoitering point for trade with the British for many years, until they finally occupied Con Son in 1861, calling the main island Poulo Condore and building their first prison to house insurgents and revolutionaries, names applied to anyone who didn't like being colonized. Prison riots and revolts were many; some even successfully took over the island at one period in 1862, and the French magistrate on the island was murdered in 1919. But the sounds of clanking shackles and suffering would ring out over the desert expanses of Con Son, under both the French and the Americans, until full liberation in 1975. The United States demolished the island's open-pit cells, called tiger cages, in 1970, but accommodations on the island were never plush.

Fourteen islands comprise this remote archipelago, the largest of which, Con Son, hosts a population of less than 5,000, mostly in the small port areas on the east and south ends of the island. The other 13 islands are uninhabited but for the national park observers who stand watch on rocky outcrops. **Giant sea turtles** come in large numbers to breed on the beach of nearby Hon Bay Canh, just a few clicks offshore from the main island of Con Son. The World Wildlife Foundation has pumped lots of grant money into the protection program for Con Dao's turtles, and efforts at conservation are paying off. Also due to WWF's largesse, the large national forest area and bird breeding grounds are well managed and maintained, and the island's park office hosts a helpful museum and trekking information center where visitors can get permits and information for one of the island's short jungle treks.

Just getting here by plane is an adventure: The open cockpit of a Russian Antonov 38 lets you look out the front window and the side portals over the blue sea and sweeping swirls where coastal estuaries spill into the briny sea on the delta. You fly low enough to see farmers in their field, and this short flight from Ho Chi Minh City brings you to a laid-back, remote island, almost like its own little banana republic. Con Son is one of those quirky remote destinations where you can get to know the whole expat community in a few handshakes, and where you'll be raising glasses with the very pilot who just flew you in that morning—and the same guys who'll fly you out (hopefully after some sleep and a cup of coffee). The central port area is a long concrete sea wall—none too picturesque—but the waters of the bay are pleasing and the views are good from the island's small clutch of budget resorts. Con Son Island is also a great place to explore secluded beaches, jungle scenery in the large Con Dao National Park, or remote islands and dive sites by joining a 1-day diving and snorkeling trip.

There isn't much to the port town on Con Son, but the town's old colonial buildings, some with French street names still neatly carved in the stucco of antique cornices, lend to the general atmosphere of this little bleached beach outcrop. Houses in town are often made from old prison walls: lean-tos built against the aging bulwarks or occupying whole prison buildings or administration buildings. The tiny central market area is where you'll find what little action there is, and a stay on Con Dao is a good way to unwind from busy city life in Ho Chi Minh. There are also a number of quiet, secluded beaches, the likes of **Bai Dat Doc** near the airport. Don't miss the small temple dedicated to Gia Long's Royal Concubine, **Lady Phi Yen,** who was imprisoned on the island after exile and a sad lover's tale of deceit—see "Attractions," below.

Cool sea winds make the island rather temperate year-round, but note that, because of wind conditions and poor visibility, **diving** is not possible in the winter months from November to January (the very opposite of Nha Trang, which is in high season for diving at that time).

Getting There

Once reached only by chartered helicopter from Vung Tau, Con Dao now connects with Ho Chi Minh City by regular fixed-wing flight. **Vasco Airlines** (Vietnam Air Service Co.), a division of Vietnam Airlines, flies a 30-seater Russian Antonov 38, a twin-engine turbo prop plane left over from years when Russia and Vietnam shared both technology and ideology. The ride itself is part of the adventure of visiting Con Dao. The operation is reliable, however small-time it may look when you are boarding. Flights leave from **Ho Chi Minh City's Ton Sa Nhat Airport** early every morning (one-way flights cost 761,000 VND).

Buy tickets through any Ho Chi Minh travel agent for a fee, or contact **Saigontourist** at 49 Le Thanh Ton St. (© **08/3827-9279**), just adjacent to the People's Committee Building at the city center. You can also contact **Vasco** directly by phone to their offices at 114B Bach Dang Rd. (© **08/3844-5999** or 3842-2790), and they can drop off a ticket at your hotel for cash payment.

There are regular boats that connect Con Dao and Vung Tau, but they leave at 5pm and take 12 hours for the overnight ocean crossing (costing just peanuts). Not recommended.

Be sure to arrange transport from the airport to your hotel before arriving on the island. If you arrive without prearranged accommodations, you'll be refreshingly free of the pushy taxi drivers and hotel touts who crowd your arrival in most tourist areas of Vietnam, but you'll realize how much easier these guys make travel in-country. Prearranging your accommodations from Vung Tau means perhaps paying a higher price, though, so if you want to try to save some money, arrive without a reservation, hop on one of the buses loaded with Vietnamese tourists going to the port area, and go to a hotel front desk to negotiate, or walk to the next hotel. Car or motorbike connection from the airport is 20,000 VND.

Orientation

The airport is on the far southern tip of the island, and a 15-minute ride by van—arrange with your hotel before arrival—brings you to the central town area with its crumbling prisons. The growing town is set around the old prisons. A commercial port sits on the north end of the island, and a few beaches are along the rocky coast.

FAST FACTS There are no banks on the island, and Visa is the only credit card accepted—for a room only—at the Saigontourist Con Dao Resort. Bring cash. There are a few little Internet cafes, but the connection is so slow it's just not worth it. The **post office** is at 48 Nguyen Hue (© **064/383-0226**) next to the radio tower.

Where to Stay & Dine

Even the best choices in town are quite affordable, but easiest on the budget is little **Phi Yen Hotel** (© **064/383-0168**), where simple air-conditioned rooms start at just 180,000 VND for a single. The staff at Phi Yen doesn't speak English, but the place is good for a simple flop and for arranging your day trips elsewhere.

Keep an eye out for the new Evason Hideaway from the **Six Senses** group, the popular developers of Evason Hideaway Ana Mandara (p. 272). A soft opening for their new property is planned for sometime in 2010.

Dining on Con Dao is rather limited. The best is at the Saigon Con Dao Resort (see below), where you can pick from a good English menu. Choices range from Vietnamese dishes to the likes of burgers and fries. Go for the fresh seafood and the delicious hot pots. This is pretty much where everyone on the island eats, which means that the place gets overcrowded—particularly on weekends—with big groups of domestic tourists.

There are the standard stalls serving *pho* and *com* (noodle soup and rice dishes) near the small central market, but few other options remain.

ATC Resort What you get here is colonial appeal. The four basic guesthouse rooms in this converted French administration building are clean, hung with heavy rafters, covered in wicker, and surrounded by a balcony. It's the perfect place to "take over" with a small group, just across the road from the wide bay (though no real views from rooms). You'll find hammocks out front, but the place is rustic, with fans only, and spaces are open at the top, meaning you'll need to sleep under a mosquito net (provided by the resort). They also have a clutch of wooden bungalows farther along the strip. You won't find any dining options on the property, but the rooms in the main block are charming, and you can get into the slow pace of island life here.

16B Ton Duc Thang St. ✆ **064/383-0456.** Fax 064/383-0111. 24 units. 500,000 VND–700,000 VND double. No credit cards. **Amenities:** Restaurant. *In room:* A/C, TV, fridge, minibar, Wi-Fi.

Con Dao Resort The newest of the island resorts, Con Dao Resort (not to be confused with government-run Saigon Con Dao Resort) is at the far southern edge of town. Don't expect much more than large, clean, tile rooms and large public spaces. But what sets this resort apart is the picturesque (though not really swimmable) beach out front, and the fact that the resort was recently finishing some grouting and landscaping the area around a small beachside pool.

8 Nguyen Duc Thuan. ✆ **064/383-0939.** Fax 064/393-0979. condaoresort@vol.vnn.vn. 45 units. $45–$55 double; $60–$120 suite. No credit cards. **Amenities:** Restaurant and bar; outdoor pool; tennis court. *In room:* A/C, TV, fridge, minibar.

Saigon Con Dao Resort ★ Housed in renovated prisoner administration buildings from the 1930s, the Saigon Con Dao Resort is managed by government-run Saigontourist, which accounts for the rather drab feel here. Most guests at Saigon Con Dao Resort book their trip and tours on the island through the Saigontourist office in Ho Chi Minh (49 Le Thanh Ton St., District 1; ✆ **08/3827-9279**), and big discounts are available from the rack rates listed below (you can usually show up at the front desk and haggle a low price when the resort is not full). Further development in this mellow, low-lying compound is limited by the hotel's historical landmark status (they'd love to put a pool in the open lawn area at the back but are restricted from doing so). Rooms are simple, cozy, and clean. They're decorated in bright white tile with rattan furnishings; it's not luxe, but very livable. Bathrooms are oversize and very clean. Larger suites are not worth the upgrade. Large balcony common areas face the main seaside street and port area. Dining at the hotel restaurant is about as good as it gets on Con Dao (at least you can read the menu), and the hotel's tour services are extensive.

18/24 Ton Duc Thang St. ✆ **064/383-0155.** Fax 064/383-0567. www.saigoncondao.com. 106 units. $48 double; $88 suite. MC, V (with 5% service charge). **Amenities:** Restaurant; pool; motorbikes. *In room:* A/C, TV, fridge, minibar, Wi-Fi.

Attractions

At press time, the Con Dao Museum had only one English speaker on staff, so chances are, you'll visit the prison areas with large Vietnamese groups. Fortunately, Saigon Con Dao Resort has English-speaking guides who can accompany groups for a fee. Try to go with an English-speaking guide; otherwise, it's a long and dull tour, punctuated by a few brief descriptions like "This is prison toilet," when pointing at a very obvious hole in the ground. The main prison sights are all in the center of town, as is the Con Dao Museum.

Con Dao Museum Located in the center of town adjacent to the longest jetty where early prisoners first caught sight of the island, the Con Dao Museum was once the home of island governors—whether French, South Vietnamese, or American. The building was converted to a museum after the island prisons were overrun and liberated by Viet Cong troops in 1975, and this is now the place to begin any exploration of the island's brutal history. Aimed mostly at Vietnamese visitors, it's a very important patriotic sight and a pilgrimage, really, for the many who were held here or who lost loved ones. Be respectful of the Vietnamese groups at the museum.

The collection tells the tale of the prison isle, from grisly photos of emaciated prisoners shackled together, to artwork by past internees of their desperate conditions, to the very rifle butts and clubs that were used to torture prisoners. The last room in a clockwise loop through the building tells of the liberation of Con Dao, chronicles the reconciliatory returns of the many prisoners who were housed here, and has a rather faded collection of German and Russian state gifts to the people of Vietnam. Many members of the current Hanoi administration did tenure in these horrific halls, and the museum has their pictures and information in the entrance. There are good English-language descriptions of the island's history, lists of official French and U.S. policies toward prisoners, and information about the many uprisings and incidents of armed resistance by prisoners to their jailors.

To visit the actual prison sights below, you'll have to wait for a group to coalesce and for one of the docents to walk you to the two nearby prison sights. More comprehensive tours of island sights include a visit to the few surviving French **"tiger cages"** where, from 1940 to 1955, prisoners were kept in open pits and monitored from above by jailors.

Entrance to the museum is just 20,000 VND. Guided tours of the prisons (below) start at the museum entrance and are included in the price of your entry—but you will have to wait to join one of the large Vietnamese tour groups (most likely in the late morning or after lunch).

To arrange a private tour with an English-speaking guide, contact the tour desk at Saigon Con Dao Resort (✆ **064/383-0155**).

Lady Phi Yen Temple This small local temple was built in homage to Lady Phi Yen, wife of Nguyen Emperor Gia Long, who was sequestered on the island. Just north of town, the temple is a 1958 remake of a late-19th-century original (destroyed by the French). The story goes that Phi Yen accompanied her husband in exile after defeat at the hands of the Tay Son. Under threat and desperately seeking French support—help that he would receive, but with many concessions to the French that heralded the beginning of Vietnam's French colonization—his wife expressed doubt, preached peace, and was suspected by Gia Long of treason. Lady Phi Yen was thrown into an isolated cell and left to die after he left the island—fleeing Tay Son—but she survived with the help of mythical creatures (a monkey and a tiger), only to commit suicide later. The temple honors her tragic tale, her fortitude, and her love of peace.

On the southern end of the central port area of Con Son.

Trai Phu Hai Prison The door opens with a clang and a creak as your docent unhitches the heavy hasp on the massive door out front—my guide was petite and wore a white *ao dai* dress that just didn't match the surroundings. Low guard towers loom over the open courtyard, and thick, high walls are topped in shards of glass. The guardhouse still has a chalkboard with smudges on it from the lists of names of the last residents. At the center of the broad space is a small Christian chapel built later in 1963, a bit of irony really, considering the atrocities committed here. Comprising the bounds of the courtyard are the sloping terra-cotta-tiled roofs and shaded walkways of cellblocks. Where elsewhere in Vietnam the faded yellow plaster, heavy timbers, and umber tile work of French colonial architecture looks quaint and inviting, here it takes on a rather sinister aspect.

The first cell on the left, number 9, is set up like the prisons in their heyday, when over 5,000 men were held here, with 80 to 100 shackled together in large common cells. Concrete mannequins, disturbingly lifelike, are rendered in all manner of contorted positions, just as the inmates were: one leg shackled to a long steel rod, one prisoner crammed against the other, surrounding an open area at center. Docents light a handful of joss sticks, and visitors are invited to make an offering at a small Buddhist altar at the center of the room.

Built in 1862, the prison is the oldest of the island prisons. Originally Bagne 1 (or Prison 1) under the French, the South Vietnamese called it Camp II and, later, Phu Hai. Closest to the Con Dao Museum. Contact the museum directly or Saigontourist's Con Dao Resort for guided tours and information.

Trai Phu Son Just adjacent to Trai Phu Hai, this prison is more of the same: a large courtyard surrounded by large common rooms of high yellowed walls. The prison's claim to fame is its most notorious revolutionary prisoners—the likes of early revolutionary Le Hong Phuong, and later Le Duan, who succeeded Ho Chi Minh as the president of Vietnam at the end of the Vietnam War. Plaques listing the names of famous internees are next to each door. At Trai Phu Son, your guide will take you into a small isolation cell and will proceed to close the door, shutting out all light, leaving just the smell of wet cement and blinding dark to give you an idea of what solitary is like. Vietnamese tour groups scream wildly. Most tours include a visit to both large prisons.
At the town center, just adjacent to Trai Phu Hai. Contact Saigontourist at the Con Dao Resort for entry.

Outdoor Activities

Diving

Rainbow Divers (© **09/0557-7671;** www.divevietnam.com), with an office on the main street right next to the Con Dao Museum, is a franchise of the same popular dive operator in Nha Trang and Phu Quoc. The friendly expat owners and staff are very helpful with arranging great diving and snorkeling trips, as well as tours to other parts of the island and any other advice or assistance you might need. Con Dao Rainbow Divers is pretty much the tourist information center on the island, and their cozy veranda is a good place to meet up with other travelers. ***Note:*** Diving is allowed only from February to October; there's poor visibility in winter months.

Rainbow here in Can Dao is a well-run, PADI-certified operation, offering anything from open-water certification to dive master courses. They're relatively new to the island, and along with some well-scouted dives, they'll take folks out to unexplored areas of this picturesque little archipelago. (In fact, the day that I was there, a dive team freed a small reef shark from a net and named it the "Lucky Shark Reef.") Underwater are some nice reefs, and sights comparable to popular Nha Trang. A number of decompression chambers are accessible to Con Dao, thanks to nearby Vung Tau's large offshore oil operations and many professional divers, quite unique for such a remote diving destination. A 3-day open-water course costs $350; a discover scuba dive costs just $60; and three dives in a 1-day trip will cost you $125.

For just $20, you can tag along with the dive crew for a day of **snorkeling** and **island cruising** on their large, shaded dive boat. Dive sights are many, and more are found each year. You can also swim from the dive boat to deserted islands where solitary park rangers keep watch over bird-breeding sights. The elusive **Dugong,** a large sea mammal something like a manatee, is said to swim these waters, but few are seen and only in the early mornings. You might spot **giant sea turtles,** which come to breed on the Con Dao archipelago, mostly on Hon Bay Canh just offshore and on a secluded beach away from the main island of Con Son.

Trekking

Trekking in Con Dao National Park provides good glimpses of jungle and a few remote bays and beaches. For information on arranging your day in the mountain, start at the **Con Dao National Park Office,** which is just a few kilometers inland from the port area at 29 Vo Thi Sau St. (✆ **064/383-0669**). The park administrator, Mr. Hung, can explain day-trip options and issue the requisite free permits for entrance to protected areas of the preserve. The office is open during normal island business hours, from 8 to 11:30am and 1 to 5pm.

The park office features a small museum, funded by the World Wildlife Fund. Peruse natural artifacts and information on the park's wildlife, including the breeding patterns of the protected island turtles, which come to breed on the archipelago's beaches from May to October. Park rangers stand vigil on islands to protect the turtle eggs (and the bird eggs) from the many sea poachers.

Good **short hikes** start just up the road from the park entrance (go by motorbike) and carry you down to a small bay just across from **Ba Island.** The downward track is well marked and even has Vietnamese signs urging guests to behave properly (translated into English, they say something like "Don't take anything besides pictures, don't leave anything beside footprints"). Other funny little signs point out the obvious, like, "Hey, stop here and see how many birds you can hear!" or "Stop! Look down. How many ants can you count?"

A longer trek explores the knoll and remote beaches near the airport, best attempted with a guide hired at the park entrance. Other trips include day boat trips to outlying islands, particularly to **Bay Canh** just off the west coast, where you can trek to the old French lighthouse.

A SIDE TRIP TO CAT TIEN NATIONAL PARK (VUON QUOC GIA CAT TIEN)

145km (90 miles) N of Ho Chi Minh City; 195km (121 miles) S of Dalat

Covering a massive area of more than 70,000 hectares (173,000 acres) shared by three provinces—Lam Dong, Binh Phuoc, and Dong Nai—the Cat Tien National Park was first established in 1978 and enlarged (nearly doubled) in 1992. It's one of the top bird- and game-spotting preserves in the region, important not only as one of the last standing evergreen and semi-evergreen old-growth forests in the south of Vietnam, but as a habitat for some of the region's most endangered species, particularly the Javanese rhinoceros. Once ranging widely throughout Southeast Asia, the rhinos were thought completely extinct until a few were spotted in 1999 by tripwire cameras in the park. The sad fact is that these are the last few of a nearly extinct breed, but part of the park's importance is to create the right conditions of wide grasslands and damp, swampy wallows so that the rhinos will see resurgence in numbers. Other rare animals—including tigers, sun bears, and Asian wild dogs—are known to range freely, and the park has been quite successful in growing a population of the threatened Siamese crocodile. You're unlikely to see anything too rare, but even the shortest walk in the dense forest or along the park access road means sightings of squirrels and monkeys and small game like civets and miniature forest deer.

Con Dao by the Bells

For Vietnamese, a visit to Con Dao is something akin to standing in front of the Liberty Bell in Philadelphia or the Magna Carta in the British Library. As such, old Communist cadre decorum is the rule, and like back in the days when the state ruled every move for citizens, there is a system of bells and announcements telling you what to do. Starting at 5am, you'll hear wake-up music and announcements. At 5:30am, music and instructions follow for exercise time. The lunch bell sounds at 11am, and 1pm is the end-of-lunch (or wake-up-from-siesta) bell. The bell at 5pm signals an end to the workday, and at 6pm you'll hear the news. You will become regimented, cadre.

But the park's birds bring most visitors here. You could meet anyone from eccentric amateur birders to professors of **ornithology.** The park's canteen, in fact, looks something like a panel in one of Gary Larson's *Far Side* cartoons, with peculiar scientists comparing eyeglass prescriptions and zoom lenses, and swapping their experiences in spying all that is ruby-crested, struts, and shows plumage. The birds are interesting, and the park publishes a comprehensive guide listing the many rare species here. I had the good fortune to see a massive yellow hornbill, as well as various large egrets, heron, and rare water fowl.

The park is sponsored by the folks at the World Wildlife Foundation and, under their tutelage, Vietnamese rangers have reduced the number of people living in the park to a dwindling 9,000 (subsistence farmers are given good incentives to move, and support thereafter), and steps are being taken to eliminate dangerous detritus, the kind that is not just an eyesore, but can harm animals, like fishing nets and rope traps. The park now supports over 100 varieties of mammals, 350 species of bird, over 100 types of fish, 79 reptile species, 41 amphibians, 457 butterflies, and thousands of insects. The tally of protected animals is as follows: 18 mammals (including the endangered Indo rhino), 20 birds, 12 reptiles, 1 amphibian, and an orange-necked partridge—which is endangered—in the proverbial pear tree. The nice part is, unlike other parks in Vietnam, the animal population density is high and you're sure to spot some critters. You might not see the big rare guys, but certainly you'll spot a few civets, monkeys, and funky birds. You're also sure to see some great specimens of massive, ancient ficus trees on many of the park's hiking trails. The grasslands and wetlands that give life to the park's animals and plants drain into the **Dong Nai River,** which runs near the park entry.

The park area was also home to ancient Oc Eo settlements from Vietnam's early history, and you can find some information about them, and the ancient Phu Nam dynasty, at the visitor center.

The best news is that Cat Tien National Park is very organized. Just wash up on the shores of the information counter, and you can organize tours, borrow bicycles, rent jeeps, and hire guides at very reasonable rates. Start with the **night viewing** by jeep for 200,000 VND per person, with descending rates per person for larger groups.

Be sure to visit **Bai Sau,** otherwise known as **Crocodile Lake,** largest of the park's wetland areas and the best opportunity for seeing larger game. (I saw a small herd of Sambar deer, civets, and, yes, crocodile eyes glowing on the lake at night.) The lake is 10km (6¼ miles) from the park office, and the lakeside ranger station is a stunning 5km (3-mile) forest walk. You must hire a guide for the trip. You can overnight at the lake for the best chance to see wildlife at night, but the experience is very basic; imagine an aging Boy Scouts' camp minus any frills.

For further information, contact the park office at Tan Phu District, Dong Nai Province (© **061/366-9228;** fax 061/366-9159; cattien_nationalpark@yahoo.com).

Getting There

Hiring a car for the one-way trip from either Dalat or Ho Chi Minh is the best option. Expect to pay $60 to get you to the park gate, but it'll save you some hassle.

The park is located 24km (15 miles) north of Hwy. 20 between Dalat and Ho Chi Minh (the turnoff to the park is 125km/78 miles from Saigon and 175km/109 miles from Dalat). You can arrange a ride to kilometer 125 from Ho Chi Minh or Dalat, but you'll have to keep an eye out for the turnoff and remind the driver before you get there. Budget tourist cafe buses also follow these routes daily and are good about dropping you off in the right spot.

The motorbike taxi drivers at the turnoff are some of the hungriest bunch of crocodiles I've ever met, and the sad news is that once you hop off the bus, they have you over a barrel. The bargaining starts at 400,000 VND. These guys are delusional, and persistent, and you're the only game in town. Dig deep for a bit of patience. Sit and have a coffee. Have a laugh. And laugh hard at the price. Locals pay about 40,000 VND. Anything near that is reasonable. Be ready to make like you're going to walk to the park yourself (they'll follow). I got tired of it and paid 70,000 VND and thought I was done with it, but know that from the moment you enter the park, *everyone* will ask you how much you paid to get there. It is like a badge that defines you, so try to get a good deal (or lie).

Park entrance is 50,000 VND. Walk 100m (328 ft.) down the road to the free ferry, and then to the park information and check-in center, where the very helpful folks will help you sort things out.

Where to Stay & Dine

Accommodations near the park entrance are quite good. A clean, tile room with air-conditioning is just 180,000 VND. Cheapest are the little wood-and-thatch huts for 90,000 VND. The entrance area is a cozy little campus, and there is a fun fraternal vibe among the many visitors here, most of whom are avid birders and eager to connect with fellow members of that rare species. Dining at the canteen is reasonable and quite good; they also have a selection of local wines that really gets the conversation flowing. Expect to meet people here and be able to arrange shared tours to the woods together.

One other option is to spend the night out at Bai Sau, Crocodile Lake. Accommodations here are spartan, but they do have running water and toilet facilities. Rooms have no fan and just a hanging mossie net, but the less-than-basic, rustic comforts ensure a good chance to spot rare animals at lakeside in the early morning or at night.

13

The Mekong Delta

Don't leave without seeing the Mekong Delta, one of Vietnam's most interesting and scenic regions. An organized tour, even the most low-budget version, offers action-packed days with bus and boat trips to small craft villages, mangrove swamps, island orchards, and spectacular **floating markets.** A 1-day trip isn't quite enough to fully delve into the delta, so plan on an overnight—best in the delta's urban centers of Can Tho or Chau Doc near Cambodia (try to stay at the Victoria in either location). For more specific advice on tour options, see p. 350.

The delta is a web of Mekong River waterways covering an area of about 60,000km (37,200 miles) across three provinces. The region is densely populated with 18 million souls, most engaged in farming and fishing. Called the "rice basket" of Vietnam, the Mekong Delta accounts for more than 50% of all rice and produce in the country, exporting between 4 million and 5 million tons of rice per year. The land is tessellated with bright green rice paddies, fruit orchards, sugarcane fields, and vegetable gardens, and its waters stay busy with boats and fish farms. Rice production and harvest still involves water buffaloes instead of tractors, as well as backbreaking hand planting of rice shoots, weeding, and hand harvesting.

Impoverished under socialist agricultural programs, the region benefited greatly from the 1980s Doi Moi reforms, and rice paddies that once yielded just one crop now produce three crops per year, an important part of Vietnamese economic self-sufficiency.

The delta was a hotbed for Viet Cong guerillas during the war with the U.S., and some tours will take you to the vestiges of old Viet Cong hide-outs, complete with hideaway ambush holes and a ride among the mangrove swamp where stealth forces disappeared after raids in Saigon.

1 VISITOR INFORMATION

To cope with necessary logistics in the Mekong Delta, use a tour agent, who can offer everything from day trips to long adventure tours and longer homestays. Cycling the delta has become a popular option, and many of the tour operators (I recommend Exotissimo and Ann Tours) are now offering a cycling option that takes you along the dusty paths that line the area's canals and that link rice paddies between small towns. Again, even on a bike, go with a tour operator to avoid the crowded roads in the region and get to the back of beyond. Many tours conclude in Chau Doc, and travelers make their way to Phnom Penh from there—and more and more travelers are punctuating their Mekong Delta adventure with some toes-in-the-sand time on Phu Quoc Island. Tour operators are flexible and can accommodate any special plans.

TOUR OPERATORS

My pick for classic tours to the Mekong Delta is **Ann Tours,** 58 Ton That Tung St., District 1 (✆ **08/3833-2564;** fax 08/3832-3866; www.anntours.com). Their custom tour takes you off the beaten path (from $45 a day with a group) on homestays and to more remote areas with experienced local guides. Another excellent operator is **Exotissimo,** 9 Dinh Tien Hoang St., District 1 (✆ **08/3825-1723;** fax 08/3829-5800; www.exotissimo.com). Their prices are steeper than Ann's, but their guides are incredibly knowledgeable and their level of professionalism is unrivaled. They arrange private, customized tours, which means you travel away from groups and on your own time schedule.

Saigontourist, in Ho Chi Minh City at 49 Le Thanh Ton St., District 1 (✆ **08/3829-8914;** fax 08/3822-4987; www.saigon-tourist.com), is a large government-run operation that runs regular bus schedules and tours for groups large and small. Tour quality—and price—is much higher than what's offered by budget tourist cafes (see below).

Victoria Hotels (main office: Ho Chi Minh City, second floor, 101 Tran Hung Dao St., District 1; ✆ **08/3837-3031;** fax 08/3836-4108; www.victoriahotels-asia.com) runs the two finest hotels in the region (in Chau Doc and Can Tho). If you book through this hotel company directly, consider taking advantage of their excellent tour services—all with private driver and guide transfers and good local tours using one—or both—hotels as a base. They have luxury day-cruisers in Can Tho and offer a standard course of floating market tours from both Can Tho and Chau Doc. Also check out their high-speed connection—on board a zippy runabout—between Chau Doc and Phnom Penh, Cambodia.

You'll also find many **eco-tour options** in the delta, with trips that combine cultural touring and cycling trips (the area is mercifully flat). Contact **Buffalo Tours,** a Hanoi-based tour group (✆ **04/3828-0702;** fax 04/3926-3126; www.buffalotours.com), which runs comprehensive group and private cycling tours of the delta. On the budget end, **Delta Adventure Tours** (267 De Tham, District 1; ✆ **08/3920-2112**) runs lots of unique routes and houses you in their private resort near Chau Doc.

The **tourist cafes** all run standard, affordable tours. Contact **Sinh Café,** 246–248 De Tham St., District 1 (✆ **08/3837-6833;** www.sinhcafevn.com), or **TNK,** 230 De Tham St. (✆ **08/3837-8276;** www.tnktravelvietnam.com), in the Pham Ngu Lao area of Ho Chi Minh City. All of the budget cafe tour companies offer 2- and 3-day tours starting at $10 per day (with optional connection to Cambodia), and for that low, low price, expect little in the way of good tour leading and explanation. Accommodations on these trips are very basic, and one gets the sense of being on a cattle drive (as cattle, not cowboys), and though they do hit all of the relevant sights, I highly recommend going with a more upmarket tour (see Exotissimo or Ann Tours, above) to see the delta in style and with informed guides and tour leaders that are helpful and supportive (not cattle drivers).

TYPICAL ITINERARIES

The trips below are the most common itineraries on bus tours. Custom itineraries offer myriad deviations from these now well-tracked paths, including options for **homestays** with rural families, as well as more-off-the-map destinations like **Ben Tre** and other parts of **Vinh Long Province.** Generally, the more you pay—such as with **Exotissimo** or through **Ann Tours** private tours—the better the trip.

Many travelers make their Mekong Delta trip a one-way adventure, going **on to Cambodia** overland from the town of **Chau Doc.** For information about this and tours that will take you directly to Cambodia's capital, Phnom Penh, check with Saigon's many **tourist cafes** (see "Visitor Information & Tours" in chapter 12).

Tours can also be extended to include some beach time at **Phu Quoc Island,** which lies just off the coast of the delta to the west, near Chau Doc. You'd have to overland (by car or

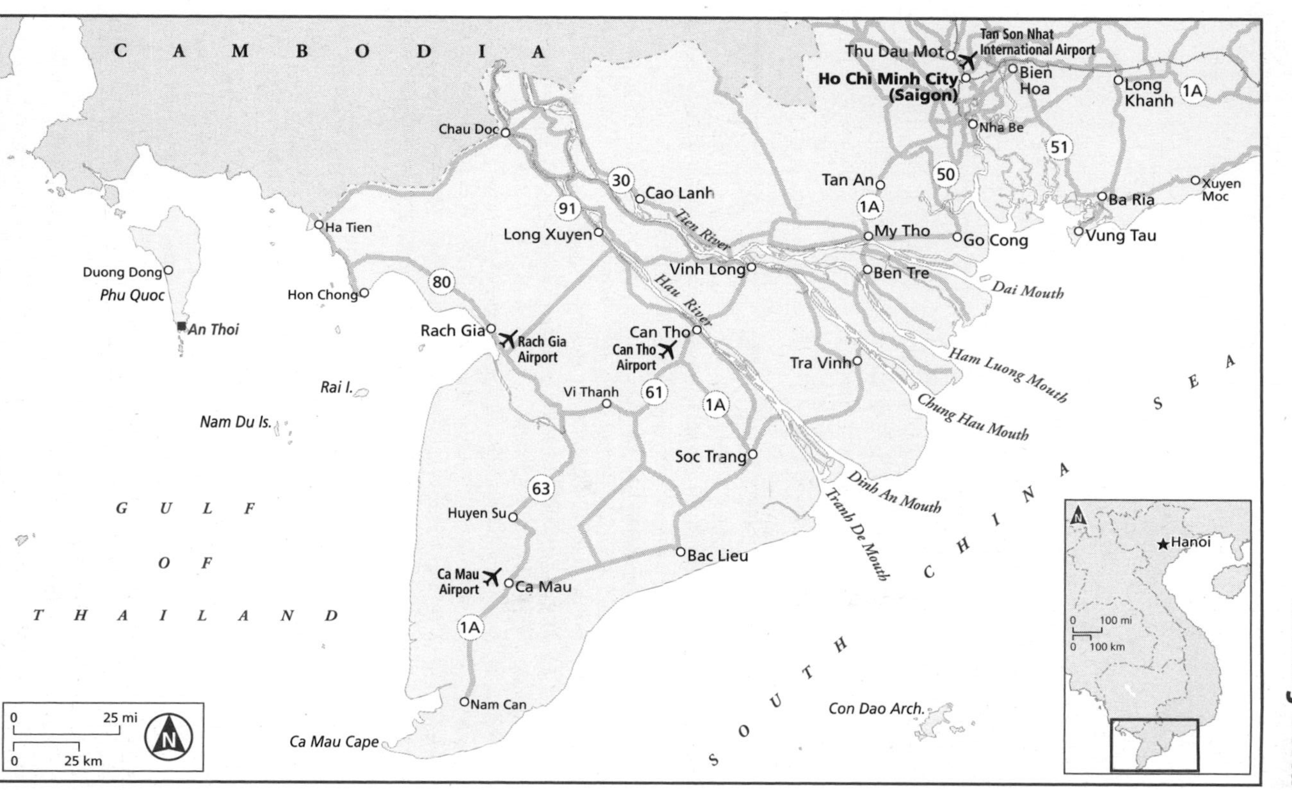
CAMBODIA
GULF OF THAILAND
SOUTH CHINA SEA
Thu Dau Mot
Tan Son Nhat International Airport
Ho Chi Minh City (Saigon)
Bien Hoa
Long Khanh
1A
Nha Be
51
50
Tan An
Xuyen Moc
Ba Ria
Vung Tau
Chau Doc
30
Cao Lanh
91
Tien River
Long Xuyen
1A
My Tho
Go Cong
Ha Tien
Vinh Long
Ben Tre
Dai Mouth
Duong Dong
Phu Quoc
Hon Chong
80
Hau River
An Thoi
Rach Gia
Rach Gia Airport
Can Tho
Can Tho Airport
Tra Vinh
Ham Luong Mouth
Rai I.
Vi Thanh
61
1A
Chung Hau Mouth
Nam Du Is.
Soc Trang
Dinh An Mouth
63
Huyen Su
Tranh De Mouth
Bac Lieu
Hanoi
Ca Mau Airport
Ca Mau
1A
0 100 mi
0 100 km
Nam Can
Con Dao Arch.
0 25 mi
0 25 km
N
Ca Mau Cape

King Rice

Space isn't wasted in the densely populated Mekong Delta—any empty plot is used for farming, mostly of lowland "wet rice," which is grown in flooded paddies separated by dikes. Technology, from industrial pumps to spring-loaded hand scoops, is used to irrigate the fields. Rice is king in Vietnam. More than the country's staple food and economic backbone, it's part of the Vietnamese character.

First, seeds are planted in flooded paddies and then replanted to avoid rot. Everything is done by hand, and even harrowing and plowing is still done at the back of a buffalo. The Communist model of cooperation, particularly by way of sharing water resources, has served the Vietnamese well, and since the inception of the Doi Moi economic reforms, which made Mekong growers personally accountable for their output (in other words, it hit them in the pocketbook), the country has made great leaps in catching up with rice-growing giants like nearby Thailand, Japan, and the western United States. Now, due to high productivity and improved technology, the only concerns are keeping salinity levels down and avoiding contamination from fertilization. Rice exports from Vietnam reached nearly 1 million metric tons in 2006. Shipments to the Asian destinations totaled 550,000 tons, with 415,000 tons alone going to the Philippines.

local bus—ouch) from Chau Doc to the coastal town of **Rach Gia** and then go by boat or a very short flight to Phu Quoc. There are daily flights between Phu Quoc and Saigon.

2-DAY TOUR Start in the early morning from Saigon, with a visit to the **Cai Be Floating Market** near My Tho, and then various handicraft sights. The trip to **Vinh Long Market** is done by boat, with stops at island orchards and rural villages—including a walk over a shaky "Monkey Bridge" across a canal—and the first day ends in the city of **Can Tho,** where you'll spend the night.

On the second day, take a 3-hour boat trip—with plenty of stops and photo ops at places like a rice vermicelli factory, a raw-rice-processing plant, and rural orchards, as well as a stop at the large **Cai Rang Floating Market**—before returning to Saigon in the evening (around 7pm). These 2-day itineraries are jampacked, and you're always on the go by bus, boat, and foot.

3-DAY TOUR A 3-day tour expands on the 2-day itinerary to include far-flung **Chau Doc,** set on the Bassac River (a tributary of the Mekong) and one of my favorite little towns. Lots of travelers call this their last port of call in Vietnam and carry on into Cambodia by boat from here.

The **first day** basically mirrors the first day of the 2-day tour, but the morning of **day 2** takes you to floating houses and ethnic Cham villages near Chau Doc. You'll then travel up little **Sam Mountain,** a little knob of a pilgrimage peak that gives you a great vantage over the wide, flat delta, and then you return to **Can Tho** for an overnight.

The morning of **day 3** takes you to the **Cai Rang Floating Market** near Chau Doc (a bonus is that you'll be there early in the middle of the action), with stops at more local cottage-industry workshops before making your way back to Saigon in the evening.

2 MY THO

70km (43 miles) SW of Ho Chi Minh City; 104km (65 miles) N of Can Tho; 179km (111 miles) N of Chau Doc

As the closest Mekong Delta town to Ho Chi Minh City, My Tho—capital of Tien Gang Province—is your best bet for short day trips to the Mekong Delta, and some tours make an overnight here on the way to or from cities deeper in. The city is just a small riverside grid along the Mekong. Most boat trips from My Tho include a visit to **Thoi Son Island,** with its sprawling fruit orchards, as well as **Cai Be Floating Market.** You could conceivably visit My Tho on your own by arranging transport from Ho Chi Minh City, and from My Tho organize a boat tour through local **Tien Giang Tourist** (63 Trung Trac; **© 073/387-2105;** www.tiengiangtourist.com). My Tho also makes a good base for an exploration of **Ben Tre,** farther to the east.

3 CAN THO

175km (109 miles) SW of Ho Chi Minh City; 104km (65 miles) SW of My Tho; 75km (47 miles) NW of Chau Doc

With a population of over two million, Can Tho is the largest city on the Mekong Delta and the fifth-largest city in Vietnam, just behind Danang. Set at a confluence of two smaller Mekong tributaries (the Hao Giang and the Can Tho rivers), it makes a great base for canal tours to the surrounding countryside. Can Tho's quaint riverside location has given rise to a few new semiluxe hotels, and it has become a popular honeymoon destination for Saigon couples. A visit to the floating markets, the city's massive central market, or outlying riverside towns is memorable. Travel in and around Can Tho is best arranged with a tour group or good private guide who can take you to all the right places: the impressive floating market, rice-paper-making and weaving villages, small factories, and picturesque rural canals.

A fine park on the riverside promenade showcases a large, shiny statue of Ho Chi Minh overlooking the busy water's edge and large neon advertisements for local beer—would he approve? Check out the small Chinese Temple across from Ho Chi Minh's statue, a good example of the places of worship for Can Tho's large Chinese community, who faced heavy recrimination in the late 1970s when China and Vietnam butted heads over Vietnamese involvement in Cambodia. At press time, the city was also putting the finishing touches on a large covered riverside market.

GETTING THERE

All of the tour agents (see "Visitor Information," above) provide extensive services to Can Tho. There is no airport in Can Tho, so travel is by road only. From Ho Chi Minh City, you will travel on Hwy. 1 to Vinh Long. The highway was recently widened and speed limits were increased, so travel time is a mere 3½ hours, without bathroom breaks. Local buses—should you be so brave and patient—arrive and depart from Can Tho's roadside bus station about 1km (half a mile) north of the town center (take a motorcycle taxi to or from the riverside for 10,000 VND). Can Tho is 3½ hours by bus from Ho Chi Minh City by road (and about 3 hr. to/from Chau Doc, which is in the other direction). **Mai Linh Express** (**© 0710/357-3999**) runs regular connections on reliable shuttle buses to

 Ho Chi Minh City (70,000 VND) and Chau Doc (50,000 VND). They also offer free pickup and transport from your hotel to their office and departure area in the busy Can Tho bus station.

GETTING AROUND

The busiest part of sprawling Can Tho is along the riverside area, all of which, including taking in the town's museums and shopping, can be done on foot. You can also hop on motorbike taxis.

VISITOR INFORMATION & TOURS

Most travelers come to Can Tho on group or private tours out of Saigon. If you've got plenty of time and need a break from the 3½- to 4-hour ride to Can Tho, I recommend stopping at Vinh Long for a **bike ride** through the orchards and gardens on Anh Bin Island. Most outfitters can arrange for bike rentals and lunch along the way.

If you're on your own and hoping to set up trips to Can Tho's nearby floating markets and mangrove swamps, contact **Can Tho Tourist Company** (20 Hai Ba Trung, along the riverside at the center of town; ✆ **0710/382-1852;** www.canthotourist.com.vn). They can help you arrange boat trips to the markets, as well as unique homestays. Prices are a bit higher than the tourist cafes, but the service is better. And if you need help with your onward travel, these folks can help with that, too. All tours take you to **Ninh Kieu** or **Cai Rang** floating markets. The nearest market to town, if you're short on time, is little **Phong Dien.**

Private boat tours gather at the riverside and approach you like they're trying to sell you something illegal—and they are. The government, in collusion with Can Tho Tourist (above), has put the kibosh on local independent tour operators, claiming that they were getting bad reports from tourists and need to standardize programs to minimize tourist impact (good reasons, of course, but the truth is more about government monopoly). Private boat hire starts at around $15 for half-day trips, and these guys are eager for work and very accommodating. If you have your own group, this is a good choice; and don't listen to anyone telling you that you'll be arrested—it's the boat driver who'll have trouble with police, not you.

Fast Facts Can Tho

Banks & Currency Exchange Look for the **Vietcombank** branch, where you'll find international **ATM service,** at 7 Hoa Binh (✆ **0710/382-0445;** daily 8–11am and 1:30–4pm).

Internet Service Try **Duong Truyen,** at 36 Hai Ba Trung, which has decent service and is generally less crowded than Internet cafes near the riverside area (daily 7:30am–10pm).

Post Office The large central post office is near the bank and museum area, just a few hundred meters from riverside, at 2 Hoa Binh St.

WHERE TO STAY

Golf Hotel Can Tho The star of the Golf chain (there are three hotels in Dalat; see p. 242), this one in Can Tho is quite popular with newlyweds. Right along the river, it looks a bit like a big wedding cake. Rooms try to be fancy, with high ceilings, built-in cabinetry, and heavy filigree, but the thin office carpet is a letdown. Bathrooms are tidy, with granite tile, but lower rooms have showers only (no tub). Large deluxe rooms are done in the same decor, but with lots more space. And the best rooms have balconies with great views of the riverside and harbor—worth the upgrade. There's a quiet pool area, extensive massage facilities, a basement club, and a very kind and helpful front-desk staff.

02 Hai Ba Trung St., Ninh Kieu District. ✆ **0710/381-2210.** www.vinagolf.vn. 107 units. $162–$198 double; $85 family room; $430–$528 suite. MC, V. **Amenities:** 3 restaurants; 2 bars; pool; room service. *In room:* A/C, TV, fridge, hair dryer, minibar, Wi-Fi.

Saigon Can Tho Saigon Can Tho is best for a quick overnight in a pinch. Everything's a bit run-down. Deluxe rooms are huge—like the Golf Hotel—but it almost feels like too much space really, and bland. Rooms with balconies are great but come with lots of street noise. The place is affordable, and Saigontourist runs a helpful tour desk in the lobby.

55 Phan Dinh Phung St., Ninh Kieu District, Can Tho. ✆ **0710/382-5831.** Fax 0710/382-3288. www.saigoncantho.com.vn. 46 units. $49–$62 double. MC, V. **Amenities:** 2 restaurants; sauna; steam. *In room:* A/C, TV, fridge, minibar, Wi-Fi.

Victoria Can Tho ★★ After more than a decade of operations, the Victoria Can Tho still offers the best digs in this bustling Mekong city. Like all Victoria properties, rooms here are large, upscale, and charming, with natural woods, elegant silk hangings, and a puffy comforter on a big, sumptuous bed. River-view rooms are the best choice and have balconies overlooking busy river traffic. Bathrooms are a bit dated, but plans are in the pipeline to renovate and model them in the same style as the sleek rain-shower and glass cubicles found at Victoria Hoi An (p. 219). The hotel is just a short trip from the city by bicycle or taxi, but better to arrive in style aboard the hotel's wooden sampan boat, a free shuttle service, which drops you off at the Can Tho Market.

Cai Khe Ward, Can Tho City. ✆ **0710/381-0111.** Fax 0710/382-9259. www.victoriahotels-asia.com. 92 units. $195–$210 double; $290 suite. AE, MC, V. **Amenities:** Restaurant; bar; bikes; concierge; fitness center; Internet; riverside pool; room service; spa. *In room:* A/C, TV, fridge, minibar, Wi-Fi.

WHERE TO DINE

Dining at the Victoria Hotel's **Spices Restaurant** comes at a price, but everything is good. In town, restaurants are along the riverside; most are just open-air storefronts serving good local cuisine and seafood.

Note: For good snacks to take on day trips, look for the **Coop Mart** (1 Hoa Binh Blvd., near the Can Tho Museum; ✆ **0710/376-3586**), an extensive supermarket, open daily 8am to 10pm.

Mekong Restaurant VIETNAMESE The food here—at this quiet little storefront with an air-conditioned room—is hearty and healthy. You'll find good vegetarian options and a laid-back "diner" feel to the place.

38 Hai Ba Trung, at riverside right next to Nam Bo. ✆ **0710/382-1646.** Main courses 25,000 VND–70,000 VND. No credit cards. Daily 8am–2pm and 4–10pm.

Nam Bo ★ VIETNAMESE/INTERNATIONAL Set in a riverside corner colonial that's the coolest perch in town, the picturesque upstairs dining area of Nam Bo is always booked by group tours. Make a reservation for a small balcony table. Service is friendly and as efficient as it can be with all the griping hoards. The restaurant serves lunch, but

Finds Sleeping on the Mekong

Skip the landlubber hotel options and spend the night aboard ***Les Bassac*** ★, a classic, two-deck wooden boat. The luxury junk, run by TransMekong, is the only option for cruising the Mekong Delta in style. You can board *Les Bassac* at Can Tho or Cai Be, depending on the day of the week. I took the cruise from Can Tho to Cai Be (if you can, travel in the opposite direction—on day 2 of the cruise, you can visit the Cai Rang market, which is a busier, livelier market than the Cai Be market). Cabins are cozy spaces smelling of fresh wood. Bathrooms are small and lack separate shower units, but they come with stylish Art Deco taps and the amenities of a first-class hotel. The 2-day itinerary consists of sailing along the Mekong, stopping at villages and floating markets along the way, and eating sumptuous meals on deck. Overnight tours start at $204.

TransMekong also runs affordable breakfast and sunset cruises on small wooden sampans for $11 to $15. Contact Trans Mekong (97/10 Ngo Quyen, Can Tho; ✆ **071/382-9540;** www.transmekong.com) for further details, or book through major outfitters like Exotissimo or Saigon Tourist.

mainly for groups, and the kitchen closes promptly at 1pm, sending individual walk-in guests packing. They do have a good menu of familiar fare, from pizzas to Thai dishes, and the set menus feature everything from snake specials, to Vietnamese courses, to Italian dishes. If the place is full, and it usually is, try Mekong Restaurant (above), a more down-to-earth stop with no big groups, or the Sao Hom (see below), which has better views of the river from its second floor.

50 Hai Ba Trung. ✆ **0710/382-3908.** Main courses 55,000 VND–120,000 VND; set menus from 100,000 VND per person. MC, V. Daily 9am–10:30pm.

Sao Hom ★ WESTERN/VIETNAMESE Run by the same people that opened Nam Bo, this restaurant has an idyllic riverside location. They're located inside the old Can Tho Market Hall and occupy prime real estate next to the pier where the luxury boat *Les Bassac* docks (see the box "Sleeping on the Mekong," above). It's an open restaurant with cheerful yellow paint and outdoor seating. This is a good place to come when you're looking for some Western comfort food or a safe experience of Vietnamese dishes.

Old Can Tho Market Hall, Ninh Keu Pier. ✆ **0710/381-5616.** Main courses 70,000 VND–110,000 VND. MC, V. Daily 7am–9pm.

ATTRACTIONS

The real attractions in Can Tho are the floating markets and riverside life. Most days in this part of the delta begin early, around 6am. You'll go by boat on a circuitous route to a number of rural sights, including the large **Cai Rang Floating Market,** where you're not sure who's watching whom as your tiny long-tail boat makes its way among busy sellers in packed sampan-style boats—great photo opportunities and best early in the morning. A number of handicraft villages are in the area, and boat trips make stops at some rather canned tour attractions, the likes of a weaving village, rice-paper factory, vermicelli-production plant, rice mill, and cool "monkey bridge" made of vines as well as a large island orchard. The riverside scenery is beautiful and the sights, though touristy, are quite interesting. Other floating markets include **Phong Dien** and **Phong Hiep,** both slightly farther afield and part of an all-day loop with stops at a small mangrove swamp. If you arrive in the city in the midafternoon and have some free time on tour or while in transit back to Saigon, check out the few sights below:

Army Museum The Army Museum is an interesting visit and just across Hoa Binh Street (away from the river) from the Can Tho Museum (see below). An interesting display of weaponry, maps, photos, stained glass, and memorabilia from Vietnam's long struggles are on display. At the center is a small "hooch," or thatched building, housing a mannequin meeting of high-level Viet Cong guerrillas on the delta. Outside are a rusty missile, a crashed "Huey" helicopter, a U.S. recon plane, and a few Peugeot cars up on blocks (not sure if they are an exhibit or a repair project).

Note that the upper floors are closed and locked. Wonder what goes on up there?

On Hoa Binh just across from the City Museum. Free admission. Daily 7–11am and 2–5pm.

Can Tho City Museum ★ A comprehensive and colorful museum of local history, industry, custom, Chinese population, and the region's role during colonial repression, as well as during the war years with the United States. Maps are detailed but indecipherable. You won't find any signs in English, but that doesn't matter, as most exhibits, like the scenes and images of the delta's history, are interesting and self-explanatory. Go with a guide if you want to get background information. The second floor is a patriotic display of war remnants. There's also a model Chinese apothecary and temple in homage to the region's large Chinese population, local musical instruments, and a large diorama of a wedding procession. You'll see a bust of Ho Chi Minh and other Vietnamese patriots in the lobby. A visit here combined with a tour of the Army Museum (see above) is a good little city walk.

06 Phan Dinh Phung St. Free admission. Daily 7–11am and 2–5pm.

Riverside Market and Can Tho Market Hall Riverside market is a typical, local wet market located near the center of town. Come here to wander through the stalls with the locals and see the varied aquatic life (turtles, fish, and snakes, oh my!) and veggies on offer in the Mekong Delta. It's located next to the river, but unfortunately everything is indoors, so there's not much of a view and pretty much no ventilation. If you're squeamish about dirty feet, wear closed-toe shoes when you visit. Next door to Riverside is the old Can Tho Market Hall, which dates back to 1913. It's a dry market selling mostly clothes and trinkets. The market is housed in a bright, cheery yellow building and is very neat and tidy. It's geared for tourists. The Sao Hom restaurant (see above) at the back of the market is my top choice for a coffee break.

71 Ha Ba Trung St. Free admission. Daily 7am–midafternoon.

4 CHAU DOC

285km (177 miles) SW of Saigon; 75km (47 miles) SW of Can Tho; 180km (112 miles) SW of My Tho

This little riverside border town—worth a visit in and of itself—is the main stopover for travelers going to and from Cambodia (see "Getting There," below). Chau Doc is a bustling center of trade and river transport, yet also a lazy, riverside burg and a throwback to another time. You'll still see old-style Ho Chi Minh surreys, called *xe loi,* a two-wheel cart on the back of a regular bicycle, instead of the standard cyclo. And though most boats have long-tail motors, many fishermen and small-time traders still row their own boats in the standing, forward-pushing style. A large floating market and nearby ethnic Cham villages are popular for early morning tours (usually part of a larger Mekong Delta package), as well as the small pilgrimage peak called **Sam Mountain** just outside of town. There are a few good hotel options (best is the Victoria), and dining is at alfresco eateries near the market, as you take in the busy comings and goings.

GETTING THERE

Contact a tour agent in Ho Chi Minh City (see "Tour Operators," p. 349). Chau Doc is 285km (177 miles) southwest of Saigon, and the all-day bus ride combines visits to other hamlets in the delta, boat trips, and lunch stops—it's a fun, full day.

Local **buses** leave and arrive from the busy station a few kilometers north of town on Le Loi (connect by motorbike taxi for about 15,000 VND). **Mai Linh Express** (✆ **076/356-2812**) runs regular connections on reliable shuttle buses to Ho Chi Minh City (105,000 VND) and Can Tho (50,000 VND). You can buy Mai Linh tickets at the bus station or have your hotel book them ahead of time.

Boats from Chau Doc to Phnom Penh (and vice versa) leave at 7am, arriving at 4:30pm, and cost $8 (plus $26 for a Cambodian visa). Contact any local tour operator in Saigon or make arrangements with tour operators in Chau Doc (see below), or, coming from Cambodia, with Capitol Tours in Phnom Penh.

VISITOR INFORMATION & TOURS

Should you be crossing over from Cambodia and looking for onward connection by cafe bus, tiny **Mekong Tours** (10 Quang Trung, ✆ **076/386-8222;** or 14 Nguyen Huu Canh, near the central market, ✆ **076/356-2828;** www.mekongvietnam.com) runs a terrible guesthouse but offers good tours and bus connections to other parts of the delta or with Saigon.

Fast Facts Chau Doc

Banks & Currency Exchange There are a few small banks in little Chau Doc, but your best bet for currency exchange is at the Victoria Hotel. Best to bring enough money for on-tour incidentals (usually few) and carry a few U.S. dollars if you're coming from Cambodia.

Internet On the post office grounds (see below), find **Diem Truy Cap,** a small Internet storefront with rather slow service at 6,000 VND per hour. In the center of town near the market, try **Saigon Net,** at 40 Nguyen Van Thoai (✆ **076/356-1491**), with similar service.

Post Office The main branch is at 73 Le Loi St. (✆ **076/386-7900**), just adjacent to the large riverside park. The main office is open from 6am to 10pm.

WHERE TO STAY

There are a few minihotels around town. If you come on a budget tour with **Sinh Café,** you'll stay at 77 **Than Tra Hotel,** 77 Thu Khoa Nghia St. (✆ **076/386-6845**), or something similar: cellblock basic, but cheap, with air-conditioning.

Song Sao Hotel This is just a basic minihotel overlooking the town's main square. Some rooms are pretty stinky with disinfectant and others are a bit beat-up, so ask to see the room first before ponying up with any loot. Bathrooms are clean but of the guesthouse bathroom style (with shower in room).

12–13 Nguyen Huu Canh St., on the main square in town. ✆ **076/356-1776.** Fax 076/386-8820. 24 units. $11–$15 double. No credit cards. *In room:* A/C, TV, Wi-Fi.

Trung Nguyen Hotel This minihotel gets kudos for its clean, basic rooms stacked high above the marketplace. They have no services to speak of, but the staff is friendly as all get-out, and basic rooms—at the same price as some of the grittier choices in this category, have cable TV, working air-conditioning, and no bad odors (yet).

86 Bach Dang St., near the market. ✆ **076/386-6158.** Fax 076/386-8674. trunghotel@yahoo.com. 15 units. $13–$17 double. No credit cards. **Amenities:** Bikes; Internet. *In room:* A/C, TV, fridge.

Victoria Chau Doc ★ The riverside Victoria Chau Doc stands proud on the banks of the Bassac, a busy but captivating stretch of the Mekong. The 10-year-old resort is beginning to look worn around the edges, but it is still your best option in Chau Doc and the staff remains friendly and eager to please. Rooms are a good size, with wood floors and fine detail throughout—a tidy, comfortable colonial copy. Prices are based on the view (an extra $15 for a view of the river). Bathrooms are nice black-and-white-tile affairs and are large, though taps and shower heads are starting to show their age. The beds are similarly grand in size, but getting a tad lumpy. Halls are done in a comfortable antique tile, and the general atmosphere of this old riverside dandy is quite pleasant. There's a small pool and decks with great views. They have a private boat for tours or connections to Cambodia, and the helpful front-desk staff can arrange any local tours.

32 Le Loi St., Chau Doc Town, An Giang. ✆ **076/386-5010.** Fax 076/386-5020. www.victoriahotels-asia.com. 92 units. $127–$143 double; $187 suite. MC, V. **Amenities:** Restaurant; bar; free bikes; concierge; fitness center; Internet; riverside pool; room service; spa. *In room:* A/C, TV, minibar, fridge, Wi-Fi.

WHERE TO DINE

The fine **Bassac Restaurant** at the Victoria Chau Doc (above) serves fine Vietnamese and Western cuisine in an air-conditioned dining room or on a picturesque deck. Beyond the otherwise bland **Thuan Loi Hotel** (18 Tran Hung Dao St.; ✆ **076/386-6134**) lies a charming floating restaurant serving basic Vietnamese fare. The restaurant is made up of a trio of thatched huts balanced on sticks over the river. Be sure to book ahead, as even a small tour group can take over the entire place; have your hotel concierge reserve the corner table in the main hut for unobstructed views of the river.

Chau Doc's other local dining options are in and around the market, particularly at the end near the city center and busy square, or in one of the town center's basic storefront eateries that serve good local fish, among other Vietnamese specialties. Try **Hong Phat** (77 Chi Lang St.; ✆ **076/386-6950**) for Chinese and European facsimiles (daily 9am–9pm).

ATTRACTIONS

The sprawling riverside market at the town center, a crossroads for goods to and from is a feast for the eyes (and the nose), and there are some small temples to visit in the small downtown area. Even the most budget tour will take you to the **floating villages ★★** in wooden sampans rowed in the unique "forward stroke" Vietnamese style (give it a try).

You'll get to see a unique way of life and visit one of the many catfish farms that, collectively, are taking the world market by storm.

About 7km (4¼ miles) out of town to the north, and not a bad day trip by bicycle, is the **Sam Mountain ★**, a popular local pilgrimage peak. There's a colorful temple at the base of the mountain, and the path up is dotted with smaller spots for worship and shade-giving awnings where you can buy a Coke, stretch out in a hammock, and enjoy the view. It's a tough hike that might have you saying, "What in the Sam Hill?" But this is the only high spot—some 230m (755 ft.)—for miles and the view is like looking at a map of the Mekong's overflowing tributaries.

Easily arranged at any hotel or tour desk in Chau Doc, a visit to **Tuc Dup Hill** is a revisiting of some of the delta's worst history. Here, U.S. forces tried—but failed—to put a stop to small-time insurgencies and logistical support from Cambodia. Called the "Two Million Dollar Hill" for the kind of resources the U.S. poured into taking the hill, Tuc Dup was successfully defended by the Viet Cong throughout a 4-month U.S. assault. Near Tuc Dup, you'll see graves and memorials to later skirmishes, some very bloody, between Vietnamese and Cambodian soldiers and villagers.

CHAU DOC AFTER DARK

Just west of the market, the town's central square lights up like a wonderland at night, with hanging Christmas lights on the trees and faux electric fireworks atop poles around a central temple area and a lit-up Buddha of Compassion. The square is a good place to strike up a friendly conversation with locals. Grab a lawn chair at one of the many coffee bars serving the sweet local gelatin called *che,* and say *"Chao chi/em/anh"* to the person sitting nearest you (see chapter 16 to find out which is best for whom).

5 PHU QUOC ISLAND

120km (75 miles) W (over sea) from Rach Gia (Rach Gia is 250km/155 miles S of Saigon by road)

The same size as Singapore, the island of Phu Quoc lies off the west coast of Vietnam's Mekong Delta. At times claimed by Cambodia and Thailand, the island is now like an armed fortress of the Vietnamese navy, and 80% of the island is protected as the Phu Quoc National Forest. Exploring the dirt-track byways of the forested isle, among picturesque pepper plantations and long stretches of deserted beach, is a hoot. A visit to Phu Quoc is a good, affordable opportunity to relax, spend time on the beach, and snorkel or scuba-dive. Get there soon and someday you'll be able to say, "I went there before it was touristy."

The pepper industry on Phu Quoc has just gotten back up to speed after a long gap since the days when every French table had a shaker of Phu Quoc's finest. Phu Quoc is most famous for production of *nuoc mam,* the noxious fish sauce that is part of any meal in Vietnam. U.S. pilots flying over the island during the Vietnam War joked that the fumes from *nuoc mam* factories of Phu Quoc were enough to blow out the torch on a jet engine. Find a guide on the island, and you'll be able to get up-close and personal with the aromatic production of Vietnam's most versatile condiment.

Phu Quoc was for many years an off-the-map tourist destination, but the developers, led by Saigontourist's large Saigon Phu Quoc Resort, are coming in droves. Still, services remain limited, and dining is more or less available only at small seaside resorts on Long

A Unique Breed: The Phu Quoc Ridgeback

Found only on the island of Phu Quoc, the medium-size Phu Quoc Ridgeback is a bit taller and sturdier than the average curly-tailed street mutts you find elsewhere in Vietnam. Tenacious hunters, intelligent, and loyal, Ridgebacks are credited with nearly completely ridding the island of all things that crawl, walk, or creep. Locals still employ the dogs to hunt small game. Usually black, and with a slightly blunted pointy nose and perky ears, Ridgebacks are not under any specific control or pedigree breeding, so they come in all shapes and sizes.

As elsewhere in Vietnam, dogs roam free and travel in packs, which means you should be mindful if out on the beach or rural roads late at night. I saw one of the worst dogfights I've ever seen in my life on this island. If leaving by boat or visiting the pier area in far southern An Thoi town, keep an eye out for the small kennels where local entrepreneurs sell Ridgebacks. I got one guy down to about $30, and a strong, healthy pup goes for a whopping $100 in Saigon—a fortune in a country where dogs are more or less meat on feet. The dogs are said to breed only on the island, and controlled breeding on the mainland has been unsuccessful.

Beach. The quiet, undeveloped quality of this beach escape—just a short, easy hop from Saigon—is the real attraction.

The Six Senses group, popular developers of Evason Ana Mandara Resort and Evason Hideaway Ana Mandara in Nha Trang (see chapter 11), plans on having a large resort here in the near future, and developers are lined up, wringing their hands and ready to build. Thanks to red tape, this quiet island is still a dirt-track backwater, with bungalows and little in the way of infrastructure. But plans are underway for expanding the airport and including international flights.

Weather on the island, thanks to cool ocean breezes, is always temperate and thus a great escape from sultry Saigon. The coolest time to go to Phu Quoc is from December to February. ***Note:*** The island is quite rainy and exposed to monsoon storms, from May to November.

GETTING THERE

Vietnam Airlines offers daily flights from both Ho Chi Minh City and Rach Gia, a small coastal town adjacent to Phu Quoc on the Mekong Delta mainland. Some flights actually hop from Ho Chi Minh to Rach Gia and then on to Phu Quoc. From Ho Chi Minh, the flight is about 45 minutes on a midsize turboprop plane. The cost is 830,000 VND for the one-way trip. Flights leave Saigon's **Tan Son Nhat** domestic terminal daily at 9, 10:20, and 11:50am, and 12:45pm. Return flights from **Phu Quoc Airport** to Saigon leave daily at 8:35, 10:50, and 11:55am, and 1:25 and 2:20pm. Contact Vietnam Airlines in Ho Chi Minh directly at their office at 116 Nguyen Hue, District 1 (✆ **08/3824-4482**), across from the Rex Hotel, or call their reservations office at ✆ **08/3832-0320.** ***Note:*** Try to book at least a week in advance; residents of Phu Quoc often travel to Ho Chi Minh City for daily shopping trips and errands, so these flights fill up fast.

Any travel agent can make arrangements for a small fee. A motorbike taxi from the airport to Long Beach is just 10,000 VND, but drivers eager to adopt you and be your guide for your time on the island means that these guys will make the trip for 5,000 VND, or even free, if you promise to rent their bike from them (a popular way to explore the island). An international airport is in the works, but for now there's nothing more than blueprints and a model. It is expected to be up and operational by 2012.

There are regular high-speed ferryboats that connect Phu Quoc with Rach Gia on the mainland. The 3-hour, 140km (87-mile) trip is relatively smooth (in the low season) and costs just 240,000 VND. Boats connect with the island by the far southern port town of An Thoi; it's a 30,000 VND motorbike taxi or 12,000 VND bus ride between An Thoi and the Long Beach area; expect to pay 180,000 VND for a taxi between An Thoi and Duong Dong Beach. **Tramaco Boat Tours** (12 Tu Do St., ✆ **077/387-8655** in Rach Gia; Khu Pho 1, Duong Dong, ✆ **077/398-0666** on Phu Quoc) and **Duong Dong Express** (18 Nguyen Cong Tru, ✆ **077/387-9765** in Rach Gia; 4 Tran Hung Dao, Duong Dong, ✆ **077/398-1648** on Phu Quoc) are the two main companies; both have early morning departures. Be sure to buy boat tickets at least 1 day in advance.

Be warned that the boat can get overcrowded and may have the unfortunate lingering odor of previous passengers' weak stomachs. The journey is pleasant and smooth during the low season but is often beset by jarring waves during the high season; hotel staff can advise you of ocean conditions. Taxis and motorbikes congregate outside the ferry port and can shuttle you to the bus terminal (some 6km/3¾ miles out of town). From there, public buses can take you onward to Ho Chi Minh City, Can Tho, or Chau Doc. **KienGiang Tourist** (36 Pham Hong Thai; ✆ **077/386-2081**), a small tour operator in Rach Gia, can help arrange onward travel, but you may end up spending a night in the busy port town. I recommend flying directly from Ho Chi Minh City to Phu Quoc, but another good option is a multiday trip on the Mekong Delta ending in Chau Doc; from there, arrange with your tour operator for passage to oceanside Rach Gia and hop one of the short flights or (gulp) the crowded hydrofoil on to Phu Quoc before returning by flight to Ho Chi Minh.

There's also the "Super Dong," which connects between Phu Quoc's southern An Thoi Port and Rach Gia. The Dong departs in the afternoon and, unless you arrange your own transport from the pier at Rach Gia, that means an overnight there. Buy tickets on the Dong for 240,000 VND or 220,000 VND (8am and 1pm departure, respectively) at their offices on Phu Quoc (34 Tran Hung Dao; ✆ **077/398-0111**) or in Rach Gia (14 Tu Do; ✆ **077/387-7742**). The **local bus station in Rach Gia** is at 260A Nguyen Binh Khiem St. Buses connect regularly with Chau Doc, Can Tho, and on to Ho Chi Minh's Mien Tay Bus Station. Head to **Mai Linh Express** (✆ **077/382-9292**) for comfortable shuttle buses to Ho Chi Minh City (105,000 VND) or Can Tho (55,000 VND). There's also a minibus stand—with cozier, air-conditioned vans that have assigned seats—on Tran Quoc Toan Street. For all ground transport, you can also contact the office of helpful **KienGiang Tourist** (36 Pham Hong Thai; ✆ **077/386-2081**).

Boats also run from Phu Quoc's eastern port of Ham Ninh to Ha Tien, a small town just adjacent to the Cambodia border, but departures are irregular and, especially in dry season because of low river water, they require a small boat to take you from the ferry to a point some distance from the Ha Tien area. Stick to the boats between An Thoi and Rach Gia, or fly.

ORIENTATION

The island is over 50km (31 miles) in length and just 20km (12 miles) wide at its center. The Phu Quoc Airport is near **Duong Dong,** the island's largest town, a fishing port on the western shore. From Duong Dong, Tran Hung Dao Street connects with Long Beach, where you'll find most of the island resorts. Ong Lang Beach is about 6km (3¾ miles) north of Duong Dong. At the northernmost point of the island, you're just 15km (9⅓ miles) from Cambodian waters.

GETTING AROUND

Taxis wait just outside the **Phu Quoc Airport** (✆ **077/384-6742**) arrival terminal. Starting rates are 12,000 VND for the first 2km (1¼ miles) and 2,000 VND per 200m (656 ft.) thereafter. **Mai Linh Taxi** (✆ **077/397-9797**) is a reliable company. Phu Quoc is also a great place to putter around on a motorbike—the dirt roads are mostly smooth and there is hardly any traffic. An all-day motorbike rental will set you back 200,000 VND.

Fast Facts Phu Quoc

Bank & Currency Exchange The **Vietcombank** branch on 20 Duong 30/4 Street (✆ **077/398-1036;** Mon–Sat 7–11am and 1–4pm; www.vietcombank.com.vn) has comprehensive services, including traveler's check cashing, currency exchange, and now an **ATM** compatible with most international cards (MAC, Cirrus, and so on). Just across the street from Vietcombank is a branch of **Western Union** (✆ **077/384-8621**), where you can make that important SOS call back home for a few bucks.

Internet There's decent **Internet** service next to the post office.

Post Office The **post office** is in the town center, just down the Duong 30/4 from the Vietcombank (✆ **077/384-6177**). It's open from 6:30am to 9pm (closed Sun).

WHERE TO STAY & DINE

If, for whatever reason, you hanker for in-town living, **Long Beach Hotel** (Cua Lap, Duong To Commune; ✆ **077/398-1818**) is a basic minihotel in the heart of Duong Dong, but considering that you can bag yourself a seaside resort for just peanuts more, there's little reason to stay here.

Dining is best at your resort. In Duong Dong, you'll find the usual host of local fare, but nothing spectacular. Saigon Phu Quoc Hotel has good seafood and is the ritziest joint on the island. Rainbow Divers' **Rainbow Bar** (✆ **0913/400-964**), on the main beach access road, has a little beachside place serving good burgers and familiar Western fare. At the entrance to Kim Hoa Resort, **Carole's** (✆ **077/384-8884**) serves excellent seafood specialties and familiar Western fare such as wood-oven pizzas.

Long Beach

Long Beach is where you'll find the island's best accommodations. The beach is getting busier with touts and sellers, but a friendly, laid-back atmosphere prevails. Ong Lang Beach (see below) is just to the north of Duong Dong town and is slated for large-scale resort development.

Beach Club ★ So far the farthest south of the many budget resorts along Long Beach, budget Beach Club is a great choice for a few days of quiet and fun in the sun. British owner Mike and his Vietnamese wife, Thien, are the most gracious and helpful hosts. Accommodations are basic—large, tidy, fan rooms with mosquito nets in a small block set back from the beach, and a similar standard in free-standing bungalows at beachside—but the friendly staff and laid-back feel of this hideaway draws you in. There are hammocks in every spot of shade, and the hotel's dogs, fine specimens of the Phu Quoc Ridgeback (see the box, "A Unique Breed: The Phu Quoc Ridgeback," above) are friendly and playful (quite unique in a land where dogs are normally abused or neglected if they aren't eaten). The food here is tops, and this is a good place to meet other travelers. Mike is a wealth of information on the area; he can happily provide maps and arrange any rentals or tours.

On the south end of Long Beach. ✆ **077/398-0998.** www.beachclub-vietnam.com. 10 units. $20 for hotel block room; $25 for bungalow. No credit cards. **Amenities:** Restaurant; bar; motorbikes. *In room:* Fan only (w/mosquito netting), no phone.

Saigon Phu Quoc Resort ★ Large and with all the fixin's of a big self-contained beach resort, the tatty edges and indifferent "big government hotel" service of the Saigon Phu Quoc is a real turnoff. That said, this hotel keeps the highest standard on the island (for now). About 7 years old, some units are getting musty and need to be renovated; newer rooms, though in larger multistory blocks, are the better choice. Saigon Phu Quoc is a sprawling campus on a hillside overlooking the sea. Lounging in the hotel's large central pool and bar area, and lying under one of their large, beachside thatched awnings are great ways to spend the day. They have extensive services, including a spa area, small gym, tennis courts, and golf driving net and putting green—though everything is well used and a little rough around the edges. Rooms aren't anything special—just large, bland, clean spaces, some with "standing Jacuzzi" power showers in tidy bathrooms, others with small tubs. Free-standing "Star Cruise" bungalows at seaside are worth the upgrade, but for my money, nearby budget stops (the others listed here) are comfortable options, and you can use Saigon Phu Quoc's services as an outside guest for a small negotiable fee. ***Note:*** The rack rates listed here are just guidelines; the hotel offers real discounts, particularly in low season from April to November, and it's not a bad idea to visit the front desk in the afternoon, when they have lots of empty beds, and see what you can finagle.

1 Tran Hung Dao, Long Beach, Phu Quoc (just a few clicks south of Duong Dong Town). ✆ **077/384-6999.** Fax 077/384-7163. www.sgphuquocresort.com.vn or www.vietnamphuquoc.com. 83 units. Apr–Oct $79–$109 double, $149–$189 family rooms and suites; Nov $99–$149 double, 209–$259 family rooms and suites; Dec–Mar $124–$347 double, $407–$501 family rooms and suites. MC, V. **Amenities:** 2 restaurants; 3 bars; babysitting; bikes; children's center and small playground; golf pitching net and putting green; health club; Internet; room service; tennis court; watersports rentals (kayaks). *In room:* A/C, TV, fridge, hair dryer, minibar, Wi-Fi.

Sao Bien—Sea Star Resort ★ New to the beach, Sea Star is one of those little workhorse resorts that has found its own by not trying to be too much. It's just rooms—basic, two-unit, free-standing concrete bungalows with tile floors, hard but cozy beds, air-conditioning, TV, and plain bathrooms, all clean, square, and without much style. Who needs style when your room opens right onto the sandy beach? (All of the rooms do.) Large rattan rockers are great for putting your feet up and diving into that novel you've been carrying around.

Ba Keo—Khu Pho 7—Duong Dong, Phu Quoc (on the southern end of the dusty Long Beach access road). ✆ **077/398-2161.** 37 units. $30–$55 double. No credit cards. **Amenities:** Restaurant; bar; bikes and motorbikes. *In room:* A/C, TV, fridge, minibar, Wi-Fi.

Duong Dong Beach

Grand Mercure La Veranda ★★ This is, hands down, the best resort on the island. Resort bungalows are laid out around a small natural garden or oceanside; I highly recommend springing for the latter. Beachside bungalows come with the added bonus of hearing ocean waves as you drift off to sleep. They also have bigger bathrooms (equipped with separate tubs) than the other units. All bungalows come with private balconies and cozy four-poster beds dressed with luxurious feathery soft sheets. Art Deco is the theme throughout, though with a twist of modernity, such as bright purple walls offset by lime-green curlicue borders—it's cheeky without being cheesy. The main house is a classic colonial mansion with a restaurant on the second floor serving a fine selection of French fare and sumptuous Vietnamese food at affordable prices. Dining at the resort is an excellent choice not only for the food, but also for the view and the relaxing ambience created by the sound of live jazz piano from the downstairs bar.

Tran Hung Dao St., Duong Dong Beach. ✆ **077/398-2988.** Fax 077/398-2998. www.mercure-asia.com. 43 units. $160–$215 room/villa; $330 La Veranda suite. AE, MC, V. **Amenities:** 2 restaurants; bar; Jacuzzi; outdoor pool; room service; spa. *In room:* A/C, satellite TV/DVD, movie library, hair dryer, minibar, Wi-Fi.

Ong Lang Beach

Just 6km (3¾ miles) north of Duong Dong town, a little turnoff leads to this collection of bungalows. Go before it becomes a giant resort area (soon).

Phu Quoc Resort or **Thang Loi** (✆ **077/398-5002;** www.phu-quoc.de) is a little budget enclave of simple, rustic bungalows starting at $10 (down the northern fork of the turnoff on the main road; south is Mango Bay, see below). The resort is in a shaded grove high above the beach, and the central dining area is a good place to pick up a game of cards and meet some fellow travelers.

Mango Bay Resort ★ Billed as a "low-density resort" with an eye to the environment and in harmony with the surroundings, Mango Bay is a cool off-the-track collection of cozy bungalows along a picturesque, rocky bay. Sandy paths connect simple, spacious, free-standing units, each separated from the next by a good distance, which affords you privacy. It's boutique rustic, with finely molded colored concrete in pale yellow set against dark wood and high ceilings of thatch. Bathrooms are enormous outdoor areas with floors done in aggregate, just simple fixtures in a partly covered outdoor space with a low bamboo fence for privacy. Room details are stylish, with funky designer lamps, and in wood with tile and concrete inlay on floors in some units. Older rustic wooden units are more atmospheric. All rooms have fans. There are also budget hotel-block rooms. All have big balcony areas.

Ong Lang Beach, Phu Quoc Island. ✆ **077/398-1693.** www.mangobayphuquoc.com. 30 units. $42 for hotel block double; $49 for older wood bungalows; $56–$70 for newer concrete and wood bungalows. No credit cards. **Amenities:** Restaurant; bar. *In room:* Fan, no phone.

EXPLORING THE ISLAND

Phu Quoc's quiet dirt roads are a great place to get your motor runnin' and ying ying ying all over the island. Motorbike rental for 1 day costs 200,000 VND and can be arranged at any hotel front desk or from the motorbike taxi lads themselves at the airport.

Heading north along the west coast of the island, roads of thick red dust connect villages set along salty inlets crowded with small fishing boats. You'll first come to the beach area of **Ong Lang,** which hosts a small clutch of resorts and services along a quiet stretch of sand; a small turnoff from the main road takes you there. Continuing north, follow long stretches of open beach lined with fish and squid out to dry on large bamboo mats. There are lots of opportunities along the way for complete seclusion. The coastal road reaches **Gan Dau,** a small town of busy *nuoc mam* (fish sauce) factories. ***Note:*** Don't buy bottles of *nuoc mam* as souvenirs; the pungent sauce is banned from Vietnam Airlines and virtually all flights out of the country! Farther out on the peninsula area, you'll find a few local hangout spots with hammocks under shade trees by the beach.

From Gan Dau, you can turn inland and make a long clockwise loop. It's 13km (8 miles) along jungle road to the town of Rach Vieu, and another 6km (3¾ miles) east brings you to the **Suai Cai Crossroad.** From there you can go 13km (8 miles) to the beaches of Bai Thom (a military base on the far north end of the island), or even get motocross for the long trip down the treacherous trails on the island's east side; most take the short loop inland, some 16km (10 miles) heading back to Duong Dong town.

Going south from central Duong Dong town, toward the An Thoi Port area on the far southern tip of the island, are a few attractions. The west coast road is unpaved and bumpy, but far more interesting than the paved central road (though that's a good way to head back to your hotel).

Along the coast, **Phu Quoc Pearl Farm** (Duong To Village, 10km/6¼ miles south on the western coastal road, Tran Hung Dao; ✆ **091/399-3201**) is a relaxed roadside stop overlooking a long stretch of open beach along the dusty coastal road, as well as a small museum with good explanations about the complex process of pearl farming and a very high-end boutique with some very unique colored and clear pearls in fine gold and silver settings. Stop here if you're heading to Sao Beach (Bai Sao) in the far south.

Nha Tu Phu Quoc is the old jail where the French housed Vietnamese dissidents. The sight is just an enclosed field with old fallen-down sheet metal Quonset huts, but there is a little adjoining museum with some photos and information (daily 7–11:30am and 1:30–4pm).

The town of **An Thoi** in the far south is little more than a turnaround point, a busy little port worth a wander, though.

One-day **boat trips** from Phu Quoc to the **An Thoi Archipelago** off the southern tip of the island are fun. Saigontourist runs regular junkets to this chain of 15 small islands and islets surrounded by deep blue waters, and every hotel works with the same boat-trip consolidators to arrange the $15 all-day tour, which includes a lunch and snorkeling gear rental.

Saigon Phu Quoc Resort also runs evening **squid fishing trips.** You're sure to see the lights of squid fishermen far out on the horizon each evening; it looks like a small city out there at certain times of year. The tour leaves at 4:30pm and you motor out to join the large fleet. Fishermen catch squid by attracting them with a light and hooking them near the surface, a fun and playful jigging technique. Kids love it.

Not far from the ferry terminal of An Thoi, some 25km (16 miles) south of central Dong Duong town, lies beautiful **Khem Beach,** a long white-sand stretch lined with palms and with some actual pounding surf. On clear days, it's great for snorkeling. The beach is still free of the developers' shovels, which means no resorts (yet). You'll just spot a few lazy beachside sugar shacks with low tables under umbrellas and lots of hammocks in the shade where you can sip a cool drink, order lunch, and watch the day go by. It's a popular beach for domestic tourists, though, so it gets pretty crowded on the weekends.

SCUBA & SNORKELING

As in their other locations in Vietnam (Nha Trang, Whale Island, and Can Dao Island), **Rainbow Divers** (✆ **0913/400-964;** www.divevietnam.com) runs a very professional outfit here on Phu Quoc. Check out their small office near the boat-booking offices just south of Duong Dong town, at their popular **Rainbow Bar** on the road near the resorts south of Duong Dong, or at their beachside **Rainbow Restaurant**—as well as at most hotel front desks (as in Nha Trang, the Rainbow Divers folks are already going a little overboard with exposure and advertising). There are other small dive companies on Phu Quoc, but Rainbow is the most professional and, unlike the others, has access to all of Phu Quoc's coral dive sites in the north, as well as in the south at the An Thoi Islands. The diving season is from October to May, depending on currents.

14

Cambodia

Cambodia is unpredictable—very unpredictable—but that's the allure for many travelers who come here. Traffic is chaos. Corruption is law. Poverty is endemic. Less than half of Cambodians have access to clean water and sanitation facilities. Children suffer from malnutrition and inadequate immunizations against polio, measles, and diphtheria. The political situation is uncertain. And although the good news is that years of rampant violence and anarchy are over and a stable coalition government is now in power, strong destabilizing elements remain and a powerful criminal underworld still exists—which means that things are never as they seem.

The sign on the ride from the airport reads: "Abuse a child in this country, go to jail in yours," and speaks of multilateral participation with foreign governments to crack down on child abusers, but foreign "sexpats" and fugitives from the law still find Cambodia a nice, cozy place to crawl under the rug. Ownership is tenuous, at best, and many foreign investors have their investments just evaporate. Illegal logging of old-growth teak is still common practice, despite the best efforts of regional and international bodies.

In Cambodia you can pay to fire heavy weaponry that's left over from the recent past of violence. It's a place where sometimes you have to just keep dialing in the hopes of getting a phone connection that works—and where everything is going to happen in "just 15 minutes," which inevitably stretch into hours. What brings so many here is their desire to help; humanitarian-aid workers are the majority in places like Phnom Penh, but tourists flock here also for the incredible temples of Angkor Wat and rural journeys that were too dangerous until only recently.

The situation is grim in this small agrarian kingdom, but things are improving. Following years of war, the chaos and genocide of Pol Pot's Khmer Rouge, and a long period of civil and political instability, Cambodia was for years an armed camp, closed to foreign visitors (except maybe travelers of the danger-seeking variety). The first wave of intervention troops from the United Nations did as much to bolster vice in country as they did to establish order; armed anarchy and banditry ruled until very recent years.

Fortunately, Cambodia is now beginning to heal, and, though this process will take years, the country is enjoying a period of relative stability. Strict gun laws and more tenacious policing of offenders mean that disarming of Cambodia has sped up. Cambodia offers travelers a host of experiences—from the legacy of ancient architecture to a growing urban capital and beautiful countryside. Even the shortest visit is a window into a vibrant ancient culture and a chance to meet with very kind and resilient people.

What brings so many to this Buddhist land of smiles is **Angkor Wat,** the ancient capital and one of the man-made wonders of the world. The temple complex at Angkor is stunning, a monumental Hindu/Buddhist temple compound of behemoth block temples, towering spires, giant carved faces, and ornate bas-reliefs. It's a pilgrimage point for temple aficionados and a place of spiritual significance to many—seeing Angkor is a once-in-a-lifetime experience. Most travelers limit their visit to a few days at the temples and major sites in the growing capital, **Phnom Penh,** which is tatty but charming, with crumbling French colonial architecture and a splendid palace.

Travel in rural Cambodia, once unheard of, is improving, but you still need some tolerance for bumpy roads and rustic accommodations—and getting off the track in Cambodia is a glimpse of a beguiling, unpredictable land. Cambodia is resplendent with natural gifts such as the **Mekong River**—the country's lifeline that connects with **Tonle Sap (Great Lake),** Southeast Asia's largest lake, surrounded by fertile lowlands.

Bouncing around the hinterlands of Cambodia still begs caution, though, and travelers should be aware of the massive amount of UXO (unexploded mines) and the absence of proper medical services. Any of the larger tour operators are a good bet for arranging trips to the likes of mountainous **Rattanakiri** in the northeast, the Thai border area, or rural riverside towns along the Mekong. The country's only port, **Sihanoukville,** is a popular beach destination. Intrepid travelers commonly rent motorcycles or brave rattletrap buses.

Known for warm, beguiling smiles that have weathered great hardship, Khmer people are very friendly, approachable, and helpful; but be warned that the hard sell is on in Cambodia, and you're sure to be harried, especially by the persistent young sellers at Angkor Wat. Nevertheless, travelers here are sure to meet with great kindness.

Tourism is growing in leaps and bounds. Many **nongovernmental organizations (NGOs)** here do their part to rebuild and support the growing nation. Their activities, centered in offices in Phnom Penh, are what keep social services and the infrastructure at subsistence levels. If you're interested, volunteer opportunities abound and you can effect great change as a volunteer or through donations. The number of foreign aid workers means increased quality of services; hotels and restaurants in Siem Reap and Phnom Penh are on par with any in the region, although outside of these two centers, they are sparse.

If only to see the Angkor temples, the trip to Cambodia is worth it. This beguiling land that's shaking off the shackles of a devastating recent history is an exciting, emerging tourist destination.

1 GETTING TO KNOW CAMBODIA

THE LAY OF THE LAND

About the size of Missouri, some 181,035 sq. km (69,898 sq. miles), Cambodia's 20 provinces are bordered by Laos in the north, Vietnam in the east, Thailand to the west, and the Gulf of Thailand to the south. The marine port in Cambodia, Sihanoukville, is connected to the capital and largest city, Phnom Penh, via a major U.S.-built highway.

The mighty Mekong enters from Laos to the north and nearly bisects the country. The river divides into two main tributaries at Phnom Penh before it traces a route to the delta in Vietnam, and most areas of population density lie along the river valleys and fertile plains of this great river and its tributaries. Near Siem Reap, the Tonle Sap (Great Lake) is the largest lake in Southeast Asia. In the monsoon summer months, when the Mekong is swollen from the snows of Tibet, the river becomes choked with silt and backs up on the Mekong Delta. The result is an anomaly: The Tonle Sap River relieves the pressure by changing the direction of its flow and draining the Mekong Delta hundreds of miles in the opposite direction and into the Tonle Sap Lake.

The northeast of the country, Rattanakiri Province, and areas bordering Vietnam are quite mountainous and rugged, as are the Thai border areas defined by the Dangrek Mountains in the northwest and the Cardamom Mountains in the southwest. These jungle forest regions are a rich source for timber in the region, and steps toward preservation come slow.

A LOOK AT THE PAST

Some 2 millennia ago, a powerful people known as the Khmer ruled over much of present-day Southeast Asia, including parts of what is now eastern Thailand, southern Vietnam, and Laos. Theirs was a kingdom that seems to have been created in a dream: wondrous temples, magnificent cities rising from steamy jungles, and glorious gods.

The story of Khmer civilization is one of a slow decline from the zenith of the powerful Angkor Civilization of the 11th century. War and years of alternating occupation by neighboring Thailand to the west and Vietnam to the east, later by the French and Japanese, had Cambodia bouncing like a strategic Ping-Pong ball, and the Khmer kingdom's size was chiseled away considerably. Remaining is what we know today as Cambodia, a tiny land half the size of Germany.

The name Cambodia is an Anglicized version of the French *Cambodge,* derived from the tribe of northern India from which the Khmer are said to descend. Citizens are alternately referred to as Khmer or Cambodian; the language is Khmer. Whatever the origins, the name Cambodia hardly evokes thoughts of ancient glory: Especially in the West, Cambodia suggests instead a history of oppression, civil war, genocide, drug running, and coup d'état. Constant political turbulence, armed citizenry, bandits, and war fallout, such as unexploded mines and bombs, have given the country a reputation as one of the world's most dangerous places to travel rather than a repository of man-made and natural wonders. It's important to have perspective on the country's troubled history in order to understand the present. Only then can we appreciate the present civil order and the fact that citizens have been or are being disarmed, and that Cambodia is making the slow push into this new century.

A TURBULENT POLITICAL PAST

Cambodia is populated by people of the **Mon-Khmer** ethnic group, who probably migrated from the north as far back as 1000 B.C. It was part of the kingdom of Funan, a Southeast Asian empire that also extended into Laos and Vietnam, to the 6th century, when it was briefly absorbed into a rebel nation called Chenla. It then evolved into its glorious Angkor period in the 8th century, from which sprung many of Cambodia's treasures, most notably the lost city of Angkor.

By the late 12th century, however, the Angkor kingdom began a decline, marked by internal rebellions. Angkor was lost to the Kingdom of Siam in 1431, and Vietnam jousted with Siam and also had a hand in controlling the kingdom, to some degree, beginning in the early 17th century. The French took over completely in 1863, followed by the Japanese and then the French again. Cambodia finally regained independence in 1953 under the leadership of **Prince Norodom Sihanouk.**

Vietnamese Communist outposts in the country, however, drew Cambodia into the Vietnam War. It was heavily bombed by U.S. forces in the late 1960s. A U.S.-backed military coup followed in 1970, but in 1975 the infamous **Khmer Rouge,** led by the tyrannical **Pol Pot,** took over Cambodia, renamed it Democratic Kampuchea,

and established a totalitarian regime in the name of communism. Opposition—even imaginary opposition—was brutally crushed, resulting in the death of over two million Cambodians. The civil and Vietnam wars decimated Cambodian infrastructure. It became, and still is, one of the world's poorest nations, with a mainly agrarian economy and a literacy rate of about 35%.

In response to Khmer Rouge infractions in its country, Vietnam invaded Cambodia in 1978 and occupied it until 1989, installing a puppet regime led by Hun Sen as prime minister. When Vietnam departed, the United Nations stepped in and engineered a fragile coalition government between the Sihanouk and Hun Sen factions. There was never full agreement, however, and Hun Sen took over in a violent 1997 coup. The Khmer Rouge subsequently waned in power, and Pol Pot died in 1998.

In November 1998, a new coalition government was formed between the two leading parties, leading to relative political peace. Cambodia is now leaning toward a war-crimes tribunal for Khmer Rouge perpetrators, but it still has not decided how to confront its vicious and bloody past and move forward.

Saloth Sar, aka Pol Pot

Known by many names—Pouk, Hay, Pol, "87," Grand-Uncle, Elder Brother, First Brother, and later as "99" and Phem—he might have just one name really: monster. A man who rose from relative obscurity to the highest post in Cambodia, riding on the rungs of a growing socialist movement that, somewhere along the line, and mostly due to his leadership, became genocide, Saloth Sar is responsible for the deaths of untold numbers—estimates range from one million to two million.

Born Saloth Sar (1925) in Kompong Thom, south of Cambodia, Pol Pot's path to power was tangential. He attended some of Cambodia's finest schools and studied abroad in France, where he came in contact with Marxism and socialist ideals that he later bent to create his chaotic kingdom. He worked as a teacher briefly and then took up the mantle of revolutionary, working first alongside and then separately from the Vietnamese Communists. Pol Pot lived on the jungle fringes between Cambodia and Thailand, carrying on his violent ideological revolution until his death in 1998.

THE PRESENT

July 2003 elections went off without incident, but it took nearly a year for negotiation of a government coalition. Hun Sen still reigns as prime minister. In the fall of 2004, King Norodom Sihanouk, Cambodia's longtime standard-bearer through the many violent regime changes and trying times, abdicated, selecting his son Norodom Sihamoni, a retired ballet dancer, to take up the symbolic post of king.

Cambodia's economy is experiencing a 5% annual growth rate, mostly spurned by tourism, but the scene in rural Cambodia is bleak. Basic medical services are nonexistent; education and job training are out of reach for rural peasantry; and international monitors and aid organizations look to this young population (some 60% under the age of 20), the survivors and the next generation after genocide, to foster peace and productivity. The forecast is not good. The proliferation of new AIDS cases in Cambodia, and the inability to treat patients, is a major concern. Rural travel entails following safety precautions to the letter (see "Safety," below) and staying abreast of the political situation—instability being the hallmark—but know that the Cambodia of today is a much safer and saner land than only a few years ago. And tourist dollars are a big help.

THE KHMER PEOPLE

Ninety percent of Cambodia's 11 million people are ethnic Khmer, the remainder a mix of ethnic Vietnamese, Chinese, hilltribes, and a small pocket of Cham Muslims. Cambodia's history is a road map of incursions and invasion. Cambodia is a geographic and cultural crossroads of the two powers, India and China, that shaped Southeast Asia and, more than any country in the region, reflects the French term *Indochine.* Khmer culture, like nearby Laos, is defined by Theravada Buddhism.

ETIQUETTE

Traditions and practices in Cambodia, like neighboring Thailand and Laos, are closely tied with Theravada Buddhism. Modest dress is expected of all visitors, and bare midriffs or short shorts are an offense to many and will cause a stir. Men and women should go easy on public displays of affection. As in all Buddhist countries, it is important to respect the space around a Buddhist monk; women especially should avoid touching and even speaking to the men in orange robes outside the temple.

In personal interaction, keep it light and friendly, especially when bargaining or handling any business affairs. If Khmer people are confused, misunderstand, or disagree, they do what many Westerners find inconceivable: smile, nod, and agree while whole in the knowledge that they will do something different. This is difficult to understand, but try to remember that if you're angry and lots of people around you are smiling, you're unlikely to have achieved your desired aim (in short, you're doomed). Direct discourse is certainly not standard procedure here, and many Western visitors can feel cheated by that misunderstanding. Be clear in what you expect from someone—whether a guide, a motorbike driver, or a business associate—and get firm affirmation of that fact. Listen closely to what comes after the *but* in "Yes, but . . . ."

On the line of cultural "no-nos," remember that the feet are considered dirty and that the head is sacred and pure. This means that even pointing the feet in the direction of another or stepping over someone, thus exposing the souls of the feet, is impolite. Touching someone's head, even tussling a child's hair, should be avoided.

Hospitality has its own elaborate rules, and, like in any culture, it is important to accept when possible, or comfortable, and say thank you, *"Awk koun."*

CUISINE

A crossroads of culture, Cambodia is also a crossroads of cuisine, with a mixture of Thai, Laotian, and Vietnamese, as well as newcomers Chinese and French. Just like its neighbors, rice is the staple of the Khmer diet, but not even the devastating cultural purge of Pol Pot, in which all foreign food and customs were banned, could remove the French-infused tradition of eating good baguettes and specialty breads with good milk coffee at outdoor cafes (you'll even see folks still playing boulle in provincial towns). Don't pass up a snack at one of the many glass-sided bread carts that roam city streets, particularly in Phnom Penh; mostly sweet breads, but also good baguettes, bought at these trucks are good to have on all-day bus rides and long 1-day trips. You can find lots of stands selling Vietnamese baguettes stuffed with pâté as well.

Dining Khmer style is a long, jocular affair, with cover-the-table spreads of various dishes shared by many over long hours of drinking and chat. Fish is the most prized entree, and Khmer *amok,* a dish of fish steamed in bamboo leaf with coconut milk and curry, is not to be missed. Fried veg and meat dishes abound, some with fiery spices and chili, similar to Thai fare.

Dessert is good sweet cakes and breads or treats made of glutinous rice, or sticky rice, in coconut milk. The list of good local fruit is long, topped by mangos (when in season), papaya, mangosteens *(mankut),* durian, rambutan, jackfruit, and lots of citrus treats, and all kinds of spiky, horned things you're sure to see at the market. Just ask how much and ask the vendor to cut it open for you.

LANGUAGE

The language of Cambodia is called *Khmer,* a term that refers to the ethnic majority of the country but is used to describe all things Cambodian: Khmer people (the Khmer), Khmer food, culture, and so on. Unlike in neighboring Thailand and Laos, the Khmer language is not tonal and is thus more merciful to the casual learner. Basic pronunciation is still frustrating and difficult, though. Khmer script is based on a south Indian model and is quite complex.

Khmer has many loan words from French, Chinese, and now English, especially technical terms. Older Khmers still speak French, and young people are keen to learn and practice English. In the major tour centers, speaking slowly and clearly in basic English phrases will do the trick, but a few choice phrases in Khmer will get you far.

USEFUL KHMER PHRASES

English	Khmer	Pronunciation
Hello	**Soa s'day**	Sew sadday
Goodbye	**Lia haoy**	Lee howie
Thank you	**Awk koun**	Awk coon
Thank you very much	**Awk koun chelan**	Awk coon chalan
How are you?	**Sohk sabai?**	Sook sabai?
I am fine.	**Sohk sabai.**	Sook sabai.
Yes (man)	**Baat**	Baht
Yes (woman)	**Jaa**	Jya
No	**Te**	Tay
I'm sorry	**Sohm To**	Sum too
Do you have _______?	**Men awt men?** (lit. do you have or don't you?)	Men ought men?
Water?	**Tuhk?**	Took?
Toilet?	**Bawngku uhn?**	Bangku oon?
How much?	**Th'lai pohnmaan?**	Tlai bawn mahn?
Can you make it cheaper?	**Som joh th'lai?**	Sum joe tlai?

2 PLANNING YOUR TRIP TO CAMBODIA

VISITOR INFORMATION

You'll find a wealth of information at www.gocambodia.com, or click on "Cambodia" at www.visit-mekong.com. The Cambodian Embassy to the United States sponsors www.embassyofcambodia.org.

- **In the U.S.:** 4500 16th St. NW, Washington, DC 20011 (✆ **202/726-7742;** fax 202/726-8381; www.embassyofcambodia.org). **In New York:** 866 U.N. Plaza, Ste. 420, New York, NY 10017 (✆ **212/421-7626;** fax 212/421-7743).
- **In Australia/New Zealand:** No. 5 Canterbury Crescent, Deakin, ACT 2600, Canberra (✆ **02/6273-1259;** fax 02/6273-1053; www.embassyofcambodia.org.nz).
- **In Thailand:** No. 185 Rajdammri Rd., Lumpini Patumwan, Bangkok 10330, Thailand (✆ **02/254-6630;** fax 02/253-9859).

WORKING WITH A TOUR OPERATOR

Many visitors choose to see Cambodia with the convenience of a guided tour, which is a good idea: It's not only safer and easier, but it also means that you won't miss the finer details of what you're seeing and can visit rural Cambodia in as much comfort as possible. Being part of a larger group tour is a good, affordable option. Even if you travel independently, you might want to sign up with a local tour operator (like Diethelm or Exotissimo, below) once you're there.

Recommended Tour Operators

International

- **Abercrombie & Kent.** 1520 Kensington Rd., Ste. 212, Oakbrook, IL 60523-2141 (✆ **800/554-7016;** fax 630/954-3324; www.aandktours.com).
- **Asia Transpacific Journeys.** 2995 Center Green Court, Boulder, CO 80301 (✆ **800/642-2742** or 303/443-6789; fax 303/443-7078; www.asiatranspacific.com).

Regional

These regional agents are reputable operators with foreign management and a high level of service—whether transport and rooms or all-inclusive tour itineraries. All three act as on-the-ground operators for international travel agents.

- **Diethelm Travel.** No. 65 Street 240, P.O. Box 99, Phnom Penh, Cambodia (✆ **023/219-151;** fax 023/219-150; www.diethelmtravel.com). **In Siem Reap:** House No. 470, Krous Village, Svay Dangkum Commune, Siem Reap, Cambodia (✆ **063/963-524;** fax 063/963-694).
- **Exotissimo.** 46 Norodom Blvd., Phnom Penh (✆ **023/218-948;** fax 023/426-586; www.exotissimo.com). **In Siem Reap:** New Building B, 2021 Street 60MK, Siem Reap (✆ **063/964-323;** fax 063/963-621).

Also, just as Vietnam has its budget "traveler cafes," Cambodia hosts a roster of good budget tour options. The folks at **Capitol Tour** (No. 14 Road 182, Phnom Penh; ✆ **023/217-627**) offer affordable, no-frills tour and transport options. Most trips leave early in the morning from their offices in Phnom Penh or Siem Reap. Also try **Mekong Express** for reliable ground transport.

ENTRY REQUIREMENTS

All visitors must carry a passport and visa. Applying online (http://evisa.mtaic.gov.kh) for a 1-month e-visa costs $25. The procedure is simple, straightforward, and will save you time and energy at the airport/border crossing. Visas can also be issued on arrival at the Phnom Penh or Siem Reap airports for $20, as well as at almost all border crossings. For example, an overland visa-upon-arrival is available from both Thailand (overland from Poipet) and Vietnam (by boat from Chau Doc or by bus through Moc Bai) for $23. Bring one 4×6-inch passport photo for your application.

Tourist visas can be extended three times for a total of 3 months. Any travel agent can perform the service for a small fee. Business visas, for just $25 upon entry, can be extended indefinitely.

CUSTOMS REGULATIONS

For visitors 18 years and older, allowable amounts of goods when entering are as follows: 200 cigarettes or the equivalent quantity of tobacco, one opened bottle of liquor, and a reasonable amount of perfume for personal use. Currency in possession must be declared on arrival. Cambodian Customs on the whole is not stringent. With a long, sad history of theft from the Angkor temples, it is forbidden to carry antiques or Buddhist reliquary out of the country, but Buddhist statues and trinkets bought from souvenir stalls are fine.

MONEY

Cambodia's official currency is the Riel, but the Cambodian economy is tied to the fate of its de facto currency, the U.S. dollar. Greenbacks can be used anywhere. The exchange rate at the time of publication was **4,100 Riel = $1.** It's important to have Riel for smaller purchases, but there's no point in exchanging large amounts of foreign currency. Prices for all but the smallest purchases are in U.S. dollars and are thus listed in this chapter. The **Thai Bhat** is widely accepted in the western region of the country. You'll commonly receive small change in Riel. The Riel comes in denominations of 100, 200, 500, 1,000, 2,000, 5,000, 10,000, 50,000, and 100,000. You cannot change Cambodia's Riel outside the country, so anything you carry home is a souvenir.

ATMS **ANZ Bank** and **Canadia Bank** have ATMs throughout Cambodia with reliable international service.

CURRENCY EXCHANGE You can change traveler's checks in banks in all major towns. Because the U.S. dollar is the de facto currency, it's not a bad idea to change traveler's checks to dollars for a 1% or 2% fee and make all purchases in U.S. cash.

TRAVELER'S CHECKS Traveler's checks are accepted in most major banks for exchange, but not commonly at individual vendors. American Express is a good bet and is represented by **Diethelm** (p. 375).

CREDIT CARDS Cambodia is a cash economy, but credit cards are becoming more widely accepted. Most large hotels and high-end restaurants accept the majors, but you'll want to carry cash for most transactions, and certainly in the countryside.

WHEN TO GO

CLIMATE Cambodia's climate falls into the pattern of the southern monsoons that also hit neighboring Thailand and Vietnam from May to November. The seasonal temperature varies little, meaning that it's always hot (a yearly mean of about 82°F/28°C), and the best time to go is in the dry season from December to April. Wear light, loose clothing, preferably cotton, and bring a hat.

PUBLIC HOLIDAYS & EVENTS **Independence Day** is November 9 (1953) and is celebrated throughout the country like the American Fourth of July. October 31 is **King Sihanouk's Birthday,** and **Khmer New Year** is in the middle of the month in April. There are water festivals and boat races at the end of November, and the **Angkor Festival** is held at the end of July.

SAFETY

Check with your home country's overseas travel bureau or with the **United States Department of State** (click "Travel Warnings" at www.state.gov) to keep abreast of travel advisories and current affairs that could affect your trip.

The days of the Khmer Rouge taking backpackers hostage are long gone, and the general lawlessness and banditry that marked Cambodia as inaccessible and dangerous only a short time ago has abated. Gun-toting thugs, once a common sight in any town, have been disarmed, but old habits die hard and, in general, travelers should take caution. Poverty in rural areas breeds desperation and a volatile climate. Below are some good guidelines.

Warning! Some Important Safety Tips

- Remember that the police and military of Cambodia are not there to protect and serve. Any interaction with the constabulary usually results in frustration and/or you coming away short a few dollars. Contact your embassy for major problems, and call for police assistance only in cases of theft or extreme danger. Demand a ticket if threatened with a fine of any sort, although often, especially for small traffic infractions, it's best to just cough up a buck or two.
- Rural travel is opening up, and you'll find a hearty welcome in even the most remote hamlet, but travelers may find some roads a bit rough. Know, too, that you're really on your own out in the sticks, with no hospitals and limited support services. Banditry has lessened, but still be sure to travel by day (also because of road conditions).
- Especially at night, travelers should stay aware, not unlike in any big city at night; purse snatching is not uncommon in Phnom Penh, and pickpockets are as proficient here as anywhere in the region, so take care.
- Land mines and unexploded ordinances (UXOs) can be found in rural areas in Cambodia, but especially in Battambang, Banteay Meanchey, Pursat, Siem Reap, and Kampong Thom provinces. Don't walk in heavily forested spots or in dry rice paddies without a local guide. Areas around small bridges on secondary roads are particularly dangerous.

Drugs

Cambodia is one of the world's biggest producers of cannabis—not to mention heroin, amphetamines, and other substances—and peddlers abound. You might be tempted to buy or sample substances offered, but if caught, you could face a lengthy jail sentence, which is guaranteed to be uncomfortable. Enough said.

Health Concerns & Vaccinations

In chapter 3, I outline the health essentials for Vietnam, which are quite similar to Cambodia. Health considerations should comprise a good part of your trip planning for Cambodia, even if you're going for only a few weeks. You'll need to cover all the bases to protect yourself from tropical weather and illnesses, and you will need to get special vaccinations if rural areas are on your itinerary. You should begin your vaccinations as necessary (ask your doctor how many weeks before your trip you need to allow to give them time to take effect). If you follow the guidelines here and those of your doctor, however, there's no reason you can't have a safe and healthy trip.

Malaria is not a concern in Phnom Penh or any of the larger towns, but upcountry and even in and around Siem Reap and Angkor Wat, it's quite common. Many travelers take preventative medication. Check with the Centers for Disease Control and Prevention (CDC) at www.cdc.gov for current information. An **antimalarial prophylaxis** is recommended everywhere but in Phnom Penh. Take atovaquone proguanil (brand name

Malarone), doxycycline, or mefloquine (brand name Lariam). If you plan to travel extensively in the rural areas on the western border with Thailand, primaquine is the only effective preventative.

Other mosquito-borne ailments, such as **Japanese encephalitis** and **dengue fever,** are also prevalent. Your best protection is to wear light, loosefitting clothes from wrist to neck and ankles, wear a bug repellent with DEET, and be particularly careful at sunset or when out and about early in the morning.

Hepatitis is a concern as anywhere (see chapter 3), and reliable statistics on **AIDS** are not out, but with rampant prostitution and drug abuse, Cambodia is certainly fertile ground for the disease. Recent efforts to educate needle users about the dangers of the substance and the importance of clean needles, as well as increased condom use, are positive signs, but recent statistics show that the tide of new AIDS cases is rising.

Foreign Embassies in Cambodia

If you encounter problems during your visit, go to your embassy. Addresses for embassies in Phnom Penh are as follows:

- **U.S.:** 1 Street 96, at the corner of Street 95 and Street 51 (✆ **023/728-000;** http://cambodia.usembassy.gov).
- **Canada:** Villa #9, Senei Vinnavut Oum (Street 254; ✆ **023/213-470;** www.canadainternational.gc.ca/thailand-thailande). ***Note:*** The Canadian Embassy in Phnom Penh does not have a regular consular service; instead, contact the Consular Section at the Australian Embassy (see below) for general consular assistance.
- **Australia** (also serves New Zealanders): Villa #11 Senei Vinnavut Oum (Street 254; ✆ **023/213-470;** www.cambodia.embassy.gov.au).
- **U.K.:** No. 27–29 Street 75 (✆ **023/427-124;** http://ukincambodia.fco.gov.uk).

GETTING THERE

BY AIR International flights to Cambodia from neighboring countries are many and affordable. Cambodia's two main hubs, **Siem Reap Airport** and **Phnom Penh International Airport,** are served by the following: Bangkok Airways from Thailand; Malaysia Airlines from Kuala Lumpur; Lao Airways from Vientiane; Vietnam Airways from Ho Chi Minh City and Hanoi; and Silk Air from Singapore and Shanghai Air, EVA, President, and China Southern connections between Phnom Penh and points in China.

Note: There's a **$25 international departure tax** ($13 for children 11 and under).

BY BOAT Daily boat connections run between Chau Doc in Vietnam and the town of Neak Loeung, some 2 hours east of Phnom Penh in Cambodia. You can arrange the trip through any budget travel agent in Vietnam, and many include the onward boat

Warning! Medical Safety & Evacuation Insurance

The Cambodian medical system is rudimentary at best and nonexistent at worst. Make sure that you have medical coverage for overseas travel and that it includes emergency evacuation. For details on insurance, see chapter 15. There are a few clinics in Phnom Penh and Siem Reap, but for anything major, evacuation to Bangkok is the best option.

connection to Phnom Penh as part of a multiday Mekong Delta trip. ***Note:*** Budget tour operators **Sinh Café** (✆ **08/369-420** in Ho Chi Minh City) and **Capitol Tour** (No. 14 Road 182, Phnom Penh; ✆ **023/217-627**) are now working together, so when you cross borders, the other company adopts you. It's an all-day journey in a diesel-belching tour boat, but views of life on the wide, lazy Mekong are worth it. ***Also note:*** A visa is available on arrival when entering Cambodia, but you have to have a prearranged visa for entry to Vietnam.

For a luxury option, the **Victoria Chau Doc Hotel** (✆ **076/865-010**) offers an expensive private transfer from Chau Doc to Phnom Penh on a speedy runabout boat.

BY BUS Buses connect with neighboring **Vietnam** at the Moc Bai border area—at the town of Svay Rieng on the Cambodian side. From Saigon in Vietnam, contact **Saigon-tourist** (✆ **08/829-8914**) or **Sinh Café** (✆ **08/369-420**) for direct connection to Cambodia—Sinh Café and Capitol Tour (also called Capitol Guesthouse) are in cahoots, and one carrier takes up your transport at the border. Going in either direction (to or from Cambodia), you'll cross the border around noontime and the $6 bus drops you at your destination sometime after 3pm. The overland border procedure is quick and easy going into Cambodia. You just have to fill out some forms and pay the 2,000 VND tax (payable in any currency). The Capitol/Sinh office is just across the border and has nice "chill-out chairs" (low lawn chairs) where you can get a coffee and wait for the buses to fill. Sinh buses are clean and have air-conditioning now, and some even make a quick stop at Psah Goki, a sprawling marketplace on the road between the one-time enemy countries. Going from Cambodia to Vietnam, ask at any travel agent or hotel, or the Capitol Guesthouse (discussed later), and be sure that you have a prearranged visa for Vietnam. Visa is available on arrival at any land crossings in Cambodia. It's a manageable route but draining, and I highly recommend **going by air in or out of Phnom Penh or Siem Reap from Vietnam or Thailand.**

GETTING AROUND

BY AIR Connection between Phnom Penh and Siem Reap is frequent and regular on Siem Reap Airways. ***Note:*** There's a $6 domestic departure tax in both Phnom Penh and Siem Reap.

Warning! Border Hassles: Thailand to Cambodia Overland

I don't recommend going by prearranged tours arranged on Thailand's Khao San Road or Sukhumvit Road with dodgy tour agents. Scams abound: overcharging, price fixing at remote border points with extortive fees, and arriving late in Siem Reap in the hopes that you'll stay at the company guesthouse. If you're game for the overland route from the Thai capital, take a local bus from Bangkok's Mo Chit (Northern) Bus Station to Aranyaprathet, follow the border procedures (do not enlist the help of anyone who will charge you later); then, once across the border, go by a Toyota Camry taxi for 1,000 Thai baht ($25) to Siem Reap. Best to fly, though.

For good, constantly updated information about crossing the Thai border, check the useful website **www.talesofasia.com**.

Tips Krama Chameleon

All things to all people, it's a scarf, a towel, a curtain, a headband, a headdress, a sling for a baby, a belt, a sash, a mask to cover the nose and mouth on dusty roads, an over-the-shoulder satchel, a carrier for a fighting rooster, a cushion for carrying water jars on the head, a bandage, a hanky, and a shawl. The *Krama,* a woven cotton scarf, usually of a two-tone checked pattern but in many variations, is essential for rural travel. They're convenient and make great gifts. If you don't have a *Krama,* the young sellers at the temple sites in Angkor or on the streets of Phnom Penh are sure to remind you that you need one (or another one).

BY BUS Most travelers find local buses rough but a great way to connect with local people (maybe even sit on their laps). Most routes depart from Phnom Penh.

Mekong Express connects Phnom Penh and Siem Reap with daily luxury buses for just $11 (87 Sisowath Quay, Phnom Penh; © **023/427-518**) and runs various routes (also boats) throughout Cambodia. Bus rides come with an edible snack, and there's a bathroom onboard. They make good time: 5½ hours stopping for one 15-minute break only. ***Tip:*** Earplugs are your friend on this bus ride (and any bus ride, really), as they play Khmer karaoke songs and various Asian pop music videos.

Capitol Tour (No. 14 Road 182, Phnom Penh; © **023/217-627**) is a long-popular choice for inexpensive seat-in-coach connections and tours throughout the country. Buses leave early from the busy Capitol tour offices in Siem Reap and Phnom Penh (at their office in the capitol, they serve good cheap breakfasts, are open 6am to 9pm, and a loudspeaker lets you know when the bus is leaving with something like, "For the traveler who him going to Siem Reap, please get on the bus now!").

BY CAR/MOTORBIKE Hiring a car with a driver, driving yourself, or going by rented motorbike is a great way to see Cambodia's rural highways and byways. Rough country roads mean that you'll need to hire the most durable of vehicles, with good suspension. Hiring a driver is recommended; traffic is unpredictable. Contact hotels and travel agents. In Phnom Penh, **Lucky! Lucky!** (413 Monivong Blvd.; © **023/212-788**) is the best place to rent quality motorbikes ($7–$8 a day) and other vehicles. You'll have to leave your passport, but these folks are reliable and trustworthy. Next door is **New! New!,** a friendly competitor copycat.

BY BOAT Speedboats make the 5-hour trip between Phnom Penh and Siem Reap. The cost is $30 to $35, and any hotel can arrange a ticket. Boats leave from the pier near 106 Street in the north end of town or connect with Siem Reap's Tonle Sap docks by taxi.

TIPS ON ACCOMMODATIONS

Be warned that accommodations often fill up in the winter high season, especially the finer hotels nearest Angkor Wat. ***Note:*** There's a 10% VAT charge at most major hotels. Expect discounts in the low season. Phnom Penh and Siem Reap both have the highest concentrations of comfortable accommodations at international standards, but there are developments in small towns as well. Sihanoukville, Cambodia's little seaside resort south of the capital, boasts a fine high-end resort, the Sokha Beach, but in rural stops like Battambang, you'll find only budget rooms. Some of the most convenient choices are the smaller, foreign-owned guesthouses where you're likely to meet up with other travelers and can get the inside scoop on what's going on in the area.

TIPS ON DINING

In this old French colony, the cuisine is heavily French, all affordable, and often quite good. You'll also find tasty Thai, and tourist centers are chockablock with storefronts that serve up reasonable facsimiles of Western favorites.

TIPS ON SHOPPING

You'll find antiques stores and boutiques in the major centers, but shopping for trinkets and memorabilia is best at the big markets: the Russian Market and Central Market in Phnom Penh, and the Old Market in Siem Reap. The temple town of Siem Reap is fashioning itself as a chic international destination, and along with the many luxurious hotels and fine dining comes good boutique shopping and galleries. In Siem Reap, you'll find fine art photography by noted expatriate artists and some good original artwork and pleasing reproductions from the temples, a far cry from refrigerator magnets and collector spoons (but you can find those along the road to the temples).

Important note: The treasures and carvings of Angkor and Cambodia have been looted for centuries, and those treasures are still being sold. **Do not buy any antique stone carving or temple reliefs in Cambodia.** Even some reputable galleries are willing to arrange backroom deals for authentic Khmer antiquities, even make it look legitimate. For more information, go to www.heritagewatch.org.

Fast Facts Cambodia

Business Hours Vendors and restaurants tend to open at about 8am and close at 9 or 10pm. Government offices, banks, travel agencies, and museums are usually open from 8am to 4 or 5pm, with an hour break for lunch.

Crime Where violence and banditry was once an everyday occurrence, Cambodia has become much safer. The civilian population is more or less disarmed and civil authorities have firm control, but stay on your toes. Try not to be on the roads late at night, and be careful to lock your valuables in hotel safes. In the event of trouble—as in a holdup—comply and report it to local officials.

Drug Laws Availability might look like permission, but that's not the case. It's a time-tested rule that you can bribe your way out of (or into) anything in corrupt Cambodia, but it's best not to test it. Police are crooked and may be the ones selling the drugs (out of uniform) in order to collect the bribe. Dabbling in this arena makes you friends in all the wrong places, and Cambodia is not a good place to have the wrong friends.

Electricity Cambodia uses 220-volt European standard electricity, with rounded, two-prong plugs requiring an adaptor. Bring a surge protector for delicate instruments.

Emergencies In Phnom Penh, dial ✆ **117** for police, or ✆ **119** for an ambulance.

Hospitals You'll want to take care of any medical or dental issues before arriving in Cambodia. The **SOS Clinic** in Phnom Penh (No. 161 Street 51; ✆ **023/216-911**) is your best bet in a pinch.

Internet Reliable service can be found in the major centers; prepaid wireless connections have recently become available. Prices for connections range from 50¢ per hour at budget Internet cafes to $3 per hour for wireless DSL connections. Note that local Internet cafes can be a bit frustrating; without the proper protective software, bothersome pop-ups and very slow connections are common. Pay more and get more is the rule.

Language The Cambodian language is Khmer. English, French, and Mandarin are also widely spoken.

Police Khmer police exist to harass and collect, not to protect and serve. Contact them only in the event of a major emergency, at ✆ **117** or the expat hot line, ✆ **023/724-793.**

Post Office Hotels usually sell stamps and send postcards. See individual chapters in this book for specific post-office locations.

Publications The ***Cambodia Daily*** and the twice-monthly ***Phnom Penh Post*** are good local rags with nitty-gritty news from Cambodia, as well as stories from international wire services. You can also find Thailand's *Bangkok Post* and the *Nation,* as well as the *International Herald Tribune* and the standard array of international news mags (*Time, Newsweek,* and the *Economist*). Free local magazines are chock-full of good insights. Look for the useful ***Asia Life Phnom Penh,*** a free listings-and-entertainment monthly geared to English-speaking expats, and ***Pocket Cambodia Guide,*** a free guide published in each of the tourist areas of Cambodia and updated regularly.

Telephone & Fax Phones in the major centers are reliable, and international direct-dial is common. See "Telephone Dialing Information at a Glance," below.

Time Zone Cambodia is 7 hours ahead of Greenwich Mean Time, in the same zone as Bangkok. It's 12 hours ahead of New York City and 3 hours behind Sydney.

Tipping Tipping is not obligatory but appreciated. A blanket 10% to 20% is exorbitant. Best to just round up any check or leave a buck or two.

Toilets Public toilets are a little rough—mostly of the Asian "squatty-potty" variety—and rather grungy, with an attendant at the door charging a small fee for entrance and a few squares of gritty paper. Not a bad idea to bring your own roll and some germ-fighting hand sanitizer. Facilities in Western accommodations are more familiar.

Water No tap water is potable. Buy bottled water, available everywhere.

Telephone Dialing Information at a Glance

- **To place a call from your home country to Cambodia:** Dial the international code (011 in the U.S., 0011 in Australia, 0170 in New Zealand, or 00 in the U.K.), plus the country code **855,** the city code (**23** for Phnom Penh, **63** for Siem Reap), and the phone number (for example, 011+855+23/000-000). ***Important note:*** Omit the initial 0 in all Cambodian phone numbers when calling from abroad.
- **To place a call within Cambodia:** Dial 0 before the city code (as numbers are listed in this book). All phone numbers are six digits after the city code.
- **To place a direct international call from Cambodia:** Most hotels offer international direct-dialing, but with exorbitant surcharges of 10% to 25%. Faxes often have high minimum charges. To place a call, dial the international access code **(001)** plus the country code, the area or city code, and the number (for example, to call the U.S., you'd dial 001+1+000/000-0000).
- **Here are international country codes:** Australia 61, Myanmar 95, Canada 1, Hong Kong 852, Indonesia 62, Laos 856, Malaysia 60, New Zealand 64, the Philippines 63, Singapore 65, Thailand 66, U.K. 44, U.S. 1, Vietnam 84.
- Post offices and Internet cafes all rent time on direct lines. If you can manage the static and the delays, affordable Internet phone service is available at Internet cafes. Also keep your eyes open for the many streetside stalls with mobile phones on loan, a good choice for regional calls.

3 PHNOM PENH

Founded in the mid–14th century by the Khmers as a monastery, Phnom Penh replaced Angkor Thom, a city at the Angkor temples, a century later as the country's capital. The city has long been a vital trading hub at the confluence of three rivers: the Mekong, Tonle Sap, and Bassac. Perhaps the city's most auspicious period was actually when it lay vacant; following an eviction order from Pol Pot, the city was deserted in a period of hours, and almost all of Phnom Penh's residents moved to the countryside in 1975, not to return until 1979 under the authority of Vietnamese troops.

It has been a long road to the peaceful and growing Phnom Penh of today. There were many years of frontier-style anarchy after the city was repopulated in 1979. Drugs and prostitution remain a big downtown commodity, but it's unlikely that you'll be caught in the crossfire, which you couldn't say 7 or 8 years ago. The notorious brothel village of Svay Pa just north of the city has finally been put out of commission. Today Phnom Penh enjoys its own kind of harmony of opposites and offers visitors peaceful moments of a sunset at riverside, as well as its dusty, motorbike-choked labyrinthine alleys and busy markets. The city is an incongruous cluster of crumbling French colonials, and the central riverside area has a pace all its own that's great for wandering.

There's also much of historical interest in Phnom Penh. Its **Royal Palace** is a stone showpiece of classical Khmer architecture, and the **Silver Pagoda,** on the palace grounds, is a jewel-encrusted wonder. Throughout the city, you'll see the faded glory of aged **French colonial architecture.** There are also many notable *wats,* Buddhist temples with resident monks. Of more grisly interest is the **Tuol Sleng,** or Museum of Genocide, a schoolhouse-turned-prison where up to 20,000 victims of Pol Pot's excesses were tortured before being led to the **Choeung Ek,** otherwise known as "The Killing Fields," about 16km (10 miles) from Phnom Penh.

It's a town certainly worth exploring for a few days. Phnom Penh has a pace all its own, and you'll find a lot to catch your eye, whether it is the glut of luxury vehicles, anything from big sport utility vehicles to European sports cars all rolling around with tinted windows and no license plates, or sprawling local markets.

VISITOR INFORMATION & TOURS

Deluxe

- **Diethelm Travel,** No. 65 Street 240, P.O. Box 99, Phnom Penh, Cambodia (✆ **023/219-151;** fax 023/219-150; www.diethelmtravel.com). In Siem Reap: House No. 470, Krous Village, Svay Dangkum Commune, Siem Reap, Cambodia (✆ **063/963-524;** fax 063/963-694).
- **Exotissimo,** 46 Norodom Blvd., Phnom Penh (✆ **023/218-948;** fax 023/426-586; www.exotissimo.com). **In Siem Reap:** New Building B, 2021 Street 60MK, Siem Reap (✆ **063/964-323;** fax 063/963-621).

Budget

- **Capitol Guesthouse Tours,** No. 14A Street 182, Sangkat Beng Prolitt (✆ **023/217-627**). This is the town's budget travel cafe and a good place to arrange inexpensive rural and local tours and onward connections by bus and boat. Remember that you get what you pay for, but the services are convenient.
- Small tour operators and ticket shops abound along Sisowath. For flights and other services, try **K.U. Travel and Tours** (✆ **023/723-456;** www.kucambodia.com), at No. 77 on Street 240 (in the cafe and gallery area).
- For buses and onward land and water connections, contact your hotel front desk, who, in turn, will likely contact one of the following consolidators: **Mekong Express** (87Eo Sisowath Quay; ✆ **023/427-518**), which offers the most deluxe services at slightly higher rates, but their air-conditioned buses are clean and very efficient; **Neak Krorhrom Travel and Tours** (127 Eo Street 108, on the Wat Phnom end of Sisowath Quay; ✆ **023/219-496**); **PTM Travel and Tours** (200 Eo Monivong; ✆ **023/986-363**); or **World Express Travel and Tours** (14 Eo Street 169; ✆ **023/884-574**). These are just a few of the many. ***Note:*** Avoid booking full-package-tour connections to Bangkok.

GETTING THERE

BY AIR All major airlines in the region connect here. **Phnom Penh International Airport** is just a 15-minute drive from the city center, and a cab costs $7, a ride on the back of a motorbike just $2. Buy tickets from the taxi stand outside the departure terminal under the archway to your left.

BY BOAT Speedboats connect Phnom Penh with Siem Reap and leave every morning from the main dock on the north end of town. Tickets are available just about anywhere

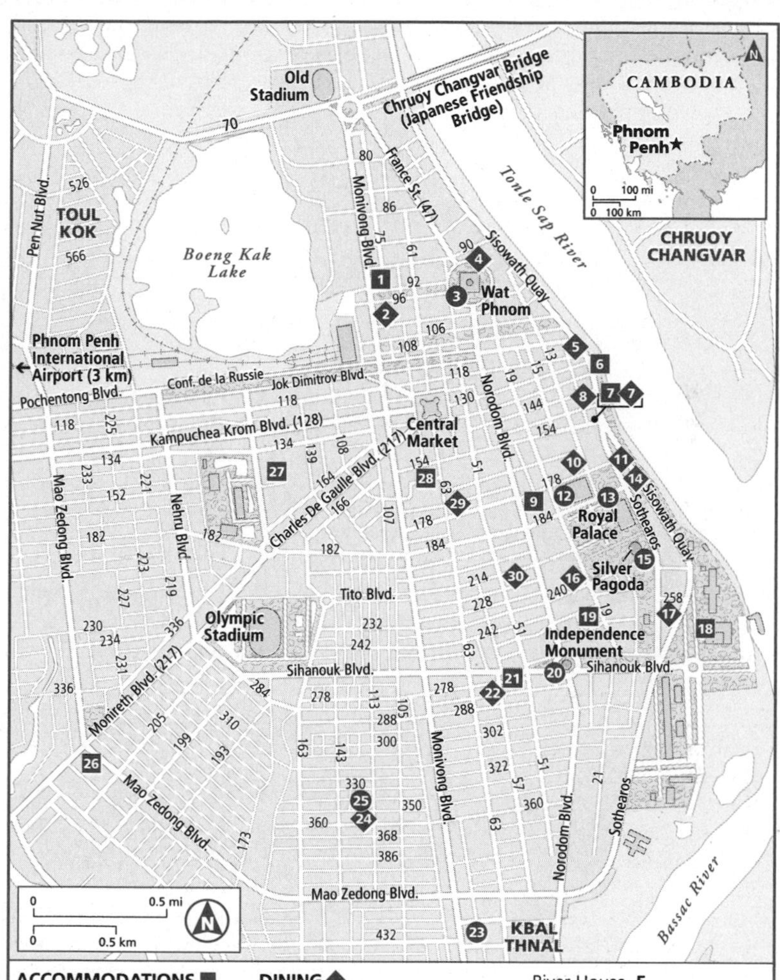

ACCOMMODATIONS ■
Amanjaya Hotel **7**
The Billabong **28**
Blue Lime **9**
Golden Gate Hotel **21**
Goldiana **20**
Hotel Cambodiana **18**
Hotel InterContinental Phnom Penh **26**
Juliana Hotel **27**
The Pavilion **19**
The Quay **6**
Raffles Hotel Le Royal **1**

DINING ◆
Boddhi Tree Umma **24**
Café Metro **8**
Comme à la Maison **22**
Foreign Correspondents Club (FCC) **11**
Friends (Mith Samlanh) Restaurant **10**
K West **7**
La Résidence **30**
Le Deauville **4**
112 Restaurant **2**
Origami **16**
Pacharan **14**
River House **5**
Romdeng **29**
Topaz **17**

ATTRACTIONS ●
Independence Monument **20**
The Killing Fields & Choeung Ek Memorial **23**
National Museum **12**
Royal Palace **13**
Silver Pagoda **15**
Tuol Sleng, Museum of Genocide **25**
Wat Phnom **3**

in town. The price is $25 from most hotels or the Capitol Guesthouse (see above). **Mekong Express Tour Boat** charges $35 for the 5-hour trip on a larger, more comfortable boat. Contact them just across from the ferry terminal (87 Sisowath Quay; ✆ **023/427-518**). See the "Getting There" section at the beginning of this chapter for information about boat connections from Vietnam.

BY BUS Phnom Penh is a hub for buses throughout the country—best are the many budget tourist companies offering affordable daily connections to anywhere from the far south to Siem Reap. A tourist bus to Siem Reap takes 6 to 7 hours and costs $5. **Sorya Transport** (✆ **023/210-859**), with an office just west of the central market, sells tickets to all the major stops and minor hamlets in the country. **Mekong Express** (see "By Boat," above) has daily connections to Siem Reap on an air-conditioned bus for $11. Their buses make the trip in about 5½ hours.

GETTING AROUND

Phnom Penh's downtown is accessible on foot, and it's easy to find your way because the streets are arranged in a numbered grid. For sites farther afield, like the Killing Fields or any temples, you'll need wheels. Metered taxis are around, and any hotel can arrange daily car rental (with driver).

Motorcycle taxis, called ***motodups,*** can be hired anywhere and cost about $1 for short trips in town. Bargain hard. These guys are everywhere, especially on the riverside, and the competition is in your favor. Then again, what the heck is $1? Tip and you'll have a friend for life.

Tuk-tuks are the best choice and available anywhere. The name is taken from the Thais, but these tuk-tuks have nothing to do with the noisy Bangkok three-wheeler. Cambodia's tuk-tuks are a two-wheeled surrey pulled by a standard motorbike. They are shaded, and the padded seat is great for two. There's a small shelf at the front of the cart, usually with laminated maps and advertisements, and, in a pinch, you can seat two more, but it's not very comfy. Pay between $2 and $3 for trips around town; a ride farther out, say, to the Killing Fields, will set you back $15.

Lucky! Lucky!, at 413 Monivong Blvd. (✆ **023/212-788**), rents high-quality motorbikes for rural touring (available for long-term rental), as well as jeeps and even luxury cars. Next door is **New! New!,** a friendly competitor. Rates are $5 to $9 per day.

Fast Facts Phnom Penh

American Express For basic American Express services, contact **Diethelm Travel** (No. 65 Street 240, P.O. Box 99, Phnom Penh; ✆ **023/219-151;** www.diethelm travel.com).

Banks & Currency Exchange **ANZ Bank** has many reliable international ATMs in town, the most convenient being at their riverside branch, 265 Sisowath Quay (✆ **023-726-900**). **Canadia Bank,** at No. 265–269 Street 114 (✆ **023/215-286**), and **Mekong Bank,** at 1 Street 114 (✆ **023/217-112**), are also in the downtown area and can cash traveler's checks and give cash advances. A **Western Union** office is at 327 Sisowath Quay (✆ **023/990-688**).

Clinics The **International SOS Medical and Dental Clinic,** at No. 161 Street 51 (✆ **023/216-911**), is the best place to handle minor emergencies. **Naga Clinic,** at No. 11 Street 254 (✆ **011/811-175**), is another. For any major emergency or injury, however, you'll want to arrange medical evacuation.

Emergency For police, dial ✆ **117;** for fire, dial ✆ **118;** and for the expat hot line, dial ✆ **023/724-793.**

Internet Internet outlets line riverside Sisowath Street. Hourly access starts at $1. **Friendly Web,** near Capitol Guesthouse, has good access from its office at No. 199 EO, Street 107 (at the corner of Road 182; ✆ **012/843-246**). **Sunny Internet Cafe** has several flatscreen computers serving up fast ADSL connections in a bright location at 351 Sisowath Quay (✆ **023-986-629**). **KIDS** is an NGO where American owner Bill Herod brings Internet technology to Khmer students. They have good, inexpensive access in their offices at No. 17A Street 178 (✆ **023/218-452;** kids@camnet.com.kh).

Post Office The post office is in the north end of town on Street 13, east of Wat Phnom. It's open daily from 6:30am to 5pm and has standard delivery service and an international phone. **DHL** has an office on No. 28 Monivong Rd. (✆ **023/427-726**), and **FedEx** is at No. 701D Monivong (✆ **023/216-712**). There's also a post office at the airport in the outdoor archway between arrivals and departures (across from the Dairy Queen).

Telephone The local code for Phnom Penh is **23.** International direct-dialing is available in most hotels and at the post office. Storefront Internet cafes along Sisowath do inexpensive Internet calls or direct-dialing. Cellphones are very popular, and you'll find streetside stalls on wheels where you can make local and international calls for next to nothing, with a good cellular connection.

WHERE TO STAY

There are some choice hotels in town, from old, upscale gems to budget minihotels and even a few small boutique properties. I recommend spending a little more for bargain luxury because the midrange properties of Phnom Penh are run-down, at best. Always ask about seasonal rates.

Very Expensive

Hotel InterContinental Phnom Penh ★ This luxury behemoth has every amenity and in-room convenience—from wireless and in-room Internet to fine fitness, health, and beauty services. The downside is the location; the self-contained hotel is pretty far from the city's action. Rooms are done in tidy carpet, dark-wood furnishings, patterned couches, striped raw silk curtains that match the spreads on the king-size beds, and marble detailing in the entryways. Everything is large and luxe, and beds are fluffy and comfortable. Well-appointed bathrooms have separate showers and tubs with Art Deco faucets. Oak desks and floor-to-ceiling windows give guests that "power broker" feel (even if you're just a small fish). The large outdoor pool has an Angkor Wat water park theme, with stone carving decorations, a centerpiece red stone fountain of three elephant heads, and an elegant water-level bar.

296 Blvd. Mao Tse Toung. © **023/424-888.** Fax 023/424-885. www.ichotelsgroup.com. 346 units. $150–$190 double; $300 Executive/Regency suite; $3,000 Regency/Royal suite. AE, MC, V. **Amenities:** 2 restaurants; bar; 2 snack bars; babysitting; children's playroom; concierge; great fitness center; Internet; outdoor pool; room service; sauna; spa. *In room:* A/C, TV, fridge, minibar, ADSL or Wi-Fi.

Raffles Hotel Le Royal ★★★ This is my favorite high-end hotel in Phnom Penh. Built in 1929, this is the city's most atmospheric hotel, an authentic Art Deco and colonial classic. Everything from the vaulted ceilings in the lobby to the classic original central stairs breathes history and charm. Walking down the arched hallways, with sunlight bouncing off the black-and-white floor tiles and streaming in through stone columns, is like walking smack into the extravagance of Indochina. Rooms are done with fine tiled entries, high ceilings, indirect lighting, a sitting area with inlaid furniture, and ornate touches like antique wall sconces and fine drapery. Landmark rooms, just one step above the standard, are a good choice in the old wing and are larger, with nice appointments like claw-foot tubs and Art Deco faucets. The central pool area is a tranquil oasis divided by a unique pavilion, and the amenities throughout, such as the fine spa facility, are luxe. The staff is attentive and very professional.

92 Rukhak Vithei Daun Penh (off Monivong Blvd.), Sangkat Wat Phnom. © **023/981-888.** Fax 023/981-168. www.raffles.com. 172 units. $300–$340 double; $390–$2,500 suite. AE, MC, V. **Amenities:** 3 restaurants; 2 bars; babysitting; children's club; concierge; health club; Internet; Jacuzzi; 2 outdoor pools; room service; sauna. *In room:* A/C, TV, fridge, hair dryer, minibar, Wi-Fi.

Expensive

Amanjaya Hotel ★★ Riverside at Sisowath Quay, this three-story corner building is a true house of style. The porous laterite walls of the lobby—the same stone used in Angkor—and Buddhist statues throughout contribute to a cool boutique vibe. Though sparse in services and amenities, rooms are spacious, done in rich red silk hangings and bedspreads, in bold contrast with dark-wood trim and floors. All rooms have king-size beds. For the same price as the standard suites at the Quay nearby (see below), Amanjaya's deluxe suites are far more spacious and come with a small balcony. All bathrooms are immaculate affairs done in wood and tile, with neat tub/shower units in deluxe suites and separate shower and tub in the more expensive suites, delineated by unique large-stone gravel paths in concrete. Rooms vary in size and shape; best are the corner suites with panoramic views of the river and busy street below. Noisy traffic is the only drawback.

No. 1 Street 154, Sisowath Quay. © **023/214-747.** Fax 023/219-545. 21 units. Apr–Sept $120–$175 deluxe suites, $220 suites; Oct–Mar $155–$215 deluxe suites, $250 suites. MC, V. **Amenities:** Restaurant; room service. *In room:* A/C, TV, fridge, minibar, Wi-Fi.

Hotel Cambodiana ★★ With a convenient location, atmosphere, and all the amenities, this is a good jumping-off point for the sites downtown. The building looks like a giant gilded wedding cake, and its vaulted Khmer-style roofs dominate the sky in the southern end of downtown. The lobby is abuzz with activity, whether it's visiting dignitaries or disembarking tour buses, but the helpful staff handles it all with grace. The large riverside pool is great, and there are some fine choices in international dining. Everything is tidy, but decoration is a chain-hotel style in plain wood and office carpet; it's a bit dull, and some floors reek of pungent deodorizers. The high-end suites are richly decorated and unique, and executive privileges on the top floors are luxe. They have wireless Internet (with prepaid cards) available in all public spaces. All rooms have picture windows and good views of town or the river.

313 Sisowath Quay. © **023/218-189.** Fax 023/426-392. www.hotelcambodiana.com. 230 units. $170–$180 double; $400–$500 suite. AE, MC, V. **Amenities:** 4 restaurants; bar; concierge; executive-level

rooms; small health club; Internet; Jacuzzi; outdoor pool; room service; sauna; tennis court. *In room:* A/C, TV, fridge, minibar.

The Quay ★★ This chic new riverside hotel is giving nearby Amanjaya a run for its money. I advise skipping the small, windowless (though, admittedly, still very stylish) standard rooms and booking yourself into a panorama suite. For the extra $50, you get a room twice the size, with large balconies with unobstructed views of the river and a cozy sitting area with Arne Jacobsen swan chairs. The decor of light wood, champagne-color textiles, and cream walls and furniture creates a truly soothing escape from the chaos of Phnom Penh. Bathrooms in all units are sleek and outfitted with stylish sinks and shower cubicles; suites come with large stone tubs. The rooftop Jacuzzi is luxurious, if a bit uncomfortable, as there is also a popular rooftop bar, so you may have to shimmy your way past patrons for a soak.

277 Sisowath Quay. ✆ **023/992-284.** Fax 023/224-893. www.thequayhotel.com. 16 units. $130 standard suite; $185 panoramic suite. AE, MC, V. **Amenities:** Restaurant; rooftop Jacuzzi; room service. *In room:* A/C, TV, fridge, minibar, Wi-Fi.

Moderate

Blue Lime ★★ Blue Lime is the latest oasis from the group that brought the Pavilion (see below) to Phnom Penh. Rooms are spacious, especially if you bump up to the superiors; the extra $5 also gets you a nice private balcony. Bathrooms are a good size, with stylish sinks and separate rain shower areas. The hot water comes from solar panels, so there is a bit of waiting involved, but really, you'll rarely need a hot shower in these tropical climates! The pool is surrounded by four-poster daybeds and tall, leafy tropical trees. Staff here is friendlier than at Pavilion, and extremely efficient and thoughtful. A room on the top floor offers lovely views of the curved rooftop of the National Museum in the distance. Rooms are, on balance, spotless, but there was an ant problem in mine, so be sure to throw food and sweets in the fridge. Blue Lime is already popular with travelers in the know, so book far in advance.

42 Street 19Z (in the alley off Street 19; btw. 181Eo and 179B Street 19). ✆ **023/222-260.** www.bluelime.asia. 14 units. $40–$50 double (Dec–Jan add $10). MC, V. **Amenities:** Restaurant; bar; nice-size outdoor salt pool. *In room:* A/C, TV, fridge, hair dryer, minibar, no phone, Wi-Fi.

Juliana Hotel ★ The Juliana is a good distance from the center of town and popular with group tours. Rooms are situated around a luxuriant central pool shaded by palms and with a terrace and lounge chairs: a bright spot in an otherwise dull landscape. The hotel is Thai owned and managed, and popular with regional businessmen. Standard rooms aren't especially attractive and have aging red carpet and the nicks and scrapes of heavy use. That said, superior and deluxe rooms are large and well appointed in tidy carpet and light wood trim. Regal headboards top large beds, and there are nice rattan furnishings throughout. Be sure to request a nonsmoking room, and check it out before checking in. Billing as a "city resort" kind of comes up short, but the Continental restaurant is inviting and the pool is a standout.

16 Juliana 152 Road, Sangkat Vealvong. ✆ **023/880-530** or 885-750 www.julianacambodia.com. 82 units. $60–$70 double; $200 suite. AE, MC, V. **Amenities:** 2 restaurants; lobby bar; babysitting; small health club; Internet; outdoor pool; room service. *In room:* A/C, TV, fridge, minibar.

The Pavilion ★★ This is a very popular boutique hotel, so make sure to book ahead and get confirmation of it in writing or by e-mail. The Pavilion—hidden behind big, heavy wooden doors and long white walls—is an absolute oasis in this city of honking, jostling tuk-tuks and motorcycles. Stepping into the central courtyard garden is incredibly calming.

Daybeds with overstuffed pillows, friendly staff, and a compact outdoor pool offer much needed comfort after touring the city. Double rooms are basic, with firm beds and a few silk decorations. The bathrooms are a real plus in this price category, as they come with separate shower cubicles, stylish sinks, and Art Deco tile. For a splurge, book one of the pool rooms, which come with nice private toe dippers. ***Note:*** The Pavilion's sister hotel, the **Kabiki** (22 Street 264; ✆ **023/222-290**), was built specifically for families. It has a very similar ambience and level of service.

227 Street 19. ✆ **023/222-280.** www.thepavilion.asia. 20 units. $40–$75 double; $85 suite or pool rooms. MC, V. **Amenities:** Restaurant. *In room:* A/C, TV, fridge, minibar, Wi-Fi.

Inexpensive

The Billabong ★ This hotel attracts the laid-back group of travelers who want something a little more luxe than the basic $15 backpacker deal. Everything is done in navy blue and white and feels a bit like an old-fashioned cabana or low-key country club. Rooms are basic, with navy sheets and red silk bed throws. Bathrooms do not have a separate shower unit, but they are clean and tidy. Staff is ultra friendly here, and the outdoor pool is an excellent little oasis after a day of touring the city. Spring for a room with a poolside view; it's worth the extra $3.

5 Street 158. ✆ **023/223-703.** Fax 023/998-472. www.thebillabonghotel.com. 10 units. $36–$39 double; $58 superior; $62 deluxe. MC, V. **Amenities:** Restaurant; Internet. *In room:* A/C, TV, fridge, minibar.

Golden Gate Hotel Standard rooms here are basic but clean and quite livable. Deluxe rooms are larger but just as plain. This is a popular spot for long-staying expat business visitors and NGO folks, and the suites, with kitchenette and small living room, are like one-room apartments. Rooms are done in either tile or office carpet and have mismatched but tidy cloth and rattan furniture. The best choice is a deluxe room on a higher floor (with view). Be sure to ask to see the room first, as they really vary.

No. 9 Street 278, Sangkat (just south of the Independence Monument). ✆ **023/427-618.** Fax 023/721-005. www.goldengatehotels.com. $28 standard double; $35 deluxe; $45 suite (monthly rates available). MC, V. **Amenities:** Restaurant; room service; Wi-Fi. *In room:* A/C, TV, fridge, Internet (in deluxe and suite only), minibar.

Goldiana ★ A labyrinthine complex, the result of many construction phases, the Goldiana is one of the best budget choices in the Cambodian capital. It is also another top choice for NGO workers and those working in diplomatic circles. The hotel is just south of the Victory Monument and a short ride from the main sites. It's low-luxe but squeaky-clean. Rooms are large and have either carpet or wood flooring. The hotel's maintenance standard, unlike similar hotels in town, is meticulous. Bathrooms are smallish but comfortable, with a tub/shower combo and granite tile. The third-floor pool is a real bonus in this category. The staff is kind and helpful and is used to the questions and concerns of long-staying patrons, tourists, and business clients.

No. 10–12 Street 282, Sangkat Boeng Keng Kang 1. ✆ **023/219-558.** Fax 023/219-490. www.goldiana.com. 148 units. $48 double; $68–$98 suite. MC, V. **Amenities:** Restaurant; gym; Internet; outdoor rooftop pool; room service. *In room:* A/C, TV, fridge, hair dryer, Internet, minibar.

WHERE TO DINE

Between remnants of French colonialism and the recent influx of humanitarian-aid workers, international cuisine abounds in the Cambodian capital. Some restaurants themselves are actually NGO (nongovernment organization) projects designed to raise money for local causes or provide training. Ask Khmer folks where to eat, and you'll certainly be pointed to any of the streetside stalls or storefront Chinese noodle shops south of the Central Market, but good eats can be had from one of many options along riverside Sisowath or in and among the lazy alleys of the town center.

For an interesting evening of local fun and frolic, cross the Cambodian–Japanese Friendship bridge on the Tonle Sap River in the north end of town and follow the main road a few short clicks to the town of **Prek Leap,** a grouping of large riverside eateries always crowded with locals on the weekend. Some of these places put on popular variety shows: It's the universal language of slapstick in play here and a good chance to eat, talk, and laugh with locals. All the restaurants serve similar good Khmer and Chinese fare. Go by taxi and pick the most crowded place; the more, the merrier.

Expensive

Foreign Correspondents Club (FCC) ★ CONTINENTAL With a long history as Phnom Penh's place to see and be seen, the FCC is as much a tour stop as a restaurant. Once the gathering place of the dust-caked, camera-toting, intrepid breed who came to chronicle the country's troubled times, the FCC is now a multifloor affair of restaurant, bar, and shops done in dark wood and terra cotta. There are low reclining chairs in the cafe area, a fine dining room, and a dark bar as the stalwart centerpiece. The whole second floor is oriented to the fine views of the river and busy Sisowath below. The food is uninspired Western, but you come here more for the atmosphere than a fine meal. The pizza is particularly bland (no tomato sauce and bad cheese), but try the snacks like nachos and enchiladas. The upstairs bar is popular in the evening and often has cover bands playing live music.

No. 363 Sisowath Quay. ✆ **023/724-014.** Main courses $4–$13. MC, V. Daily 7am–midnight.

112 Restaurant ★ FRENCH You found it—the new French restaurant highly favored by the expats in this area of town. The decor is a bit busy, with brown and white embroidered table settings and chairs, wrought-iron lamps and light covers everywhere, and tall potted trees curving around the arched ceilings. Music is also hit and miss: One moment it's Ella Fitzgerald and *My Funny Valentine,* the next moment it's the Carpenters' *Yesterday Once More.* But the food is excellent. They have signature French dishes like steak tartare and an impressive salad menu. The green salad with goat cheese on toast and walnuts is crisp and tangy, and a meal unto itself.

1A Street 102 (Colonial Mansions). ✆ **023/990-880.** Reservations recommended. Main courses $12–$27. AE, MC, V. Daily 11am–2pm and 6–10pm.

La Résidence ★★ FRENCH If you splurge on only one meal in Phnom Penh, do it here. Housed in a former imperial mansion, this is fine dining at its best. Waitstaff are discreet and attentive, the setting is romantic without being stuffy, and the food is fantastic. Book ahead to get a table by the garden window. The chef previously worked in Michelin two- and three-star restaurants. The menu consists of classic and modern French food. Anything from the foie gras list is rich and decadent, but I suggest the stuffed ravioli with duck liver in Parmesan cream sauce, a dish worthy of the zillion-calorie intake. A three-course dinner will likely set you back at least $50; if money is tight, opt for a more frugal three-course set lunch menu.

22–24 Street 214. ✆ **023/224-582.** www.la-residence-restaurant.com. Reservations recommended. Main courses $8.50–$80 (average is about $25); set lunch menu $16–$29. AE, MC, V. Mon–Fri 11:30am–2pm and 6:30–10pm; Sat–Sun 6:30–10pm.

Origami ★★ JAPANESE Sushi in Cambodia? Go figure. There are a number of Japanese restaurants in town, in fact, but Origami serves fine sushi and all manner of good, authentic Japanese that'll have you saying *"Oishi!"* From *tonkatsu* (deep-fried pork over rice) to real Japanese ramen (noodle soup), Ms. Kimura, the genial proprietor, covers all the bases. Essential ingredients are imported from Japan, and everything is well priced. The sushi is the real deal; the presentation and decor of this little park-side gem could have been lifted straight out of Tokyo. Popular with Japanese expats on humanitarian assignment, the restaurant is an NGO offering Khmer kids training in Japanese language and culture.

No. 88 Sothearos St. (near the main downtown sites). ✆ **012/968-095.** Main courses $3–$12; set menu $10–$20. V. Mon–Sat 11:30am–2pm and 5:30–9:30pm.

River House ★★ FRENCH/CONTINENTAL One of many along the riverside, this bar and restaurant stands out by virtue of size and style. A classic corner colonial, its downstairs is an open-air bar area with quaint cushioned chairs under canvas umbrellas; there's now an elegant air-conditioned dining room. Elegant rattan chairs, two stately bars in wood and glass, and the fine linen and silver presentation are luxe far beyond the price tag. The food is excellent, characterized by fine French specials like duck done as you like, coq au vin, and a popular chateaubriand with Morilles mushrooms. Come for a romantic dinner and stay for dancing.

No. 6 Street 110 (corner of Sisowath). ✆ **023/212-302.** Reservations recommended. Main courses $7–$32. AE, MC, V. Daily 10am–11pm.

Topaz ★★ FRENCH/CONTINENTAL Good familiar food and atmosphere that's sophisticated but not stuffy are the hallmarks of Topaz, an 8-year-old French bistro. In air-conditioned comfort, diners choose from informal booth seating near the comfortable bar or at elegant tables with fine linen, silver, and real stemware in a formal dining room unrivaled in town. The menu features great steaks, pasta, and salad. The Caesar salad is noteworthy. Daily specials are contingent on the day's imports of fish or fine steaks. Wine racks line the dining room walls, with some great choices. Everything's good. *Bon appétit!*

182 Eo Sothearos Blvd. (near the downtown sites). ✆ **023/221-622.** Reservations recommended. Main courses $10–$35. MC, V. Daily 11am–2pm and 6–11pm.

Moderate

Café Metro ★ ASIAN/INTERNATIONAL This stylish, contemporary restaurant serves excellent food in a corner-side location overlooking the river. The food is excellent, mostly seafood and Australian beef. They've got a nice selection of "small plates" for those who want lighter portions. On the large-plate menu, the grilled tenderloin served with a side of fries will knock out any hunger pangs. There's free Wi-Fi access and an extensive martini menu, to boot.

271 Street 148 (on the corner with Sisowath Quay). ✆ **023/222-275.** Main courses $8–$17. MC, V. Daily 7am–1am.

Comme à la Maison ★ CONTINENTAL Expats love this place. It's quiet—no honking. They have great bread; in fact, on a weekend morning there's a steady stream of deliveries leaving their bakery. Light fare tops the bill: good soups and salads sopped up with something freshly baked. Comme à la Maison also features heartier French entrees, meats, and cheese platters, as well as good pizzas and pastas. Follow up with fresh yogurt, fruit, and good desserts. The quiet courtyard area is at the top of the list for escaping the chaos of busy Phnom Penh.

No. 13 Street 57 (around the corner from the Goldiana, southwest of the town center). ✆ **023/360-801.** www.commealamaison-delicatessen.com. Main courses $4–$10. No credit cards. Daily 6am–3pm and 6–10:30pm.

K West ★★ WESTERN/KHMER In the lobby of the Amanjaya Hotel, one of Phnom Penh's coolest boutique properties, this chic little international bar and bistro is French owned and managed. The menu features an array of savory salads. Fine pastas are made fresh and cooked to order, and you'll find good meat and poultry entrees, seafood specials, and a host of good Khmer dishes. Dessert is a cornucopia of cakes and pies, a lime-and-lemon torte, and brownies, as well as ice cream, banana splits, or a dish called "The Colonel" of lemon sherbet and vodka. The air-conditioned double-height interior has cozy wooden booths for privacy and is flanked by a long wooden bar area, popular among expats. The place is a busy catwalk in the evening.

1 Street 154, Sisowath Quay, Phnom Penh. ✆ **023/214-747.** Main courses $5–$30. MC, V. Daily 6:30am–midnight.

Le Deauville ★ FRENCH This open-air French bar and brasserie is a good, mellow choice. On the north end of the Wat Phnom roundabout, the folks at Le Deauville serve fine, affordable French and Khmer dishes. The atmosphere is unpretentious and cozy, with a large open bar at center, tables scattered in the streetside courtyard, and a wall of potted greenery shielding you from traffic. Daily lunch set menus give you a choice of salad and entree, and you can choose from local specialties like filet of Mekong fish with lime or medallion *de boeuf.* The restaurant serves good pizzas and spaghetti and has a wine list that fits any taste and budget. Be sure to ask about Le Deauville II, the large dining barge that makes regular city cruises or can be chartered; aboard the ship, you can enjoy similar fine French cuisine as in this casual bistro. Le Deauville is a popular spot for a casual drink in the evening.

Street 94 (just north of Wat Phnom). ✆ **012/843-204.** Main courses $4.50–$12. V. Daily 11am–10pm.

Pacharan ★ SPANISH This hip place serves up reliable tapas. They've got all the favorites: patatas bravas, cured meats, Spanish tortillas . . . the list goes on. In keeping with tapas spirit, portions are small and you're meant to order many different plates to share among friends. The calamari is excellent, but I advise you to skip the lackluster chicken croquettes. They also have a fine selection of Spanish wines.

389 Sisowath Quay. ✆ **023/224-394.** Tapas $2–$10. MC, V. Daily 11am–11pm.

Inexpensive

Boddhi Tree Umma ★ ASIAN/KHMER Include lunch here with a trip to nearby Tuol Sleng (see "Attractions," below), a sight that doesn't inspire an appetite, really, but the Boddhi Tree is a peaceful oasis and not a bad spot to collect your thoughts after visiting vestiges of Cambodia's late troubles. Named for the tree under which the Buddha "saw the light," this verdant little garden courtyard and rough-hewn guesthouse has comfy balcony and courtyard seating and seems to serve up as much calm as the coffee, tea, and light fare that make it so popular. There are daily specials and often visiting chefs. All the curries are good, and they have great baguette sandwiches. Established in 1997 as a way to drum up funds and support to help Khmer kids and families in challenging circumstances, the folks here welcome your suggestions and invite visitors to get involved in their important work.

 No. 50 Street 113, Beong Keng Kong (across from Tuol Sleng museum). © **023/211-397.** www.boddhitree.com. Main courses $2–$4. No credit cards. Daily 7am–9pm.

Friends (Mith Samlanh) Restaurant ★★ KHMER/INTERNATIONAL Not to be missed is this friendly little gem, an NGO project where Khmer street kids are given shelter and taught useful skills for their reintegration into society. The food is great, an ever-changing tapas menu of local and international favorites like spring rolls, fried rice, good salads, and a host of desserts. I had delicious sweet sticky rice with a nice mix of local fruit. This is a great spot to cool off and have a light bite while touring the city center (right across from the "must-see" National Museum); the place is a cozy open-air colonial in a courtyard done up in primary-color murals of the kids' drawings. The name of the restaurant means "Good Friends," and you might meet some here as you find yourself giving English lessons, laughing, and smiling with these young survivors.

No. 215 Street 13 (across from the entrance to the National Museum). © **023/426-748.** www.mithsamlanh.org. Main courses $2.50–$4.75. V. Daily 11am–9pm.

Romdeng ★★ KHMER Romdeng serves tasty Khmer food in an original, atmospheric French colonial house. Run by the same NGO as Friends Restaurant (see above), the menu is similar, but the decor is a bit cozier, with small, separate dining areas, and alfresco seating set around a small outdoor pool and garden. Try the fish and pumpkin curry in coconut sauce, a delicious savory dish that packs just the right amount of spice and is big enough for two.

No. 74 Street 174. © **092/219-565.** www.mithsamlanh.org. Main courses $4.50–$6.25. V. Daily 11am–10pm.

Snacks & Cafes

Java Café and Gallery, No. 56 Sihanouk Blvd. (© **023/987-420**), is a good spot in town to relax and escape the midday heat. Just south of the main sights (near the Independence Monument), this popular second-story oasis has casual seating on a large balcony and an open gallery interior. They serve coffee, cappuccino, and good cakes and other baked goods; they sometimes feature live music in the evening. It's open 7am to 10pm.

The **Deli,** at No. 13 Street 178 (© **012/851-234**), is a favorite among the expats in town for a good sandwich and excellent pastries.

The **Shop** is a stylish cafe on popular Street 240 (© **023/986-964**), with a newer, equally comfortable location on the north end of Sisowath Quay. Come here for baked goods (try the raspberry chocolate tart), filling paninis and toasted sandwiches, tea, and coffee. There are neat details like butcher-block tables and fresh flowers, and they can arrange picnic lunches for day trips from Phnom Penh.

Chocoholics *must* visit **Chocolate by The Shop ★** (35 Street 240; © **023/998-638**), next door, which serves fantastic Belgian truffles, chocolates, and frozen bonbons all for reasonable prices.

Sugar Palm (No. 19 Street 240; © **023/220-956**) serves good Khmer dishes at streetside or from their upstairs balcony. It's a gallery that features good local crafts and a good place to relax and enjoy real Khmer atmosphere and good treats.

Pizza can be found at any number of storefronts on the crowded riverside; **Happy Pizza,** at No. 223 Sisowath Quay (© **012/559-114**), is among them. Beginning with the name, there are cute little codes in play here, so to cut through it all, say "Please don't put marijuana on my pizza," unless you want it. Same drill at **Ecstatic Pizza,** 193 Norodom Blvd. (© **023/365-089**); both are good and will deliver, pot or not.

ATTRACTIONS

All sights in the city center can be reached on foot, but you'll want to hire a car with a driver or, for the brave, a motorbike taxi to reach sights outside the city center. **Tuol Sleng** and the **Killing Fields** can be visited together, and arrangements can be made at any hotel lobby.

Central Market This Art Deco behemoth, built in 1937, is a city landmark and, on any given day, a veritable anthill of activity. The building is a towering rotunda with busy wings extending in four directions. The eastern entrance is the best spot to find T-shirts, hats, and all manner of trinkets and souvenirs, as well as photocopied bootlegs of popular novels and books on Cambodia. Goldsmiths and watch-repair and -sales counters predominate in the main rotunda, and you can find some good deals. Spend some time wandering the nooks and crannies, though, and you're sure to come across something that strikes your fancy, whether that's a chaotic hardware shop, a cobbler hard at work with an awl, or just the cacophony and carnival-barker shouts of salesmen and haggling shoppers. Be sure to bargain for any purchase. The **Russian Market** in the south end of town is comparable and equally worth a visit (it's a good stop on the return trip from the Killing Fields).

Btw. streets 126 and 136 in the town center. Daily 5am–5pm.

Independence Monument Built in the late 1950s to commemorate Cambodia's independence from the French on November 9, 1953, this towering obelisk is crowned with Khmer Nagas and is reminiscent of Angkor architecture and Hindu influence. The area is at its most majestic when all lit up at night (or from afar while squinting).

South of the town center at the intersection of Norodom and Sihanouk.

The Killing Fields & Choeung Ek Memorial ★★ Originally a Chinese cemetery before becoming the execution grounds for the Khmer Rouge during their maniacal reign under Pol Pot from 1975 to 1979, the site is a collection of mounds, mass graves, and a towering monument of cataloged human skulls. The monument is 17 stories high, reminding visitors of April 17, 1975, the day the Khmer Rouge took over Cambodia. As a sign of respect, you take your shoes off before mounting the steps to view the monument up close. Human skulls, arranged by age and gender, are arranged at eye level, while other bones are placed on higher levels. The Killing Fields are often visited in conjunction with a tour of Tuol Sleng (see below).

15km (9¼ miles) south of Phnom Penh. Arrange a private car or motorbike. Free admission, but guides are available (highly recommended) in exchange for donations. Daily 7:30am–5:30pm.

National Museum ★★★ What the British Museum is to the Elgin Marbles of Greece's Parthenon, the National Museum of Phnom Penh, opened in 1920 by King Sisowath, is to the statuary of Angkor Wat. This important storehouse holds artifacts and statuary from all regions of Cambodia. The sad fact is that many pieces didn't make it here—they were plundered and smuggled out of the country. Nevertheless, this grand red sandstone edifice has a beautiful and informative collection of Khmer pieces. From the entrance, begin on your left with a room of small prehistoric artifacts. A clockwise loop around the central courtyard walks you through time, from static, stylized pieces of stiff-legged, standing Buddhas, to contra-posed and contorted forms in supplication. There are good accompanying descriptions in English, but this is not a bad place to have a knowledgeable guide (ask in the lobby). The central courtyard features a shiva lingum and large temple fragments. At the more significant works—the statue of Jayavarman VII, for example—elderly ladies, looking like museum docents, hand out incense and flowers and instruct visitors to place them on makeshift altars. Don't feel obliged, but feel free to do so and just drop a few Riel or even $1.

Just north of the Royal Palace at Street 178, a short walk from the river. Admission $3. Daily 8am–5pm.

Royal Palace and Silver Pagoda ★★★ Don't miss this glittery downtown campus, the ostentatious jewel in the crown of Cambodia's monarchy. Built in the late 1860s under the reign of Norodom, the sight is comprised of many elaborate gilded halls, all with steep tile roofs, stupa-shape cupolas, and golden temple nagas denoting prosperity. The grand **Throne Hall** at the center is the coronation site for Khmer kings and the largest gilded cathedral in the country. Don't miss the many royal busts and the gilded umbrella used to shade the king when in procession. The French built a small exhibition hall on the temple grounds, a building that now houses the many gifts given to the monarchy, among them cross-stitch portraits of the royal family and all manner of bric-a-brac. Just inside the door, don't miss an original by Cézanne that has suffered terrible water damage and hangs in a ratty frame like an unwanted diploma: a shame. The balcony of the exhibition hall is the best bird's-eye view of the gilded temples. The facade of the neighboring **Royal Residence** is just as resplendent and is still the home of the now-abdicated King Sihanouk and his son and successor.

The **Silver Pagoda** is just south of the palace, and entrance is included with the same ticket. The floors of this grand temple are covered with 5,000 blocks of silver weighing more than 6 tons. The temple houses a 17th-century Buddha made of Baccarat crystal, and another made almost entirely of gold and decorated with almost 10,000 diamonds. That's not exactly what the Buddha had in mind, perhaps, but it's quite beautiful. The temple courtyard is encircled by a covered walkway with a contiguous mural of Cambodia's history and mythology. On the southern end of the complex is a small hill covered in vegetation and said to model the sacred Mount Meru; there's a large Buddha footprint and a small temple that provokes devout practice in Khmer visitors.

Btw. streets 240 and 184 on Sothearos. The entrance is on the east side facing the river. Admission $6.50. Daily 7:30–11am and 2–5pm.

Tuol Sleng, Museum of Genocide ★★ The grounds of this former high school are just as they were in 1979 at the end of Cambodia's bloody genocide. During the violent recent history in Cambodia, the two-story compound became one of the most notorious concentration camps, essentially a torture chamber before people were slaughtered in the Killing Fields. A visit here is a visceral revisit of some horrible events, too much for some visitors. From 1975 until 1979, an estimated 17,000 political prisoners, most just ordinary citizens, were tortured at Tuol Sleng and died, or were executed in the nearby Killing Fields. If you don't come with a guide, you'll certainly want to hire one at the entrance, although you're free to roam the grounds on your own. Local guides often have personal experience with the prison and are vital sources of oral history. They are open to questions, but go easy on any debate. Recrimination against the arbiters of these horrible events is an important issue here; just as Cambodians hope to move on into the future, they fear revisiting the past in the current international tribunals. The prison population of Tuol Sleng, also known as S-21, was carefully cataloged; in fact, the metal neck brace employed for holding subjects' heads in place for the admitting photograph is on display. There are some written accounts in English, paintings done by a survivor, and gory photos of the common torture practices in the prison, but perhaps what is most haunting is the fear in the eyes of the newly arrived; one wing of the buildings is dedicated to these very arrival photos. This sight is a bit overwhelming, so be prepared.

South of town at the corner of streets 350 and 113. Admission $2; guide fees vary (usually $2–$3 per person). Daily 8am–noon and 1–5pm.

Wat Phnom ★★ This is Cambodia's "Church on the Hill." Legend has it that sometime in the 14th century, a woman named Penh found sacred Buddhist objects in the nearby river and placed them here on the small hill that later became a temple. *Phnom,* in fact, means "hill," so the name of the city translates to "Penh's Hill."

The temple itself is a standard Southeast Asian *wat,* with Naga snakes on the cornered peaks of the roof and didactic murals of the Buddha's life done in Day-Glo allegories along interior walls. Don't miss the central ceiling, which, unlike the bright walls, is yet to be restored and is gritty and authentic.

The hillside park around the temple was once a no-go zone peopled by armed dealers and pimps, and in the evening you should still be careful, but now it's a laid-back little park. You're sure to meet with some crafty young salesmen who'll offer you the chance to show your Buddhist compassion by buying a caged bird for a dollar and letting it go; if you stick around long enough, you'll see the bird return to the cage.

Intersection of Street 96 and Norodom Blvd.

SHOPPING & GALLERIES

The best shopping in town, for everything from souvenirs and trinkets to the obligatory kitchen sink, is at any of the large local markets. The **Central Market** (see "Attractions," above) shouldn't be missed, but the **Russian Market** between streets 440 and 450 in the far south of town is where the real deal on souvenirs can be had (go by cab). It takes hard haggling to get the good deals on neat items like opium paraphernalia, carvings, and ceramics. It's all authentic-looking, even if made in China.

Shops and galleries are growing in number in the developing capital. All along Street 178, interesting little outlets are springing up and include a few affordable silk dealers like **Sayon Silkworks,** just west of the National Museum on Street 178. **Asasax Art Gallery,** No. 192 Street 178 (✆ **012/217-795;** www.asasaxart.com.kh), features unique local works. **Silk & Pepper,** at 33 Eo Street 178 (✆ **023/222-692**), has some great silk accessories and kimonos. Take a stroll along Street 240, which is home to a fantastic cafe culture and a few antiques shops and boutiques like **Bliss,** No. 29 Street 240 (✆ **023/215-754**), which sells some unique beaded and embroidered cushions and quilts; or **Le Lezard Bleu** (61 Street 240; ✆ **023/986-978** or 012/406-294), which features traditional and contemporary artworks and top-notch framing.

Bazar, at 28 Sihanouk Blvd., near the Independence Monument (✆ **012/776-492**), has a small but refined collection of Asian antiques and furniture.

For upscale, original clothing, **Ambre ★**, at 37 Street 178 (✆ **023/217-935;** closed Sun), is a two-story store that carries the whimsical, beautifully cut designs of Cambodian-born, France-raised Romyda Keth. Keth has a love affair with jersey and often layers clothing with funky embroidery or gorgeous swaths of organza.

For CDs, DVDs, and cool T-shirts and hip-hop fashions, stop by the **Boom Boom Room,** on Street 93, in the backpacker area near Boeung Kak Lake, or at a newer location across from the Golden Gate Hotel (No. 1C Street 278; ✆ **012/709-096**).

For essentials and Western groceries, stop by the **Lucky Market,** No. 160 Sihanouk Blvd. (✆ **023/215-229**), the most popular shopping center for Phnom Penh's many expats. "The Lucky" is just west of the Victory Monument traffic circle. For fresh, organic produce and fine canned goods, **Veggy's** is at No. 23 Street 240 (© **023/211-534**) and carries a similar line of familiar comfort foods from back home, whether home is Arkansas, Tokyo, Paris, or Seoul.

Monument Books, No. 111 Norodom Blvd. (© **023/217-617**), has a great selection of new books; it's a good spot to find books on the Khmer language and culture. Upstairs you'll find Monument Toys for the kiddies. There are also stores at 53 Street 426 (© **023/217-617**) and in the airport at the international departure level. Also check out the **Sorya Shopping Centre** (© **023/210-018**), just south of central market, which carries brand-name international goods as well as discount copies.

PHNOM PENH AFTER DARK

Phnom Penh is notorious for some of the seediest nightlife in all of Southeast Asia. There are some good, friendly bars in town, though many are the "hostess bar" variety.

The downtown area along the riverside is chockablock with small storefront bars and a few upscale spots. The **Rising Sun,** No. 20 Street 178 (© **012/970-719**), is a comfy English pub, a dark wooden stopover great for a few pints and a game of darts near the town center. **Green Vespa** (95 Sisowath Quay; © **012/887-228;** www.greenvespa.com) is a funky bar decked out in a Vespa theme—dig the cool green Vespa on display over the door. It's popular with expats and open daily from 6pm until late. **Chow** (277 Sisowath Quay; © **023/224-894**), the rooftop bar at boutique hotel the Quay, is a personal favorite. Sip a proper cocktail perched on tall riverside bar stools, or curl up in one of the chic daybeds that line the wall. Drinks are half-price during happy hour (4–8pm).

SPA SERVICES

Senses Salon and Spa (157 Sisowath Quay; © **023/990-244**) is along the riverside just next to the popular River House (p. 392). With a limited number of luxury treatment rooms, this Thai-French-owned facility specializes in all kinds of massage, with a focus on traditional Thai and relaxing oil massages, as well as aromatherapy, facials, skin care and scrubs, soaks, wraps, and waxing. It's the best spa in town.

Comparable, though with a focus on European techniques, is **In Style,** at No. 63 Street 242 (© **023/214-621**), near the town center at riverside. Popular among expats is **Bliss Spa** (29 Street 240; © **023/215-754**).

Budget **Island Massage** (© **023/991-950**), a small storefront at 329 Sisowath Quay with air-conditioned comfort, offers excellent foot massages for a great break after a day of city touring, as well as a list of basic health and relaxing body massage at low cost. They also have two other locations at Street 94 (© **023/992-282**) and 43 Street 86 (© **023/991-250**).

DAY TRIPS FROM PHNOM PENH

Oudong

Following defeat at Angkor by the Thais, the Khmer capital moved to Oudong, and kings ruled from there for more than 100 years until the power center shifted to nearby Phnom Penh in 1866. The area was a monastic center, and the 13th-century temples, like most others, pale in comparison to those of the Angkor complex. Still, the hills of Oudong offer breathtaking views. It's 1 hour west of Phnom Penh and is best reached by rented vehicle.

Phnom Chisor & Tonle Bati

If you've been to or are going to Angkor Wat, these temples will pale in comparison, but the ride through the countryside and among rural villages makes for a good day. Tonle Bati (33km/21 miles south of Phnom Penh) is a small collection of Angkor-style temples.

Entrance costs $3. Nearby Phnom Chisor is a group of 10th-century ruins atop a picturesque hill. Phnom Penh travel agents can make all the arrangements.

4 SOUTHERN CAMBODIA

When you think of Cambodia, visions of tranquil beaches probably aren't the first thing that comes to mind, which is a shame. It isn't much when compared with the quality and quantity of beach living in nearby Thailand, or even along the coast of Vietnam, but the southern coast of Cambodia boasts some fine sandy stretches worthy of putting your feet up for a few days, especially after some heavy-duty temple touring or bouncing around the roads of rural Cambodia.

Route 4, which connects Phnom Penh with Cambodia's only port at Kompong Som, or **Sihanoukville,** after the former king, was built by the United States to facilitate Cambodian trade and the influx of aid starting from the mid-1960s. Just adjacent to the busy Sihanoukville port, you can find some lovely little beach areas, most of which are speckled with budget bungalows and groovy bars owned by Western expatriates, as well as a fine little resort called the Sokha Beach Resort (see "Where to Stay," under "Sihanoukville," later). The town of **Kampot** is a lazy little river town, just a grid of mostly colonial-style houses along a quiet, lazy river, but another good place to kick back. You might also visit nearby **Kep,** which was a French colonial vacation spot whose 1950s/1960s-era villas lay in ruin. **Bokor Mountain,** a short ride from Kampot, was the cool mountaintop retreat of the French but is now closed for renovations. Connections by bus with Sihanoukville are convenient, and many choose to do this region in a rented vehicle or even by affordable local taxicab. So if you're stuck in Phnom Penh for a few days waiting out a Vietnam visa, hit the beaches. You'll be surprised.

KAMPOT & KEP

148km (92 miles) S of Phnom Penh; 112km (70 miles) E of Sihanoukville

The French colonists built many luxury vacation homes along the coast here. Development continued in the high plateau of Bokor Mountain with a large hotel, casino, even a church and school. The two towns are some 25km (16 miles) apart, and today most choose to stay in Kampot and make a side trip to Kep. Kampot is just a quiet riverside town with views of the mountains and a lazy grid of old colonial houses. There are a few nice little hotels and little to do but wander, chat with locals and expats at cafes, and peep the sunset over Bokor. Kep has a large crab market sitting on a busy bay of fishing vessels; hit Kep to check out the classic colonial homes (someday they'll probably all be boutique resorts or private dwellings again). This area is a laid-back stop on your way to Sihanoukville.

Essentials

Getting There

The road from Phnom Penh is good, a thin ribbon of asphalt. Your best bet is to arrange a taxi from Phnom Penh. There are no tourist bus services directly to Kampot or Kep. Connection with Sihanoukville by taxi costs about $20 for a 3-hour ride.

Getting Around

Kampot is a tiny riverside town, all easily traversed on foot (if you can pull yourself from the guesthouse hammock). Kep is just 25km (16 miles) east of Kampot, easily reached on rented motorbike, motorbike taxi, or motorbike with trailer (called tuk-tuk).

If you're off to Kep beach or the caves near Kampong Trach, take a motorbike with driver for just $4 per day trip, or $2 one-way if you stay in Kep overnight. Renting your own little 100cc Devo machine is just $3; the 250cc Honda Degree bike, which has good suspension and can take the bumpier roads, is $11. Maintenance at the town's two rental agents is limited. The price is quite low, but so is the quality. Say a prayer and contact **Sean Ly Motor Rental Shop** at No. 27 DSoeng Ngoc Rd. (✆ **012/944-687**), just south of the central traffic circle; it's your best bet for picking up a motorbike. Next door, nearer the traffic circle, **Cheang Try** (✆ **012/974-698**) looks less efficient but offers the same bevy of beat-up bikes at the same price. It's $3 for a 100cc putt-putt mobile, and $5 for a 250cc Honda Degree with heavy suspension. The same offices also rent cars or even four-wheel-drive vehicles for $20 per day.

For more extensive tour services, **Art Suriya Travel** (✆ **012/501-742**) offers custom tours of the surrounding area or other parts of the region. Costs are higher than the storefront tour offices, but you get the full custom treatment. Contact **Mr. Sok Lim** at his tour offices on the north end of Kampot (at riverside, north of the central bridge; ✆ **012/719-872**) for adventure trips and jungle-trekking tours around Bokor.

From **Kep,** check out the $10 day trips out to **Rabbit Island** ★, which has pretty, quiet beaches good for swimming.

Where to Stay

Kampot

Blissful Guesthouse Welcome to Hotel California. An old colonial villa fashioned with heavy wooden beams, Blissful Guesthouse has hammocks swinging from every veranda and under every tree, a quiet upstairs sitting area, and lots of cozy papasans and couches to curl up with a book and rest. Rooms are guesthouse basic, with hard beds and small shower-in-room bathrooms, but everything's clean. Angela, the friendly Danish owner, is a font of local information. The bar hops late and this is a great place to meet up with other travelers, perhaps arrange an onward taxi share, or get metaphysical late into the night.

Just a short walk east of the river, past the "2000" monument. ✆ **012/513-024.** www.blissfulguesthouse.com. 10 units. $4–$8 double. No credit cards. **Amenities:** Restaurant; bar; motorbikes. *In room:* Fan only, no phone.

Bokor Mountain Lodge This old colonial lined with cool travel photos on the riverside is the best location in town. Open colonnaded walkways overlook the busy street below and river beyond. Breakfast is included and there's a good in-house tour company that can arrange excursions. They've got Wi-Fi access but it can be finicky.

Riverfront Dr. (riverside at the center of Kampot). ✆ **033/932-314.** www.bokorlodge.com. 6 units. Oct–Apr $35–$45 double, $60 family suite; May–Oct $30–$40 double, $50 family suite. Rates include breakfast. MC, V. **Amenities:** Restaurant; bar. *In room:* A/C, TV, Wi-Fi.

Little Garden Guesthouse The place is just that: a little garden area with an upstairs block of clean, basic, affordable rooms. Go for a top-floor unit adjoining a cool open sitting area shared by a few rooms. The rooftop terrace has wonderful views of the river (on clear days you can see neighboring Vietnam's Phu Quoc Island) and is a terrific place to collapse on hot days. These folks are involved with the local orphanage and can get you connected to offer some service during your trip.

River Rd. (just north of the bridge). ✆ **012/256-901.** www.littlegardenbar.com. 15 units. $10–$25 double; long-term rates available. No credit cards. **Amenities:** Restaurant. *In room:* TV, A/C, fan, no phone.

Knai Bang Chatt ★★ Knai Bang Chatt marks the arrival of luxury in Kep. This seaside property is made of one new and three renovated villas, built in what was called the New Modern Khmer style of the 1960s. Rooms are spacious and done in mellow, neutral colors like champagne and beige mixed with subtle mauves and khaki green. Beds are extremely cozy. Everyone gets a huge private terrace overlooking the garden or ocean. The outdoor infinity pool faces some stiff competition from the nearby ocean, where you can take a midnight dip among phosphorescent plankton.

Phum Thmey Sangkat Prey, Thom Khan Kep. ✆ **012/879-486.** www.knaibangchatt.com. 11 units. Apr–Sept $150–$225 double; Oct–Mar $200–$450 double. MC, V. **Amenities:** Restaurant; bar; outdoor pool; spa. *In room:* A/C, TV, fridge, minibar, Wi-Fi.

Veranda Natural Resort ★ On a hilltop high over the tiny town of Kep, Veranda is the best budget choice out this far. In fact, the rooms have a certain boutique flavor that's quite attractive. On stilts overlooking the sea far below, rustic thatch and wood units are compact but tidy, with small but clean bathrooms (shower only) attached. Go for an oceanview room with an outdoor daybed, and you've got a little low-luxe private oasis. If you're splurging, check out the Residence House, which has newer, more luxe rooms that come with private balconies. The bar is a popular spot for sunset views over Bokor Mountain in the distance. The restaurant serves good faux-Western and Khmer—a good thing, because you're pretty much stranded up here (expect to pay $5–$10 for main courses).

Opposite ASPECA orphanage and far up the hillside overlooking town. ✆ **012/888-619.** www.veranda-resort.com. 29 units. $30–$75 double; $195 villa. MC, V. **Amenities:** Restaurant; bar; motorbikes. *In room:* A/C (some rooms), TV (some rooms), no phone, Wi-Fi.

Where to Dine

Just north of the Bamboo Light Café (below), past the bridge on the riverside road, check out the **Little Garden Bar** (✆ **012/602-661;** www.littlegardenbar.com). Its expat owner serves up good Western cuisine. They also run trips and sponsor programs for a local orphanage. Stop in, and you're likely to meet up with other like-minded travelers (whether that "like mind" is drinking all night or motorbiking up Bokor).

For good Khmer food, stop by the open-air **Restaurant Phnom Kam Chay Thmey** (✆ **012/602-505**), an affordable joint right next to the bridge.

After dinner and a brief walk around town, the only thing going on is the bar at Blissful Guesthouse. Grab a wholesome **fruit shake** for 1,000 Riel at one of the stalls just west of the central monument area. Ask for no sugar unless you like it super sweet.

Bamboo Light Café ★ SRI LANKAN With cheap and tiptop eats, this ranks up there with my favorite Indian restaurant back home. Curries are red or yellow, mild or fiery—prepared to your tastes. The mutton dishes are especially good, as are the Sri Lankan Kottu roti dishes (pancakes cut up and mixed with potato and curry). The very clean interior has cool, indirect lighting in bamboo stanchions. The balcony area is where you're most likely to meet the groovy dudes you saw out on the road in the day. Great breakfasts of bacon and eggs, as well as good sandwiches and Western meals, are served all day. With an Internet cafe upstairs, this is a good place to beat the heat.

River Rd. (near the bridge) in central Kampot. ✆ **012/681-530.** bamboo_vana@yahoo.com. Main courses $2.50–$4. No credit cards. Daily 7am–10pm.

SIHANOUKVILLE

230km (143 miles) S of Phnom Penh; 112km (70 miles) W of Kep

A popular summertime spot for Khmers, Sihanoukville is really a port town, but the beaches are good, there are some good accommodations choices, and it's very affordable. Trips to outlying islands for scuba diving and snorkeling are attracting more and more Western tourists.

Essentials

Getting There

BY CAR The U.S.-built Route 4 between Phnom Penh and Sihanoukville is a long, straight, smooth ribbon of highway; if this sounds ideal, it just means that people go like the dickens on this road, and accidents are many, as are fatalities at roadside, in villages where the relative danger of this high-speed road is not yet understood. Be extremely careful should you choose a self-drive option along this stretch. Renting a private taxi is your best bet, and the 3-hour ride to or from Phnom Penh goes for about $30 per vehicle. The cost jumps up to $40 to $50 if you depart Phnom Penh in the late afternoon. Taxi connection with Kampot to the east (see the section above) is $20 for the 3-hour ride. Contact any hotel or guesthouse front desk.

BY BUS Frequent, convenient buses connect Sihanoukville and Phnom Penh. The 3-hour ride costs $5 (including a snack) in an air-conditioned bus with **Mekong Express** (✆ **023/427-518**), and $3 to $4 with other budget carriers. **Capitol Tours** (✆ **023/217-627**) and **Sorya Transport** (✆ **023/210-859**), among others, offer daily connections to and from Phnom Penh, usually leaving in the morning.

Orientation

Sihanoukville is set on a wide peninsular area jutting south and east into the Gulf of Thailand. The peninsula is shielded by islands—Koh Rong, Koh Rong Sam Leuem, Koh T Kiev, and Ko Ses are among the many. Starting on the north end of the peninsula, find the busy port area, just south of which, tracing the coast, you'll find Victory Beach, Independence Beach, Sokha Beach, and Ochheuteal Beach to the far south. Ekareach Street turns inland at the terminus of Route 4, just past the busy port, and cuts a path across the peninsula to the downtown market area before ending at the Golden Lion Monument near Ochheuteal Beach. Signs point the way from Ekareach to the beaches along its length.

Getting Around

Motodups, the ubiquitous motorcycle taxis, are everywhere in Sihanoukville and your best bet for ferrying to and from the beaches. Bicycle and motorbike rentals are also available. Distances and the many hills along Ekareach Street make hopping a moto or renting one worthwhile, but once at the beach, you can easily walk around town.

FAST FACTS **Canadia Bank** (✆ **034/933-697**) and **Mekong Bank** (✆ **034/933-867**) both have convenient branches, with cash exchanges, in the downtown area along Ekareach Street. The telephone code for Sihanoukville is **34,** and IDD phone services, as well as cheap Internet phone connection at the Internet cafes, abound. **Ocean Mart** is in a convenient location close to the major beaches and next to the main traffic circle (beside Golden Lions Traffic Circle), and you'll find terminals aplenty at local restaurants and bars. Emergency services in Sihanoukville are nonexistent, and any major medical issue means evacuation to Phnom Penh or on to Bangkok. The **International Peace**

Clinic (✆ **012/794-269**), at the center of town on Ekareach Street, offers basic first aid, and the **Sokha Beach Resort** (Oceanside at Sokha Beach; ✆ **032/935-999**) has a doctor on call at their own private clinic.

Where to Stay

Expensive

The Independence Hotel ★ This restored hotel has an excellent location on a private strip of sand on Independence Beach. The hotel used to be a showpiece of the Royal family and once played host to elite dignitaries. Former King Norodom Sihanouk himself was responsible for the interior design of the hotel back in the 1960s, but don't expect royal appointments. The rooms have a musty smell and bland decor. The layout of the deluxe rooms is awkward: There's a large entranceway, but the bed is tightly crammed between two walls—you may have to turn sideways to get into bed. The views, however, are amazing; many rooms overlook the ocean. There's also a beautiful garden walkway at the base of a rocky outcrop along Independence Beach. Staff is also very friendly and very eager to please.

Street 2 Thnou, Sagkat No. 3, Khan Mittapheap. ✆ **034/934-300.** Fax 034/933-660. www.independencehotel.net. 52 units. $140–$160 double; $250–$450 suite. MC, V. **Amenities:** Restaurant; bar; concierge; Internet; outdoor pool; room service; spa. *In room:* A/C, TV, fridge, hair dryer, minibar.

Sokha Beach Resort ★ Kids Where the Independence is all cool and modern architecture, Sokha Beach Resort is finely executed kitschy Khmer. You can see the traditional, winged red-tile roofs from a distance, and the public spaces are decorated with carved stone reliefs and Khmer statues. Room decoration is functional, with bamboo rattan chairs and tables, and terra-cotta floors. Club suites have swanky '70s-style circular beds, and all suites have an ocean view. If you're looking for something special, rent one of their 10 villas. The villas bear '50s/'60s box-style architecture and were originally military housing units. The exterior is done in unfinished gray brick and white stone walls, and a small driveway leads to a private entrance. The bedrooms have the same decor as those in the hotel. Each villa has a small living room and a separate garden space, so you're really set apart from other hotel guests.

Tip: If you're on a luxe budget, book a room at the affiliated **Sokha Inn.** It lies at the northern end of the property, about a 2-minute walk from the main entrance, but golf carts will shuttle you back and forth. Rooms are $85. Sure, it kind of feels like you're staying in the "servants' quarters," but you have access to all the hotel's amenities for about a third of the price.

Street 2 Thnou, Sangkat 4, Mittapheap District, Sihanoukville. ✆ **034/935-999.** Fax 034/935-888. www.sokhahotels.com. 166 units (Sokha Inn: 24 units). $250–$300 double; $350–$380 villa; from $500 suite. MC, V. **Amenities:** 2 restaurants; 3 bars; babysitting; bikes; children's play area and planned activities; health club; room service; spa; tennis courts; watersports equipment rentals; Wi-Fi. *In room:* A/C, TV, fridge, hair dryer, minibar.

Inexpensive

Malibu Bungalows ★ Owned and operated by Ms. Lina, a Khmer-born U.S. resident and friendly raconteur, Malibu is a cool collection of beach bungalows on a steep hillside overlooking the beach. There's also a small hotel block farther back. The hotel is at the crest of a dynamic promontory, such prime turf that the Khmer government decided they would like to commandeer the land for their own use; Ms. Lina and her connections with Khmer royalty keep the area—there are a few nearby guesthouses—from being gobbled up. There's a cozy little sitting area near the entry, and the hotel's restaurant offers great views of Sokha Beach below and the vast sea beyond. The breakfast buffet is delicious, and Ms. Lina can, upon request, arrange for a unique Khmer-style royal meal. The rooms are simple, free-standing bungalows lining the precipitous steps along a verdant hillside path; at the bottom is a cool bar area and small private beach. There are also comfy air-conditioned apartment blocks near the entry at the top of the hill. Rooms are rustic, and electricity can be erratic here. Mosquito nets and bamboo furnishings give the place a certain Robinson Crusoe feel.

Group 14, Mondol 4, Sangkat 4, Khan Mittapheap, Sihanoukville (on a small rise above the Sokha Beach Resort). ✆ **012/733-334** or 016/770-277. 19 units. $40–$45 double; $35–$45 bungalow. No credit cards. **Amenities:** Restaurant. *In room:* A/C (in rooms only, bungalows have fans), TV, fridge, minibar, no phone.

Orchidee Guest House This guesthouse is popular with expats and returning guests. Simple rooms have air-conditioning and satellite television, but very basic tile bathrooms with a shower-in-room setup. It's affordable, and a fun party vibe pervades. The $30 standard rooms are big, with white tiles, and the best choice (better than the red-carpet rooms). Bathrooms are large, plain affairs with tubs. Get a room next to the pool, and you're likely to make lots of friends over oversize drinks with umbrellas.

23 Tola St. (1 block back from Ochheuteal Beach), Sihanoukville. ✆ **034/933-639** or 012/380-300. www.orchidee-guesthouse.com. 72 units. $13–$28 double; $30–$40 family room. No credit cards. **Amenities:** Restaurant; motorbikes; outdoor pool. *In room:* A/C, TV, fridge, minibar.

Reef Resort This small guesthouse is casual and laid-back. Rooms are neat and tidy, and the bamboo furniture, silk lamps and wall hangings, and knit blankets give the place a very charming appeal. Each room comes with a small poolside terrace. The bar has a proper pool table and a large flatscreen TV for movies or sports events. It is a great place to while away the evening with a couple beers.

Road from Golden Lion to Serendipity. ✆ **012/315-338.** www.reefresort.com.kh. 11 units. $35–$65 double; $70–$80 family room. MC, V. **Amenities:** Restaurant; bar; small outdoor pool. *In room:* A/C, TV, DVD (family rooms only) fridge, minibar, no phone, Wi-Fi.

Where to Dine

Dining in Sihanoukville means mostly good seafood for little cash, and there are lots of oceanside budget stops. Expats are putting up shingles around town advertising tastes of home and cocktails. Sokha Beach Resort (see above) has a fine seafood restaurant.

Bamboo Light Café ★ SRI LANKAN Like their popular restaurant in Kampot, the folks at Bamboo Light serve great Sri Lankan fare, including hot curries (or tempered to your taste) with chapatti or nan bread, as well as Sri Lankan Kottu roti, a dish of roti pancake mashed up with potato, curry, and vegetable. Everything is delicious, and they can even put together a good packed lunch for any day trips.

78 Ekareach St., in the downtown area. ✆ **012/925-707.** bamboo_vana@yahoo.com. Main courses $2.50–$4. No credit cards. Daily 7am–10pm.

Mick and Craig's ★ WESTERN These guys are the real originals in Sihanoukville, and backpackers and expats alike flock here. Some of the best food in town is here, served in a casual open-air setup with good tunes, a busy bar, and a billiards area. You can sign up for trips with their in-house eco-tour company, pick up a book in their casual book corner, or even stay in their new guesthouse (the whole place has just moved to a new location near Serendipity Beach, just behind the Lion traffic circle, and they're calling it a "sanctuary" now). They offer lots of favorites from home: pizza, sandwiches made with bread baked on-site, snacks like nachos and potato skins, steaks, bangers and mash (sausage with mashed taters), grilled fish, and good veggie offerings (including a yummy veggie burger), as well as lots of good Khmer dishes. Dessert is apple crumble or ice cream. Extensive breakfasts are the best cure for that Sihanoukville hangover: muesli and fruit or the full-on hangover fry-up.

Just adjacent to the Golden Lion Traffic circle at the head of the road leading to Serendipity Beach. ✆ **012/727-740.** Main courses $5–$9. No credit cards. Daily 7am–11pm.

Snakehouse INTERNATIONAL Here's a fun night out. Part restaurant, part menagerie of jungle with snakes, turtles, and crocs. The animals are well taken care of in stylish displays, and the restaurant has a cool, laid-back feel. The food is good (the animals are for viewing, not eating). Snakehouse serves up a good selection of local dishes and standard international fare, anything from spaghetti to steak and sandwiches. The place is up on a hill above town and makes for a fun evening.

Soviet St., on the hilltop near Sihanoukville's busy backpacker ghetto. ✆ **012/673-805.** Main courses $4–$9. No credit cards. Daily 8am–11pm.

Starfish Café INTERNATIONAL Set up as an NGO to train and employ people with physical disabilities, many of whom are victims of antipersonnel mines, the Starfish Café gives hope to a group of people who are systematically shunned by Khmer society, funding local literacy programs and serving as a drop-in point for clients of the Starfish Project (see their website for more information). The place offers a time-tested formula of good sandwiches, baked goods, and light local fare. The friendly staff can offer good information about local tours and travel. There's an upstairs reading area and a shaded courtyard. They sell popular T-shirts, as well as products from the Snar Dai Project, which sells goods made by mothers of street kids.

Just behind the Samudera Market at the town center. ✆ **012/952-011.** www.starfishcambodia.org. Main courses $3–$4.50. No credit cards. Daily 7am–6pm.

Attractions

Apart from sticking your toes in the sand and sipping cocktails, tours to outlying islands are the main attraction in Sihanoukville. Contact the friendly folks at **EcoAdventures** (Samudera Market, Town Center, Sihanoukville; ✆ **012/654-104;** www.ecosea.com). They arrange great day tours with stops in remote coves where clients can snorkel or take a scuba course. The diving is mostly shallow and the visibility varies, but EcoAdventures is a very professional outfit, and a day on their boat—whether diving, snorkeling, or taking in the scenery over their tasty lunch buffet (or diving off the top deck)—is alone worth the trip down to Snooky.

For tours to outlying hills, contact the friendly folks at **Eco-Trek Tours Cambodia,** next to Mick and Craig's Sanctuary, Serendipity Street (✆ **012/987-7073** or 016/876-200; ecotrektourscambodia@yahoo.com). For car and taxi service on to any other parts of the area, contact any hotel front desk.

5 SIEM REAP & ANGKOR WAT

The ruins of the ancient city of **Angkor,** capital of the Khmer kingdom from A.D. 802 until 1295, are one of the world's marvels. The "City of Kings," Angkor boasts some of the largest religious monuments ever constructed; it's a vast and mysterious complex of hulking laterite and sandstone blocks. Unknown to the world until French naturalist Henri Mouhot literally stumbled onto it in 1861, the area of Angkor existed for centuries only as a myth—a wondrous city (or cities, to be exact), its exact location in the Cambodian jungle unknown. After Mahout in 1861, archaeologists flocked here, only to be foiled by years of conflict that left the temples in the hands of the Khmer Rouge. Many temples were damaged and pillaged. Tourists were the subsequent invaders, from the late 1990s. Today the sight is mobbed, but you can still find those quiet moments in communion with this amazing man-made wonder.

The temple complex carries the remains of passageways, moats, temples, and palaces that represent centuries of building in the capital. Days spent scrambling about and exploring the temples are memorable, and this is a great place to bring adventurous kids who like to get their play clothes dirty.

The temples are served by the nearby town of Siem Reap, some 6km (3¾ miles) to the south. Siem Reap means "Victory over the Thais" and refers to the 16th-century victory that solidified the Khmer kingdom—though animosity between the two neighbors remains to this day. All of western Cambodia was once under Thai control, and Khmer people are very proud of their survival in the face of so many invaders, the very reason that an image of Angkor Wat graces the national flag.

Siem Reap, once just a dusty track with a few storefronts, now supports a host of large five-star hotels and resorts, fine-dining options aplenty, and the kind of good services, shops, galleries, and spas that make the little city a new oasis of luxury in parched western Cambodia. The town's central market is a great stop for souvenir purchases, and the nearby downtown area is abuzz day and night with fine-dining options and quaint bars and party spots.

A 3- or 4-day visit will suffice (though many do it in less time) to come away with a newfound love for ancient cultures, Asian religions, and sunsets. Good options abound for visiting more far-flung temple ruins (in fact, one of the most common complaints is about the large crowds that now visit Cambodia's "Disneyland of Temples"), and trekking or boat trips to remote mangrove swamps and a large bird sanctuary are enough to keep you busy. Bring your sense of adventure, your camera, and a youthful sense of wonder. You won't be disappointed by amazing Angkor.

Give of "Yourself" in Siem Reap

They want your blood in Siem Reap. Many humanitarian-aid agencies use Siem Reap as a base for raising funds and treating rural peoples. The **Kantha Bopha Hospital,** on the main road to the temples, and the **Angkor Hospital for Children** (contact them through www.fwab.org or ✆ **063/963-409**) are always looking for blood donors to help young patients through the most trying periods of acute dysentery and hemorrhagic fever. Patients often make it to these centers from rural parts in dire circumstances and need immediate blood transfusions to make it through their first days. Just show up at either clinic to make a donation of blood, time, and/or money—all of which are desperately needed.

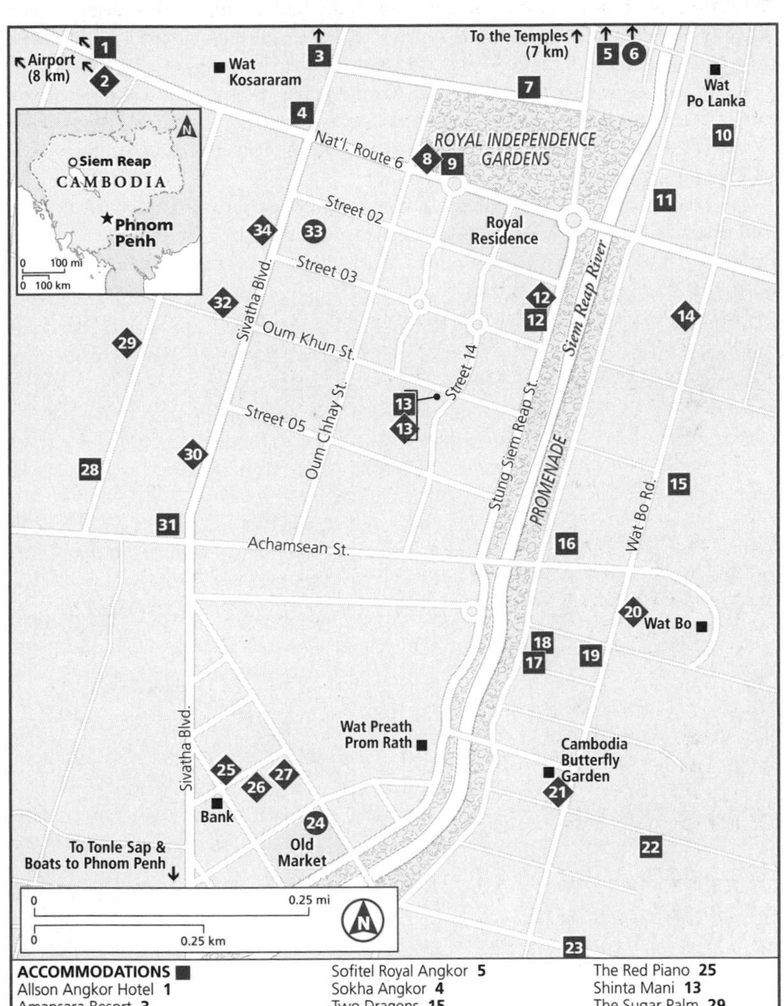

ACCOMMODATIONS ■
Allson Angkor Hotel **1**
Amansara Resort **3**
Angkor Palace Resort and Spa **1**
Angkor Village Hotel **22**
Angkor Village Resort **5**
Auberge Mont Royal D'Angkor **28**
Bopha Angkor **18**
City River Hotel **17**
FCC Angkor **12**
Hôtel de la Paix **31**
La Noria **11**
La Résidence d'Angkor **16**
Le Meridien Angkor **1**
Passaggio **23**
Pavillon d'Orient **10**
Pavillon Indochine **3**
Raffles Grand Hotel d'Angkor **7**
Shinta Mani **13**
Sofitel Royal Angkor **5**
Sokha Angkor **4**
Two Dragons **15**
Victoria Angkor Hotel **9**
Viroth's Hotel **19**

DINING ◆
Abacus **32**
Blue Pumpkin **27**
Butterflies Garden Restaurant **21**
Cafe Indochine **34**
Chivit Thai **14**
FCC Angkor (Foreign Correspondent's Club) **12**
Kama Sutra **26**
Khmer Kitchen Restaurant **27**
Le Bistrot de Siem Reap **8**
Madame Butterfly **2**
Meric **31**
The Red Piano **25**
Shinta Mani **13**
The Sugar Palm **29**
Taj Mahal **27**
Tell Restaurant **30**
Viroth's Restaurant **20**

ATTRACTIONS ●
Land Mines Museum **6**
New Market **33**
Old Market **24**

GETTING THERE

BY PLANE **Bangkok Air** (in Phnom Penh: ✆ **023/426-624;** in Siem Reap: ✆ 063/ 380-191; www.bangkokair.com) is currently the only airline running the 1-hour connection to Siem Reap from Phnom Penh. One-way fares are $70.

If you just want to see the great temples at Angkor, the process is simplified with international arrivals: Vietnam Airlines flies directly from Ho Chi Minh City, Bangkok Airways flies directly from Bangkok, and you can check flights by Silk Air and Lao Aviation for other routes.

I highly recommend flying into town. The international airport is relatively new and beautifully designed, using traditional Cambodian architecture. ***Note:*** The international departure tax (from both Phnom Penh and Siem Reap) is $25; the domestic tax is $6.

BY BOAT A ride on the 5-hour boat connection between Phnom Penh and Siem Reap costs $30 to $35. Contact any hotel or travel agent (they all sell the same tickets at the same price). The scenic trip connects to Siem Reap via the great Tonle Sap Lake. Siem Reap also connects with Battambang, to the south and west, via the Tonle Sap and the Sangker River. The trip shows you life in fishing villages along the river as you trace the banks of the Sangker. In the rainy season, the ride is 6 to 8 hours, but in the dry season (Feb–May) it can take 8 to 10 hours or more and isn't recommended. Book your ticket at any tour agent or your hotel or guesthouse. The price is $14.

A new option is the weeklong cruise between **Angkor Wat** and either **Can Tho** or **My Tho** in Vietnam's Mekong Delta aboard one of the luxury, shallow-draft **Pandaw Cruise Boats** (www.pandaw.com). Shared rooms on the vessel start at $780.

BY BUS Your hotel front desk can arrange bus transportation for you at no additional cost. **Mekong Express** (✆ **023/427-518**) connects Phnom Penh and Siem Reap with daily luxury buses ($11 for the 5½-hr. ride). Bus rides come with water and an edible snack, and there's a bathroom on board. ***Tip:*** A set of earplugs is your friend on this bus ride (and any bus ride really), as they play Khmer karaoke songs and various Asian pop-music videos. **Capitol Tour** (No. 14 Road 182; ✆ **023/217-627**) also runs daily minivans between Phnom Penh and Siem Reap ($5 for the 5-hr. ride), as well as to destinations farther afield such as Battambang or Poipet at the Thai border. **Neak Krorhorm Travel and Tour** (in Phnom Penh, ✆ **023/219-496;** and in Siem Reap near the Old Market, ✆ **063/964-924**) provides similar services.

GETTING AROUND

You'll need some kind of wheels to make your way around Siem Reap and to and from the temples. Any hotel front desk or travel agent can make arrangements for you.

A rented **car with driver** is about $25 (double that with a guide). This is your best bet if hitting the temples farther afield, but if just doing the main temple circuits, I recommend one of the open-air options below.

Tuk-tuks are the best choice and available anywhere. The name is taken from the Thais, but these tuk-tuks have nothing to do with the noisy Bangkok three-wheeler. These are a two-wheeled surrey pulled by a standard motorbike. They are shaded, and the padded seat is great for two. There's a small shelf at the front of the cart, usually with laminated maps and advertisements, and, in a pinch, you can seat two more, but it's not very comfy. Pay $16 for the whole day, $1 to $2 for short trips in town.

A **motorcycle taxi,** called a *motodup,* is a good, cheap option for between $6 and $8 per day. Helmets are generally available, though few wear them (I recommend wearing one). This is a good choice for solo travelers going to the temples without a guide. For sights farther afield, it can be a bit tiring. If going way out, ask for a helmet with a wind screen, as it's safe and saves a day of squinting. Riding **your own motorbike** was once the most popular choice, but local officials put a stop to it, citing many road accidents.

The temple roads are flat and well paved, so **bicycles** are a popular choice. You can rent one for $2 to $3 per day from guesthouses and hotels. Take care in the scorching midday heat, and drink plenty of fluids. On a bike, you can go where you please, as you please. When parking at temples, vendors implore you to park near them and they'll mind your bike. Agree to nothing, but tell them that maybe you'll buy something later; when you do need the inevitable bottle of water, buy from your new friend.

VISITOR INFORMATION & TOURS

Siem Reap is full of helpful traveler services and information. In fact, most hotels and guesthouses can help you arrange all of the essentials. Below are a few service providers I'd recommend, among the many others you'll see in the area.

Expensive

- **Diethelm,** House No. 470, Krous Village, Svay Dangkum Commune, Siem Reap (**© 063/963-524;** fax 063/963-694; www.diethelmtravel.com). Providing all local and regional services, Diethelm is a top international tour operator, offering classic tours in Angkor, as well as anywhere in the region.
- **Exotissimo,** New Building B, 2021 Street 60MK, Siem Reap (**© 063/964-323;** fax 063/963-621; www.exotissimo.com). Like Diethelm (see above), Exotissimo is a large conglomerate, with offices throughout the region that can arrange any inevitability. Mostly for larger budgets.
- **Osmose,** at Sam Veasna Center for Wildlife Conservation (**© 063/963-710;** www.osmosetonlesap.net). Offering high-end tours to the far-flung coastal areas of the Tonle Sap Lake, Osmose levies high fees for its popular eco-tours in order to maintain high standards of low environmental impact, and to fund its efforts at encouraging sustainable development and preservation in the region.
- **Terre Cambodge,** 668 Hup Guan St. (**© 092/476-682;** www.terrecambodge.com). Catering to many of the French tourists who flock to Siem Reap and have deeper pockets, Terre Cambodge arranges adventure trips to the farther-flung reaches in the area, ranging from off-the-map destinations along Tonle Sap to little-known jungle temples far from Angkor.

Budget

Here are a couple of the more reliable, less expensive companies. Hotel or guesthouse front desks can, for free or a small fee, arrange tickets with one of the companies listed below. In fact, popular **Capitol Guesthouse** and more upscale **Mekong Express Tours** don't even have offices in town and must be booked through hotel front desks.

- **Neak Krorhrom Travel and Tours,** just adjacent to the Old Market (east side; **© 063/964-924**), is a good one for onward bus connections to rural stops like Battambang. In fact, book with one of the other operators and you'll likely end up waiting for the bus out in front of these offices.
- **PTM,** right in the heart of the bar street near the Old Market (**© 063/964-388;** fax 063/965-486; www.ptm.com.kh), offers basic bus services and can book flights.

Fast Facts Siem Reap

Banks & Currency Exchange **Canadia Bank,** on the western side of the Old Market (© **063/964-808**), and **ANZ Royal Bank** (566–570 Tep Vong St. © **023/726-900**) are the best options for services. **ANZ** has several ATMs around town, including one at the central branch and two 24-hour ATMs in the heart of the backpacker district just south of Red Piano Bar. You can change traveler's checks in some hotels and in any bank.

Emergency There's a tourist police station near the entrance to the temples. For local police, dial © **117.** In the event of a medical emergency, contact **International SOS Clinic** in Phnom Penh (© **023/216-911**).

Internet Small storefront offices surround the central market area. On the main street, try **E-Café,** No. 011 Siwatha Blvd., an air-conditioned facility with speedy connections, for just over $2 per hour, by far the best in town. **Phsar Chas Netweb,** on the northwest corner of the Old Market (© **012/461-849**), is typical of the many others in the Old Market area. It's just $1 per hour for relatively speedy dial-up service, and they can connect you to your home country with Internet phone for next to nothing, or you can borrow a mobile phone for in-country calls. Almost all Internet shops can burn CDs if you need to empty your camera's memory card. Also try the shops just adjacent to the Red Piano. Most are open early to late (7am–midnight). If you have a Wi-Fi-capable laptop, you can connect using prepaid PIC cards at the **FCC** restaurant, the **Raffles Grand** and **Sofitel** hotels, as well as at the **Angkor What?** bar among others. The **Blue Pumpkin** and **Molly Malone's** offer free Wi-Fi access to customers.

Post Office The post office is on Pokambor Avenue at riverside near the town center (next to the FCC; see "Where to Dine," later in this chapter). It's open daily 7am to 5:30pm and can handle foreign and domestic regular and parcel post.

Telephone The city code for Siem Reap is **63.** Most hotels have international direct-dialing (IDD), but many of the Internet cafes around the Old Market have better rates and offer callback service or Internet phone services.

WHERE TO STAY

Tourist numbers are high, and development is revved up in tiny Siem Reap. Visitors can choose from some of the finest upscale accommodations in the region.

For midrange hotels (below $100), there are a handful of nice boutique choices in town. In the high season, high-end accommodations often fill up, so be sure to book ahead. In low season, be sure to ask for a discount. Most hotels levy a 10% VAT.

Very Expensive

Amansara Resort ★★ *Aman* means "peace" in Sanskrit, and the suffix *sara* refers to Khmer Apsara dancers. Set downtown in an old guest villa once owned by King Sihanouk, the suites of the Amansara are done in a cool, contemporary, minimalist design of white stucco and dark timber all surrounded by shade trees. The outside world melts away when you step into this complex. Large bedrooms with adjoining sitting areas lead to a private outdoor courtyard area. Decor is simple; the bedroom wall has a white stone bas-relief of a banyan tree, the courtyard has a lotus pond with goldfish. The services at Amansara are unrivaled: private driver and guide, personalized excursions to the temples and town, high tea with freshly baked cookies and cake, stocked bar, wine and cheese cellar, and the list goes on. The idea is that Amansara is your home, so you can wander into the central house and mix yourself a gin and tonic or grab a cookie whenever you fancy. Unfortunately, the compulsory daily $100 "half-board charge" per person *on top* of the rather steep room fees feels like you're being nickel-and-dimed (or Benjamin Franklin–ed!) here. That said, service is in its own category here and it is a remarkable experience for Siem Reap.

Road to Angkor, Siem Reap, Kingdom of Cambodia. ✆ **063/760-333.** Fax 063/760-335. www.amanresorts.com. 24 units. $750 suite; $950 pool suite. AE, MC, V. **Amenities:** Restaurant; bar; complimentary bikes (with or without guide); library; 2 large outdoor salt pools; room service; luxurious Aman spa. *In room:* A/C, TV, bar, fridge, hair dryer.

Angkor Palace Resort and Spa ★★ The acres and acres of open space afforded by the Angkor Palace Resort's location—far from the action—wins this one kudos. Plenty of elbowroom, fine gardens, a large pool, and unique tennis courts in a town where real estate is at a premium are quite unique. This high-end resort offers a friendly and casual atmosphere, again unique in a town of more and more haughty, high-end addresses. The pool area is large, open, and inviting, with bridges connecting walkways; the spa is tops, and you'll find extensive services, including a fine Italian restaurant, in-house Internet services, and any kind of tour services or vehicle rental you might need. Rooms are enormous and done in dark wood with white silk spreads on the beds and fine local hangings on the walls. First-floor rooms have direct access to the pool area. Bathrooms are large, with wood floors connecting the main bedroom to a small dressing area; then large Italian tile covers the bathroom floor, where rosewood and granite accent every inch of the walls and counter. The resort's spa has a host of fine massage and facial treatments, but planning and construction are underway for a much larger project. You'll find a good sauna and steam area, as well as a Jacuzzi at poolside.

No. 555 Phum Kruos, Khum Svay Dang Khum, Siem Reap. ✆ **063/760-511.** Fax 063/760-512. www.angkorpalaceresort.com. 259 units. $350–$400 deluxe; $600 suite; $1,500 villa. AE, MC, V. **Amenities:** 2 restaurants; babysitting; concierge; driving range; health club; Internet; outdoor pool; room service; smoke-free rooms; fine spa facilities; tennis courts. *In room:* A/C, TV, fridge, Internet, minibar.

Hôtel de la Paix ★★★ This chic, modern hotel is a personal favorite in Siem Reap. The original design—a sort of Art Deco meets minimalist meets Khmer decor—is a refreshing change from the colonial-heavy influence of popular hotels like the Raffles or the Victoria (see below). Staff is incredibly friendly and appears invested in providing a wonderful experience for guests. Spacious deluxe rooms come with black-and-white color schemes, accent pillows in deep purple, and silver wall hangings and lamps. A white marble bathtub lies a couple feet away from the foot of the bed. Around the corner is the funky stone shower console with tropical shower head. If you decide to splash out on the two-story spa suite, get the corner unit (room no. 346), which comes with a huge balcony equipped with a private stone tub, lounge chairs, a love seat with a pretty Boddhi tree bas-relief carving behind it, and a cozy dining table. There's a large, partially outdoor pool with an indoor enclave at one end. If you are around at noon, make sure to glance at the marble Apsara statue in the main lobby—a single ray of light filters through a cleverly placed hole in the ceiling and shines on the statue's head. The moving design is a good indication of the thoughtful touches throughout the hotel that pay tribute to the architecture found at nearby Angkor Wat.

Sivatha Blvd. ✆ **063/966-000.** Fax 063/966-001. www.hoteldelapaixangkor.com. 107 units. $300 double; $420–$650 suite. AE, MC, V. **Amenities:** Restaurant; lounge; cafe; babysitting; concierge; fitness center; Jacuzzi; nice outdoor pool; sauna; spa. *In room:* A/C, TV, DVD (in suites), iPod/MP3 docking station, fridge, hair dryer, minibar, Wi-Fi.

La Résidence d'Angkor ★★ This stylish, self-contained sanctuary is managed by luxury Orient-Express. Cross a small moat to enter the cool interior of the steeply gabled, dark-wood lobby with its grand Angkor-inspired reliefs. The tranquil central courtyard is lined with palms and dominated by a small but stylish pool fed by the font of stylized Shiva-lingum. The resort area is small, but everything from the gardens to the room decor is tidy and designed for quiet privacy. Rooms are large, well appointed, open, and elegant, with cloth divans, retro fixtures, and nice local touches. Large bathrooms connect with bedrooms by a unique bamboo sliding door, and another glass slider opens to a small private balcony with cool lounges and views of the courtyard. The lobby restaurant is good fine dining, and there are some great open sitting areas for drinks, as well as a library with books, chess, and a conference table.

River Rd., Siem Reap. ✆ **063/963-390.** Fax 063/963-391. www.residencedangkor.com. 62 units. $218–$406 double; $330–$642 suite. AE, MC, V. **Amenities:** Restaurant; bar; motorbikes; outdoor saltwater pool; room service. *In room:* A/C, TV, fridge, hair dryer, minibar, Wi-Fi.

Le Meridien Angkor ★★ The massive monolith of the Le Meridien looks something like a spaceship landed on the road running north to the temples. Three stories and square, the building is beveled, with the larger edge at the top, and is surrounded by a moat and large open areas, all stylistic nods to the temple architecture nearby; accents of culture include fine Apsara sculptures in each room and tinted photos of the temples. Done in dark wood, rooms are clean and elegant, with silken comforters on the beds, cane matting on the floors, and Khmer-style contemporary divans near the window. Deluxe and Superior rooms differ only slightly in size. Bathrooms connect to the main bedroom via a shuttered window, and all are done in a sparkly black tile, with granite counters and glass showers separate from tubs. Dining options range from buffet to a fine Italian restaurant, all set in large glassed-in spaces overlooking a lush central courtyard where a many-headed Ganesha statue holds court. The pool is a unique esplanade of smaller, tiered pools connected with waterfalls and traversed by interlocking raised pathways and Greek-style colonnaded arches.

Vithei Charles de Gaulle, Khum Svay Dang Kum, Siem Reap (on the temple road, just north of town and the Kantha Bopha Hospital). ✆ **063/963-900.** www.lemeridien.com or www.angkor.lemeridien.com. 223 units. $270 superior; $300 deluxe; $410–$520 suite. AE, MC, V. **Amenities:** 2 restaurants; bar; concierge; health club; outdoor pool; room service; spa. *In room:* A/C, TV, high-speed Internet, minibar.

Raffles Grand Hotel d'Angkor ★★★ Right in the center of town, this is simply the best hotel in Siem Reap; it remains unrivaled for luxury, charm, and service. The imposing colonial facade gives way to a marble lobby, connected by Art Deco black-and-white-tile halls to the many rooms and fine services. If arriving by air, hotel staff will pick you up and escort you to a waiting limo while your visa, immigration, and luggage issues are magically taken care of. At the hotel, a doorman outfitted in the old hat and uniform of the Royal Guards whisks you past the cool lobby and into the Conservatory, a bright alcove restaurant overlooking the expansive outdoor pool. Staterooms are large, with classic French doors and windows, beautiful black-and-white-tile entries, fine furnishings, and antique standing lamps, and most come with a balcony. Landmark rooms, the next-higher standard, have four-poster beds, wooden floors spread with rugs, a balcony with rattan furniture, and nice touches like porcelain bathrooms and more antique detail. Personality suites are gems. Each has a unique theme, color, and decor. Bathrooms have claw-foot bathtubs as well as separate showers, and the balconies are large enough to hold a table and chairs for two and a cozy daybed. The courtyard pool (lit by fairy lights and tiny candles in the evening) is large and inviting, and the nearby spa facilities are indulgent.

1 Vithei Charles de Gaulle, Khum Svay Dang Kum, Siem Reap. ✆ **063/963-888.** Fax 063/963-168. www.raffles.com. 131 units. $360–$410 double; $510 suite; $2,500 2-bedroom villa. AE, MC, V. **Amenities:** 4 restaurants; 2 bars; children's club; concierge; health club; Jacuzzi; big outdoor pool; spa; 2 tennis courts; Wi-Fi. *In room:* A/C, TV, fridge, hair dryer, minibar.

Sofitel Royal Angkor ★★ Sofitel is famed in the region for bringing life back to classic hotels of old Indochina, but in Siem Reap they started fresh, with a project limited only by the designer's imagination. The lobby is an old-world Indochine replica with antique Khmer pagoda and a menagerie of overstuffed European furniture. Design and decor nicely marry Khmer and French styles, with vaulted Naga roofs high above the sculpted central garden and tranquil pond area. The courtyard pool is large, open, and fun—great for kids, with a short river meander crossed by a small bridge. The spa is tops, and the private massage areas are uniquely resplendent, with private bathrooms. Rooms are spacious, with dark-wood floors and rich touches like designer throw rugs and elegant built-in cabinetry. All bathrooms are large, with tubs and large granite counters. Spring for a superior room with a balcony and view of the central courtyard: It's worth it. Be sure to take a moment, preferably near the magic hour of sunset (but any time will do), and take it all in from the island pagoda in the central pond.

On the way to the temples, just north of the town center. Vithei Charles de Gaulle, Khum Svay Dang Kum, Siem Reap. ✆ **063/964-600.** Fax 063/964-609. www.sofitel.com. 238 units. $340–$360 double; $420–$605 suite. AE, MC, V. **Amenities:** 5 restaurants; 3 bars; bikes; concierge; 18-hole golf course; health club; Jacuzzi; large outdoor pool; room service; sauna; smoke-free floor; spa. *In room:* A/C, TV w/in-house movies, fax, fridge, hair dryer, minibar, Wi-Fi.

Sokha Angkor Maybe this is what Angkor Wat would have looked like if it was a pleasure resort rather than a place of worship. The lobby is gigantic, with big columns framing a bronze-and-sheer-glass chandelier. A blown-up photograph of a Banteay Srei temple is plastered over the elevator doors. In the courtyard, a large stone pediment with a waterfall empties into the outdoor pool. Big stone lions at the back and lingas at the front are mini fountains, spitting out streams of water that also empty into the pool. Rooms are, thank goodness, more subtle. Blond-wood furniture gives things a light feeling, and a floral spritzer gives everything a springtime-fresh smell. Bathrooms are reasonable size, with tallow stone tubs and separate glass shower consoles.

Road No 6 and Sivatha St. ✆ **063/969-999.** Fax 063/969-992. www.sokhahotels.com. 276 units. $250–$300 double; from $500 suite. AE, MC, V. **Amenities:** 3 restaurants; bar; lounge; concierge; health club; outdoor pool; room service; spa. *In room:* A/C, TV, fridge, hair dryer, high-speed Internet, minibar.

Victoria Angkor Hotel ★★ Victoria Angkor is a tasteful replica of a French colonial–era hotel, but with the amenities and functionality of a modern resort. Public spaces are done in earth tones, rattan and wood accents, and Art Deco floor tiles in mustard-yellow tones. A large central atrium with period-piece elevator and towering courtyard staircase greets the visitor to this downtown campus, just a stone's throw from the Raffles (see above). The central pool is a private oasis surrounded by a mini jungle, with massage salas nestled in the flora. Rooms are large, luxurious, and decorated with retro oil paintings of peaceful jungle scenes and framed photographs of everyday life in Siem Reap.

Floors are wood with a border of fine tile that matches luxurious woven bedspreads. All rooms have balconies. Colonial suites have individual themes, and the best ones are the corner suites, with large, covered outdoor balconies. Fine dining at their Le Bistrot (see below) is tops.

Central Park, P.O. Box 93145, Siem Reap. ✆ **063/760-428.** Fax 063/760-350. www.victoriahotels-asia.com. 130 units. $328–$368 double; $494 colonial suite (breakfast is an additional $18–$20). AE, MC, V. **Amenities:** 2 restaurants; bar; babysitting; bikes; children's center; concierge; Jacuzzi; spacious outdoor saltwater pool; room service; spa. *In room:* A/C, TV, fridge, hair dryer, minibar, Wi-Fi.

Expensive

Angkor Village Hotel ★★ In a quiet neighborhood not far from the main market, this peaceful little hideaway is a unique maze of wood bungalows connected by covered boardwalks surrounding a picturesque ivy-draped pond. Rooms are rustic wooden affairs with high bamboo catay ceilings, wood beams, built-in cabinetry, comfortable beds, and decorative touches like traditional Khmer shadow puppets and statuary. Top units have balconies overlooking the central pond. Bathrooms are all large, with a tub/shower combo and sinks set in unique oversize ceramic cauldrons. The pool is small but picturesque in a verdant courtyard at the rear. The Auberge de Temples Restaurant is on a small island in the central pond and serves fine French and Khmer cuisines. The hotel's **Apsara Theater Restaurant,** just outside the gate, has Khmer-style banquet dining and performances of Khmer Apsara dancing nightly. The whole place is infused with Khmer culture and hospitality, and so popular is the original that they've expanded (see **Angkor Village Resort,** below). Angkor Village is often full, so be sure to book ahead.

Wat Bo Rd., Siem Reap. ✆ **063/965-561.** Fax 063/965-565. www.angkorvillage.com. 52 units. $169 (off-season discounts available). AE, MC, V. **Amenities:** Restaurant; bar; bikes; Internet; small library; outdoor pool; room service. *In room:* A/C, TV, fridge, minibar, Wi-Fi.

Angkor Village Resort ★ This campus of luxury rooms is located a few steps closer to the temples (it all counts when you're racing for the sunrise). The resort offers the same standard of comfort and style as its sister hotel (see above), but with a fun pool as well as large ponds of Japanese koi, fountains, and lush landscaping. The resort does a good job of creating a sanctuary far away from town, but unfortunately the loud music from nearby developments occasionally overpowers the tranquil buzzing of cicadas. Rooms are stylish but lean more to the cozy than to the austere, with firm four-poster beds completing the cozy effect. All rooms have balconies overlooking the pool. Baths are large, with raised shower units open to a tile room with a one-piece wooden counter set with two bright, free-standing porcelain sink bowls; pale-green tile and cool, indirect lighting are quite pleasing. The toilet area is separate. The staff is as friendly as they come. Breakfast of fresh breads and crepes by the pond is a treat.

Phum Traeng (on the north end of town nearer the temples), Siem Reap. ✆ **063/963-561.** Fax 063/963-363. www.angkorvillage.com. 40 units. $199 double. AE, MC, V. **Amenities:** Restaurant; bar; bikes; Internet; small library; outdoor pool; room service. *In room:* A/C, minibar, fridge, Wi-Fi.

FCC Angkor ★ This hotel is located beside the popular restaurant of the same name. Located behind high walls and shaded by towering tropical trees, the FCC is the best moderately priced oasis in town. All the rooms have names (Basil, Lychee, and so on), not numbers, to give things a personal feel. Rooms have low beds on wooden frames and modern amenities such as flatscreen TVs and hip furniture. The decor is similarly cool, with pale-yellow tile floors paired with fun block-color paintings hanging on the walls. The long and narrow outdoor pool is great for an afternoon cool-off.

Pokambor Ave. (next to the Royal Residence and just north of the post office). ✆ **063/760-280.** Fax 063/760-281. www.fcccambodia.com. 31 units. May–Sept $130–$150 double, $280 suite; Oct–Apr $170–$190 double, $340 suite. MC, V. **Amenities:** Restaurant; bar; outdoor saltwater pool. *In room:* A/C, satellite TV/DVD, fridge, minibar, Wi-Fi.

Pavillon d'Orient ★★ Another Art Deco colonial hotel arrives in Siem Reap, but this one stands out for its newness and boutique charm. Pavillon is a great choice in this price range, as it comes with nice perks such as free tuk-tuk transportation to the temples. Rooms are large, and all have private balconies overlooking the central garden. Bathrooms come with tubs and rain showers. This buzz-worthy place is often full, so make sure to call ahead; if it's booked, you'll find similar standards of service and friendliness at its sister hotel, Pavillon Indochine (below).

Road 60, Siem Reap (on the new road to the temples). ✆ **063/760-646.** www.pavillon-orient-hotel.com. 18 units. $85–$110 double. AE, MC, V. **Amenities:** Restaurant; bar; nice outdoor pool; room service; spa. *In room:* A/C, TV, fridge, minibar.

Shinta Mani ★ A member of the Sanctuary Resorts group, a Hong Kong–based hotel organization dedicated to sustainable tourism, environmental stewardship, and holistic practices, Shinta Mani is both a small boutique hotel and a school of hospitality—creating opportunities in health, beauty, and hospitality for the next generation of underprivileged kids in Siem Reap. While public spaces are done on a small scale—the pool is quite tiny—fine rooms and cool minimalist decor sets this hotel apart. Each unit is stylish, with cool tile and buff-polished wood features. Lower-priced rooms (and their bathrooms) are quite compact, so if you need your space, I strongly suggest upgrading to a deluxe. Bathrooms connect to the main room via large sliding doors. The overall effect is chic, clean, and luxurious. Their dining space has won international awards.

Junction of Oum Khum and 14th St. (near the FCC). ✆ **063/761-998.** Fax 063/761-999. www.shintamani.com. $100–$110 double; $125–$140 deluxe. MC, V. **Amenities:** Restaurant; bar; small outdoor pool; room service; spa. *In room:* A/C, TV, fridge, minibar, Wi-Fi.

Moderate

Allson Angkor Hotel ★ Of the many hotels along the airport road, Route 6, the Allson Hotel is the best (and only slightly more expensive than the rest). Popular with group tours, the hotel is large and ostentatious, with high, Khmer-style roofs and large reproductions of temple statuary in the entry. Everything is clean and comfortable, if a bit sterile. Ask for a room in the new building in the back. Guest rooms are bland but large, with crown molding, clean carpet, and good, familiar amenities like a minibar and safe. The bathrooms are a little small. This is a good, comfortable step down from the glitzier hotels in town, and the best choice if they're full. The lobby is always busy with tour groups, but the staff remains friendly and expedient. The hotel is sufficiently self-contained, with good basic amenities, an outdoor pool in the courtyard, a good restaurant, and all necessary services. The two caged bears in the hotel's garden are enough to make you cry, though.

Rte. 6, Phum Sala Kanseng. ✆ **063/964-301.** Fax 063/964-302. www.angkor-hotel-cambodia.com. 193 units. May–Sept $70 double, $74 deluxe, $150 suite; Oct–Apr $75 double, $85 deluxe, $160 suite. AE, MC, V. **Amenities:** Restaurant; bar; basic gym; Internet; outdoor pool. *In room:* A/C, TV, fridge, hair dryer, minibar.

Bopha Angkor With their popular nightly dance show and Khmer restaurant, there's a certain "cultural theme park" vibe to this place, but Bopha Angkor is tidy and affordable, and genuinely offers a culturally infused visit to Siem Reap. Rooms are arranged in a U-shaped courtyard around a lush central garden. Private spaces are large but not luxe and feature fun local accents like mosquito nets and souvenir-shop trinkets on the walls. The staff is friendly and the hotel is close to the old market area.

No. 0512 Acharsvar St. (across the canal from the market). ✆ **063/964-928.** Fax 063/964-446. www.bopha-angkor.com. 38 units. $55–$87 double; $180 suite. MC, V. **Amenities:** Restaurant; bar; outdoor pool. *In room:* A/C, TV, fridge, minibar, Wi-Fi.

City River Hotel Here are simple accommodations near the town center. Popular with bus tours, the tidy new City River Hotel handles it all with ease. Shiny lacquered wood in the lobby is as bright and airy as the friendly staff, who snap to in their starchy uniforms, quite a rarity in this category. As the name suggests, you're right on the Siem Reap River, a short walk from the popular Old Market area. Rooms are spartan, with no real decoration to speak of, but are clean and quiet; the bus tours haven't had at them yet, so this is one to get to before that. And the price is reasonable, though there are few amenities. They do, however, offer guests access to the nearby Bopha Angkor hotel (see above), with use of the pool.

No. 0511 Achasva St., Wat Bo, Siem Reap. ✆ **063/763-000.** Fax 063/963-963. www.cityriverhotel.com. 60 units. $68–$99 double; $150 suite. AE, MC, V. **Amenities:** Restaurant; room service. *In room:* A/C, TV, fridge, hair dryer, Internet, minibar.

Pavillon Indochine ★ This converted traditional Khmer house and garden is the closest you'll get to the temples and is quite peaceful, even isolated, in a quiet neighborhood. The upscale guesthouse is charming and surprisingly self-contained, with a good restaurant and a friendly, knowledgeable French proprietor whose staff can help arrange any detail in the area. Rooms are large, clean, and airy, in terra-cotta tile and wood trim, but they're not particularly luxe. There's a fine line between rustic atmosphere and necessary comforts, like hot water and air-conditioning (though many choose to go with a fan). The courtyard area is a picturesque garden dotted with quiet sitting areas with chairs or floor mats and comfy pillows.

On the back road to the temples, Siem Reap. ✆ **012/804-952.** www.pavillon-indochine.com. $60–$65 double; $85 suite. 24 units. AE, MC, V. **Amenities:** Restaurant. *In room:* A/C, mobile phone available upon request.

Viroth's Hotel ★★ Value I dare you to find another hotel that is this chic and this affordable. A small boutique affair, this spot provides a private, intimate experience. The rooms are minimalist and modern, with sleek geometric furniture, but soft touches like a floor vase filled with large pieces of dried palm leaves, dark brown leather desktops, and coffee-colored coverlets and accent pillows keep it warm and inviting. Most rooms have private balconies. The best room in the house is room no. 3, on the ground floor. It comes with a large poolside corner terrace equipped with cozy lounge beds. There's a small outdoor pool surrounded by cream-colored sun beds. Breakfast is served on the rooftop restaurant. It's lit with fairy lights at night and is an excellent place to spend the evening, looking out over the rooftops of Siem Reap.

0658 Wat Bo Village (behind City River Hotel). ✆ **063/761-720.** Fax 063/760-774. www.viroth-hotel.com. 7 units. $75–$80 double. AE, MC, V. **Amenities:** Restaurant; bar; rooftop Jacuzzi; saltwater outdoor pool; room service; small spa. *In room:* A/C, TV, no phone, Wi-Fi.

Inexpensive

The downtown area of Siem Reap, on either side of the main road, is brimming with budget accommodations.

Auberge Mont Royal d'Angkor Down a lazy lane just to the west of the town center, Auberge is a cozy choice for budget travelers. Terra-cotta tile covers all open areas and rooms, and there are atmospheric touches like canvas lamps, carved wood beds, cushions, and traditional hangings, curtains, and bedspreads. The walls could use a fresh coat of paint, but the hotel is overall neat and tidy. The traditional decor is pleasant and inviting. Bathrooms are done in clean tile and have tiny bathtubs. Pool villa rooms are well worth the upgrade.

West of the town center. ✆ **063/964-044.** www.auberge-mont-royal.com. 26 units. $30–$50 double; $60 pool villa. AE, MC, V. **Amenities:** Restaurant; bar. *In room:* A/C, TV, fridge, minibar, no phone.

La Noria ★ La Noria is a mellow group of bungalows connected by a winding garden path. The guesthouse is near the town center, but you wouldn't know it in the hush of this little laid-back spot. Rooms are basic but have nice local touches. Terra-cotta floors, wooden trim, and small balconies are all neat and tidy, and fine hangings and details like shadow puppets and authentic Khmer furniture round out a pleasing traditional decor. Bathrooms have no separate shower consoles, but are small and clean. The place is light on amenities but has a small pool and makes up for any deficiency with gobs of charm. The open-air restaurant is a highlight, serving good Khmer and French cuisine. The hotel is affiliated with Krousar Thmey, "New Family," a humanitarian group doing good work, and there's a helpful information board about rural travel and humanitarian projects.

Down a small lane off Rte. 6, to the northeast of town. ✆ **063/964-242.** Fax 063/964-243. www.lanoria angkor.com. 28 units. $39 with fan; $49 with A/C. No credit cards. **Amenities:** Restaurant; outdoor pool. *In room:* A/C (optional).

Passaggio ★ This unpretentious hotel is convenient to downtown and adjoins its own helpful travel agent, Lolei Travel. Rooms are large and tidy, but not much more; the three floors here are something like a motel in the U.S., complete with tacky art. The one suite has a bathtub; all others have stand-up showers in bathrooms that are nondescript in plain tile but are neat and new. The friendly staff can arrange any detail and is eager to please.

Watdamanak Village (across the river to the east of town). ✆ **063/760-324.** Fax 063/760-163. www. passaggio-hotel.com. 17 units. $32–$52. AE, MC, V. **Amenities:** Restaurant; free airport transfers; free Internet. *In room:* A/C, TV, fridge, minibar, no phone, Wi-Fi.

Two Dragons ★ Two Dragons is the best budget spot for picking up good information on the temples and onward travel, as well as for meeting up with other travelers. Run by American Gordon Sharpless, a longtime Asian traveler, writer, and photographer, the guesthouse hosts many young backpackers who read Gordon's popular Tales of Asia website (http://talesofasia.com), which is packed with useful information about the rigors and rip-offs of crossing overland with Thailand regional travel. Rooms are spartan but very clean and with either air-conditioning or fans. A little patio area is on the second floor, and free tea and coffee are available 24 hours a day. Good camaraderie pervades this place. The restaurant serves terrific Thai and Khmer cuisine. The staff is as friendly as they come and can help arrange good guides to the temples.

1 Wat Bo Area (on the east side of the river, adjacent to the post office). ✆ **063/965-107.** http://tales ofasia.com/cambodia-twodragons.htm. 14 units. $17–$27 double. AE, MC, V. **Amenities:** Restaurant; bar; bikes. *In room:* A/C, fridge (in some), no phone, Wi-Fi.

WHERE TO DINE

Dining in Siem Reap is not a pricey affair. The major hotels all have fine upscale eateries, and there are also several good free-standing spots. The area around the Old Market is a cluster of storefronts, most of little distinction from one another, but all are affordable and laid-back.

Expensive

Le Bistrot de Siem Reap ★★ FRENCH The atmosphere in this restaurant is wonderfully charming, with old French music playing lightly in the background, light gray walls with the ceiling trim and accent walls painted warm maroon, and black lacquer tables with mixed wooden and rattan chairs. The walls are adorned with old posters advertising voyages to the Far East, but the cuisine is a superb culinary trip to France. The wine list is a work in progress, so ask for a recommendation. They also have a good selection of Cuban cigars. It's a wonderful, tasty slice of old Indochine.

Central Park, P.O. Box 93145, Siem Reap. ✆ **063/760-428.** Reservations recommended. Main courses $15–$26. AE, MC, V. Daily 6:30am–midnight.

Meric ★★ KHMER This is a slick, trendy restaurant located in the equally stylish Hôtel de la Paix. I prefer the Western dishes to the Khmer tasting menu, but both are constantly changing, with the latter often offering off-the-beaten-path specials such as mashed snake or frog. The steaks here are the best in town, and service is tops. There is outdoor dining around a stately Boddhi tree in the central courtyard, or indoor tables near the open kitchen.

Sivatha Blvd. ✆ **063/966-000.** Reservations recommended. Main courses $18–$26. AE, MC, V. Daily 6–10:30am, noon–3pm, and 6–10:30pm.

Moderate

Abacus ★ ASIAN/FRENCH This restaurant, set in a traditional Cambodian stilt house, is a refreshing change from the eateries along Pub Street. There are a central bar made of volcanic stone and a few tables with rattan chairs on the first floor, underneath the house. Terrace seating upstairs is divided among various small, cozy rooms. The menu is written on a chalkboard, and you can choose from a good selection of either Asian rice bowls or Western mains with a couple of side dishes.

Oum Khun St. ✆ **012/644-286.** Main courses $5–$17. No credit cards. Daily 11am to late.

Cafe Indochine ★★ ASIAN On the north end of the busy central road that leads to the temples, Cafe Indochine is a cool, old Indochina throwback. Set in an old wooden building that's been newly renovated, this little perch is a cool place to watch life go by on the busy street out front and unwind from a busy day at the temples. The menu is an eclectic list of Thai, Cambodian, Vietnamese, and French dishes: true Indochina. Start with fine, light spring rolls, either fried or fresh. Salads are savory, and they serve good Thai spicy soups like Tom-Yam, as well as French bouillabaisse. Try a shared set menu for $9 per person and get a short course in local cuisine like beef done in savory *loc lac* style; fine curries; *amok* fish; a number of whole-fish dishes; and beef, chicken, or vegetable stir-fries. Follow up with good ice cream or coffee.

44 Sivatha Rd. ✆ **012/804-952.** Main courses $5–$9. AE, MC, V. Daily 10am–3pm and 5–11pm.

FCC Angkor (Foreign Correspondent's Club) ★★ INTERNATIONAL The glowing white, modern cube of the FCC would be at home in a nouveau riche California suburb or a Jacques Tati film, but it is a bit jarring canalside in the center of Siem Reap. The first floor offers some of the finest boutique shopping in the city, and the second floor is an elegant open space with high ceilings: a modern colonial. There's an Art Deco bar, low lounge chairs at the center, and standard dining space on the balcony. The main room is flanked on one end by an open kitchen. The FCC is the town's runway and holds numerous functions and hosts live music. The menu is the same as the original FCC in Phnom Penh, with soups, salads, and Western standards, like pasta, steaks, and wood-fired pizzas. The staff can't seem to believe they work here, and service is hot and cold but very friendly. They have wireless Internet and are the de facto Starbucks in Siem Reap. Also, don't miss the cool billiards room, a modernist installation behind glass, or the big-screen TV surrounded by large lounge chairs at poolside.

Pokambor Ave. (next to the Royal Residence and just north of the post office). ✆ **063/760-283.** Main courses $8–$22. AE, MC, V. Daily 7am–midnight.

Madame Butterfly ★ THAI/KHMER Serving the finest authentic Khmer- and Thai-influenced cuisine in town, the setting is very pleasant and alone worth a visit. In a converted traditional wooden home, seating is in low rattan chairs, and the decor is characterized by a tasteful collection of Buddhist and Khmer artifacts. Candlelight mingles with mellow indirect lighting, and the whole effect is casual and romantic. There are daily specials, and the menu is heavy on good curries and hot-pot dishes. I had a delicious dish of poached fish in coconut sauce with sticky rice. The Masaman curry is divine, and the *mchou pous,* a chicken-and-shrimp bisque, is rich and tasty.

A short ride west on No. 6, airport road. ✆ **016/909-607.** Main courses $6–$15. V. Daily 6am–11pm.

The Red Piano ★ INTERNATIONAL Angelina Jolie and cast and crew of the film *Tomb Raider* made this atmospheric bar their second home while filming at the temples. Imported steaks, spaghetti, sandwiches, salads, and international specialties like good Indian samosas or chicken *cordon bleu* round out a great menu of familiar fare. Everything is good, and this place is always hoppin' late into the evening. Due to popular demand (it's sometimes hard to get a seat), they've expanded onto a second floor, and renovations throughout give the place a tidy, upscale charm.

50m (164 ft.) northwest of the Old Market. ✆ **063/963-240.** Main courses $4–$6. No credit cards. Daily 7am–midnight.

Shinta Mani ★★ INTERNATIONAL Shinta Mani is uniquely refined for Cambodia. Dining indoors is cool, referring to both the air-conditioning and the decor. Outdoors is a small open bar area and a few tables set under a heavy wooden lattice thatched roof. Service is professional, but the staff seems slightly nervous, often worrying over the details a bit too much, and you might even catch yourself rooting for them. Prices are high for this part of the world, but everything that comes out of the kitchen has panache. Elegant presentations on white china enhance the experience of fine Khmer and Western dishes made with local ingredients. Popular entrees include a fine beef sirloin, a savory stuffed chicken breast, and comfort foods like spaghetti and fried rice (which are a bit easier on the budget). In a town where you can eat for so cheap, Shinta Mani is carving its niche and attracting rave reviews from international critics, but the backpackers are kept at bay. The wine list is exhaustive, the drink list doesn't stop, and whether dining in the cool, intimate inside or among the humming cicadas outdoors, you can enjoy a slow-paced savory meal with good conversation.

Junction of Oum Khum and 14th St. (near the FCC). ✆ **063/761-998.** Reservations recommended. Main courses $8–$20. AE, MC, V. Daily 6:30am–10:30pm.

Inexpensive

Chivit Thai ★ THAI You've found it! Authentic Thai in an atmospheric streetside restaurant, with both air-conditioning and outdoor dining. The food is great, the price is low, and there's casual floor seating and a rustic charm to the place, quite romantic in candlelight. Name your favorite Thai dish, and they do it here. The Tom Yum (sweet, spicy Thai soup) is excellent, and they have good set menus comprised of many courses that are much finer than their low price tag. Enjoy!

130 Wat Bo Rd. (across the river from the FCC, near the intersection of Rte. 6 going out of town). ✆ **012/830-761.** Main courses $2.50–$5. No credit cards. Daily 7am–10pm.

Kama Sutra ★ INDIAN This restaurant serves excellent Indian food in the heart of Pub street. It's covered outdoor seating, so dining is informal, and there's the option of refreshing air-conditioned seating upstairs. The fare is hearty, and the atmosphere is loud and happy.

E161 Bar St. ✆ **063/761-225.** Main courses $2.50–$7.50. No credit cards. Daily 11am till late.

Khmer Kitchen Restaurant ★ KHMER This busy little storefront hides itself down an alley on the north end of the Old Market but draws a nightly crowd for big portions of simple, delicious Khmer fare. Good curries and stir-fries share menu space with unique dishes like baked pumpkin. It's about the food here, not the service, but these folks are friendly enough, considering how busy they usually are.

Down an alley just north of the old market. ✆ **063/964-154** or 012/763-468. Main courses $2–$3. No credit cards. Daily 10am–10pm.

The Sugar Palm ★★ TRADITIONAL KHMER This is where food and beverage managers from nearby five-star hotels come to feast. Co-owner Kethana serves old-fashioned, flavorful, and hearty Khmer food. The restaurant has a warm and inviting ambience with subdued, covered lighting, a wall painted in sunny yellow, and vaulted ceilings. The furniture and bar are done in dark sugar palm wood. Staff walks around barefoot on spotless wooden floors. Most of the seating is on the wraparound balcony, partially covered from the outside world with roll-down bamboo blinds. On the menu, the pomelo salad is excellent. Fleshy pomelo tendrils are played off the sharp taste of dried shrimp and crunchy chopped peanuts. Strips of spicy red pepper give it an extra kick. For mains, I recommend the chicken stir-fried with ginger. The meat is tender and the sauce is loaded with tender slices of sautéed ginger.

Ta Phul Rd. (400m/1,312 ft. south of the Caltex gas station). ✆ **063/964-838.** Main courses $4–$6. MC, V. Daily 11am–3pm and 5–10pm. Bar till late.

Taj Mahal ★★ NORTHERN INDIAN It has become almost obligatory where young tourists gather to have an Indian restaurant be the flame for the travel-weary and empty-bellied moths, and Taj Mahal is, in fact, a bright light. It serves a range of northern Indian cuisine—from heaping *talis* with curries, lentils, and rice to delicious tandoori, fiery curries (unless otherwise specified), and good nan breads to sop it all up, plus beer to wash it down. Cozy and clean Taj Mahal is an old Siem Reap standby and packs 'em in nightly. Seating is best at streetside as you face the north end of the market, with its many busy street stalls. Ask for your samosa cooked to order, and you'll be bowled over. I promise, everything is good.

North Old Market. ✆ **063/963-353.** Main courses $1.50–$4.50. No credit cards. Daily 8am–11pm.

Tell Restaurant ★★ GERMAN/INTERNATIONAL Tell Restaurant serves hearty German fare, catering to the many expats and travelers longing for a bit of home (mostly a German and Scandinavian home). Savory entrees like goulash and Vienna schnitzel, German sausages, *cordon bleu,* stroganoff, and a signature raclette special or enormous cheese fondue (priced at $27 and expected to be shared by two or more) are quite impressive. You walk away with a bit of a heavy belly into the steamy Khmer evening, but after a day touring the temples (and usually another one planned), a hearty meal might be just the ticket. They also have a whole roster of good salads and lighter fare, from Mexican to Indian and Italian, as well as good Khmer entrees. Don't miss the choice of "Hangover Breakfasts," comprised of a shot and a beer and a pile of good fried food, great after sampling the many and exotic cocktails on offer. The restaurant is just a busy storefront on central Sivatha Road alongside the likes of Dead Fish Tower, a popular bar, and lots of small storefronts catering to backpackers.

No. 374 Sivatha Rd. (200m/656 ft. north of the Old Market). ✆ **063/963-289.** Main courses $3–$9. V. Daily 10am–2pm and 5:30–10pm.

Viroth's Restaurant ★★ KHMER This is my favorite restaurant in Siem Reap. Like its sister hotel two streets down (p. 416), Viroth's Restaurant boasts a sleek and stylish interior. The French and Khmer were the original owners of popular Angkor Café (see "Dining at the Temples," below). Unlike the hotel, which is still a secret among those in the know, the restaurant is well known and well loved. The food is traditional Khmer cuisine and is mighty tasty. The amok fish is a perfect blend of coconut milk and lemon grass, and unlike at other restaurants, the fish is completely deboned. The spacious dining area is on a raised wooden platform, and ceiling and floor fans keep a cool breeze going and send ripples through the strips of sheer saffron sheets suspended from the ceiling and hanging between tables.

246 Wat Bo St. (behind La Résidence Hotel). ✆ **063/760-774.** Main courses $3.30–$7. MC, V. Daily 10:30am–2pm and 5:30–10pm.

Snacks & Cafes

Blue Pumpkin This is a stylish, all-white cafe with Wi-Fi access on the northeast end of the Old Market. Blue Pumpkin is a longtime local favorite, serving great pastries, coffee, and entrees like burgers and sandwiches. They'll pack you a lunch for the temples, too. Next door is Kokoon, a fine shop for trinkets and souvenirs.

365 Mondol 1. ✆ **063/963-574.** MC, V. Daily 6am–11pm.

Butterflies Garden Restaurant ★ Don't miss this netted enclosure with a butterfly farm and meticulous menagerie of local flora and fauna, including a pond filled with Japanese carp. There are detailed descriptions of all plants and some individual butterflies. They serve Khmer and international cuisine. Vegetarians will also enjoy an extensive selection here.

Across the Siem Reap River north of the Old Market. Entrance $2. No credit cards. Daily 8am–5pm.

Dining at the Temples

Across the busy parking lot closest to Angkor Wat, the snazzy **Angkor Café** (✆ **063/380-300**) is a little gallery and souvenir shop that serves, for a mint by Khmer standards, good coffee, tea, and sandwiches, all provided by **Blue Pumpkin** (see "Snacks & Cafes," above). It's the best thing going on the Angkor compound, and, apart from the good food, the building is air-conditioned, great for a break at midday. The attached boutique offers high-end silver and stone reproductions of the temples, as well as silk and other souvenirs. Open daily from 8am to 5:30pm. No credit cards.

In and among all the major temples, you'll see lots of small **thatch-roofed eateries,** and all will implore you to enter. The competition means that you have more leverage when haggling: "Are you sure this Coke is $2? Someone over there said it was . . . ." You get the picture. You'll be swarmed by vendors when you approach these restaurants. Just pick one quickly, and the rest will split. Prices are slightly inflated, but it's a tourist sight and folks need to make a living (and probably have to pay some heavy kickbacks). A few bucks will get you fried rice, noodles, or vegetables. Most of these places have shaded hammock areas out back (mostly for drivers, but a good place to rest) and basic toilets. Carrying your own antiseptic hand sanitizer is a good idea.

ATTRACTIONS

Angkor Wat is the Disneyland of Buddhist temples in Asia. The temple complex requires a few busy days to get around the major sights thoroughly. Everyone has a favorite, but I've highlighted a few must-sees below. Plan carefully and catch a sunrise or sunset from one of the more prime spots; it's a photographer's dream. ***Note:*** The temples are magnificent, and days spent clambering around the temples are inherently interesting, but be careful not to come away from a visit to ancient Angkor with a memory of an oversize rock collection or jungle gym. There's much to learn about Buddhism, Hinduism, architecture, and Khmer history; it's useful to hire a well-informed guide or join a tour group. There are also subtleties to temple touring, and a good guide is your best chance to beat the crowd and catch the intricacies or be in the right place for the magic moments of the day. Contact any hotel front desk or the tour agencies listed earlier. Hiring a guide for 1 day costs $20.

The Temples

Entrance fees for Angkor Wat are as follows: A 1-day ticket is $20, a 3-day ticket is $40, and a 1-week ticket is $60. The tickets were recently restructured, extending the validity of 3-day passes to 1 week instead of 3 consecutive days. Similarly, 1-week passes are now valid for 1 month. Tickets are good for all sights within the main temple compound, as well as Banteay Srei, to the north, and the outlying temples of the Roluos Group. Other sights, such as Beng Melea or Ko Kur, require an additional fee. The temples open at dawn, and you can buy a ticket as early as 5am to get there for sunup. At dusk, around 6pm, temple attendants start gently nudging visitors out of the park.

My strongest recommendation is to get a guide, at least for 1 day of temple touring. A guide not only provides the most useful information that will serve as a background for your further exploration, but makes the logistics of that first day much easier. Contact any hotel front desk or tour office, and they can arrange something for you. The cost of a guide is $20 per day. Guides are certified and come from the same school, and so dispense nearly the same information, but, of course, some are better than others. Ask around for recommendations.

Tip: The temple sites listed below are more or less in the usual order you might visit them on tour. A visit to Angkor is now a noisy romp among large Korean, Thai, Chinese, and European groups. An average guide will take you along in the heart of the herd, following the standard temple routine, but a good guide knows how to get you out of the pack. Insist on it.

Important note: The Angkor complex is currently undergoing massive restoration. Most of the temples noted below are included in the extensive project, and as such, certain sections are hidden behind scaffolding or closed off to visitors. While it is disappointing, the restoration is not so invasive as to warrant canceling your trip here. Work should wrap up sometime in 2010.

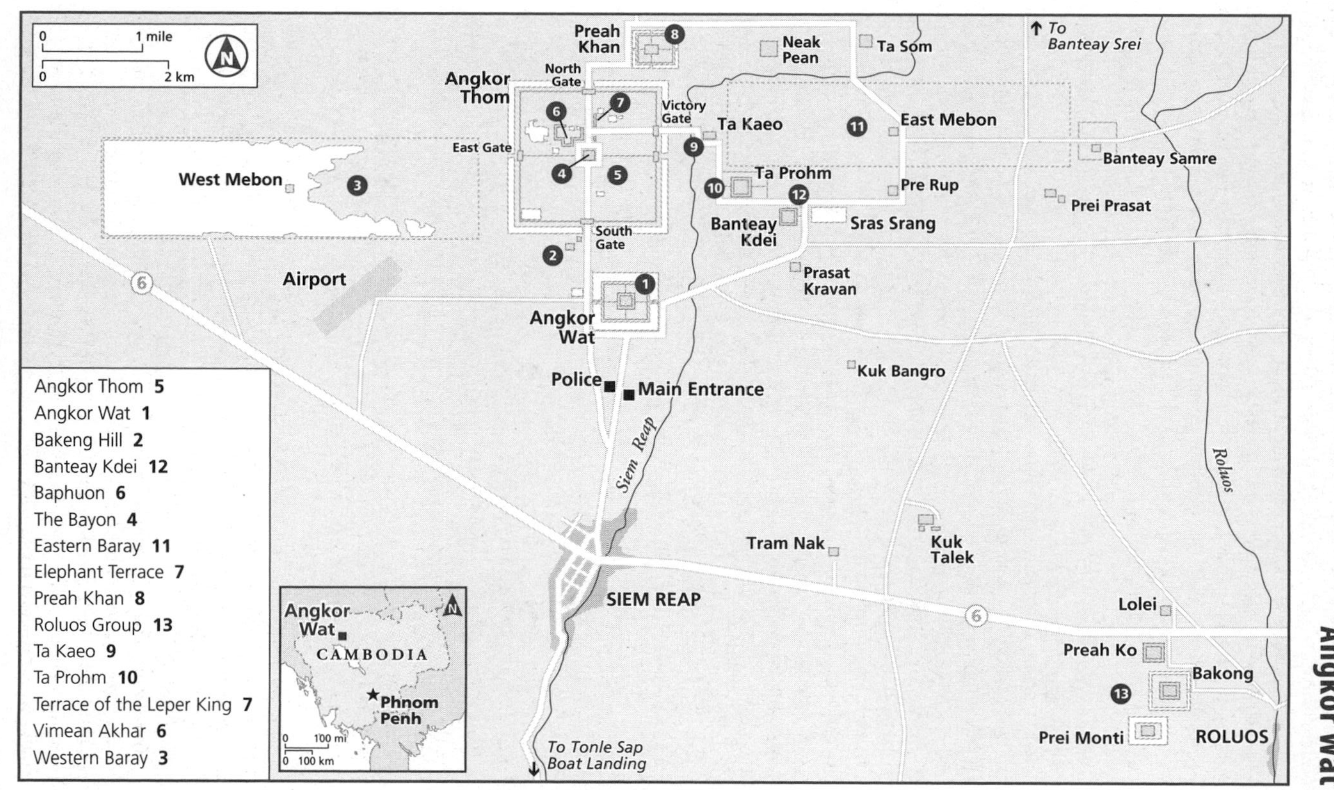
0 1 mile
0 2 km
Preah Khan
Neak Pean
Ta Som
To Banteay Srei
Angkor Thom
North Gate
Victory Gate
Ta Kaeo
East Mebon
East Gate
West Mebon
Banteay Samre
Ta Prohm
Pre Rup
Prei Prasat
South Gate
Banteay Kdei
Sras Srang
Airport
Prasat Kravan
Angkor Wat
Police
Main Entrance
Kuk Bangro
Siem Reap
Roluos
Tram Nak
Kuk Talek
SIEM REAP
Lolei
Preah Ko
Bakong
Prei Monti
ROLUOS
To Tonle Sap Boat Landing
Angkor Thom 5
Angkor Wat 1
Bakeng Hill 2
Banteay Kdei 12
Baphuon 6
The Bayon 4
Eastern Baray 11
Elephant Terrace 7
Preah Khan 8
Roluos Group 13
Ta Kaeo 9
Ta Prohm 10
Terrace of the Leper King 7
Vimean Akhar 6
Western Baray 3
Angkor Wat
CAMBODIA
Phnom Penh
0 100 mi
0 100 km

Angkor Wat ★★★ The symbol of Cambodia, the five spires of the main temple of Angkor are known the world over. In fact, this is the most resplendent of the Angkor sites, one certainly not to miss even in the most perfunctory of tours.

Built under the reign of Suryavarman II in the 12th century, this temple, along with Bayon and Baphuon, is the very pinnacle of Khmer architecture. From base to tip of the highest tower, it's 213m (699 ft.) of awe-inspiring stone in the definitive, elaborate Khmer style. The temple moat is 1.5×1.3km (1×¾ miles) around and 90m (295 ft.) wide, crossed by a causeway with long naga statues on each side as railings from the west; in fact, Angkor is the only temple entered from the west (all others from the east). Angkor Wat is the only Angkor monument that is a mausoleum—all others are temples or monasteries. Angkor's main temple is dedicated to Vishnu.

Approaching the temple, you'll first cross the causeway over the main moat—restored in the 1960s by the French. Enter the compound across the first gallery, the Majestic Gallery, with some carvings and Brahma statuary, and then pass into the large, grassy courtyard housing the main temple. This next causeway is flanked on either side by two small library buildings, as well as two small ponds. (***Hint:*** Hop off the causeway and take a photo of the temple reflected in the pond on the right.)

An outdoor staircase sits at the approach to the main temple. From there, you'll enter the richest area of statuary, galleries, and bas-reliefs. The famous bas-reliefs encircling the temple on the first level (south side) depict the mythical "Churning of the Ocean of Milk," a legend in which Hindu deities stir vast oceans in order to extract the elixir of immortality. This churning produced the Apsaras, Hindu celestial dancers, who can be seen on many temples. Other reliefs surrounding the base of the main temple show Khmer wars, and corner towers depict Hindu fables.

The most measured and studied of all the sites, Angkor Wat is the subject of much speculation: It's thought to represent Mount Meru, home of Hindu gods and a land of creation and destruction. Researchers measuring the site in *hat,* ancient Khmer units of measure, deduce that the symmetry of the building corresponds with the timeline of the Hindu ages, as a map or calendar of the universe, if you will. The approach from the main road crosses the baray (reservoir) and is an ascending progression of three levels to the inner sanctum. The T-shirt hawkers are relentless, and the tricky steps and temple height are a challenge to those with vertigo, but the short trip is awe-inspiring and the views from the top are breathtaking. ***Note:*** There's a guide rope on the southern face (and often a long line up).

It's a fair walk up to the second level, a flat, open space that overlooks the main temple square, the famed Angkor *prangs* or parapets on each corner. From here, it's a steep climb (use the staircase with roped handrail on the south side of the temple) up to the third and final level (at the time of writing, this level was closed to visitors). There are four large courtyards surrounded by galleries, and balcony overlooks from the base of the prangs at each corner. These high perches are great for watching the sunset over Bakeng Hill (though, lately, the guards try to get more folks down earlier and earlier).

Angkor Wat is the first temple you pass when entering the temple complex, but depending on your guide, you might save it for the evening and head directly to nearby Angkor Thom.

Bakeng Hill ★★ Just past Angkor Wat, Bakeng Hill is meant to resemble Mount Meru, the center of the earth in the Hindu cosmology. The hill makes a great spot for sunrise- or sunset-viewing and gets crowded like a mosh pit in high season. The hike up is a good way to limber up and break a sweat predawn, but the crumbled steps and slippery mud are a bit much for some. Consider taking the trek in style high upon an elephant's back in a houda. Elephants for hire start at about $20 and wait at the bottom of the hill.

Angkor Thom ★★★ The temple name means "The Great City" in Khmer and is famed for its fantastic 45m (148-ft.) central temple, **Bayon,** and nearby **Baphuon.** The vast area of Angkor Thom, over a mile on one side, is dotted with many temples and features; don't miss the elaborate reliefs on the Bayon's first-floor gallery or of the **Terrace of the Leper King** and the **Terrace of Elephants.** The **Angkor Thom Gates,** particularly the south gate, are good examples of the angelic carving of the Jayavarman head, a motif you find throughout the temple sites. The bridge spanning the moat before the south entrance is lined with the gods and monsters said to have been in competition to churn the proverbial sea of milk that would cause creation of the world. The line of statues with the gate in the background is a classic Angkor scene.

The Bayon ★★★ The **Bayon** is the very centerpiece of the larger Angkor Thom city and, with its classic carved faces, is one of the best loved of the Angkor temples. Bayon is a Buddhist temple built under the reign of prolific Jayavarman VII (A.D. 1190), but the temple was built atop a previous Hindu site and adheres to Hindu cosmology; with its central tower depicting Meru and its oceanic moat, it can be read as a metaphor for the natural world. The Bayon is famous for its huge stone faces, usually set in groups of four around a central *prang,* or tower, and each face indicating an ordinal direction on the compass. The curious smiling faces are done in deep relief at Bayon—and also in different forms at the entrance gates to Angkor Thom, at Ta Prom, and at Banteay Kdei—and the image is the enigmatic Mona Lisa of Southeast Asia, at once recognizable as an image of compassion and equanimity. The face is also said to depict Jayavarman VII, the temple's very builder and benefactor. You approach the Bayon along a forested area at the city center, cool and misty, where streams of light come through in visible rays and the drone of cicadas is deafening (you might even see some monkeys). Elephant trekkers also line the road to the temple.

The three-level Bayon is nearly square. The first level is surrounded by an intricate **bas-relief gallery** depicting stories of Khmer conquests and battles, as well as daily life and ritual among the early Khmers. A good guide can lead you to the juicy bits of the fun story, and you can spend a good bit of time sorting out the details for yourself, too (kids love it). Look for the unique pairs of Apsara dancers on columns near the gallery (Apsaras usually dance alone). On the South Wall, find three tiers depicting Khmer battles with the Cham from 1177 to 1181, a battle that took place on the waters of the Tonle Sap Lake in boats—look for the grisly images of crocodiles eating the carcasses of the fallen. Also note the Chinese figure with beard, top knot, and lance on a horse. Khmer soldiers ride elephants and have short hair, a spear, and a magic string for invincible fighting; they also carry shields and banners. A good guide can point out details like a lady crouching and getting burned on a fire, a man handing a turtle to a chef, and a scene of a cockfight and soldiers sacrificing a buffalo to ensure good luck in battle. There's a real sense of humanity to these images.

The second level has some Apsara reliefs and porticos with lingum, but the third level is the most interesting, where you can get up close with the many **Apsara Faces** thought to resemble a serene Jayavarman. Each of the 54 small towers is adorned with a face, or a number of faces, and you can have a ball with your zoom lens. There are a number of porticos with small lingum statues, and elderly matrons sell incense sticks and a chance to make merit by making an offering. The large central tower, or prang, is 25m (82 ft.) in diameter, with 16 small coves for meditation of kings and high priests. In 1933, French archaeologist George Groslier excavated the main prang, only to find a massive statue of Jayavarman hidden underneath. The statue, called **Jaya Bot Mohania,** is a seated Jayavarman with a seven-headed naga snake looming over him; it is now on display at a small temple near the **Victory Gate** (just east of the Bayon).

One of the greatest views of the many faces of the Bayon is from the ground at the northern end of the temples, just before a large snack, refreshment, and shopping area. Stop here on your way to the Baphuon (reviewed below) by foot.

Baphuon Just north of the Bayon is the stalwart form of the **Baphuon,** a temple mount built in 1066 and an important Khmer capital. Early French archaeologists sought to restore the crumbling mount and began to disassemble the temple block by block, but their efforts were interrupted by war, and it would be some years before archaeologists would return to find a confused jigsaw puzzle of a dismantled temple, and, *mon dieu!,* someone had misplaced the plans. Bilateral efforts are underway to solve the puzzle and put the temple back together, and these ongoing efforts give visitors an idea of what original temple construction might have been like. The Baphuon was the last capital in the Angkor period.

The east gate of the Baphuon is the only remaining part of what was once a large laterite wall. A narrow causeway with moats on either side connects the gate with the main temple. The temple has five levels that are all the same height, which makes the site more like a pyramid and unique among Angkor temples. ***Note:*** From the Baphuon, you can make a clockwise loop, first to Vimean Akhar, then to the Terrace of the Leper Kings and the Terrace of Elephants (all on foot), before you return to the vendors' area and your awaiting chariot to go on to Preah Khan or via the east gate to Ta Prohm.

Pre Rup ★ With its three central spires, **Pre Rup** looks a bit like a mini Angkor Wat. Pre Rup was built by King Rajeindravarmen II in 961 and was dedicated to Shiva. The best views are from the Hindu temple's south side. It is made of gray sandstone, which is a less durable material than the pink sandstone of Banteay Srei. As such, time and weather have had their way with the temple, and many of the intricate carvings and details have been worn away by rain and erosion, but it's still completely awesome in size and structure. Plants have begun to grow on the central towers, and you can see bright green leaves working their way through the stone. You'll be scrambling over the fallen rock and debris near the bottom of the temple, and you'll still feel like a humble, insignificant mortal. Climb to the top of the temple and look west; on a clear day, you can see Angkor Wat's spires (roughly 12km/7½ miles away) peeking out over the treetops.

Vimean Akhar ★ Continuing north of the Baphuon—and still within large Angkor Thom—you reach the "Palace of Air," or **Vimean Akhar,** which was a royal palace built by three successive kings (Jayavarman II and V and Suryavarman I) over a period of time from 944 to 1045. This Hindu temple dedicated to Shiva is some 12m (39 ft.) high with three levels; each of the three levels represents one of the kings who helped build it. Each side has steep steps, and the shallow moat is full in rainy season. The top of the temple is a narrow pillared gallery. The steep climb is best attempted to the left (west) when approaching from the Baphuon (there's a handrail). Have a drink or a fresh coconut in a shaded area at the bottom of the other side.

Adjacent to the Baphuon are two large ponds: The biggest is 125m (410 ft.) long and was where the king himself bathed; the smaller ponds were for the king's courtiers.

Note: The eastern entrance of the Vimean Akhar has a Sanskrit inscription with a brief history of construction and orientation. Most are in museums, and this is one of just a few that you can still find on the temple site.

Moments The Magic Hours at Angkor Wat

The skies over Angkor always put on a show. With just a bit of prior planning, you can see the dawn or the day's afterglow framed in temple spires, glowing off the main *wat* or reflected in one of the temple reservoirs. Photographers swoon. Here are a few hints for catching the magic hours at the temples.

The sunrise and sunset views from the upper terraces of **Angkor Wat,** the main temple, are some of the best, though it's a tough climb for some. At dusk, temple staffers start clearing the main temple area just as the sun dips. Smile, avoid them, and try to stay for the afterglow.

For the classic photographer's view of Angkor Wat at sunset—with the image reflected in a pool—enter the first wall of the temple compound, walk halfway down the front gangway, and then take a right or left down the set of stairs and out into the field. The view from the water's edge, with warm light bouncing off the temple, is stunning. The pond on the right nearly disappears in dry season but has natural edges, not stone, and makes for a nicer shot.

It's a bit crowded, but views from **Phnom Bakeng (Bakeng Hill),** a short drive past the entrance to Angkor Wat, are stunning at both sunrise and sunset. It's a good climb up the hill, and those so inclined can go by elephant for about $20.

The open area on the eastern side of **Banteay Kdei** (see Angkor Wat map, above) looks over one of Angkor's many reservoirs, **Sras Srang,** which serves as a great reflective pool for the rising glow at sunrise. See the "'Get High' at Angkor" box, below, for other options.

If money is no object, contact **Helicopters Cambodia Ltd.** ★ at their office just north of the Old Market at No. 217 (✆ **012/814-500**). For a fee, you can see the sights from any angle you choose. Be sure to specify your needs and interests, and they can create an itinerary that suits.

More affordable is a ride with **Angkor Balloon.** Just $15 gets you a 10-minute ride up to 250m (820 ft.) above the ground. The balloon basket is large, good for walking around and taking in the view from different sides. The balloon is controlled from the ground by tether, a very sophisticated contraption brought to Cambodia by French developers. It's a bit like an amusement park ride really. The takeoff is 1km (half a mile) west of the main entrance to the temples (you're sure to see them from afar throughout the day). Flights start at 5:30am and end at 6pm, and the prime sunrise and sunset spots fill up quickly. Call them at ✆ **012/520-810** to book a ride. In the middle of the day, it's first-come, first-served.

The Terrace of the Leper King ★★ Built by Jayavarman, this section is the northern half of a long north-south shelf (the Elephant Terrace, below, is the southern half) of what was supposedly a main viewing stage for the king and his entourage to watch elaborate shows in the open area out front. Approach the terrace from its most northern point. Outside you'll find an image of the guardian of hell, because the area site was a crematorium. The top of the terrace is a statue of the king with leprosy (a copy of the original). The long terrace is made of two walls, and visitors pass through a shaded walkway on the interior. The whole site is lined with rich relief carving and has been lovingly restored and propped up with a new concrete wall that maintains the integrity of the original. ***Note:*** There are toilets (porta-potties) at the far north end of the Terrace of the Leper King.

The Elephant Terrace This terrace is the south end (near the Bayon) of a long performance terrace of the king, so named because of its elaborate reliefs of elephants, whose trunks make decorative columns. The long concourse (about 350m/1,148 ft.) depicts images of circus acrobats, wrestlers, and elephant hunters in the wild.

Preah Khan Built by Jayavarman VII in 1191, the name of the temple means "Sacred Sword." It's rumored that this was where Jayavarman called home during the building of the Bayon. You approach the Preah Khan through a walkway lined with low lantern towers (note that the Buddhist reliefs were changed to divine vultures during the iconoclastic period). The compound is surrounded by wall and moat. The moat represents the ocean, the wall is a mountain, and the temple is Mount Meru—the mother mountain of Hindu creation. Four gates face the ordinal directions, and each gate has a God and Demon statue–like entry to Angkor Thom, but just a tower, no Apsara face. Stop in at the small visitor center for information about preservation. The temple is a monastery, like Ta Prohm and Banteay Kdei, and is thought to have been built in homage to Jayavarman's father. The site plan is much like Ta Prohm. The temple passage has lots of meandering galleries and side rooms with statues (most broken or missing) and Shiva Lingum. Many Buddha reliefs here have been chiseled off. Interior walls are lined with cross-legged, bearded forest hermits in relief. The central tower is a stupa for ashes of a later king, dating from the 16th century and replacing a large Buddha statue of Jayavarman VII that

"Get High" at Angkor

Like many of the world's great monuments, the temples of Angkor are laid out over massive spaces, with miles of temple wall on the side of each temple, as if a sign to the gods. Visitors approaching temples on foot experience the temple like Khmers of the Angkor period would have, in procession from one side to the other, but we see only one section of the main gate, for example, or experience only the inner sanctum of the temples without being able to see the whole. It is important to remember that the Angkor temples were each self-contained cities or large monasteries, with populations in the hundreds of thousands. Now choked with jungle, these wider areas are best appreciated from above, where the scope of the building at Angkor is best understood. The rule is that there's a 1km (half-mile) "no fly" radius around the temple compound, and the trips below know just where that is and can take you as close as they are allowed.

was found by the French in 1943, then summarily lost. One side room has a headless Buddha perfect for that canned "Put your head on the seated Buddha" photo. The many empty pedestals and lintels are courtesy of the Khmer Rouge and many tomb raiders.

Enter the temple from the west, and then make the long and winding walk along the central axis, exiting through the east gate where you see a massive Spoong tree (like a Banyan tree). From here, make your way back to the west entrance and your transport.

Ta Prohm ★★★ The jungle foliage still has its hold on this dynamic temple, which was left in a ruinous state when early archaeologists freed the temples from the jungle. Ta Prohm is a favorite for many; in fact, those very ruinous vines appeal to most. As large around as oak trees, the Khmer Spoong tree is something like a banyan tree, and it's often encased in the wandering tendrils of the *charay,* a thick vine. The powerful Spoong and the charay vines cleave massive stones in two or give way and grow over the top of temple ramparts. It's quite dynamic, and there are a few popular photo spots where the collision of temple and vine are most impressive. Sadly, Ta Prohm was looted quite heavily in recent years, and many of its stone reliquaries are lost. The temple was built in 1186 by Jayavarman VII as a monastery dedicated to the king's mother and spiritual teacher. There are 39 towers connected by numerous galleries. The exterior wall of the compound is 1km×600m (½ mile×1,968 ft.), and entrance gates have the classic Jayavarman face. Most visitors enter from the west gate—some drivers will pick you up on the other side. A line of small open-air eateries is just outside the main entrance to Ta Prohm, popular places for a snack or lunch.

Ta Kaeo ★ What's most interesting about Ta Kaeo is that it was never completed. Legend has it that the temple was struck by lightning during its construction, and all work was abandoned at a stage where the main structure was complete, but no adornment had been added; as such, it serves as "Temple Structure 101." Also unique is the fact that Ta Kaeo is made of a rich green sandstone (elsewhere it's a deeper brown or grayish color). Built in the 10th century by Jayavarman V, the temple was dedicated to Shiva. The central prang once housed a lingum, and the three levels are all encircled by sandstone galleries. The climb to the top is very steep, a bit of "four-points" rock climbing, really, but the view is well worth it.

Banteay Kdei The first temple built by Jayavarman VII in 1181, Banteay Kdei is just opposite the large **Sra Serang Reservoir,** a lovely lily pond that is 300×700m (984×2,296 ft.) and surrounded by sandstone steps of Khmer Vintage—the reservoir is a popular place to watch the sunset gleaming off the water's surface. Sra Serang once housed a small island temple where the king liked to meditate—now local folks bathe here or steer the water to local rice farms. The four gates of Banteay Kdei have Jayavarman's iconic smiling face—like those at the famed Bayon. The east entrance brings you past an area lined with lions and nagas along an open terrace once used for performances. There's a moat around the second interior gate. The Buddha at the entrance is an original, intact statue, quite unique to the Angkor compound where so many pieces have been stolen or destroyed (beheaded).

Some portions of the main interior temple area are held together with strong rope and cable. Look for a small offering house with columns just inside on the right used to gain merit through gift-giving. Also watch for the refined Apsara carvings on the main temple. Exit via the west gate—look for more Jayavarman heads—and walk the verdant fields around the side of the temple back to the east gate and your wheels, or take a short walk, through a gauntlet of young hawkers, to the Sra Serang Reservoir.

Banteay Srei ★★ True temple buffs won't want to miss this distinct complex. Some 32km (20 miles) north of the main temples, the 10th-century buildings of Banteay Srei are done in a style unique to the high spires of Angkor. The collection of low walls surrounds low-rise peaked structures of deep red sandstone. It is the only building to have been built with pink sandstone, a high-quality mineral that can withstand tougher elements. As such, the carvings and bas-reliefs on this temple are some of the most intricate, best-preserved carvings you'll find in Angkor. Translated as "The Citadel of Women," it has relief carvings on the squat central buildings and intricate tellings of ancient Hindu tales. Walking through the temple, there's a real feeling of "work in progress." Some of the doorways flanking the central pathway were originally framed in wood and have weakened with age. As such, the sandstone pediments that once stood on top crashed to the ground and broke into large pieces. They've since been reassembled and lie at the foot of the doorways like some ancient jigsaw puzzle. After the first gate and walkway, you'll come to a small entranceway that has a square pedestal with a round piece in the middle that used to hold a linga (it was stolen some years ago). Look at the frame of the square. It isn't smooth and straight, as you would expect, but completely warped and oddly worn away. The Khmer Rouge used to sharpen their knives here. The hallmarks of the temple are the three temples. The middle one is dedicated to Shiva and is flanked by temples honoring Vishnu and Brahma. I highly recommend you go with a guide who can explain the finer details of temple inscriptions. ***Tip:*** The colors are best before 10am and after 2pm, but there are fewer visitors in the afternoon.

Beng Melea ★★ Truly the temple aficionado's temple, Beng Melea is where to go if the Angkor temples seem tame, if you are longing to go "Tomb Raider" and clamber around the crumbling stones of an undiscovered (work with me here) jungle temple that has been claimed back by the jungle. Squint or use your imagination, and you can feel like Indiana Jones. The kids will love it. Beng Melea is 60km (37 miles) east of Siem Reap and often arranged as a day trip after a stop at the Roluos Group. The road is paved and smooth until just after the Roluos Group, where you turn north at the town of **Dom Dek,** which has a local market that's worth a stop. From there, follow a dusty, bumpy road. If you go by motorbike—good luck—wear a *Krama* or a good mask. The temple has three gallery walls and a moat at entry. No one has ever found the Sanskrit inscription on the temple, but Angkor Wat's builder, Suryavarman, supposedly put it up in the 12th century. The interior temple area is a big, fun pile of rubble, great for trouncing around. The area has just been cleared of mines, and the temple, long a secret enclave for temple buffs, is now attracting more visitors. There was a film recently produced on the temple site, and the filmmakers have left their handy ramps, making it a bit easier to get around. The east entrance is closed because of the many rocks fallen here, but enter just to the right of this main entrance and look for the relief images of the god of fire over the first door as you approach the gallery by the first ramp, and then an image of a three-headed elephant born of the mythical churning of the ocean of milk Hindu creation legend. A small library is inside this first gallery area. From here, plunge into the temple center. The platform path takes you through a covered, dark gallery. Between sections, you'll have to do some clambering and rock hopping. ***Warning:*** Be careful of the slippery moss. The path exits the opposite (west) side of the temple, and from there you can either wend your way back through, following a different course to the rocks, or walk around the outside. Get here as early as you can, and you'll have the place to yourself. The ride is

1 hour by car at a cost of about $50 with a driver, and about 1½ hours by motorbike, about $20 to $25 with a driver. North of Beng Melea is **Koh Ker,** another popular off-the-map temple.

Kabal Spean ★★ Finds Known as the "River of a Thousand Linga" (a *linga* is a phallic symbol representing the Hindu god Shiva), Kabal Spean lay undiscovered by Westerners until a French researcher stumbled across it only recently. Dating from the early 11th century, the relief carvings that line the streambeds are said to purify the water before it fills the reservoirs (called *barays*) of Angkor. It's the journey here that's really interesting—on some rough roads through rural villages north of Banteay Srei—and there's a fun forest hike (about 30 min. to the first waterfall). Khmer folks come to picnic, and it's a good spot to swim or follow the path that trips along at brookside; from there, you can view the many carvings in relief on the banks and creek bed.

5km (3 miles) north of Banteay Srei. Admission $3.

Land Mines Museum You won't find signs leading you to this seemingly impromptu museum; Cambodian officials prefer their own rhetoric to that of the owner and curator, Mr. Akira. The museum itself is just a corrugated-roof area stacked high with disarmed ordinance and detailed data about the use, effects, and statistics about UXO (unexploded ordinance) in the country. Most interesting is the small grove out back, an exhibit of how mines are placed in a real jungle setting. The museum is a call to action for demining in the country. Resist any temptation to volunteer (unless properly trained), but you're sure to have a chance to chat with Mr. Akira, peruse his recent book on the subject, and sign a petition (he's hoping to achieve NGO status).

On the main road to the temples, just before the checkpoint and a few clicks east. Go by motorbike or taxi. www.cambodialandminemuseum.org. Admission $1. Daily 7am–5pm.

Roluos Group About 13km (8 miles) east of the town center, these three are best viewed in context of Angkor architecture's progression, as the forefathers of the more dynamic of Angkor's main temples. A visit to these temples is included in the temple ticket but will cost you a bit extra for transport.

Tonle Sap Lake Day trips on the Tonle Sap Lake fall into two categories, so be careful what you're signing up for. First, avoid the 1½-hour tours out of the boat ferry jetty, Chon Khneas. These trips sound like fun, and for just $15 per boat or $10 per person, you can go with a driver and guide out onto the Tonle Sap. You do glimpse a bit of river life, the net-twirling fishermen, floating schools donated by Korean NGOs, and the commercial boat traffic on the Tonle Sap's main inlet, but once out on the water of the lake, you get a quick ride among ethnic Vietnamese, Khmer houseboats, and fisherman; then stop at a large tourist-trap barge with crocodile pits, small fish farms, and perhaps an aquarium with some sickly looking turtles, snakes, and fish choking on dirty water. It's all about the $1 Coke or souvenirs you might buy. Not worth the trip, so be sure to avoid rides to just Chong Khneas. The only exception to this is the fine upmarket evening cruises along this same route through the company **Terre Cambodge** (see below). The cost is $20 per person and doesn't include the fine cocktails you might enjoy while watching the sun dip into the cool lake.

The best day trips are one of the full-day options that take you to far-flung floating villages like **Kampong Phluk** in canoes among low mangrove or to a lush bird sanctuary, called **Preak Toal.** Following these routes with the larger tour operators comes with a hefty price tag for Cambodia, from $80 or so per day, but it's worth it.

Contact **Terre Cambodge** (www.terrecambodge.com) or talk with any of the budget tour operators in town (or your hotel's tour desk). All services are consolidated through the same providers, so you get the same trip wherever you buy it. Be sure and specify the exact sights you want to see and any inclusions you'd like, such as lunch. One unique find is the folks at **OSMOSE** (www.osmosetonlesap.org), whose main focus is conservation but who run fine tours as well.

These trips are best in rainy season because the mangrove swamps are dried up at other times. The birds at the bird sanctuary are best viewed from December to April. The Tonle Sap basin is lush and green when the water recedes in the dry season, but the water is so low that getting around on the lake, which drops from 12m (39 ft.) down to 4m (13 ft.) in depth—a third of its rainy-season size—is quite difficult.

If you're connecting onward with Siem Reap or Battambang by boat, you'll get a glimpse of life along the aquatic byways of Cambodia. The road heading south to the lake follows the Siem Reap River and gives you a glimpse into communities of precarious stilt houses that look ready to totter any second and farmers herding groups of domesticated ducks along canals. To get to the boat, you follow a long dirt causeway lined with shanty houses and elbow among trucks overloaded with minnows and small fish caught in the lake, squishing and leaking and bouncing precariously. Out on the open water on the speedboat to or from Phnom Penh, it's just hot sun and blue water—not especially picturesque, but fun when the water is high in the rainy season.

IN SIEM REAP TOWN

Angkor National Museum This new museum beckons visitors from the main road to the temples. It houses an impressive collection of artifacts from Angkor, many of which are on loan from the National Museum and the Conservation d'Angkor, a treasure trove that was heretofore closed to the public. Highlights include a room displaying 1,000 Buddhas, and an Angkor Wat exhibition with a model of the famed temple. It's a good place to see carvings and statue details up close and with decent explanations on hand. But visit only if it is pouring rain or you need a respite from walking around in the blistering heat; otherwise, your time and money are better spent at the temples. Historians and conservationists have criticized the lack of history (most of the "1,000 Buddhas" date back to the 20th c. only), and local Cambodians are smarting at the fact that the private Thai company behind the museum appears to be profiting from national treasures. (To be fair, it has agreed to transfer control to the Cambodian government after 30 years.) The museum is unfortunately housed in a sterile retail mall that looks like it was beamed in from the suburbs of America.

968 Vithei Charles de Gaulle, Khrum 6. ✆ **063/966-601.** Admission $15. Daily 8:30am–6:30pm.

SHOPPING

Shopping in the Angkor temple town has boomed, and new boutiques pop up daily. The old standbys, like the market and smaller boutiques, are also benefiting from increased numbers of tourists and expats.

You can find good **reproductions of temple statuary** anywhere in town, but it's a pretty cumbersome buy unless Siem Reap is your last stop before, say, Bangkok and a flight home. **Rubbings** of temple bas-relief can be found anywhere and are easily transported, best in a light poster tube. Original artwork and photography are available at every turn. Silk hangings and clothing are on sale in many boutiques, but "buyer beware" of price and quality before making a big investment. The vendors below are the best of many, and the Old Market area, where most are concentrated, is within easy walking. Don't miss the chic FCC compound and its upmarket shops and galleries.

Beyond This place is indeed "beyond," and parents should certainly heed the warning at the door that within they will find explicit material. The artwork of owner Jerry Swaffield, an Irishman and longtime expat, is wonderfully bizarre, a piss-take on Asian travel and the state of the world in expressive pen and ink drawings, like refined political cartooning, of the bizarre and sometimes a bit vulgar. Not to be missed. Swaffield also prints his own comic book about the typical visitor in Cambodia (check the website at www.cheapcharliecomics.com). Swaffield also has a collection of bizarre and extreme photographs, set in a chaotic yet stylistic display, in the back room. Images of Khmer Rouge cannibalism and atrocities, as well as diseased figures, are a bit much for some. All in all a very unique collection not to be missed (but maybe just stay in the front room). Open daily from 9am to 9pm. MasterCard and Visa accepted. At the FCC Angkor, Pokambor Ave. ✆ **063/760-609.** beyondart@online.com.kh.

Carnets d'Asie Bookstore, boutique, gallery, and tea shop all in one, Carnets d' Asie features some rare finds, including works by local artists, as well as fine temple reproductions and statuary. The large, tinted photographs of **Pier Poretti** (also see his gallery in Siem Reap; ✆ **012/925-684**) features large in the collection, with some classic views of the temples, as well as scenes of life in rural Cambodia. The large, open tea area at the back of the gallery is a good place to meet with friends and have a look at your finds. Open daily from 10am to 10pm. No. 333 Sivatha. ✆ **063/746-701.** www.carnetsdasie-angkor.com.

Colors of Cambodia Here's a fun one. A project set up to fund Cambodian schools, the shop sells framed artwork of young Khmer kids who visit the temples or depict their daily life in Technicolor crayon. Some of the work is quite expressive, and a purchase here certainly goes a long way to helping out. Open daily from 8am to 7pm. No credit cards. House No. 270, Mudull 1 Village (northwest side of the Old Market). ✆ **063/965-021.** colorsofcambodia@yahoo.com.

John McDermott Photography Just next door to the FCC, American John McDermott displays his stunning silver gelatin prints, some very classic images of the temple, in a cool, tiled contemporary space. The gallery is inspiring for more amateur photographers shutter-bugging at the temples, and these fine prints make great gifts. Small postcards are available for $2, larger reproductions just $35, and poster-size prints start at $300. Due to popularity, a beautiful two-story second gallery has opened in the heart of the backpacker district. The second floor features exhibitions by other artists. Both open daily from 10am to 10pm. MasterCard and Visa accepted. On the north end of the FCC compound on Pokambor Ave., ✆ **012/615-695,** and on the Passage, near the Old Market. ✆ **012/274-274.** www.mcdermottgallery.com.

Monument Books An expansion of the popular Phnom Penh outlet, Monument Books carries the best in new volumes about the temples, from coffee-table tomes to guidebooks and histories, as well as international newspapers. Their new Old Market–area location is large and carries an extensive collection. Another location, inside Lucky Mall on Sivatha St., is open daily 8:30am to 10pm. Open daily 8am to 8:30pm. MasterCard and Visa accepted. Inside Angkor National Museum.

New Market Recently rebuilt, the New Market is distinct from the old, in that it caters more to local tastes, which makes it good for a wander and for taking some photos. Open daily from dawn to dusk. On the north end of Sivatha St.

Psar Chas, the Old Market The very heart of tourist Siem Reap, this is the best place to find Buddhist trinkets and souvenirs like T-shirts, as well as good books on the temples. The market is a fun wander, and friendly folks here are used to foreign visitors, so you can easily haggle in English (or by passing a calculator back and forth to display your offer on an item). The many food stalls on the north end of the market are a good way to sample local cuisine for next to nothing. Most businesses in town give their address in relation to the Old Market, so it's a good place to know for orientation purposes. Open daily from dawn to dusk. Riverside in the south end of town.

Senteurs d'Angkor Carrying good contemporary Khmer arts and crafts, statuary copied from Angkor's greats (a good place to pick up that Jayavarman VII bust), traditional leather shadow puppets, silver jewelry, Khmer silks, *Kramas* (Khmer scarves), traditional local spices (pepper and lemon grass), potpourri, local teas, rice brandy, and fragrant handmade soaps, Senteurs d'Angkor is a good stop to satiate your shopping appetite before a flight back home. Open daily 7am to 9:30pm. Great souvenirs at reasonable prices. No. 275 Psaa Chas, cater-cornered to the northeast end of the busy Old Market. ✆ **063/964-801** or 012/954-815.

Tara and Kys Art Gallery A stunning collection that ranges from comically stylized caricatures of Khmer and Vietnamese life (they also have a gallery in Ho Chi Minh City) to expressive paintings and prints from the temples, Tara and Kys gallery is a fun visit. Open daily 9am to 9pm. 105 Mondol 1, opposite the Provincial Hospital north of the market. ✆ **012/679-011.**

Large, mall-style souvenir venues line the road just north of town on the way to the temples and are a good stop for the obligatory collector's minispoon or plastic replica of the temples, but are mostly set up for bus tours.

You'll find lots of small **convenience stores** in and around town. Star Mart is a familiar convenience store open 24 hours (on the airport road), though just one among many. It's not a bad idea to stock up on a few snacks before a day of temple touring.

SPAS & MASSAGE

After a day of scrambling, sweating, and climbing the temples, there's nothing like a bit of pampering to round things out, and with the tidal-wave rise in tourism in Siem Reap, all kinds of services are popping up. On the high end of the scale, contact the **Sofitel Hotel** (on the way to the temples on Vithei Charles de Gaulle; ✆ **063/964-600**), the **Raffles Grand Hotel d'Angkor** (at the very town center; ✆ **063/963-888**), or the **Angkor Palace** (✆ **063/760-511**).

In town, try **Visaya Spa** at the plush FCC complex (Pokambor Ave. just north of the post office; ✆ **063/760-814**), which has three stylish treatment rooms and a roster of high-end services, including body scrubs, wraps, facials, aqua therapy, and massages, all at high prices for this part of the world (a 90-min. massage is $40) but worth it. Contact them to make a reservation, or just stop in. Open daily from 10am to 10pm.

Frangipani, a small storefront spa just down a little alley opposite the Blue Pumpkin in the area north of the Old Market, offers a fine roster of treatments, from facials and aromatherapy to oil massage and traditional massage. A good little find with a professional staff offering services starting at just $18 per hour for a traditional massage. For booking, call ✆ **012/982-062.**

Body Tune Spa, in the very heart of Bar Street (btw. the Red Piano and the Soup Dragon restaurant; ✆ **012/444-066**), is in the midmarket range (about $10), with good affordable services and some burgeoning style.

On the lower end of the scale, where you can expect to pay as little as $6 for an hour of massage, try any of the small storefronts just north of the Old Market, in the popular tourist area. Services vary at these little storefronts, now numbering five and growing. For good Khmer massage, similar to Thai massage, try **Islands Traditional Khmer Massage** (north of Psar Chas; ✆ **012/757-120**). The most affordable massage in town, and a great way to support local enterprise, is at one of the many massage schools for the blind. Trained by international volunteers, blind masseuses—who in Khmer society might have little other chance in life than to rattle a cup or string flowers onto leis as temple offerings—are able to make a comfortable living. One convenient and very professional location is **Seeing Hands IV** (✆ **012/286-316** or 286-317), on central Sivatha near the Tell Restaurant and the Dead Fish Tower bar. Trained by Japanese and endorsed by Aus Aid and the Blind Care Foundation, masseuses are professional, and for only $5, you can't go wrong. Most folks tip heavily here and come away with a unique connection. Call or just stop in.

SIEM REAP AFTER DARK

Siem Reap is a town where most visitors are up with the sun and out visiting the temple sites, but there are a few good evening options.

Apsara dance is an ancient art in Cambodia. Dancers in traditional gilded costume practice their slow art: elegant contortions of a dancer's wrists. Contact the folks at the **Angkor Village** (✆ **063/963-561**) to make reservations for the nightly show, combined with a fine set Khmer menu in the traditional indoor banquet-house theater. Dinner begins at 7pm, and the show starts at 7:30pm (tickets cost $22).

The Raffles Grand Hotel d'Angkor has a similar show in an open pavilion on the lawn at the front of the hotel ($32, including dinner). Times and performances vary, so be sure to call ✆ **063/963-888** in advance. Most hotels have a performance space, and many small restaurants have shows of varying quality.

Okay, admittedly, this one is pretty kitschy, but the kids might like it: **Cambodia Cultural Center,** far west of Siem Reap on the airport road (Svay Dongkum; ✆ **063/963-836**), holds a host of shows and all-day events, including a mock Khmer wedding and Apsara dance. Call for current offerings, as the program varies. If you don't like the performance, you can walk the grounds, set around a large central pond, spend some time in Cambodia's only wax museum, walk among all of Cambodia's sights done in miniature, or visit various exhibits of village life and rural skill. You can even get around in an electric car. This one's most popular with Asian tour groups.

Dr. Beat (Beatocello) Richner plays the works of Bach and some of his own comic pieces between stories and vignettes about his work as director of the **Kantha Bopha Foundation,** a humanitarian hospital just north of the town center. Admission is free, but donations are accepted in support of their valiant efforts to serve a steady stream of destitute patients, mostly children, who suffer from treatable diseases such as tuberculosis. Dr. Richner is as passionate about his music as he is about his cause. You're in for an enjoyable, informative evening. Performances are every Saturday at 7:15pm just north of the town center on the road to the temples.

Bars & Clubs

There are a few popular bars near the Old Market in Siem Reap. Below are just a few. Most nightlife centers around what has become the de facto "Bar Street" in the center of the Old Market area, where lots of hip little spots hop into the late evening (usually till

2am and sometimes later). It's a great place to swap tales of temple touring and meet up with other travelers.

The **Angkor What?** (Pub St., 1 block west of the Old Market; ✆ **012/490-755**) was the first—and still the most popular—bar here, more or less where it's at in Siem Reap. Sign your name on the wall and say "Hi" to all the folks you met that day at the temples or on highways and byways elsewhere. **Easy Speaking Café and Pub,** next to the busy Angkor What?, handles the spillover. A similar crowd stays late. **Buddha Lounge** (✆ **012/865-332**), in the same area, also rocks late and has a free pool table.

Ivy Bar, on the northwest corner of the market (✆ **012/800-860**), is a popular expat haunt. Works of local photographers line the wall, and it's the office away from the office for travel writers and correspondents. **Dead Fish Tower** (✆ **063/963-060**), on the main road heading toward the temples, is set up like the rigging of a tall ship, with precarious perches, funky nooks, and unique drinks. **Laundry** (✆ **016/962-026**) is the funky side of Siem Reap. When the temple town gets psychedelic and stays up really late, this is where it happens. On a side street to the north of the Old Market, it's open nightly but usually hosts special events that you'll see promoted all around town.

Linga (North of Old Market; ✆ **012/246-912**) is a gay bar that attracts a decent mixed crowd to a corner location overlooking the small side street and the traffic on Mundul 1 Village St. The walls have psychedelic paintings of Buddhist monks.

Molly Malone's (Bar St., across the street and west of Red Piano Bar; ✆ **063/965-576**) is the hippest pub in town. They've got local expats playing live music, a mix of original songs and covers of crowd-pleasers like old Beatles and Roberta Flack numbers. The bar is fully stocked with a fine selection of Irish whiskey, and they've got a good stock of imported beer.

6 BATTAMBANG

180km (112 miles) from Siem Reap; 290km (180 miles) from Phnom Penh; 150km (93 miles) from Poipet

The west of Cambodia is made for the hearty traveler, a place to get off the track if you have the gumption. The far west, areas like the southwestern Cardamom Mountains and the northern border region with Thailand, are virtually off-limits to all but the most hearty vehicles, but Battambang is quite accessible and boasts a few interesting sights, offering a glimpse into the daily rhythms of rural Cambodia.

Travel west of Siem Reap means bumpy, dusty roads, best in a rented taxi (cheap to share). Where once it was just dusty pickup trucks along a pitted track notorious for banditry, the road east of Siem Reap to Phnom Penh, National Hwy. 5, is wide and paved, and means just a few hours of air-con cruising to the dulcet tenor of a bus DVD player churning out Khmer pop videos before you make the capital. How far things have come.

Poipet, the border town where most overland travelers enter or exit Cambodia with Thailand, is just a collection of dodgy casinos and persistent touts circling like hawks over the cattle-chute of tourists who pass through this bottleneck daily (see the "Border Hassles: Thailand to Cambodia Overland" box at the beginning of this chapter). Avoid Poipet at all costs, or just fly through on your way to or from Cambodia.

From Sisophon, to the west of central Tonle Sap Lake, the road splits; National Hwy. 6 connects with Siem Reap and National Hwy. 5 goes south to Battambang, both roads reconnecting a few hundred kilometers away in Phnom Penh.

After visiting the temples of Angkor, you can connect with Battambang by boat or bus, and from there carry on to Phnom Penh, via Pursat, or directly to the Thai border via Sisophon. It is some beautiful countryside, in places a flat plain dotted with palms and cattle grazing what appears to be sand; in others, especially near Battambang, it is lush and green, a bread basket of Cambodia.

Second only to Phnom Penh in size, little Battambang is third in per-capita income, eclipsed by the rising star of Siem Reap. Over the centuries, the town switched hands between Thailand and Cambodia, and was under Thai control as late as the 1940s. The people of Battambang did resist the initial coup d'état of the Khmer Rouge in the late 1970s but succumbed under heavy fighting, and the area became a Khmer Rouge stronghold.

Battambang sits on the west bank of the Sangker River, which connects with the Tonle Sap; daily boats carry tourists along this picturesque route (best to avoid in the dry season, though). The city is also the heart of one of the country's most productive farmlands, and the surrounding area is lush with growth. Fields of mango, papaya, jackfruit, and milky fruit, as well as peanuts, corn, and green beans, are well irrigated (note the long green hoses connecting fields), and a tour out into the countryside by car or motorbike is what is really on offer here. Battambang also has a strong colonial history, evident in the town's many French-style villas and storefronts, and there's a certain cozy ease to this riverside burg.

At the traffic circle on the eastern end of the city, find a large statue of Ta Dumbong, the legendary Khmer King who founded order and security in the town and surrounding area with what is the town's namesake, a *Bat Dambang,* or a "Disappearing Stick."

Important warning: Battambang was heavily mined during Cambodia's late troubles, and many of the NGO folks you'll meet out this way are here in support of teams who do the very dangerous jobs of removing land mines from rural areas. As such, do not venture too far afield in the countryside, at least not by yourself, and stick to well-worn paths wherever possible.

ESSENTIALS

Getting There

Though government sources are projecting an air connection to Battambang, at press time, flights weren't going there. The nearest air connection is at Siem Reap.

BY BUS Daily air-conditioned tourist buses connect Battambang with Siem Reap, east to Phnom Penh via Pursat, or west to Poipet and the Thai border area via Sisophon. All buses leave between 6 and 8am. Bus companies are near the Psah Boeung Choeuk on the east end of Battambang, and most buses arrive near there. Contact **Capitol Tour** offices in Phnom Penh (14AE0 Road 182, Sngkat Beng Prolitt; ✆ **023/217-627**), or near the Psah Boeung Choeuk in Battambang. **Neak Krorhorm Travel and Tour** (in Phnom Penh, ✆ **023/219-496;** in Siem Reap near the Old Market, ✆ **063/964-924;** or in Poipet, ✆ **012/627-271;** neaktour@yahoo.com) also has regular buses and an office near the market in Battambang (✆ **053/953-838**). You can book bus tickets at your hotel's front desk. It's $4 between Siem Reap and Battambang, and $5 between Battambang and Phnom Penh.

BY RENTED TAXI OR MINIVAN You can commandeer a Toyota Camry or a Japanese or Korean minivan just about anywhere in Cambodia; it's just a question of ponying up a big fee for one-way use. Expect to pay $40 to $50 for a car from Siem Reap to Battambang, for example, but more common routes, from the Thai border to Siem Reap or from

Phnom Penh to Kampot or Sihanoukville in the south, come at reasonable rates of about $20 to $25 for a 3- or 4-hour cruise. All-day car rentals at Angkor or for day trips from certain areas start at around $20 per day. If you're looking to keep your costs low, you can usually find other travelers looking to share expenses; just pop in at a cafe or a bar and meet a possible travel companion. Contact your hotel front desk or any tour agent in Siem Reap or Phnom Penh to make arrangements.

BY BOAT Boat connection between Battambang and Siem Reap makes for a pleasant morning when the water is high but should be avoided in dry season. Starting at the ferry docking area on the Tonle Sap nearest Siem Reap, boats depart in the early morning, from 7am, and the 6-hour trip (some 8–9 hr. when navigating narrow canals in the dry season) costs $20 to $25. Book a boat ride through your guesthouse or a tour company such as Capitol Tour or Neak Krorhorm Travel (see above).

Orientation

The town lies on the north side of the Sangker River. A new bridge connects National Route 5 with the south bank of the river, and a smaller iron bridge, built by the French, crosses at the center of town. On the south bank, at the intersection of Route 5 and the airport road, you can see a statue of the town's founder holding the stick that is the town namesake. Hotels and services are clustered at the town center. Bus company offices are in the east of town near the Psah Boeung Choeuk. Nearby Psah Nath is another large market good for a wander.

Getting Around

You can walk around the town center, but for sights farther afield, hiring a motorbike taxi driver, or *motodup,* is the easiest and most affordable way; the downside is that, short of the highways, Route 5 from Sisophon and Route 10 going to Pailin, roads are very dusty. If you do take a motorbike, be sure to bring a scarf or a Khmer-style *Krama,* or ask the driver to stop at a streetside stall for a 500 Riel (10¢) mask. Find drivers in front of the main hotels; try to find someone who can speak a bit of English, as you'll be together for a long day. Most of the younger drivers are well informed about the area's temples and flora and fauna, and are keen to practice their English. Expect to pay about $3 per sight or $8 per day for transport. All-day rentals of a Toyota Camry start at $20. Contact any hotel front desk.

FAST FACTS Bring cash to Battambang, best in U.S. dollars. The Thai Bhat is accepted widely, and at a rate better than you'll get in Siem Reap (usually about 40B for $1). ANZ Royal, Canadia Bank, and UCB are located in front of Phsar Nath (the main market), and all have ATMs.

WHERE TO STAY & DINE

Among Battambang's dining options, the popular **White Rose** (in the very heart of town, just 1 block from the river; House No. 102 on Street No. 2; ✆ **053/952-862**) is a worthy find and makes good use of the surrounding countryside's abundant produce. Serving good, authentic Khmer and a laundry list of Chinese-style stir-fries, Thai soups and treats, and some Western cuisine, the White Rose is the most popular choice among humanitarian workers visiting Battambang. Prices are from 75¢ to $1.50. Just across the street from White Rose is **Smokin' Pot** (✆ **012/821-400;** vannaksmokinpot@yahoo.com), a German-owned restaurant (the name refers to the pot you put on a stove, not in a pipe), which offers daily cooking courses and good Khmer and Western cuisine. **La**

Villa (✆ **053/730-151**) is the upscale choice for Western dining in town, also offering reliable Asian food.

La Villa ★ This is the best option in Battambang, and most people know it, so make sure to book ahead. The charming hotel is set in a 1930s colonial house done in sunny yellow with white shutters over arched windows. Rooms are spacious and come with gorgeous Art Deco tile and four-poster beds. Suites come with balconies or terraces overlooking the river. Tall guests should stay on the first floor, as second-floor rooms come with sloping ceilings that are charming only when you aren't accidentally bashing your head on them. Bathrooms are large and modern; some come with awkward, though sizable, tubs.

N 185 Pom Romchek 5 Kom Rattanak Srok, Battambang. ✆ **053/730-151.** Fax 053/730-151. 7 units. $60 double; $85 suite. MC, V. **Amenities:** Restaurant; bar; Internet; outdoor pool. *In room:* A/C, TV/DVD, fridge (suites only), hair dryer (suites only), minibar (suites only).

Teo Hotel Large, clean, air-conditioned rooms are the hallmark of this hotel, the top choice among the NGO set. In fact, their 87 rooms are often sold out. They have a wide selection starting at just $11 for a clean, simple room with a guesthouse-type bathroom (with shower and toilet area combined). Their more upmarket rooms are just larger versions of the same, but with better bathrooms and tidier furnishings. For such a provincial post, the staff is especially sophisticated in dealing with the wants of its power-driven customers, most of whom arrive in big, white Land Rovers and demand all kinds of assistance. Luggage storage boxes behind the counter, Internet access, car rentals, and guide or interpreter services, as well as useful information about the surrounding areas, are available on request. However convenient, the Teo is just a tidy business hotel with no frills.

Road No. 3, Kamakor, Khum Svay Por, Battambang. ✆ **053/952-288** or 012/857-048. Fax 053/953-288. 87 units. $11–$44 double. MC, V. **Amenities:** Restaurant; room service. *In room:* A/C, TV.

ATTRACTIONS

A wander among Battambang's classic crumbly colonials, all of which are colored a deep yellowish tan that lights up in the morning and evening light, makes for nice city walking. A few Buddhist temples are scattered around town, and south of the city is the large statue of a kneeling **Ta Dambong,** the legendary founder of peace and stability in the region, holding the "Disappearing Stick" from which Battambang gets its name.

The real sights in this area are the rural temples and beautiful countryside. A 1-day trip can get you to all of them, and as much fun are the rural stops in between: a visit to a farmer's field, perhaps, or to roadside juice stands. A trip to Wat Phnom Sampeou and Wat Banang is a good circuit, beginning at Route 10 on the west end of town and then returning along the river. For $5, most motorbike drivers will try to talk you into a trip back on a small metal-and-bamboo, motor-driven platform that sits on top of the train tracks, a common form of transport, considering that the train passes only once each day. A visit to Wat Phnom Ek is an additional trip in the other direction.

Just a short 8km (5-mile) drive from Wat Phnom Sampeou (see below) and included in most day trips out of Battambang, the Angkor-era ruins of **Wat Banang** are nothing in comparison with the stunning temples of Angkor, of course, but for temple buffs or burgeoning archaeologists, Wat Banang's five Angkor-style towers, which predate the penultimate Angkor era, are a unique insight into the development of building styles. Reached by a long, steep staircase of 298 laterite steps, the temples themselves are hewn in rough laterite, with some of the original sandstone facing and Apsara decorations, many with the faces chipped off during one of Angkor's iconoclastic revolutions, still intact. Views from the top are lovely.

Wat Phnom Ek, on the north end of town, is another pre-Angkorian ruin. The hilltop temple of Wat Phnom Ek is, like Wat Banang above, in relatively good condition, with some carving intact.

Wat Phnom Sampeou A 2002 reconstruction of a Buddhist temple built in 1964, Wat Sampeou is a dynamic little hilltop temple, its towers jutting out of the top of a steep hill, one of the only high points in a wide, flat plain. The temple is best known as Battambang's "Killing Fields," like Choeung Ek outside of Phnom Penh, where thousands of concentration-camp victims of the Khmer Rouge were killed. At Sampeou, victims were slaughtered and thrown into deep caves, two of which now house small temples and monuments. A visit here follows a circuit, first to the caves and a small temple that was once the prison building of the concentration camp here, and then to the nearby hilltop temple. The temple itself is not incredibly interesting—just a few spires and some shaded meditation areas and statuary—but the views across the plain are stunning and the monks are quite friendly and talkative. The path then leads back down a steep path to the entrance.

When you arrive at the base, you'll be swarmed by a group of young guides. For just $1, one of the lads can take you the easy way up the hill and point out the poignant sights, saving you some time scouting around on your own. Most speak just a bit of English but are happy to talk with you and can tell you some details about the temple legend, a very confusing and ambling tale meant to be told over hours and hours about a girl named Rumsay Sok, who was courted by the Khmer king and—through a series of magical events and the intervention of chickens, crocodiles, and a storm at sea—used her magical hair to dry up the valley and create the mountains that represent characters in the legend. Your guide can point out the nearby Crocodile Mountain, as well as a small statue of the magic lady.

16km (10 miles) from Battambang. Admission $2. Guide hire $1. Daily dawn–dusk.

Fast Facts

15

1 FAST FACTS: VIETNAM

AREA CODES The area codes for the provinces of Vietnam are as follows: An Giang 076, Bac Can 0281, Bac Giang 0240, Bac Lieu 0781, Bac Ninh 0241, Ben Tre 075, Binh Dinh 056, Binh Duong 0650, Binh Phuoc 0651, Binh Thuan 062, Ca Mau 0780, Can Tho 0710, Cao Bang 026, Da Nang 0511, Dac Lac 0500, Dong Nai 061, Dong Thap 067, Gia Lai 059, Ha Giang 0219, Ha Nam 0351, Hai Duong 0320, Haiphong 031, Hanoi 04, Ha Tinh 039, Ho Chi Minh 08, Hung Yen 0321, Hoa Binh 0218, Khanh Hoa 058, Kien Giang 077, Kontum 060, Lai Chau 0231, Lam Dong 063, Lang Son 025, Lao Cai 020, Long An 072, Nam Dinh 0350, Nghe An 038, Ninh Binh 030, Ninh Thuan 068, Phu Tho 0210, Phu Yen 057, Quang Binh 052, Quang Ngai 055, Quang Ninh 033, Quang Tri 053, Soc Trang 079, Son La 022, Tay Ninh 066, Thai Binh 036, Thai Nguyen 0280, Thanh Hoa 037, Thua Thien Hue 054, Tien Giang 073, Tra Vinh 074, Tuyen Quang 027, Vinh Long 070, Vung Tau 064, Yen Bai 029.

BUSINESS HOURS Vendors and restaurants tend to be all-day operations, opening at about 8am and closing at 9 or 10pm. People are up and about very early in the morning in Vietnam—in fact, some towns still follow the old socialist bell system over outdoor speakers that start with waking bells at 5am, exercise regimen at 5:30am, siesta bell at 11am, return-to-work bell at 1pm, finish-work bell at 5pm, and the news piped in at 6pm (this mostly in remote areas). Note that locals eat an early lunch, usually just after 11am, and some restaurants are all but closed at 1pm. Government offices—including banks, travel agencies, and museums—are usually open from 8 to 11:30am and 2 to 4pm. Streets are often very quiet during the siesta hours of the day, when the sun is most merciless. Restaurants usually have last orders at 9:30 or 10pm, and, with the few exceptions of city clubs, bars are rarely open much past midnight.

DRINKING LAWS There are virtually no age restrictions limiting when or where you can buy or consume drinks. Laws against drinking and driving are not enforced, so it is not uncommon to find that your motorbike or taxi driver has had a few. Be cautious, especially at night.

DRIVING RULES See "Getting There & Getting Around," p. 23.

ELECTRICITY Vietnam's electricity carries 220 volts, so if you're coming from the U.S., bring a converter and adapter for electronics. Plugs have either two round prongs or two flat prongs. If you're toting a laptop, bring a surge protector. Big hotels will have all these implements.

EMBASSIES & CONSULATES Embassies are located in Hanoi at the following addresses: **Australia,** 8 Dao Tan (✆ 04/3831-7755); **Canada,** 31 Hung Vuong (✆ 04/3734-5000); **European Union,** 83B Ly Thuong Kiet (✆ 04/3946-1702); **New Zealand,** 63 Ly Thai To (✆ 04/3824-1481); **United Kingdom,** 31 Hai Ba Trung (✆ 04/3936-0500); **United States,** 7 Lang Ha (✆ 04/3772-1510).

EMERGENCIES Nationwide emergency numbers are as follows: For police, dial ✆ **113;** for fire, dial ✆ **114;** and for ambulance, dial ✆ **115.** Operators speak Vietnamese only.

HOLIDAYS Banks, government offices, post offices, and many stores, restaurants, and museums are closed on the following legal national holidays: New Year's Day (Jan 1), Tet holiday (usually a few days in Jan/early Feb on the Gregorian Calendar—see "Vietnam Calendar of Events," in chapter 3), Gio To Hung Vuong Day (1 day, usually in Apr on the Gregorian Calendar—see "Vietnam Calendar of Events," in chapter 3), April 30 (Saigon Liberation/Reunification Day), September 2 (National Day).

For more information on holidays, see "Vietnam Calendar of Events," in chapter 3.

HOSPITALS In Hanoi, the expatriate choice for comprehensive services is the **Hanoi French Hospital,** south of the town center at 1 Phuong Mai (✆ **04/3574-0740**). For emergencies or minor medical issues in Hanoi, stop in at the convenient **International SOS** medical center at 31 Hai Ba Trung St., just south of Hoan Kiem Lake; call the 24-hour service center for emergencies at ✆ **04/3934-0555.** They have both Vietnamese and foreign doctors on call. Also in Hanoi, find the **Hanoi Family Medical Practice** at Van Phuc Diplomatic Compound at 298 Kim Ma (✆ **04/3843-0748**).

In Ho Chi Minh City, **International SOS** is at 167 Nam Ky Khoi Nghia St., District 3 (24-hr. hot line ✆ **08/3829-8424**). The **International Medical Center,** at 1 Han Thuyen, District 1 (✆ **08/3865-4025** for emergencies), offers services similar to what you'll find at International SOS.

INSURANCE Travel insurance is a very good idea for Vietnam. In the event of, say, a motorbike accident or a stomach ailment, seeking treatment at the international hospitals is very expensive. A consultation with a doctor at International SOS alone will set you back close to $200, let alone medicine and fees for setting broken bones or treating an acute case of diarrhea.

For information on traveler's insurance, trip cancellation insurance, and medical insurance while traveling, please visit www.frommers.com/planning.

INTERNET ACCESS Internet cafes are found in cities throughout Vietnam, especially in popular guesthouse and hotel areas. At cafes, rates are dirt-cheap—usually around 4,000 VND per hour. In rural areas and at hotel business centers, rates are usually much more expensive. Take a short walk and you can find affordable service.

LANGUAGE Vietnamese is the official language of Vietnam. Older residents speak and understand French, and young folks are busily learning Chinese these days. While English is widely spoken among folks in the service industry in Hanoi and Saigon, it is harder to find in other tourist destinations. Off the beaten track, arm yourself with as many Vietnamese words as you can muster (see chapter 16) and a dictionary.

LEGAL AID The legal aid system in Vietnam is tenuous for its own citizens, let alone international travelers. If you find yourself on the wrong side of the law, contact your embassy or consulate immediately.

MAIL A regular airmail letter will take about 10 days to reach North America, 7 to reach Europe, and 4 to reach Australia or New Zealand. Mailing things from Vietnam is expensive. A letter weighing up to 10 grams costs 13,000 VND to North America, 11,000 VND to Europe, and 9,000 VND to Australia/New Zealand; postcards, respectively, cost 8,000 VND, 7,000 VND, and 6,000 VND. Express mail services such as FedEx and DHL are easily available and are usually located in or around every city's main post office.

NEWSPAPERS & MAGAZINES *Viet Nam News* (http://vietnamnews.vnanet.vn) is the country's English-language daily newspaper. You can find copies at bookstores around town.

PASSPORTS See www.frommers.com/planning for information on how to obtain a passport. See "Embassies & Consulates," above, for whom to contact if you lose your passport while traveling in Vietnam. For other information, please contact the following agencies:

For Residents of Australia Contact the **Australian Passport Information Service** at ✆ **131-232,** or visit the government website at www.passports.gov.au.

For Residents of Canada Contact the central **Passport Office,** Department of Foreign Affairs and International Trade, Ottawa, ON K1A 0G3 (✆ **800/567-6868;** www.ppt.gc.ca).

For Residents of Ireland Contact the **Passport Office,** Setanta Centre, Molesworth Street, Dublin 2 (✆ **01/671-1633;** www.irlgov.ie/iveagh).

For Residents of New Zealand Contact the **Passports Office** at ✆ **0800/225-050** in New Zealand or 04/474-8100, or log on to www.passports.govt.nz.

For Residents of the United Kingdom Visit your nearest passport office, major post office, or travel agency, or contact the **United Kingdom Passport Service** at ✆ **0870/521-0410** or search its website at www.ukpa.gov.uk.

For Residents of the United States To find your regional passport office, either check the U.S. State Department website or call the **National Passport Information Center** toll-free number (✆ **877/487-2778**) for automated information.

POLICE You won't find a helpful cop on every street corner. Count on them only in cases of dire emergency, and learn a few words of Vietnamese to help you along. Moreover, police here can sometimes be part of the problem. Especially in the south, you and your car/motorbike driver might, for instance, be stopped for a minor traffic infraction and "fined." If the amount isn't too large, cooperate. Corruption is the rule, and palm-greasing and graft pose as police process. Be aware.

SMOKING "No smoking" areas are rare in Vietnam, and even those that exist are often not well ventilated. Like other countries in the region, Vietnam is a smoker's paradise, and complaining about secondhand smoke is often met with confusion.

TAXES A 20% VAT was instituted for hotels and restaurants in January 1999, but expect variation in how it's followed. Upscale establishments might add the full 20%, and some might even tack on an additional 5% service charge. Others might absorb the tax in their prices, and still others will ignore it entirely. Inquire before booking or eating.

TELEPHONES For domestic calls, visit the post office, where public phone service is offered at affordable rates, or buy a domestic phone card at any post office or phone company branch, usually at a rate of about 1,000 VND per minute. Local calls from hotels come with exorbitant surcharges and are best avoided.

The best way to make international calls from Vietnam is using an international calling card program, the likes of AT&T or MCI. Most hotels offer international direct-dialing, but with exorbitant surcharges of 10% to 25% on already inflated rates. International calls from any post office are more affordable, but without a calling card it is usually over $1 per minute.

Internet phone service is available at most little Internet storefronts. You can buy a card that gives you rates as low as 3,000 VND per minute, but many Internet shops don't allow you to use cards purchased elsewhere and levy a small surcharge on top of the 3,000 VND per minute. Internet phone quality ranges widely, best from the larger cities, and there is always a slight "walkie-talkie" delay, but it is the most affordable way to stay connected.

If you have a GSM cellphone that accepts SIM cards, you can buy an affordable plan at any post office or telecommunications center. The trick here is that receiving calls from anywhere is free of charge, so you can buy someone back home an affordable international phone card and arrange times when they can call you.

To call Vietnam: If you're calling Vietnam from the United States:

1. Dial the international access code: 011.
2. Dial the country code: 84.
3. ***Important Note:*** City codes are listed in this book with a 0 in front of them, as is required when dialing domestically. Do not dial the city code's prefix of 0 when dialing from abroad. When dialing a number (as listed in this guide), such as ✆ 04/555-5555, from abroad, you dial as follows: ✆ 011 (for international), + 84 (for Vietnam), + 4 (the city code minus the 0) + 555-5555. Looks like ✆ 011-84-4-555-5555.

To make international calls: To make international calls from Vietnam, first dial 00 and then the country code (U.S. or Canada 1, U.K. 44, Ireland 353, Australia 61, New Zealand 64). Next you dial the area code and number. For example, if you wanted to call the British Embassy in Washington, D.C., you would dial 00-1-202-588-7800.

For directory assistance: Dial ✆ **116** if you're looking for a number inside the country.

For operator assistance: If you need operator assistance in making a call, dial ✆ **110.**

Toll-free numbers: Calling a 1-800 number in the States from Vietnam is not toll-free. In fact, it costs the same as an overseas call.

TIME Vietnam is 7 hours ahead of Greenwich Mean Time. There's no daylight saving time in Vietnam, meaning that in the summer months, it's 12 hours ahead of the U.S. East Coast, in winter months 11 hours ahead; it's 14 or 15 hours ahead of the U.S. West Coast, and 3 or 4 hours ahead of Sydney, Australia.

TIPPING Tipping is common in Hanoi and in Saigon. In a top-end hotel, feel free to tip bellhops anywhere from 10,000 VND to 15,000 VND. Most upscale restaurants throughout the country now add a service surcharge of 5% to 10%. If they don't, or if the service is good, you might want to leave another 5%. Taxi drivers will be pleased if you round up the bill (again, mainly in the big cities). Use your discretion for tour guides and others who have been particularly helpful. Contrary to rumor, boxes of cigarettes as tips don't go over well. The recipient will say regretfully, "I don't smoke," when what he really means is "Show me the money." Exceptions to this are chauffeurs or minibus drivers.

TOILETS You won't find public toilets or "restrooms" on the streets in most cities in Vietnam but they can be found in hotel lobbies, bars, restaurants, museums, department stores, railway and bus stations, and service stations. Be sure to carry tissues, as many of the restrooms in the railway and bus stations do not have toilet paper. Large hotels and fast-food restaurants are often the best bet for clean facilities. Restaurants and bars in resorts or heavily visited areas may reserve their restrooms for patrons.

VISAS For information about Vietnamese visas, go to **www.vietnamembassy-usa.org** and click on "Visa—Consular Services." Or go to one of the following websites:

Australian citizens can obtain up-to-date visa information from the **Vietnam Embassy** at 6 Timbarra Crescent, Malley, Canberra, ACT 2606 (✆ **2/6286-6059;** www.vietnamembassy.org.au), or at the **Consulate General of Vietnam** at 489 New South Head Rd., Double Bay, Sydney, NSW 2028 (✆ **2/9327-2539;** www.vietnamconsulate.org.au).

British and **Irish** subjects can obtain up-to-date visa information by contacting the **Vietnam Embassy** at 12–14 Victoria Rd., London W8-5RD, U.K. (✆ **0171/937-1912;** fax 0171/937-6108) or by visiting the "Vietnam Visa" section of the website at **www.vietnamembassy.org.uk**.

Canadian citizens can obtain visa information from the **Vietnam Embassy** at 470 Wilbrod St., Ottawa, ON K1N 6M8 (✆ **613/236-1398;** www.vietnamembassy-canada.ca).

Citizens of **New Zealand** can obtain up-to-date visa information by contacting the **Vietnam Embassy,** Level 21 Grand Plimmer Tower, 2-6 Gilmer Terrace, Wellington (✆ **4/473-5912;** www.vietnamembassy-newzealand.org).

VISITOR INFORMATION In Hanoi and Ho Chi Minh City, head to the **Tourist Information Center** (7 Dinh Tien Hoang St. in Hanoi; ✆ **04/3926-3366;** or 4G-4H Le Loi St., District 1 in Ho Chi Minh City; ✆ **08/3822-6033**) for detailed free tourist maps and general information. These centers also have a couple of computers offering free (but agonizingly slow) Internet access. In the north, Sapa's new **Tourism Information Center** (✆ **020/387-1975**) is a good resource for local hiking conditions and decent maps. Recent stats and general information on the country and local holidays can be found at the state-run tourism site www.vietnamtourism.com.

WATER Water is not potable in Vietnam. Outside of top-end hotels and restaurants, drink only beverages without ice, unless the establishment promises that it manufactures its own ice from clean water. Bottled mineral water, particularly the reputable La Vie and A&B brands, is everywhere. Counterfeits are a problem, so make sure you're buying the real thing, with an unbroken seal. Beware of big typos: "La Vile" water speaks for itself.

2 AIRLINE, HOTEL & CAR RENTAL WEBSITES

MAJOR AIRLINES

Air France
www.airfrance.com

Air New Zealand
www.airnewzealand.com

American Airlines
www.aa.com

British Airways
www.british-airways.com

China Airlines
www.china-airlines.com

Delta Air Lines
www.delta.com

Japan Airlines
www.jal.co.jp

Korean Air
www.koreanair.com

Lufthansa
www.lufthansa.com

Northwest Airlines
www.nwa.com

Qantas Airways
www.qantas.com/au

Philippine Airlines
www.philippineairlines.com

Thai Airways International
www.thaiair.com

United Airlines
www.united.com

Vietnam Airlines
www.vietnamairlines.com

BUDGET AIRLINES

Jetstar (Australia)
www.jetstar.com

MAJOR HOTEL & MOTEL CHAINS

Hilton Hotels
www.hilton.com

Hyatt
www.hyatt.com

InterContinental Hotels & Resorts
www.ichotelsgroup.com

Life Resorts
www.life-resorts.com

Mövenpick Hotels
www.moevenpick-hotels.com

Sofitel Hotels
www.sofitel.com

Sheraton Hotels & Resorts
www.starwoodhotels.com/sheraton

Victoria Hotels & Resorts
www.victoriahotels-asia.com

CAR RENTAL AGENCIES

Budget
www.budget.com.vn

TNK Travel Vietnam
www.tnktravelvietnam.com

16

The Vietnamese Language

The ancient Vietnamese language, though not complex structurally (subject, object, verb with no plurals), is tonal and therefore difficult for Westerners to master. In its earliest written form, Vietnamese was based on the Chinese pictographic writing, called ***Chu Nom,*** and you'll see remnants of that tradition on temple walls—in fact, young people still study written Chinese in school. But in the 17th century, a French missionary named **Alexandre de Rhodes** developed ***Quoc Ngu,*** the Romanized Vietnamese alphabet that's used today. Unlike other languages in the region, many of which use Sanskrit as a base, Vietnamese looks almost readable to a Westerner, and though the easy recognition of Romanized letters makes finding street addresses much easier, the system of accent marks is complex and pronunciation is difficult. There are no dialects of Vietnamese, but regional accents are quite distinct.

To really learn Vietnamese, you'll need to work with a pronunciation coach, and the best part about traveling in Vietnam is the willingness of people to listen, laugh, and correct or model for you as you bludgeon their precious language. Learning just a little goes a long way.

Today most city dwellers seem to speak at least a little English, and the older generation speaks some French. With increased influence from China—the Chinese comprise well over 50% of international visitors in Vietnam—younger people are increasingly studying Mandarin. Students especially will be eager to practice English with you (as well as French or Mandarin). Solo travelers, being less intimidating, are at an advantage; you'll have many opportunities (and invitations) to have a squat on a street corner, drink a *bia hoi* (local draft beer), and practice pronunciation.

Note: For useful **food terms** and names of popular dishes, see chapter 17.

1 THE BASICS

USEFUL VIETNAMESE PHRASES

English	Vietnamese	Pronunciation
Hello	**Xin chaøo**	Seen chow
How are you?	**Em/Anh/Chi/Ong Khoe Khong?**	Em/Ahn/Chi/Ong Kwe kong?
I am very well, thank you.	**Rat khoe, cam on.**	Rek kwe, kam un.
Good morning	**Chaøo buoåi saùng**	Chow boy sang
Good afternoon	**Chaøo buoåi chieàu**	Chow boy chew
Good evening	**Chaøo buoåi toái/ ñeâm**	Cho boy toy/dem

English	Vietnamese	Pronunciation
Thank you	**Caùm ôn**	Cahm un.
You're welcome/ Not at all	**Khoâng coù chi**	Kawng kaw chi
Goodbye	**Taïm bieät**	Tam bee-et
Please	**Laøm ôn**	Lahm un
Yes	**Vaâng**	Vung
No	**Khoâng**	Kawng
Excuse me	**Xin loãi**	Seen loy
May I take a picture?	**Toâi coù theå chuïp hình ñöôïc khoâng?**	Doi kaw tay joop ayn khong?

NUMBERS

English	Vietnamese	Pronunciation
0	**Khoâng**	Kawng
1	**Moät**	Mawt
2	**Hai**	Hi
3	**Ba**	Bah
4	**Boán**	Bawn
5	**Naêm**	Nam
6	**Saùu**	Sow
7	**Baûy**	Bay-ee
8	**Taùm**	Tam
9	**Chín**	Cheen
10	**Möôøi**	Mooey
11	**Möôøi moat**	Mooey mot
12	**Möôøi hai**	Mooey hi
20	**Hai möôi**	Hi mooey
21	**Hai möôi moat**	Hi mooey mot
30	**Ba möôi**	Baw mooey
100	**Moät traêm**	Mot jam
243	**Hai traêm boán möôi ba**	Hi jam bawn mooey ba
1,000	**Moát ngaøn**	Mot ngun
10,000	**Möôøi ngaøn**	Mooey ngun
100,000	**Moät traêm ngaøn**	Mot jam ngun
1,000,000	**Moät trieäu**	Mot true

Note: Numbers up to 20 continue with Möôøi plus ordinal numbers. In other words, 12 is "ten two" and 19 is "ten nine."

EMERGENCY

English	Vietnamese	Pronunciation
I need a doctor.	**Toâi caàn baùc só.**	Toy kahn back see
Hospital	**Beänh vieän**	Ben vee-in
Antibiotic	**Thuoác khaùng sinh**	Dook kahng shin

Tips Who Do You Think You're Talkin' To?

It's important to know who you're speaking to, especially in Vietnam, where the pronoun *you* is used widely and denotes the relationship of the two people speaking. If you're just saying "Hello" to someone, you need to say the equivalent of "Hello older man" or "Hello young person." In fact, when peers meet, there's a moment of figuring out who is older/younger—sometimes folks even ask so that they know what to call you. The second-person pronouns are important and easy to learn. Say hello as follows:

- Use *Chao ong* for a man significantly older, an elder or grandfather.
- *Chao ba* is polite for a married woman older than you, an auntie or grandma.
- *Anh* is the word for a young man (only if older than you) or brother; if you're elderly, everyone is *Em* and *Anh* to you.
- Say *Chao chi* to an older or middle-age lady.
- Use *Chao co* when referring to an older single lady or teacher.
- *Chao em* is the proper pronoun for someone younger than you, male or female. ***Note:*** A man saying this to a woman is considered too informal—as if it were a come-on—so the more neutral *Chi* or *Co* is better. Also note that shouting *"Em"* or *"Em oi!"* is the best way to get a waitress's attention. If the waitress is much older, though, be sure to use *"Ba oi!"* instead.

GETTING TO KNOW SOMEONE

English	Vietnamese	Pronunciation
What is your name?	**Anh teân laø gì?**	Ayn ten la zee?
Where are you from?	**Anh töø ñaâu ñeán?**	Ayn nuoc now den?
I am . . .	**Toâi laø ngöôøi . . .**	Toy la noo-ai . . .
(an) American.	**Myõ.**	mee
(an) Australian.	**Uùc.**	ook
British.	**Anh.**	ayn.
(a) New Zealander.	**Taân Taây Lan.**	tan tay lan.
Have you had a boyfriend yet?	**Anh/Chòo baïn trai/ gaùi chöa?**	Kaw ban dray/ ban guy chew-uh?
Have you had a wife/ husband yet?	**Anh/Chò coù choàng/ vôï chöa?**	Kaw vuh/cham choo-ah?
Which part of Vietnam are you from?	**Baïn ôû thaønh phoá naøo?**	Ayn ou (pronounced like "ou" in *should*) tan fo now?
I am studying Vietnamese.	**Toâi ñang hoïc tieáng Vieat**	Toy howp tee-un Vietnam.
I like . . .	**Toâi Thích . . .**	Toy tick . . .
studying Vietnamese.	**Ñang hoïc tieáng Vieät.**	howp tee-en Viet.
ice cream.	**AÊn kem.**	ahn kem.
traveling.	**ñi du loch.**	dee zoo lick.

English	Vietnamese	Pronunciation
How long have you been in Vietnam?	**Anh/Chi ôû Vietnam ñöôïc bao laâu?**	Ayn ou Vietnam nuoc bow low?
One week/ month/year	**Moät tuaàn/ thaùng/name**	Mot too-ang/tang/nan
What is your job?	**OÂng/Baø/Anh/Chi laøm ngheà gì?**	Lam ngay zee?
I am . . .	**Toâi laø . . . Toy la . . .**	
a writer.	**nhaø vaên.**	nya van.
an artist.	**hoïa só.**	ho-a see.
a teacher.	**giaùo vieân.**	gee-ow vee-en.
in business.	**thöông gia.**	too-ong zee-a.
a student.	**sinh vieân.**	seen vee-en.
retired.	**veà höu.**	vay hoo.
Good	**Toát**	Tawt
You are clever!	**Anh thoâng minh laém!**	Ayn tong min lem!
Oh, my gosh!	**OÂi trôøi ôi!**	Oh zoi oi!
How old are you?	**OÂng/Baø/Anh/Chò bao nhieâu tuoåi?**	Bow nyew too-ee?
I am 34 years old.	**Toâi ba möôi boán tuoåi.**	Toy la ba mooey bawn too-ee.
See you again.	**Heïn gaëp laïi.**	Hen gup lie.

TALKING ABOUT LANGUAGE

English	Vietnamese	Pronunciation
Could you speak English?	**OÂng/Baø/Anh coù noùi ñöôïc tieáng Anh Khoâng?**	Ayn kaw noi nook tieng ayn kong?
I speak a little Vietnamese.	**Toâi noùi ñöôïc chuùt chuùt.**	Toy noy duck choot eet.
How do you say . . . in Vietnamese?	**Caùi naøy/chöõ naøy . . . noùi tieáng Vietnam laø gi?**	Che ne tieng Vietnam la zee?
I don't understand.	**Toâi khoâng hieåu.**	Toy kawng hew.
I understand.	**Toâi hieåu.**	Toy hew.
Please speak slowly.	**Xin oâng/baø noùi chaäm laïi.**	Seen owng/ba noy chum lie.
Please repeat that.	**Xin oâng/baø noùi/ laäp laïi.**	Seen owng/ba noi lie.

2 GETTING AROUND

GETTING THERE

English	Vietnamese	Pronunciation
Where is . . .	**. . . ôû ñaâu?**	. . . er dow?
the bus station?	**Traïm xe buyùt?**	Chram say bwit?
the train station?	**Traïm xe löûa?**	Chram say loo-a?
a hotel?	**Khaùch saïn?**	Kak san?
a guesthouse?	**Nhaø nghæ?**	Nya Ngee?
a restaurant?	**Nhaø haøng?**	Nya hahng?
the toilet?	**Nhaø veä sinh?**	Nya vay shin?
a hospital?	**Beänh vieän?**	Nya too-wong?
my embassy?	**Toøa ñaïi söù Anh?**	Toa lahn soo ayn?
the road to . . .?	**Ñöôøng ñeán . . .?**	Doo-ang dee . . .?
Where can I buy a map?	**Toâi coù theå mua baûn ñoà ôû ñaâu?**	Doi kaw tay mua ban do ou do?
Turn right.	**Reõ phaûi.**	Ray fie
Turn left.	**Reõ traùi.**	Ray chrai
Where are you going?	**OÂng/Baø/Anh/Chò ñi ñaâu?**	Owng/ba/ayn dee doe?
I am going from . . . to . . .	**Toâi ñi töø . . . ñeán . . .**	Doy di two . . . den . . .
I want to go to . . .	**Toâi muoán ñi . . .**	Toy Moo-an dee . . .
When?	**Luùc naøo?**	Look now?
Yesterday	**Hoâm qua**	Home gwaa
Today	**Hoâm nay**	Home ngai
Tomorrow	**Ngaøy mai**	Ngay my
What time do we leave?	**Maáy giôø thì khôûi haønh?**	May zuh tee khoy hawn?
What time do we arrive?	**Maáy giôø thì ñeán?**	May zuh tee den?
Is it far?	**Xa khoâng?**	Saa kawng?
Very far	**Xa laém**	Saa lum
Fast	**Nhanh**	Nuan
Slow	**Chaäm**	Jam

TOURING

English	Vietnamese	Pronunciation
I want to see . . .	**toâi muoán xem . . .**	doi moo-an same . . .
temple	**ñeán**	den
pagoda	**chuøa**	choo-uh
church	**nhaø thôø**	nya thuh
mountain	**nuùi**	nu-y

English	Vietnamese	Pronunciation
cave	**hang ñoäng**	hang dong
river	**soâng**	song
lake	**hoà**	ho
beach	**baõi bieån**	bye byen
It is very beautiful!	**Ñeïp quaù!**	Dep gwa!
I'm tired.	**Toâi meät**	Toy kaw mut

TRANSPORTATION

English	Vietnamese	Pronunciation
airport	**phi tröôøng**	fee kang
taxi	**taéc xi**	taxi
I want to rent a car.	**Toâi muoán thueâ tac xi.**	Toy kaw tay mun say hoy u do
motorbike	**Xe may**	Say my
motorbike taxi	**Xe oâm**	Say ohm
bicycle	**Xe ñaïp**	Say dap
bus	**Xe buyùt**	Say bwit
train	**Xe löûa**	Say loo-ah
baggage	**Haønh lyù**	Han lee
backpack	**Ba loâ**	Balo
pedicab	**Xích loâ**	Sick low

RESTAURANT & SELF-CATERING

English	Vietnamese	Pronunciation
Please bring me . . .	**Laøm ôn cho . . .**	Lam on chuh . . .
It is delicious, thank you.	**Raát Ngon, caùm ôn.**	Wreck ngawn kam un.
bread and butter	**Baùnh mì vaø bô**	Bun me vuh bo
egg	**Tröùng**	Chrung
vegetable	**Rau**	Rau
beef/chicken/fish	**Thòt boø/Thòt gaø/caù**	Tit baw/ Tit ga/ cha
fried/boiled/grilled	**Chieân/luoäc/nöôùng**	chi-yen/loo-uk/noo-wong
one cup of coffee/tea	**Moät taùch caø pheâ/traø**	Mot tak kafay/cha
I can't eat spicy food.	**Toâi khoâng aên cay ñöôïc.**	Toy khong ahn kyai doo-uk.
Check, please!	**Tính Tieàn.**	Tin tee-un

HOTEL

English	Vietnamese	Pronunciation
Do you have any available rooms?	**OÂng/Baø coøn phoøng troáng khoâng?**	Owng/ba kaw foam kawng?

I want a . . .	**Toâi muoán moät**	Doi moo-an mot foam
single room. (Please)	**phoøng cho moät ngöôøi**	cho mot ngoo-ai.
double room.	**moät phoøng cho hai ngöôøi.**	Mot foam cho hi ngoo-ai.
I want a room with . . .	**Toâi muoán moät phoøng coù . . .**	Doi moo-an mot foam cho . . .
hot water.	**nöôùc noùng.**	noo-uc nawng.
air-conditioning.	**maùy laïnh.**	my la-n.
a bath.	**phoøng taém.**	fawng tam.
a phone.	**ñieän thoaïi.**	di yen twye.
Can I see the room?	**Coù theû xem phoøng ñöôïc khoâng?**	Kaw tay same foam kawng?
I need a . . . pillow.	**Toâi muoán . . . goïi.**	Toy moo-an . . . goy
blanket.	**meành.**	men.
towel.	**khaên taém.**	kawn tam.

SHOPPING

English	Vietnamese	Pronunciation
Please give me . . .	**Cho toâi . . .**	Jya toy . . .
Do you have . . .?	**Coù khoâng . . .**	Kaw kawng . . .
mineral water?	**nöôùc suoái?**	nook kwang?
iced tea?	**traø ñaù?**	chaa da?
a beer?	**bia?**	bee-ah?
soap?	**xaø phoøng?**	sa phong?
How much does it cost?	**Bao nhieâu tieàn?**	Baugh nyew tyen?
Expensive!	**Maéc quaù! (south)**	Mak gwa!
(Too much!)	**Ñaét quaù! (north)**	Dat gwa!
Cheap!	**Reû!**	Ray!
Do you have something . . .	**Coù . . .**	Kaw . . .
better?	**toát hôn?**	tawt hawn?
bigger?	**lôùn hôn?**	lawn hawn?
smaller?	**nhoû hôn?**	nyaw hawn?

Fun Facts Laugh from Your Mistakes

The Vietnamese language, with its six tones, has an enormous capacity for puns, and Vietnamese people get a kick out of foreigners' mistakes. Words that mean "progress with sales," if pronounced incorrectly, come out as "very hungry." Bawdy mistakes by foreigners who think they're ordering pork but are naming a human body part, for example, send Vietnamese people into a tizzy.

17 Vietnamese Cuisine

Dining in Vietnam is one of the highlights for visitors, and the secret is out, thanks to a proliferation of good, affordable, authentic Vietnamese restaurants springing up in the West. Characterized by the light, subtle nature of this cuisine, where ingredients are left alone to work their magic, Vietnamese gastronomy is getting the international kudos it well deserves. Take places like New York and Los Angeles, for example, where you can find an authentic bowl of *pho* (noodle soup) or fresh spring rolls, and where Vietnamese ingredients—from rice paper and green papaya to rice whiskey and *nuoc mam* (pungent fish sauce)—are influencing some of the finest Pacific fusion restaurants. Gourmets have discovered Vietnam, and many are making their own long-haul flights to experience the real deal.

The 1990s saw a resurgence of French-influenced cuisine after years of harsh restrictions on Western influence. A few staples like good baguettes and some French dishes survived the purges, but it took the cultural reopening of Vietnam under the Doi Moi policy to see a real resurgence of international cuisine and all kinds of creativity come into the better kitchens of the land.

Vietnam relies on wet rice cultivation—and short-grained white rice is more than a staple; it defines the Vietnamese soul and is the backbone of the economy. Because of the nation's heavy population density, it seems like every piece of arable land is farmed, mostly for rice paddies as well as fruit orchards and vegetable farms. "South ships north" is the old adage about food production, as the Mekong Delta is the nation's breadbasket, providing most of the country's rice and much of its produce. The diversity of a chef's palate in tropical Vietnam—with its many herbs, spices, and fruit that just falls from the trees—makes for some great dining adventures. In this chapter I offer a short primer in some of the basic dishes. Dine out with locals wherever possible. Even if you foot the bill for the whole table, the cost is still a pittance.

1 TYPICAL INGREDIENTS

Vietnamese cuisine relies heavily on fresh ingredients and the right mix of herbs and spices. Look for the following in any dish you experience in the country: *Mang* (bamboo shoots) are the tender young stalks of a thick bamboo that's usually sliced thin and served fresh, dried, boiled, or as pickles; *bap chuoi* (banana blossom) is a red flower bud used in salads or as garnish; *la chuoi* (banana leaves) are used to wrap small portable meals of cakes or meats; and *kho qua* (bitter gourd) is used as a garnish. *Ot* (red chilies) are a common ingredient and add a real zing to any Vietnamese dish.

Fresh fish is available anywhere in Vietnam—you're never very far from the sea or a river—and meat and poultry are locally farmed.

Herbs and fresh vegetables are used both in cooking and as condiments at the table. With most Vietnamese meals, you'll be offered a plate of *rau que* (raw basil), which comes in several varieties, as well as *ngo* (coriander) and lettuce. The use of lemon grass, mint, coriander, ginger, basil, and garlic creates light, fresh, and flavorful fare. Vietnamese foods are also part of the intricate system of Chinese medicine, and the many herbs and spices in Vietnamese cooking serve multiple purposes. Ginger and garlic are part of many remedies, and aromatic teas, roots, and herbal poultices come with doctor's orders.

Sadly, MSG (monosodium glutamate) is used widely in Vietnamese fare. In fact, the *Agi No Moto* ("More Taste") brand from Japan is offered on some local tables as a condiment. If you have a hard time processing MSG (that is, you get headaches, shortness of breath, or MSG "seasickness"), ask for food without it.

Nuoc mam is the famous—or notorious—Vietnamese fish sauce; its pungent flavor (and more pungent aroma) sets Vietnamese food apart. *Nuoc mam* is olive oil, soy sauce, and ketchup all rolled into one: the universal condiment of Vietnam. What is it? Simply put, it is fish that has been fermented in salt water, but the subtleties to *nuoc mam* production are as calculated as the making of fine wine or olive oil. Sadly, touring production facilities in places like the island of Phu Quoc to the far south and the town of Phan Thiet near Saigon is not as rewarding—pretty stinky really—as visiting a vineyard or an olive grove. The taste and smell of *nuoc mam* is overwhelming to the Western palate, but a true appreciation of Vietnamese food brings understanding of *nuoc mam*'s importance. Did someone say "acquired taste"? ***Nuoc cham*** is the most popular tabletop alternative, and mixes the pungent standard *nuoc mam* with sugar, vinegar, and seasonings for a more pleasant introduction to this unique Vietnamese flavor—you gotta try it once.

2 DINING & ETIQUETTE

Vietnamese are very hospitable, and there's a good chance you'll be invited to eat with a local family or join a Vietnamese group at a restaurant—you don't want to pass up the opportunity if it presents itself.

Etiquette is a rather casual affair—meaning that there are few "no elbows on the table" kinds of restrictions—but there are a few things to remember. The order of who is served, of who is given the choicest delicacies, and of who eats first is very important. When in doubt, wait. It's best to see that the eldest member of the group is served first and given the choicest fare—a whole egg from the top of a hot pot, a shrimp, or piece of steak.

Meals are slow, friendly affairs surrounding a banquet, usually on the floor, with everyone sitting in a circle. Courses come out of the kitchen in succession, and don't expect to get away with just eating like a bird—mom or grandma is sure to be a full-on food pusher and it's hard to say no (once a friendly host just kept filling small bowls and shoving them my way). Expect lots of comings and goings and lively discussion. Shared dishes are picked up with either chopsticks or forks—both are okay—and eaten in a small hand-size bowl. It's okay to sip or slurp from the bowl, and shovel the last bits of a meal using your chopsticks. ***Also note:*** It's okay—customary even—to wipe utensils before eating.

POPULAR DISHES

Authentic Vietnamese cuisine is best enjoyed alfresco at streetside, where food is cooked fresh and served, without any pomp and circumstance, on squat stools at a low table, often under an umbrella—a great way to meet local people (folks will be amazed/excited/appalled that you're there) and pick up some language. The food does the talking in

Vietnam, though. Below are a few of the kinds of dishes you can sample. Get adventurous. Go where locals go. Look for stalls that are packed, or storefront restaurants that have a line out the door, and walk in, smile, and point or just say, "One, please," holding up a finger. The entry fee is low, usually $1 or less per dish. Order up!

PHO This classic Vietnamese noodle soup has become a staple all over the world. Vietnamese—and increasingly their Western visitors—are almost fetishistic about their interest in the intricacies of its preparation. ***Pho bo*** (noodle soup) is a dish of wide rice noodles done in a beef broth; flavored with ginger, black pepper, lemon, and shallots; and topped with thin slices of roast beef and fresh greens like basil or coriander. ***Pho ga*** (noodle soup with chicken) is the same as *pho bo,* but with shredded chicken on top. *Pho*'s simple formula keeps people searching the length of Vietnam looking for just the right combination (see "Quest for the Perfect Noodle," p. 319). Everyone is loyal to a favorite stall, though, so ask for a recommendation. Locals eat *pho* any time—for breakfast, lunch, or dinner, and as a midnight snack after a night on the town.

COM The very definition of "eating" is to *an com,* or "eat rice." Vietnam's staple plays a part in nearly every meal, whether as whole kernels or mashed and processed into rice paper, rice noodles, or fermented into rice wine. And Vietnamese *com* shops (the *o* in *com* is pronounced like the elongated *ou* in the word *should*) line every street. *Com* restaurants serve all manner of stir-fries or curries, often quite spicy in the south, along with a bowl of "Vietnamese bread." If you're out in the sticks a lot, you'll want to learn to say the likes of *com trung,* or "rice with egg" and *com chien* or "fried rice."

BUN Vietnamese *bun* (the *u* in *bun* is pronounced like a shortened *oo* in *wood*) is rice vermicelli, a fresh, light rice noodle with a slightly pungent aroma to it. Bun-style dishes are many, usually a mix of herbs and spices served with broth as a one-dish meal. ***Bun bo*** is rice vermicelli with shredded beef, usually in a fiery sauce. ***Bun rieu*** is a hearty stew of paddy crabs cooked in curry and shrimp paste and served with fresh rice vermicelli and greens. Avoid the various pig intestine varieties of bun dishes, the likes of *bun moc* or *bun gio heo,* and if you're eating at a local stall—unless you're an aficionado—ask the owner to go light on the *nuoc mam.*

NEM RAN (CALLED CHA GIO IN THE SOUTH) This is the classic fried Vietnamese spring roll, a delicious appetizer of ground meat or fish mixed with shrimp paste, mushrooms, spices, and some greens, folded into a thin rice wrapper and dipped into a sweet and sour sauce. It's an especially popular dish during the Tet holiday.

BANH XEO A thin pancake of rice flour folded with chicken or pork and topped with onions, sprouts, and greens, *banh xeo* is a popular treat in the south.

BANH CUON *Banh cuon* is a variant of the standard spring roll. Made with a thick rice wrap, like a heavy crepe cooked in fat, *banh cuon* are stuffed with chicken, beef, or shrimp (lots of varieties) and steamed. A Hanoi specialty.

CHA CA A classic Hanoi specialty that has found its way into restaurants along the length of Vietnam, *cha ca* is a delicious meal of delicate whitefish, fried at high heat in gobs of peanut oil with dill, turmeric, lemon shrimp paste, and a dash of rice whiskey. You prepare the dish yourself over a small brazier of coals that heat the frying pan. In a small rice bowl, diners each add a portion of the flash-fried fish to fresh *bun* (rice vermicelli) and fresh greens and peanuts. The best place to sample *cha ca* is at Hanoi's famed Cha Ca La Vong (p. 90).

NEM NUA These are my favorite: fresh spring rolls you make yourself, popular all over Vietnam and a great light, low-budget snack. You're given a plate of rice wraps, bowls of condiments like pickles and sour eggplant, and a dish of pork, shrimp, or vegetables (your choice); you're left to do the origami to put it all together. Vietnamese people get a real kick out of watching unpracticed Westerners fumble with this, and someone is always on hand to show you how to put it all together and dip it in the spicy sauce.

DAOFU CHIEN Here's a popular dish available just about everywhere—a good one to learn by heart and order when you're out in the boonies. It's a basic dish of fried tofu with lemon grass, delicious with rice and a side of ***rau mouang xao chau,*** fried morning glory (a kind of stringy spinach) with oyster sauce.

CHA TOM Popular in tourist restaurants, this sweet, savory dish appeals to the foreign palate. *Cha tom* is ground, seasoned shrimp grilled on a stick of cut sugar cane. It's a delicious appetizer.

BO BAY MON This is "beef served seven ways." A Saigon specialty, this succession of beef dishes includes fondue, fried, barbecued, and soup. It's a real treat.

GOI NGO SEN A lotus root salad served with pomelo.

CA HAP Steamed fish served as you like. Always look for regional specialties. **Hue cuisine,** for example, is famous for its light specialties, such as *bun bo hue* and good spring rolls. In **Hoi An,** try the Vietnamese raviolis, and in **Hanoi** the great *pho,* dog-meat dishes, and *cha ca* (see above). Keep your eyes open for the fish sauce of Phan Thiet and Phu Quoc; duck dishes and spicy curries in **Saigon;** and many other regional favorites. Explore. Ask what's good. Make sure it's not guts or frogs, unless you want to try guts or frogs, and *bon appétit!*

DRINKS

You can find tea, whiskey, beer, coffee, delicious shakes, and fruit juices—hot or cold, sweet or mellowing—anywhere in Vietnam.

Small cups of hot, **bitter Chinese tea** (called ***tra***) are de rigueur for a first meeting, for a business situation, and for just killing time—say, during check-in at a hotel. The cups just keep getting filled up, and this casual offering of Chinese tea is an important component of hospitality. ***Note:*** When pouring more, fill your host's cup first and your cup last.

Tea follows hundreds of years of Chinese tradition—under Chinese tutelage—in the provinces of Thai Nguyen and Lao Cai, for example, where estates date back centuries. Vietnam's plantations produce all varieties, standard black and green as well as fine jasmine tea, and fine teas are imported from China.

Tra da is iced tea, a standard pot of bitter Chinese tea poured over ice, usually unsweetened. Local restaurants serve *tra da* gratis from large pitchers. It's a great way to cool down on a hot day (although you should beware of drinking ice that's made from unfiltered water, especially if you have a sensitive stomach).

Local ***bia hoi,*** a cheap draft beer of watery lager made in every region, is served cold on tap in every town, usually in small storefronts crowded with squat stool tables and lots of revelers. You can expect a fun night of *"Chuc mung!"* ("Cheers!" or "Good luck!") all around.

Tips For Vegetarians

Just say *"An chay"* ("I eat vegetarian"), and you'll be met with approving nods, as vegetarian cooking is the province of tonsured Buddhist monks and, like anywhere, the health-conscious. Any dish can be altered for vegetarians, and good vegetable dishes like ***rau mouang xao chau*** (fried morning glory with oyster sauce) or the standard ***rau xau*** (mixed fried vegetables) are available anywhere. That said, strict vegetarians, the likes of vegans, will find themselves trying to convince chefs not to include fish sauce, eggs, and cheese, for example, which are considered permissible for monks and Vietnamese vegetarians.

Vietnamese whiskey, called ***ruou,*** comes in many varieties, and most of it could thin paint and is sure to cross your eyes in due time—go easy with the stuff. I've had offers at dawn, and traveled with locals who knocked the stuff back all day long. Hospitality is one thing, but it's also okay to say, "No, thank you." *Nep moi* is the standard variety, and it's sold in stores throughout the country, as well as in most *bia hoi* bars and roadside restaurants. In the Central Highlands, don't miss an opportunity to slurp from a long reed straw from a massive pot of ***ruou can,*** a particularly potent local brew made by ethnic-minority groups.

The hills of Vietnam's Central Highlands, from Dalat all the way up to Kontum, look something like a Colombian landscape, with high, rolling hills as far as the eye can see sprouting coffee like a giant Chia pet—you almost expect a grinning Juan Valdez to pop from behind a bush with a steaming cup any minute. Vietnam is the second-largest **coffee grower** in the world—just behind Mr. Valdez's cohorts—and though roasting techniques are primitive, choice Vietnamese Robusta coffee is delicious.

Small coffee joints can be found on every corner. Look for the **Trung Nguyen** brand, Vietnam's Starbucks of coffee. And because coffee is made with boiled water, it's okay to drink. Trung Nguyen stores might look like a chain, but franchising in Vietnam is limited to getting a free sign (you will see TRUNG NGUYEN everywhere) in exchange for buying and serving Trung Nguyen coffee, so individual outlets are all independent and distinct. Also look for the fine **Highland Coffee** outlets in Hanoi and Ho Chi Minh City.

Filter coffee is served in small cups with stainless-steel filters of coffee over the top. You pour your own hot water and wait for the slow filtration process—part of the experience really, and a good lesson in patience (the Vietnamese even have a saying about the patience required to sit and watch a filter coffee drip).

Vietnamese coffee is usually served with ***sua,*** or very sweet condensed milk. Say *"Ca phe sua chut-chut"* if you want only a little of the saccharine sweet stuff (a bit too much for some), or order a *"café den"* for black coffee. Rarely will you find *sua tuoi* (fresh milk)—only in the big cities—but you'll always find *duong* (sugar) on the table. Ordering ice coffee at a local alfresco stand just means the same rig as above, accompanied by a glass of ice—all very do-it-yourself—just say *"Ca phe sua da"* and wait for the drip and pour it on ice.

Nuoc Khoang is Vietnamese for "drinking water," which is available in bottles everywhere. Just say ***"Cho toâi nuoc khoang"*** (pronounced *Jya toy nook kwang*). Even locals drink bottled water (tap water is never potable), and all ice or drinking water provided is

Eew, What's That?!

Vietnam is home to some of the world's most exotic fare, with the likes of dog, snake, deer, jungle animals, and frogs gracing menus at the finer local restaurants, as well as any sea creature that moves—one man's bait is another man's dinner.

***Thit co* (dog meat)**—a delicacy of the north—is reputedly prepared by beating the animal with a rubber hose to tenderize its flesh before it's slaughtered. A meal of dog is usually eaten family style, almost exclusively by men to celebrate business deals (the meat is said to increase one's virility). Similarly, ***thit ran* (snake meat)** is a popular dish in Hanoi and is served in the Le Mat section north of Hanoi—now a popular tourist night out (see the box, "Have You Tried the Snake?" in chapter 5).

In the mountain towns of the Central Highlands and far north, you'll find such delicacies as wild boar, venison, and goat. Chinese restaurants everywhere serve the likes of frog and eel.

One of Vietnam's rarest culinary oddities is ***cafe cut chon,*** a beverage made from average Vietnamese coffee beans that have passed through the most bizarre process. The beans of this coffee are served after being digested and passed—I choke on that euphemism—by a civet, something like a jungle fox (in reality, a relative of the mongoose). The taste? Earthy, they say, and strong. There are lots of shops in the Central Highlands towns that claim to have the real deal, but who knows if this fox poop is genuine?

usually boiled or filtered and is just fine. Kids love the popular ***nuoc mia,*** or sugar-cane juice. Also popular are cool drinks with lemon: ***Nuoc chanh*** is lemonade and ***soda chanh*** is a lemon soda. Ask for it with or without sugar *(duong).* This is the hip expat drink of choice.

DESSERT

Che is a popular dessert dish of rice gelatin sweetened with Chinese litchi fruit and sugar. ***Kem*** (ice cream) is available everywhere, both Western-style ice cream (as taught by French colonists) and the local variety made with soy and coconut.

Sinh to is a delicious soy-based sweet shake made with the fruit of your choosing. Find little *sinh to* stands just about everywhere, popular at night market areas, and enjoy this sweet treat on the go, slurping it through a straw from a plastic bag. Shakes are made with *sua,* the same ultrasweet condensed milk that's popular in coffee. Ask for *khong sua* (no *sua*) or *sua chut-chut* (just a little).

Tropical Vietnam offers a wide variety of fruit, sometimes served with *da ua* (fresh yogurt). Find the likes of *chuoi* (banana), *tao* (apple), *xoai* (mango), *du du* (papaya), *mang cut* (mangosteen), *nhan* (longan, a sweet palm-size fruit), *vu sua* (the star apple or star fruit), *dua hau* (watermelon), *buoi* (grapefruit, which comes in many varieties), *chom chom* (rambutan, which is like a litchi with a spiky rind), *dua* (pineapple), and *sau rieng* (durian, the "smelly jackfruit" of renown), among others. Fresh fruit is affordable and available everywhere.

INDEX

AARP, 40
Abercrombie & Kent, 46, 375
Absolute Asia, 46
Academic trips and language classes, 43
Access-Able Travel Source, 38
Accessible Journeys, 38
Accommodations, 49–51
Ba Be Lake and Cho Ra Town, 153
Bach Ma National Park, 203
best, 4–6
Buon Ma Thuot, 251–252
Cambodia, 380–381
Battambang, 438–439
Kampot and Kep, 400
Phnom Penh, 387–390
Siem Reap, 410–417
Sihanoukville, 403–404
Can Tho, 354–355, 358–359
Cao Bang, 154
Cat Ba Island, 168–169
Cat Tien National Park, 348
Con Dao Archipelago, 342–343
Dalat, 240–243
Danang, 208–210
Dien Bien Phu, 149–150
environmentally friendly, 42
Haiphong, 158, 160
Halong City, 162–163
Hanoi, 77–88
Ho Chi Minh City, 300–313
Hoi An, 213–220
Hue, 188–192
Lai Chau, 151
Lang Co Beach, 205
Lang Son, 155, 156
Mai Chau, 143
Mekong Delta, 356
My Lai, 267
Nha Trang, 271–276
Ninh Binh, 174
Phan Thiet, 286–289
Phu Quoc, 363–365
Pleiku and Kontum, 257
Quy Nhon, 264–265
Sapa, 136–138
Son La, 146
Vinh, 180–181
Vung Tau, 337, 339–340
A Dong Photo Company (Hanoi), 122
Adventure and wellness trips, 43–45
AIDS, 31, 378
Air quality, 32
Air travel
Buon Ma Thuot, 250
Cambodia, 378–379, 384
Siem Reap, 408
Dalat, 236
Danang, 206
Dien Bien Phu, 149
environmentally friendly, 42
Hanoi, 67
Ho Chi Minh City, 294
Hue, 186
Nha Trang, 268
Phu Quoc, 361–362
Quy Nhon, 262
to Vietnam, 23–24
within Vietnam, 24–25
Alexandre Yersin Museum (Nha Trang), 279
Allez Boo (Ho Chi Minh City), 333
Alphana Jewelry (Ho Chi Minh City), 332
Amazing Internet (Hanoi), 75
Amber Room (Ho Chi Minh City), 333
Ambre (Phnom Penh), 397
American Express, Phnom Penh, 386
American Foundation for the Blind (AFB), 37
Ana Mandara (Nha Trang), 282
Anam QT Spa (Ho Chi Minh City), 329
Angkor Hospital for Children (Siem Reap), 406
Angkor National Museum (Siem Reap), 432
Angkor Thom (Cambodia), 425
Angkor Thom Gates (Cambodia), 425
Angkor Village (Cambodia), 435
Angkor Wat (Cambodia), 368, 405–406, 424–429
restaurants, 421–422
shopping, 432–434
Angkor What? (Siem Reap), 436
Annam (Ho Chi Minh City), 331
Ann Tours, 68, 297, 349
An Phu Tourist, 188, 207, 208, 212, 239, 271
An Phu Tours (Hanoi), 70–71
An Thoi, 366
An Thoi Archipelago, 366
Antiques
Hanoi, 117
regulations, 117
A-1 Hill (Dien Bien Phu), 150
Apocalypse Now (Hanoi), 123
Apricot Gallery
Hanoi, 120
Ho Chi Minh City, 329
Apsara dance (Cambodia), 435
Apsara Faces (Cambodia), 425–426
Area codes, 441
Army Museum (Hanoi), 108
Art galleries
Hanoi, 120–121
Ho Chi Minh City, 329–330
Phnom Penh, 397
Artista Cafe (Dalat), 245
Art Suriya Travel (Phnom Penh), 400
Art Vietnam (Hanoi), 120
Asasax Art Gallery (Phnom Penh), 397
Asiana Travel Mate (Hanoi), 69

Asia Transpacific Journeys, 43, 46, 375
ATMs (automated-teller machines), 27
Hanoi, 74
Australia
customs regulations, 23
embassy of
in Cambodia, 378
in Vietnam, 75
passports, 443
visas, 445
Authentique Interiors (Ho Chi Minh City), 332
Avian influenza (bird flu), 32
Avis Rent a Car, 38
A-Z Queen Salute Café Travel (Hanoi), 69, 75

Ba Be Lake, 152–153
Ba Be National Park, 153
Ba Be Street (Hanoi), 121
Bacchus Corner (Ho Chi Minh City), 331
Bac Ha Market (Sapa), 139–140
Bach Dang (Ho Chi Minh City), 319
Bach Ma National Park, 203–205
Bach Ma Temple (Hanoi), 107
Backroads, 46
Ba Dinh District (Hanoi), 71, 108–110
Ba Hung (Halong Bay), 167
Bai Chay (Halong City), 162
Bai Dat Doc, 341
Bai Sau (Crocodile Lake), 347–348
Ba Island, 346
Bai Tu Long Bay, 164
Bakeng Hill (Cambodia), 424–425
Bamboo Forest (Truc Lam) Zen Monastery (Dalat), 249
Bambou Company
Hoi An, 230
Hue, 194
Nha Trang, 282
Ban Don, 254
Ban Gioc waterfalls, 154–155
Banks and ATMs
Buon Ma Thuot, 251
Cambodia, 376
Siem Reap, 410
Sihanoukville, 402
Can Tho, 354, 358
Cao Bang, 154
Dalat, 239
Danang, 208
Dien Bien Phu, 149
Haiphong, 158
Halong City, 162
Hanoi, 74
Ho Chi Minh City, 298
Hoi An, 212–213
Hue, 188
Kontum, 257
Lang Son, 155
Nha Trang, 271
Phan Thiet, 285–286
Phnom Penh, 386
Phu Quoc, 363
Quy Nhon, 264
Sapa, 136
Son La, 146
Vung Tau, 336
Ban Lac, 143
Banteay Kdei (Cambodia), 429
Banteay Srei (Cambodia), 430
Bao Dai's Palace (Dalat), 246
Bao Khan Street (Hanoi), 122, 124–125
Bao Quoc (Hue), 198
Baphuon (Cambodia), 426
Barbara's Backpackers (Quy Nhon), 264
Bat Dan Street (Hanoi), 104
Battambang (Cambodia), 436–440
Bat Trang, 127
The Bayon (Cambodia), 425
Bazar (Phnom Penh), 397
Beaches. ***See also specific beaches***
best, 3
Cat Co, 171–172
Nha Trang, 280
Beng Melea (Cambodia), 430
Ben Thanh Market (Ho Chi Minh City), 318–319, 321
Beyond (Angkor), 433
B-52, Downed (Hanoi), 109
Bia hoi **stands**
Hanoi, 124–126
Ho Chi Minh City, 335
Bich Dong Temple (near Ninh Binh), 176
Biking
Can Tho, 354
Hanoi, 74, 115
Ho Chi Minh City, 296
Siem Reap, 409
Binh Chau Hotsprings (near Vung Tau), 340
Binh Dinh Museum (Quy Nhon), 266
Binh Tay Market (Ho Chi Minh City), 326
Bird flu (avian influenza), 32
Bird-watching
Cat Ba Island, 171
Cat Tien National Park, 347
Bliss (Phnom Penh), 397
Bliss Spa (Phnom Penh), 398
Blue Diving Club (Nha Trang), 281
Boat-building operation (Quy Nhon), 266
Boat travel and cruises, 24
Cambodia, 378–380
Battambang, 438
Siem Reap, 408
Can Tho, 354, 358
Cat Ba Island, 167–168
Con Dao Archipelago, 342
Haiphong, 158
Halong Bay, 164–166
Ho Chi Minh City, 296, 333
Mekong Delta, 356
Nha Trang, 281–282
Phnom Penh, 384, 386
Phu Quoc, 362, 366
Vung Tau, 336
Body Tune Spa (Siem Reap), 434
Bokor Mountain, 399
Bonsai Cruise (Ho Chi Minh City), 333
Bookstores
Hanoi, 121–122
Ho Chi Minh City, 330
Bookworm (Hanoi), 121
Boom Boom Room (Phnom Penh), 397
Bridge of the Rising Sun (Hanoi), 103, 111
Brown Eyes (Hue), 194
Bru people, 235
Buddha Lounge (Siem Reap), 436
Buffalo Tours, 44, 68, 126, 135, 166, 173, 350
Bunker of Colonel Christian De Castries (Dien Bien Phu), 150
Buon Ma Thuot, 249–255
Business hours, 441
Bus travel
Cambodia, 380, 386
Battambang, 437
Siem Reap, 408
Sihanoukville, 402
Can Tho, 358
Dalat, 236, 238
Danang, 207
Haiphong, 158
Hanoi, 68
Ho Chi Minh City, 295

Bus travel *(cont.)*
Hue, 186
Nha Trang, 270
Phan Thiet, 285
Quy Nhon, 262
Sapa, 135
within Vietnam, 25–26
But Thap Pagoda, 127

Café Central (Ho Chi Minh City), 319
Café Galy (Dalat), 245
Cafe Latin (Ho Chi Minh City), 333
Café l'Opera (Ho Chi Minh City), 320
Cafe 333 (Ho Chi Minh City), 320
Cage (Ho Chi Minh City), 333–334
Cai Be Floating Market (My Tho), 353
Cai Rang Floating Market (near Chau Doc), 352, 356–357
Calendar of events, 19–21
Cambodia, 368–440
accommodations, 380–381
business hours, 381
crime, 381
cuisine, 373
customs regulations, 375
drug laws, 381
electricity, 382
emergencies, 382
entry requirements, 375
etiquette, 372–373
foreign embassies in, 378
getting around, 379–380
health concerns and vaccinations, 377–378
history of, 370
hospitals, 382
Internet access, 382
Khmer people, 372
language, 373–374
lay of the land, 369–370
planning your trip to, 374–383
police, 382
post office, 382
publications, 382
restaurants, 381
safety, 377
shopping, 381
southern, 399–405
suggested itinerary, 63–64
telephone, 382, 383
toilets, 382
tour operators, 374–375
traveling to, 378
visitor information, 374
Cambodia Cultural Center (Siem Reap), 435
Camp Fuller and the Rockpile, 201
Cam Ranh Airport (Nha Trang), 268
Cam Ranh Bay, 283
Canada
customs regulations, 23
embassy of
Cambodia, 378
Vietnam, 75
passports, 443
visas, 445
Can Gio Island, 327
Can Tho, 353–357
Can Tho Tourist Company, 354
Cantonese Assembly Hall (Quang Trieu/Guangzhou Assembly Hall; Hoi An), 226
Cao Bang, 153–155
Cao Dai Holy *See* Temple (near Ho Chi Minh City), 327–328
Cao Dai sect, 210
Cao Dai Temple (Danang), 210
Capitol Guesthouse Tours (Phnom Penh), 384
Capitol Tour (Cambodia), 375, 379, 380, 408, 437
Carnets d'Asie (Angkor), 433
Car travel
Buon Ma Thuot, 250
Cambodia, 380
Sihanoukville, 402
Can Tho, 353
Cat Tien National Park, 348
Dalat, 236, 238
Danang, 207
Hanoi, 72
Ho Chi Minh City, 295
North-Central Vietnam, 173
Phan Thiet, 285
Sapa, 135
to Vietnam, 24
within Vietnam, 25
Cat Ba Island, 167–172
Cat Ba National Park, 170–171
Cat Cat Village (Sapa), 140
Cat Co beaches, 171–172
Cathedral of Saint Joseph (Phat Diem), 179
Catherine Denoual-Maison (Ho Chi Minh City), 332
Cat Tien National Park, 346–349
Cau Lac Bo Nhac Jazz Club (Hanoi), 126
Cave of Stakes (Do Go; Halong Bay), 166
Cave of the Prehistoric Man (Cuc Phuong National Park), 178
Caves, Marble Mountains, 211
Cellphones, 48–49
Centers for Disease Control and Prevention, 27
Central Circus (Hanoi), 123
Central Coast, 18
Central Highlands, 18, 232–260
ethnic minority hilltribes, 234–235
Central Market
Hoi An, 227
Phnom Penh, 395
Central Vietnam, 184–231
brief description of, 53–54
Cha Ca Street (Hanoi), 106
Cham Island, 228
The Cham Museum (Danang), 210–211
ChamPa (Hoi An), 231
Cham people, 206, 228
Cham Tower (near Phan Thiet), 290
Chapel of St. Pierre (Phat Diem), 179
Charlie Hill, 259
Cha Tam (Ho Chi Minh City), 326
Chau Doc, 357–360
Chicken Village (Lat Village; near Dalat), 248
Children, families with, 38–39
Chi Linh Star Golf and Country Club (near Hanoi), 115
China
embassy of, 75
Lao Cai as gateway to, 132
China Beach, 206
accommodations, 213–214
Chinese people in Vietnam, 8
Chinese rule in Vietnam, 10–11
Cho 19-12 (19-12 Market; Hanoi), 122
Cho Da Lat (Dalat Market), 246

Choeung Ek Memorial (Phnom Penh), 395
Cholera, 30
Cholon ("Chinatown" of Ho Chi Minh City), 325–326
Cho Ra Town, 152–153
Chow (Phnom Penh), 398
Christmas, 21–22
Chua Phap Hoa (near Vung Tau), 340
Chua Quan Am Temple (Ho Chi Minh City), 326
Chuong Vang Theater (Hanoi), 107
Church Street (Nha Tho; Hanoi), 125
Cinemas, Hanoi, 124
The Citadel & Imperial City (Hue), 195–199
City Hall (Ho Chi Minh City), 321
Climate
- Cambodia, 376
- Vietnam, 18–19

Clothing. *See also* Silk fabrics and clothing
- Ho Chi Minh City, 330–331
- packing tips, 20

Coc Ly Market (Sapa), 140
Colors of Cambodia (Siem Reap), 433
Co Luong Communal House (Hanoi), 107
Communal houses (Hanoi), 101, 104, 106, 107
Communist Party, Anniversary of the Founding of the, 20
Con Dao Archipelago, 340–346
Con Dao Museum, 344
Con Dao National Park, 346
Connection kit, 49
Con Son Island, 340–346
Cooking classes, Hoi An, 230
Council Travel, 41
Country codes, 383
Craft Link (Hanoi), 116
Crazy Kim Bar (Nha Trang), 282
Credit cards, Cambodia, 376
Crocodile Lake (Bai Sau), 347–348
Cua Dai Beach, 228
- accommodations, 218–220

Cua Lo Beach (Vinh), 179, 183
Cua Ngo Mon (The Noon Gate; Hue), 196
Cu Chi Tunnels, 328
Cuc Phuong National Park, 127, 177
Cuc Phuong National Park Endangered Primate Resource Center, 177
Cuisine, 90
- Cambodia, 373
- snake meat, 99

Culture of Vietnam. *See* History and culture of Vietnam
Currency and currency exchange. *See also* Banks and currency exchange
- Cambodia, 376
- Vietnam, 26–27

Customs regulations
- Cambodia, 375
- Vietnam, 23

Cyclos, Hanoi, 73

Dakbla River, 256
Daklak Tourist, 250, 251
Dakrong Bridge, 200, 201
Dak To, 259
Dalat, 232–249
- accommodations, 240–243
- attractions, 245
- cafes, 245
- getting around, 236, 238–239
- post office, 240
- restaurants, 243–245
- telephone, 240
- traveling to, 236
- visitor information & tours, 239

Dalat Market (Cho Da Lat), 246
Dalat Railway Station (Cremaillaire Railway), 246
Dalattourist, 239
Damsan Tourist (Buon Ma Thuot), 250
Damsan Tours (Buon Ma Thuot), 251
Danang, 205–211
Dao Duy Tu Street (Hanoi), 106
Dao people, Sapa, 140–141
Dao (Zao) people, 131
Da River (Song Da) Reservoir, 142, 146
Dead Fish Tower (Siem Reap), 436
DEET insect repellent, 28
Delta Adventure Tours (Ho Chi Minh City), 350
Delta Deco (Hanoi), 117
Demilitarized Zone (DMZ), 199–202
Dengue fever, 29, 378
Diamond Department Store (Ho Chi Minh City), 331
Dien Bien Phu, 148–150
Dien Bien Phu Cemetery, 150
Dien Bien Phu loop, 141–152
Dien Bien Phu Museum, 150
Dietary red flags, 30–31
Diethelm Travel, 46, 375, 384, 386, 409
Disabilities, travelers with, 37–38
Discrimination, dealing with, 36
Diving
- Con Dao Archipelago, 341, 345
- Nha Trang, 280–281
- Phu Quoc, 367

DMZ (Demilitarized Zone), 199–202
DMZ Café (Hue), 194
Doc Let Beach, 283
Do Go (Cave of Stakes; Halong Bay), 166
Dom Dek (Cambodia), 430
Dong Da District (Hanoi), 71, 110–111, 155
Dong Da River Valley, 151
Dong Duong (Comtoir De L'Indochine; Ho Chi Minh City), 332
Dong Ha, 200
Dong Khoi (Ho Chi Minh City), 329
Dong Kinh Nghia Thuc Square (Tonkin Free School Movement Sq.; Hanoi), 103, 108
Dong Nai River, 347
Dong Son culture, 11
Dong Xuan Market (Hanoi), 122
Do Son Buffalo Fighting Festival (near Haiphong), 21
Dragon's Pearl, 166
Dray Sap and Gia Long Waterfalls, 253–254
Dr. Beat (Beatocello) Richner (Siem Reap), 435
Drinking laws, 441
Drug laws, Cambodia, 381
Drugs, Cambodia, 377
Drum and Virgin Cave (Halong Bay), 166–167
Duong Dong Beach, 365

E **asy Riders (Dalat), 44–45, 238–239**
Easy Speaking Café and Pub (Siem Reap), 436
E-Café (Siem Reap), 410
EcoAdventures (Sihanoukville), 405
Ecotourism, 41–43
Halong Bay, 164
Mekong Delta, 350
Eco-Trek Tours Cambodia (Sihanoukville), 405
Ede people, 235
Ede Village, 253
Elderhostel, 40
ElderTreks, 40
Electricity
Cambodia, 382
Vietnam, 441
The Elephant Terrace (Cambodia), 428
Embassies and consulates, 75, 441
***The Emeraude,* 165**
Emergencies, 442
Cambodia, 382
Emperor Jade Pagoda (Phuoc Hai; Ho Chi Minh City), 324
Encephalitis, Japanese, 29, 378
Entry requirements
Cambodia, 375
Vietnam, 22–23
Escorted general-interest tours, 46–48
Eté (Hanoi), 125
Ethnic Hilltribe Museum (Kontum), 259
Ethnic minorities. *See* Hilltribes
The Ethnographic Museum (Buon Ma Thuot), 252
ET Pumpkin Tours, 69, 128
European buildings (Hanoi), 101
European Health Insurance Card (EHIC), 33
European Union, embassy of, 75
Exhibition of the Resistance Against the American Invader (Hue), 196
Exotissimo, 46–47, 68, 297, 350, 375, 384, 409
Extreme weather exposure, 32–33

F **amilies with children, 38–39**
Fansipan, Mount, 134
Ferries. *See* Boat travel and cruises
Festival at the Perfume Pagoda (near Hanoi), 20
Festivals and special events, 19–21
54 Traditions Gallery (Hanoi), 120
Five Lakes Trail, 204
The Flag Tower (Hue), 195
Floating villages, 359–360
Flying Wheels Travel, 38
Flying with Disability, 38
Food and wine trips, 45
The Forbidden Purple City (Hue), 195
Frangipani (Siem Reap), 434
French colonial rule, 13–14
The French Quarter (Dalat), 246–247
Friends of Vietnam Heritage, 70
Fukian Assembly Hall (Phuc Kien; Hoi An), 226–227
Funky Monkey (Hanoi), 125

G **alerie Lotus (Ho Chi Minh City), 329**
Galerie Royal (Hanoi), 118
Gan Dau, 366
Gaya (Ho Chi Minh City), 330
Gays and lesbians, 36–37
Ghenh Rang Landscape Park (Quy Nhon), 266
Giac Lam Pagoda (Ho Chi Minh City), 326–327
Giai Dieu (Hanoi), 117
Gia Long Waterfalls, 253, 254
Gio To Hung Vuong, 20–21
Global Spectrum, 45
Golf
Hanoi, 115
Ho Chi Minh City, 328
Phan Thiet, 290
Vung Tau, 338
Go2 Bar (Ho Chi Minh City), 334
Gougah Falls (Dalat), 248
Gourmand Shop (Hanoi), 123
Green travel, 41–43
Green Vespa (Phnom Penh), 398
Groove Shack (Nha Trang), 282
Groovy Gecko Tours (Dalat), 239
Guava (Nha Trang), 282

H **ahn's Green Hat Boat Tour (Nha Trang), 281**
Hai Ba Trung District (Hanoi), 71
Haiphong, 157–161
Hai Scout Cafe (Hoi An), 231
Hai Van Pass, 202–203
Halong Bay, 126, 163–167
Halong City, 161–163
***Halong Ginger,* 164–165**
Hamburger Hill, 201
Handspan Travel, 44, 68–69, 97, 135, 166
Hang Bac Street (Hanoi), 107
Hang Buom Street (Hanoi), 107
Hang Chieu (Hanoi), 106
Hang Da Market (Hanoi), 104
Hang Dao (Hanoi), 108
Hang Dau Street (Hanoi), 118
Hang Dieu Street (Hanoi), 104
Hang Duong Street (Hanoi), 106
Hang Gai Street (Hanoi), 103–104
Hang Nga Guest House and Art Gallery (Dalat), 247
Hang Phen Street (Hanoi), 104
Hang Thiec Street (Hanoi), 101
Hang Vai (Hanoi), 101, 104, 106
Hanh Hung (Hoi An), 230
Hanoi, 65–127
accommodations, 77–88
banks and currency exchange, 74
business hours, 74
climate, 74
day trips from, 126–127
doctors and hospitals, 74–75
embassies and consulates, 75
exploring, 100–114
founding of, 66
getting around, 72–74
layout of, 71
medical services, 442
neighborhoods, 71
newspapers and magazines, 76

nightlife, 123–126
outdoor activities and other fitness pursuits, 114–115
pharmacies, 76
police, 76
post office, 76–77
restaurants, 88–100
safety, 77
shopping, 116–123
snacks and cafes, 97–100
spas and fitness, 115
telephone, 77
traveling to, 67–68
visitor information and tours, 68–71
Hanoi Art Contemporary Gallery, 121
Hanoi Cinematique, 124
Hanoi Cooking Centre, 45
Hanoi Family Medical Practice, 75
Hanoi French Hospital, 75
Hanoi Gallery, 120
Hanoi Hilton (Hoa Lo Prison; Hanoi), 111
Hanoi Language and Culture Tours, 43
Hanoi Moment, 117
Hanoi Opera House, 111, 123
Hanoi Railway Station, 67
Hanoi Silk, 116
Hanoi Traditional Opera, 123
Hash House Harriers (Hanoi), 124
Health concerns
Cambodia, 377
Vietnam, 27–33
Hepatitis, 29–30, 378
Hidden Hanoi, 69
Highland Coffee (Ho Chi Minh City), 320
Highlands Tour (Nha Trang), 271
Highway 4 (Hanoi), 125
Hiking
Bach Ma National Park, 203–204
Con Dao National Park, 346
Cuc Phuong National Park, 177–178
Sapa, 140
Hilltribes (ethnic minorities), 38–39
Cao Bang area, 154
Central Highlands, 234–235
Kontum area, 259, 260
in northern Vietnam, 130–131
Sapa, 140–141
Seminary and Ethnic Hilltribe Museum (Kontum), 259
Historical Museum (Buon Ma Thuot), 253
History and culture
Cambodia, 370–372
Vietnam, 7–17
HIV, 30
Hmong, 131
Hmong people, Sapa, 140–141
Hmong Spring Festival, 20
Hoa Binh, 142
Hoa Binh Noodle Shop (Ho Chi Minh City), 324
Hoa Lo Prison (Hanoi Hilton; Hanoi), 111
Hoa Lu, 127, 176
Hoang Silk (Ho Chi Minh City), 332–333
Hoang Tru Village, 182–183
Hoan Kiem District (Hanoi), 71, 111
Hoan Kiem Lake (Hanoi), 103, 111–112, 114–115
Ho Chi Minh, 13
biographical sketch of, 180–181
birthday of, 21
Hoang Tru Village, 182–183
home in Hue, 199
Kim Lien Village, 183
mausoleum (Hanoi), 108–109
museum
Hanoi, 108
Ho Chi Minh City, 322
Hue, 199
Pac Bo (Ho Chi Minh's Hide-Out), 155
residence (Hanoi), 109
statue of (Vinh), 182
Ho Chi Minh City (Saigon), 291–348
accommodations, 300–313
banks and currency exchange, 298
budget tourist cafes, 298
consulates, 299
day trips from, 327–328
dentists, 298
districts of, 297
emergencies, 299
exploring, 320–327
getting around, 296
hospitals and clinics, 299
Internet access, 299
medical services, 442
nightlife, 333
post office, 299
restaurants, 313–320
safety, 299–300
shopping, 329–333
side trips from, 335–348
snacks and cafes, 318–320
spa and massage facilities, 329
telephone, 300
toilets, 300
traveling to, 294–296
visitor information & tours, 297–298
Ho Chi Minh City Campaign Museum, 323–324
Ho Chi Minh City Museum, 321–322
The Ho Chi Minh Fine Arts Museum (Ho Chi Minh City), 329–330
Ho Chi Minh Municipal Theater (Saigon Opera House), 323
Ho Chi Minh Trail, 201
Kontum area, 259–260
Ho Chi Minh Trail Museum (Hanoi), 114
Hoi An, 211–231
accommodations, 213–220
attractions, 224–228
banks and currency exchange, 212–213
cooking courses, 230
excursion to My Son, 228–229
getting around, 212
Internet access, 213
nightlife, 231
post office, 213
restaurants, 220–224
shopping, 229–230
telephone, 213
traveling to, 212
visitor information & tours, 212
Hoi An Cathedral, 227
Hoi An Cloth Market, 229
Hoi An Tourist Guiding Office, 212
Hoi An Tourist Service Company, 212
Holidays, 442
Cambodia, 376
Hong Gai (Halong City), 162
Hong Hoa (Hanoi), 117
Hospital Cave, 172

Hospitals
Cambodia, 382
Vietnam, 442
Ho Than Tho (Lake of Sighs), 247
House of Hoi An Traditional Handicraft, 227–228
Hue, 184–199
accommodations, 188–192
attractions, 195–199
cafes, bars & nightlife, 194
getting around, 186, 188
Internet access, 188
post office, 188
restaurants, 192–194
shopping, 194
telephone, 188
traveling to, 186
visitor information & tours, 188
Hue Festival, 189
Hue Monuments Conservation Center, 196
Hung Long Art Gallery (Hoi An), 230
Hun Tiep Lake (Hanoi), 109
Huong Giang Tourist Company (Hue), 188
Huong Nghia Communal House (Hanoi), 106
Huong Tuong Communal House (Hanoi), 107

I Love Vietnam (Hanoi), 69
Imaginative Traveller, 47
Imperial City (Hue), 195–199
Independence Day (Cambodia), 376
Independence Monument (Phnom Penh), 395
India, embassy of, 75
Indigo (Sapa), 141
Indochina Corner, 260
Infostones (Hanoi), 122
In Style (Phnom Penh), 398
Insurance, 442
International Association for Medical Assistance to Travelers (IAMAT), 27–28
International Gay and Lesbian Travel Association (IGLTA), 37
International Labor Day, 21
International SOS (Hanoi), 74
International Student Identity Card (ISIC), 41
International Youth Travel Card (IYTC), 41
Internet access, 49, 442
Cambodia, 382
Intimex (Hanoi), 122
Intrepid, 46, 47
Ipa Nima (Ho Chi Minh City), 330–331
Ipa Nima and Tina Sparkle (Hanoi), 118–119
Ireland
passports, 443
visas, 445
Island Massage (Phnom Penh), 398
Islands of the Hon Mun Marine Park, 280–281
Islands Traditional Khmer Massage (Siem Reap), 435
Itineraries, suggested, 54–64
Cambodia, 63–64
in 14 days, 59–61
by motorcycle or jeep, 62–63
UNESCO World Heritage Sites, 61–62
Ivy Bar (Siem Reap), 436

Japan, embassy of, 75
Japanese Covered Bridge (Hoi An), 227
Japanese encephalitis, 29, 378
Jarai people, 235
Jasmine (Ho Chi Minh City), 329
Java Café and Gallery (Phnom Penh), 394
Jaya Bot Mohania (Cambodia), 426
Jean Lou Coiffure De Paris (Nha Trang), 282
Jeremy Stein's Rainbow Divers (Nha Trang), 281
***Jewel of the Bay,* 165–166**
Jibe's (Phan Thiet), 290
John McDermott Photography (Siem Reap), 433
Jungle Beach, 283
Jun Village, 254

Kabal Spean (Cambodia), 431
Kampong Phluk (Cambodia), 431
Kampot, 399–401
Kangaroo Cafe (Hanoi), 69
Kantha Bopha Foundation (Siem Reap), 435
Kantha Bopha Hospital (Siem Reap), 406
Karl Marx Mountain, 155
Karst, in Halong, 164
Kayaking, 164
Kenh Ga, 127, 176–177
Kenly Silk (Ho Chi Minh City), 333
Kep, 399–401
Khai Dinh's Tomb (Hue), 197
Khai Silk (Hanoi), 116
Khai Silk (Ho Chi Minh City), 333
Khem Beach, 366–367
Khe San, 201–202
Khmer New Year (Cambodia), 376
Khmer people, 372
Kids, 38–39
Kien-Giang Tourist (Phu Quoc), 362
The Killing Fields (Phnom Penh), 395
Kim Giao Forest, 171
Kim Giao Peak, 171
Kim Lien Village, 183
King Sihanouk's Birthday (Cambodia), 376
King's Island Golf Resort and Country Club (near Hanoi), 115
Koh Ker (Cambodia), 431
Konica Digital Photo Center (Hanoi), 122
Konkoitu, 260
Kontum, 255–260
Kontum Tourist, 257
***Krama,* 380**
K.U. Travel and Tours (Phnom Penh), 384

La Bella (Ho Chi Minh City), 331
Labor Day, International, 21
La Casa (Hanoi), 117
La Cave (Hanoi), 123
Lady Phi Yen, 341
Lady Phi Yen Temple (Con Son), 344
La Fenêtre Soleil (Ho Chi Minh City), 320
Lai Chau, 151
Lake of Sighs (Ho Than Tho), 247
Lak Lake, 254
La Louisiane (Nha Trang), 280–282

Lam Ty Ni Pagoda (Home of Thay Vien Thuc; Dalat), 247–248
Land Mines Museum (Cambodia), 431
Lang Co Beach, 204–205
Lang Hai, 339–340
Lang Son, 155–156
Language
- Cambodia, 373–374
- Vietnam, 442

Lan Ong Street (Hanoi), 106
Lao Cai, 128–132
Laos
- embassy of, 75
- traveling to Vietnam from, 24

L'Apothiquaire (Ho Chi Minh City), 329
La Salsa (Hanoi), 125
Lat Village (Chicken Village; near Dalat), 248
Laundry (Siem Reap), 436
Legal aid, 442
Legend of the Lake of the Recovered Sword (Hanoi), 111
Legise de Pierre (Stone Chapel; Phat Diem), 179
Le Lezard Bleu (Phnom Penh), 397
Le Mat ("Snake Village"), 99
Lenin River, 155
Le Pub (Hanoi), 125
Les Epices (Ho Chi Minh City), 332
Level 23 (Ho Chi Minh City), 334
Lien Khuong Airport (Dalat), 236
Life Photo Gallery (Hanoi), 121
Linga (Siem Reap), 436
Ling Ong Pagoda (near Danang), 211
Linh Phuoc Pagoda (Dalat), 248
Littering, 35
Long Beach, 363–365
Long Son Pagoda (Nha Trang), 279
Louisiane (Nha Trang), 278
Love Planet Tours and Books (Hanoi), 121
Lucky! Lucky! (Phnom Penh), 386
Lucky Market (Phnom Penh), 397
Lunar New Year Festival (Tet Nguyen Dan), 20
Ly Dynasty (Hanoi), 123

McDermott, John, 433
Mai Chau, 142–145, 148
Mai Gallery (Hanoi), 120
Mail, 442–443
Malaria, 28–29, 377–378
Malaysia, embassy of, 75
Ma May Street (Hanoi), 107
Mango Rooms (Hoi An), 231
Maps, Hanoi, 76
Marble Mountains, 207, 211
Markets
- Cao Bang area, 154
- Hanoi, 122
- Hoi An, 227
- Phnom Penh, 395, 397
- Sapa, 139–140

Mavena Hanoi, 116
MC Decoration (Ho Chi Minh City), 332
Medical services, 442
MedjetAssist, 33
Mekong Delta, 349–367
- typical itineraries, 350, 352
- visitor information and tours, 349–350, 352

Mekong Express Tours, 358, 380, 384, 386, 402, 408, 409
Metropole Hotel (Hanoi), 115
Mid-Autumn Festival, 21
Mieu Island, 281–282
Mi Indochine (Ho Chi Minh City), 331
Minh Dam, 340
Minh Mang, Tomb of (Hue), 197
Mirror Mirror (Hanoi), 119
Miss Vy's School of Cooking (Hoi An), 230
M'Lieng Village, 254–255
M'nong people, 235
M'nong-style jugs of whiskey, 255
Mobility-Advisor.com, 38
Mobiphone, 48
Mojo (Ho Chi Minh City), 320
Molly Malone's (Siem Reap), 436
Money and costs, 26–27
- Cambodia, 376

Monsoon seasons, 18
Monument Books (Angkor), 433
Monument Books (Phnom Penh), 398
Morning Glory Restaurant and Cooking School, 45
Mosaique (Hanoi), 119
Mosquitoes, 28–29
MossRehab, 37
Mot Island, 281
Motorcycle taxis
- Cambodia
  - Siem Reap, 408–409
  - Sihanoukville, 402
- Danang, 208
- Hanoi, 73
- Ho Chi Minh City, 296
- Phan Thiet, 285
- Phnom Penh, 386
- Quy Nhon, 262

Motorcycle travel and rentals, 144–145
- Buon Ma Thuot, 250–251
- Cambodia, 380
  - Siem Reap, 409
- Dalat, 238–239
- Hanoi, 73, 144–145
- Ho Chi Minh City, 296
- Hue, 188
- Kampot, 400
- packing tips, 145
- safety, 145
- suggested itinerary, 62–63

Mr. Cuong's Motorbike Adventure (Hanoi), 73, 144
Mr. Hung's Vietnam Adventure Tour
- Hanoi, 73
- Mai Chau, 144–145

Mui Ne Sailing Club (Phan Thiet), 290
Mun Island, 281
Muong people, 131
Museum of History and Culture (Hoi An), 225
Museum of Trade Ceramics (Hoi An), 225
Museums, best, 3
Myanmar, embassy of, 75
My Khe Beach, 206
- accommodations, 210

My Lai, 267
My Lai Massacre, 267
My Son, 228–229
My Tho, 353

Nagu (Hanoi), 119
Nam Nguyen, 255
National Day, 21
National Museum (Phnom Penh), 395–396

National Museum of Vietnamese History (Hanoi), 112
National Oceanographic Museum of Vietnam (Nha Trang), 279
Neak Krorhorm Travel and Tour (Cambodia), 384, 408, 409, 437
New Collection: Hoa Sua Embroidery and Sewing Showroom (Hanoi), 116
New Market (Siem Reap), 433
Newspapers and magazines
- Cambodia, 382
- Vietnam, 443
  - Hanoi, 76

New Year's Day, 20
New Zealand
- customs regulations, 23
- embassy of, 75
- passports, 443
- visas, 445

Ngoc Son pagoda (Hanoi), 103, 111
Nguom Ngao Cave, 155
Nguyen Cau Digital Camera Lab (Hanoi), 122
Nguyen dynasty, 65, 186, 196, 197, 323
Nguyen Hue, 261
Nguyen Hue Plaza (Ho Chi Minh City), 321
Nguyen Sieu Street (Hanoi), 107
Nha Tho (Church Street; Hanoi), 125
Nha Tho Street (Hanoi), 117, 118
Nha Trang, 268–283
- accommodations, 271–276
- attractions, 279–280
- banks and currency exchange, 271
- cafes, 278
- crime in, 270
- getting around, 270–271
- nightlife, 282–283
- post office and mail, 271
- restaurants, 276–278
- shopping, 282
- side trips and overnights from, 283
- telephone, 271
- traveling to, 268, 270
- visitor information & tours, 270–271

Nha Trang Sailing Club, 280–283
Nha Tu Phu Quoc, 366
Nightlife
- Hanoi, 123–126
- Hoi An, 231
- Hue, 194

Nine Dynastic Urns (Hue), 196–197
19-12 Market (Cho 19-12; Hanoi), 122
Ninh Binh, 173–179
Ninh Binh area, 127
Noi Bai International Airport (Hanoi), 67
The Noon Gate (Cua Ngo Mon; Hue), 196
North-Central Vietnam, 173–183
Northeastern coast, 157–172
Northeastern highlands loop, 152–156
The northern highlands, 128–156
Northern Vietnam, 18
- brief description of, 53
- hilltribes, 130–131

Notre Dame Cathedral (Ho Chi Minh City), 322
Nui Ba Den, 328
Nung people, 131

O'Briens (Ho Chi Minh City), 334
Ocean Dunes Golf Course (Phan Thiet), 290
Off-road adventures, 44–45
The Old House of Phun Hung (Hoi An), 225
The Old House of Tan Ky (Hoi An), 225–226
Old Quarter (Hanoi), 71
- nightlife, 124
- sights and attractions, 100–114
- street name translations of Old Quarter trades, 102
- walking tour, 103–108

Old Wooden Church and Orphanage (Kontum), 258–259
One-Pillar Pagoda (Hanoi), 109
163 Cyclo Bar (Ho Chi Minh City), 334
Ong Lang, 366
Ong Lang Beach, 365
"Open tours," 26, 70
Oriental Gallery (Hanoi), 121
Orient Gallery (Hanoi), 121
Osmose (Cambodia), 409, 432
Oudong (Cambodia), 398
Outdoor activities, best, 3–4

Pac Bo (Ho Chi Minh's Hide-Out), 155
Pac Bo Caves, 154
Pacharan (Ho Chi Minh City), 334
Packing tips, 20
- motorcycle travel, 145

Pak Kaw, 153
Paradise Ocean Noon Golf Club (Vung Tau), 338
Parasailing, 282
Paris Peace Accords, 16
Particular Art Gallery (Ho Chi Minh City), 329
Pa So, 151, 152
Passports, 22, 443
Peace Cafe (Dalat), 238, 239, 245
Perfume Pagoda (near Hanoi), 127
- Festival at the, 20

Perfume River, 186
Petro Express (Vung Tau), 336
Phan Thiet, 285–290
Phat Diem, 127, 178
Phat Tire Ventures, 44, 58, 239
The Philippines, embassy of, 75
Phnom Chisor (Cambodia), 398
Phnom Penh (Cambodia), 383–399
- accommodations, 387–390
- attractions, 395
- clinics, 387
- day trips from, 398–399
- emergencies, 387
- getting around, 386
- Internet access, 387
- nightlife, 398
- post office, 387
- restaurants, 390–394
- shopping and galleries, 397–398
- snacks and cafes, 394
- spa services, 398
- telephone, 387
- traveling to, 384, 386
- visitor information and tours, 384

Phnom Penh International Airport, 378
Phong Nha-Ke Bang National Park, 183
Phsar Chas Netweb (Siem Reap), 410
Phuc Kien (Fukian Assembly Hall; Hoi An), 226–227
Phung Hung Street (Hanoi), 104
Phuoc Hai (Emperor Jade Pagoda; Ho Chi Minh City), 324
Phu Quoc Island, 350, 352, 360–367
Phu Quoc Pearl Farm, 366
Phu Quoc Ridgeback, 361
Planning your trip
- to Cambodia, 374–383
- to Vietnam, 18–51
  - accommodations, 49–51
  - calendar of events, 19–21
  - customs regulations, 23
  - entry requirements, 22–23
  - escorted general-interest tours, 46–48
  - getting around, 24–26
  - health concerns, 27–33
  - money and costs, 26–27
  - packing tips, 20
  - safety concerns, 33–36
  - special-interest trips, 43–45
  - specialized travel resources, 36–41
  - staying connected, 48–49
  - sustainable tourism, 41–43
  - traveling to Vietnam, 23–24
  - when to go, 18–19

Pleiku, 255–260
Police, 443
Polite Pub (Hanoi), 125
Pol Pot, 372
Pom Coong, 143
Pomten's Bar (Hue), 194
Po Ngar Cham Towers (Nha Trang), 280
Pongour Falls (Dalat), 248
Poretti, Pier, 433
Preah Khan (Cambodia), 428–429
Preak Toal (Cambodia), 431
Prenn Falls (Dalat), 248
Pre Rup (Cambodia), 426
Prescription medications, 33
Press Club (Hanoi), 125
Psar Chas, the Old Market (Siem Reap), 434
PTM Travel and Tours (Cambodia), 384, 409

Q Bar (Ho Chi Minh City), 334
QT Salon and Spa (Hanoi), 115
Quan Chuong Gate (Hanoi), 106
Quang Ngai, 267
Quang's Ceramics (Hanoi), 117
Quang Trung, Emperor, 21, 261
Quang Trung Museum (Quy Nhon), 266
Quan Kong Temple (Hoi An), 227
Quan Su Pagoda (Hanoi), 112–113
Quan Thanh Temple (Hanoi), 110
Queen's Beach (Quy Nhon), 266
Queen Travel (Hanoi), 69
Quy Hoa Leper Colony (Quy Nhon), 266
Quy Nhon, 261–267

Rabies, 30, 32
Rainbow Bar (Nha Trang), 278
Rainbow Divers, 345–346, 367
Rainfall, monthly, 19
R & R Tavern (Hanoi), 126
Red Beer (Hanoi), 126
Red Bridge Cooking School (Hoi An), 230
Red Door Deco (Ho Chi Minh City), 332
Red Dunes, 290
Red River, 126–127
Regions of Vietnam, 53–54
Religion, 9
- hilltribe, 130

Respiratory illnesses, 32
Responsible tourism, 34–35
Restaurants
- Ba Be Lake and Cho Ra Town, 153
- best, 6
- Buon Ma Thuot, 252
- Cambodia, 381
  - Kampot and Kep, 401
  - Phnom Penh, 390–394
  - Siem Reap, 417–422
  - Sihanoukville, 404–405
- Can Tho, 355–356, 359
- Cao Bang, 154
- Cat Ba Island, 169–170
- Con Dao Archipelago, 342–343
- Dalat, 243–245
- Danang, 210
- environmentally friendly, 42
- Haiphong, 160–161
- Hanoi, 88–100
- Ho Chi Minh City, 313–320
- Hoi An, 220–224
- Hue, 192–194
- Lang Son, 156
- Le Mat, 99
- Mai Chau, 143
- Ninh Binh, 174
- Phan Thiet, 289–290
- Phu Quoc, 363–365
- Pleiku and Kontum, 258
- Quy Nhon, 265–266
- Son La, 146–147
- Vinh, 179
- Vung Tau, 338

Reunification Palace (Ho Chi Minh City), 322–323
Revolutionary Museum
- Buon Ma Thuot, 253
- Hanoi, 113

Rex Hotel (Ho Chi Minh City), dinner theater, 335
Rhododendron Trail, 204
Rice, 352
Rising Sun (Phnom Penh), 398
Roch Chapel (Phat Diem), 179
Rock climbing, 164, 239, 429
The Rockpile, 201
Roluos Group (Cambodia), 431
Romy's Ice Cream and Coffee Bar (Nha Trang), 278
Route 6, 147, 148
Royal Palace and Silver Pagoda (Phnom Penh), 396
Royal Theater (Hue), 195
Royal Traditional Theater (Hue), 195
Russian Market (Phnom Penh), 395, 397

Safety concerns, 33–36
Cambodia, 377
motorcycle travel, 145
The Sa Huynh Culture Museum (Hoi An), 225
Saigon. *See* Ho Chi Minh City
Saigon Crafts (Ho Chi Minh City), 332
Saigon Liberation Day, 21
Saigon Opera House (Ho Chi Minh Municipal Theater), 323
Saigon Saigon (Ho Chi Minh City), 334
Saigon Square (Ho Chi Minh City), 331–332
Saigontourist, 297, 342, 350
Sailing
Hoi An, 228
Nha Trang, 282
Sam Mountain, 360
Sapa (Ho Chi Minh City), 132–141, 332
accommodations, 136–138
attractions, 139–141
banks and communication, 136
restaurants, 138–139
shopping, 141
traveling to, 134–135
visitor information and tours, 135–136
SARS, 32
SATH (Society for Accessible Travel & Hospitality), 37
Sayon Silkworks (Phnom Penh), 397
Scuba diving
Con Dao Archipelago, 341, 345
Nha Trang, 280–281
Phu Quoc, 367
Sea kayaking, 164
Sea turtles
Con Son, 346
Hon Bay Canh, 341
Sedang people, 235
Seductive (Hue), 194
Seeing Hands IV (Siem Reap), 435
Seminary and Ethnic Hilltribe Museum (Kontum), 259
Senior travel, 40
Senses Salon and Spa (Phnom Penh), 398
Senteurs d'Angkor (Siem Reap), 434
Serepok River, 253
17th Parallel, 200
Sexually transmitted diseases (STDs), 30
Sheridan's (Ho Chi Minh City), 334
Shopping, Cambodia, 381
Siem Reap (Cambodia), 405–436
accommodations, 410–417
attractions, 422–427
emergencies, 410
getting around, 408–409
Internet access, 410
nightlife, 435–436
post office, 410
restaurants, 417–422
shopping, 432–434
spas and massage, 434–435
telephone, 410
traveling to, 408
visitor information & tours, 409
Siem Reap Airport, 378
Sihanoukville, 399, 402–405
Silk & Pepper (Phnom Penh), 397
Silk fabrics and clothing
Hanoi, 116–117
Ho Chi Minh City, 332–333
Hoi An, 229
Hue, 194
Phnom Penh, 397
Silver Lake, 290
Silver Pagoda (Phnom Penh), 396
Single travelers, 41
Sinh Balo (Ho Chi Minh City), 297–298
Sinh Café, 24
Dalat, 239
Hanoi, 70
Ho Chi Minh City, 298, 350, 379
Hue, 188
Phan Thiet, 285
Sinh Café II (Ho Chi Minh City), 298
Sinh Café III (Nha Trang), 271
Sinh Café IV (Hoi An), 212
Sin Ho, 151
Smoking, 443
"Snake Village" (Le Mat), 99
Snorkeling, Phu Quoc, 367
Society for Accessible Travel & Hospitality (SATH), 37
Solace (Hanoi), 126
Song (Hanoi), 119
Song Da (Da River) Reservoir, 142, 146
Son La, 146–147
Son La Prison, 147
Sorya Shopping Centre (Phnom Penh), 398
Sorya Transport (Phnom Penh), 386
South-Central Vietnam, 261–290
Southern Cambodia, 399–405
Southern Vietnam, 19
brief description of, 54
South Korea, embassy of, 75
Spas and massage
Cambodia
Phnom Penh, 398
Siem Reap, 434–435
Hanoi, 115
Ho Chi Minh City, 329
Special events and festivals, 19–21
The Spotted Cow (Hanoi), 126
Squid fishing trips, 366
Sra Serang Reservoir (Cambodia), 429
STA Travel, 41
Stone Chapel (Legise de Pierre; Phat Diem), 179
Student travel, 40–41
Studio (Hanoi), 126
Suai Cai Crossroad, 366
Summit Trail (Bach Ma National Park), 204
Sun exposure, 32–33
Sunset Bar (Hanoi), 126
Surprise Cave (Halong Bay), 166

Ta Dambong, statue of (Battambang), 439
Ta Kaeo (Cambodia), 429
Tam Coc (Three Grottoes; near Van Lam), 127, 174
Tam Duong, 152
Tam Island, 281
Tam-Tam Café (Hoi An), 231
Tam Thuong Alley (Hanoi), 104
Tan Dinh Cathedral (Ho Chi Minh City), 325
Tan Dinh Market (Ho Chi Minh City), 325
Tan My (Hanoi), 117
Tan My Design (Hanoi), 119
Tan Son Nhat airport (Ho Chi Minh City), 294
Taoi people, 235

Ta Phin Village and Cave (Sapa), 140
Ta Prohm (Cambodia), 429
Tara and Kys Art Gallery (Siem Reap), 434
Tashunco (Nha Trang), 282
Taxes, 443
Taxis, Hanoi, 72
Tay people, 131
Tay Son Rebellion, 184, 261
Telephone, Cambodia, 382, 383
Telephones, Vietnam, 443–444
Temperatures, average daily, 19
Temple of Literature and National University (Van Mieu-Quoc Tu Giam; Hanoi), 110–111
Temples and archaeological sites, best, 2–3
Terrace of the Leper King (Cambodia), 428
Terre Cambodge (Cambodia), 432
Terre Cambodge (Siem Reap), 409
Tet holiday, 19, 21
Tet Nguyen Dan (Lunar New Year Festival), 20
Tet Offensive, 16
Tet Trung Nguyen, 21
Thai Binh Reading Pavilion (Hue), 195
Thai Hoa Palace (Hue), 196
Thailand
  embassy of, 75
  traveling to Cambodia overland, 379
Thai people, 131
Thang Long (Hanoi), 121
Thang Long Water Puppet Theater (Hanoi), 123–124
Thanh Gia (Hanoi), 115
Thanh Ha Communal House (Hanoi), 106
Thanh Ha Silk (Hanoi), 116
Thanh Mai (Hanoi), 121
Thapba Mud Bath and Hot-spring Resort (near Nha Trang), 282
Thap Doi Cham Towers, 267
Thap Rua (Hanoi), 112
Thay Vien Thuc, Home of (Lam Ty Ni Pagoda; Dalat), 247–248
Theater, Hanoi, 123–124
Thic Ca Phat Dai (Vung Tau), 338
Thien Cung Grotto (Heavenly Cave; Halong Bay), 166
Thien Hau-The Lady Temple (Ho Chi Minh City), 326
Thien Mieu Temple (Hue), 196
Thien Mu Pagoda (Hue), 198
Thien Ngan (Ho Chi Minh City), 330
Thien Vuong Pagoda (Dalat), 248
Things of Substance (Hanoi), 119
Thoi Son Island, 353
Three Grottoes (Tam Costs of cruises; near Van Lam), 127, 174
Three Trees (Hanoi), 119
Thuan An Beach (Hue), 199
Thua Thien-Hue region, 184
Time zones
  Cambodia, 382
  Vietnam, 444
Tipping
  Cambodia, 382
  Vietnam, 444
TM Brothers (Dalat), 239
TM Brother's Café (Nha Trang), 271
TNK Travel, 69, 350
To Hieu, tree of (Son La), 147
Toilets
  Cambodia, 382
  Vietnam, 444
Tombo (Ho Chi Minh City), 332
Tomb of Minh Mang (Hue), 197
Tomb of Tu Duc (Hue), 197–198
Ton Dao Church (Phat Diem), 178
Tonle Bati (Cambodia), 398–399
Tonle Sap Lake (Cambodia), 431
Topas Adventure Travel, 69, 135
Tours and tour operators. *See* Visitor information and tours
Tours of Peace (TOP), 44–45
Train travel
  Danang, 208
  Haiphong, 158
  Hanoi, 67–68
  Ho Chi Minh City, 295–296
  Hue, 186
  Lang Son, 155
  Nha Trang, 268, 270
  Quy Nhon, 262
  Sapa, 134–135
  to Vietnam, 24
  within Vietnam, 25
Trai Phu Hai Prison (Con Son), 344–345
Trai Phu Son (Con Son), 345
Tram Ton, 150
Tram Ton Pass, 152
The Tran Family Home and Chapel (Hoi An), 226
Trang Bang, 328
Trang Tien Bridge (Hue), 186
Trang Tien Plaza (Hanoi), 118
Trang Tien Street (Hanoi), 121
Tran Quoc pagoda (Hanoi), 110
Travel CUTS, 41
Traveler's checks, Cambodia, 376
Traveling to Vietnam, 23–24
Travel insurance, 442
Treat's Same Same Café (Hoi An), 231
Treat's Same Same Not Different Bar (Hoi An), 231
Trekking, Con Dao National Park, 346
Tropical illnesses, 28–29
Truc Lam (Bamboo Forest) Zen Monastery (Dalat), 249
Trung Nguyen, 255
Trung Trang Cave, 171
Tuan Giao, 147
Tube house (Hanoi), 101
Tuberculosis, 30, 32
Tuc Dup Hill, 360
Tu Duc, Tomb of (Hue), 197–198
Tu Hieu (Hue), 198–199
Tuk-tuks
  Phnom Penh, 386
  Siem Reap, 408
Tulico Trains, Sapa, 135
Tuol Sleng, Museum of Genocide (Phnom Penh), 396–397
Typhoid, 30

United Kingdom
  customs regulations, 23
  for disabled travelers, 38
  embassy of, 75
    Cambodia, 378
  passports, 443
  visas, 445

United States
customs regulations, 23
embassy of
Cambodia, 378
Vietnam, 75
passports, 443
USIT, 41

Valley of Love (Dalat), 249
Van Gallery (Hanoi), 121
Van Hoa Viet (Hanoi), 117–118
Van Loi (Hanoi), 118
Van Mieu-Quoc Tu Giam (Temple of Literature and National University; Hanoi), 110–111
Vasco's Bar (Ho Chi Minh City), 334
Veggy's (Ho Chi Minh City), 331
Veggy's (Phnom Penh), 398
Vets with a Mission, 45
Victoria Hotels (Ho Chi Minh City), 350
Victoria's Orient Express, 134
Viet Fine Arts Gallery (Hanoi), 120–121
Vietnam Airlines, Hanoi, 67
Vietnamese House (Hanoi), 118
Vietnamese people, 7–9
Vietnam Ethnology Museum (Hanoi), 114–115
Vietnam Explorer (Nha Trang), 281
Vietnam Golf and Country Club (Ho Chi Minh City), 328
Vietnam History Museum (Ho Chi Minh City), 323
Vietnam National Museum of Fine Arts (Hanoi), 109–110
***Vietnam News*, 76**
Vietnam Vespa Adventure, 43, 45, 285, 298
Vietnam War, 14–16
Vietnam War veterans, 39–40, 292–293
tours for, 44–45
Viet Silk (Hue), 194
Vimean Akhar (Cambodia), 426
Vina Express (Vung Tau), 336
Vinaphone, 48
Vinh, 179–183
Vinh Moc, tunnels of (DMZ), 200
Vinh Moc Tunnels, 202
Vinh Nghiem Pagoda (Ho Chi Minh City), 324–325
Visas, 22, 445
Visaya Spa (Siem Reap), 434
Visitor information and tours
Buon Ma Thuot, 251
Cambodia, 374
Can Tho, 354, 358
Dalat, 239
Danang, 208
Hanoi, 68–71
Hoi An, 212
Hue, 188
Mekong Delta, 349–350, 352
Nha Trang, 270–271
North-Central Vietnam, 173
Pleiku and Kontum, 257
Quy Nhon, 264
Sapa, 135
Siem Reap, 409
Volunteer travel, 42
Vung Tau, 335–338

Warehouse (Hanoi), 123
War Remnants Museum (Ho Chi Minh City), 325
Wat Banang (Battambang), 439–440
Water, drinking, 30–31
Cambodia, 382
Wat Phnom (Phnom Penh), 397
Wat Phnom Ek (Battambang), 440
Wat Phnom Sampeou (Battambang), 440
Weather, 18–19
Western Canned Foods (Hanoi), 122
West Lake (Hanoi), 110
Whale Island, 284–285
Why Not Bar (Nha Trang), 283
Wi-Fi access, 49
Wildlife. *See also* Bird-watching
Cat Ba National Park, 171
Cuc Phuong National Park, 177
Women's Museum (Hanoi), 113–114
Women travelers, 39
World Express Travel and Tours (Phnom Penh), 384

Xu (Ho Chi Minh City), 334–335
Xuan Dieu Street (Hanoi), 118
Xuan Huong Lake (Dalat), 249
Xuan Thu (Ho Chi Minh City), 329

Yaly Couture (Hoi An), 230
Yen Bai, 152
Yen Thai Communal House (Hanoi), 104
Yen Thai Street (Hanoi), 104
Y-Not? Salon (Hanoi), 115
Yok Don National Park, 250, 251, 254